Introduction to Intellectual Property
Theory and Practice

KLUWER LAW INTERNATIONAL

Introduction to Intellectual Property Theory and Practice

World Intellectual Property Organization
(Geneva, Switzerland)

Wolters Kluwer

Law & Business

AUSTIN   BOSTON   CHICAGO   NEW YORK   THE NETHERLANDS

Published by:
Kluwer Law International
PO Box 316
2400 AH Alphen aan den Rijn
The Netherlands
Website: www.kluwerlaw.com

Sold and distributed in North, Central and South America by:
Aspen Publishers, Inc.
7201 McKinney Circle
Frederick, MD 21704
United States of America
Email: customer.care@aspenpubl.com

Sold and distributed in all other countries by:
Turpin Distribution Services Ltd.
Stratton Business Park
Pegasus Drive, Biggleswade
Bedfordshire SG18 8TQ
United Kingdom
Email: kluwerlaw@turpin-distribution.com

Printed and bound in Great Britain by
CPI Antony Rowe, Chippenham and Eastbourne

reprinted in June, 2008

ISBN 978-90-411-0938-5

©2008 Kluwer Law International BV, The Netherlands

PREFACE

The World Intellectual Property Organization (WIPO), an intergovernmental organization with a membership of 157 States as of July 1, 1996, is one of the specialized agencies of the United Nations system of organizations. WIPO is responsible for the promotion of the protection of intellectual property throughout the world through cooperation among States, and for the administration of various multilateral treaties dealing with legal and administrative aspects of intellectual property.

One of the mandates of WIPO is the preparation and publication of books, manuals and other teaching aids in the field of intellectual property. The study of intellectual property is frequently rendered difficult by the insufficiency of readily available teaching material. It was in order to fill the need for more teaching material that WIPO published, in 1988, a volume entitled *Background Reading Material on Intellectual Property.* The present book is a revision of that popular work, with updated information and a greatly expanded scope.

Consisting of a collection of texts on all aspects of intellectual property law and administration, this book is an essential reference work for government officials, lawyers, intellectual property agents and businessmen, and, of course, students.

The reading material consists of papers and lectures prepared by the International Bureau of WIPO, or by lecturers engaged by WIPO for various meetings, symposiums and training courses. The materials presented are identified by the document or publication number of WIPO.

This book is intended as a general introduction to intellectual property. Particular attention has been paid to the subject of international cooperation in intellectual property, including a discussion of the principal multilateral treaties which deal with the protection of intellectual property. The role of intellectual property in cultural, economic and technological development and the interaction between industrial property offices and the various users of the intellectual property system are also outlined.

Originally published by WIPO in loose-leaf form, this book is the result of a cooperation agreement between Kluwer Law International and WIPO.

Arpad Bogsch
Director General
World Intellectual Property Organization

CONTENTS

PART I

Introduction to Intellectual Property

CHAPTER 1

The System of Intellectual Property

A. THE CONCEPT OF INTELLECTUAL PROPERTY

1.1   Very broadly, intellectual property means the legal rights which result from intellectual activity in the industrial, scientific, literary and artistic fields. Countries have laws to protect intellectual property for two main reasons. One is to give statutory expression to the moral and economic rights of creators in their creations and such rights of the public in access to those creations. The second is to promote, as a deliberate act of Government policy, creativity and the dissemination and application of its results and to encourage fair trading which would contribute to economic and social development.

1.2   Creations of the mind, such as an idea for an invention, a piece of music or a trademark, can not, like physical objects, be protected against other persons' use of them by the mere possession of the object. Once the intellectual creation is made available for the public, its creator can no longer exercise control over the use made of the creation. This basic fact, that is, the inability to protect something by the mere possession of an object, underlies the whole concept of intellectual property law.

1.3   Generally speaking, intellectual property law aims at safeguarding creators and other producers of intellectual goods and services by granting them certain time-limited rights to control the use made of those productions. Those rights do not apply to the physical object in which the creation may be embodied but instead to the intellectual creation as such.

1.4   Intellectual property is traditionally divided into two branches, "industrial property" and "copyright."

1.5   "Industrial property" embraces protection of inventions by means of patents, protection of certain commercial interests by means of trademark law and law on trade names, and the law on protection of industrial designs. In addition, industrial property embraces the repression of unfair competition.

1.6   "Copyright" grants authors and other creators of works of the mind (literature, music, art) certain rights to authorize or prohibit, for a certain limited time, certain uses made of their works. Copyright, broadly speaking, embraces the provisions on the protection of copyright in the strict sense of the word and also the protection of what is usually referred to as "neighboring rights."

1.7   The Convention Establishing the World Intellectual Property Organization (WIPO), concluded in Stockholm on July 14, 1967 (Article 2(viii)) provides that "'intellectual property' shall include rights relating to:

(1) literary, artistic and scientific works;
(2) performances of performing artists, phonograms, and broadcasts;
(3) inventions in all fields of human endeavor;
(4) scientific discoveries;
(5) industrial designs;
(6) trademarks, service marks, and commercial names and designations;
(7) protection against unfair competition;

and all other rights resulting from intellectual activity in the industrial, scientific, literary or artistic fields."

1.8   The areas mentioned under (1) belong to the copyright branch of intellectual property. The areas mentioned in (2) are usually called "neighboring rights," that is, rights neighboring on copyright. The areas mentioned under (3), (5) and (6) constitute the industrial property branch of intellectual property. The area mentioned under (7) may also be considered as belonging to that branch, the more so as Article 1(2) of the Paris Convention for the Protection of Industrial Property (Stockholm Act of 1967) (the "Paris Convention") includes "the repression of unfair competition" among the areas of "the protection of industrial property"; the said Convention states that "any act of competition contrary to honest practices in industrial and commercial matters constitutes an act of unfair competition" (Article 10*bis*(2)).

1.9   The expression "industrial property" is sometimes misunderstood as relating to movable or immovable property used for industrial production, such as factories, equipment for production, etc. However, industrial property is a kind of intellectual property and thus relates to creations of the human mind. Typically, such creations are inventions and industrial designs. Simply stated, inventions are new solutions to technical problems, and industrial designs are aesthetic creations determining the appearance of industrial products. In addition, industrial property includes trademarks, service marks, commercial names and designations, including indications of source and appellations of origin, and the protection against unfair competition. Here, the aspect of intellectual creations—although existent—is less prominent, but what counts here is that the object of industrial property typically consists of signs transmitting information to consumers, in particular, as regards products and services offered on the market, and that the protection is directed against unauthorized use of such signs which is likely to mislead consumers, and misleading practices in general. The Paris Convention (Article 1(2)) provides that "the protection of industrial property has as its object patents, utility models, industrial designs, trademarks, service marks, trade names, indications of source or appellations of origin, and the repression of unfair competition".

1.10 The area mentioned in the WIPO Convention under (4)—scientific discoveries—belongs to neither of the two branches of intellectual property. According to one opinion, scientific discoveries should not have been mentioned among the various forms of intellectual property since no national law or international treaty gives any property right in scientific discoveries. Scientific discoveries and inventions are not the same. The Geneva Treaty on the International Recording of Scientific Discoveries (1978) defines a scientific discovery as "the recognition of phenomena, properties or laws of the material universe not hitherto recognized and capable of verification" (Article 1(1)(i)). Inventions are new solutions to specific technical problems. Such solutions must, naturally, rely on the properties or laws of the material universe (otherwise they could not be materially ("technically") applied), but those properties or laws need not be properties or laws "not hitherto recognized." An invention puts to new use, to new technical use, the said properties or laws, whether they are recognized ("discovered") simultaneously with making the invention or whether they were already recognized ("discovered") before, and independently from, the invention.

B. COPYRIGHT AND NEIGHBORING RIGHTS

1.11 Copyright relates to artistic creations, such as poems, novels, music, paintings, cinematographic works, etc. In most European languages other than English, copyright is called author's rights. The expression "copyright" refers to the main act which, in respect of literary and artistic creations, may be made only by the author or with his authorization. That act is the making of *copies* of the literary or artistic work, such as a book, a painting, a sculpture, a photograph, a motion picture. The second expression, "author's rights" refers to the person who is the creator of the artistic work, its author, thus underlining the fact, recognized in most laws, that the author has certain specific rights in his creation, for example, the right to prevent a distorted reproduction, which can be exercised only by himself, whereas other rights, such as the right to make copies, can be exercised by other persons, for example, a publisher who has obtained a license to this effect from the author.

1.12 "Neighboring rights" is an abbreviated expression. The full expression would be "rights neighboring on copyright." It is generally understood that there are three kinds of rights, which are covered by the concept of neighboring rights: the rights of performing artists in their performances; the rights of producers of phonograms in their phonograms; and the rights of broadcasting organizations in their radio and television broadcasts.

1.13 The protection of authors' interests does not consist merely in preventing the unauthorized use of their works. Their works are intended to be made available to the public at large. The various categories of works are made accessible to the public in different ways. A publisher reproduces the manuscript of a literary work in its final form without adding to the expression of the work as created by the author. The interests of book publishers are protected on the basis of the rights assigned or licensed to them by authors.

1.14 The situation is slightly different in the case of dramatic and musical works. Where such works are to be communicated to the public, they have to be performed or recited with the aid of performers. In such cases, also the interests of the performers themselves should be taken into account in relation to the use of their individual interpretations of the works concerned.

References for Section A
International Bureau of WIPO, *WIPO's Development Cooperation Activities*, WIPO/CNR/ABU/93/9
H. Olsson, *Introduction to Intellectual Property Law*, WIPO/CNR/S/93/1
International Bureau of WIPO, *The Elements of Industrial Property*, WIPO/IP/WDH/93/1

1.15 The development of sound recording techniques and the possibility of relatively easy reproduction of such recordings have also raised the need for protection of producers of phonograms. The easy availability in the market of increasingly efficient recording devices created the growing problem of record piracy, which by now has become a worldwide problem. Furthermore, records are frequently used by broadcasting organizations; while such a use may provide publicity for the records and for their producers, they also have become an essential ingredient of the daily programs of broadcasting organizations. Consequently, just as the performers were seeking their own protection, producers of phonograms began to pursue the case of their protection against unauthorized duplication of their phonograms, and also for a right to remuneration for the use of phonograms for purposes of broadcasting and other communication to the public.

1.16 Finally, there are the interests of broadcasting organizations as regards their broadcasts. The broadcasting organizations require their own protection against the unauthorized retransmission of their broadcasts by other broadcasting organizations and against such reproduction thereof.

1.17 Generally speaking, it is the expression of the author's ideas that is protected rather than the ideas themselves. For example, if an author makes an exposé of his ideas on how to build a radio receiver, the copyright he has in his exposé when published in the form of an article in a review will not prevent a third party from using the author's ideas to build such a receiver, but the copyright will protect the author against the reproduction of copies of his article without his consent. As for the invention itself, it does not enjoy copyright protection but may be protected on other grounds in the industrial property context. A fundamental point is that ideas, as such, are not protected by copyright. Unless he has patent protection, a person who has made his ideas public, for example in a public lecture, has no means of stopping others from using it. But once that idea has been expressed in tangible form, copyright protection exists for the words, musical notes, drawings, etc., in which it is clothed. For a work to enjoy copyright protection, however, it must be an original creation.

1.18 The final fixation of a work in a material form (writing, printing, photography, sound or visual recording, sculpture, construction, painting, graphic reproduction, etc.) is not necessarily a prerequisite of protection. However, certain countries, notably those that follow the Anglo-American legal system, require, mainly for reasons of proof, some fixation of the work before protection is assured.

1.19 Copyright protection is independent of the quality or the value attaching to the work—it will be protected whether it be considered, according to taste, a good or a bad literary or musical work—and even of the purpose for which it is intended, because the use to which a work may be put has nothing to do with its protection.

1.20 Rights are made to be respected and, if they are not, there are sanctions. Any unauthorized use of works protected by copyright, when authorization of such use is required by law, constitutes what is called a copyright infringement (for instance, reproduction, public performance, broadcasting or any other communication to the public effected without permission, adaptation in any other form without the consent of the author, plagiarism, etc.). Legislation specifies sanctions to remedy the prejudice caused by such infringements, and the sanctions may be civil or criminal depending on the importance of the infringement or violation.

1.21 Finally, it is generally accepted that the whole set of prerogatives that constitute copyright has to be recognized and protected at least throughout the life of the author. After his death, his work continues in principle to be protected for a certain time. The period is generally 50 years after the death of the author. This is regarded as being a fair balance between the preservation of the economic rights conferred on the author and society's need to have access to the expression of a culture whose essential aspects will have a more lasting effect than transitory successes. On expiry of the term of protection, the work falls into the public domain, that is, it can be used by anyone without any authorization.

C. PATENTS AND RELATED CONCEPTS

(a) Patents for Invention

1.22 An invention is an idea which permits the practical solution of a specific problem in a field of technology. Inventions are characteristically protected by patents, also called "patents for invention." Every country which gives legal protection to inventions—and there are over 140 such countries—gives such protection through patents, although there are a few countries in which protection may also be given by means other than patents, as will be seen below.

1.23 The basic function and role of the patent system is simple and reasonable. It is desirable in the public interest that industrial techniques should be improved. In order to encourage improvement, and to encourage also the disclosure of improvements in preference to their use in secret, any person devising an improvement in a manufactured article, or a method of making it, or a new substance and/or the process of making that substance, may, upon disclosure of the details to the Patent Office of a country, be given a set of exclusive rights for a certain period of time. After that period expires, the invention passes into the public domain. The exclusive rights are justified on the grounds that if it had not been for the inventor who devised and disclosed the improvement, nobody would have been able to use it at that or any other time since it and the manner of producing it may have remained unknown. In addition, the giving of the monopoly encourages the putting into practice of the invention, since the only way the applicant can make a profit is by putting the invention into practice, either by using it himself and deriving an advantage over his competitors by its use, or by allowing others to use it in return for royalties.

1.24 Not all inventions are patentable. Generally, laws require that, in order to be patentable, the invention must be new, it must involve an inventive step (or it

References for Section B
International Bureau of WIPO, *The Elements of Industrial Property*, WIPO/IP/WDH/93/1
International Bureau of WIPO, *International Protection of Copyright and Neighboring Rights*, WIPO/CNR/ABU/93/2
International Bureau of WIPO, *Copyright in the Light of the Fundamental Notions Concerning its Origin, its Development, its Protection, its Scope and its Limits*, STC/ZU/CNR/I/4

must be non-obvious), and it must be industrially applicable. These three requirements are sometimes called the requirements or conditions of patentability. Furthermore, the laws of some countries exclude certain specific kinds of inventions from the possibility of patenting: for example, inventions which comprise substances obtained by nuclear transformation.

1.25 It is customary to distinguish between inventions that consist of products and inventions that consist of processes. An invention that consists of a new alloy is an example of a product invention. An invention that consists of a new method or process of making a known or new alloy is a process invention. The corresponding patents are usually referred to as a "product patent" and a "process patent," respectively.

1.26 Under the protection conferred by a patent for invention, anyone who wishes to exploit the invention must obtain the authorization of the person who received the patent—called "the patentee" or "the owner of the patent"—to exploit the invention. If anyone exploits the patented invention without such authorization, he commits an illegal act. Such protection is limited in time. In most countries, it is about 20 years from the date of filing the application for patent protection.

1.27 The rights conferred by a patent are described in the patent law of the country in which the patent for invention was granted. The rights, usually called "exclusive rights of exploitation," generally consist:

(1) in the case of product patents for invention, of the right to make, use, sell and import the product that includes the invention, and

(2) in the case of process patents for invention, of the right to use the process that comprises the invention as well as the right to make, use, sell and import products which were made by the process that comprises the invention.

1.28 It has been mentioned earlier that if anyone exploits the patented invention without the authorization of the owner of the patent for invention, he commits an illegal act. However, as already stated, there are exceptions to this principle, because patent laws may provide for cases in which a patented invention may be exploited without the patentee's authorization, for example, exploitation in the public interest by or on behalf of the government, or exploitation on the basis of a compulsory license. A compulsory license is an authorization to exploit the invention, given by a governmental authority, generally only in very special cases, defined in the law, and only where the entity wishing to exploit the patented invention is unable to obtain the authorization of the owner of the patent for invention. The conditions of the granting of compulsory licenses are also regulated in detail in laws which provide for them. In particular, the decision granting a compulsory license usually has to fix a remuneration for the patentee, and that decision usually may be the subject of an appeal.

(b) Utility Models

1.29 A second form of protection for inventions consists in the registration, or the granting, of a patent for a "utility model." The expression "utility model" is merely a name given to certain inventions, namely—according to the laws of most countries which contain provisions on utility models—inventions in the mechanical field. This is why the objects of utility models are sometimes described as devices or useful objects. Another type of protection which may be considered similar to utility model patents is referred to as a "petty patent."

1.30 Utility models usually differ from inventions for which ordinary patents for invention are available mainly in three respects: *first*, in the case of an invention called "utility model," the inventive step required is smaller than in the case of an invention for which a patent for invention is available; *second*, the maximum term of protection provided in the law for a utility model is generally much shorter than the maximum term of protection provided in the law for an invention for which a patent for invention is available; and *third*, the fees required for obtaining and maintaining the rights are generally lower than those applicable to ordinary patents. Moreover, in certain countries there is also a substantial difference in the procedure for obtaining protection for a utility model: this procedure is generally shorter and simpler than the procedure for obtaining patents for invention.

1.31 Utility models can encourage inventors and investors to invest in and protect technical developments which do not fulfill the requirements of patentability and to obtain protection both at a lower cost and more quickly. Consequently, utility models are of particular interest to small and medium-sized industries and can promote technical development in developing countries. Utility models can fill a gap in the protection of inventions which occurs when the requirements relating to inventive step for patents mean that certain inventions which do not comply with those requirements cannot be protected. Moreover, this form of protection prevents the patent system from being devalued by being applied to minor technical inventions.

D. INDUSTRIAL DESIGNS

1.32 Generally speaking, an industrial design is the ornamental or aesthetic aspect of a useful article. The ornamental aspect may consist of the shape and/or pattern and/or color of the article. The ornamental or aesthetic aspect must appeal to the sense of sight. The article must be reproducible by industrial means, which is why the design is called "industrial." If this latter element is missing, the creation may rather come under the category of a work of art that is protected by copyright law rather than by a law on industrial property.

1.33 In order to be protectable, an industrial design must, according to some laws, be new and, according to other laws, original.

1.34 Industrial designs are usually protected against unauthorized copying or imitation. The protection usually lasts five, ten or 15 years.

References for Section C
H. Olsson, *Introduction to Intellectual Property Law*, WIPO/CNR/S/93/1
International Bureau of WIPO, *The Elements of Industrial Property*, WIPO/IP/WDH/93/1
P. Smith, *Introduction to Patent Law and Practice: The Basic Concepts*, WIPO Pub. No. 672(E) (1989)
International Bureau of WIPO, *Different Titles of Protection for Inventions*, WIPO/LAC/CCS/89/2

1.35 The document that certifies the protection of an industrial design may be called a registration certificate or a patent. If it is called a patent, one must, in order to distinguish it from a patent for invention, always specify that it is a patent for an industrial design.

1.36 With the remarkable evolution in design art in recent years, consumers have become more and more interested in a combination of utility and pleasing aesthetic appearance in the articles they buy. This tendency results in an increasing investment by manufacturers in design development and in a corresponding necessity to protect the result of their creative work through the registration of the relevant designs.

E. TRADEMARKS, TRADE NAMES AND GEOGRAPHICAL INDICATIONS

(a) Trademarks

1.37 The concept of a mark is not a new one. For centuries, merchants and manufacturers in various parts of the world have labeled their products with signs of one kind or another to distinguish them from those of their competitors. However, the use made of marks long remained a limited phenomenon relating only to certain types of goods that were sold far from their place of production. Most goods were consumed at the place they were produced and no marks were used. The modern concept of a mark, that is to say the mark as we know it today, first appeared in the 18th century as a result of the increased possibilities for communication and the adoption of laws guaranteeing freedom of commerce and industry. As from that time, trade became more developed, both within States and between States, and the increased circulation of goods of all kinds made it necessary to place marks on those products so that they could be identified, both in the interests of producers and traders and also those of the consumers.

1.38 Since the end of the Second World War, the unprecedented development of international trade has led to an even greater use of marks in all countries and in all fields of activity. Although we are not always aware of the fact, marks today assume an ever greater place in our day-to-day life and we enter into contact with a host of marks, not only in supermarkets and public places where we are faced with posters, but also in the press, on radio and on television, that enter into the home.

(i) Functions of Marks

1.39 A trademark serves several purposes. From the viewpoint of the person who is interested in buying goods, the trademark serves the purpose of guiding him in his decision to buy. Such a decision is based on the expected characteristics or other properties of the goods (size, weight, color, fragrance, taste, durability, degree of efficiency in the operations in which the goods are used, etc.). In a

References for Section D
International Bureau of WIPO, *General Aspects of Industrial Property*, WIPO/IP/THR/91/1
International Bureau of WIPO, *Other Elements of Industrial Property*, ISIP/86/4

single word, one may say that what the prospective buyer is looking for is a certain quality or other characteristic of the goods. So, one of the functions of a trademark is to convey a feeling of that quality or characteristic. One of the functions of a trademark is to distinguish the goods with that quality or characteristic from other comparable goods. While it is often said that a trademark must enable anyone to distinguish the goods of one enterprise from goods of the same kind produced by another enterprise, the consumer does not necessarily know the name of the firm that manufactures or markets the product, apart from which the mark may yet serve to distinguish goods from other goods that come from the same firm.

1.40 A second function of the trademark is to allow the manufacturer to identify goods manufactured by him once they are no longer in his possession but already in the possession of others, for example the shops that sell it.

1.41 A third function of the trademark is to allow the authorities responsible for controlling the quality or other characteristics of the goods sold under a trademark to do their job.

1.42 But enterprises do not only deal with goods, they also render services. Services may be of almost any kind: travel, advertising, transport, insurance, treatment of materials, etc. A "service mark" is thus a sign used by enterprises offering services (hotels, restaurants, airlines, travel agencies, car-rental agencies, laundries and dry-cleaners) in order to identify their services on the market.

(ii) Economic Importance of Marks

1.43 Marks are nowadays widely used in practically all countries—whether developing or industrialized countries, market-economy or planned-economy countries—and they play an important economic part in marketing and trade. Marks serve equally the purposes of those who offer goods or services on the market—such as manufacturers, producers, distributors, wholesalers and retailers—and the interests of consumers, public authorities and the economy in general.

1.44 A mark enables the enterprise that uses it to draw the attention of possible consumers to the existence of the goods bearing that mark, to hold their attention once they have become acquainted with the products and, finally, to distinguish them from products of the same type that are offered on the market. An enterprise may, in this way, acquire a reputation for the products it offers under a given mark. The value represented by the mark derives from this association between a mark and a product and thereby enables demand for the goods bearing that mark to be maintained and expanded and to compete with other enterprises that offer goods of the same type. Once a mark has already acquired a firm reputation it also makes it easier to penetrate new markets and thus to stimulate export activities.

1.45 Marks also meet the interests of consumers, in various ways and to a not inconsiderable extent. The use and promotion of marks helps to make consumers aware of the goods and services available on the market, to more readily identify their origin and to effect a choice between similar goods and services. These are all factors that stimulate competition. In the long term, this may lead to an increase in the number and types of consumer goods and bring about an eventual drop in prices. The use of marks may also stimulate competition between users in respect of quality, which, in the long term, can help to improve the overall quality of goods and services.

1.46 An effective trademark system likewise contributes to the protection of consumers against various forms of unfair trading practices (for example, the use of misleading marks or of confusingly similar marks). Many countries do not have specific legislation on consumer protection or, where such legislation does exist, the consumers are frequently not in a position to assert their rights. In such cases, trademark legislation can constitute one of the rare sources of law available to protect the consumer.

1.47 Marks are equally useful to the national authorities, particularly to those responsible for verifying the quality and other characteristics of goods and services. The use of marks may assist them, for example, in identifying, as a result of complaints that have been received or of tests that have been carried out, those goods and services that do not comply with the statutory requirements, from amongst the goods and services that are identical or that belong to the same category. Finally, the registration of marks constitutes a useful source of statistical and economic information for the national authorities.

1.48 Every country has therefore an interest in setting up an effective system to ensure that marks are protected and used in a way that satisfies the legitimate interests of producers and consumers and which enables the best use to be made of the contribution trademarks can make to economic development.

(b) Trade Names

1.49 Trade names are generally names, terms or designations which serve to identify and distinguish an enterprise and its business activities from those of other enterprises. Whereas marks distinguish the goods or services of an enterprise, a trade name identifies the entire enterprise without necessarily any reference to the goods or services it puts on the market, and symbolizes the reputation and goodwill of the business as a whole. Thus, a trade name is a valuable asset for the enterprise it identifies. It is also a useful source of information for consumers. Therefore, it is in the interest of both business enterprises and consumers that trade names be protected and that legal measures be adopted to prevent the use of trade names in ways that are likely to confuse or mislead consumers.

1.50 Trade names are protected under most national laws. However, the legal regimes governing trade names vary considerably from country to country. They are typically determined by a combination of provisions of civil, commercial, company, trademark and/or unfair competition laws and/or special laws on trade names. Many countries provide for a registration system of trade names, although the systems vary significantly both as to their territorial scope (local and/or national) and the legal consequences of registration.

(c) Geographical Indications

1.51 Among the types of commercial designations are indications of source and appellations of origin. Indications of source and appellations of origin together form what are referred to as "geographical indications."

1.52 An indication of source is constituted by any denomination, expression or sign indicating that a product or service originates in a country, a region or a specific place (for instance, "made in ..."). As a general rule, the use of a false or deceptive indication of source is unlawful.

1.53 An appellation of origin is constituted by the denomination of a country, a region or a specific place that serves to designate a product originating therein, the characteristic qualities of which are due exclusively or essentially to the geographical environment, in other words, to natural and/or human factors. The use of an appellation of origin is lawful only for a certain circle of persons or enterprises located in the geographical area concerned and only in connection with the specific products originating in that area (for instance, "Bordeaux," "Champagne," etc.).

1.54 Indications of source and appellations of origin both serve to identify the source or origin of the products or services for which they are used. Appellations of origin, however, have an additional function. Whereas an indication of source shows only from where a product comes, an appellation of origin indicates, in addition, the characteristic qualities of a product which are determined by the geographical area from which it comes and to which the appellation refers. Furthermore, while any expression or sign evoking the geographical source of a product may constitute an indication of source (e.g., a national emblem), an appellation of origin is always a geographical name (generally the name of the country, region or place from which the product originates, although, in some cases, it can refer to a specific geographical area without actually indicating its name).

1.55 The legal recognition and protection of indications of source and appellations of origin are in the general interest. They convey very important information to consumers on the geographical origin of goods and services and, indirectly, on their inherent quality and characteristics. Therefore, if properly used, geographical indications can help the public in its purchasing decisions and frequently exercise a strong influence thereon. However, the wrongful use of geographical indications can mislead consumers as to the geographical source of goods or services, sometimes thereby causing serious damage to consumers.

1.56 Furthermore, an enterprise which wrongfully uses a geographical indication might not only mislead the public but might also gain an unfair advantage over its competitors, including those from the geographical area covered by the indication, who, over a period of time, may lose the whole or part of their custom and the goodwill and reputation symbolized by such indication.

References for Section E
International Bureau of WIPO, *The Protection of Trademarks and Service Marks; History and Functions of the Trademark System*, ISIP/92/3
World Intellectual Property Organization, *Introduction to Trademark Law & Practice* (second edition), WIPO Pub. No. 653(E) (1993)
International Bureau of WIPO, *The Elements of Industrial Property*, WIPO/IP/WDH/93/1
International Bureau of WIPO, *Other Elements of Industrial Property*, ISIP/86/4

F. UNFAIR COMPETITION

1.57 Protection against unfair competition has been recognized as forming part of industrial property protection for almost a century. It was in 1900, at the Brussels Diplomatic Conference for the Revision of the Paris Convention for the Protection of Industrial Property (hereinafter referred to as "the Paris Convention"), that this recognition was first manifested by the insertion of Article 10*bis* in the Convention. In its original version, as adopted at the Brussels Diplomatic Conference, that Article read as follows: "Nationals of the Convention (Articles 2 and 3) shall enjoy, in all the States of the Union, the protection granted to nationals against unfair competition." As a result of the subsequent revision conferences, the Article now reads as follows (in the Stockholm Act (1967) of the Paris Convention):

"(1) The countries of the Union are bound to assure to nationals of such countries effective protection against unfair competition.

(2) Any act of competition contrary to honest practices in industrial or commercial matters constitutes an act of unfair competition.

(3) The following in particular shall be prohibited:

1. all acts of such a nature as to create confusion by any means whatever with the establishment, the goods, or the industrial or commercial activities, of a competitor;

2. false allegations in the course of trade of such a nature as to discredit the establishment, the goods, or the industrial or commercial activities, of a competitor;

3. indications or allegations the use of which in the course of trade is liable to mislead the public as to the nature, the manufacturing process, the characteristics, the suitability for their purpose, or the quantity, of the goods."

1.58 An additional 12 practices are identified as unfair competition in the commentary to the Model Law for Developing Countries on Marks, Trade Names, and Acts of Unfair Competition. They are:

(1) bribing the buyers of a competitor, to secure or retain their patronage;

(2) obtaining the business secrets or trade secrets of a competitor by espionage, or by bribing his employees;

(3) using or disclosing, without authorization, the secret technical "know-how" of a competitor;

(4) inducing employees of a competitor to violate their employment contracts or to leave their employer;

(5) threatening competitors with suits for patent or trademark infringement, if done in bad faith and for the purpose of reducing trade by them and hindering competition;

(6) boycotting trade to prevent or hinder competition;

(7) dumping, that is, selling below cost, with the intent and effect of hindering or suppressing competition;

(8) creating the impression that the customer is being offered an opportunity to make purchases under unusually favorable conditions, when such is not the case;

(9) slavishly copying goods, services, publicity, or other features of the trade of a competitor;

(10) encouraging or utilizing breach of contract by competitors;

(11) effecting publicity which makes comparisons with goods or services of competitors;

(12) violating legal provisions not directly concerning competition to obtain, through such violation, an unfair advantage over other competitors.

1.59 Whereas industrial property rights, such as patents, are granted on application by industrial property offices and confer exclusive rights with respect to the subject matter concerned, protection against unfair competition is based not on such grants of rights but on the consideration—either stated in legislative provisions or recognized as a general principle of law—that acts contrary to honest business practices are to be prohibited. Fair play in the marketplace cannot be ensured only by the protection of industrial property rights. A wide range of unfair acts, such as misleading advertising and the violation of trade secrets, are usually not dealt with by the specific laws on industrial property.

1.60 The link between the two kinds of protection is clear when certain cases of unfair competition are considered. For example, in many countries unauthorized use of a trademark that has not been registered is considered illegal on the basis of general principles which belong to the field of protection against unfair competition (in a number of countries such unauthorized use is called "passing off"). There is another example of this kind in the field of inventions: if an invention is not disclosed to the public and is considered to constitute a trade secret, the unauthorized performance by third parties of certain acts in relation to that trade secret may be illegal. Indeed the performance of certain acts in relation to an invention that has been disclosed to the public and is not patented or in respect of which the patent has expired, may under very special circumstances also be illegal (as an act of "slavish imitation").

1.61 What is unfair or dishonest largely depends on the economic and social realities at a given time and place. This makes unfair competition law particularly adaptable to changing circumstances and realities. Unfair competition law can furnish a solid legal framework and yet provide a sufficiently flexible standard for formulating and applying measures which can be at the same time sensitive to the particular and ever-changing social and economic conditions in a particular country and effective to combat the specific types of dishonest trade practices which give rise to concern.

References for Section F
International Bureau of WIPO, *Protection Against Unfair Competition: Analysis of the Present World Situation*, WIPO Pub. No. 725(E) (1994)
BIRPI, *Model Law for Developing Countries on Marks, Trade Names, and Acts of Unfair Competition*
International Bureau of WIPO, *The Elements of Industrial Property*, WIPO/IP/ACC/86/1

CHAPTER 2

The History and Evolution
of Intellectual Property

A. THE HISTORY AND EVOLUTION OF PATENTS

2.1   Three periods stand out as important in the history and evolution of patents:

(1)   Privileges (15th to 18th centuries): the sovereign grants a monopoly only
      where he sees fit; the concept of utility and sometimes that of favoritism play
      an important part;
(2)   National Patents (1790 to 1883): every inventor is entitled to apply for a
      patent, the grant of which depends solely on objective conditions; protection
      of domestic inventions abroad is not entertained;
(3)   Internationalization (1883 to the present): protection of inventions outside
      their country of origin is developed along with international trade; worldwide
      or regional conventions assist this development.

(a)   Privileges

2.2   A privilege is an instrument by which the sovereign affords a special right
to an individual. These privileges could contain rights of very differing kinds for
the beneficiary, in particular exemption from the guild rules, exemption from
taxation, allocation of land, interest-free loans, naturalization or even titles of
nobility. The reasons for granting them were also very varied. The privileges
granted for the working of mining deposits are held to be the forerunners of the
industrial privileges. The earliest privileges conferred for the working of a new
technique made no distinction between an inventor in the modern sense of the
word and the person who introduced a technique already known abroad. The
concern of the sovereign was that the innovation replaced imports by a new
domestic industry. The Republic of Venice was the first to adopt a statute for this
form of privilege, the "Parte Veneziana" of 1474.

2.3   That statute already laid down the principles on which today's patents were
to be built: the usefulness of new inventions for the State, the exclusive rights of
the first inventor for a limited period, penalties for infringement.

2.4   The practice of transferring technology and setting up new industries in
England began to grow in the 12th century, and by the 14th century grants of
special privileges were being made by the Crown to individuals to protect them
whilst they established new industries based on imported technology. This

protection took the form of granting the introducer of new technology the sole right to use it for a period sufficiently long for him to establish it and train others in its use. This sole right shielded him during the difficult formative years and gave him a head start, as compensation for providing the State with a new industry and greater independence.

2.5   Such temporary rights were often granted by Letters Patent, which means an "open letter", so called because it carried a seal at the bottom as opposed to being sealed closed. It was by way of an official notice to the public of the rights granted. While originally designed to encourage new industries, the system of granting such rights became abused as a means of augmenting the royal income. Complaints were made in parliament and the Crown promised that patents should be subject to trial by law.

2.6   One of the most famous of such trials occurred in the case of "Clothworkers of Ipswich," in 1615, during which it was said: "But if a man hath brought in a new invention and a new trade within the kingdom in peril of his life and consumption of his estate or stock, etc., or if a man hath made a new discovery of anything, in such cases the King of his grace and favor in recompense of his costs and travail may grant by charter unto him that he shall only use such a trade or traffic for a certain time, because at first people of the kingdom are ignorant, and have not the knowledge and skill to use it. But when the patent is expired the King cannot make a new grant thereof."

2.7   The abuse of grants of special rights continued until, in 1628, the Statute of Monopolies was passed. This declared all monopolies, dispensations and grants to be void except:

"any letters patent and grants of privilege for the term of fourteen years or under, hereafter to be made, of the sole working or making of any manner of new manufactures within this realm, to the true and first inventor of such manufactures which others at the time of making such letters patent and grants shall not use."

2.8   The system of privileges developed, in England, through the action of the Courts, towards a system of grants based solely on procedural conditions of which some, such as submission of a detailed "specification" required as of 1711, gave a foretaste of today's patents.

2.9   From 1760, the number of patents granted in England grew rapidly in direct relation to the Industrial Revolution. In the other countries, however, where industrialization began at a later date, the number of patents remained low; in France, the discredit expressed in general in respect of all hindrances to the freedom of production and trade, together with the poor results generally obtained by the owners of "letters patent," led the monarch to decide that these beneficiaries would lose their rights if they had not put their invention into application within a period of one year (declaration of 1762) and to reject a large number of requests for privileges.

(b) National Patents

2.10 Almost simultaneously, the United States (1790) and France (1791) adopted patent laws based on the grant of a patent to all inventors provided that certain objective conditions were met. Article 1 of the French Law of January 7, 1791, was particularly significant: "any discovery or new invention, in all kinds of industry, shall be the property of its author; consequently, the law shall guarantee to him the full and complete enjoyment thereof, in accordance with the conditions and for the time to be determined hereafter."

2.11 However, the lawmaker also expressed nationalist concerns: a 1793 amendment to the law in the United States afforded patents to citizens only; in France, the person introducing foreign techniques was treated on an equal footing with the true inventor; an inventor who obtained a patent for his invention abroad after having obtained a French patent lost enjoyment of the latter!

2.12 The new system was extended throughout the early decades of the 19th century, particularly as a result of French law being applied in the countries conquered by Napoleon. In the monarchies, either those that had been maintained or had been restored after 1815, the principle of privileges continued, but, in practice, the right to a patent was acknowledged everywhere. As the Industrial Revolution extended to further countries, a quantitative explosion in the number of patents took place: in the years 1815 to 1820, the United States, France and Britain were the only countries that granted more than 100 patents a year. Between 1850 and 1854, these three countries each exceeded 1,000 and several other countries granted some hundreds. At the same time as this quantitative development took place, qualitative improvements were introduced. Simple importers of techniques ceased to be treated in the same way as inventors, the concept of novelty was developed, formalities were redefined and in some cases simplified. Almost everywhere, except in the United States, where substantive examination had been introduced in 1836, a system of registration predominated. Although foreigners were generally able to obtain domestic patents, it remained fairly rare for one and the same invention to be patented in a number of countries, partly because the need did not arise and partly because the complexities of procedure made multiple protection a complicated matter and one of uncertain effectiveness.

2.13 However, the existence of patents was felt to constitute a hindrance to international trade. In the member States of the Zollverein, the Customs Union of the German States prior to the constitution of a unified Empire in the 19th century, the patentee lost his right to oppose imports of goods covered by the patent where they were produced in another member State of the Zollverein. With the success of free trade, for which England had given the example, it seemed that the patent system would be abandoned at the same time as the customs barriers. However, the inventors and their associates, the industrialists of the technically most developed countries, reacted and launched the idea of international protection for inventions. At the 1873 Universal Exposition in Vienna, a patent congress submitted various ideas in that respect. At the same time, an economic crisis led to a retreat in the idea of free trade and caused any idea of abolishing patents to be rejected. At Paris, during a further universal exposition, an international congress began with drawing up a solution for the international protection of industrial property. Developments continued in 1880 and a diplomatic conference finally led, on March 20, 1883, to the signing of the convention that created the Union for the Protection of Industrial Property.

(c) Internationalization

2.14 With the signing of the Paris Convention, a period began of internationalization of industrial property and, in particular, of the patent system. The Paris Union provided the framework within which progress was achieved, by means of the periodical revisions of the Convention, rendering the protection of inventions originating in one member country of the Union more readily obtainable and more effective in the other member countries.

2.15 At the Stockholm Diplomatic Conference in 1967, an agreement was concluded to create the World Intellectual Property Organization (WIPO) (which has become a specialized agency of the United Nations), providing the industrial property and copyright Unions with a permanent structure. The special needs and aims of the developing countries have been one of the major features of WIPO's activities.

2.16 Ever since its creation, the Paris Convention provided the possibility for member States to conclude "special agreements" between themselves as regards industrial property. This possibility has been extensively used, particularly for the conclusion of the Patent Cooperation Treaty (PCT) (1970; administered by WIPO) and the European Patent Convention (1973; administered by the European Patent Office (EPO)). These special agreements enable progress to be achieved within a restricted framework where not all member States of the Paris Union feel the need to increase their international commitment; except where such agreements have a geographical basis, they are accessible to all member countries of the Union.

B. THE HISTORY AND EVOLUTION OF TRADEMARKS

2.17 Trademarks are not a creation of our times, even though their current omnipresence is of rather recent origin.

2.18 Trademarks, as marks of origin, were affixed by the makers of bricks, leather, books, weapons, cooking-ware and other things even in the ancient cultures. These marks were either letters, usually initials, or other symbolic signs stamped on the goods to signify the maker of the product. Certainly these marks did not exercise their present-day function of facilitating distribution of goods in a complex economy. Nevertheless, they signify an important element in trademark law, still valid today, namely, that marks create a relationship between goods and their maker. Such markings were also used as signs of ownership. The English word "brand," often used synonymously with "trademark" even today, reflects this usage: "brand" was the marking placed on cattle by farmers with hot irons.

References for Section A
D. Vincent, *The Role and Functions of Patents, Industrial Designs and Utility Models as Tools of Technology Transfer*, TMP/KL/9
Y. Plasseraud, *Historical Insights Into Industrial Property Rights*, WIPO-CEIPI/IP/SB/93/1

2.19 Trademarks—although not yet called by that "term of art", a word created only in the 19th century—continued to play a similar role throughout the greater part of history, including medieval times and the centuries beyond.

2.20 Marks were of particular significance in the growing production of goods for export. Thus, metal goods were made in England long before the industrial age and the production of steel, and weapons and cutlery carried the traditional signs of their English makers. This is true also of goods made of precious metals. Even today, the marks affixed by the makers of silver teapots or trays in Augsburg, Braunschweig, London, Paris, Amsterdam or Petersburg (the old name of Leningrad) in the 16th and 17th centuries still serve as the guidelines for ascertaining the quality and origin of such goods.

2.21 The guilds constituted the principle form of craft production from the time at which town life began to be reorganized, based on trades, headed by master craftsmen, who achieved that status only following apprenticeship and the completion of a masterpiece. The conditions of manufacture were verified by the guilds' inspectors. Various marks were used: the guild mark, the master craftsman's mark chosen once and for all when his master's status was conferred upon him; occasionally, a journeyman's mark or a local mark. These marks could take the shape of seals attached to pieces of material, or hallmarks on articles of precious metal.

2.22 The aim was to check that the organization of the profession was respected both as regards the rules of manufacture and compliance with the distribution of tasks as between the various trades. These marks, aimed at making the craftsmen feel responsible, were mostly compulsory and do not seem to have played any significant part in winning customers.

2.23 It was forbidden to use a mark belonging to someone else and the severity of penalties laid down in the 16th century for counterfeits shows that the transgression of the rules spread with the decline of the guilds. Examples are the 1544 Edict of Charles V, which dictated exclusion from the trade and severance of the right hand, and the 1564 Royal Edict of France which imposed the death sentence for counterfeit marks on gold cloth.

2.24 In France, the guilds were abolished by the Law of March 17, 1791, and the privileges of the English guilds disappeared in 1835. However, well before those dates, the guild system was already declining, losing ground to non-regulated professions, to international trade and, starting with the Industrial Revolution, to large scale undertakings. The disappearance of the guild rules led to that of the guild marks, which were replaced by more modern types of trademarks in the 18th century.

2.25 Trademarks began to assume their present-day role in the course of the last century. The advent of mass production, the establishment of a more complicated system of distribution of goods from the producer to the buyer, the growing trade in goods, all brought with them the need for a universally applicable identification of the goods: the goods had to be called something in addition to having their natural name, such as tools, matches, beer, etc.

2.26 With the increasing use of trademarks, there also came an increase in copying. Cheap knives and forks could be passed off as cutlery from, for example,

Sheffield by copying the marks of the makers of Sheffield. The cases were numerous. Usually, the rightful users of the marks had no means of stopping the counterfeiters. The marking of their goods provided them with no legally recognized right, and the general law was hardly developed anywhere to such an extent that such counterfeiting could be pursued as an act of deceit or, in our present language, as an act contrary to honest business practices. Commercial morality usually also did not consider such acts as wrong. However, in the course of time, remedies were developed by the courts, or the legislatures acted to stop the infringement of trademark rights.

2.27 In England, a remedy against such infringement was developed by the courts beginning in the middle of the last century. It is sufficient to point out that a time came when the user of a trademark was seen as entitled to exclude others from willfully taking away the reputation he had developed under the mark. This was the birth of the famous action of passing off: no person is entitled to pass off his goods as those of another.

2.28 British law at that time was in force in many countries, including the region of North America which became the United States of America.

2.29 After the independence of the United States of America in 1776, it was only a slow process which resulted in separate legal development in that country. Presently, of course, the legal system of the United States, while still having many things in common with the legal system of the United Kingdom, is totally separate and independent. In the field of trademarks, similar court decisions developed as in the United Kingdom. Eventually, the coalition of trademark owners became strong enough to convince the federal legislature, the Congress, to pass a trademark act. This was done in 1870, but that act lasted only for seven years, when it was declared unconstitutional. In any event, it took until 1905 before a new comprehensive trademark act was enacted. This was, interestingly enough, the same year that the United Kingdom adopted a new trademark act.

2.30 On the European continent, as a result of the absence of a system like the British common law, trademark protection could be adopted only by the legislatures. One of the first countries to enact a comprehensive law was France, whose 1857 law remained in force for more than 100 years. Many European countries, such as Germany and Italy, still had to find their national unity. Thus, in Germany, the first legislative protection provided for registered trademarks was a Prussian ordinance of 1874. The first "Reichsgesetz" of 1874, only three years after the formation of the German Reich, was quite limited in scope and allowed only pictorial marks to be registered. The first comprehensive enactment in Germany was that of 1896. The development in the neighboring countries was quite similar.

2.31 The development in trademark law in this century can be summarized under a few headings: use or registration as the basis for the creation of rights; recognition of modern ways of exploiting trademarks (assignment, licensing); recognition of new theories of trademark protection.

2.32 These developments were not only those by legislatures; very often the significant lines were established by court decisions.

2.33 As far as the recognition of new theories of trademark protection in this century is concerned, reference could be made to the British Act of 1938 and the Benelux Trademark Act of 1970.

2.34 The British Act for the first time created new rights for the trademark owner, namely the right to exclude any trademark use whatever, regardless of whether there was likelihood of confusion or not. Thus, in the British law, it seems that where a competitor refers to a trade marked product in order to present the advantages of his own product he could be enjoined for trademark infringement. The Benelux Act has also created a new right, namely, the right to enjoin any use which is causing damage to the trademark owner, regardless of similarity of goods. These examples show that the traditional notion of trademarks as signs indicating origin, and nothing else, is no longer quite true, even as far as present trademark legislation is concerned.

2.35 National developments in trademark law have been influenced to a substantial degree by developments in the international field. Particular reference should be made to the Paris Convention. The Paris Convention is the basic international convention in the field of industrial property, including trademarks. It is supplemented by the Madrid Agreement on the International Registration of Marks, signed in 1891, a special union for members of the Paris Convention. The important point under the aspect of the history of trademark law is that the ratification of these international treaties and their transformation into national legislation has contributed substantially to making the field of industrial property law as international as it is today. The international conventions embody the common views of the international community in industrial property law, and the standards of these treaties were carried into national legislation again and again, especially when the conventions were revised.

C. THE HISTORY AND EVOLUTION OF COPYRIGHT

2.36 The idea of copyright protection only began to emerge with the invention of printing, which made it possible for literary works to be duplicated by mechanical processes instead of being copied by hand. This led to the appearance of a new trade—that of printers and booksellers, in England called "stationers". These entrepreneurs invested considerable sums in the purchase of paper, in buying or building presses, and in the employment of labor, involving an outlay which could be recouped with a reasonable return over a period of time. In this situation, without any form of protection against competition from the sales of unauthorized copies, the investment in the printing and selling of books was a precarious and speculative venture; and many were ruined. The pressures grew for some form of protection; and this came in the shape of privileges granted by the various authorities; in England and in France by the Kings; and in Germany by the Princes of the various States. These privileges gave the beneficiaries exclusive rights of reproduction and distribution, for limited terms, with remedies available for enforcement by means of fines, seizure, confiscation of infringing copies, and possibly damages. The resulting situation exhibited many of the basic features of the copyright system as we know it today.

References for Section B
Y. Plasseraud, *Historical Insights Into Industrial Property Rights*, WIPO-CEIPI/IP/SB/93/1
A. Krieger, *Theory and History of Trademark Law*, BTMC/2

2.37 By the end of the 17th century the system of privileges—i.e. the grant of monopoly rights by the Crown—was being more and more criticized and the voices of authors asserting their rights began increasingly to be heard. This led in England in 1709 to what is acknowledged to be the first copyright statute—The Statute of Anne. The object of this law was expressed in the long title of the Bill as being for the encouragement of learning and for securing the property of copies of books to the rightful owners thereof. Its principal effect was to provide that the author or a book enjoyed the sole right to print and publish it for 14 years from the date of its first publication; he could, of course, sell that right, and usually did, to a bookseller. The Act also provided that at the end of that first period of 14 years a second protection period commenced which again belonged initially to the author, if living; so that the overall effect was to create a period of copyright protection running for 28 years from the date of the first publication. In the case of books already printed when the Act was passed, there was a single period of 21 years protection. The emphasis of the Act was therefore on the protection against unauthorized copying of published works, and in practice the principal beneficiaries were the publisher/booksellers. It should be noted that the Act imposed both a registration and a deposit condition; published books had to be registered at Stationers Hall, and copies had to be deposited for the use of universities and libraries (rising ultimately to a total of nine).

2.38 In the 18th century there was continuous dispute and litigation over the relationship between copyright subsisting at common law and copyright under the Statute of Anne. This was finally settled by the House of Lords in the case of *Donaldson* v. *Beckett* in 1774 which ruled that at common law the author had the sole right of printing and publishing his books, but that once a book was published the rights in it were exclusively regulated by the Statute. This common law right in unpublished works lasted until the Copyright Act 1911, which abolished it; and today in England copyright subsists solely by statute.

2.39 In France the evolution from the system of privileges to a system of copyright was part of the general changes in French life brought about by the Revolution which abolished privileges of all kinds including the privileges of publishers. In 1791 and 1793 the Constituent Assembly passed two decrees which laid the foundations for the French copyright system. The Decree of 1791 secured for the author a right of public performance throughout his lifetime, and for 5 years after his death for the benefit of his heirs or assigns, and the Decree of 1793 gave the author an exclusive right to reproduce his works throughout his lifetime and for 10 years after his death for the benefit of his heirs or assigns. We can see immediately a difference in approach from that of the Statute of Anne. In France these rights are described as "authors' rights" and they are enjoyed throughout the author's lifetime and do not depend upon either publication or upon compliance with formalities such as registration.

2.40 However, both in England and in France, the rights were seen essentially as property rights, simply securing for the author or his heir or assignee the economic value of the work protected.

2.41 The next development to note was the appearance in Germany of philosophic concepts by philosophers such as Kant, who saw in copyright or authors' rights not merely a form of property securing an economic benefit for the author or right owner. They regarded an author's literary and other creative work as an extension of, or reflection of, the author's personality, in respect of which he was entitled by natural justice to be protected as a part of his personality. This concept greatly influenced the development of copyright in continental Europe and, in particular, led to the development of the *droit moral* or moral rights (the non-economic rights of authors).

2.42 To complete this brief historical survey one should turn to the United States of America and observe that until 1976, when the current United States Copyright Act was enacted, the law of copyright in the United States was closely based upon the original provisions in the English Statute of Anne. Thus, the first federal American law, enacted in 1790, provided for the protection of books, maps and charts for a period of 14 years from the first publication, which could be renewed for a further term if the author was still alive on the expiry of the first term, and subject to strict requirements of registration and deposit. Those features remained in the United States law until 1976 when the present law was enacted which changed the duration of protection to the life of the author plus 50 years, thus bringing it into line with virtually all other countries with copyright laws; however, the 1976 Act still retains the requirements of registration and deposit which have their origins in the Statute of Anne of 1709.

2.43 The essence of the conceptual differences between the common law and civil law systems is as follows: the common law countries treat copyright, in effect, as a form of property, capable of being created by an individual or a corporate author, and once created, susceptible to commercial exploitation in the same way as any other form of property, the component rights being exclusively directed to securing enjoyment of the economic potential of the property. In civil law countries the author's right is also regarded as having "property" characteristics, and the copyright law seeks to protect the economic content of that property to the same extent as does the common law system; but, and herein lies the difference, there is an added dimension to authors' rights—i.e. the intellectual or philosophical concept that the work of an author is an expression of his personality which by natural justice requires protection just as much as the economic potential of the work.

2.44 The international period of copyright protection began with the signing of the Berne Convention for the Protection of Literary and Artistic Works in 1886. Subsequent revisions of the Berne Convention have continued to improve the international system of protection of copyright in the light of continued technological development affecting authors' and related rights.

References for Section C
D. de Freitas, *The Main Features of Copyright Protection in the Various Legal Systems*, WIPO/CR/ KL/86/5

CHAPTER 3

The World Intellectual Property Organization and International Cooperation in Intellectual Property

A. THE WORLD INTELLECTUAL PROPERTY ORGANIZATION (WIPO)

(a) History

3.1 The World Intellectual Property Organization (WIPO) is one of the 16 specialized agencies of the United Nations (UN) system of organizations. The "Convention Establishing the World Intellectual Property Organization" was signed at Stockholm in 1967 and entered into force in 1970. However, the origins of WIPO go back to 1883 when the Paris Convention was adopted, and to 1886 when the Berne Convention was adopted. Both of these conventions provided for the establishment of international secretariats, and both were placed under the supervision of the Swiss Federal Government. The few officials who were needed to carry out the administration of the two conventions were located in Berne, Switzerland.

3.2 Initially there were two secretariats (one for industrial property, one for copyright) for the administration of the two conventions. In 1893, the two secretariats united. The name of the organization now known as WIPO has undergone several changes in the course of its history. The most recent of its names, before it became WIPO, was BIRPI, the acronym of the French language version of the name: United International Bureaux for the Protection of Intellectual Property (in English). In 1960, BIRPI was moved from Berne to Geneva.

3.3 At the 1967 diplomatic conference in Stockholm, when WIPO was established, the administrative and final clauses of all the then existing multilateral treaties administered by BIRPI were revised. The said clauses had to be revised because member States wished to make the Organization (WIPO)—which is, of course, an organization of Governments—independent of the Swiss Government, to give it the same status as all the other comparable intergovernmental organizations, and to pave the way for WIPO to become a specialized agency of the United Nations system of intergovernmental organizations.

3.4 Among the specialized agencies, some of the best known are the International Labour Organization (ILO), the United Nations Educational, Scientific and Cultural Organization (UNESCO), the World Health Organization (WHO) and the Food and Agriculture Organization (FAO). They are called "specialized agencies" because each of them has specialized knowledge and expertise, and has accumulated vast international experience in a particular subject or field of activity of importance to the international community. Thus, ILO is specialized in labor, UNESCO in education, science and culture, WHO in health, FAO in food and agriculture and WIPO in intellectual property.

3.5 Most of the intergovernmental organizations now called specialized agencies did not exist before the Second World War. They were created for the specific purpose of dealing with a particular subject or field of activity at the international level. However, some intergovernmental organizations, such as the ILO, the Universal Postal Union (UPU) and the International Telecommunication Union (ITU) were in existence, and had become the responsible intergovernmental organizations in their respective fields of activity, long before the establishment of the United Nations. After the United Nations was established, these organizations became specialized agencies of the United Nations system of organizations.

3.6 Similarly, long before the United Nations was established, BIRPI was the responsible intergovernmental organization in the field of intellectual property. WIPO, the successor to BIRPI, became a specialized agency of the United Nations when an agreement was signed to that effect between the United Nations and WIPO and came into effect on December 17, 1974. An intergovernmental organization can only become a specialized agency of the United Nations pursuant to such an agreement.

3.7 A specialized agency, although it belongs to the family of United Nations organizations, retains its independence. Each specialized agency has its own membership. All member States of the United Nations are entitled to become members of all the specialized agencies, but in fact not all member States of the United Nations are members of all the specialized agencies. Each State decides for itself whether it wants, or does not want, to become a member of any particular specialized agency. For example, although Switzerland is not a member of the United Nations, it is a member of WIPO. Each specialized agency has its own constitution, its own governing bodies, its own elected executive head, its own income, its own budget, its own staff, its own programs and activities. Machinery exists for coordinating the activities of all the specialized agencies, among themselves and with the United Nations, but, basically, each agency remains the master of its own destiny, responsible, under its own constitution, to its own governing bodies which consist, of course, of States members of the organization.

3.8 The agreement between the United Nations and WIPO recognizes that WIPO is, subject to the competence of the United Nations and its organs, responsible for taking appropriate action in accordance with its basic instrument, treaties and agreements administered by it, inter alia, for promoting creative intellectual activity and for facilitating the transfer of technology related to industrial property to the developing countries in order to accelerate economic, social and cultural development.

(b) Structure

3.9 The constitution, the "basic instrument," of WIPO is the Convention signed at Stockholm in 1967. In describing WIPO, the following questions will be answered in very general terms: why is an intergovernmental organization needed? What are the Unions administered by WIPO? Which states are members of WIPO? What does WIPO do? How is it governed and managed?

3.10 Why is an intergovernmental intellectual property organization needed? Intellectual property rights are limited territorially; they exist and can be exercised only within the jurisdiction of the country or countries under whose laws they are granted. But works of the mind, including inventive ideas, cross frontiers with ease, and, in a world of interdependent nations, should be encouraged to do so. Moreover, with growing similarity in the approach and procedures governing intellectual property matters in various countries, it makes eminent sense to simplify practice through international standardization and mutual recognition of rights and duties among nations. Therefore, governments have negotiated and adopted multilateral treaties in the various fields of intellectual property, each of which establishes a "Union" of countries which agree to grant to nationals of other countries of the Union the same protection as they grant to their own, as well as to follow certain common rules, standards and practices.

3.11 The Unions administered by WIPO are founded on the treaties. A Union consists of all the States that are party to a particular treaty. The name of the Union is, in most cases, taken from the place where the text of the treaty was first adopted (thus the Paris Union, the Berne Union, etc.). The treaties fall into three groups.

3.12 The first group of treaties establishes international protection, that is to say, they are treaties which are the source of legal protection agreed between countries at the international level. For instance, three treaties on industrial property fall into this group. They are the Paris Convention, the Madrid Agreement for the Repression of False and Deceptive Indications of Source on Goods and the Lisbon Agreement for the Protection of Appellations of Origin and their International Registration.

3.13 The second group consists of treaties which facilitate international protection. For instance, six treaties on industrial property fall into this group. They are the Patent Cooperation Treaty which provides for the filing of international applications for patents, the Madrid Agreement Concerning the International Registration of Marks, the Lisbon Agreement which has already been mentioned because it belongs to both the first and second groups, the Budapest Treaty on the International Recognition of the Deposit of Microorganisms for the Purposes of Patent Procedure and the Hague Agreement Concerning the International Deposit of Industrial Designs.

3.14 The third group consists of treaties which establish classification systems and procedures for improving them and keeping them up to date. Four treaties, all dealing with industrial property, fall into this group. They are the International Patent Classification Agreement (IPC), the Nice Agreement Concerning the International Classification of Goods and Services for the Purposes of the Registration of Marks, the Vienna Agreement Establishing an International Classification of the Figurative Elements of Marks and the Locarno Agreement Establishing an International Classification for Industrial Designs.

3.15 Revising these treaties and establishing new ones are tasks which require a constant effort of international cooperation and negotiation, supported by a specialized secretariat. WIPO provides the framework and the services for this work.

(c) Functions

3.16 The activities of WIPO are basically of three kinds: registration activities, the promotion of intergovernmental cooperation in the administration of intellectual property, and substantive or program activities. All these activities serve the overall objectives of WIPO, to maintain and increase respect for intellectual property throughout the world, in order to favor industrial and cultural development by stimulating creative activity and facilitating the transfer of technology and the dissemination of literary and artistic works.

3.17 The registration activities of WIPO involve direct services to applicants for, or owners of, industrial property rights. These activities concern the receiving and processing of international applications under the Patent Cooperation Treaty or for the international registration of marks or deposit of industrial designs. Such activities are financed normally from the fees paid by the applicants, which account for about three-fourths of the budget of WIPO.

3.18 The main activities in intergovernmental cooperation in the administration of intellectual property are concerned with the management of collections of patent documents used for search and reference, and devising means for making access to the information which they contain easier; the maintenance and updating of international classification systems; the compilation of more and more sophisticated statistics; regional surveys of industrial property and copyright law administration.

3.19 WIPO maintains comprehensive collections of industrial property and copyright laws, which are available to the public, and are published in WIPO's monthly publications and on the CD-ROM called "IPLEX."

3.20 The substantive or program activities of WIPO, which constitute the major part of its activities, include promoting the wider acceptance of existing treaties, updating—where necessary—such treaties through their revision, concluding new treaties, and organizing and participating in development cooperation activities.

(d) Administration

3.21 The Convention establishing WIPO provides for four different organs: the General Assembly; the Conference; the Coordination Committee; and the International Bureau of WIPO (or Secretariat).

3.22 The General Assembly is the supreme organ of WIPO. Among its other powers and functions, the General Assembly appoints the Director General upon nomination by the Coordination Committee; it reviews and approves the reports and activities of the Coordination Committee as well as the reports of the Director General concerning WIPO; it adopts the financial regulations of WIPO and the biennial budget of expenses common to the Unions; it approves the measures proposed by the Director General concerning the administration of the international agreements designed to promote the protection of intellectual property; it determines the working languages of the Secretariat taking into consideration the practice of the United Nations; and it also determines which States not members of WIPO and which intergovernmental and international non-governmental organizations shall be admitted to its meetings as observers.

3.23 The General Assembly consists of all the States which are members of WIPO and are also members of any of the Unions.

3.24 Unlike the General Assembly, the Conference consists of all the States which are members of WIPO whether or not they are members of any of the Unions. The main functions of the Conference could be divided into five groups. First, the Conference constitutes a forum for exchanges of views, between all States members of WIPO, on matters relating to intellectual property, and, in this context, the Conference can, in particular, make any recommendations on such matters, having regard to the competence and autonomy of the Unions. Secondly, the Conference is the body that establishes the biennial development cooperation program for developing countries and, thirdly, adopts a budget for that purpose. Fourth, the Conference is also competent to adopt amendments to the Convention establishing WIPO. Proposals for the amendment of the Convention may be initiated by any State member of WIPO, by the Coordination Committee or by the Director General. Fifth, the Conference, like the General Assembly, can determine which States and organizations will be admitted to its meetings as observers.

3.25 The Coordination Committee is both an advisory organ on questions of general interest and the executive organ of the General Assembly and the Conference. The Coordination Committee gives advice to the various organs of the Unions and WIPO on matters of common interest to two or more of the Unions or to one or more of the Unions and WIPO itself, in particular regarding the budget of expenses common to the Unions. The Coordination Committee also prepares the draft agenda of the General Assembly and of the Conference, as well as the draft program and budget of the Conference.

3.26 The fourth organ of WIPO is the International Bureau of WIPO or Secretariat. It is headed by the Director General, and, at the present time, its permanent staff comprises some 450 persons, from nearly 60 different countries, recruited according to the principle of equitable geographical distribution established in the United Nations system.

(e) Membership

3.27 The Convention establishing WIPO declares that membership shall be open to any State which is a member of any of the Unions, and to any State which is not a member of any of the Unions, provided that it is a member of the United Nations, any of the specialized agencies of the United Nations, or the International Atomic Energy Agency, or is a party to the Statute of the International Court of Justice or is invited by the General Assembly of WIPO to become a member. Thus, only States can be members of WIPO or, indeed, of any other specialized agency of the United Nations.

3.28 To become a member, a State must deposit an instrument of ratification or accession with the Director General of WIPO at Geneva. States party to the Paris or Berne Conventions may become members of WIPO only if they are already bound by, or concurrently ratify or accede to, at least the administrative provisions of the Stockholm (1967) Act of the Paris Convention or of the Paris (1971) Act of the Berne Convention.

3.29 One hundred and fifty seven States were party to the Convention Establishing the World Intellectual Property Organization (WIPO) as of October 1, 1996: Albania, Algeria, Andorra, Angola, Argentina, Armenia, Australia, Austria, Azerbaijan, Bahamas, Bahrain, Bangladesh, Barbados, Belarus, Belgium, Benin, Bhutan, Bolivia, Bosnia and Herzegovina, Brazil, Brunei Darussalam, Bulgaria, Burkina Faso, Burundi, Cambodia, Cameroon, Canada, Central African Republic, Chad, Chile, China, Colombia, Congo, Costa Rica, Côte d'Ivoire, Croatia, Cuba, Cyprus, Czech Republic, Democratic People's Republic of Korea, Denmark, Ecuador, Egypt, El Salvador, Estonia, Fiji, Finland, France, Gabon, Gambia, Georgia, Germany, Ghana, Greece, Guatemala, Guinea, Guinea-Bissau, Guyana, Haiti, Holy See, Honduras, Hungary, Iceland, India, Indonesia, Iraq, Ireland, Israel, Italy, Jamaica, Japan, Jordan, Kazakstan, Kenya, Kyrgyzstan, Laos, Latvia, Lebanon, Lesotho, Liberia, Libya, Liechtenstein, Lithuania, Luxembourg, Madagascar, Malawi, Malaysia, Mali, Malta, Mauritania, Mauritius, Mexico, Monaco, Mongolia, Morocco, Namibia, Netherlands, New Zealand, Nicaragua, Niger, Nigeria, Norway, Pakistan, Panama, Paraguay, Peru, Philippines, Poland, Portugal, Qatar, Republic of Korea, Republic of Moldova, Romania, Russian Federation, Rwanda, Saint Kitts and Nevis, Saint Lucia, Saint Vincent and the Grenadines, San Marino, Saudi Arabia, Senegal, Sierra Leone, Singapore, Slovakia, Slovenia, Somalia, South Africa, Spain, Sri Lanka, Sudan, Suriname, Swaziland, Sweden, Switzerland, Tajikistan, Thailand, The former Yugoslav Republic of Macedonia, Togo, Trinidad and Tobago, Tunisia, Turkey, Turkmenistan, Uganda, Ukraine, United Arab Emirates, United Kingdom, United Republic of Tanzania, United States of America, Uruguay, Uzbekistan, Venezuela, Viet Nam, Yemen, Yugoslavia, Zaire, Zambia and Zimbabwe.

B. THE DEVELOPMENT COOPERATION PROGRAMS OF WIPO

(a) Objectives

3.30 A very important sphere of WIPO's activities concerns assistance in the development of developing countries. "Development cooperation" is the expression used in the United Nations system to describe what used to be called "aid" or "assistance to developing countries" or "legal-technical assistance". What is WIPO's principal aim in this field? It is to promote respect for intellectual property inside each developing country and in the international relations of that country, because experience shows that national creativity in the

References for Section A
International Bureau of WIPO, *Introduction to WIPO: Objectives, Organizational Structure and Activities; Development Cooperation Program*, WIPO/ACAD/E/94/2
International Bureau of WIPO, *The Organization, Functions and Activities of the World Intellectual Property Organization*, WIPO/IP/SUV/93/3(a)
International Bureau of WIPO, *WIPO, What it is and What it Does*, TMP/KL/4
International Bureau of WIPO, *General Information*, WIPO/400(E) (1994)

field of technical inventiveness and in the literary and artistic field is considerably enhanced and, in fact, is really only possible if it is accompanied by the protection of inventors and the authors of literary or artistic works, and if such protection extends to investors who are ready to invest in creativity.

3.31 The main aim of the development cooperation program is to make a special contribution to the development process within the developing countries in the field of intellectual property, thereby calling for a whole range of multiple activities. There are indeed enormous differences between the various developing countries as regards their degree of industrialization and their productivity in the fields of technical inventiveness and literary and artistic creativity. Many of them lack specialists in the field of intellectual property. Many of them also have a need for national laws better suited to their development objectives. Those that have not as yet enacted new legislation since their independence still apply provisions which are not suited to their real needs and are outmoded. Finally, a large number of them have need of a national infrastructure enabling the laws to be administered more efficiently and permitting greater exploitation of the possibilities that improved laws and improved infrastructures could offer them for their industrialization as well as their cultural expansion.

3.32 The main objectives of WIPO's development cooperation program are to assist developing countries in the establishment or modernization of intellectual property systems suited to their development goals through developing human resources; to facilitate the creation or improvement of national or regional legislation (embodying internationally acceptable standards and principles) and their effective enforcement; to encourage domestic inventive and creative artistic activity and the exploitation of its results; to facilitate the development of indigenous technologies and the acquisition of foreign patented technology; to facilitate access to foreign works protected by copyright; to facilitate access to and the use of technological information contained in patent documents; to promote the exchange of experience and information among legislators in the field of intellectual property; to promote the exchange of experience and information among members of the judiciary concerning the enforcement of the protection of intellectual property; and to facilitate the management and exploitation by local enterprises of their intellectual property rights.

3.33 The WIPO Program and Budget for the 1994-95 Biennium sets out the following objectives for assisting developing countries in the establishment or modernization of intellectual property systems suited to their development goals:

(1) developing human resources;
(2) facilitating the creation or improvement of national or regional legislation and its effective enforcement;
(3) encouraging adherence to WIPO-administered treaties;
(4) facilitating the creation or improvement of governmental and other institutions for the administration and effective implementation of national or regional legislation;
(5) encouraging local inventive activity and the commercial exploitation of inventions, and encouraging local creative artistic activity and the exploitation of its results;

(6) developing the teaching of and research in intellectual property law, with particular emphasis on the use of that law for economic development;
(7) developing the profession of intellectual property lawyer and agent;
(8) promoting the exchange of experience and information among legislators in the field of intellectual property;
(9) promoting the exchange of experience and information among members of the judiciary concerning the enforcement of the protection of intellectual property;
(10) facilitating access to and use of technological information contained in patent documents, especially for diversification and accumulation of technology;
(11) facilitating the acquisition of foreign, but locally protected, technology through licensing contracts;
(12) facilitating the management and exploitation by local enterprises of their intellectual property rights;
(13) consulting the two Permanent Committees for Development Cooperation;
(14) facilitating participation in certain WIPO meetings.

3.34 In order to carry out activities to fulfill these aims, WIPO has set up permanent programs specifically designed to organize technical assistance to developing countries.

3.35 Each Permanent Program is directed by a Permanent Committee that reviews the progress made under the Permanent Program and discusses activities to be proposed to the Member States for the following year or years. The Permanent Committee meets every two years. In addition, a Working Group also meets every two years in the year in which the Permanent Committee does not meet.

3.36 The Permanent Committee consists of all States members of WIPO which have informed the Director General of their desire to be members of this Committee; on October 1, 1996, 121 countries were members of the Permanent Committee for Development Cooperation Related to Industrial Property, and 108 were members of the Permanent Committee for Development Cooperation Related to Copyright and Neighboring Rights.

(b) Development Cooperation in Relation to Industrial Property

3.37 WIPO's development cooperation activities in the field of industrial property, which are carried out within the framework of the WIPO Permanent Program for Development Cooperation Related to Industrial Property, are aimed at helping developing countries in the following respects:

(1) training of government officials and representatives of the private sector, such as lawyers and industrial property agents;
(2) providing legal advice and assistance in drafting new, or revising existing, industrial property legislation;
(3) establishing or strengthening industrial property offices and institutions;
(4) promoting indigenous innovative and inventive activities;
(5) using the technological information contained in patent documents;
(6) establishing programs for legislators and the judiciary; and
(7) promoting awareness of intellectual property protection in local enterprises.

(i)   Training

3.38 WIPO's training program consists of various regular general and specialized courses organized each year, in a number of developed and developing countries, for the collective training of government officials, and periodic seminars, workshops and other types of meetings at the national, sub-regional and regional levels in which government officials and other personnel from developing countries participate. In addition, attachments to industrial property offices and institutions in developed or developing countries for practical training are often organized for government officials, as well as observation visits to such offices for middle and senior level officials. WIPO also organizes on-the-job training in some countries by international experts. Practical training attachments abroad and on-the-spot training at home usually involve very specific tasks, such as state-of-the-art searching, examination of trademarks and patents, etc.

3.39 In recent years, training programs have been extended to new categories of beneficiaries, in addition to the government officials working in the national industrial property administration. The training program is open for private lawyers and practitioners, staff of R&D institutions and enterprises, representatives of the judiciary, ministries of trade and foreign affairs and other persons dealing with questions related to industrial property matters.

3.40 The aim of the training activities is to enable government officials and other personnel from developing countries to acquire knowledge and practice in the various aspects of industrial property so that they may effectively organize and administer the industrial property system of their own countries. Training activities occupy a preeminent place within WIPO's development cooperation program because laws and institutions, however good they may be, are of little use without qualified staff to administer them.

(ii)   Legal Advice and Assistance

3.41 In recent years, there have been many instances of a growing interest, on the part of governments of developing countries in various parts of the world, in making industrial property an effective tool in the economic and technology development process. The existence of an industrial property law suited to the needs of the country concerned is a precondition of an effective industrial property system.

3.42 For this reason, WIPO has received many requests for advice in drafting industrial property laws where they do not exist, and in revising existing laws which are inadequate for the country's economic needs and priorities.

3.43 At the request of a government, WIPO comments on draft legislation prepared by the government or prepares draft legislation with due regard to the wishes of the government and the needs of the country concerned. These wishes and needs would have been ascertained through consultations and surveys made on the spot by WIPO experts. The draft texts are then submitted to the authorities for study and comment. What follows is often an exchange of letters and visits between the authorities and WIPO experts to clarify and improve the texts.

3.44 In addition, WIPO has produced several model laws or guides for developing countries dealing with such subjects as patents, trademarks, industrial designs and industrial property licensing.

(iii)   Establishment or Strengthening of Industrial Property Institutions

3.45 A law is not an end in itself for the country concerned. It provides an important framework within which its industrial property system will function. The law must be administered and used, and for that purpose suitable administrative machinery and procedures are required.

3.46 Here again, WIPO has considerable expertise to offer to governments and institutions. WIPO experts are sent to countries, at their request, in order to give on-the-spot advice, on such matters as the establishment or streamlining of procedures, preparation of organigrams, acquisition of appropriate equipment, acquisition of the required documentation, establishment of linkages with external institutions, assessment of staff requirements and training needs, utilization of office space, and the determination of suitable fee (revenue) schedules. WIPO has sent many expert missions to countries to provide help and advice along such lines.

3.47 Often, such administrative improvements and changes are planned, for implementation over a period of time, by WIPO in consultation with the authorities concerned, depending on priorities and available resources.

3.48 For an industrial property administration system to be useful, it must serve the public. In many countries, the industrial property system has not been used to full advantage partly because the public, including business circles, are unaware of the advantages the system has to offer, and its role in the development process, for example, the role and functions of trademarks and patents, why they should be protected, and so on. WIPO therefore organizes seminars which aim at building, to start with, awareness of industrial property by answering such basic questions as what is industrial property, what are its constituent elements, how does industrial property help trade and technological development, and in what way do trademarks help consumers, what is a patent and why should inventions be protected.

(iv)   Promotion of Indigenous Innovation and Inventiveness

3.49 As observed earlier, the role that the industrial property system can play in technological and economic development has long been recognized in developed countries and is now being recognized in an increasing number of developing countries as well. The protection afforded by industrial property laws, especially patent and utility model laws, results in more innovations and inventions, more investment and effort in research and development (R and D), leading to technological improvements and thereby to improvement in the quality of industrial output.

3.50 Without a national industrial property system and, more particularly, a patent system, it will be difficult for a country to stimulate and protect the results of indigenous innovation. Once a national industrial property system is established, however, governments can, with the help of WIPO experts, if they so wish, devise ways and means of encouraging local entrepreneurs and enterprises to evolve their own innovations and inventions as well as to adapt imported technology and know-how. WIPO also assists in the creation of national associations of inventors. Legal advice on patenting, financial support and incentives, public recognition of inventors, award of prizes through competitions, etc. are measures that governments are encouraged to adopt. Through mass participation in nation-wide inventors competitions, and in invention clubs in schools, public consciousness and use of the patent system is stimulated and ensured. Since the late seventies, WIPO has established an award scheme (a WIPO gold medal and certificate) for inventors and innovators that is widely used by developing countries to encourage inventive activity.

(v) Use of Patent Information

3.51 One of the activities of WIPO in assisting the development process in developing countries is directed at improving access by those countries to the technological information contained in patent documents. The usefulness of patent documents as sources of technological information is widely acknowledged in the industrialized countries. The principal aim of WIPO's assistance to developing countries in this area is to improve their access to technological information contained in patent documents by the provision of the necessary patent documentation and training in methods of retrieval and dissemination.

3.52 The WIPO Program for Patent Information and Documentation Services began in 1975. Its aim is to provide free-of-charge patent information services to institutions in developing countries under agreements concluded between the International Bureau of WIPO and contributing industrial property offices in industrialized countries.

3.53 WIPO gives assistance and advice, and is the executing agency for several UNDP projects, concerning the planning and establishment of patent information and documentation centers which serve the needs of national or regional institutions in developing countries. Such centers may be created within an existing or planned industrial property office, or within a scientific and technological information center.

3.54 The assistance and advice is given following a request addressed to WIPO by the competent authorities concerned. The form of the assistance offered depends upon the circumstances prevailing in the developing country or region, and includes a preliminary written assessment of the needs, addressed to the competent authorities, and the organization of a detailed fact-finding mission to the developing country or region by officials of WIPO and/or outside consultants. If the recommendations made to the competent authorities are accepted by them, WIPO can assist in their implementation.

(vi) Programs for Legislators and the Judiciary

3.55 WIPO cooperates in promoting the exchange of experience and other information among legislators so that they are better prepared to consider the needs, and find solutions to such needs, of their own countries when engaged in the adaptation of their intellectual property legislations to the changing economic and technological situation on the domestic level and in international relations. This cooperation may take the form of national and regional seminars and study trips.

3.56 In addition, WIPO works to promote the exchange of experience and information among members of the judicial branch (judges of courts of all levels) so that they are better prepared to interpret and apply domestic laws and international treaties in the field of intellectual property law and to order measures that would prevent the continuation of infringement of intellectual property rights. Such cooperation may take the form of national and regional seminars, simulated trials and study trips.

(vii) Local Enterprises

3.57 WIPO also cooperates in promoting awareness, in local enterprises, of the importance of having their inventions patented, their trademarks registered and their industrial designs deposited, in their own country, in other countries or with international organizations. It will give advice on how to obtain protection in the most expeditious and cost effective way, and on how to exploit their industrial property rights. Such cooperation may take the form of seminars and, at the request of any government, the preparation of case-studies and guidelines on the establishment of industrial property departments or focal points in selected enterprises.

(c) Development Cooperation in Relation to Copyright and Neighboring Rights

3.58 Within the framework of its Permanent Program for Development Cooperation Related to Copyright and Neighboring Rights, and at the request of governments of developing countries and regional organizations, WIPO has undertaken the training of specialists, and has been providing advice and assistance to national authorities in connection with preparation of legislation or updating of legislative texts, and the establishment or strengthening of national or regional institutions concerning copyright and neighboring rights.

3.59 It is generally accepted that without the necessary laws, the necessary infrastructure to implement them and, most importantly, the necessary knowledge and skills, it is not possible for a newly developing country to stimulate its scholarship, research or cultural development. Without the establishment and strengthening of the necessary infrastructure in developing countries, the cultural exchange and mutual protection of intellectual values between them and the developed countries can also not be enhanced. Laws cannot be implemented and institutions cannot exist without skilled personnel and, therefore, WIPO has been giving its training programs the priority they deserve.

3.60 The general objectives of the development cooperation with developing countries are to assist those countries in the establishment or modernization of intellectual property systems suited to their development goals, in particular in the following ways:

(1) developing human resources;
(2) facilitating the creation or improvement of national or regional legislation and its effective enforcement;
(3) encouraging adherence to WIPO-administered treaties;
(4) facilitating the creation or improvement of governmental and other institutions for the administration and effective implementation of national or regional legislation;
(5) encouraging local creative artistic activity and the exploitation of its results;

(6) developing the teaching of law relating to copyright and neighboring rights;
(7) developing the profession of copyright lawyer;
(8) promoting the exchange of experience and information among legislators in the field of copyright and neighboring rights;
(9) promoting the exchange of experience among members of the judiciary concerning the enforcement of the protection of copyright and neighboring rights.

3.61 The activities carried out under the Permanent Program are the following: (i) training courses, (ii) information meetings and seminars, (iii) drafting of model laws specially designed for the developing countries concerning copyright and neighboring rights, (iv) assistance in the setting up and modernization of institutions responsible for administering copyright and neighboring rights, and (v) publication of guides, manuals and glossaries.

(i) Training

3.62 Training under the WIPO training program is designed to instruct and inform officials from developing countries in the field of copyright and neighboring rights, with the main purpose of assisting those countries in having specialized staff necessary for the efficient functioning of the national copyright and neighboring rights administration. The training program comprises (a) training afforded to officials who are or would be responsible for the administration of copyright; this is more in the nature of refresher or specialization courses; and (b) a general introductory course to afford basic training.

3.63 In recent years, training programs have been extended to new categories of officials in addition to the representatives of national copyright administrations and collective administration, the scope of human resources development programs will include also representatives of the judiciary, the enforcement of agencies, such as police, customs and the ministries of foreign affairs, ministries of trade and diplomatic staff involved with questions related to copyright and neighboring rights matters.

3.64 It is also desirable that the teaching of intellectual property law should be developed in a number of universities in developing countries. The International Bureau has already awarded fellowships for this purpose to university teachers from developing countries to enable such personnel to examine the course and curriculum content in order to introduce or strengthen teaching at the university level. This means a more intensive involvement for training of "trainers."

3.65 WIPO provides specialized meetings, seminars and regional courses to provide participants with information concerning different aspects of the protection of copyright and neighboring rights, with special regard to the actual needs to be complied with as well as the development of relevant legislation and its implementation in the countries concerned. They are of a very varied nature and deal with differing subjects; some concern subjects related to the WIPO program of activities, others are general information meetings and seminars on copyright and/or neighboring rights.

3.66 In the first decade of development cooperation activities of the Permanent Program in the field of copyright and neighboring rights, over fifty courses and regional, subregional or national meetings have been organized, primarily designed to increase the awareness of copyright and neighboring rights, their role in development, the impact of new technologies and the desirability of increased multilateral cooperation in these areas. The above-mentioned courses and meetings have been attended by more than 3,000 participants from nearly 100 developing countries.

3.67 Special attention is being given to training in questions of patent information for officials of developing countries. Such training takes three different forms. First, specialized group training courses lasting between two to four weeks are organized each year at industrial property offices in industrialized countries and at the European Patent Office. Second, individual training is offered at the industrial property offices of some industrialized, and some developing, countries. Third, WIPO organizes, on a country or regional basis, seminars on patent information in developing countries.

(ii) Legislative Assistance

3.68 Legal assistance is provided by the International Bureau in two forms: the drafting of model laws and assistance in the drafting of national legislation. The International Bureau has already drawn up a number of model laws for the use of the developing countries. These texts are prepared by meetings of experts from developing countries and developed countries, working on the basis of drafts prepared by the International Bureau and, in all cases, submitted for their comments to the States and subsequently adopted by meetings of governmental experts.

3.69 In the field of copyright and neighboring rights at the moment there exists the Model Law on Neighboring Rights (Rome Convention), published in 1974. The following have also been discussed and finalized:

(1) model provisions for the implementation of the Satellites Convention;
(2) guiding principles covering the problems posed by the practical implementation of the licensing procedures for translation and reproduction under the copyright conventions;
(3) model provisions for the protection of expressions of folklore, as a result of the work of a Committee of Governmental Experts.

3.70 As part of this legal assistance, meetings are held in Geneva or in the country concerned between officials responsible for drafting national legislation and officials of WIPO. In addition, WIPO provides comments on draft laws submitted to it by countries before these are finalized.

(iii) Institutional Assistance

3.71 WIPO also provides technical assistance for all developing countries members of the United Nations in the setting up or reorganization of their administrative structures for copyright.

3.72 The cornerstone of a copyright system is a well-established and widely respected copyright organization which undertakes safeguarding of the rights and interests of authors, the collection and distribution of their royalties, and which can contribute also to the promotion of education and culture, as well as assist in the participation in international cultural exchange.

3.73 In 1986, WIPO organized an International Forum on the Collective Administration of Copyrights and Neighboring Rights in Geneva, which allowed a very useful exchange of information and views within the framework of the Berne Convention, particularly between representatives of governments, intergovernmental and non-governmental organizations. Among the latter were leading federations and other organizations representing authors, performers, publishers, film makers, television and radio broadcasters and phonogram producers. The participants at the Forum considered it desirable, *inter alia*, that WIPO continue to pay particular attention to rendering assistance in the setting up or strengthening of collective administration systems in developing countries.

3.74 In the framework of strengthening and modernizing of institutions for the collective administration of authors' rights, WIPO has undertaken a program of assistance in coordination with the International Confederation of Societies of Authors and Composers (CISAC) and the Swiss Society for Authors' Rights in Musical Works (SUISA) to provide small and medium authors' societies of developing countries with the standard software "COSIS" (Copyright Societies Information System). In August 1992, the authors' society of Burkina Faso was the first one to be equipped with such software. The program of WIPO's assistance provides for the equipment of authors' societies of developing countries with a computerized system, including COSIS, and particular attention has been given, towards this aim, to the training of specialists who would thereafter train local staff of authors' societies concerned.

3.75 In all these activities under the Development Cooperation Program it is kept in mind that the developing countries face the challenge of economic development with limited economic resources. Likewise the priorities given to education, the shortage of trained personnel and resources required on the one hand, and during an interim period, easier access to works of foreign origin, in particular in the scientific and technological fields, and on the other, in the long term the need to develop indigenous creativity and authorship, are essential for improvement of educational standards which are the very basis of the developmental process. So is the need for an effective copyright system to nurture national intellectual creativity in order to sustain the developmental process itself. Again in order to assist in the developmental process in developing countries, national laws on copyright, established by independent national governments, in step with the character of the people, and the national, social, economic and political structure, are essential for encouraging intellectual creativity.

(iv) Publications

3.76 The International Bureau publishes surveys, guides, glossaries and/or manuals to facilitate the understanding of intellectual property, and of its Conventions. Mention in this connection may be made of the following:

(1) Guide to the Rome Convention and to the Phonograms Convention, published in several languages;
(2) a Glossary of terms used in copyright and neighboring rights legislation was published in 1980 in three languages (English/French/Spanish) and subsequently in English/French/Arabic; English/French/Russian;

English/French/Portuguese; and English/French/Japanese; that Glossary is under revision;

(3) a collection of texts of copyright and neighboring rights laws and regulations is being kept by the International Bureau, including texts on the CD-ROM product "IPLEX."

(d) The WIPO Academy of Intellectual Property

3.77 In the framework of its training program for developing countries, WIPO, in 1993, began offering an Academy of Intellectual Property, held at its headquarters in Geneva. The sessions of the WIPO Academy are held in different languages, currently English, French and Spanish (with other languages to be added in the future). Each session lasts two weeks, and involves a program of lectures, discussions and field trips. Each year two or three Academy sessions will be offered to the attention of senior level government officials of developing countries who are instrumental in policy formulation or implementation in their respective countries.

3.78 The objective of the Academy is to present to the participants the main elements and current issues in the field of intellectual property, focusing on the policy considerations behind them. This approach is intended to enable the participants, after returning to their respective countries, to become active in the formulation of government policies on intellectual property questions, particularly the impact of those questions on cultural, social, technological and economic development.

3.79 The participants in the Academy are typically middle or senior level government officials who, in the field of intellectual property, are instrumental in the policy-making process of their countries.

3.80 The lectures are delivered by outstanding outside specialists from industrialized and developing countries, and by WIPO officials. A Course Coordinator, experienced in teaching of intellectual property subjects, is assigned to each session to stimulate interactions and exchange of experience among the participants and between the participants and the lecturers.

References for Section B
International Bureau of WIPO, *WIPO and its Program of Development Cooperation in the Field of Copyright and Neighboring Rights*, WIPO/CR/GE/93/7
International Bureau of WIPO, *WIPO and International Cooperation in Relation to Patents*, WIPO/PA/CB/86/5
International Bureau of WIPO, *Review and Evaluation of Activities Under the Permanent Program Since the Last Session of the Permanent Committee (November 1992); Main Orientations for the Permanent Program in 1994 and 1995*, PC/IP/XVI/2
The Director General of WIPO, *Draft Program and Budget for the 1994-95 Biennium; Plan for the Medium Term of 1996 to 1999*, AB/XXIV/2

PART II

The Role of Intellectual Property in Promoting Economic and Technological Development

CHAPTER 4

The Effect of Intellectual Property Protection on Economic and Technological Development

A. DEVELOPMENT OBJECTIVES OF DEVELOPING COUNTRIES

4.1 The development objectives of a developing country are aimed at the solution of its specific problems. These problems have been identified by governments of developing countries in various national and international fora and can also be identified by an examination of the social and economic development objectives set down by governments in developing countries. In listing some of these problems and development objectives, no order of priorities is attempted since priorities differ from country to country and from region to region.

4.2 Developing countries have set themselves the target of establishing a sound agricultural and industrial base. This includes the desire to improve agriculture and to progress towards food self-sufficiency and to stimulate commercial activity and economic growth. It also embraces the desire to establish appropriate small, medium and large scale industries in priority sectors, and to develop the manufacturing sector in order to achieve import substitution, thereby reducing the present dependence on imported products. It also includes the increased use of local raw materials as inputs in the manufacturing sector, and the promotion of exports including exports of finished products rather than only of raw materials. Since many developing countries are rich in traditional art and folklore, which is often the basis of interesting and unique creations of local craftsmanship and textile designing, they aim at encouraging and gaining the maximum economic benefit from such indigenous creations.

4.3 As regards rural development, developing countries are determined to take measures aimed at improving the general infrastructure in rural areas, providing better living conditions and improved amenities for the rural population and the development of low cost technology, including agricultural technology, suitable for rural areas.

4.4 In the science and technology sector, the objectives include the establishment and implementation of a science and technology policy aimed at ensuring the acquisition of appropriate technology, or technologies suited to local conditions, on fair and reasonable terms, the unpackaging and adaptation of foreign technologies, the promotion and development of indigenous technologies and of the indigenous innovative capacity and the upgrading of technology in the informal production sector (e.g., handicraft and village industry). With regard to energy, developing countries place emphasis on the need to develop new and renewable sources. Similarly, other objectives for the improvement of existing infrastructures have been set in the areas of health, housing, communications, and the development of human resources.

4.5   In most developing countries there exist practical problems which impede the achievement of development objectives. Such practical problems include a lack of equipment, infrastructure and amenities which are taken for granted in developed countries. Fortunately, these practical problems are being tackled and substantial progress has been made in many such countries.

B. INDUSTRIAL PROPERTY AND DEVELOPMENT

(a) The Definition of Technology

4.6   Technology has been defined as systematic knowledge for the manufacture of a product, or the rendering of a service in industry, agriculture or commerce, whether that knowledge be reflected in an invention, a utility model, an industrial design, a plant variety, or in technical information in the form of documentation, or in skills or experience of experts, for the design, installation, operation or maintenance of an industrial plant or its equipment or for the management of an industrial or commercial enterprise or its activities.

4.7   It should be noted that, in this definition, technology consists of knowledge. But not all knowledge is included. It must be knowledge that is systematic, that can be communicated, that can be applied to meet a problem or a need that arises in a particular kind of human activity in industry, agriculture or commerce. There are thus three criteria in this definition of technology.

4.8   First, the knowledge must be systematic. By systematic is meant organized with a view to its providing a solution to a problem.

4.9   Second, the knowledge must exist in some place, as in a writing or in the mind of a person, and it must be disclosed or be capable of being disclosed and thus communicated or communicable by one person to another in some way.

4.10   Third, the knowledge must be directed to an end, that is, to serve a useful purpose in industry, agriculture or commerce.

4.11   In this respect, it may be knowledge which will be used to manufacture a product, as for example, a television set, or to make the picture tube that is one part of the set, or to manufacture a machine, as for example, a machine that will make the bolts or nuts that will be needed to fasten the base of the picture tube to the frame of the television set.

4.12   The knowledge may be used in the application of a process, as for example, the process for annealing or coating the wire that will be needed to connect the picture tube to other parts of the television set.

References for Section A
International Bureau of WIPO, *The Role of Industrial Property in Economic Development*, WIPO/IP/ACC/86/5

4.13 It may be knowledge that can be used in the extraction of natural resources from the earth, as for example, the mining of iron ore or coal, or the exploration and drilling for oil, or from the sea, as for example, the drawing of salt from water, or in preventing pollution of the air.

4.14 It may be knowledge that is useful in planting seeds, as for example, what kind and what amount of fertilizer, or in the growing of plants, as for example, the kind and amount of insecticide, or in the harvesting of a crop, such as when and with what mechanical means.

4.15 It may be knowledge which is useful in the operation of a machine or in its maintenance. It may be knowledge which is helpful in packaging the product that is manufactured or the crop that is grown. It may be knowledge which explains the advantages of the product or crop to its user or consumer and thus helps to promote its sale.

4.16 An invention is an example of systematic knowledge, that is, knowledge organized with a view to giving a solution to a technical problem.

4.17 In the case of the patented invention, the solution to the problem is described in a written form. That written form is the patent document issued and published by the government authorities. That document also confers the exclusive rights to the solution upon its owner. The document also constitutes the means by which the description of the solution can be communicated to others. The utility model certificate and the specimen or photographic or other graphic representation of an industrial design for which a patent is granted or which, under some laws, is registered, serves a similar function. Such an invention, utility model or industrial design is thus specific technology which is described and disclosed in a particular way and form.

(b) Inventions, Technology and Development

4.18 Inventiveness and creativity are features which have favored the differentiation of mankind in the course of evolution from all other living species. The capacity to put these features to productive use continues to be of fundamental importance within the social and economic structures of human society. Indeed, the survival of any enterprise, organization, or even nation, may be said to depend essentially on its capacity to keep pace with development and progress.

4.19 Inventions and innovations are the most important and specific and least predictable of the intellectual creations of man, but they make development and progress possible.

4.20 Inventions and innovations are the logical results of the combined effects of wants and accumulated knowledge. In the past the opinion prevailed that invention and innovation were spontaneous events initiated and created by an endowed individual who experienced a flash of inspiration. Today, it has become more and more apparent, however, that invention and innovation may be provoked or stimulated.

4.21 Experience has shown that national creativeness can considerably contribute to technological progress only if it is matched by a legal security and protection for inventors, innovators and those who have invested in invention and innovation.

4.22 One of the major institutions which contributes to the stimulation of invention and innovation is the industrial property system. In the family of UN organizations, the World Intellectual Property Organization (WIPO) has a mandate to encourage creativity, inventiveness and respect for intellectual property all over the world.

(i) Invention, Innovation and Economic Progress

4.23 Economic progress requires a constant stream of new ideas and products in order to improve conditions of life and efficiency of production. New products and processes are equally important to the regeneration or replacement of declining industries, and thus to the full utilization of the productive sectors of an economy.

4.24 The most widely used measure of economic progress (whether for a country or for an individual enterprise) is productivity, i.e. output per unit of input. While productivity is dependent on a wide variety of economic and social factors, technological innovation is widely held to be the single most important contributor to improvements in productivity. Technological innovation can lead to more effective use of labor, capital and natural resources, thus enabling an enterprise to produce the same amount of output with less of input.

4.25 The principal significance of improved productivity is, of course, that it facilitates economic growth. If less inputs are required to produce the same amount of output, the resources which are liberated by the use of a more efficient process may be put to other productive uses, thus allowing overall expansion of output and economic growth to occur.

4.26 Given the contribution of innovation to improved productivity and economic growth, it is hardly surprising that the promotion of inventive and innovative activity constitutes an important part of the development process in most countries, whether developed or developing, which have the ambition to benefit from technological and economic progress.

4.27 Within the context of the general policy of promoting innovation, the creation of inventions and other technological innovations (including the adaptation of existing technology) by a country within its own territory and through its own nationals assumes particular importance. Indigenous inventiveness is an indispensable element of economic self-reliance. A pool of talent to facilitate such indigenous inventiveness exists in every nation. What is needed is a means of harnessing this pool of talent which encourages the use of all inventive talent and all forms of new technological innovation without discrimination—in other words, regardless of whether the innovation in question is a simple gadget for daily use, a sophisticated invention using high technology, or a new technical solution capable of use by a particular enterprise or an entire industry.

4.28 During the last 10–20 years, in many countries, increasing attention has been paid to the encouragement of creativity and inventiveness not only in big enterprises, but also among small and medium-sized business and individual inventors. Those who have recognized that innovative thinking is of crucial importance for successfully effecting social and technological change, have opened the door to new technological, managerial and social approaches to master the new economic circumstances.

(ii) Evolution of Innovation Policy

4.29 The relationship between invention and innovation (as important elements of the more common terms "science and technology") and economic development has been particularly underlined in the past two decades during which in both developing and industrialized countries innovation has become a priority policy objective. In developing countries, scientific and technological development has been advocated and put in hand as an explicit and indispensable component of accelerated development policies.

4.30 The approach of governments towards promoting inventive and innovative activity has undergone a historical evolution. In the early years of industrialization, in the 18th and 19th centuries, when the classical patent protection was introduced, the granting of exclusive patent rights was considered by economists such as Adam Smith, David Ricardo and John Stuart Mill as "the best and most efficient form of promotion of invention by the State." Not only because that did not imply any cost to the State, but mainly because the remuneration and reward of the inventor depended exclusively on private initiative and the market success of the invention, a fact that was completely in line with the classical economic theory and practice.

4.31 Scientific research and discovery in those years, using very modest means, did not need special governmental support. The patent law granted inventors a special position, a monopoly on the market, but the whole innovation process, from research and development to industrial application and commercialization, was left to the free rules of the market. The only exception related to the development of inventions in the military field, where the State engaged itself more and more as from the beginning of this century.

4.32 As the world advanced further into this century, and more particularly after the Second World War, governments assumed broader involvement in the promotion of inventive and innovative activity. The role of each government in this respect has depended on the nature of the social, economic and political system prevailing in the specific country as well as on national priorities, objectives and interests. In many countries the involvement of governments in promoting inventive and innovative activities has increased significantly in recent decades, not only through the adoption of measures aimed at inducing the private sector to play a more dynamic role in that respect, but also through financing of research and development (R&D) activities and even, in some cases, through direct engagement in such activities by creating State-owned research and development centers and laboratories. At the same time, the individual inventor has given way to teams of researchers and inventors, employed by private industry and government.

4.33 Today in many countries increasing attention is being paid to the importance of technological innovation, promotion of creativity and inventiveness not only in big enterprises, but also among small and medium sized business and individual inventors in order to achieve structural change and continuing economic growth. Countries which delayed to incorporate innovation policies at different stages of industrial production were faced with a slow-down in the rate of productivity, difficulties in adapting to fluctuating prices of energy and raw material resources, weaknesses in their international competitiveness and economic stagnation. In contrast, the experience of some other countries which have been successful in the past in effecting technological change shows clearly that the present economic environment, especially as it concerns the increased cost of natural resources and basic materials, requires new technological and managerial approaches, increased inventive and innovative activity in order to master the new circumstances and enable the attainment of social and economic goals.

4.34 The options for technological change and innovation are numerous and, as further advances are made in science, so is the opening of new opportunities and possibilities to all countries. Technological innovation is becoming far more multi-disciplinary: thus, for example, technological developments in one field, such as electronics, communications and aerospace research, or in genetic engineering, may have far-reaching implications in many other fields, like agricultural production, for example. The rising trend in research costs and related investments obliges governmental authorities and private companies to make responsible choices and sound management decisions in directing science, technology and innovation policy to ensure an optimal contribution to the solution of both new and old problems.

(iii) Invention, Innovation and the Patent System

4.35 One of the important elements in the sound management of a science and technology policy based, *inter alia*, on encouraging invention and innovation is, undoubtedly, the patent system. An efficient patent system contributes to the stimulation of innovation in three main ways.

4.36 First, the existence of the patent system, with the possibility of obtaining the exclusive right to work an invention for a limited period of time, constitutes an important incentive to inventive and innovative activity. Research and development today require substantial human and material resources. If the inventions which are the fruit of R&D were not protected by the grant of patents, they would be available for exploitation by all, including those who have not invested in R&D. The inventive organization or person would, under these circumstances, be placed at a substantial competitive disadvantage, since the cost of its products would contain an element reflecting the cost of R&D, absent in the price of the products of those who have merely appropriated the invention. By allowing the inventor the exclusive use of an invention for a limited period of time, the patent system enables the inventor to exact a premium for, and thus recover, initial R&D costs, and thus acts as a stimulus to the undertaking of further research and development.

4.37 Second, the limited period of time during which the holder of a patent is entitled to the exclusive use of his invention creates an environment which facilitates the efficient development and utilization of patented inventions. It protects the inventor against uncontrolled competition from those who have not taken the initial financial risk. It thus creates conditions in which risk capital can be safely advanced for the transformation of an invention into an innovation. The inventor will be at ease to further develop the invention into a final, commercially polished, product or process that could be marketed and produce a benefit.

4.38 Third, the patent system provides the framework for the collection, classification, and dissemination of the richest store of technological information existing in the world today. In other words it contributes to the dissemination of new knowledge since the right of the inventor to the exclusive use of his invention for a limited period is not granted freely. In return for the grant of a patent, the inventor must disclose the details of his invention to society. Thus the information contained in a patent is available for research and experimental purposes (although not, of course for commercial use) by all during the term of the patent grant. After the expiration of the patent term, the information falls into the public domain and is freely available for full commercial use by all. The patent system thereby contributes to the evolution of the technological base of industry.

4.39 It should be mentioned that, while the patent system is a vital element in the stimulation of invention and innovation, many other factors in practice combine to contribute to successful innovation. External factors such as economic, technical or regulatory matters, which are beyond the control of the innovator, may affect the success or failure of the innovation.

4.40 Studies of the factors affecting technological innovation which are susceptible to management and control have shown that the great majority of successful innovation is demand-led. In other words, successful inventions usually result from identified market needs. Successful inventions are made "just-in-time", to meet a specific market demand. Innovation, by definition, must include business success, since innovation is an idea of invention that becomes business success.

(iv) Government Support for Inventive Activity

4.41 Today governmental authorities in the great majority of countries, developed or developing, demonstrate an increasing awareness of the importance of promoting inventive and innovative activity and of the role of creative individuals—inventors and innovators—in the all-round development process. A great variety of approaches, mechanisms and specific measures are being experimented and adopted in the different countries having one common aim, to foster and boost technological, economic and social progress for the benefit of their people.

4.42 It is only natural that governments support inventors, their role in the development process being essential and vital. For their inventions, be they important or modest, contribute to the birth and improvement of technology, the progress of industry and the increasing betterment of life.

4.43 Government support to inventors and inventive activity depends much on the level of development. Government support cannot be the same in a country with hardly any industry and a highly-industrialized one. The importance of the support clearly depends on the nature of the socio-economic system prevailing in any given country. The nature and level of government support will depend on political choices, based on other conditions, such as national priorities, objectives and interests.

4.44 Government policies related to technological innovation can be placed in two categories. In the first category there are those policies which are directed towards contributing to the achievement of broad socio-economic objectives and priorities and which only indirectly influence technological innovation, invention and innovative activities in particular. Typical of such policies are those aimed at furthering industrial activities, trade and regional development, or influencing domestic consumption patterns, etc. In the second category are government policies which directly relate to and influence the process of technological innovation—such as creating a favorable innovative climate, including promoting the awareness of the importance of technological innovation for industrial and economic development at all levels (schools, including specialized and technical schools, universities, industry, agriculture, public administration, etc.) and by various means (publication of books and magazines, radio and television programs and films on science and technology, technological museums, lectures and workshops, etc.).

4.45 It may further include establishing appropriate R&D facilities, including support facilities such as technological documentation centers, attaching more importance and giving recognition to national inventors and innovators, protecting and assisting them technically and financially to develop their inventions and innovations, favoring more efficient coordination between research and industry and extending assistance beyond R&D activities strictly speaking, to cover also testing of new products and processes and marketing, or directly promoting production and commercialization.

4.46 As already mentioned, the major government policy in support of inventors and inventive activity is the legal framework which it provides for the protection of the rights and interests of inventors. The protection of industrial property is the best stimulus for inventiveness because patents and utility models or certificates offer to the inventor a double incentive: material and moral; money received as contractual payment or reward, and recognition now and for posterity that something unusual, something springing from the creator's intellect, has been achieved.

4.47 However, the responsibilities of governments towards their inventors do not end with laws and treaties securing substantive protection of inventions. Their administration must be effective and not over-expensive, in order to avoid unnecessary obstacles between an inventor and his legal rights.

4.48 With regard to governmental institutions offering assistance to inventors and support to inventive activity, the situation also differs very much from country to country. In some countries, the industrial property administration is the only governmental institution engaged directly in this respect, while in other countries, in addition to the industrial property administration ministries or departments, dealing with industry, trade and economy, science and technology, could be involved in such activities. Certain countries have established special systems or structures to assist individual inventors, small enterprises and non-profit organizations in obtaining protection for their inventions and their effective management (e.g. the payment of the different kinds of fees, free consultancy services, etc.).

4.49 Some provisions contained in financial or tax laws creating favorable conditions for inventors and inventive activity could be summarized as follows:

(1) reduced taxes in respect of income stemming from licensed patents and know-how;
(2) reduced fees for acquisition and maintenance of industrial property rights by individual inventors;
(3) special loans or subsidies, including interest-free or low interest loans;

(4) grants for development of certain inventions and innovations;

(5) possibilities for concluding governmentally or publicly financed "research contracts."

4.50 In an increasing number of countries, specialized governmental institutions have been created to encourage inventive activity and also to promote the development, exploitation and to some extent the commercialization of local inventions, by providing the inventor with the relevant support.

4.51 For instance, in some countries individual inventors may get assistance and their inventions may be tested in government-owned or government-financed research and test laboratories and institutions. Usually it is done on a non-profit basis and in some cases restitution of the expenses is required if the invention has been successful on the market.

(v) Rewards and Recognition for Inventors

4.52 An important means of action by governments for promoting inventive activity is the direct encouragement of inventors by public recognition. Non-material rewards (medals, diplomas) and sometimes financial rewards are granted not only to meritorious inventors, but also to potential inventors in the framework of youth science and invention contests. In some countries such moral awards and celebrations have even been established by governmental acts.

4.53 Another important support to inventors are exhibitions of inventions in as much as they highlight the inventions and facilitate the establishment of contacts with industry. In several countries, government agencies—including in some cases the industrial property administrations—organize or participate in the organization of such promotion activities. In other countries, moral support is lended by government authorities, who accept to afford their "patronage" to exhibitions and shows organized by private entities.

4.54 Inventiveness and creativity are specific human talents, that could be developed or lost in the course of life. Education is an important factor in that process. In many countries the promotion and encouragement of inventive activity among the youth enjoys increasing attention. With a view to creating better opportunities for development of those talents as early as possible, several countries organize special exhibitions and contests for inventions made by schoolchildren, students. and young people.

(vi) Cooperation among Inventors

4.55 However important government support to inventors may be, it is necessary for the inventors themselves to realize better that they need to act collectively. They will be better heard, and their wishes will be better satisfied, if they form associations, if they are active in those associations and if their associations maintain closer relations with each other on the regional or international level.

4.56 In fact several governments have given assistance to their local inventors' association or have supported the inventors of their countries in creating such an association. Inventors' associations exist already in over 60 countries, including in over 30 developing countries. Most inventors' associations have similar objectives: in an initial stage limited to the immediate needs of inventors, those objectives have been subsequently broadened to reflect the associations' desire to contribute to the development of their countries, the ultimate aim being always, and above all, the justified satisfaction of the inventor.

4.57 At the international level the cooperation between organizations of inventors is either bilateral or in the framework of international organizations of inventors. Today there exist two international organizations of inventors: one global, IFIA (International Federation of Inventors' Associations) which today has already among its members more than 40 national associations, and one regional: the African Federation of Inventors' Associations (AFIA) which counts today associations from ten African countries among its members.

(c) Industrial Property Protection and Development

(i) Introduction

4.58 Industrial property has long been recognized and used by industrialized countries, and is being used by an ever increasing number of developing countries, as an important tool of technological and economic development. Many developing countries are aware that it is in their best interest to establish national industrial property systems, where they do not exist, and to strengthen and upgrade existing systems which, inherited from their historical past, are no longer adequately responding to new needs and priorities.

4.59 Countries have laws to protect industrial property for two main reasons, related to each other. One is to give statutory expression to the moral and economic rights of creators in their creations, and the other is to promote, as a deliberate act of government policy, creativity and the dissemination and application of its results, and to encourage fair trading: this contributes to economic and social development.

4.60 For example, the right to obtain a patent for an invention encourages the investment of money and effort in research and development; the grant of a patent encourages investment in the industrial application of the invention; the official publication of the patent adds to the world's supply of documentary sources of technological information. Trademark rights protect enterprises against unscrupulous competitors seeking to make profit out of deceiving the public.

(ii) Patents and Patent Information

4.61 An equitable and modernized patent system, by providing recognition and material benefits to the inventor, constitutes an incentive for inventiveness and innovative activity. It also creates a favorable climate for the transfer of technology by means of the security it provides for the patentee.

4.62 Patent laws require that an application for a patent for invention describe the invention with such clarity and completeness of all the technical details that anyone having ordinary skill in the art should, by merely reading the description, be able to carry out the invention, and that granted patents for invention be published. In other words, at the latest when the patent for invention is granted, the invention will be "disclosed," that is, its essence and mode of exploitation will be brought to the knowledge of anyone who cares to know.

4.63 The utilization of information available through this disclosure avoids wasteful duplication of effort and the multiplication of costs that research aimed at finding solutions to technical problems can entail; it acts as an inspiration or catalyst for further inventions and this contributes to the advance of science and technology.

4.64 From the point of view of its information aspect, the patent system is a useful aid for developing countries wishing to have access to the technological information required for their various developmental purposes. This statement takes into account the fact that the legal protection that patents enjoy is subject, *inter alia*, to a time limitation and a territorial limitation. In this respect, the patent system—where appropriately used through an adequate administrative infrastructure—benefits not only the public sector, but also the parastatal entities and the private sector. Each of these sectors can derive substantial advantages wherever patent information services operate efficiently and are integrated with other technological information schemes existing in the respective countries or regions.

4.65 Technological information based on patent documentation is of prime importance and usefulness. The functions of patent documentation include:

4.66 Since in technical literature, such as books or periodicals, patent documentation is sometimes badly neglected, any information taken exclusively from those sources may be incomplete as far as the state of development in a certain field of technology is concerned. Also there is often information contained in patent documents which is useful as an indication of the direction to be taken by the research worker on a particular technological problem. Information on the state-of-the-art as may be found in recently published patent documents, in combination with his own specific scientific knowledge, will enable the researcher either to develop subjects already known or to proceed in new directions, thus creating new and progressive technologies and products. The utilization of such information would thereby save time, money and effort by avoiding the repetition of work that has been accomplished by others elsewhere;

4.67 Patent documentation is useful for identifying alternative technologies which could replace known technology in order to provide economic or environmental benefits. For example, information may be obtained about the advantages to be gained by employing a new, essentially improved, device, by using cheaper raw materials, by using fewer manufacturing steps or parts and perhaps even by the use of by-products of existing processes that previously had been considered to be of no use. Another possibility would be that an invention described in patent literature offers a shorter or faster process and therefore offers a higher return on invested capital and also higher productivity. In any event, patent documents will identify enterprises already active in a specific field of technology and from which further information thereon could be obtained;

4.68 Another aspect is the evaluation of a specific technology which is being considered for acquisition or which is being offered for license. In this regard, a state-of-the-art search using patent documents would provide information on the different technologies available on the market, or currently being developed, and such information would allow a better evaluation and analysis of the technology which is being offered under license;

4.69 This question may arise, for example, in the planning of a new branch of a specific type of production or of the improvement of already existing procedures or processes. This could be of great importance if local instead of imported raw materials could be utilized or if by-products of an already existing process were to be processed to useful products instead of being wasted. In such cases, patent literature could give valuable information which would enable the interested party to choose the most favorable options before entering into negotiations with firms offering the technology or the complete plants for production;

4.70 A state-of-the-art search through patent documents will usually identify those solutions to a technical problem that have been proposed in the past. Patent literature will often discuss disadvantages and difficulties that can be avoided by using a particular process or design or will discuss advantages or benefits of a particular process or design.

4.71 These advantages which may be derived from the information aspect of the patent system, can be gained if such use is adequately incorporated in the administrative infrastructure of the countries concerned. In this respect it is essential that the patent system, and the patent information aspect of it, be adequately understood and accepted as a necessary component of the development efforts of the government. The awareness of the usefulness of the patent system for technological development purposes, and the existence of an adequate industrial property system providing patent information services are essential elements. Equally essential is the need to coordinate the said system and its patent information services with other branches of the government administration related to aspects of technology transfer and technological development.

4.72 In this connection, it is necessary that the development objectives of the country concerned be reflected in the patent system of that country. In particular, the administration entrusted with patent matters must have the required capabilities and the mandate for undertaking and achieving the tasks and results provided for in the patent legislation. Legislation will in many instances also be useful, if not indispensable, for the establishment of formal linkages between the different administrative branches or bodies of the government, in order that they appropriately coordinate and cooperate with each other's efforts with a view to obtaining the best results in the national interest. It may be mentioned that in many instances the inadequate utilization of the patent system in developing countries is merely a consequence of the lack of appropriate cooperation between the patent administration and the other relevant governmental bodies. The existence of appropriate linkages with the various related sectors mentioned above could ensure the effective contribution of the patent system (patent laws and patent administration) towards the development process.

(iii)   Utility Models

4.73 One of the main advantages of a patent system is the encouragement of indigenous inventiveness and the stimulation of creativity among the peoples of the country. Such encouragement and stimulation could result in a large number of inventive products some of which might not, however, meet all the stringent requirements for patentable inventions. Creativity of this kind, nevertheless, deserves reward and should be encouraged. The protection of utility models serves this purpose by providing for a type of industrial property with less stringent requirements and a relatively shorter duration in comparison with a patent.

(iv) Industrial Designs

4.74 Many developing countries are extremely rich in traditional art and folklore which stimulates creation of local craftsmanship. These creations usually fall within the ambit of the term "industrial designs". By providing recognition and material benefits to the creator of an industrial design, an effective system of protection stimulates creative activity.

(v) Trademarks

4.75 A well-selected trademark is an asset of substantial economic importance to an enterprise because it enables that enterprise to establish a market position based on the trademark. Thus, the effective protection of trademarks is an important aspect of commercial activity in any given country.

4.76 Developing countries are increasingly concerned about what consequences the advertising and promotion of marks might have on consumption patterns in their countries.

4.77 In formulating and applying industrial property policy and laws, the competent public authorities must, of course, as in any other field, take into account the particular realities of their country and the public interest at large, which, in the case of industrial property, must include the interests of consumers.

(vi) Concluding Observation

4.78 No industrial property system, however elegantly its basic laws are drafted and however efficiently they are implemented, can make an effective contribution to economic and technological development unless the system is known to, and used by, those for whose benefit it was established. An industrial property system is established to serve the needs of traders, manufacturers, industrialists, researchers, businessmen and consumers. The list of potential users and beneficiaries is inexhaustible, and the benefits to be derived from an effective use of industrial property cut across sectoral lines within an economy.

4.79 An essential task is to promote, among owners and users, as well as among potential owners and users, of industrial property, within the government and in the private sector, awareness of the nature of industrial property, and of how its main components can be developed and successfully exploited in commerce and industry to enable the industrial property system to serve better the national interest and national goals of development.

(d) Implications of Industrial Property Protection for the Management of Individual Businesses

4.80 The growth, indeed the very survival, of any company, and even of entire nations depends essentially on their ability to progress, not only in the national context but also internationally. As a result of the ever-growing pace of technological development which is the fruit of man's innovative activity, competitors are constantly launching new products and/or processes on a market in a perpetual state of progress, improvement and renewal. Any company unwilling to compete in the modern marketplace is therefore bound to stagnate gradually until the day when it becomes vulnerable to challenges from national or international competitors in what it might have once thought was its own backyard.

4.81 Industrial property rights make it possible for the creators of innovations (goods, processes, apparatus, etc.) to establish themselves more readily, to penetrate new markets with a minimum of risk, and to amortize the investments made in the research that led to the innovations in the first place. In a practical sense, these innovations become the spearhead of some of the most advanced technology. This is becoming more and more apparent in a modern world increasingly dominated by technology.

C. COPYRIGHT AND DEVELOPMENT

4.82 Copyright has a special role in the context of development. Particularly during the last three decades when the political map of the world changed considerably, and several States progressively became independent and other States were newly created, developing countries have had to cope with the enormous problems of educating the vast masses of their peoples. Some developing countries, racing against time in order to provide mass education by methods both formal and non-formal, are facing acute challenges in respect of encouraging and fostering intellectual creativity, and satisfying the urgent need for promoting knowledge, in particular, knowledge in the field of science and technology, in their countries.

4.83 Most developing countries, on attaining independence, have given priority to the training of their peoples and to education, in order to meet the need for staff and management personnel to design and implement development policies and plans. In the early stages, this priority involved drawing heavily on expatriate administrators and resorting abundantly to foreign works (including technical documents, and manuals), and consequently to foreign methods and precedents. In order to remedy that situation, emphasis had to be placed on the need to give an essentially national character to the training of the people.

4.84 It is indeed important that people be trained in a manner that is in keeping with their natural environment. Consequently, teaching material, including literary, artistic and scientific works, has to be created by authors originating in

References for Section B
International Bureau of WIPO, *The Elements of Industrial Property*, WIPO/IP/WDH/93/1
International Bureau of WIPO, *Promotion of Inventive Activity and Technological Innovation*, WIPO/IP/SUV/93/8
International Bureau of WIPO, *Industrial Property, Enterprises and Development*, WIPO-CEIPI/IP/SB/92/25
International Bureau of WIPO, *The Role of Industrial Property in Economic Development*, WIPO/IP/ACC/86/5
International Bureau of WIPO, *Guide on the Industrial Property Activities of Enterprises in Developing Countries*, WIPO Pub. No. 649(E) (1983)

the community to which the works are addressed, and the community has in turn to see and recognize its reflection in them, as the author is the spokesman for his period and the mirror held up to his fellow citizens. Until that takes place, and it can only really take place gradually, in step with the advancement of the development process, recourse to foreign works remains essential. Even in the long run, a reasonable level of recourse to foreign works will continue to remain desirable, in order to facilitate cultural interchange and the reciprocal flow of ideas.

4.85 In many developing countries, there is a shortage of specialists in certain areas of knowledge. Incentives and subsidies are required for the purpose of encouraging national authorship both in a language in general use and in the local language. Also required is education of the public in the laws of copyright.

4.86 Development of national authorship and creativity cannot be set in motion without guarantees to the author of adequate remuneration for his efforts, to enable him to devote his time and attention fully to the need for producing educational material. Copyright protection involves ensuring not only payment of attractive and reasonable royalties to the authors, but also suitable protection for publishers, for the opportunity available to an author to have his works disseminated depends equally on the laws protecting publishers. This process of dissemination cannot be confined to national boundaries. Hence the need to protect one's authors and creators both nationally and internationally. This calls for adequate legislation.

4.87 Developing countries may wish to introduce such legislation also in order to protect the traditional manifestations of their culture which are the expression of their national identity. Copyright legislation has to be framed with due regard to national needs and in a manner that best serves the national interests. Without laws protecting copyright effectively national creativity cannot be nurtured and sustained.

4.88 Once the law has been enacted, the infrastructure for its application has to be established. It is essential to have a proper administrative infrastructure tailored to suit the needs of the particular domestic situation.

References for Section C
International Bureau of WIPO, *Intellectual Creation as an Incentive for the Development and Cultural Promotion of Nations*, WIPO/CNR/CA/85/2

CHAPTER 5

Licensing and the Transfer of Technology

A. INTRODUCTION

5.1   One means for accomplishing economic development through the transfer of technology is the commercial transfer and acquisition of technology. Of course, technology can also be transferred and acquired by other than commercial methods. Personnel can be educated or trained at research and development institutions, technical institutes or centers of high learning. Such personnel can in turn study books, periodicals or other publications on special scientific and technical subjects, or read patent documents, and in that way acquire knowledge of specific technology. But these methods will inevitably fall short of enabling those personnel or others to apply that knowledge, especially the inventions described in patent documents, to manufacture products, produce goods or render services.

5.2   This is true for two reasons. First, the exclusive rights to work an invention belong to the owner of that invention. Without the authorization of the owner, his or its invention can not be put into practice by others. Second, as has been mentioned, not all the knowledge—the know-how—which facilitates or is otherwise useful for the working of the invention is set forth in the description of the invention that is found in the patent document. Hence, it becomes necessary to buy those rights, or to buy the permission to use the invention, or to buy the know-how that enables the invention to be put into practice in the most efficient way.

B. THE COMMERCIAL TRANSFER AND ACQUISITION OF TECHNOLOGY

(a) In General

5.3   The commercial transfer and acquisition of technology, that is, the selling and buying of the exclusive rights to a patented invention or of the permission to use the invention or of the know-how, takes place through certain legal methods.

5.4   Those legal methods give rise to legal relationships between the owner of the exclusive rights or the supplier or the know-how who transfers the exclusive rights or gives the permission or supplies that know-how—called the transferor— and the person or legal entity which acquires those rights or that permission or receives that know-how—called the "transferee." Those legal relationships are essentially contractual in nature.

5.5   By "contractual" in nature it is meant that the transferor of the technology consents to transfer and the transferee consents to acquire the rights, the permission or the know-how in question.

5.6   There are three principal legal methods that can be used to bring about a commercial transfer and acquisition of technology.

(b)   The Sale: Assignment

5.7   The first legal method is the sale by the owner of all his or its exclusive rights to a patented invention and the purchase of those rights by another person or legal entity.

5.8   When all the exclusive rights conferred by the grant of a patent for invention are transferred, without any restriction in time or other condition, by the owner of the patented invention to another person or legal entity, it is said that an "assignment" has taken place. The word "assignment" is a typically English expression that covers the legal concept that has just been described. That concept is recognized in the laws of many countries. It applies also to the exclusive rights in utility models, industrial designs and trademarks, as well as other objects of industrial property. For the sake of simplicity, however, the further explanation of this legal concept will be confined to the principles and characteristics of the assignment of the patented invention. Similar principles and characteristics apply to the assignment of other objects of industrial property.

5.9   The legal act whereby the owner of the patented invention transfers those rights to another is evidenced by a writing in the form of a legal document generally referred to as an "instrument of assignment of patent rights" or "assignment of patent rights" or, more simply yet, as an "assignment." The transferor, that is the owner of the patented invention, is called the "assignor" and the other person or entity, the transferee who or which acquires all the exclusive rights, is called the "assignee." When an assignment takes place, the transferor—the so-called "assignor"—no longer has any rights in respect of the patented invention. The transferee—the so-called "assignee"—becomes the new owner of the patented invention and is entitled to exercise all the exclusive rights conferred by the grant of the patent for invention.

(c)   The License Contract

5.10   The second legal method is through a license, that is, the giving by the owner of a patented invention to another person or legal entity of the permission to perform, in the country and for a limited period of time, one or more of the acts which are covered by the exclusive rights of the owner of the invention patented in that country. When that permission is given, a "license" has been granted. It may be recalled that those acts are the making or using of a product that includes the invention, the making of products by a process that includes the invention, or the use of the process that includes the invention. Here, again, the word "license" is a typically English expression that covers the legal concept that has just been described. That concept is also recognized in the laws of many countries. It applies also to the exclusive rights in other objects of industrial property. Again, for the sake of simplicity, the remaining explanations of the principles and characteristics of the license will be limited to the patented invention. Similar principles and characteristics do apply, however, to the license of other objects of industrial property.

5.11 Where a license is granted, the legal document evidencing the permission given by the owner of the patented invention is usually referred to as a "license contract" or, more simply yet, as a "license." The owner of the patented invention who gives that permission is referred to as "the licensor." The person or legal entity who or which receives that permission is referred to as "the licensee."

5.12 It is formally called a "license contract" because two types of legal acts or transactions are usually involved. First, there is the *giving* by the owner of the patented invention to another person or entity *of the permission* to perform one or more of the acts covered by the exclusive rights of the patented invention. That permission or authorization is referred to as "a license." Second, the license is usually granted subject to certain conditions which will be set out in the written document by which the license is granted to the licensee.

5.13 One of the conditions will obviously be related to the payment by the licensee of money in return for the license that is granted. Thus, the licensee may promise to pay a fixed sum of money at a stated time or at stated times in the future or the licensee may promise to pay a sum of money, the amount of which will depend on the degree of working of the patented invention.

5.14 Another condition might be that the invention will be used by the licensee only for the manufacture of products destined for a specific use, as for example, the manufacture of a pharmaceutical product for use in humans but not for use in animals. Another condition might be that the licensee work the invention in certain factories only or sell the product embodying the invention in certain defined areas only.

5.15 The conditions that have just been mentioned call for promises to be made or action to be taken by the licensee. It is also possible that the conditions may relate to promises to be made or action to be taken by the licensor. For example, the licensor may promise to defend in court a lawsuit brought by a third person against the licensee in which that third person claims that the working of the invention by the licensee violates the exclusive rights already conferred by the grant of another—a separate or distinct—patent for invention which is owned by that third person.

(d) The Know-How Contract

5.16 The third of the three principal legal methods for the transfer and acquisition of technology concerns know-how.

5.17 It is possible to include provisions concerning know-how in a writing or document that is separate from a license contract. It is also possible to include such provisions in a license contract. In the case where the know-how relates to a patented invention or a registered trademark or industrial design, the provisions are usually found in the license contract that deals with that patented invention or other object of industrial property. This is particularly so when the owner of the patented invention or other object of industrial property is also the developer and holder of that know-how. For a variety of reasons, however, even in such a case, the provisions concerning the know-how might be placed in a separate or distinct writing or document.   Whenever provisions concerning know-how appear in a separate or distinct writing or document, that writing or document is normally called a "know-how contract."

5.18 Through such provisions, one party—the supplier of the know-how—undertakes, that is, promises, to communicate the know-how to another party—the recipient of the know-how—for the use by that other party.

5.19 The know-how may be communicated in a tangible form.   Documents, photographs, blueprints, computer cards, and microfilm, among others, are illustrations of tangible forms.   Examples of know-how that could be transmitted in such forms are architectural plans of the factory buildings, the diagrams of the layout of the equipment in the factory, drawings or blueprints of machines, lists of spare parts, manuals or instructions for the operation of machines or the assembly of components, lists and specifications of new materials, labor and machine time calculations, process flow charts, packaging and storing instructions, reports on stability and environmental aspects, and job descriptions for technical and professional personnel.   Such know-how in tangible form is sometimes referred to as "technical information or data."

5.20 The know-how might also be communicated in an intangible form. Examples of the transmittal of know-how in such a form would be an engineer of the supplier of the know-how explaining a process to an engineer of the recipient or the manufacturing engineer of the recipient witnessing a production line in the enterprise of the supplier.   Another example would be training in the factory of the recipient, or at the enterprise of the supplier, of personnel of the recipient.

5.21 Know-how in intangible form relating to the demonstration of, or advice on, manufacturing and other operations is sometimes referred to as "technical services."   Know-how in intangible form relating to training is sometimes referred to as "technical assistance."   Where the know-how in intangible form is to consist of the actual direction of manufacturing operations or other operations, such as planning, or financial and personal administration, or marketing, it is sometimes referred to as "management services."

5.22 The provisions on these various forms of know-how can be rather lengthy and may refer to annexes, schedules or tables that are attached to the contract document and which set forth in detail the technical information or data, or the service or assistance that is agreed to be provided.

5.23 The provisions concerning the transmittal of know-how in tangible form, on the one hand, and in intangible form, on the other, might be subject of separate writings or documents.   Indeed, under the laws of certain countries, such provisions must be the subject of distinct contracts or agreements, each covering separately, the different forms, commonly called, respectively, "the technical information contract" (or more loosely, "the know-how contract"), "the technical services contract (or agreement)" the technical assistance contract (or agreement)" and "the management contract (or agreement)."

5.24 The provisions concerning the know-how to be communicated are not limited, however, to a description of the know-how and the means by which it will be transmitted. They will extend as well to the price to be paid by the recipient for that know-how and to certain other matters relating to its disclosure to third persons.

5.25 The possibility that the know-how to be communicated by the supplier to the recipient might be disclosed, accidentally or otherwise, to third persons, is a very real concern to the supplier of the know-how.

5.26 The know-how of the supplier has usually been acquired or developed by the supplier in the course of research and development activities and through experience in the application of industrial and business techniques in the operations of the supplier's enterprise. The know-how may very well be the reason for the current competitive position, if not leadership, of the supplier in the technology field concerned. As such, it is a valuable asset of the supplier to be preserved. At the same time, it is a resource which the supplier is willing to part with in exchange for an agreed price from the recipient and others who may wish to use it. Its supply to the recipient is consequently the result of a bargain. The price is not just the payment by the recipient of a monetary remuneration fixed by agreement between the supplier and the recipient. It is also the commitment by the recipient not to disclose the know-how to third persons except under certain conditions or with the consent of the supplier.

5.27 The provisions concerning know-how will thus cover various measures to safeguard against the disclosure of the know-how to unauthorized persons. Certain safeguard measures may even have to be taken prior to, as well as during the negotiations. Those measures will thus have to be agreed to even before the execution of the know-how contract itself.

5.28 In a number of countries, the legal form of the document evidencing an assignment or a license contract and other formalities and requirements concerning an assignment or license are prescribed by the patent law or by the commercial law.

5.29 Thus, a requirement may be imposed that an instrument of assignment of patent rights be executed in a particular manner, as for instance, it may be required that the instrument be signed not just by the assignor but also by the assignee.

5.30 Further, a requirement might be imposed that a public official certify, in the case where the assignor is a physical person, that the signature affixed as the signature of the assignor is the signature of the person who purports to be the assignor. In the case where the assignor is a legal entity, the law might require that the representative of that legal entity give evidence to a public official that the representative has the authority to sign on behalf of the legal entity.

5.31 Similar requirements might be imposed by the law in respect of the license contract and the licensor and the licensee.

5.32 In addition, in a number of countries, the patent law may require that an instrument of assignment of patent rights or a license contract be presented to the patent office for registration. By the act of registration, the assignee or the licensee is recognized by the Government as the transferee or holder of the rights transferred by the assignment or of the rights conferred by the license contract.

5.33 In addition, in a number of countries, the law may require that the terms and conditions set forth in the instrument of assignment or in the license contract be reviewed or examined and approved by one or more designated government authorities. For instance, where technology is to be acquired from abroad or where payments in foreign exchange must be made, the law might require the foreign investment commission or the central bank or both review and approve the provisions of the assignment or the license contract.

5.34 As in the case of the assignment and the license contract, the law may require that the know-how contract—or the separate contracts or agreements covering the different forms of know-how—be signed in a specified way. So also, law may require that the know-how contract—or those separate contracts or agreements—be registered or reviewed or examined and approved by one or more designated government authorities.

(e) Sale and Import of Capital Goods

5.35 The commercial transfer and acquisition of technology can take place with the sale, purchase and import of equipment and other capital goods. Examples of capital equipment are machinery and tools needed for the manufacture of products or the application of a process.

5.36 Raw materials, for example, crude oil or phosphoric acid, can also be considered as capital goods in that although they are products in themselves, they may be necessary for the manufacture of another product, such as gasoline or fertilizer, respectively. So also, intermediate goods, such as cotton or polyester fibre, or woven cloth and leather, which is to be cut and sewn into clothing, and parts or other components, such as tires, batteries, radiators and engines, which are to be assembled into an automobile, may be considered in the nature of capital goods in that they are needed in the manufacture of other products.

5.37 Such sales and purchases of capital goods and their import into the country can be considered, in a sense, technology transfer transactions. They are often accompanied by documentation containing technical information, as for instance, manuals on the installation, operation and maintenance of machinery or other equipment, specifications giving size, quality, color, density and other characteristics of the raw material or intermediate goods in question, or instructions on the assembly of parts or other components of a product. Such documentation contains knowledge essential to the use of capital goods.

5.38 Contracts covering the sale and purchase and the import of capital goods are sometimes associated with a license contract or with know-how provisions or a know-how contract. In certain instances, provisions concerning the sale and purchase and the import of capital goods may be found in the license contract or the know-how contract itself.

(f) Franchising and Distributorship

5.39 The commercial transfer of technology may also take place in connection with the system of the franchising or distributorship of goods and services.

5.40 A franchise or distributorship is a business arrangement whereby the reputation, technical information and expertise of one party are combined with the investment of another party for the purpose of selling goods or rendering services directly to the consumer.

5.41 The goods in question may be durable, as in the case of automobiles or home appliances. The goods in question may be consumable in use, as, for example, prepared food or beverages. The services may extend to the rental of capital equipment, for example, automobiles, trucks or other power equipment, or to hotel operations, or dry cleaning facilities, or secretarial help.

5.42 The outlet for the marketing of such goods and services is usually based upon a trademark or service mark or a trade name and a special decor or design of the premises. The license of such a mark or name by its owner is normally combined with the supply by that owner of know-how in some form, either technical information, technical services, technical assistance or management services concerning production, marketing, maintenance and administration. The owner of such a mark or trade name and know-how is called a "franchisor" or "licensor." The party to whom the license is granted and the know-how is supplied is called the "franchisee," "distributor" or "dealer." The franchisee, distributor or dealer may own the premises or contribute money and time as an investment in the business firm. Other aspects of their business relationship, including sharing of the profits of the franchise or distributorship will be agreed to between the franchisor or licensor and the franchisee, distributor or dealer and set forth in a writing or document called a "franchise agreement" or "distributorship agreement."

5.43 As in the case of the assignment, the license contract and the know-how contract, the law may require that such franchise or distributorship agreements be registered and reviewed or examined and approved by one or more designated government authorities.

5.44 The complexity of many business arrangements and technology transfer transactions, however, often presents problems for the enterprises or other entities and the officials of their government which wish to acquire technology. Their experience in acquiring technology may not be as extensive as those of the enterprises that own technology and are willing to transfer it. Therefore, it may be necessary or advisable for the technology acquirer to seek the assistance of others in planning for and acquiring a given technology. It may even be necessary or advisable to cooperate in a more extensive manner with the technology transferor than the degree of cooperation which normally results from, for instance, the license contract or the know-how contract.

5.45 This leads to the explanation of three other kinds of business arrangements that the technology acquirer may resort to. These are "the consultancy arrangement," the "turn-key project" and "the joint venture arrangements."

(g) The Consultancy Arrangement

5.46 The help of an individual consultant or a firm of consultants that will give advice and render other services concerning the planning for, and the actual acquisition of, a given technology can be useful, if not indispensable, for such enterprises, entities and governments that wish to acquire technology from enterprises in other countries.

5.47 In such a business arrangement not only is help received in acquiring the technology but the experience gained and the lessons learned in engaging and working with the individual consultant or firm of consultants will be valuable knowledge that can serve to better carry out future projects.

5.48 As concerns planning, the advice or services may relate to the choice of the product to be manufactured or improved upon and the technology to be used, to the investment required, to the type of business organization or other relationships to be established, and to the suitability of each for the objective or objectives to be attained.

5.49 The planning advice or services may extend to recommendations on the type of product to be manufactured, the choice of the technology to be used in that manufacture and its possible sources.

5.50 The services might include general surveys of the geographical area or areas under consideration to determine the suitability of the area for the installation of a factory or for the marketing of the product.

5.51 The services could include studies of the availability of labor, raw materials, intermediate goods, parts or components. They might include assessments of the impact of the technology on the environment, including field testing and laboratory analysis. Investment estimates, the identification of sources of financing and other pre-investment type services might also be provided. The consultancy services could also include an evaluation of the types of business relationships that are possible and which should be entered into. In this connection, recommendations could be made on which of the different legal methods for the acquisition of the technology selected should be used.

5.52 The consultancy services might extend also to the implementation of a project. "Design and engineering" services are a typical example. Such services concern the preparation of the plan for the site of the plant, the design of the factory building, the design of machinery and other equipment, the preparation of tender documents for the construction of the building or the equipment and for civil engineering works, the evaluation of bids and advice on the award of contracts, the supervision of the construction of the factory, including the installation of the equipment, the supervision of the start-up and testing of the equipment and making findings on the state of performance of the process utilized, as well as giving advice in the initial period on the operation of particular equipment or the entire factory.

5.53 The consultancy services could extend further to actual research and development with a view to improving the product being manufactured or the process being applied or to determining possible uses of by-products or to creating new or related products or processes.

5.54 One or more individual consultants or firms of consultants might be engaged to render the services in question. Usually, however, such an individual or firm specializes in a particular type of service, such as investment planning, design and engineering, environmental impact, marketing or business organization and management. In a sense, the consultancy services are forms of know-how. They can thus be considered within the framework of the know-how contract, more particularly, the technical services contract or agreement.

(h) The Turn-Key Project

5.55 In certain instances, two or more of the business arrangements, and hence the legal methods that they reflect, can be combined in such a way as to entrust the planning, construction and operation of a factory to a single technology supplier, or to a very limited number of technology suppliers.

5.56 Thus, the "turn-key project" may involve a comprehensive arrangement of certain of the legal methods, whereby one party undertakes to hand over to his client—the technology recipient—an entire industrial plant that is capable of operating in accordance with agreed performance standards. More usually, the turn-key project involves the undertaking by one party to supply to the client the design for the industrial plant and the technical information on its operation. In the latter event, supplementary arrangements might also be made for the acquisition of rights to the technology, for civil engineering work and for provision of technical services and assistance concerning the construction of the plant, the purchase and installation of equipment, raw materials or parts and components, training, and supervision of the operation of the plant, at least in its initial stages.

5.57 It is called a "turn-key" project because the end result is to "turn" over to the client the "key" to the door of the industrial plant. That is a symbolic way of expressing the completion of the tasks agreed to between the parties.

5.58 Of course, it is also possible, depending upon the experience and resources of the technology recipient, that the technology recipient undertake one or more specific tasks, such as part of the civil engineering work, the construction of the factory building and the purchase and installation of equipment, and even the design of that factory and equipment.

5.59 Both the consultancy arrangement and the turn-key project arrangement have their shortcomings. The first does not usually entail the responsibility of the consultant for the results. In the second, the technology supplier or suppliers are so responsible. Neither the first or the second provide means for a continuing involvement of the technology supplier so that access to later advances in its technology can be more readily facilitated. This is because neither contains a commitment to the technology acquirer to provide further advice or services or to provide improved or additional technology. Neither contains measures to provide money or other resources that may be needed for further growth.

5.60 Because of these shortcomings and for other reasons, joint venture arrangements can be more attractive means of industrial or commercial cooperation.

(i) Joint Venture Arrangements

5.61 The following will explain what is meant by a "joint venture," describe the two forms of arrangements, give examples of the use of the two forms, and how the different legal methods can be used in those arrangements.

5.62 First of all, some explanations must be made in connection with what is meant by "joint venture arrangements." In essence, a joint venture arrangement, or as it is more simply termed "a joint venture" is, in a broad sense, as the words imply, the doing together by two or more persons or enterprises of an activity which may or may not succeed. In the sphere of business, it is one kind of business relationship or form of business organization. It consists of an agreement between two or more persons or between two or more enterprises or even between one or more persons and one or more enterprises to combine, in a specified way, a certain kind and amount of their resources in order to manufacture, to produce or to sell a product or to render a service and to share in a specified way the profits that result and the risks that occur.

5.63 There are two fundamental forms of joint venture: the equity joint venture and the contractual venture.

5.64 The equity joint venture is an arrangement whereby a separate legal entity is created in accordance with the agreement of two or more parties. The parties undertake to provide money or other resources as their contribution to the assets or other capital of that legal entity. That entity is usually established as a limited liability company and is distinct from either of the parties which participated in its creation. That company becomes the owner of the resources that are contributed by each party. Each of the parties in turn become the owners of the company, that is, each is said to have "an equity" in the company.

5.65 Where one or more of the parties is a foreign enterprise or entity, such a party is, or such parties are called a "foreign participant" or "the foreign participants." The parties or participants, as they are called, will agree on the purposes and functions of the limited liability company, the proportion of the capital each will contribute to, and the share of each in the profits of, the limited liability company, and on such other matters as its management, operation, duration and termination. One or more of these matters may be governed as well by a joint venture law or by company law and related laws, including laws on taxation and labor relations.

5.66 On the other hand, the contractual joint venture might be used where the establishment of a separate legal entity is not needed or where it is not possible to create such an entity. This may be the case where the project involves a narrow task or a limited activity or is for a limited time or where the laws of the country in which the business operation is to be conducted do not recognize the ownership of property by foreigners. The relationship between the parties will be set forth in the contract or agreement concluded between them.

5.67 The different legal methods for the commercial transfer and acquisition of technology can be used in either form of joint venture arrangement.

5.68 An assignment of the exclusive rights to a patented invention, a utility model, industrial design or trademark by one of the participants could constitute a portion of that participant's contribution to the capital of the joint venture company. It is also possible, of course, for one of the participants to grant a license of a patented invention or other object of industrial property or to supply know-how as part of that participant's contribution to the joint venture company. More commonly, however, such a license or the supply of know-how in one or more of its forms will be the subject of one or more contracts made after the joint venture company is established. Those contracts will be concluded between one of the participants as the transferor of the technology in question and the joint venture company. Through such contracts the technology in question can be transferred to the joint venture company which will thus acquire the means to enable it to carry out its operations.

5.69 Whether one or more of the legal methods will be used in the establishment of the joint venture company or whether one or more of those legal methods will be used and when so as to enable the joint venture to carry out its operations will be matters for negotiation between the prospective participants. The result of their negotiations will be reflected in the joint venture agreement. The license contract, the know-how contract, the technical services or the technical assistance contract, the franchise contract, and contracts covering other commercial matters, might even form annexes to the joint venture agreement. They would be signed once the joint venture company was established.

5.70 Needless to say the joint venture agreement, whether it be for the establishment of a limited liability company or not, and the different contracts of the various legal methods that may be used, must be concluded in accordance with laws and regulations applicable to such companies and to the tax laws concerning those companies or to the laws relating to agency or partnership, as well as to other economic laws, including laws relating to labor, the sales of goods, insurance and to foreign economic and trade contracts.

C. NEGOTIATION OF LICENSING AGREEMENTS

(a) Introduction

5.71 Any technical licensing contract may be analyzed in respect of the following basic elements:

(1) the subject of the contract;
(2) the licensor's obligations;
(3) the obligations common to both parties.

5.72 In reality, these elements are frequently spread out through the contract or are even intermingled. Nevertheless, examining a contract from these points of view has the advantage of providing a clear and logical analysis of the essential aspects that have to be considered when negotiating a contract.

5.73 The following topics are typically the subject of the negotiations leading to the conclusion of the license contract or which require special attention in drafting its provisions. These provisions are discussed from the point of view of the licensing of patents but they apply also to the other forms of intellectual property.

(b) Identification of the Parties

5.74 One of the first points of concern to the negotiators of the license contract will be the identification of the entities or persons which or who will become the

References for Section B
International Bureau of WIPO, *Licensing of Patents: Methods and Arrangements for the Commercial Transfer and Acquisition of Technology*, WIPO/IP/WDH/93/6

parties or, in other words, will sign the license contract and become legally bound to carry out its provisions.

5.75 The objective in describing the parties to a license contract is to identify each of them with sufficient certainty, such that the identity of each entity or person from which or whom a given performance can be expected or to which or whom it will be rendered, will not later become a subject of controversy.

5.76 This objective assumes particular significance in complex business transactions in which there is more than one entity or person on either side. This is quite likely to be the situation in a licensing and know-how arrangement between entities or persons in different countries.

5.77 For example, one side in the negotiations leading to the conclusion of the license contract may be a grouping of legal entities, all organized and located in one foreign country or each organized and located in separate countries, but in either case, with a common ownership, control or other interest. In such cases, it may be contemplated that the patent license will be given by one of the legal entities in the group (or perhaps even by a legal entity outside the group) and that other performances will be undertaken or received by one or more of the other legal entities in the group.

5.78 Similar questions will arise where the other side to the negotiations is likely to involve a number of government authorities—ministries, commissions, bureaus or administrations or other government units—or public entities, state enterprises or private entities, including those established as a result of a joint venture with a foreign legal entity.

5.79 Further, consideration will have to be given to whether one document setting forth all the terms and conditions and commitments should be prepared and executed between all the parties on both sides or whether several documents, each containing distinct terms and conditions and commitments, should be drawn up and signed by the different parties on each side.

(c) Objectives of the Parties; Scope of the License

5.80 When the parties are negotiating a license contract, they usually proceed on the basis that certain technology is necessary for the manufacture of a particular product or the application of a particular process from which a product or other result is to be obtained. In other words, the ultimate objective of the parties in concluding a license contract is the transfer by the licensor, and the acquisition by the licensee, of a given technology and of the right to exploit that technology in the making, or in the use or sale of a given product or in the application of a given process through which a product or other result will be obtained.

5.81 This objective of the parties will be expressed both generally and specifically in the license contract.

5.82 Their objective will be reflected in a general way either in a preambular part of the license contract, consisting of a series of provisions often referred to as "recitals" or "whereas clauses," or directly in an operative element of the license contract, consisting of a particular article entitled "background information."

5.83 The objective of the parties to the license contract will be expressed more specifically in subsequent provisions that delineate the "scope" of the license contract. One set of those provisions identifies the technical subject matter of the license contract (that is, the product or the process, the invention or inventions and the know-how and technological advances, if any). Another group of those provisions will determine which of the parties may perform one or more acts of exploitation, set forth the place or places where that act or those acts may take place, and establish the duration of the exploitation, and specify the purpose or purposes for which the technology may be exploited. Other provisions will prescribe the level of working of the invention or inventions, specify the means, if any, to assist in the exploitation, fix the remuneration for the exploitation and state the consequences of a failure or of an interference with the exploitation of the technology or with other commitments agreed upon.

(d) Subject Matter

5.84 The provisions of the license contract that define its technical subject matter in effect identify the technology which will be the subject of exploitation, and ultimately, if the license contract is fulfilled, that will be transferred from the licensor and acquired by the licensee.

5.85 These provisions describe the product to be made, used or sold, or the process to be applied and from which a product will be obtained and in turn used or sold; identify the invention or inventions included in that product or process; describe the know-how, if any, that is to be supplied; and identify the technological advances of one party or the other, and the conditions under which those advances will be made available by that party to the other.

(e) Identification of Product or Processes

5.86 Since the ultimate objective of the licensee concerns a product or process, one of the provisions in the license contract will identify in concise terms that product or process. In the typical case, that provision is set forth in the part of the license contract dealing with definitions.

5.87 The product might be identified somewhat broadly, as for example, "instruments for the purpose of writing," which would include, for instance, fountain pens, ball-point pens and felt-tipped pens. The product might be defined more specifically, as for example, only one or more but not all of those kinds of pens.

5.88 The process might be identified as a chemical formula according to which certain chemical substances interact when a specified catalyst is introduced resulting in a specified product.

5.89 The title and the abstract set forth in the application for the grant of a patent for the invention that is included in the product or the process may be a useful starting point in providing the requisite information to describe the product or the process.

(f) Identification of the Invention

5.90 The provision that identifies the invention or inventions included in the product or process usually refers to the number of the patent for invention or the application for the grant of a patent for invention, the country where the patent was granted or registered or where the application was filed, the date of the patent grant or the filing date of the application, and in some cases, the title of the invention and the status of the application. Where the product or the process in question includes a number of inventions, the relevant information in respect of each invention is usually grouped together and set forth in a schedule attached to the license contract.

(g) Description of the Know-How

5.91 Under the standard requirements of most patent laws, the description of the invention claimed in an application for the grant of a patent for invention must disclose the invention in a manner sufficiently clear, detailed and complete to permit a person having ordinary skill in the art to carry out the invention. Some patent laws go further, and require also that the best mode contemplated by the inventor for carrying out the invention be set forth. But those patent laws do not extend to requiring a description of additional means that may facilitate the carrying out of the invention. Such additional means may consist of the use of technical information and expertise acquired through long experimentation with the invention.

5.92 More frequently, the technical information or expertise is not disclosed because it is not known at the time of putting the description together as part of the documentation to be submitted to obtain the grant of a patent for invention. The description of the invention claimed in the application for the grant of a patent for invention is often based on research work carried out under laboratory or small-scale conditions. Commercial production or even production on a pilot scale may not come until a later stage. It may then be too late for it to be incorporated in the description of the invention in the form of an amendment to the application as filed because the patent for invention has long since been granted. Further, as to whether the invention will be cost-competitive or not, this may not be known at the time of the filing of the application. Commercial costing may not be determinable until commercial production commences and optimum production runs can be reached.

5.93 For the foregoing reasons, it will be useful, if not indispensable, that the potential licensee acquire from the licensor or, with its or his assistance, from others, the technical information, data or knowledge resulting from experience or skills, in other words, the "know-how," which is or may in the future be applicable in effectively exploiting the invention or inventions included in the product or process in question.

5.94 As regards the description of such know-how, technical information can be identified in terms of the relevant documentation, as for example, diagrams of the layout of the plant, drawings or blueprints of machines, lists of spare parts, manuals or instructions for the operation of machines or the assembly of components, specifications of raw materials, labor and machine time calculations, packaging and storing instructions and information on stability and environmental aspects. Job descriptions can be drawn up for each expert whose technical or professional expertise is needed. This information can be set forth in one or more annexes, appendixes or schedules attached to the license contract.

(h) Confidentiality

5.95 Know-how is acquired or developed by the licensor in the course of research and development activities or through the application of industrial and business techniques in the operations of the licensor's enterprise. The know-how may often be the reason for the current competitive position, if not superiority, of the licensor in the technology field concerned. As such, it is a valuable asset of the licensor to be preserved. At the same time, it is a resource which the licensor is willing to part with in exchange for an agreed price from the licensee or others who wish to use it. Its supply to the licensee is consequently the result of a bargain in which the price is not just the payment of a monetary remuneration fixed by the license contract but also the commitment by the licensee not to disclose that know-how to third persons except under certain conditions or with the consent of the licensor.

5.96 Turning to the terms and conditions of the license contract itself, the parties will need to define which portions of the know-how, whether developed by one or the other, and at what times, should or should not be disclosed, to whom, and for what duration. The parties will also need to state the effects if an unauthorized disclosure should occur, accidentally or otherwise, including the consequences in the event that the license contract expires or, because of a default of one or the other of the parties, it comes to an end before its stated expiration, including the period agreed upon for non-disclosure.

(i) Access to Technological Advances

5.97 The technological advance of immediate concern to the parties to the license contract will normally be one which significantly or substantially affects, for example, in the case of a given product, the volume of its production, the cost of its manufacture or the efficiency of its use, or, in the case of a given process, the material conditions under which that process is applied, or the cost of its application, or the efficiency of its application.

5.98 Various approaches can be taken by the parties to the license contract to provide information about and to define their respective rights in technological advances which either may have made or acquired.

5.99 The parties might decide that the mutual exchange of information on technological advances is in their best interests, and that each shall be free to exploit, free of charge, the technological advance of the other. This is called cross licensing. They might also decide that if either party makes available the technological advance of the other to a third person for a remuneration, then the other shall be entitled to share in that remuneration in some agreed manner and amount. It is usually provided further that the party making the technological advance should apply for patent protection. In the event that it does not elect to do so, the other party may apply, in the name of either and at the expense of the party applying.

(j) Territorial Exclusivity

5.100 Which of the parties to the license contract will be able, by virtue of its provisions, to perform what act or acts of exploitation, in what territory or territories, and with what effects on arrangements with third persons in relationship with the licensor or the licensee who are also interested in exploiting the technology are distinct but related questions. They are related because each concerns the exclusive right of the licensor under the patent for invention granted to the licensor and which will be the subject matter of the license contract. A decision on each of these questions must be clearly reflected in the license contract.

(k) Permitted Field of Use

5.101 A provision on the field or fields of use or activity specifies the purpose or purposes for which the invention or the know-how may be applied. It serves to define the scope of that application by the licensee. At the same time, depending on that defined scope, the licensor may be able to grant a license or supply know-how to each of a number of other licensees, each specializing in different applications of the invention or the know-how in question. That permits the most practical way of exploiting the invention or know-how, given the capabilities of each particular licensee.

5.102 It should be noted that the amount to be paid by the licensee for the technology may vary according to the purpose or purposes for which the technology is sought to be exploited. The licensor may be willing to authorize the exploitation of the invention or supply the know-how for application in terms of a given field of use or activity. On the other hand, the licensor may be willing to authorize that exploitation in respect of all the purposes for which the invention or the know-how may be applied. In the latter event, it is likely that the price asked for will be higher than where a more limited field of use or activity is agreed upon. In the long run, though, it may be desirable for the licensee to have the opportunity to apply the technology for all purposes. The price asked for in that case, however, must be compared to the lower price which may be asked for if a limited purpose is agreed to. The comparison becomes all the more relevant if the licensee is not currently, nor in the future likely to be, in a position to exploit the technology beyond the limited purpose.

(l) Exploitation

5.103 The licensor expects that the licensee will not only exploit the invention and apply the know-how but will do so to the fullest extent permitted by the terms and conditions of the license contract.

5.104 The parties might wish to specify that the licensee will make, use or sell the product that includes the patented invention or will apply the know-how in a certain manner with a view to obtaining a certain result and to exploiting the technology at a certain level. The parties might wish also to set forth the commitments of the licensor the performance of which will assist the licensee in achieving the expected manner and extent of working or other exploitation.

5.105 The questions that usually arise in respect of the manner and extent of exploitation are concerned with the following matters: the quality of the product; the volume of production; the making of part of the product by third persons to be authorized by the licensee; the import of the product to meet local demand in the absence of sufficient working in the country itself; and the use of the distribution channels of the licensor.

5.106 The quality of the product is a factor in promoting the sale of the product, in establishing the goodwill of the licensee and in maintaining the licensee's competitive position in the market.

5.107 Further, the quality of the product may be linked to the reputation of the licensor where the product is to be marketed bearing the trademark of the licensor. From the point of view of the public, a product bearing a trademark carries with it a certain symbol of quality and consistency, for which someone, whether identified or not, holds himself responsible.

5.108 Consequently, the standard of quality of the product, the know-how to be imparted to meet that standard and the requisite quality will be matters which are usually reflected in appropriate provisions in the license contract.

5.109 The license contract might stipulate an agreed quality standard for the product. In that case, the license contract usually includes also a provision that the licensor will inform the licensee of the way in which the product is to be made so that the required quality standard can be attained.

5.110 Other ways, although indirect, exist to assure that a given standard of quality for the product is achieved. It might be stipulated that certain production personnel designated by the licensor will be employed by the licensee to supervise certain phases of production.

5.111 The licensee might wish to have certain assurances from the licensor concerning the actual working of the patented invention and the application of the know-how. The licensee might wish to have an assurance from the licensor that, by working the patented invention of the licensor and applying the know-how supplied by the licensor, the licensee will be able to fulfill its or his expectations under the license contract to make a given product that includes the patented invention or know-how. The licensee might wish to have the assurance that by such working and application the licensee will be able to obtain a given product or other result through the process that includes the patented invention or the know-how.

5.112 Also of concern to the licensee in respect of the effective exploitation of the patented invention is whether the know-how supplied by the licensor will be adequate or suitable in attaining the objective of the licensee to make the patented product or to obtain a given product or other result through the patented process.

5.113 The approach to this question consists essentially of the licensor giving to the licensee an assurance as to the know-how to be supplied. Such an assurance is referred to as a guarantee of know-how.

5.114 In this context, a guarantee is an assertion that a given fact or event concerning the know-how exists or that a given performance will take place if the know-how is applied; that assertion is accompanied by a promise that if the fact or event does not exist or the performance does not take place, a correction will be made or some other act will be done in its place.

5.115 The guarantee provision of the license contract might be phrased in terms of the conformity of the know-how supplied to the agreed description of what was promised to be supplied. It might be phrased in terms of the results to be attained by the application of the know-how. It might be phrased in terms of the suitability of the know-how to meet the technological requirements of the licensee.

(m) Settlement of Disputes

5.116 When non-performance is likely, or does occur, and there is no provision in the license contract which fixes the agreed consequences in respect of that failure of performance, one party might propose a solution that is satisfactory to the other. That solution might be the allowance of additional time to render the performance or the substantial correction of the flaw or flaws in question. It might mean that some other performance in lieu of the defective performance would be acceptable. In these ways, an amicable way of settling the dispute between the parties could be arrived at without recourse to legal remedies in the courts or other tribunals.

5.117 Yet circumstances could arise when the party injured by the default in the performance of the other is not offered a satisfactory solution. It could be also that the party alleged to have defaulted, denies that there has been a failure to perform as agreed. In either event, some machinery for the settlement of the dispute should be provided for before recourse is had to the courts or other tribunals. Thus, recourse might have been to the advice of independent experts, or the findings and recommendations of a group consisting of representatives of each side, or to conciliation or to arbitration proceedings or, ultimately, to the courts or other tribunals competent in the matter. In particular, a clause designating the WIPO Arbitration Center as the forum for settling disputes may be added to a license contract.

D. REMUNERATION

(a) Introduction

5.118 One of the most critical and complex issues to be negotiated between the prospective transferor and the potential transferee is the "price" or the "cost" of the industrial property to be acquired whether outright or by license, and of the technology to be transferred.

5.119 The "price" or the "cost" is dependent upon a number of factors, including the nature of the industrial property rights and the technology and the relative bargaining power of the two parties. The prospective transferor usually makes a careful assessment in terms of value or the need for the particular technology, the alternative technologies available, the prospect of technological advances and the likely production and profitability of the potential transferee. The prospective transferor also makes detailed projections of production and consequent income flow from other potential licensees or technology recipients.

References for Section C
F. Dessemontet, *Intellectual Property in Licensing and Franchising Contracts*, ISIP/86/8
International Bureau of WIPO, *Licensing of Industrial Property Rights—Patents*, WIPO/IPE/IR/93/9

5.120 The potential transferee assesses the total payments that it is likely to make for a particular technology and for advances in that technology against the profitability of the enterprise over a period of time and also evaluates such payments in relation to costs of alternative technology or payments made with respect to similar transactions.

(b) Direct Monetary Compensation

5.121 Direct monetary compensation for industrial property rights or for technology may take different forms: (a) "lump-sum payment"—a pre-calculated amount to be paid once or in installments; (b) "royalties"—post-calculated, recurring payments, the amount of which is determined as a function of economic use or result (production units, service units, sales of the product, profits); (c) "fees"—compensation for services and assistance rendered by technical or professional experts, fixed at a specified amount or calculated per person and per period of service.

5.122 These forms of remuneration may be combined in a given industrial property license or technology transfer agreement. In some instances, the lump-sum payment form may replace the system of royalties altogether, while in other instances the two might be combined one way or another, as where the licensee or technology recipient may elect to make a lump-sum payment in lieu of one form of royalty or another. In other instances, the licensee or technology recipient may be given the opportunity to elect to pay royalties on production units rather than on sales. The fees for technical services and assistance may be determined separately, either stipulated in advance or negotiated as rendered.

5.123 It is to be noted, however, as elaborated below, that under the laws in certain countries governing the transfer of technology the various rights or elements of technology may have to be separately priced or valued and even made the subject of distinct licenses or agreements.

(i) Lump-Sum Payment

5.124 The lump-sum amount may be paid, in the case of a transfer or assignment of industrial property rights, at the time of the transfer or assignment of industrial property rights or, in the case of an industrial property license or a technology transfer agreement, upon the conclusion of the license or agreement or shortly or sometime thereafter, either in a single payment or in a series of instalment payments. The latter may be staggered in relation to certain events such as the execution of the license or the agreement, or on the delivery of certain technical information.

5.125 The lump-sum payment is often made for the outright acquisition of industrial property rights, whether by sale or assignment, as well as in the case of the license of industrial property rights or the transfer of know-how, where the technology can be transferred all at once and the licensee or technology recipient can readily and fully absorb it. Such payment is made for the transfer of rights and know-how concerning technology which is less sophisticated and may be quite appropriate from the viewpoint of the licensee or technology transferee if a continuing supply of technical information concerning technological advances or the marketing of the product or technical services and assistance in support of the licensee or technology recipient is not required of the licensor or technology supplier. For example, a lump-sum payment may be made to obtain the rights in a patented product, or to a patented process or to sets of drawings, specifications or other technical information that are sufficient in themselves to enable the licensee or technology recipient to manufacture and sell certain products.

5.126 Under the laws in certain countries governing the transfer of technology, recourse to the form of lump-sum payment for the acquisition of industrial property rights or technology is subject to certain conditions. Under one of these laws, it is provided that, subject to the authorization of a specified governmental unit, a lump-sum amount may be paid if it is determined in advance on the basis of the estimated volume of sales during the period of the license or agreement and provided, further, that the amount is within the maximum limits which may be established for the sector, activity or product. Under another of these laws, a lump-sum payment is permitted in the case of the acquisition of patent rights by transfer or purchase and for certain types of technical services and assistance; otherwise, the remuneration must take the form of royalties in the case of a patent or trademark license or an agreement for the supply of know-how to be applied in the production of consumer goods or materials in general or in the manufacture of machinery, equipment or other capital goods. In the latter cases, however, although a lump-sum amount may be fixed for the technical information initially supplied, it must represent an advance on the royalty remuneration.

(ii) Royalties

5.127 As indicated previously, royalties are post-calculated, recurring payments, the amount of which is determined as a function of economic use or result.

5.128 In order to establish this functional relationship between the recurring amounts and the economic use or result, the provision in the license or agreement may refer to the volume of production, to the sales price of the product that is manufactured incorporating the technology (or, in the case of the trademark license, that is sold bearing the trademark) or to the profits of the licensee or technology recipient.

5.129 As noted previously, under the laws in certain countries governing the transfer of technology, royalties are the only form of remuneration which may be provided for in specified types of industrial property licenses or technology transfer agreements. In particular, these laws require that the royalties be ascertained either on a percentage basis or as a fixed value per product unit, but in either case imposed or related to the sales price, or, when applicable, also linked to the profits earned from the sales of the product.

(iii) Lump-Sum Payment Compared with Royalties

5.130 The lump-sum payment is characterized by the fact that the obligation is fulfilled immediately or fairly shortly. Further, the parties do not have to make continuous accounts or control the calculation or the remittance, as in the case of royalties.

5.131 The lump-sum payment, when compared with royalties, may or may not have certain tax advantages. The continuous payment of royalties is considered to be income to the licensor or technology supplier from the viewpoint of taxation and, as such, royalties are subject to income taxes. The single lump-sum payment, and even the lump-sum payable in instalments, may be considered the counterpart to, or the financial result of, a sale or purchase operation, with the assignment or transfer of the industrial property rights and the supply of the know-how considered analogous to the sale of commercial goods. The licensor or technology supplier will also have to pay taxes on the lump-sum payment. The single lump-sum payment, however, may be subject to a different (often higher) tax rate than income in the form of royalties. Under some tax laws, it may be possible to alleviate the higher or progressive rates on the lump-sum payment if it is split into instalments and paid over several tax years and thus subject to lower tax rates.

5.132 Where a more or less single performance is the counter value, the lump-sum payment may lead to results economically more justified between the parties. If, for example, unexpected high sales are reached, especially under the influence of monetary fluctuations or other economic circumstances, the system of royalties leads to unexpected and unjustified returns to the licensor or technology supplier. Upon the payment of a lump-sum, the licensor or technology supplier would receive only the counter value of its single performance of the licensor or technology supplier. Upon the payment of a lump-sum, the licensor or technology supplier would receive only the counter value of its single performance which it thought was justified at the time the agreement was concluded.

5.133 On the other hand, the lump-sum payment may also entail risks for the licensee or technology recipient if production or sales of the product lag behind expectation and if the lump-sum payment is disproportional to the economic value of the performance of the licensor or technology supplier.

(iv) Lump-Sum Payment and Royalties Combined

5.134 In many cases, the remuneration for industrial property rights or know-how is a combination of a lump-sum payment and royalties.

5.135 The lump-sum payment is often treated as an initial payment for disclosing information that enables the potential licensee or technology recipient to evaluate the technology. The licensor or technology supplier frequently views this payment as the initial remuneration for basic research and development in respect of technology. The actual initial payment varies a great deal from transaction to transaction and may range from a small sum for the delivery of initial technical information to a very large amount for sophisticated technology that has required much research and development. In some instances, the initial lump-sum payment may be viewed as a minimum payment or regarded as a down payment or advance against royalties. Further, the licensee or technology recipient may be given the opportunity to make an additional lump-sum payment, stipulated in advance or negotiated at the time of the election to make that payment, in lieu of royalties, with a credit against the payment of the royalties already made.

5.136 In negotiating remuneration in the form of a combined lump-sum payment and royalties, the licensee or technology recipient will need to evaluate carefully the total outflow and incidence of the payments that may be likely for various combinations. The burden of interest charges, for example, is important in determining the size of the lump-sum figure, while projections of production estimates and of cash-flow from sales during the period of the license or agreement are essential in assessing the percentage rate of royalties.

(v) Fees for Technical Services and Assistance

5.137 Specific technical services and assistance, to be provided by the licensor or technology supplier, may be necessary in connection with the transfer of the technology or the marketing of the product under a trademark, and may have to be paid for separately.

5.138 The fees for specific technical services and assistance related to a patent or trademark license or a technical know-how agreement include: (a) the cost of training programs for the personnel of the licensee or technology recipients; (b) fees for technical services and assistance to be rendered by technical experts of the licensor or technology supplier to the licensee or technology recipient at the latter's industrial plant during the period of the license or agreement; (c) fees for technical services and assistance which concern machinery, equipment or other capital goods needed in the utilization of the technology at the industrial plant of the licensee or technology recipient.

(c) Indirect and Non-Monetary Compensation

(i) Income from Related Operations

5.139 The licensor or technology supplier may receive income from various operations, such as commissions on the sales of the product made on behalf of the licensee or technology recipient through the distribution channels of the licensor or technology supplier, profits from the sale of the product supplied to the latter under exclusive purchase arrangements, profits from the sale to the licensee or technology recipient of related products which complete its marketing program, profits from the sale to the licensee or technology recipient of raw materials, intermediate goods, parts or other components and rentals from machinery, equipment or other capital goods released by the licensor or technology supplier to the licensee or technology recipient.

(ii) Dividends

5.140 If the licensor or technology supplier assumes a financial participation in the enterprise of the licensee or technology recipient or if they enter into a joint venture, the licensor or technology supplier will obtain, in the event of successful commercial operations, dividends from the financial participation. If an essential part of the commercial operations depends upon the industrial property rights or technology of the licensor or technology supplier, there may be a direct dependency between the amount of the royalties and the amount of the dividends: the higher the royalties the lower the dividends, and vice versa. The degree of participation and financial and tax factors may dictate the relevant amount to be assigned to each and the formation of reserves or the holding back of profits, which may lead to an increase in the value of the financial participation.

5.141 In this context, attention is directed to the laws in certain countries governing the transfer of technology which treat as profits payments in respect of the price of industrial property rights or technology made between a subsidiary and its parent, or between subsidiaries; or where there exists economic unity or community of interests between the parties, or where effective technical, administrative, financial and commercial management of the technology transferee is exercised by the technology transferor; or where the technology transferor supplies raw materials or intermediate products used in the process in an amount equal to more than a specified percentage of the total cost of the product. Some of these laws also provide that in such cases the lump-sum payment or royalties may neither be treated as a contribution to capital nor constitute shares in the profits or in the capital of the enterprise of the licensee or technology recipient nor be deducted for the purpose of calculating the tax on its income.

5.142 Under the laws in certain other countries governing the transfer of technology, although royalties may be paid by the licensee or technology recipient to the licensor or technology supplier even where the latter has a financial participation in the former, the amount of the royalty payments must be reduced substantially in the event that the licensor or technology supplier has a majority participation in the licensee or technology recipient; in addition royalty payments by a wholly owned subsidiary to its foreign parent company are ordinarily not permitted.

(iii)   Cost Shifting or Sharing Measures

5.143 Certain cost shifting or sharing measures, for example, the expenses in maintaining or defending rights under the patent or the trademark, that are adopted may have the effect of reducing the expenses of the licensor or technology supplier and increasing the cost to the licensee or technology recipient of the technology transfer transaction.

(iv)   Feed-back of Technical Information

5.144 The technical know-how of the licensee or technology recipient which is to be turned over to the licensor or technology supplier can also constitute a form of income to the latter.

(v)   Acquisition of Market Data

5.145 The licensor or technology supplier may benefit from data provided by the licensee or technology recipient concerning the marketing of the product in the local area, including new sales promotion techniques, which may prove useful to the marketing of the product in other areas.

(vi)   Cost Reductions and Savings to the Licensee or Technology Recipient

5.146 Some elements of a given technology transfer transaction may have the effect of reducing the operating expenses of the licensee or technology recipient or otherwise lead to savings on the part of the technology transferee.

5.147 Mention may be made of such measures as the utilization by the licensee or technology recipient of the channels of sales distribution of the licensor or technology supplier, the use without payment of the trademark of the licensor or technology supplier, the access of the licensee or technology recipient to information concerning improvements to existing inventions, or developments in know-how, or new inventions of the licensor or technology supplier or rights in respect of such technological advances, and the opportunity to benefit from the marketing information and other technical services and assistance of the licensor or technology supplier.

(d) Description of the Currency of the Obligation and of Payment

5.148 It is necessary to distinguish two aspects of the question of currency designation. The first concerns the determination of the currency which will serve as the measure of the obligation to pay, and the second relates to the choice of the currency in which payments will be made to discharge that obligation. The currency of obligation and the currency of payment may be one and the same but they need not necessarily be, and in fact may be different, as is often the case in an international commercial transaction.

(i) Currency of Obligation

5.149 The currency of the obligation in the case of the lump-sum payment may be the currency of either the country of the licensor or technology supplier, or the country of the licensee or technology recipient or a third country.

5.150 In the case of royalties, if the royalty amount is linked to the volume of production, and does not depend on the value of the unit produced, the currency chosen may be either that of the country where production takes place or that of another country. If the royalty amount is linked to sales, the currency chosen may be that of the country where sales take place. If export sales are likely, more than one currency may be chosen—the currency of the country of the licensee or technology recipient where production and domestic sales occur, and the currency or currencies of the country or countries where the export sales are made. If royalties are linked to the profits of the enterprise of the licensee or technology recipient, then the currency of the country where that enterprise is legally organized may be chosen.

5.151 As concerns fees for technical services and assistance, the determination will most likely be between the currency of the country of the expert and the currency of the country where the services are performed; however, in the case of services performed by experts sent to the country of the licensee or technology recipient, the amount of the fees will normally be determined in the currency of the country of the expert, with payment in whole or in part in the currency of that country and the remainder, if any, plus the portion attributable to living expenses and other facilities in the country of the licensee or technology recipient.

5.152 Under the laws in certain countries governing the transfer of technology, it is provided that the currency of the obligation must be currency of the country of the licensee or technology recipient, though remittance abroad may be made in the equivalent foreign currency; whereas, under the laws in some other of these countries, though the currency of the obligation may be expressed in a foreign currency at least the expenses connected with the maintenance of experts in the country of the licensee or technology recipient must be paid in the currency of that country.

5.153 Many factors may play a role in the choice of the currency of payment, such as whether the currency of obligation can be utilized in the country of that currency by the licensor or technology supplier; the inflation rate in the country of the currency of obligation; the stability in the international money markets of that currency in relation to other currencies; the existence of currency exchange controls in the country of the currency of obligation or where the income of the licensee or technology recipient is generated; and the applicability of tax laws which may provide special benefits to one party or the other.

(ii) Rate of Exchange

5.154 In the event that the currency of payment chosen differs from the currency of obligation, the rate of conversion will normally figure as a provision in the license or agreement. Any one of a number of different exchange rates may be selected; for example, the official rate established by national or international monetary authorities, or an average of the said rates or a commercial rate, such as the telegraphic transfer selling rate or other selling rate or other rate of a specified domestic or foreign commercial bank.

E. TYPES OF INTELLECTUAL PROPERTY LICENSES

(a) Introduction

5.155 The typical provisions of an intellectual property license are discussed above in general terms. Some provisions are particular to the type of intellectual property being licensed. Some of the more important of these provisions are listed below.

(b) Patent Licenses

5.156 Under a patent license, the purpose of the contract is to authorize the use of an invention protected by a patent. The patent involved is identified by stating the name of the country in which it has been granted, together with its number. Generally, the technical subject matter of the invention is briefly stated in the preamble or in the article defining terms used in the contract. Reference is also frequently made to a separate annex when the license concerns a number of patents issued in differing countries. It is advisable to state exactly those countries in which patent applications are still pending and to stipulate which of the parties is responsible for complying with the administrative and legal formalities required for the upkeep of the patent.

5.157 A patent affords a set of exclusive rights: to use the invention, to manufacture it, to sell it or place it on the market. Generally, a license provides an authorization for the licensee to carry out all those acts.

5.158 A license may be an exclusive license, a sole license or a simple license. An exclusive license guarantees that the licensee will have no competition, not even that of the licensor or of the latter's subsidiaries. This must be stipulated in the agreement. A sole license guarantees the licensee that the licensor will afford

References for Section D
International Bureau of WIPO, *Licensing Guide for Developing Countries*, WIPO Pub. No. 620(E) (1977, 1992)

no licenses to other manufacturers within the contractual territory. A simple license provides no guarantees in that respect, but simply constitutes an authorization to use the invention.

5.159 In such cases, it is recommended to include in the contract what is know as the "most favored licensee clause". Such a clause ensures that the licensee will enjoy the most favorable conditions that may subsequently be granted to a second licensee (for the same territory). This clause thus avoids any distortion of competition that would result from differing contractual conditions for the supply of technology.

(c) Trademark Licenses

5.160 Trademark licensing is of fairly recent origin in trademark history. Since the original function of a trademark was to indicate trade origin, goods emanating from a source other than the trademark owner could not, without deception, carry a licensor's mark. Indeed the grant of a trademark license rendered a licensor vulnerable to the claim of non-user and expungement of its mark. The exercise by a licensor of quality control over the products sold by a licensee to which the mark was affixed opened the door to the fiction that such control was a form of user avoiding expungement of the mark. This fiction formed the basis of the registered user provisions inserted into most trademark statutes in the last forty years.

5.161 Most registered user provisions require the license parties to submit their agreements to the Registrar who scrutinizes them to ascertain the nature and extent of the quality controls to be exercised by the licensors. The Registrar is obliged to ensure that registration of such agreements accord with the national interest, and the Registrar is required to refuse registration to agreements which appear to him to facilitate trafficking. It should be noted, however, that registration has been considered not to be essential for validity of a trademark license. The registration provisions have been described as permissive and not mandatory. Provided a licensor maintains control over the quality of the licensed products and the licensor is perceived as retaining a connection with the licensed products expungement can be avoided.

5.162 Trademark licenses may be granted as adjuncts to or separately from patent and know-how licenses. Among the provisions particular to most trademark licenses are the following:

5.163 *Permission to Use*. The grant of permission to use the relevant mark or marks is the first-stated provision of most license agreements. The particulars of the mark or marks are usually listed in a schedule to the license agreement, together with the products in respect of which the mark is to be used.

5.164 *Number of Licensees*. It will be important for the licensee to know how many other licensees will be appointed to service the license territory. It will also be important to ascertain whether the licensor intends to distribute within the territory. Finally, it will be important to a licensee where others are to be appointed to ensure that its rivals are appointed on comparable terms.

5.165 *Quality Control*. As mentioned above, at the heart of any registered user agreement is a provision that the licensee will not use the marks on products which do not attain the standard of quality prescribed by the licensor. Quality control provisions will provide that the user receives, on a confidential basis, all specifications, technical data and know-how of the licensor to allow the prescribed quality standards to be met. Policing of this clause will usually require the user to send sample products to the licensor and to permit inspections of the user's factory and warehouses and of methods of production, materials used, storage and packing of finished products. The agreement should permit the user to dispose of products which do not meet the quality standard provided they do not carry the trademark.

5.166 *Marketing.* The license will designate the territory in which the trademark may be used. This will usually contain prohibitions against trading outside the designated territory as well as provisions keeping the licensor out of the license territory. Advertising material employed by the licensee may have to receive the licensor's approval.

5.167 *Financial Arrangements.* In addition to a fee or royalties for being permitted to use its trade marks, a licensor may also require payment in respect of the provision of skilled persons to instruct employees of the licensee in the materials required to achieve the prescribed quality standards required in the agreement. Arrangements also have to be made to allocate the cost of the sampling procedure. Finally, the licensee is usually required to keep detailed books and records of sales of the trademarked products.

5.168 *Infringements.* The licensee is normally required to report to the licensor all particulars of infringements which occur and the licensor usually has conduct of all infringement proceedings.

(d) Copyright Licenses (Publishing)

5.169 In the case of a publishing contract, the owner of copyright does not need and usually does not intend to part with his copyright or even his right to control the publication of his work. Under certain copyright laws, which consider the author's economic rights inseparable from his moral rights, assignment of the author's right to publish the work may not even be possible. When entering into a publishing contract, the owner of the copyright usually only undertakes to restrict the exercise of his right in the work to be published and restrict it to the extent necessary for the publisher to be able to use the work. At the same time, the ownership of copyright does not change but remains with the author or other owner of the copyright.

5.170 Thus, a characteristic publishing contract is a mere license granted to the publisher by the owner of copyright. To be of value to the publisher, a license must also enable him to protect his publishing activity against third persons.

5.171 A license is generally understood in the field of copyright as the authorization given by the author or other owner of copyright (licensor) to the user of the work (publisher or other licensee) to use it in a manner and according to conditions agreed upon between them.

5.172 The publisher should be granted a license comprising all the rights necessary for optimum realization of the planned publication. Generally, he acquires an exclusive license (providing him with an exclusive right) to reproduce and publish the work concerned—or, if appropriate, to provide, reproduce and publish its translation—in a standard trade edition, comprising a reasonable number of copies.

5.173 The license can be granted for one edition only, or also for subsequent ones. The size of a single—or the first—edition is usually determined in the contract either by fixing the number of copies it should comprise, or by stipulating a minimum and/ or maximum number of copies ("the print run.") The agreement on the size of a single—or the first—edition usually takes into account the need to comply with the presumable demand of the public, at costs permitting sales at the usual retail price per copy prevailing in the given book market as regards similar publications.

5.174 In the case of a license to publish the work in translation, the language (or languages) of the authorized edition (or editions) must be specified.

5.175 In order to promote the dissemination of the work published, and with regard to possible further exploitation of the publication under the contract, the licensee may acquire also certain so-called "subsidiary rights." Such rights serve the purpose of reproducing or communicating to the public, or licensing others to reproduce or communicate to the public, the work (or its translation) in specified forms other than the standard trade edition.

5.176 Such subsidiary rights may for instance comprise: the right of previous and subsequent publication in the press of one or more extracts from the work; serial rights, that is, the right to publish the entire work or parts of it in one or more successive issues of a newspaper or periodical, before or after publication of the work in the standard trade edition; the right to read extracts from the work in sound or television broadcasting; the right to include the published work or a part of it in an anthology; the right to arrange for pocket book or book club editions subsequent to the standard trade edition.

5.177 Publishers often request the licensor to confer on them, in the framework of subsidiary rights, the right also to license the reproduction of the published work by means of making microfilms or other reprographic reproductions thereof, for purposes beyond the limits of fair use allowed by the law. The publisher may also request the right to license storage of the work in a computer, accessible to the public. Again, publishers may request the licensor to entitle them to license the reproduction of the work in the form of sound recordings as well. Sometimes, also the right of licensing the reproduction of filmstrips is requested. All these kinds of reproduction by means of modern technology are often referred to in contemporary publishing contracts as "mechanical reproduction" of the work, and the rights involved as "mechanical reproduction rights." This term should not be confused with the notion of the "musical mechanical right," which means the right to reproduce a musical work in the form of sound recordings.

5.178 It is a reasonable and usually accepted position not to confer upon the publisher rights to exploit the work in any manner involving its adaptation, such as dramatization rights for stage or film production, or for sound or television broadcasting, or translation rights in general. Strictly speaking, the exploitation of such rights goes beyond the scope of the promotion or direct exploitation of the publisher's own publication of the work.

5.179 The grant of "digest rights" (the right to publish an abridgement or shortened form of the work), or of the so-called "strip cartoon rights," is often made subject to special authorization in each case, in view of the moral interests of the author relating to the integrity of his work.

5.180 With regard to the integrity of the work to be published, special stipulations can be incorporated in the contract. This may prove useful especially in countries where no appropriate "moral rights" provisions are established by legislation. For example, it may be agreed that "the publisher shall reproduce the work without any amendment or abbreviation thereof, or addition thereto."

5.181 As regards translation of the work, it is usual to agree that "the publisher shall have a precise and faithful translation made at his own expense. The title of the translation is subject to the written approval of the Copyright Licensor. Upon request, the final text of the translation shall also be submitted to him for approval."

5.182 It can also be stipulated that "the Publisher shall ensure that the title of the work and the name of its author shall appear with due prominence on every copy produced." Depending on the circumstances, it also can be added that "the Publisher undertakes to print the name of the original publisher (that is, ...) as well as the year(s) of the previous edition(s) of the work on the verso of the title page."

5.183 With regard to certain formalities required in a few States (mainly in the United States of America) as a condition of the full enjoyment of copyright in published works, it is generally stipulated in publishing contracts that an appropriate notice of copyright shall be printed on the title page. The notice consists of the symbol C, the year of the first publication of the work and the name of the owner of the copyright in the work.

5.184 As regards distribution of the copies published, it is often stipulated that "the Publisher shall provide for efficient promotion of the work at his own expense." In cases where his license has not been confined to one edition only, it is often added that "he shall see to it that the book is continuously available, and that new editions are printed in due time, so as to comply with actual demand."

F. GOVERNMENT CONTROL OF LICENSING AGREEMENTS

5.185 In many developing countries, the inflow of technology is subject to a variety of controls as a means of ensuring that contracts concerning transfer of technology are consistent with the economic aims of the government. In some countries, these controls are part of a more comprehensive system of laws dealing with foreign investment in the country. In others, the controls result from the foreign exchange regulations which are directed at the flow of payments abroad, whether as dividends, royalties, or income in other forms or as the return of

References for Section E
F. Dessemontet, *Intellectual Property in Licensing and Franchising Contracts*, ISIP/86/8
M. Blakeney, "Licensing Foreign Marks", 12 *Intellectual Property in Asia and the Pacific* 4
International Bureau of WIPO, *Basic Notions and Related Practices About Publishing Contracts Between Parties Belonging to Different Countries*, B/CR/3

capital. Indirectly, import regulations, particularly lower tariff rates or exemptions on products embodying needed technology, may also have an effect on the inflow of technology. In still other developing countries, legal systems have been devised specifically to control the transfer of technology to, or within, the country. These systems include the requirement that industrial property licenses and technology transfer agreements be notified to government authorities or be registered or approved by them in accordance with criteria established by the legislation or set forth in regulations or guidelines issued by appropriate governmental bodies.

5.186 The failure of the responsible party to submit for registration or approval an industrial property license or technology transfer agreement or its modification, amendment, extension or termination, to the appropriate government authorities within the time limits and under the other conditions prescribed has a number of legal consequences. Under the relevant laws, the failure to comply may render the license or agreement void or unenforceable and subject the party responsible to a penalty or to the suspension of its right to trade or to loss of its business organization status. The registration or approval of the license or the agreement may be a prerequisite to giving evidence of actual exploitation of a patent or actual use of a trademark in the country, or obtaining an authorization from the fiscal authorities to make payments abroad or to receiving fiscal or other benefits designed to encourage or promote investment in certain sectors or industries.

5.187 The WIPO Model Law for Developing Countries on Inventions (Volume II), contains provisions establishing a legal and administrative framework for the examination and registration of such contracts in accordance with the policy of ensuring that such contracts do not impose unjustified restrictions upon the acquirer of the technology ("the transferee") which would have the consequence that the contract, as a whole, would be harmful to the economic interests of the country.

5.188 The intent is not only to protect the local enterprise that is contracting to acquire the technology—which, frequently, is in a relatively weak bargaining position—but also—and even to a higher degree—to prevent the economic policy of the government being frustrated by certain contracts. It is of vital importance to a developing country that—even though badly needed—the acquisition of foreign technology should not impose an undue burden on its economy. If the cost of technology should exceed its value to the local economy, there may be serious consequences; for example, a decline in the industrial growth rate, depletion of natural resources, unfavorable balance of trade, misallocation of financial resources, etc.

5.189 The Model Law provides that the examination and registration of contracts is a task of the Patent Office. According to the organizational structure of the government, instead of the Patent Office, another government agency could be entrusted with this task.

5.190 In order to assist the office concerned in the examination of such contracts the Model Law establishes a list of 17 terms that the Office must particularly take into consideration. The list of 17 terms is not exhaustive: registration of a contract can be refused even if that contract does not contain any of the terms listed; this can be the case if the contract contains a term not appearing on the list but which imposes certain restrictions upon the transferee so that the contract, taken as a whole, is harmful to the economic interests of the country. Secondly, the presence in the contract of any of the 17 terms listed does not necessarily entail a refusal to register the contract; registration of the contract can only be refused if the restrictions imposed upon the transferee are unjustified and if the contract, taken as a whole, is harmful to the economic interests of the country; indeed, depending on the circumstances of the case, the presence of the term in question might not entail detrimental effects to the economic interests of the country or, if it does entail such effects, these might be offset by positive effects for the economic interests of the country brought about by the presence of other terms in the contract, since no codification of specific terms can anticipate the practically unlimited number of background factors (business, commercial, technological, etc.) which may enter into a determination of the effect a given contract will have within a given economic environment. In other words, the Office must apply the provisions without rigidity but with flexibility, while considering the particular merits of each contract in the light of the economic interests of the country.

The said terms are those the effect of which would be:

(1) to import technology from abroad when substantially similar or equivalent technology may be obtained on the same or more favorable conditions without any importation of the technology from abroad;

(2) to oblige the transferee to make payments which are disproportionate to the value of the technology to which the contract relates;

(3) to oblige the transferee to acquire any materials from the transferor or from sources designated or approved by the transferor, unless it is otherwise impossible, for all practical purposes, to ensure the quality of the products to be produced and provided that the said materials are supplied at a reasonable price;

(4) to restrict the transferee's freedom to acquire any materials from any source unless it is otherwise impossible, for all practical purposes, to ensure the quality of the products to be produced;

(5) to restrict the transferee's freedom to use any materials which are not supplied by the transferor or by sources designated or approved by the transferor, unless it is otherwise impossible, for all practical purposes, to ensure the quality of the products to be produced;

(6) to oblige the transferee to sell the products produced by him exclusively or principally to persons designated by the transferor;

(7) to oblige the transferee to make available to the transferor, without receiving appropriate payment, any improvements made by the transferee with respect to the technology to which the contract relates;

(8) to limit the quantity of the products produced by the transferee;

(9) to restrict the transferee's freedom to export or his freedom to allow others to export the products produced by him, provided that if the transferor owns, in a country to which such a restriction applies, a patent which would be infringed in case of importation of the said products into the said country; if the transferor has a contractual obligation not to allow others to export the said products to such a country; or if the transferor already supplies the market in such a country with the same products, such facts shall be taken into account;

(10) to oblige the transferee to employ persons designated by the transferor not needed for the efficient transfer of the technology to which the contract relates;

(11) to impose restrictions on research or technological development carried out by the transferee;

(12) to restrict the transferee's freedom to use any technology other than the technology to which the contract relates;

(13) to extend the coverage of the contract to technology not required to achieve the objective of the contract and to oblige the transferee to give consideration for such technology;

(14) to fix prices for the sale or resale of the products produced by the transferee;

(15) to exempt the transferor from any liability resulting from any defect inherent in the technology to which the contract relates or unreasonably to restrict such liability;

(16) to restrict the transferee's freedom to use, after the expiration of his contractual obligations, the technology acquired as a result of the contract, subject, however, to any right of the transferor under a patent;

(17) to establish the duration of the contract for a period which is unreasonably long in relation to the economic function of the contract, provided that any period which does not exceed the duration of the patent to which the contract relates shall not be regarded as unreasonably long.

5.191 The system provided for by the Model Law, although it enumerates some of the most important clauses to be considered, recommends a flexible approach which allows the examination of each contract on its merits within the general economic and technological context of the country concerned. No doubt, the approval of a contract would also depend on such considerations as foreign exchange and other controls concerning payments to be made abroad.

References for Section F
International Bureau of WIPO, *Negotiation and Control of Contracts for the Acquisition and Transfer of Technology Where Such Contracts Involve Questions of Intellectual Property*, WIPO/IP/AC/86/8
International Bureau of WIPO, *WIPO Model Law for Developing Countries on Inventions*, Vols. I and II, WIPO Pub. Nos. 840(E) and 841(E)

CHAPTER 6

The Role of Industrial Property Information and Documentation in Promoting Technological Development

A. THE ROLE OF INDUSTRIAL PROPERTY INFORMATION IN THE TRANSFER OF TECHNOLOGY

(a) Introduction

6.1 The successful transfer of technology to a given country is largely dependent on the availability of indigenous technological capacities, and the process of transferring selected imported technology should thus be complementary to national research and development efforts and the development of an indigenous technological capability. The transfer and development process involves a sequence of interlinked activities, such as the identification of technological needs in the light of development objectives; the obtaining of information on alternative sources of technology, including local sources; the evaluation and selection of the most appropriate technology; the unpackaging of technology packages in order to assess the suitability, costs, and conditions of their components; the negotiation of the best possible terms and conditions; the adaptation and absorption of imported technology and stimulation of the development of indigenous technology; and the dissemination of newly available technology to potential users.

6.2 The successful evaluation, selection, development, adaptation and application of technology requires indigenous national capacities for research and development (R & D) and the formulation of appropriate national policies in science as well as in technology. In this context the importance of scientific and technical information, for its long-term relevance to the overall process of national development, should also be properly recognized.

6.3 The exchange of technological information is essential for bridging the technological gap between and within countries and for strengthening technological capabilities of developing countries, the latter being the prerequisite for the successful adaptation of foreign technology to local conditions and for the generation of new indigenous technology.

6.4 The transfer of technological information, however efficient and selective, must be recognized in itself as being no more than an important link in the chain of the transfer of technology. The receipt of well-selected technological information by users in developing countries is only a first step towards its practical utilization; such information prepares for and supports the taking of well-founded decisions and reinforces the autonomy of those decisions.

6.5   Information about alternative technologies and sources of supply, including information about minimum costs, terms and conditions, technological specifications, guarantees, delivery and implementation schedules, resources and manpower requirements, etc. is necessary for the evaluation and selection of development projects.

6.6   Information about developments in technology-related areas both in developed and developing countries is necessary to draw up national policies relating to foreign investment, contractual arrangements for the transfer of technology, national research and development, government procurement and the initiation of large-scale public projects and other matters.

6.7   Technological information exists not only in a printed form, such as books, journals, documents, reports, directories, patent documents, standards, specifications and catalogues, but also in non-printed form such as audio-visual and machine-readable material as well as in organizational and individual expertise transferred by the interaction of people attending meetings, seminars and training.   It may also be embodied in products and services. Potentially useful technological information may be found in virtually all countries irrespective of their present level of technological development.

6.8   In spite of its availability, to obtain useful technological information is not easy for various reasons.   For instance, it is in fact difficult to obtain quick access to relevant data sources and to select the right one from a large amount of information. Another reason why information on many technologies covered by specialized literature is not fully used, in particular, by developing countries appears to be the absence of suitable local infrastructures.   At the same time, this lack of supporting infrastructure with particular reference to properly trained people may also affect the diffusion of technology developed or adapted, especially by small and medium enterprises in developing countries, which is not evaluated and made known locally and even less brought to the attention of users in other developing countries.

6.9   Industrial property information, in comparison with other technological information sources, has advantages in its availability and selectivity, since it is not only accessible to any country in the world but selected information is a reflection of current development of technology in a concise and uniform presentation.   For example, the information contained in each one of the one million patent documents published yearly is accessible to anyone situated anywhere in the world, provided he makes the effort to obtain it.   One can use patent information in a passive manner by acquiring copies of a number of selected patent documents related to the technical field he is interested in, to study their content, to choose the patent document presenting the most appropriate solution to his problem and to work the invention without referring to, or negotiating with, any third party.   This use of patent information is possible if the granted patent is no longer valid in the country in which the invention is intended to be used.

6.10   Institutions to which patent information is directly and particularly useful may be grouped into four categories, namely, governmental authorities, research and development institutions, universities and industries.

(b) Use by Government Authorities

6.11 Many different governmental authorities are potential users of patent information, particularly those authorities involved in:

(1) encouraging innovative activities;
(2) assisting national industries increase their export potential;
(3) elaborating development plans and establishing industrial priorities;
(4) generating indigenous technology aiming at increasing employment in rural areas and limiting import of consumer goods;
(5) negotiating and concluding licensing agreements.

6.12 The competent governmental authority involved in encouraging innovative activities can use patent information as a means of creating an interest in innovation in technical training courses at universities and technical colleges. Moreover, copies of national patent documents and of selected foreign documents, perhaps relating to local industries, can be provided in specialist public libraries.

6.13 The government can assist national industries to increase exports to other developing or to industrialized countries by assisting them in obtaining patent rights in those countries and by upgrading the role of its Patent Office. The government can support the efforts of big national industries to build up their own collections of patent documents and it may facilitate for them the acquisition of these documents.

6.14 When elaborating industrial development plans and establishing sectoral priorities the government could use the statistics published by its Patent Office, by other Patent Offices and by WIPO. The study in depth of patent activities in specific technical fields, particularly of foreign patents filed, may give a clear indication of industrial trends and foreign developments.

6.15 A review of patent documents concerning an indigenous technology can identify which technology is most appropriate to increase production, which technology uses less energy and which technology is capable of being used in rural areas, thus creating new jobs and reducing the importation of goods.

6.16 Developing countries operate generally from a weak position when negotiating for a licensing agreement with technology suppliers from industrially developed countries. The information that patent documents provide not only on a wide range of alternative technologies but also on alternative sources of technology enables purchasers of technology in developing countries to improve their position considerably in such negotiations. The staff of the authority in charge of technology transfer is not always technically skilled and relies on the research and development institutions to evaluate, select, and adapt foreign technology. The role of patent information in furthering the development work of these institutions has therefore a direct impact on the strengthening of capabilities for technology transfer transactions.

(c) Use by Research and Development Institutions

6.17 Every invention marks an advance in the process of technological development and at the same time the starting point for the search for new technology. The study of technological information in patents, therefore, has the effect of stimulating creative thinking and enhancing the prospects of discovering new technologies that are in advance of present knowledge.

6.18 Before embarking on a research activity, it is always beneficial to the research worker to include in the usual "library research", a study of patent information. This study of patent information enables the researcher to make the best decision as to whether to embark on his own research, or to borrow the results of research already conducted in the particular field by obtaining the appropriate licenses, or to enter into joint execution of research with others of similar interest and competence. Patent information thus facilitates the identification of important trends in research and development and also expedites the search for effective and readily applicable technical solutions to development problems.

6.19 The searcher in the research and development institution should have easy access to patent information and be well trained in exploiting this information for his research activities. A very convenient means of access would be the computer on-line service of a major data bank or a telex line which he can use in order to obtain without delay the list of patents he is interested in. Copies of these patents could be provided to him by the Patent Office or via the services of WIPO within its state-of-the-art search program.

(d)   Use by Industry

6.20 Industrial enterprises are the most important users of technological information contained in patent documents. Engineers and technical staff in industry are daily confronted with problems related to the improvement of existing products or to the introduction of a new production process. In the industrialized countries, these problems are generally solved by the staff itself, sometimes with the assistance of consultants from outside, whereas in the developing countries the management of industry relies heavily on the manufacturers of the machines to solve their technical problems. The human factor, the know-how and the motivation to create and improve should be considered as a long term investment in industry.

6.21 Industrialists in developing countries should try to solve their technical problems with the help of their own technical staff. Patent information in the form of Search Reports, copies of given patent documents or bibliographic data on sets of relevant patents, is badly needed by the engineer who is seeking a solution to his technical problems. By using patent documents as sources of solutions to technological problems, engineers working in industry become aware of the importance of their own developments and that some of their results may even be patentable.

6.22 Major industrial enterprises should build up a collection of national patents issued in the field of their activities and thus observe international developments as reflected in the patents of their competitors abroad. Large international companies typically apply for patents only after having made a detailed study of the market and having investigated the possibilities of selling its products, or after having found that the competitors are interested in that particular market. Thus the kind and the number of patent applications filed by the multinational companies can give a hint to the local industrialist about the development possibilities of his own market, and consequently he could adapt or readjust his strategy.

6.23 Finally, the needs of industry for patent information when identifying new technology, or before negotiating new technology transfer agreements, are similar to the needs of the governmental authorities or research and development institutions.

(e) Use by Universities

6.24 Many professors and students at universities believe that patents are always major technological breakthroughs and therefore do not relate directly to their research activities. This wrong approach is gradually disappearing with the realization that patents are also granted for improvements to existing devices or processes and not only for completely new ones. The breakdown of this myth concerning patents should result in the inclusion of patent documentation in the documentary sources of information available at universities. Under the auspices of WIPO, an international association of professors teaching intellectual property was created in 1980, namely, the International Association for the Advancement of Teaching and Research in Intellectual Property (ATRIP).

6.25 Universities could include in their scientific libraries collections of patent documents relevant to the activities of their technological faculties. Universities are often called upon by industry to give expert opinions or to perform specific research which requires equipment normally not available in small and medium scale industries. The role of patent information in the research done at universities is even greater than it is for research and development institutions due to the fact that students consult patent documents more willingly than the relatively more independent and experienced researcher.

6.26 Universities also play an important role in the introduction of the use of patent information at all levels within the country, because they generate the engineers and researchers who will be the future potential beneficiaries of such use. Therefore, educational material at the engineering faculties could include patent information as one of its major components.

B. THE RANGE OF PATENT DOCUMENTATION

6.27 Patent documentation is the full body of documents (or excerpts therefrom), published or unpublished, that contain data on the results of research, design, development, and pioneering programs which have been applied for and recognized as discoveries, inventions, utility models, and industrial designs; and on protection of the rights of inventors, patent-owners, and holders of diplomas and certificates of registration of industrial designs and utility models.

6.28 Therefore, patent documentation is understood as referring primarily to the official publications of Patent Offices: specifications to applications for inventions, specifications of inventions, and official patent bulletins or gazettes.

References for Section A
International Bureau of WIPO, *Guidelines for the Organization of a Patent Information and Document Center with Particular Regard to the Needs and Circumstances of Developing Countries*, WIPO Pub. No. 658(E) (1980 and 1987)
International Bureau of WIPO, *The Role of Patent Information in the Transfer of Technology*, INSPI/82/5

6.29 Patent documentation is classified into the following distinctive types:

(1) official patent bulletins (gazettes);
(2) specifications to applications for inventions (in particular, those which have or have not passed preliminary or formal examination);
(3) specifications of patents;
(4) specifications of utility models;
(5) specifications to utility certificates (France);
(6) descriptions of industrial designs;
(7) official publications on changes in the state of legal protection;
(8) official patent indexes.

6.30 The specification of a patent, that is, the document granted, and the patent application which is the basis for the patent, are, in principle, drafted by the applicant. Most laws require that the application contain "claims" and a "description." The claims state in succinct language the essence of the invention, that is, the elements which distinguish it from what is already known. The description explains the invention by indicating the "state of the art," that is, what was already known before the invention was made, describing the step forward in knowledge represented by the invention and giving additional information useful in deciding whether the invention was really new.

6.31 It is generally required that the application be sufficiently clear and complete for any person specialized in the field of technology to which the application relates to enable that person, on the basis of that application, to produce the device or to perform the process described in it ("to carry out the invention"). Also, patent rights granted on the basis of the patent document must permit a clear, unambiguous definition of the scope of protection, i.e., the exclusive right conferred by the patent. This duality of disclosure of technological information, on the one hand, and a definition of patent rights, on the other, gives patent documents not only great value as sources of the most recent information but also a particular language and structure which is initially difficult to understand. Yet understanding how patent documents are structured and the reasons for the way they are written can make this important source of technological information effective and accessible.

C. CONTENT OF PATENT DOCUMENTS

(a) Introduction

6.32 Patent documents generally convey the most recent information. This is so because applicants always try to file their applications as soon as possible;

References for Section B
R.P. Veherashni, *Problems of Technical Information, Types and Structure of Patent Documents*, MPIC/82/4.1
International Bureau of WIPO, *Guidelines for the Organization of a Patent Information and Document Center with Particular Regard to the Needs and Circumstances of Developing Countries*, WIPO Pub. No. 658(E) (1980 and 1987)
International Bureau of WIPO, *Technological Information Contained in Patent Documents and Its Use*, ISIP/93/6

usually the applicant who, among several applicants applying in respect of similar inventions, was the first to apply will be granted the patent, whereas the applications of the others will be denied; furthermore, only with a patent in his hand has an inventor the maximum legal means at his disposal for fighting against the use of his invention by others against his will; finally, an inventor having a patent usually can stipulate a higher sales price or royalty for selling or licensing his invention than if he does not, or does not yet, have a patent.

6.33 Patent documents disclose technological information by describing the inventions in accordance with the requirements of the applicable patent law and by indicating the claimed novelty and inventiveness by reference to the existing state of the art. They are thus sources of information not only on what is new (the invention) but also on what is already known (i.e. the state of the art), and in many cases furnish a history, in summary form, of the technological progress in the field to which they relate.

6.34 Patent documents have a fairly uniform presentation with respect to layout and bibliographic data, and frequently have explanatory drawings. The claims show what the essence of the invention is likely to be. Since the description must be such that the specialist is able to execute the invention on the basis of the patent document, consultation of patent documents allows of such execution, in theory always, and in practice frequently.

6.35 Patent documents have a fairly uniform structure. The claims give the essence of what is new; the description is required to show the background to the invention and to state clearly the difference between the pre-existent technology and what the invention contributes, as a step forward in technology; this means, among other things, and as distinct from scientific or technological articles, that the reader of patent documents does not first have to familiarize himself with, and adjust his mental processes to, the mental processes—different for every author—of the author of an article, in other words, this fairly uniform structure of patent documents makes their reading, once one gets accustomed to it, generally easier.

6.36 A patent document contains two types of information: bibliographic information and technical information. Some Industrial Property Offices which also publish the patent application after examination, publish additionally the search report as established by the examiners of those Offices; the search reports are generally attached to the corresponding published patent applications.

(b) Bibliographic Information

6.37 This information is presented on the first page of the patent document and includes, mainly:

(1) dates, names and addresses of the publishing authority and of the persons or companies involved in the patent, such as the inventor, the owner of the patent right, the representative or patent agent;

(2) classification symbols of the International Patent Classification (IPC), and, in some cases, also the national patent classification;

(3) title of the invention, abstract of the description and a representative drawing or a chemical formula.

6.38 Each of the bibliographic data items on the first page of a patent document is identified by a two-digit numerical code, the so-called INID-Code (Internationally agreed Numbers for the Identification of Data), which is universally adopted and which facilitates the understanding of the names, dates, addresses and classification symbols even without any knowledge of the language in which the patent document is published. The two-digit numerical code is generally printed in a small circle or between brackets and placed immediately before the bibliographic data to be coded. The presentation of the bibliographic data and the layout of the first page of most patent documents are made according to standards and guidelines elaborated by WIPO.

(c) Technical Information

6.39 Technical information contained in a patent document usually includes four elements:

(1) a short description of the state of the art of the technology as known to the inventor;
(2) the detailed description of the invention in such a manner that a technician skilled in the art is able to work the invention;
(3) one or more drawings (or chemical formulae) illustrating visually the functioning of the invention;
(4) the claims, which define the scope of the invention.

6.40 The sequence in which these four elements of information is given is not internationally standardized. However, every country maintains the same presentation for all its published patent documents. Generally, the technical content of the patent document is presented on sequentially numbered pages as follows: state of the art—detailed description—claims—drawings. The number of the pages of a patent document varies according to the complexity of the invention and to the technical field. The average length of a patent document is between 10 and 15 pages.

(d) Search Report

6.41 The Search Report is established by the patent examiner in the Industrial Property Office after consultation of the search files available in his Office. The search files consist of patent documents and other publications systematically arranged so as to group technical fields together. The search files contain the patent documents published by at least the major industrialized countries since 1920 or even earlier. The Search Report contains references to the documents which the examiner considered as describing similar or identical technical solutions as the purported invention. If one of the solutions in the Search Report is identical to the one described in the application, the invention is then considered as not being new and thus a patent would not be granted.

(e) Form of Documents

6.42 The Industrial Property Offices publish their patent documents and related data in various forms, using different information carriers. The patent information carriers which are currently available on the international market include, but are not limited to, the following:

Individual Copies of Patent Documents:

(1) in paper form;
(2) on microfiches;
(3) on CD-ROM;

Sets of Patent Documents Arranged Numerically:

(1) in bound volume;
(2) on 16mm or 35mm microfilms;
(3) on microfiches;
(4) on CD-ROM;

Bibliographic information presented in list form whereby each list comprises sets of data relating each to one patent document. The same content of each list may be arranged in various ways, and according to one of the important bibliographic data items, e.g. by classification symbol or by name of applicant. The lists can be:

(1) in paper form (official gazettes);
(2) on microfiches;
(3) on 16mm or 35mm microfilms;
(4) on CD-ROM;
(5) stored in computers which are directly accessible by on-line terminals, telephone or telex.

D. NEW TECHNOLOGIES FOR STORAGE OF AND ACCESS TO INDUSTRIAL PROPERTY INFORMATION

6.43 Modern computer technology has ushered in a new era for storage of and access to industrial property information. The focus of this new era is the technology referred to as the "CD-ROM." CD-ROM refers to Compact Disc Read Only Memory technology, in which the information is pressed on a disc of 12 cm in diameter, like the audio CDs, in the form of a series of pits, which can be read by a laser in a reading equipment (the optical disc reader). The information can then be displayed on a screen by the user. The information on a CD-ROM cannot be erased or added to (hence "read-only").

6.44 The possibilities of using CD-ROMs for industrial property documents and information introduce a new dimension into the present automated search systems. CD-ROMs offer a new information delivery mechanism which complements magnetic tape and disc storage systems or even replaces them in some

References for Section C
International Bureau of WIPO, *Guidelines for the Organization of a Patent Information and Document Center with Particular Regard to the Needs and Circumstances of Developing Countries,* WIPO Pub. No. 658(E) (1980 and 1987)
International Bureau of WIPO, *Technological Information Contained in Patent Documents and Its Use,* ISIP/93/6
International Bureau of WIPO, *The Role of Patent Information and Documentation in the Transfer of Technology,* PI.105, 1983
International Bureau of WIPO, *Patent Information — What It Is and How Useful It Is for Technology Development or Technology Transfer,* WIPO/IP/SUV/93/9

uses. CD-ROMs containing digitized texts and/or graphics in facsimile are suitable for:

(1) document archives;
(2) off-line search in bibliographic data, title, abstract and goods and services and even full text;
(3) patent document distribution.

6.45 What are the main characteristics of CD-ROMs that make their use in the field of industrial property information attractive? The following points may help to answer that question:

(1) they have an enormous storage capacity;
(2) the recordings made and the retrieval of the information, is under electronic control;
(3) the duplication of CD-ROMs is relatively cheap;
(4) CD-ROM are relatively robust and not subject to environmental effects of moisture, high or low temperatures, electric or magnetic fields;
(5) CD-ROM readers are not expensive (500 Swiss francs for a standard model), and the cost of these readers will become lower in the future;
(6) the extraction of data, e.g., by carrying out a Boolean search using several bibliographic search files, can be controlled by using a personal computer. This means that two, or more, data files stored on the disc can be manipulated in the memory of the computer as an interactive search system.

6.46 There exist two main methods for storing information on optical discs:

(1) in the form of binary-coded facsimile data (the "facsimile" or "bit-map" mode); and
(2) as character-coded data (the "digitized" mode).

6.47 In facsimile mode, the information is stored as a 'picture' comprising tiny dots that represent the image of the printed page. Each dot is represented in the computer by a 'bit' and many bits are needed to portray an image. For example, a page of information scanned at 300 dots per inch (or dpi) resolution requires about 1,050,000 bytes of storage (1 byte = 8 binary bits of information). In practice, data compression techniques reduce the storage requirements for each page, resulting in storage of 15,000 to 20,000 facsimile pages on one CD-ROM disc. On the other hand, in digitized-mode storage the number of pages stored on one CD-ROM disc varies from 150,000 to 300,000 pages, since for one printed character only one byte of storage is needed.

6.48 Further applications of CD-ROMs can be identified as follows:

(1) storage of the complete published patent documents. This application mainly acts as a publication medium either with texts and images stored in facsimile format, or in mixed mode with the text itself character coded and the images facsimile recorded, or, perhaps in the future, with text and images stored in some digitized form;
(2) in the case of patent information: storage of bibliographic data, with or without abstracts. This application provides similar possibilities to the use of the presently available on-line patent data bases;

(3) in the case of trademark information: storage of bibliographic data, with or without the list of goods and/or services and with or without images. This application provides similar possibilities to the use of the presently available on-line trademark data bases;

(4) in the case of storage related data, for example the texts of classification systems, e.g. the IPC, together with catchword indexes. This application permits the search of texts of classification systems using keywords from the catchword indexes or from the text of the classification itself, or the display of the classification using a classification symbol as a search term;

(5) a mixture of (ii) and (iv) or (iii) and (i).

6.49 A typical CD-ROM search system consists of a personal computer (PC) with a screen, a compact disc drive and a printer. The drive (also referred to as "reader") can be a stand-alone unit that is attached to the computer via a cable or a built-in unit that can be inserted in place of a second floppy disc drive. An optical disc drive can also be designed as a multi-disc-drive unit which is controlled by the PC and is designed to find the required disc from the store and to load it into the reader.

6.50 The CD-ROM package in stand-alone mode contains all the necessary search prerequisites, namely: the data base, the indexes (also called "dictionaries") and the retrieval software on the CD-ROM or on a floppy. To retrieve information, the user signs on via his work station to one of the available files on the disc, performs a search, and identifies an appropriate citation. Upon receiving the command to display the text, the computer links the command to the data identifying the location of the image encoded on the disc, down- loads image data into a temporary magnetic disc storage, and displays on the workstation screen the image of the relevant page or pages of the document. The user can print the images page by page on an appropriate printer associated with the work station.

6.51 The costs of using on-line search systems are too high for many users or potential users. The possible availability of bibliographic information concerning industrial property documents recorded in a digital mode on a CD-ROM, at a relatively low cost compared to on-line search systems, constitutes an attractive option for many users. The creation of such a CD-ROM search system allows a user to avoid being permanently connected to a remote, and expensive, data base whilst he is performing the search. Since all the information he needs to use would be stored locally in his equipment, he can search for as long and as often as he needs without incurring extra costs.

6.52 In terms of patent documentation, the storage capacity of CD-ROMs can be summarized as follows:

(1) one CD-ROM can store the complete patent documents in facsimile form, including drawings, of approximately 1,000 patent documents. The full text itself is not directly searchable, but search indexes can be added relating to document number, IPC symbols, names, words in the titles, etc., leading to the display or printing of images of the patent documents;

(2) one CD-ROM can store 3,000 complete patent documents in a mixed mode, that is, the text parts are stored in a digital mode, whilst the drawings are stored in a facsimile mode. The textual parts are directly searchable;

(3) one CD-ROM can store the digitized text, bibliographic data including abstracts but not drawings and chemical formulae, of 20,000 patent documents. This storage includes indexes of bibliographic information, including indexes from the words in titles and abstracts.

6.53 In terms of trademark information, the storage capacity is as follows:

(1) one CD-ROM can store approximately 250,000 trademark images in black and white. If the images are in grey-scales then 40,000 images can be stored, when they are in color up to 20,000 images can be stored. The images can be made searchable by mark number and Vienna classification symbols leading to the display or printing of the images of the marks.

(2) one CD-ROM can store approximately 200,000 complete trademark records in a so-called "mixed mode", that is, the text parts are stored in a digital mode, whilst the black and white images are stored in a facsimile mode. The textual parts and the images are directly searchable.

6.54 The storage of patent documents in facsimile mode on CD-ROMs offers a high density method of storage and can produce a quality image on a screen and a quality print. These products already exist, e.g. the Japanese Patent Office offers weekly distribution of newly published patent applications on CD-ROM. The European Patent Office (EPO) also offers the complete patent applications published by the EPO and WIPO, recorded on CD-ROM discs as facsimile images (e.g. the ESPACE-EP or ESPACE-WORLD discs) and also offers on CD-ROMs the front pages of published patent applications (the FIRST system).

6.55 The storage of trademark data and trademark image data on CD-ROMs offers a high density method of storage and can produce a quality image on a screen and a quality print. These products already exist, e.g. the International Bureau of WIPO offers monthly the complete international trademark file on CD-ROM discs under the ROMARIN project.

E. STATISTICS FOR PATENT DOCUMENTS AS A SOURCE OF TECHNOLOGICAL INFORMATION

6.56 According to recent statistics, the number of patent applications in the world each year is well over one million. Those applications result in the grant of over half a million patents. The number of *inventions* which are covered by those patent applications and grants is much smaller since each invention gives rise to an average of two to three patent applications in different countries. The number of patent documents published each year, both applications and granted patents, is over one million, in many different languages. Below, statistics are given for the major patenting countries.

References for Section D
International Bureau of WIPO, *New Technologies for Storage of and Access to Industrial Property Information*, ISIP/93/7

	Patents		Utility Models	
	Applications	Grants	Applications	Grants
Japan	380,035	88,400	77,101	53,400
United States of America	191,386	98,344	–	–
Germany	117,768	52,008	20,084	16,884
United Kingdom	101,242	42,586	–	–
France	82,141	44,291	–	–
Italy	65,170	32,511	3,337	1,840
Netherlands	58,822	23,264	–	–
Spain	56,733	15,815	3,492	3,279
Sweden	55,641	21,115	–	–
Switzerland	55,557	20,637	–	–
Austria	51,491	16,787	–	–
Canada	47,752	14,580	–	–
Republic of Korea	47,344	11,446	32,205	7,592
Denmark	47,088	6,629	563	453
Belgium	46,520	19,074	–	–
Russian Federation	43,717	13,214	–	–
Luxembourg	43,503	10,293	–	–
Portugal	42,932	1,694	281	83
Greece	36,907	7,835	219	188
Ireland	36,792	1,574	–	–
Monaco	32,717	115	–	–
Australia	30,729	12,728	–	–
China	19,618	6,556	47,499	46,639
Brazil	16,944	2,649	2,584	319
India	3,720	1,551	–	–
Sub-Totals	1,712,269	565,696	187,365	130,677

6.57 The above figures are based on WIPO Statistics for 1993. Where a country is a party to an international or regional arrangement, e.g. the PCT or the EPC, the figures include all international or regional applications in which that country was designated. The sub-total of patent applications given above for 25 countries represent almost 90% of the total patent applications filed in 110 countries and organizations in 1993. The sub-total of utility model applications given above for 10 countries represents more than 95% of the total applications for utility models filed in 24 countries in 1993.

6.58 There are two main reasons for this difference between the number of inventions and of the corresponding patent documents. One is that, as has been stated above, certain countries publish not only patents but also publish the applications corresponding to the patents. The other reason is that an invention must be the subject of a *separate* patent application (and of a separate patent) in each and every country in which its protection is desired. Thus, the same invention may be the subject of publication not in one but several countries. The average is somewhere between two and three.

6.59 There are no exact statistics on the number of patent documents published so far from the beginning of the times when patents were first published. They can, however, be estimated at close to 30 million. Normally, only the recent ones are of practical importance for those searching technological information; the older ones are frequently only of historical interest. Nevertheless, access to the older ones is an absolute necessity for any Industrial Property Office whose law requires it to pass a judgment on the question of whether a given patent application related to an invention is, objectively, new, since such a judgment requires looking at all the existing patent documents likely to disclose a similar invention.

F. INTERNATIONAL PATENT CLASSIFICATION (IPC)

6.60 The industrial property offices, which have to handle such enormous numbers of patent documents, are faced with two different problems, namely, the administrative processing of the patent applications and the maintenance of the search files containing the published patent documents. The search files are established for the purposes of carrying out documentary searches necessary for the examination of patent applications and for retrieving the documents relevant to specific technical fields. Special systems for arranging the patent documents are required to permit the economical handling of patent applications and patent documents within the offices, and the greater the number of patent documents, the better the system has to be.

6.61 On the one hand, patent applications have to be provided with a symbol or number for administrative purposes, that is, for registration and handling within an industrial property office. For this purpose a serial number is usually used. On the other hand, patent applications also have to be provided with special symbols which relate to the technical field or fields to which the patent application relates. These symbols are required to assist the public concerned, e.g., industry, and also

References for Section E
International Bureau of WIPO, *Patent Information—What It Is and How Useful It Is for Technology Development or Technology Transfer*, WIPO/IP/SUV/93/9

to facilitate the orderly and classified arrangement of patent documents in order to permit the search and, thus, the retrieval of documents relating to distinct technical subject matter. Industrial property offices have, therefore, been forced to develop systems for the classification of patents, in other words, systems specially adapted for the filing and fast and reliable retrieval of patent documents for the purposes of search. The development of such special classification systems for patent documents became necessary because existing classifications systems, as used in libraries for instance, proved unsuitable for the classification of patent documents. Different national classification systems were thus elaborated in different offices.

6.62 National classification systems were established as early as 1831 at the Patent Office of the United States of America, 1877 at the German Patent Office and 1880 at the United Kingdom Patent Office. The initial system of mere registration of patent applications was gradually abandoned and replaced by examination of patent applications, in the course of which the patent applications were compared with existing national patent documents. The next step was the inclusion of the universal state of the art in the area covered by the examination of patent applications, in other words, the inclusion also of patent documents published by other countries. For the purpose of this type of examination procedure, the industrial property offices were obliged to search for distinct patent documents dealing with specific technical subjects, and to locate them among a great number of foreign patent documents bearing the symbols of other national classification systems.

6.63 One means of overcoming this problem was to establish concordance tables between two different national classification systems, in other words, to devise tables which cited, for each entry in one national classification system, the corresponding entry in the other national classification system. Because of the different underlying classification principles, however, national classifications are so different that the value of such concordance tables is more than questionable. Moreover, different concordance tables would have to be set up between, on the one hand, a country's own national classification and, on the other hand, each of the other national classifications that are of interest. This method, therefore, did not offer an acceptable solution.

6.64 Another possibility for overcoming this problem was for each country to reclassify the foreign patent documents according to its own national classification. This also proved to be an unacceptable solution because of the high number of documents which would have to be reclassified, the specialists required for such high-level technical work and the linguistic knowledge required for work with foreign-language patent documents. Thus, the need for an international classification system to solve these problems became more and more apparent.

6.65 Many years of international cooperation, which started in 1956 under the auspices of the Council of Europe and the World Intellectual Property Organization (WIPO), resulted in 1971 in the Strasbourg Agreement Concerning the International Patent Classification, and provided for a worldwide forum for the International Patent Classification (IPC). As of October 1, 1996, 35 States were party to the Strasbourg Agreement: Australia, Austria, Belgium, Brazil, Canada, China, Cuba, Czech Republic, Denmark, Egypt, Estonia, Finland, France, Germany, Ireland, Israel, Italy,

Japan, Luxembourg, Malawi, Monaco, Netherlands, Norway, Portugal, Russian Federation, Slovakia, Spain, Suriname, Sweden, Switzerland, Tajikistan, Trinidad and Tobago, Turkey, United Kingdom and the United States of America.

6.66 The IPC is based on an international multi-lateral treaty administered by WIPO (the said Strasbourg Agreement). This Classification sub-divides technology into 8 sections, 20 subsections, 118 classes, 624 subclasses and over 67,000 groups (of which approximately 10% are "main groups" and the remainder are "subgroups"). Each of the sections, classes, subclasses, groups and subgroups has a title and a symbol, and each of the subsections has a title. The symbol or symbols of at least the subclass or subclasses to which the technical invention described in any patent document belongs are indicated generally on the patent document by the industrial property office of the country where the application was filed. Thus, the document will be retrievable according to its subject matter, with the help of the IPC.

6.67 The IPC exists in two authentic versions, English and French, which are published by WIPO. Complete texts of the sixth edition of the IPC have been prepared and published in, for example, the Chinese, Czech, German, Hungarian, Japanese, Korean, Polish, Portuguese, Romanian, Russian and Spanish languages.

6.68 The IPC is now applied by more than 70 countries and four international organizations, which taken together issue about 90% of the patent documents of the world. By the end of 1989, some 18 million patent documents were provided with the classification symbols of the IPC. Approximately 6.2 million of them are in Japanese, 3 million in English, 1.7 million in French and 1.8 million in German. The remainder are in various languages, mainly Dutch, Russian, Spanish and Swedish.

6.69 An intergovernmental Committee of Experts, established by the Strasbourg Agreement, keeps the IPC up to date by periodic amendments, and promotes its uniform application. The Committee of Experts, taking note of the fact that the IPC is a means for obtaining an internationally uniform classification of patent documents, has agreed that:

"(a) as the primary purpose, the IPC is to be an effective search tool for the retrieval of relevant patent documents by industrial property Offices and other users in order to establish the novelty and evaluate the inventive step (including the assessment of technical advance and useful results or utility) of patent applications;
 (b) as other purposes (equally important to developing and developed countries) the IPC is to serve as:
   (i) an instrument for the orderly arrangement of patent documents in order to facilitate access to the information contained therein;
   (ii) the basis for selective dissemination of information to all users of patent information;
   (iii) a basis for investigating the state of the art in given fields of technology; and
   (iv) a basis for the preparation of industrial property statistics which in turn permit the assessment of technological development in various areas."

6.70 WIPO made available, in May 1992, in cooperation with the German Patent Office and the Spanish Patent and Trademark Office, the first version of the IPC:CLASS (*International Patent Classification Cumulative and Linguistic*

Advanced Search System) CD-ROM. The second version of IPC:CLASS contains the first to sixth editions of the IPC in English and French, the fourth to sixth editions in German, the fifth and sixth editions in Hungarian and Spanish, catchword indexes in English, French and Spanish, the bilingual (German/English) "Stich- und Schlagwörterverzeichnis" (with the language versions separated), revision concordance data relating to the second to sixth editions of the IPC, and the IPC valid symbols data. IPC:CLASS is a simple IPC search tool that makes it possible to identify the relevant places in different editions of the IPC without having to resort to the voluminous printed publications.

G. EUROPEAN PATENT INFORMATION AND DOCUMENTATION SYSTEMS (EPIDOS) (INTERNATIONAL PATENT DOCUMENTATION CENTER (INPADOC))

6.71 To assist users in identifying primary sources of patent information, most industrial property offices publish patent gazettes (also named official gazettes or official bulletins). These gazettes usually contain a certain number of indexes, e.g., by classification symbol, by name of applicant, etc. and contain entries consisting of bibliographic data relating to, and marked also on, the newly published patent documents. Patent gazettes, therefore, are considered secondary sources of patent information. Some of these gazettes contain abstracts or reprints of the first claims and most important drawings of patent documents as well.

6.72 A truly international referral service for patent information came into existence in 1972. In that year, the International Patent Documentation Center (INPADOC) was created in Vienna by virtue of an Agreement between WIPO and the Republic of Austria. In 1990, the Center was taken over by the European Patent Office (EPO) and now provides its services under the name European Patent Information and Documentation Systems (EPIDOS). EPIDOS is located in Austria, at the Vienna sub-office of the EPO. EPIDOS stores, in a machine-readable data bank, the most important bibliographic data of each patent document, i.e., the title of the invention, its classification symbol, relevant dates, names and numbers. The said bibliographic data are either obtained from Patent Offices in machine-readable form or input by EPIDOS on the basis of the announcements published in patent gazettes.

6.73 The basic bibliographic data items are recorded by EPIDOS in respect of the patent documents published by more than 50 countries or organizations among them Argentina, Australia, Austria, Belgium, Brazil, Bulgaria, Canada, Cuba, Cyprus, Denmark, Egypt, Finland, France, Germany, Greece, Hungary, India, Ireland, Israel, Italy, Japan, Kenya, Luxembourg, Malawi, Mexico, Monaco,

References for Section F
International Bureau of WIPO, *International Patent Classification (IPC)*, MPIC/82/5 and WIPO Pub. No. 409(E) (1990)
International Bureau of WIPO, *International Cooperation in the Field of Patent Documentation and Information*, VTC/83/11
International Bureau of WIPO, *IPC:CLASS—The International Patent Classification (IPC) CD-ROM* (1993)

Mongolia, Netherlands, New Zealand, Norway, Philippines, Poland, Portugal, Republic of Korea, Romania, South Africa, Russian Federation, Spain, Sweden, Switzerland, Turkey, United Kingdom, United States of America, Yugoslavia, Zambia, Zimbabwe, the European Patent Office (applications for European patents), the International Bureau of WIPO (international applications under the PCT). The UK patents registered in Hong Kong are also recorded.

6.74 EPIDOS processes the bibliographic data and provides services to government authorities and the public. The data can be used for answering many kinds of questions, the two most important being the following: firstly, the data bank can be asked to identify all the patent documents belonging to any given group of about 64,000 technical subdivisions of the IPC. Here lies the source the main usefulness of the Center in giving the developing countries access to the achievements of modern technology; secondly the data bank can provide all the patent documents which, in the various countries, have been filed for the same invention by—usually, but not necessarily—the same person, company or enterprise. Thus, one can obtain information at a glance as to the likelihood of the invention being protected in various countries, and, which is of greater interest for the purposes of access to the technological information, as to the likelihood of the invention being described in different languages and as to the importance given to the invention by the inventor/applicant himself.

6.75 To obviate the need for users to consult all the official gazettes published by the various countries, EPIDOS publishes each week an international gazette of patents, the INPADOC Patent Gazette (IPG). This IPG is published on COM (*C*omputer *O*utput on *M*icroform) microfiche and comprises four sections, namely, a numerical section, a classification section (based on the IPC), an applicant section and an inventor section, each section containing references to all patent documents inserted in the EPIDOS data bank during the preceding week. Users can thus readily follow developments, as the weeks go by, in a given technical field, or the activities of a given firm, enterprise or applicant.

H. CAPRI SYSTEM

6.76 The CAPRI System (*C*omputerized *A*dministration of *P*atent *D*ocuments *R*eclassified *A*ccording to the *I*PC) provides for the international exchange of inventories of patent documents published before 1973, when the IPC was only used by a small number of industrial property offices, which have been reclassified according to the IPC, as well as storage and processing of the said inventories by INPADOC. The project was initiated in 1972 by WIPO and an agreement for the creation of the CAPRI database was signed with INPADOC at the end of 1975.

6.77 The characteristics of the CAPRI System are the following. In order to permit patent information centers in developing countries to establish patent document files organized or arranged according to the IPC, or to reorganize according to the IPC files of patent documents classified according to outdated

References for Section G
International Bureau of WIPO, *International Cooperation in the Field of Patent Documentation and Information*, VTC/83/11

or national classification systems, a central data bank of inventories of patent documents classified according to the IPC was gradually built up. The Patent Offices of Austria, the former Federal Republic of Germany and the Soviet Union and the European Patent Office cooperated in delivering information on the content of their files of patent documents classified according to the IPC in the form of machine-readable inventories containing an indication of the document and the classification symbols allotted to the documents. These inventories were delivered to INPADOC free of charge and were mainly for the benefit of developing countries.

6.78 The CAPRI System contains at least the PCT minimum documentation for the period covered, according to Rule 34 of the Regulations under the PCT. This means patent documents issued between at least 1920 and the end of 1972 by France, the former Federal Republic of Germany, Japan, the Soviet Union, Switzerland, the United Kingdom and the United States of America. The CAPRI Central Database contains for each document the following elements: country of publication, document number, IPC symbols and IPC edition number. Data records in the Central Database are sorted according to IPC symbols. The CAPRI Inverted File was also generated, where patent documents are listed according to country of publication and document number. Both of these databases are available on magnetic tape or COM microfiche.

6.79 The Central Database contains inventories of 613 subclasses of the IPC, totalling approximately 11 million documents and the complete SU and JP files, with approximately 0.6 million and 4 million documents, respectively.

I. STATE-OF-THE-ART SEARCH PROGRAM

6.80 The WIPO Patent Information Services for Developing Countries (WPIS) include the provision of confidential *reports on the state of the art* in response to requests received from patent information users in developing countries. Such reports identify the "state of the art" in respect of a technical problem described in the request as reflected in patent documents and non-patent literature. The search is performed by highly skilled patent examiners of industrial property offices in industrialized countries by consulting their search files which contain collections of national and foreign patents and published patent applications (90%) as well as relevant non-patent literature (10%). The search files are classified according to the International Patent Classification (IPC), which subdivides the whole technology into more than 67,000 groups. Some searches are performed in, or assisted by reference to, computerized databases hosted on internationally accessible main frame computers privately owned and located outside industrial property offices. All search reports list patent documents and relevant non-patent literature concerning the technical problem described in the request with brief descriptions explaining their relevance. Full text copies of the documents cited in the search reports are also provided free of charge.

References for Section H
International Bureau of WIPO, *International Cooperation in the Field of Patent Documentation and Information*, VTC/83/11

6.81 This program had started in 1975 in cooperation with Austria and was gradually extended to cover contributions from other donor countries. Agreements for the provision of search reports have been concluded between WIPO and the industrial property offices of the following countries: Australia, Austria, Canada, Finland, France, Germany, Japan, Norway, the Russian Federation (former Soviet Union), Sweden, Switzerland and the United Kingdom. In addition, other offices provide assistance in particular cases, and some reports are provided by WIPO itself. It should be mentioned that by August 1, 1995, some 7,500 search reports were established and transmitted free of charge to the requestors in 80 developing countries and 11 intergovernmental organizations. These reports also covered special requests for novelty search and substantive examination as to the patentability of patent applications in developing countries as well as special requests for search and examination of patent applications submitted by ARIPO (African Regional Industrial Property Organization).

6.82 The WIPO Patent Information Services for Developing Countries also provide free copies of full text of any published patent or patent application as may be specifically requested by the users from developing countries . In case a requested document is published by a country in a language not familiar to the requestor, WIPO endeavors to identify the description of the same invention contained in another corresponding patent document published by another country in English. If no corresponding patent is available in a language familiar to the requestor, WIPO seeks to identify the translation of the abstract in English wherever available. Some 30 countries provide free-of-charge copies of their patent documents; however, the main suppliers of free copies are Austria, France, Germany, Japan, Portugal, The Russian Federation, Switzerland, the United Kingdom, the United States of America, the European Patent Office (EPO) and WIPO. Since 1984, the starting date of this copy service, WIPO received some 2,000 requests from 35 developing countries and more than 30,000 copies of patent documents published by 37 countries have been supplied and mailed free of charge to the requestors.

6.83 It is estimated that the total cost of this WIPO activity for the benefit of developing countries would amount to more than 12 million US dollars had it been made on a commercial basis.

J. PATENT INFORMATION AND DOCUMENT CENTERS IN DEVELOPING COUNTRIES

(a) Introduction

6.84 The United Nations General Assembly, at its eleventh special session in September 1975, adopted resolution 3362 (S-VII) on development and international economic cooperation, paragraph 1 of Section III of which states that:

> "Developed and developing countries should co-operate in the establishment, strengthening and development of the scientific and technological infrastructure of developing countries. Developed countries should also take appropriate measures, such as contribution to the establishment of an industrial technological information bank and consideration of the possibility of regional and sectoral banks, in order to make available a greater flow to developing countries of information permitting the

selection of technologies, in particular advanced technologies. Consideration should also be given to the establishment of an international center for the exchange of technological information for the sharing of research findings relevant to developing countries."

6.85 The exponential growth of the volume of scientific and technological information generated in the world as well as the increasing complexity and inter-relationship of problems facing each country's plans for economic development make it imperative for countries to share their knowledge, experience and other resources, to facilitate the study and transfer of scientific and technological achievements, to make such achievements accessible on a mutually advantageous basis. The exchange of technological information is an essential prerequisite for developing and strengthening the national economic potential of any country, for bridging the technological gap between and within countries and for further scientific and technological progress in the world.

6.86 Given this recognition, it is clear that the establishment of a Patent Information and Documentation Center (PIDC) in a developing country will in itself constitute a very important step in the exchange and transfer of technological information in the country and hence in the transfer of technology itself.

6.87 The objectives and role of a PIDC can accordingly be expressed as follows:

(1) to provide access to technological information contained in patent documents in a manner suited to the needs of the users;
(2) to disseminate technological information contained in patent documents to the widest possible range of actual and potential users;
(3) to promote awareness of the role of patent documents in national development and the benefits to be obtained in the utilization of industrial property legislation;
(4) to assist in efforts to provide modern industrial property legislation;
(5) to provide an effective voice in matters of patent documentation in order to promote a high level of international awareness of needs of developing countries.

6.88 In meeting these objectives, the PIDC should establish clear links with scientific and research organizations, both governmental and industrial, in the developing countries and also play an active role in planning and executing national scientific and industrial development policies.

(b) Institutional Aspects

6.89 The processing of the technological information contained in patent documents should take place in the context of a national development policy aimed not only at the development of research as such, but at matters which are closely related—like the transfer of technology—which contribute to the achievement of certain general policy objectives, one of which, of course, will be that of national economic development.

6.90 In view of the above, the analysis of the institutional conditions which should govern the processing of the information contained in patent documents should be viewed as part of an integrated whole and in the light of the scientific and technological information policy, within which the institution will have to operate.

6.91 At present, for most developing countries the production of "knowledge" by way of national research, is minimal as compared with what is produced as "knowledge" by the more technologically advanced countries. This is dramatically illustrated in the field of patent documentation, since approximately 90% of the basic inventions—advancements of knowledge—are made in highly industrialized countries and the publications concerning these inventions—the patent documents—are produced in approximately the same proportion. Thus, for a developing country the dissemination of information will, for a certain number of years to come, be the main task to which a national patent information policy should be devoted.

6.92 In a developing country having a reasonably well functioning Industrial Property Office, that Office could, perhaps, be the focal point for national patent information policy. There are many reasons for this, the most important being that in almost all cases this Industrial Property Office is the only channel known (admittedly to a small number of users) as a place where at least information on knowledge (national or foreign) worth applying for a patent is available. Moreover, the Industrial Property Office has, in most cases, one or more technical specialists among its staff who can read and understand the technical content of patent documents. Last, but not least, Industrial Property Offices produce the national patent documents which, as explained below, can become the basis of the participation of the country in bilateral free exchange of patent documents.

6.93 The cost of initially establishing a PIDC, its staffing with trained personnel and its maintenance is high, and may be beyond the reach of the national budget of most developing countries. External assistance, both technical and financial, could be possible, at least initially, by, for example, the United Nations Development Programme. Regional cooperation between developing countries, linked by language or tradition, or by existing regional scientific and technological programs, serves as a good basis for the development of a regional PIDC.

(c) Organization

(i) Introduction

6.94 In the first years of its existence, the PIDC will be concerned mainly with acting as a referral center and with collecting material, organizing the services and advertising them. Training of its own staff and education of future users will be among the important initial tasks. It should be realized that the requirements, both organizational and technical, of users from the public sector and users from within the Industrial Property Office are normally different. However, whatever the size of the patent document collection, initial or planned, one should foresee the following tasks to be fulfilled which will need attention from the beginning: acquisition tasks—library tasks—file-upkeep tasks—assistance to users in general—assistance to other services in the Industrial Property Office—special assistance to the national research council—training tasks.

(ii) Acquisition and Library Tasks

6.95 The acquisition of patent documents in paper copies or on microform can be effected by way of exchange or by purchase. The purchase of collections of currently published documents on a world-wide basis is possible only if considerable funds are available. Most developing countries have no funds available for this kind of expenditure and it is thought that they do not need a world-wide collection. Thus, bilateral exchange agreements should be striven for. The negotiation of such agreements should be prepared by the "acquisition" staff, since they should, once a general policy on acquisition is set by the Director of the PIDC, be responsible for its implementation. Developing countries may also be able to acquire a patent document collection which another country makes available, e.g. for economic reasons or because paper copies are to be replaced by microform. WIPO maintains a list of such available collections.

6.96 Secondary sources of patent information, such as Official Gazettes, can also be obtained free-of-charge under certain conditions. They should always form part of a PIDC. Further secondary sources of patent information, such as specialized abstracting services or bibliographic information services for patent documents, e.g. the ones offered by EPIDOS, should also be considered for inclusion in the documentary resources of the PIDC.

6.97 Patent documents are not the only source of technological information. Therefore a certain number of "key journals" should be obtained. Unfortunately, in most cases these cannot be obtained on an exchange basis and will have to be purchased. The "key journals" should be chosen in relation to the relevance of their content. Such a list of "key journals" has been drawn up by the bodies of the Patent Cooperation Treaty (PCT) Union. In some situations, depending upon the technological fields of importance to the country or region, more general journal literature may be necessary to complement the technological information in the patent collection.

6.98 The provision of patent documents on microform is receiving increasing attention internationally. The advantages of greatly reducing storage costs, as compared with paper copies of patent documents, have to be considered together with the need to provide specialized reading and printing equipment. Maintenance of this equipment should be possible locally. Also it should not be overlooked that microform and its use need very special attention in hot and damp climates.

6.99 Once the flow of documents, including the national patent documents, is secured, they will have to be checked upon arrival and channelled to the appropriate places and people in the PIDC. A catalog will have to be established. Binding facilities for patent documents and journals will have to be organized. Some documents might be offered in microform and appropriate storage and use of these rather unusual forms of documents will have to be studied, and microform reading machines will have to be provided.

(iii) File-Upkeep Tasks

6.100 The appropriate place to which the bulk of the patent documents received has to be channelled in the PIDC is the "patent search file" section. In this section the patent documents will be organized in a manner which permits adequate access to them. The organization system which is postulated to be used is the IPC, which permits both classification of documents according to their technical content and physical organization of a collection of patent documents in files suitable for search.

6.101 Whatever the organization of the patent document collection chosen, it is inevitable that documents will constantly be added to the collection year after year and, if the PIDC operates successfully in bringing users to the collection and contents of the collection to the attention of the users, documents will constantly be removed from the collection for consultation, copying, etc. and, hopefully, be put back into the collection. Security measures will have to be taken in order to guarantee the integrity of the files because any document lost will have to be replaced by a new copy obtained from the country which had originally published it, and which will have to be paid for.

6.102 Staff will consequently be needed to assure an orderly growth of the "classified file", to keep it up to date, to draw the necessary copies, to ensure the integrity of the files and to help users to get to the files which they wish to consult.

(iv) Assistance to Users in General

6.103 Certain staff of the PIDC will have to assist users of the services provided by indicating to them:

(1) the extent of the information collections available at the PIDC;
(2) the reading, understanding and interpreting of the content of patent documents, Official Gazettes, technical journals, abstracting services, etc.;
(3) the various means of access to the information available;
(4) the use and interpretation of the IPC;
(5) the use of microform reading machines.

6.104 The assistance to users in general should be provided by technical staff with a library or documentation background. They will need to have a profound knowledge of how patent documents and patent Gazettes are written and presented. Some of them will need an excellent knowledge of the IPC. Preferably, there should be at least three of them: one for each of the three basic fields of technology-general and mechanical, chemical, electromechanical and physical. (These are typical industrial property subdivisions, which are also reflected in the approximately equal share of these fields of technology in the number of patent applications filed in any given country.)

(v) Assistance to Other Services in the Industrial Property Office

6.105 The Industrial Property Office, whether supervising the PIDC or not, would itself draw heavily on the services provided by the PIDC. In a very few years after its inception, the PIDC should enable searches to be made regarding the state of the art to establish novelty and inventive step of patent applications filed in the country.

6.106 The staff assisting users in general could also perform these tasks, but the general level of education for the former tasks would be different from the level of education required for assisting the Industrial Property Office in establishing a report enabling the said Office to make a decision on whether or not to make a grant on the basis of the application. Very often the number of applications in a given country is sufficiently high to warrant the training and education of "patent searchers" for the benefit of the patent procedure proper. "Patent searchers" should normally have a technical (university level) degree and be specialized in one of the technical fields (mentioned earlier). An excellent knowledge of the IPC as well as, possibly, of other (national) classification systems is indispensable.

6.107 New applications filed with the Industrial Property Office have to be classified according to their technical content. This is also a task which could be assigned to the above-mentioned "patent searchers" as they will be doing the search and, for this reason, have to read and understand fully the technological aspects of the purported invention.

6.108 If the Industrial Property Office, or any other governmental organization has a registry and a mechanism for controlling license contracts or if it plays, directly or indirectly, a role in the transfer of technology, or provides a technological information source for forecasting economic growth, assistance to the said Office or governmental organization dealing with these problems should be offered and continuously improved by the PIDC.

(d) Establishment of a Document Collection

6.109 In view of the great number of existing and of currently published patent documents, developing countries will, from the outset, be confronted with a high number of patent documents coming on the "information market" each year and it might, therefore, be judicious, and sometimes imperative, to reduce the number of patent documents to be acquired every year. Various methods can be used for reducing the number of patent documents in the collections and files of the PIDC, namely:

(1) selection by country of issue;
(2) selection by language of document;
(3) selection by corresponding patents;
(4) selection by period of time;
(5) replacement of the complete text of the patent document by an abstract.

6.110 There is one more method for reducing the amount of patent documents to be stored, namely, the policy which consists of limiting the acquisition of documents according to fields of interest. Such fields could be defined in terms of the priorities foreseen in the development plans of the country or of the region. The selection of "key journals" for the PIDC should be inspired by the same criteria of convenience (language, country, time, etc.) as applied for the selection of patent documents.

6.111 It is clear that for any newly established PIDC, the classification system to be used should be IPC. It should be emphasized that any newly published patent documents can, subject to a possible check on the classification, be directly inserted into the appropriate place in a search file organized according to the IPC.

(e) Services

6.112 The various services which can be developed and offered by any PIDC will have limitations only in respect of resources, manpower and the information available. The services which a technical information center can offer have been described at length and in great detail in various specialized publications. Taking into account the special characteristics of patent documents, the PIDC can offer such patent information services as:

(1) document supply: on paper or microform;
(2) Selective Dissemination of Information (SDI) Services: based on profiles of interest defined in terms of the International Patent Classification (IPC);
(3) abstract services, taking into account the language requirements of the users;
(4) translation services;
(5) bibliographic searches: by name, date, IPC symbols;
(6) state-of-the-art searches;
(7) advisory services, e.g. for those users least able to read and understand patent documents, for advising on licensing agreements;
(8) adaptation and packing of patent information in a way (monographs) which can be easily understood by the end user;
(9) public reading room.

(f) Training

6.113 The necessary infrastructure in the developing country should be built up through the training of the staff of the PIDC. Since the main task of the PIDC is to meet the requirements of the national patent information policy, it is necessary to educate and train first the staff of the PIDC. That staff, in its turn, will educate and train the end users.

6.114 Basic training in general questions of patent information should be given to all professional staff. More specialized training should be given to selected staff, as required, as part of medium-and long-term training programs.

6.115 The curriculum of the training program for the staff of the PIDC should include:

General Training:

(1) general introduction to the most important existing national and regional industrial property services, with particular emphasis on patents, inventors' certificates, utility models, and on the general concept of the scope of the protection granted and its limits;
(2) general awareness of the extent of the technological information contained in patent documents and of the various means of access to it;
(3) legal and technical content of patent documents leading to the improvement in technical knowledge disclosed in a patent document;
(4) philosophy and structure of the IPC and its relevance to searching and other forms of information retrieval based upon patent documents;
(5) the use of information contained in patent documentation in the process of concluding or controlling license agreements, and in policy and decision-making for governments and industry.

Specialized Training:

(1) in depth study of the IPC;
(2) use of secondary patent information services, such as bibliographic data services, abstracting services, etc;

(3)   storage and maintenance of documentation collections;

(4)   other specific training in relation to the services to be provided by the PIDC.

6.116 In order to make use of practical working experience gained in the patent information and documentation branch of an Industrial Property Office in a developed country and in order to provide a practical application of the theoretical knowledge acquired, the training should be complemented by substantial training in existing Industrial Property Offices which have an extensive patent information and documentation branch.

6.117 It should be emphasized that the acquisition of specialized knowledge concerning all patent information and documentation matters can take some years.   It is, therefore, indispensable that staff of the PIDC be guaranteed reasonable career prospects in the government service.

References for Section J
International Bureau of WIPO, *International Cooperation in the Field of Patent Documentation and Information*, VTC/83/11
International Bureau of WIPO, *Guidelines for the Organization of a Patent Information and Document Center with Particular Regard to the Needs and Circumstances of Developing Countries*, WIPO Pub. No. 658(E) (1980 and 1987)

PART III

Forms of Intellectual Property Protection

CHAPTER 7

Patents

A. INTRODUCTION

7.1   A patent is a document, issued, upon application, by a government office (or a regional office acting for several countries), which describes an invention and creates a legal situation in which the patented invention can normally only be exploited (manufactured, used, sold, imported) with the authorization of the owner of the patent. "Invention" means a solution to a specific problem in the field of technology. An invention may relate to a product or a process. An invention is "patentable" if it is new, involves an inventive step (i.e., it is not obvious) and is industrially applicable. The protection conferred by the patent is limited in time (generally 15 to 20 years).

7.2   In a few countries (not more than a dozen in the whole world), inventions are also protectable through registration under the name of "utility model." The requirements are somewhat less strict than for "patentable" inventions, the fees are lower than for patents, and the duration of protection is shorter than in the case of patents, but otherwise the rights under the utility model are similar to those under a patent.

7.3   Patents are frequently referred to as "monopolies", but nowhere, in most laws, is the inventor or the owner of a patented invention given the right to make, use or sell anything. The effects of the grant of a patent are that the patented invention may not be exploited in the country by persons other than the owner of the patent unless the owner agrees to such exploitation. Thus, while the owner is not given a statutory right to practice his invention, he is given a statutory right to prevent others from exploiting his invention, which is frequently referred to as a right to exclude others from making, using or selling his invention. The right to take action against any person exploiting the patented invention in the country without his agreement constitutes the patent owner's most important right, since it permits him to derive the material benefits to which he is entitled as a reward for his intellectual effort and work, and compensation for the expenses which his research and experimentation leading to the invention have entailed.

7.4   The following illustration may be helpful in trying to understand this concept. When Alexander Graham Bell received his patent for the telephone, he had the power to prevent anyone else from making, using or selling a telephone. Assume that someone else later invented a dial telephone for which that person also received a patent as an improvement on Bell's telephone. This second person would then be able to prevent anyone else, including Bell, from making, using or selling a dial telephone in accordance with that patent. This sets up the necessity and importance of licensing. In these circumstances, Bell would need a license from the owner of the dial telephone patent in order to make a dial telephone, and the owner of the dial telephone patent would need a license from Bell under Bell's basic telephone patent in order to make, use or sell the dial telephone.

7.5 It should be emphasized, however, that while the State may grant patent rights it does not automatically enforce them, and it is up to the owner of a patent to bring an action, usually under civil law, for any infringement of his patent rights. The patentee must therefore be his own "policeman."

7.6 Simply put, a patent is the monopoly granted by the State to an inventor for a limited period, in return for the disclosure of the invention, so that others may gain the benefit of the invention. The disclosure of the invention is thus an important consideration in any patent granting procedure.

B. CONDITIONS OF PATENTABILITY

7.7 An invention must meet several criteria if it is to be eligible for patent protection. These include, most significantly, that the invention must consist of patentable subject matter, the invention must be industrially applicable (useful), it must be new (novel), it must exhibit a sufficient "inventive step" (be non-obvious), and the disclosure of the invention in the patent application must meet certain standards.

(a) Patentable Subject Matter

7.8 In order to be eligible for patent protection, an invention must fall within the scope of patentable subject matter. Patentable subject matter is established by statute, and is usually defined in terms of the exceptions to patentability, the general rule being that patent protection shall be available for inventions in all fields of technology.

7.9 Examples of fields of technology which may be excluded from the scope of patentable subject matter include the following:

(1) discoveries of materials or substances already existing in nature;
(2) scientific theories or mathematical methods;
(3) plant or animal varieties, or essentially biological processes for the production of such plant or animal varieties, other than microbiological processes;
(4) schemes, rules or methods, such as those for doing business, performing purely mental acts or playing games;
(5) methods of treatment for humans or animals, or diagnostic methods practiced on humans or animals (but not products for use in such methods).

7.10 In addition, temporary exclusions from patent protection may be provided for certain kinds of products or processes for reasons of public interest, such as,

References for Section A
P. Smith, *Introduction to Patent Law and Practice: The Basic Concepts*, WIPO Pub. No. 672(E) (1989)
International Bureau of WIPO, *Revision of Paris Convention*, PR/GE/11/2

for example, pharmaceuticals, agricultural chemicals or inventions in the nuclear field. The current trend is away from such temporary exclusions.

(b) Industrial Applicability (Utility)

7.11 An invention, in order to be patentable, must be of a kind which can be applied for practical purposes. In other words, the invention cannot be purely theoretical. It must be an invention that can be carried out in practice. If the invention is intended to be a product or part of a product, that product must be capable of being made. And if the invention is intended to be a process or part of a process, that process must be capable of being carried out—"used," as it is generally said—in practice.

7.12 It is the possibility of making or manufacturing in practice, and this possibility of carrying out or using in practice, that are reflected in the word "applicability" in the expression "industrial applicability."

7.13 The word "industrial" in the same expression has a very special meaning in the terminology of patent laws. In common language, an "industrial" activity means a technical activity on a certain scale, and the "industrial" applicability of an invention means the application (making, use) of an invention by technical means on a certain scale.

(c) Novelty

7.14 Novelty is a fundamental requirement in any examination as to substance and is an undisputed condition of patentability. It must be emphasized, however, that novelty is not something which can be proved or established; only its absence can be proved.

7.15 An invention is new if it is not anticipated by the prior art. "Prior art" simply stated is all the knowledge that existed prior to the relevant filing or priority date of a patent application, whether it existed by way of written or oral disclosure. The question of what should constitute "prior art" at a given time is one which has been the subject of some debate.

7.16 One viewpoint is that the determination of prior art should be made against a background of what is known only in the protecting country. This would exclude knowledge from other countries, if it was not imported into the country before the making of the invention, even if that knowledge was available abroad before the date of the making of the invention.

7.17 Another viewpoint is based on the differentiation between printed publications and other disclosures such as oral disclosures and prior use, and where such publications or disclosures occurred.

7.18 The disclosure of an invention such that it becomes part of the prior art may take place in three ways, namely:

(1) by a description of the invention in a published writing or publication in other tangible form;
(2) by a description of the invention in spoken words uttered in public, such a disclosure being called an oral disclosure;

(3)   by the use of the invention in public, or by putting the public in a position that any member of the public may use it, such a disclosure being a "disclosure by use."

7.19 Publication in tangible form requires that there be some physical carrier for the information, a document in the broad sense of the term, and that document must have been published, that is to say, made available to the public in any manner such as by offering for sale or deposit in a public collection. Publications include issued patents or published patent applications, writings (whether they be manuscript, typescript, or printed matter), pictures including photographs, drawings or films, and recording, whether they be discs or tapes in either spoken or coded language.

7.20 Oral disclosure, as the expression suggests, implies that the words or form of the disclosure are not necessarily recorded as such and includes lectures and radio broadcasts.

7.21 Disclosure by use is essentially a public, visual disclosure such as by display, sale, demonstration, unrecorded television broadcasts and actual public use.

7.22 A document will only destroy the novelty of any invention claimed if the subject matter is explicitly contained in the document. The subject matter set forth in a claim of an application under examination is thus compared element by element with the contents of each individual publication. Lack of novelty can only be found if the publication by itself contains all the characteristics of that claim, that is, if it anticipates the subject matter of the claim.

7.23 Lack of novelty may however, be implicit in the publication in the sense that, in carrying out the "teaching" of the publication, a person having ordinary skill in the art would inevitably arrive at a result falling within the terms of the claim. Generally speaking, lack of novelty of this kind will only be raised by the Patent Office where there is no reasonable doubt as to the practical effect of the prior "teaching."

7.24 It should be noted that in considering novelty, it is not permissible to combine separate items of prior art together.

(d)   Inventive Step (Non-Obviousness)

7.25 In relation to the requirement of inventive step (also referred to as "non-obviousness"), the question as to whether or not the invention "would have been obvious to a person having ordinary skill in the art" is perhaps the most difficult of the standards to determine in the examination as to substance.

7.26 The inclusion of a requirement like this in patent legislation is based on the premise that protection should not be given to what is already known as part of the prior art, or to anything that the person with ordinary skill could deduce as an obvious consequence thereof.

7.27 The person having ordinary skill in the art is a person with appropriate technical training and practical experience. The expression "ordinary skill" is intended to exclude the "best" expert that can be found. It is intended that the person be limited to one having the average level of skill reached in the field in the country concerned.

7.28 It should be noted that novelty and inventive step are different criteria. Novelty exists if there is any difference between the invention and the prior art. The question, "is there inventive step?" only arises if there is novelty. The expression "inventive step" conveys the idea that it is not enough that the claimed invention is new, that is, different from what exists in the state of the art, but that this difference must have two characteristics. Firstly, it must be "inventive," that is, the result of a creative idea, and it must be a step, that is, it must be noticeable. There must be a clearly noticeable difference between the state of the art and the claimed invention. This is why, in some jurisdictions, there is the concept of an "advance" or "progress" over the prior art.

7.29 Secondly, it is required that this advance or progress be significant and essential to the invention.

7.30 In order to assess the nature of the differences which are relied upon as constituting an inventive step, account has to be taken of the prior art as a whole. Thus, as distinct from the assessment of novelty, the subject matter of the claim under examination is compared not with each publication or other disclosure separately, but with the combinations thereof, insofar as each such combination is obvious to the person having ordinary skill in the art. The combination may be global, whereas the claim may define a set of subject matter known separately, for instance a new form of washing machine including a particular type of motor coupled to a particular type of pump. For inventive step to be destroyed, it is necessary that not only the combination, but also the choice of the combined elements, is obvious. It is the sum of the differences that have been discovered which must be compared with the prior art and judged as to obviousness, and not each of the new elements taken individually, except where there is no technical link between them.

7.31 The evaluation of the differences should not neglect any of the three aspects that typifies all inventions, namely:

(1) a problem to be solved;
(2) a solution to that problem; and
(3) a result guaranteed by the application of that solution.

7.32 If the problem is known or obvious, the examination will bear on the originality of the solution claimed. If no inventive step is found in the solution, the question becomes whether or not the result is obvious or whether it is surprising either by its nature or by its extent. If a person having ordinary skill in the art would have been able to pose the problem, solve it in the manner claimed, and foresee the result, the inventive step is lacking.

(e) Disclosure of the Invention

7.33 An additional requirement of patentability is whether or not the invention is sufficiently disclosed in the application.

7.34 A disclosure in an application, to be complete, must contain such description and details as to enable any person skilled in the art to which the invention relates to make and use the invention as of the filing date of the application.

7.35 While the prior art setting may be mentioned in general terms in the description, the essential novelty, the essence of the invention, must be described in such detail, including proportions and techniques where appropriate, as to enable those persons skilled in the art to make and use the invention.

7.36 Specific operative embodiments or examples of the invention must be set out in the description. Examples and other descriptive passages should be of sufficient scope as to justify the scope of the claims.

7.37 Whether or not there is an examination as to substance, some jurisdictions provide for an opposition procedure which may be instituted either before or after the grant of a patent. An opposition procedure is designed to allow third parties to present objections to the grant of a patent.

7.38 So that oppositions may be filed, the public must be informed of the content of the application, and this is done by the Patent Office by publication of a notice in an official journal or gazette to the effect that:

(1)   the application is open to public inspection; and/or
(2)   the Patent Office will, unless opposition is filed within a prescribed period, grant a patent; or
(3)   a patent has been granted on the application.

7.39 The grounds upon which an opposition may be filed are limited by the relevant legislation. Generally speaking, it should be possible for an opposition to be based on non-compliance with any substantive requirement. However, the law in some countries only allows an opposition to be based on noncompliance with only certain substantive requirements. Typically these grounds are lack of novelty, inventive step or industrial applicability, insufficient disclosure of the invention, or the fact that an amendment made to a patent application has gone beyond the original disclosure in the application as filed. Some jurisdictions make it possible to file an opposition on the ground that the applicant has no right to a patent.

C.   DRAFTING AND FILING A PATENT APPLICATION

(a)   Identification of the Invention

7.40 The first task in drafting a patent application is the identification of the invention. This involves:

(1)   summarizing all the necessary features which in combination solve a particular technical problem; and
(2)   an examination of this combination to determine whether it would, according to one's own judgment, fulfill the requirements for patentability, especially inventive step.

References for Section B
P. Smith, *Introduction to Patent Law and Practice: The Basic Concepts*, WIPO Pub. No. 672(E) (1989)
International Bureau of WIPO, *The Substantive Conditions of Patentability*, BLTC/6&7

7.41 It is during this process that a full comprehension of the essence of the invention is obtained, and this is important in helping to draft the description and claims.

7.42 Generally speaking, an inventor may be so much involved in his own considerations that he may be prejudiced by the direct result of his work. The result of this is a limited understanding by the inventor of his own invention, particularly the specific problem which he attempted to solve and all the specific features which lead to the most effective solution. On the other hand there are sometimes inventors who consider their invention in such a broad light that it easily covers the state of the art.

7.43 Often the invention contains many new features. It is essential to identify the critical feature or features and to have an explanation of why they contribute to an effective solution to the problem. There are two important reasons for this. First, the claims should be as broad as possible; the broadest claim is the one restricted by the least number of features. Second, having identified the critical features and their effect, it is then necessary to ask how else may this effect be achieved, that is, can the specific features be substituted or altered while still achieving the end result. This is important not only in drafting the claims, which must be wide enough to cover these substitutes or alternatives, but also in the description of the invention which must include details of the substitutes or alternatives so that the broad claim can be supported by the description.

(b) Practical Aspects of Drafting Patent Applications

7.44 Drafting practices and requirements differ from country to country. However, there are typically three basic requirements to be complied with in the drafting of a patent application.

7.45 Firstly, there is a requirement that the application should relate to one invention only, or to a group of inventions so linked as to form a single general inventive concept. This requirement, referred to as "unity of invention," is particularly important when claims are being drafted.

7.46 Secondly, the description should disclose the invention in a manner sufficiently clear and complete for the invention to be evaluated, and to be carried out by a person having ordinary skill in the art. This is of fundamental importance, since one of the main functions of the description is to provide new technical information to third parties. An important phrase to note in this requirement is "a person having ordinary skill in the art." This allows for a simplified description since it can be assumed that the reader will be an informed reader having the background knowledge which makes it unnecessary to describe every basic detail of the invention.

7.47 Thirdly, the application must contain claims which determine the scope of the protection. The claims must be clear and concise and fully supported by the description. This third basic requirement is important since the claims are the basis of interpretation of patent protection. It is from the claims that third parties are able to know what they may do and what they may not do. The claims may not be significantly broader or different from that which has been described.

7.48 The first section of the description typically contains two elements, namely, the title of the invention and a brief statement of the technical field in which the invention lies. Usually this statement is in the form of a short introductory paragraph which commences with the phrase "This invention relates to ..."

7.49 In the second section, the background of the invention is described. In drafting this section, the patent agent usually sets out any existing problems or difficulties which the invention overcomes. Previous solutions to those problems or difficulties should be described, preferably in a way which clearly sets out the difference between the present invention and those previous solutions. This section may also describe the object of the invention, that is to say, what the invention sets out to achieve. The second section of the description is important to provide a good understanding of the invention and to put it into perspective against the prior art.

7.50 The third section of the description provides a summary of the invention in such terms that it may be readily understood. The patent agent will normally describe the invention first in general terms which correspond to those he intends to use in the main claim. By using this technique, the agent can avoid any disputes that might arise based on differences between the invention described and the invention as defined in the claims. This description of the invention in general terms is usually followed by a series of paragraphs which set out different preferred features of the invention. These paragraphs usually form the basis for dependent claims which follow the broad main claim.

7.51 In the fourth section of the description, two elements are generally found, namely a brief description of the drawings, if drawings are appropriate, and a detailed description of one or more embodiments of the invention. Extensive use of drawings can assist in describing details of the invention. If the invention relates to some form of mechanical object, for example, drawings illustrating plan, elevation and sectional views of that object could be used. Elements of the drawings which are described are numbered in the drawings and these numbers utilized in the description of the embodiment.

7.52 Where the invention is an electrical circuit, drawings can be used effectively to show the connections between the various elements or components of the circuit. Again these elements or components should be numbered for ease of reference. Normally the drawings should contain no textual matter. Exceptions, however, may be made when single descriptive words can be used where they do not interfere with the lines of the drawings. Thus in any drawing illustrating an electrical circuit, for example, standard components may be indicated in the drawings by boxes which may be labeled. Similarly, where the invention relates to a process, drawings may show a block, schematic or flow-sheet diagram, and blocks or boxes contained therein may be labeled as appropriate.

7.53 Where the invention is in the chemical field, the drawing may be a graph, and, more specifically, where the invention is of a metallurgical nature, the drawing may be a diagram such as a phase diagram.

7.54 It is usual for the description of the embodiment to include a passage which briefly describes the actual operation of the invention. If the device, for example, is a machine or an electrical circuit, the manner in which the machine or electrical circuit operates is extremely helpful in understanding the invention.

7.55 The claims are the centre or the heart of any granted patent because they define the protection which is the purpose of the patent, that is to say, they define clearly the scope of the exclusive right provided by the patent. Therefore it is the most important task within the work of the patent agent when preparing the application, to produce a wording of the claims which defines the invention in terms of the technical features disclosed in the description and which do not contain any reference to commercial advantages.

7.56 The series of claims drafted by the patent agent generally commences with a broad main claim followed by a number of claims of narrower scope. The broad claim is drafted so as to just avoid the prior art known at the time of preparing the application. The patent agent drafts the succeeding claims more narrowly, and hopefully this results in stronger claims which could withstand any anticipation by more relevant prior art which might be produced by a Patent Office during examination, or by third parties during any opposition or invalidation proceeding. It should be emphasized that there must be some element of additional invention in each succeeding claim in order for it to be stronger.

7.57 The narrower claims following the broad main claim usually refer back to one or more of the preceding claims. Because of this they are usually called dependent claims. The features introduced in each of the dependent claims must find some basis in the description. There it is usually explained that these are preferred features which produce a better technical form of the invention.

7.58 The last element of a patent is the abstract. The abstract presents a short summary of the description and the claims. It serves the purpose of enabling third parties to obtain quick information about the essential contents of the invention. It must be emphasized that it is not used to interpret the scope of protection

7.59 The guiding principle is that the abstract should be so drafted that it can efficiently serve as a scanning tool for purposes of searching in the particular art. Thus the abstract has to be as concise as the disclosure permits. Generally speaking, it contains between 50 and 150 words.

D. EXAMINATION OF A PATENT APPLICATION

(a) Examination as to Form; The Filing Date and Priority Date

7.60 It is now useful to follow the progress of an application through the Patent Office. There are three main areas of activity worthy of some comment, namely:

(1) examination as to form;
(2) search; and
(3) examination as to substance.

References for Section C
P. Smith, *Introduction to Patent Law and Practice: The Basic Concepts*, WIPO Pub. No. 672(E) (1989)

7.61 In each of these areas of activity, the normal procedure is for a dialogue to be carried out, mainly in writing, between an examiner in the Patent Office, and the applicant. The patent agent acts as a go-between in the sense that he receives communications from the Patent Office, advises the applicant as to the appropriate course of action, takes the applicant's instructions, and responds accordingly to the Patent Office's communications.

7.62 Prior to examination as to form, the application is checked to ensure that all the requirements necessary to accord the application a filing date, have been satisfied. This is a fundamental check since if a filing date is not established, the application will be treated as if it had not been filed, and it proceeds no further. The filing date is important in the general scheme of things since it constitutes the date from which certain actions are calculated, such as the term of the patent, and, where appropriate, determines the priority date of any subsequent application in another country under the terms of the Paris Convention for the Protection of Industrial Property (Paris Convention). The filing date (or priority date) is also relevant to the evaluation of novelty and inventive step.

7.63 The priority date is also important in the general scheme of things. The right of priority may be based on a national, regional or international application filed less than twelve months earlier. Its effect is to substitute the date of the earlier filing for the date of the national filing and this is particularly important with respect to the relevant prior art for evaluating novelty and inventive step.

7.64 It must be emphasized that the right of priority is only available in those countries which are party to the Paris Convention. It should be noted however, that under some national laws, priority rights are granted on a bilateral basis of reciprocity for countries not parties to the Paris Convention.

7.65 The right of priority offers great practical advantages to an applicant who seeks protection in several countries. The applicant is not required to present all applications in his own country and in foreign countries at the same time, since he has up to twelve months to decide in which foreign countries he desires protection. The applicant can use that period to organize, with due care, the steps to be taken to secure protection in the various countries of interest to him.

7.66 Examination as to form is normally carried out as soon as an application has been accorded a filing date. Basically this covers the following points: the representation, the content of the request, the statement concerning the inventor, the physical requirements governing the description, the claims and the drawings, and the inclusion of an abstract. The applicant is given an opportunity to correct any defects identified during examination as to form, and if such defects are not corrected within a specified time, the Patent Office rejects the application.

(b) Search

7.67 Depending on the examination procedure provided in the relevant law, the search will be conducted either separate from and prior to, or at the same time as, the examination as to substance. In either case, the objective of the search is to determine the prior art in the specific field to which the invention relates. In conducting the search the Patent Office checks its documentation holdings to ascertain whether any documents exist which describe a solution which is the same as or similar to that described in the application.

7.68 If the search is conducted separately to the examination as to substance, a search report will be forwarded to the applicant setting out:

(1) a list of the documents located during the search, which disclose subject matter the same as or closely resembling the invention; and
(2) the claims in the application that should be compared with each of those documents.

7.69 The report may also give an indication of the scope of the search, that is the type of documents which may have been searched, the time span covered, and the specific areas of technology searched.

7.70 The search itself is a documentary search in a collection of patent documents that is primarily arranged for search purposes according to the specific areas of technology. These patent documents may be supplemented by articles from technical journals and other so-called non-patent documents. This total collection of documents is usually referred to as "the search file".

7.71 The Patent Office conducts the search only in respect of documents in the search file. The search does not extend to disclosures other than publications and, in particular, does not seek to determine whether disclosure has taken place by public use. This type of disclosure, if any, will only be taken into account during the examination as to substance phase, and then only if that use has been brought to the attention of the Patent Office by some third party's action.

7.72 The search itself will first cover all directly relevant technical fields, and may then have to be extended to analogous fields, but the need for such extension must be judged by the examiner in each individual case, taking into account the outcome of the search in the directly relevant areas of technology. It must be realized that whilst completeness is the ideal of the search, this ideal may not necessarily be obtained because of such factors as the inevitable imperfections of any classification and information retrieval system, and may not be economically justified if the cost is to be kept within reasonable bounds.

(c) Examination as to Substance

7.73 The aim of the examination as to substance procedure is to ensure that the application satisfies certain conditions of patentability. In essence, this is to prevent the grant of a patent where:

(1) the invention is excluded from patent protection by specific provisions in the legislation;
(2) the invention is not new, does not involve an inventive step and/or is not industrially applicable;
(3) the invention is not sufficiently disclosed in a clear and complete manner in the documents filed; or
(4) some other physical requirements of the application have not been met.

7.74 As with examination as to form, the applicant is given the opportunity to remove any objections raised during the examination as to substance phase, and if he fails to do so within a specified time, the Patent Office will refuse the grant of a patent.

7.75 It is in the interest of both the applicant and the public that there exists the possibility to amend the application. Not only can deficiencies be eliminated and thus a better patent grant secured, but also amendments to clarify the disclosure will result in a better description of the invention and a more precise definition of the scope of protection.

7.76 Not all amendments are permissible. As a general rule, an amendment is not allowable if it goes beyond the original disclosure in the application.

7.77 It should be noted that since the purpose of any patent law is to protect inventions, the Patent Office will only refuse to grant a patent if the results of the examination clearly preclude the grant. Any doubt is resolved in the applicant's favor, since final adjudication on the validity or otherwise of a patent is usually possible via the courts.

(d) Grant and Publication

7.78 If and when the examination process has reached a conclusion favorable to the applicant, that is to say all the necessary requirements as to form and substance have been fulfilled, and assuming no opposition has been filed or that any opposition has been unsuccessful, the Patent Office will grant a patent on the application. This involves certain actions on the part of the Patent Office.

7.79 Firstly, when the patent is granted, the details of the patent are entered into the Patent Register. The Register usually contains bibliographic data such as the patent number, the name and address of the applicant/patentee, the name of the inventor, the original application number, the filing date, certain priority application details and the title of the invention. It does not contain any technical information.

7.80 Additionally in countries where annual fee payments are required in order to maintain the patent in force, the Register will contain details of when such fees have been paid, and may also list any details of licenses or assignments which may have been recorded.

7.81 The Register can thus be very useful to third parties especially competitors of the patentee, because it reveals the actual status of the patent. In some countries the courts accept a certified copy of an extract from the Register as being proof of the correctness of the position recorded in respect of the patent.

7.82 Secondly, the Patent Office publishes in an Official Gazette, a reference to the grant of the patent with the prescribed bibliographic data. The entry in the Official Gazette may also contain the abstract or the main claim, and if there are drawings, the most illustrative drawing.

7.83 Thirdly, a Certificate of Grant is issued to the applicant, which is the legal document establishing his ownership of the patent. A copy of the granted patent is also issued at the same time.

7.84 Lastly, the Patent Office publishes the patent document itself in printed form. Copies of the patent document are made available by the Patent Office for use by Patent Libraries, etc., as a source of technical information, and to third parties subject to the payment of a fee.

7.85 As stated above, in order to keep the patent in force, each year, for the term of the patent, a prescribed renewal or maintenance fee, usually has to be paid to the Patent Office. In some countries, where for example a deferred examination system exists, the maintenance fee is payable even before the patent is granted. In some countries the maintenance fee is not required annually but may be paid, for example, say every three to five years. A small number of countries do not require the payment of maintenance fees.

E. INFRINGEMENT

(a) Exclusive Right of a Patent Owner

7.86 Generally speaking, a patentee acquires the right, enforceable at law, to decide who shall and who shall not exploit his patented invention. He retains this right for the term of the patent, provided he pays any necessary renewal or maintenance fees.

who may not use

7.87 The patent owner's legal rights over his invention are usually limited in a number of quite different ways.

7.88 Firstly, the claims which define the monopoly may be subject to amendment or invalidation by the courts in respect of defects which were not detected prior to the grant of the patent.

7.89 Secondly, where the invention is an improvement or development of an earlier subsisting patent, the patent owner may need to obtain a license and pay royalties to the earlier patent owner.

sometimes patent needed

7.90 Thirdly, the patent owner's rights are usually limited by the patent law, quite apart from the question of validity of his patent. In most patent systems, for example, the patent owner is required to work his invention, either on his own behalf, or by licensing others to use it, if he wishes to retain his monopoly. A non-voluntary license may, for instance, be granted to third parties if it can be demonstrated that the patented invention is not worked or is insufficiently worked in the country.

work required execution demanded

7.91 Finally, a fourth legal limitation on a patent owner's right to exploit his invention is that patented inventions may often be used by Government or by third parties authorized by Government, where the public interest so requires, at terms fixed by agreement or by the courts.

subject to public interest

7.92 With the exception of the limitations just referred to, the grant of a patent allows its owner to exclude others from exploiting the patented invention. The right of the owner is called exclusive because it allows the exclusion of others from exploiting the invention and because the owner is the only one allowed to

References for Section D
P. Smith, *Introduction to Patent Law and Practice: The Basic Concepts*, WIPO Pub. No. 672(E) (1989)

exploit the invention as long as others are not given an authorization by way of license, for example, to do so. This exclusive right of the patent owner has two main applications in practice, namely protection against infringement, and the possibility of assigning of licensing the right, in part or in whole. Licensing of the patented invention will be discussed in a later chapter.

7.93 An infringement of the exclusive right of a patent owner involves the unauthorized exploitation of the patented invention by a third party. The making of the invention, in particular, its development for industrial application, usually involves considerable expense for the applicant, the future owner of the patent for invention. The patent owner thus wishes to recover this expense through exploitation of the patented invention, in particular through the sale of products that incorporate the invention.

(b) Enforcement of Rights

7.94 Initiative for enforcing a patent rests exclusively with the patent owner. It is he who is responsible for detecting infringements and bringing them to the infringer's attention. In many jurisdictions there is a strict rule that the patent owner may not threaten legal action without the possibility of incurring severe countermeasures, including damages if the threats prove to be groundless. The main purpose of such provisions in the law is to prevent patent owners threatening the customers of alleged infringers without pursuing the primary infringer. In practice, a polite letter pointing out the existence of the patent carries the implication that the patentee will sue if the infringement continues. Such a letter has proven to be quite effective in suppressing an infringement.

7.95 If the infringer is persistent, the patent owner may consider whether he wishes to offer a license. Many incipient disputes are settled through license negotiations at an early stage, the terms of the license reflecting the bargaining strength of the parties. But if the patent owner is reluctant to license on terms acceptable to the licensee, he may have recourse to legal action by suing for infringement and seeking an injunction to restrain the infringement. The invariable legal response of an infringer who wishes to pursue the contest is to petition for invalidation of the patent.

7.96 The great majority of patent infringement disputes never reach the stage of court action but are settled through negotiation. Of those that do reach the stage at which official legal action is taken, very few go beyond the pre-trial stage, the usual outcome being settlement before any court hearing, possibly with the help of an unofficial arbitrator. Settlements of this nature can take several years, especially in complicated cases, but they do not typically involve large legal costs. Such settlements almost invariably involve a license and possibly damages as well.

(c) Types of Infringement

7.97 There are several ways in which infringement of patent rights might arise. Firstly, there is the situation where a patent is deliberately infringed by a third party without any attempt to avoid the infringement, in other words deliberate pirating or counterfeiting of the patented invention. This will either be straight copying of the invention or else involve minor variations or modifications thereof. This form of infringement may occur because the third party is unscrupulous, or because he has been advised by his patent agent that the patent in question, or one or more claims thereof, is invalid.

7.98 With this form of infringement there is generally no argument as to whether or not there is infringement. If all the features of the patented invention have been copied, then there must be infringement, and the only matter to be resolved is whether the claims of the patent are valid.

7.99 The second situation which arises is where the infringement is deliberate, but some attempt has been made to avoid infringement. It frequently happens that once an invention is disclosed either by sale of the product incorporating the invention, or in a published patent document, or in some other publication, third parties are given ideas. The publication generally outlines the problem and shows a way of solving it. Third parties then may endeavor to design an alternative to do the same thing. While third parties may be genuinely trying to design around the patent whilst still making use of the basic idea of the inventor, the result does not always clearly fall outside the scope of the claims of the patent. This is probably the most common form of infringement faced by patent owners and it gives rise to the most litigation.

7.100 The last situation that arises is the case of accidental infringement. As soon as a patent owner comes across something which embodies his idea he naturally feels that his invention is being copied. This is not necessarily so, since there may be many people working to solve a particular problem at the same time. For example, research departments of different large organizations may all be working on a similar problem. Similarly there may be several companies who have been asked to tender for a contract to solve a particular problem or to achieve a certain result, and in so doing may come up with similar ideas to that which may have been involved in the patented invention. Thus, although the patent owner may feel that his invention has been copied, the third party has, in fact, arrived at a similar if not identical solution via a different route.

(d) Elements in Establishment of Infringement

7.101 To establish infringement the patent owner must prove of all the following elements:

(1) the carrying out of a prohibited act;
(2) the prohibited act must have been done after the publication of the patent application, or the issuance of the patent where no early publication occurs;
(3) the prohibited act must have been done in the country where the patent has been granted;
(4) the prohibited act must be in relation to a product or process falling within the scope of a claim of the patent.

(i) Prohibited Acts

7.102 The most important element in establishing an infringement is the carrying out of a prohibited act. Such acts are, generally speaking, set out in the patent law. A prohibited act is one which involves the making, using, selling or importing the patented product, or the use of the patented process, or the making, using, selling or importing the product directly obtained through the patented process.

7.103 To make the product means that the product described and claimed in the patent is carried out in practice. Such making is also referred to as manufacturing especially when the product is produced on a commercial scale. The method of manufacture and the quantity in which the produce is manufactured. is irrelevant so far as infringement of a patented produce is concerned. There are however, three main exceptions in most laws to infringement of exclusive rights to make a patented product, namely:

(1) where the patented product is made for the sole purpose of scientific research and experiment;
(2) where a third party had started making the product before the date when the patent application for an invention incorporated in the produce was filed; and
(3) where the patented product is made under a non-voluntary license or under an authorization granted by the Government on public interest grounds.

7.104 In respect of patented processes, only the making of products directly obtained through the patented process is a prohibited act. "Directly" in this context means "immediately" or "without further transformation or modification."

7.105 One of the difficulties in establishing infringement in respect of products directly obtained through a patented process, is that of proving that the patented process was used to produce the product. Some patent laws contain provisions which partially solve this difficulty. Such laws provide for the reversal of the burden of proof in respect of patents for processes by introducing the following presumption : if the product resulting directly from the use of the patented process was new on the filing date or priority date of the patent application, an identical product manufactured by a third party is presumed to have been obtained by the same process. Some other laws go further and eliminate the difficulty by not limiting the resulting product to one which has to be new.

7.106 The use of a patented product does not require that the use be repetitive or continuous. The rule is that use is a prohibited act irrespective of who the user of the patented product is, and for what purpose the patented product is used. The use of the patented product is a prohibited act irrespective of whether the product actually being used was made by the patent owner, with the authorization of that owner, or without the authorization of such owner.

7.107 There are, in most laws, five exceptions to infringement of exclusive rights to use a patented product, namely:

(1) where the use of the patented product is solely for purposes of scientific research and experiment;
(2) where the patented product that is used is a product which was put on the market in the country by the owner of the patent for invention, or with his authorization;
(3) where the use of the patented product occurs in vehicles in transit in the country;
(4) where the patented product is used by third parties who have the special right to continue to make the product; and

(5) where the patented product is used under a non-voluntary license or under an authorization granted by the Government on public interest grounds.

7.108 The sale of a patented product is a prohibited act irrespective of whether the product actually sold was made by the patent owner, or with or without the authorization of the owner. Any product that corresponds to the description of the invention and is claimed in the patent, even if made without the authorization of the owner, is a patented product.

7.109 Importing a product simply means that an article which constitutes or incorporates the patented product is brought into the country where protection has been conferred. Thus, importation is a physical act of transportation of the product across the border into the territory of the country. It is irrelevant which other country the product is imported from. Furthermore, it does not matter whether the importation takes place for purposes of use or sale, or for purpose of distribution free of charge. It is also irrelevant whether the imported product enjoys patent protection in the country in which it was made or in the country from which it is imported.

7.110 The principles relating to the use, sale and importation of patented products, as far as the definitions of these acts are concerned, applies, *mutatis mutandis*, also to the use, sale and importation of products directly obtained through a patented process.

(ii) After Publication of the Application or Issuance of the Patent

7.111 The second element in establishing an infringement, namely that the prohibited act must have been done after the publication of the invention in either a patent application or in the granted patent, needs little comment. It would be contrary to natural justice if third parties could be charged with committing an offense when details of the invention were not available to the public to see what it is that could not be done.

(iii) In the Country where the Patent has been Granted

7.112 The third element in establishing an infringement also requires little comment. Generally speaking, patents do not extend beyond the boundaries of the country which granted the patent. The patent law of a country has no effect in any other country. However, in a small number of countries, particularly British Commonwealth countries, it is possible to extend the coverage of a United Kingdom patent to those countries by the owner of the U.K. patent applying, generally within a period of three years from the date of grant thereof, to register such patent in the country concerned.

(iv) Within the Scope of a Claim of the Patent

7.113 The fourth element in establishing an infringement is one which is normally the decisive point in any patent litigation. The scope of protection of the patent is determined in all countries by the claims. The meaning of the claims is ultimately interpreted by the courts. The manner in which the courts will interpret a claim in turn depends upon the domestic law and to a certain extent the rules or regulations. Therefore, what a claim means will depend upon the jurisdiction in which it is being interpreted.

7.114 The courts, particularly in common law systems, attempt to determine what structure the language of the claims defines, and whether or not the alleged infringing structure corresponds to the structure defined in the language of the claims.

7.115 In attempting to answer the question as to whether a particular structure infringes a particular claim of a patent for invention, the claim should be broken down into its individual elements, and these compared with the elements of the alleged infringement to see whether they fit. If the claim can, in fact, be made to read onto the alleged infringement without stretching the words of the claim too far, then there may indeed be infringement. If, on the other hand, the claim contains a limitation to something which is not found at all in the alleged infringement, there may be no infringement.

7.116 When comparing the individual elements of a claim against the corresponding elements of the alleged infringement, the following questions have to be answered:

(1) are all the elements of the claim present in the alleged infringement?
(2) do all the elements have the same form?
(3) do all the elements perform the same function?
(4) do the elements have the same relationship to the other elements?

7.117 If the answer to each of these questions is "yes", then infringement is established, depending of course, on whether the claim in question is valid. An infringing product or process must include each and every element of the invention defined in a claim.

7.118 Of course, the establishment of infringement is not always clear cut. For example, changes in form will not avoid infringement if there is no change in the result produced. Further changing the order of steps in a process will not avoid infringement if the result is the same. Moreover the presence of additional elements in an alleged infringement does not avoid infringement if all the elements of the patent claim are also present.

7.119 One of the most difficult areas of patent claim interpretation is the determination as to whether or not there has been a substitution of equivalent elements in the alleged infringement. This is the so-called "doctrine of equivalents" which is well known in patent litigation practice in many countries. Briefly stated, the doctrine indicates that an infringer should not be allowed to continue his actions where he basically makes use of the patented invention while merely substituting a variant for an element of the invention which is equivalent technically and functionally to the element as contained in the patent claim, irrespective of whether the variant used by the infringer turns out to be an improvement or a worsening. Equivalence is restricted to those cases where the variant or variants used by the infringer function in substantially the same manner and produce substantially the same result as the element or elements contained in the claim or claims.

(e) Remedies Available to the Patent Owner

7.120 The remedies which may be available to the patent owner where infringement has been established are usually provided for in the national patent law and are generally in two forms, namely civil sanctions and criminal sanctions. These remedies are provided to ensure the respect and defense of the exclusive rights of the patent owner.

7.121 Broadly speaking, civil sanctions are available in all cases of infringement while criminal sanctions are available only under particular circumstances, namely, where the infringement was committed intentionally.

7.122 Civil sanctions normally available include the award of damages, the grant of an injunction, or any other remedy provided in the general law such as the seizure and destruction of the infringing products or the tools used for the manufacture of those products.

7.123 If the patent owner establishes in court that infringement has occurred, or is occurring, he is entitled to damages, which the court will assess. Damages will only be awarded against the infringer for infringements committed since the date of publication of the invention by the Patent Office in the patent application or the granted patent. The amount of damages may be calculated in at least two different ways. One way would be to set damages at the amount of the financial loss suffered as a result of the infringement by the patent owner. Under a second method of calculation, damages would be based on an account of profits. This does not mean that the patent owner will necessarily receive all the profits the infringer has made on the infringing articles but, nevertheless, an account of profits can be very near to the actual profits made. Damages may also be assessed by taking into account the royalty being paid by any licensees. In this case a court may decide that damages should be no less than the royalty payments per article and, as they are damages, and not royalties, it is likely that damages will be fixed at a higher figure.

7.124 Under some national laws, an infringer will not be liable to damages if he proves that at the date of infringement he was not aware, and had no reasonable ground for supposing that the patent existed.

7.125 An injunction is a prohibition of the infringing act. In such a case the court will issue a order directing the infringer to stop making further copies or infringements of the patented invention. Where the infringing act has not yet been committed but where preparations have been made by a third party with a view to committing an infringing act ("imminent infringement") the injunction means that infringement may not be started.

7.126 Criminal sanctions depend on the structure of the criminal law and the procedures applicable in the country. The usual forms of criminal sanction are punishment by imprisonment or by a fine, or both.

F. EXPLOITATION OF THE PATENTED INVENTION

(a) Exploring the Market for an Invention

7.127 New ideas or innovations have to be marketed just like any other product or property. The larger and potentially more rewarding the market for the

References for Section E
P. Smith, *Introduction to Patent Law and Practice: The Basic Concepts*, WIPO Pub. No. 672(E) (1989)

inventor's "industrial property" is, the more vigorous and professional must be his selling efforts. Major corporations and small businesses alike are well aware that the new product market is a key to their continued growth and even survival. Many companies make more than half their current sales with products developed within the past ten years, and new products and product variations are essential for continued sales growth.

7.128 The big corporation explores the potential market for a new product in a thorough and objective way and may spend millions of dollars in product planning, testing, market research and advertising. The small company can adapt the same techniques and processes to suit its own scale of operation. Above all, the independent businessman should approach the problem with the same thoroughness, patience and emotional detachment that large corporations employ. Individual inventors and innovators should do likewise.

7.129 While major companies generally try to discover what it is the public wants and then develop a product to meet the need, the independent more often dreams up a product and then sets about trying to sell it. He has probably worked lovingly on his idea for years, perhaps gone through the painstaking and lengthy procedure of obtaining a patent and has an unshakable belief in its usefulness and commercial value. This emotional relationship between the inventor and his product can easily interfere with the rationality and effectiveness of his marketing approach. One of the key qualities he must retain is objectivity. Without it, he may be tempted to rush into situations without proper evaluation and prior research.

(b) The Feasibility of an Invention

7.130 In assessing the feasibility of his product, the inventor should consider the following points:

(1) Does the product fill a need? Or, can a need be stimulated by means of clever promotion and advertising? The frisbee (a hand-tossed flying disc) wasn't needed but it caught the public imagination nonetheless.
(2) Is the product timely? Many products fail because they hit the market too soon or too late.
(3) What competition will the product have? If it will compete with similar products already on the market, is it substantially better, cheaper or otherwise more attractive?
(4) What are the economics of production? What are the problems inherent in the product's design? Can the product be made at a cost that is adequately covered by its retail selling price? How interested will financing sources be in backing it?

7.131 One of the concomitants of the size and dynamism of any large market is that successful products can be the creators of fortunes, and failures can prove unbelievably costly. One only has to consider some of the classic case histories from the US motor industry, for example, to appreciate this. Unfortunately one of the failings of many individual inventors, is their belief that their invention will have a large market.

7.132 Given that the risk of new product failure is quite high, it is understandable that businessmen may be reluctant to outlay a large sum for an invention if the probable selling price of the product when it ultimately reaches the marketplace is unlikely to exceed by a reasonable margin the expected cost of its production.

7.133 If the invention would cater to a very limited market, if well-entrenched alternative products are competitively priced, or if high marketing and distribution costs are likely to be involved, it is unlikely that the invention will be greeted with much enthusiasm by businessmen. Similarly it may not meet with a particularly good reception if it represents only a minor advance on the state of the art in a field of rapid technological development.

7.134 At all times it is necessary for the inventor to realize that what counts in any market is not the ingenuity which has found expression in the invention, its technical merit, or the aesthetics of the product, but the projected "bottom line" economic results.

7.135 It should be emphasized that every product has a life cycle. Its market reaches a peak of profitability, and sooner or later goes into a decline. Customer "brand or product loyalty" can keep some products around for years. Others, such as novelty or fad items, peak fast and are completely forgotten a few years later. Toys are a good example and most, these days, have a rapid turnover. It is said that up to forty percent of the items in a toy store at any given time have probably been introduced within the past year.

7.136 Life cycles, particularly of consumer products, are becoming shorter, and products are continually pre-empted by newer ones or beaten into a low profit generating stage by competitors with similar products.

7.137 It should be apparent from the foregoing, that one of the essential elements for consideration before marketing a product is a proper assessment of the product.

(c) Selling an Invention

7.138 It is not enough, however, to assess the product itself; the inventor should also discover whether there is an adequate market for the product covered by his invention. For example, he should consider the following questions.

7.139 Who will buy the product? The prime users of the product will have a significant effect on how it is packaged, presented and promoted, as well as its price. The potential market is a question that should be studied carefully since many product developers have jumped to conclusions, albeit the wrong ones, concerning who will buy their products, and even how they will be used.

7.140 How many people make up the potential market? This is a difficult figure to assess but is one of the keys to product survival. Statistics on local populations and potential market segments published by the relevant government agencies, as well as surveys by private firms, can provide the basis for a study of the proposed market areas by age group, marital status and so on.

7.141 In his enthusiasm for his "brain-child", the inventor often rushes to find a market for it before it has been translated from an idea on paper into at least a prototype if not a production item. Obviously the earlier the point in time from the germination of the idea, the more limited the demand will be for the particular invention. A businessman who by nature of his interests is exposed to many new product ideas is likely to be less willing to pay good money for a paper idea than he would be to compensate an inventor for an invention which has been brought to the stage of successful manufacture and marketing with many, if not all, of the design and production problems solved.

7.142 However, for some of the more sophisticated technology, research establishments, multinational corporations and the like are showing increasing interest in taking up embryo or partially developed technology with the object of completing development and thus gaining from the research effort and securing a significant lead over competitors.

7.143 "Test marketing" is a stage that many larger companies go through before commencing full scale production. They introduce the product in limited quantities to those viewed as a typical segment of their potential market. The small businessman also should consider using this technique before he commits too much time and money launching a product that ultimately may not sell.

7.144 Depending on the type of product involved, a prototype or sample might be constructed to enable the individual inventor to demonstrate the capacity and special features of the product incorporating the invention to possible buyers and users. In other instances, explicit engineering drawings are an adequate substitute.

7.145 In the case of a consumer product, a sample presented to a cross-section of retailers for their reactions can give a good indication of possible customer acceptance and sales. If the response to a widespread survey of this type is enthusiastic the inventor is ready to take the next step and consider full scale production either by himself or by someone else.

7.146 Basically, there are two methods the inventor can use to get his idea into production. He can sell or license, his product idea to a company equipped to manufacture it. Alternatively he can become a manufacturer himself, either establishing a factory or contracting out production to a job or machine shop if appropriate.

7.147 Despite the fact that almost all manufacturing companies are constantly on the lookout for new products to complement their existing line, and are dependent upon them for future profits, the independent inventor is not always welcomed with open arms. Getting to see the person with the necessary knowledge and authority to appraise and accept the proposed product often takes tact and time.

7.148 The reason why some companies receive new product ideas with coolness is many sided. Often, companies are besieged with unsolicited ideas from the public, very few of which are even worth serious consideration. Larger corporations frequently have research and development departments in which substantial sums of money have been invested. Management, naturally, favors in-house developments. Other companies are wary of inventors who may claim that their ideas have been stolen, when in fact the company may have been already working on the same idea.

7.149 Larger corporations often publish their policies and procedures regarding new product ideas from outside sources. Some have "submitted ideas departments". Most companies would prefer that the inventor merely send them a copy of his patent on a new idea. Alternatively, the inventor can submit a copy of his patent application as soon as it has been filed.

7.150 When submitting an idea which is not patentable, the inventor should be aware of the company's policy regarding unsolicited ideas before he sends it. Some companies reserve the right to make arbitrary payment for ideas as they see fit.

7.151 If a patented idea is accepted, the inventor may be able to choose whether he wishes to sell his patent outright for a lump sum, or enter into a licensing agreement with the company.

G.   COMPULSORY LICENSES

7.152 Licenses that are granted by the owner of the patent are considered "voluntary," as distinguished from "compulsory" or "non-voluntary" licenses. The beneficiary of a voluntary license has the right to perform acts covered by the exclusive right under an authorization from the owner of the patent for invention. The authorization in a contract is generally called a license contract concluded between the owner of the patent for invention and the beneficiary of the license. In contrast, the beneficiary of a non-voluntary license has the right to perform acts covered by the exclusive right under an authorization given by a government authority against the will of the owner of the patent for invention.

7.153 In countries where the grant of non-voluntary licenses is provided for, such licenses generally fall into two categories:

In Event of Abuse of Patent: Some countries provide for the grant of compulsory licenses to prevent the abuses which might result from the exercise of the exclusive rights conferred by the patent.   Under Article 5A(2) of the Paris Convention, failure to work is given as an example of such an abuse, and

In Public Interest: Some countries provide for the grant of a non-voluntary license in the case where a non-voluntary license is deemed necessary for reasons of public welfare, including health, defense, and development of the economy.

(a)   The Grant of Non-Voluntary Licenses to Remedy Abuses Resulting from the Exercise of the Patent Right

7.154 Article 5A of the Paris Convention gives countries of the Paris Union the right to legislate against the abuses which might result from the exercise of the exclusive rights conferred by the patent, for example failure to work, as provided as follows in Paragraph (2):

> "(2) Each country of the Union shall have the right to take legislative measures providing for the grant of compulsory licenses to prevent the abuses which might result from the exercise of the exclusive rights conferred by the patent, for example, failure to work."

7.155 The question as to what constitutes such an "abuse" is one left to national law. As Article 5A(2) indicates, however, failure to work is considered one type of such "abuse."

References for Section F
P. Smith, *Introduction to Patent Law and Practice: The Basic Concepts*, WIPO Pub. No. 672(E) (1989)

(i) Non-Working of a Patent

7.156 While the definition of "working" is generally a matter of national law, it usually means at least, in the case of a patent directed to a product, the making of the product and, in the case of a patent having been granted in respect of a process, the use of the process. While the laws of some countries specifically provide that the importation of a product that includes the invention does not constitute working, the current trend is away from this requirement. As a rule, the working requirement may be fulfilled through the working of the patented invention either by the owner of the patent for invention or by another entity or person under a license contract.

7.157 At the outset it should be recalled that a patent must disclose the invention in a manner such that one skilled in the art can carry it out. Thus patents, even apart from their being worked, are considered beneficial to industry, as their publication may inspire other inventions. Moreover, the inventions described in patents fall into the public domain after the expiration of their term. That is, after their expiration, the technology disclosed in a patent can be freely used by anyone without obtaining the patent owner's permission.

7.158 Despite these benefits, it is believed in some countries that, in order to be fully justified the patented invention should be worked in the country where the patent is granted, and not serve only as an exclusive right to prevent others from doing so or to control importation. The principal goal of requiring local working of a patented invention is the transfer of technology, the actual working of patented inventions in a given country being seen as the most efficient way of accomplishing such a transfer to that country.

7.159 The arguments against compulsory working of an invention in a particular country are two-fold: first, that such compulsory working of inventions may work against the goal of transferring technology and second, that it may not be economically feasible to do so.

7.160 The first argument against non-voluntary licenses is that they are less effective than voluntary licensing in encouraging the transfer of technology, and may, indeed, even be counter productive to that goal. Stated another way, voluntary licensing clearly offers one means whereby the transfer of technology can be facilitated, whereas non-voluntary licensing should not be viewed as playing such a role but should be limited to correcting abuses which may arise in the exercise of patent rights.

7.161 The transfer of technology is best done in an atmosphere of cooperation between the transferor and the transferee. In the present context, that means between the patent owner and the potential licensee. That cooperation generally leads to the disclosure of non-patented "know-how" which is necessary to make a commercially viable product, but which was not necessary to satisfy the disclosure requirement to obtain the patent. In the case of a non-voluntary license the atmosphere of cooperation, and hence the disclosure of non-patented know-how, is absent. Thus the grant of a non-voluntary license under a patent results in a bare right to work the patented invention, which is likely to be an insufficient vehicle for the full transfer of technology.

7.162 An example is the know how required to switch from the use of CFC's (which are seen as being harmful to the earth's ozone layer) as a refrigerant to other substances, which often have a lower molecular size. While the basic refrigeration cycle remains the same, devices, such as air-conditioners, using the new refrigerants would have to be redesigned to, among other things, provide tighter fits between parts which come into contact with the refrigerant so as to prevent leaks. While the patent may fully describe the new substances useful as refrigerants, and the way in which they can be made, it need not disclose the know-how needed to make air conditioners which can operate using them.

7.163 Moreover, it may not be economically feasible to require a patent owner to manufacture products in accordance with his patent in every country in which patent protection has been obtained. Such a requirement does not allow cognizance to be taken of regional or international integration of markets or of comparative advantages of countries or regions. That is, a patent owner may find that products incorporating a patented invention, or made by a patented process, may be made cheaper if production is consolidated in one facility in one country, with the demand in other countries being satisfied by importation. Indeed, the patent owner may find that individual components of his product, which are themselves protected by patents, may be best manufactured in several countries or regions, with final assembly being conducted in one facility or on a regional or national basis.

7.164 An example is the manufacture of photovoltaic cells for the conversion of light into electrical power. A significant element in the cost of production is the capital equipment used to make such cells and the training of personnel to operate the equipment. A requirement of local working with respect to patents covering photovoltaic cells, or processes for their manufacture, would, in many countries, increase the cost of such devices to a point where they would be beyond the means of local people to afford.

7.165 In response to these criticisms of non-voluntary license provisions, two points are often made. First, since in countries with such provisions they are seldom applied for and even less likely to be granted, they are of little practical importance. Secondly, such provisions do serve as a legal possibility which may encourage a patent owner to more readily enter into a voluntary license agreement, even if those provisions are seldom applied. Nonetheless, the environment of cooperation usually found in the case of voluntary licensing is more effective than the environment of coercion present in the case of non-voluntary licensing to promote the full and continuing transfer of technology.

7.166 Article 5A(2) of the Paris Convention specifically provides that countries of the Paris Union may provide for the grant of non-voluntary licenses to prevent abuses resulting from the exercise of patent rights, including failure to work. Article 5A(4) provides that compulsory licenses for failure to work or insufficient working of the invention may not be requested before a certain period of time of non-working or insufficient working has elapsed. This time limit expires either four years from the date of filing of the patent application or three years from the date of the grant of the patent for invention. The applicable time is the one which, in the individual case, expires last.

7.167 The time limit of three or four years is a minimum time limit which recognizes that it may take some time for the owner of a patent to begin working the patented invention in each country where he has obtained patent protection. The patent owner must be given a longer time limit, if he can give legitimate reasons for his inaction, for example, that legal, economic or technical obstacles prevent working, or working more intensively, the invention in the country. If that is proven, the request for a compulsory license must be rejected, at least for the time being. The time limit of three or four years is a minimum time limit also in that sense that national law can provide for a longer time limit.

7.168 Article 5A(4) further provides that the compulsory license for non-working or insufficient working must be a non-exclusive license and can only be transferred together with the part of the enterprise benefiting from the compulsory license. The patent owner must retain the right to grant other non-exclusive licenses and to work the invention himself. Moreover, because the compulsory license has been granted to a particular enterprise on the basis of its known capacities, it is bound to that enterprise and cannot be transferred separately from that enterprise. These limitations are intended to prevent a compulsory licensee from obtaining a stronger position on the market than is warranted by the purpose of the compulsory license, namely to ensure sufficient working of the invention in the country.

(ii) Procedural Safeguards and Compensation

7.169 The grant of a non-voluntary license results in the use of a very valuable property right of the patent owner. Since the grant of such a license is without the consent of the patent owner, reasonable procedural safeguards, including an effective appeal procedure, should be established to ensure that non-voluntary licenses are properly granted and executed.

7.170 In particular, the granting authority, such as a patent office, should ensure that the conditions for the grant of a non-voluntary license are met, allowing the patent owner to state his position in this regard. Moreover, the granting authority should ensure that adequate payment by the beneficiary of the non-voluntary license is made to the patent owner and provide means whereby the non-voluntary license may be canceled if the grounds for the grant of the non-voluntary license no longer exist or if the obligations under the non-voluntary license are not met by the beneficiary thereof.

7.171 The grant of a non-voluntary license does not mean that the beneficiary (the licensee) need not pay royalties. On the contrary, national laws dealing with this question generally require that the licensee make payments to the patent owner on the basis of the working of the invention.

(iii) Forfeiture or Revocation of Patent in Event of Abuses

7.172 While it is anticipated that the grant of a compulsory license would, in most instances, be sufficient to correct abuses, Article 5A(3) envisions the forfeiture or revocation of the patent in cases where the grant of such compulsory licenses is not sufficient. That paragraph further provides that "[n]o proceedings for the forfeiture or revocation of a patent may be instituted before the expiration of two years from the grant of the first compulsory license."

(b) The Grant of Non-Voluntary Licenses in the Public Interest

7.173 Some countries provide for a compulsory license when there has been no "abuse" of the patent right but where the grant of a non-voluntary license is deemed necessary to protect the public interest. In general, non-voluntary licenses granted in the public interest can be divided into those that are granted in favor of private parties and those which are granted in favor of the government itself, or in favor of a person acting on behalf of the government.

(i) Non-Voluntary Licenses Granted in the Public Interest in Favor of Private Parties

7.174 One example of a non-voluntary license granted in the public interest, but in favor of private parties, is in the case of the so-called "dependent patents." Such non-voluntary licenses are granted to remedy the situation that arises when it is not possible, without performing acts covered by one patent (the "dominant patent"), to work an invention claimed in another patent (the "dependent patent"). In such a situation, and if the owner of the dependent patent has not been able to conclude a license contract with the owner of the dominant patent on reasonable terms, the owner of the dependent patent may obtain a non-voluntary license under the dominant patent. Without that possibility, the owner of the dominant patent could prevent the working of the invention claimed in the dependent patent by refusing to grant a license. This inability to work a dependent patent is seen, in some countries, as being contrary to the public interest in having the unencumbered working of all patented inventions.

7.175 Some national laws grant such non-voluntary licenses any time a situation of dependency arises. Other national laws require that the dependent patent must serve a different purpose from that of the dominant patent or constitute a real technical advance in relation to the invention claimed in the dominant patent. That latter condition serves the purpose of avoiding abuses which could result from applicants filing patent applications on trifling inventions for the sole purpose of being able, thanks to a compulsory license, to work an important invention.

7.176 In order to introduce a certain balance between the positions of the owners of the two patents for invention, it is often provided in national laws that the owner of the dominant patent may obtain a compulsory license under the dependent patent, if the owner of the dependent patent has obtained a compulsory license under the dominant patent.

7.177 In addition to non-working, some countries provide that the use of a patent pursuant to a violation of competition (anti-trust) laws is contrary to the public interest warranting the compulsory licensing of that patent, to its unenforceability or to its invalidity, as a consequence of the anti-trust violation.

(ii) Non-Voluntary Licenses Granted in the Public Interest in Favor of the Government, or on its Behalf

7.178 A number of countries allow the government to exploit inventions without the consent of the owner of the patent, or to have third parties exploit the invention on its behalf, in the public interest. There are typically three fields in which this may occur: national defense, national economy and public health.

7.179 In most cases of public interest, it should be sufficient for the State to authorize, against the will of the owner of the patent for invention, any entity or person designated by the Government, to perform any of the acts which are covered by the patent for invention. In each specific case, the Government will decide which of those acts may be performed.

7.180 This kind of measure in the public interest suits situations that arise in cases of national emergency particularly well. To take the example of medical equipment, it might be necessary to import that equipment very quickly in case of a sudden epidemic. If the owner of the patent is not willing to import or to conclude a license contract for importation on reasonable terms, the Government might decide to ask another entity to import the apparatus or might decide to import it itself. Once the epidemic has been brought under control, however, there is no reason to maintain the measure, and the owner of the patent for invention will recover the full control of the rights attached to the patent.

(iii) Procedural Safeguards and Compensation

7.181 Because the grant of non-voluntary licenses confers the right to use a valuable property right of the patent owner, without his consent, procedural safeguards should be established to ensure that the grant of such licenses is done only when, and for as long as, the conditions warrant it. Moreover, provisions should be made for the compensation of the patent owner for the use of his property rights.

H. UTILITY MODELS

7.182 In a number of countries protection may be obtained for "utility models." In essence "utility model" is merely a name given to certain inventions, namely— according to the laws of most countries which contain provisions on utility models—inventions in the mechanical field. This is why the objects of utility models are sometimes described as devices or useful objects. Utility models differ from inventions for which patents for invention are available mainly in two respects: first, in the case of an invention called "utility model," the technological progress required is smaller than the technological progress "(inventive step")" required in the case of an invention for which a patent for invention is available; second, the maximum term of protection provided in the law for a utility model is generally much shorter than the maximum term of protection provided in the law for an invention for which a patent for invention is available. The document that the inventor receives in the case of a utility model may be called, and in several countries is called, a patent. If it is called a patent, one must, in order to distinguish it from patents for invention, always specify that it is a "patent for utility model."

References for Section G
International Bureau of WIPO, *Compulsory or Non-Voluntary Licenses in Respect of Patents for Invention*, WIPO/UNCED/CE/6

References for Section H
International Bureau of WIPO, *Definition and General Characteristics of Industrial Property Rights*, MPIC/82/2.1

CHAPTER 8

Copyright and Neighboring Rights

A. INTRODUCTION

8.1   Copyright law is a branch of that part of the law which deals with the rights of intellectual creators. Such rights are respected by the laws of most countries. The reasons for this respect of the rights of creators are the need to stimulate and foster the individual creativity of men and women and the need to make the results of that creativity available by disseminating it on the widest possible scale. Copyright law deals with particular forms of creativity, concerned primarily with mass communication. It is concerned also with virtually all forms and methods of public communication, not only printed publications but also with such matters as sound and television broadcasting, films for public exhibition in cinemas, etc. and even computerized systems for the storage and retrieval of information.

8.2   Copyright deals with the rights of intellectual creators in their creation. Most artistic works, for example books, paintings or drawings, exist only once they are embodied in a physical object. But some of them exist without embodiment in a physical object. For example music or poems are artistic works even if they are not, or even before they are, written down by a musical notation or words.

8.3   Copyright law, however, protects only the form of expression of ideas, not the ideas themselves. The creativity protected by copyright law is creativity in the choice and arrangement of words, musical notes, colors, shapes and so on. Copyright law protects the owner of rights in artistic works against those who "copy"—those who take and use the form in which the original work was expressed by the author.

B. COPYRIGHT PROTECTION

8.4   Copyright protection is above all one of the means of promoting, enriching and disseminating the national cultural heritage. A country's development depends to a very great extent on the creativity of its people, and encouragement of national creativity is a *sine qua non* for progress.

References for Section A
International Bureau of WIPO, *Introduction to Copyright: Basic Notions of Copyright*, WIPO/GIC/ CNR/GE/86/1

8.5   Copyright constitutes an essential element in the development process. Experience has shown that the enrichment of the national cultural heritage depends directly on the level of protection afforded to literary and artistic works. The higher the level, the greater the encouragement for authors to create; the greater the number of a country's intellectual creations, the higher its renown; the greater the number of productions in literature and the arts, the more numerous their auxiliaries in the book, record and entertainment industries; and indeed, in the final analysis, encouragement of intellectual creation is one of the basic prerequisites of all social, economic and cultural development.

8.6   Legislation could provide for the protection not only of the creators of intellectual works but also of the auxiliaries (the performers, producers of phonograms and broadcasting organizations) that help in the dissemination of such works, in respect of their own rights. The protection of these so-called "auxiliaries" of intellectual creators is also of importance to developing countries since the cultural harvest of some of these countries includes, in no small measure, performance, sound recording and broadcasting of different creations of their folklore as well. While developing countries are often in need of foreign books specially in the field of science, technology, education and research, they could offer to the world an abundance of their national cultural heritage, which can be protected, within the framework of copyright legislation, through protection of the rights of these auxiliaries or of neighboring rights as they are called.

8.7   Where the laws do exist, their practical value depends on the extent to which they are effectively implemented. Adoption of the law is the first step. Its effective and efficient application is imperative. This could be achieved through setting up of appropriate authors' organizations for collection and distribution of authors' fees. Copyright, if effectively implemented, serves as an incentive to authors and their assignees (the publishers) to create and disseminate knowledge. It is something that society must necessarily accept if it wishes to encourage intellectual creativity, to ensure the progress of the sciences, the arts and of knowledge in general, to promote the industry using authors' works and to render it possible to distribute such works in an organized manner among the widest possible circle of interested persons. The concept of copyright needs, therefore, to be understood, developed and propagated nationally, in the interest of economic, social and cultural development.

8.8   Copyright protection itself, however, cannot take place in a vacuum. It has no purpose without intellectual creativity, which has to be nourished and sustained. In other words, copyright protection from the viewpoint of the creator of works makes sense only if the creator actually derives benefits from such works, and this cannot happen in the absence of publication and dissemination of his works and the facilitation of such publication and dissemination. This is the essential role of copyright in developing countries.

8.9   There are several factors influencing intellectual creativity in developing countries, apart from the pecuniary condition of most of the authors and intellectual creators themselves, who need to be offered incentives and subsidies. There is the shortage of paper for the production of textbooks for the process of continuing education (both formal and non-formal), and for production of prescribed and recommended books as also general books, which are to be placed within the reach of the common man in these countries.

8.10 The role of governments in this activity can be manifold, and could include financial assistance in the creation and production of textbooks and other educational literature; inputs for training, as also help for expansion of the library system, the creation of mobile libraries to serve far-flung and remote rural areas, etc. In this whole chain, therefore, of the entire and continual process of encouraging and sustaining intellectual creativity, the various links, viz. authorship, publishing, distribution, and fostering of the library movement on a broad base, cannot be underrated, and need to be carefully nurtured and coordinated, for often individual interests need to be adjusted to the larger interests of the community.

8.11 During the eighteenth and nineteenth centuries there developed a widespread recognition of the important role played in the development of society by authors and publishers in the creation and dissemination of works, and the recognition that in the interests of society this role needs to be supported, encouraged, and adequately rewarded. In the later nineteenth and in the twentieth centuries considerable socio-economic and political changes on the one hand, and rapid strides in technological development on the other, have brought about substantial changes of outlook in relation to copyright. The freedom and expansion of the press, the gradual disappearance of the feudal order, the growth of adult training and mass education schemes, the raising of standards in higher education, the increase in the number of universities, institutions of higher learning and of libraries, the emphasis on the use of national languages, the development of science and technology, the changed map of the world with the birth of a number of newly independent developing nations—all these factors have caused conceptual changes.

8.12 The challenge in this new situation is to maintain a balance between provision of adequate rewards to creators of works and to ensure that such rewards are in harmony with the public interest and the needs of modern society. It is this balance between the public and private interests that will have to be increasingly carefully considered, specially by the developing countries, in the context of the development of their own copyright system, as well as in the context of the international protection of copyright.

C. SUBJECT MATTER OF COPYRIGHT PROTECTION

8.13 The subject-matter of copyright protection includes, every production in the literary, scientific and artistic domain, whatever the mode or form of expression. For a work to enjoy copyright protection, however, it must be an original creation. The ideas in the work do not need to be new but the form, be it literary or artistic, in which they are expressed must be an original creation of the author. And, finally, protection is independent of the quality or the value attaching to the work—it will be protected whether it be considered, according to taste, a good or

References for Section B
International Bureau of WIPO, *Intellectual Creation as an Incentive for the Development and Cultural Promotion of Nations*, WIPO/CNR/CA/85/2

a bad literary or musical work—and even of the purpose for which it is intended, because the use to which a work may be put has nothing to do with its protection.

8.14 Works eligible for copyright protection are, as a rule, all original intellectual creations. A non-exhaustive, illustrative enumeration of these is contained in national copyright laws. To be protected by copyright law, an author's works must be original. This means that the works must originate from him; they must have their origin in the labor of the author. But it is not necessary, to qualify for copyright protection, that works should pass a test of imaginativeness, of inventiveness. The work is protected irrespective of the quality thereof and also when it has little in common with literature, art or science, such as purely technical guides or engineering drawings, or even maps. This demonstrates that it is not mere ideas, as such, which are protected by copyright but it is the form of expression which is protected. Exceptions to the general rule are made in copyright laws by specific enumeration; thus laws and official decisions or mere news of the day are generally excluded from copyright protection.

8.15 Practically all national copyright laws provide for the protection of the following types of works:

(1) *literary works*: novels, short stories, poems, dramatic works and any other writings, irrespective of their content (fiction or non-fiction), length, purpose (amusement, education, information, advertisement, propaganda, etc.), form (handwritten, typed, printed; book, pamphlet, single sheets, newspaper, magazine); whether published or unpublished; in most countries "oral works," that is, works not reduced to writing, are also protected by the copyright law;

(2) *musical works*: whether serious or light; songs, choruses, operas, musicals, operettas; if for instructions, whether for one instrument (solos), a few instruments (sonatas, chamber music, etc.), or many (bands, orchestras);

(3) *artistic works*: whether two-dimensional (drawings, paintings, etchings, lithographs, etc.) or three-dimensional (sculptures, architectural works), irrespective of content (representational or abstract) and destination ("pure" art, for advertisement, etc.);

(4) *maps and technical drawings*;

(5) *photographic works*: irrespective of the subject matter (portraits, landscapes, current events, etc.) and the purpose for which made;

(6) *motion pictures ("cinematographic works")*: whether silent or with a sound track, and irrespective of their purpose (theatrical exhibition, television broadcasting, etc.), their genre (film dramas, documentaries, newsreels, etc.), length, method employed (filming "live," cartoons, etc.), or technical process used (pictures on transparent film, on electronic video tapes, etc.).

(7) *computer programs* (either as a literary work or independently).

8.16 Many copyright laws protect also "works of applied art" (artistic jewelry, lamps, wallpaper, furniture, etc.) and choreographic works. Some regard phonograph records, tapes and broadcasts also as works.

References for Section C
International Bureau of WIPO, *Introduction to Copyright: Basic Notions of Copyright*, WIPO/GIC/ CNR/GE/86/1

D. RIGHTS COMPRISED IN COPYRIGHT

8.17 The owner of copyright in a protected work may use the work as he wishes—but not without regard to the legally recognized rights and interests of others—and may exclude others from using it without his authorization.

8.18 Therefore, the rights bestowed by law on the owner of copyright in a protected work are frequently described as "exclusive rights" to authorize others to use the protected work.

8.19 The original authors of works protected by copyright also have "moral rights," in addition to their exclusive rights of an economic character.

8.20 What is meant by "using" a work protected by copyright? Most copyright laws define the acts in relation to a work which cannot be performed by persons other than the copyright owner without the authorization of the copyright owner.

8.21 Such acts, requiring the authorization of the copyright owner, normally are the following: copying or reproducing the work; performing the work in public; making a sound recording of the work; making a motion picture of the work; broadcasting the work; translating the work; adapting the work.

(a) Reproduction Rights

8.22 The right of the owner of copyright to exclude others from making copies of his protected work is the most basic right in this branch of intellectual property. The act of making copies of a protected work is the act performed by a publisher who wishes to distribute the work to the public. Therefore, the right to control this act is the legal basis for agreements between owners of copyright and publishers for the publishing of protected works.

8.23 Publishing contracts frequently deal not only with the right to authorize the making of copies of the work but also with the right to authorize other acts (for example, broadcasting, translation and so on). But the essence of a publishing contract is the authorization to make copies.

(b) Performing Rights

8.24 The second act requiring authorization is the act of public performance. A work protected by copyright may be communicated to a large number of people without being copied or reproduced. A lecture can be read aloud to an audience without copies being made. A drama or a musical work can be performed before an audience without copies being made. The right to control this act of public performance is of interest not only to the owners of copyright in works originally designed for public performance. It is of interest also to the owners of copyright, and to persons authorized by them, when others may wish to arrange the public performance of works originally intended to be used by being reproduced and published. For example, a story written originally in a particular way in order to be read at home or in a library may be transformed ("adapted") into a drama designed to be performed in public on the stage of a theater.

(c) Recording Rights

8.25 The third act to be examined is the act of making a sound recording of a work protected by copyright. Obviously, words can be communicated by sound recordings as easily as they can be communicated by writing. Copies of sound recordings can be made as easily as copies of writings. So far as music is concerned, sound recording is the most favored means of communicating a work to a wide public. Gramophone records (called "phonograms" in the technical language of copyright law) serve much the same purpose for musical works as books serve for literary works.

8.26 Sound recordings can incorporate music alone, words alone or both music and words. The right to authorize the making of a sound recording belongs to the owner of the copyright in the music and also to the owner of the copyright in the words. If the two owners are different, then, in the case of a sound recording incorporating both music and words, the maker of the sound recording must obtain the authorization of both owners.

8.27 Under the laws of some countries, the maker of a sound recording must also obtain the authorization of the performers who play the music and who sing or recite the words. This is another example of the fact that the owner of copyright in a work cannot use it or authorize the use of it in a way which is contrary to the legal rights of others. If the making of a sound recording of a performance requires, in order to be lawful, the authorization of the performers, then it is clear that the owner or owners of copyright in a work being performed cannot alone give the necessary authorization for the making of a sound recording of the performance.

(d) Motion Picture Rights

8.28 A "motion picture" is a visual recording, presenting to viewers a continuous sequence of images. In the technical language of copyright law it is often called a "cinematographic work." In some countries the word "film" is used instead of the expression "motion picture." The expression "motion picture" is perhaps preferable, because sequences of images are, today, frequently recorded by technological methods (such as magnetic tape) which do not require the use of photographic film.

8.29 A drama originally written for performance by performers to an immediately present audience ("live performance") can be visually recorded and shown to audiences far larger in numbers than those who can be present at the live performance; such audiences can see the motion picture far away from the place of live performance and at times much later than the live performance.

(e) Broadcasting Rights

8.30 The next major category of acts restricted by copyright includes the acts of broadcasting works and of communicating works to the public by means of wires or cables.

8.31 When a work is broadcast, a wireless signal is emitted into the air which can be received by any person, within range of the signal, who possesses the equipment (radio or television receiver) necessary to convert the signal into sounds or sounds and images.

8.32 When a work is communicated to the public by cable, a signal is diffused which can be received only by persons who possess such equipment linked to the cables used to diffuse the signal.

8.33 In principle, according to the Berne Convention for the Protection of Literary and Artistic Works, owners of copyright have the exclusive right of authorizing both the wireless broadcasting and the diffusion by cable of their works.

8.34 The broadcasting and diffusion by cable of works protected by copyright have, in recent years, been the subject of much discussion. New problems have arisen which may require a review by governments of their national copyright legislation.

8.35 The new copyright problems in the matter of broadcasting and diffusion by cable have arisen mainly as a result of technological advances. These advances include the use of artificial satellites in space to extend the range of wireless signals, the increasing possibilities of linking radio and television receivers to signals diffused by cable, and the increasing use of equipment able to record sound and visual images which are broadcast or diffused by cable.

(f) Translation and Adaptation Rights

8.36 The acts of translating or of adapting a work protected by copyright require the authorization of the copyright owner.

8.37 "Translation" means the expression of a work in a language other than that of the original version.

8.38 "Adaptation" is generally understood as the modification of a work from one type of work to another, for example adapting a novel so as to make a motion picture, or the modification of a work so as to make it suitable for different conditions of exploitation, for example adapting an instructional textbook originally prepared for higher education into an instructional textbook intended for students at a lower level.

8.39 Translations and adaptations are themselves works protected by copyright. Therefore, in order, for example, to reproduce and publish a translation or adaptation, the publisher must have the authorization both of the owner of the copyright in the original work and of the owner of copyright in the translation or adaptation.

(g) Moral Rights

8.40 The Berne Convention requires member countries to grant to authors:

(1)   the right to claim authorship of the work;
(2)   the right to object to any distortion, mutilation or other modification of, or other derogatory action in relation to, the work which would be prejudicial to the author's honor or reputation.

References for Section D
International Bureau of WIPO, *Introduction to Copyright: Basic Notions of Copyright*, WIPO/GIC/CNR/GE/86/1

8.41 These rights, which are generally known as the moral rights of authors, are required to be independent of the usual economic rights and to remain with the author even after he has transferred his economic rights.

E. NEIGHBORING RIGHTS

8.42 There exist rights related to, or "neighboring on" copyright. These rights are generally referred to as "neighboring rights," in an abbreviated expression.

8.43 It is generally understood that there are three kinds of rights which are called neighboring rights: the rights of performing artists in their performances, the rights of producers of phonograms in their phonograms, and the rights of broadcasting organizations in their radio and television programs. Protection of those who assist intellectual creators in communicating the message of the author or creator of a work and help to disseminate works intended by their creators and authors to be conveyed to, and enjoyed by, the public at large, is sought to be provided by what are known as neighboring rights or rights neighboring on copyright.

8.44 Works of the mind are created in order to be disseminated among as large a clientele as possible. This cannot be done generally by the author himself, for it requires intermediaries whose professional capability gives to the works those forms of presentation that are appropriate to make them accessible to a wide public. A play needs to be presented on the stage, a song needs to be performed by artists, reproduced in the form of records or broadcast by means of radio facilities. All persons who make use of literary, artistic or scientific works in order to make them publicly accessible to others require their own protection against the illegal use of their contributions in the process of communicating the work to the public.

8.45 Let us examine as to why such protection of those that thus assist intellectual creators was found necessary and how it developed. The protection of authors' interests does not consist merely in preventing the use of their creations and cannot be limited to prohibiting infringements of the rights that laws afford to the authors. Their works are intended to be made available to the public at large. Various categories of works are made accessible to the public in various ways. A publisher reproduces a manuscript in its final form without adding to the expression of the work as created by the author. The interests of book publishers are protected by means of copyright itself and laws do recognize that copyright is essential as a stimulus to creative writing as also to support the economies of publishing.

8.46 The position is slightly different with regard to dramatic and musical works, pantomimes, or other types of creative works intended for either auditive or visual reception. Where some of such works are communicated to the public, they are produced or performed or recited with the aid of performers. In such cases, there comes in the interest of the performers themselves in relation to the use of their individual interpretation in the performed work.

8.47 The problem in regard to this category of intermediaries has become gradually more acute with the tremendous and ever-increasing strides in technological development during the last few decades. Take for instance the position at the very beginning of this century. The performance of dramatists or actors ended with the play in which they performed; that of musicians interpreting a piece of music likewise was confined to the concert. Not so with the advent of the phonograph, the radio, the motion picture, the television, the videogram and the satellites. Since World War II the pace of development in these media has escalated with dazzling rapidity.

8.48 The development of the phonogram and recording devices had its effect on the performing artists' profession. The phonogram, the radio, the television and the cinema, enabled fixing of performances on a variety of material, viz., records, cassettes, tapes, films, etc. What was earlier a localized or short-lived phase of a performance in a hall before a limited audience became an increasingly permanent manifestation capable of virtually unlimited and repeated use before an equally unlimited audience that went beyond national frontiers. It enabled not only the recording and preservation of sounds, but also their prolific reproduction. With the development of the videogram, preservation of not only sounds but also of images has become possible. The performance of actors and musicians can thus be fixed on a material form that can be preserved as well as re-used and reproduced.

8.49 Similarly, the development of broadcasting and more recently, television, also had its effects on the manner in which works were used. Literary and artistic creations of the author were no longer confined to those who saw a play or observed an opera or listened to a musical performance in a given hall; it extended far beyond, to national and even international audiences able to capture the sounds and images in the privacy of their homes or in places more accessible to the public like hotels and restaurants.

8.50 The development of these technological innovations having made it possible to reproduce individual performances by performing artists and to use them without their presence and without the users being obliged to reach an agreement with them, made its own inroads, and with the consequent reduction in the number of live performances causing what has come to be known as technological unemployment among professional artists, the need for protecting the interests of performers acquired a new dimension.

8.51 Likewise by the very same token, the increasing technological development of phonograms and cassettes and, more recently, compact discs (CDs), and their rapid proliferation, was pointing to the need of protection of producers of phonograms. The appeal of the phonogram as also the easy availability in the market of the variety of increasingly sophisticated recording devices created the growing problem of record piracy, which by now has become a worldwide scourge, involving an estimated illicit manufacture of records and cassettes of a value of approximately one billion dollars a year. In addition, there is the increasing use of records and discs by broadcasting organizations; while the use of these by the latter provides publicity for the phonograms and for their producers, these also have, in turn, become an essential ingredient of the daily programs of broadcasting organizations. Consequently, just as the performers were seeking their own protection, the producers of phonograms began to pursue the case of their protection against unauthorized duplication of their phonograms, as also for remuneration for the use of phonograms for purposes of broadcasting or other forms of communication to the public.

8.52 Finally, there were the interests of broadcasting organizations as regards their individually composed programs. The broadcasting organizations required and urged for their own protection for these as well as against retransmission of their own programs by other similar organizations.

8.53 On account of the various compulsions as thus briefly outlined, the need was felt for special protection for performers, producers of phonograms and broadcasting organizations. The performers through their organizations at the international level sought a study leading to their protection with respect to the increasing recording of their performances which was making serious inroads into their income, and endangering their "live" employment opportunities. They felt that phonograms would replace them in theaters, restaurants, cafés, etc. They also feared the results of secondary use. In other words while a performer would be paid once for recording a performance, the recording of the performance could be played repeatedly for the benefit of a third party, the performers felt that they would not only not derive any income from such secondary use, but would also be placed in the awkward position of having to compete with their own recordings in respect of their employment potential for live performances.

8.54 Unlike most international conventions, which follow in the wake of national legislation and provide a synthesis of existing laws, the Rome Convention was an attempt to establish international regulations in a new field where few national laws existed. This meant that most States would have to draft and enact laws before adhering to the Convention. Since the adoption of the Convention in 1961, a large number of States (over 60) have legislated in matters related to the Convention, and a number of others are considering such legislation.

8.55 Protection of neighboring rights was thus established at the international level by the Rome Convention. Why are these referred to as neighboring rights? It is because they have developed in parallel with copyright and that the exercise of these rights is very often linked with the exercise of copyright. The development of technology resulted in the need not only to ensure protection of literary, artistic, and scientific works by means of copyright, but also to establish effective protection for the various intermediaries associated with the dissemination and broadcasting of works. (Copyright legislation could incorporate rules on neighboring rights, in a separate chapter devoted to protection of performers, producers of phonograms and broadcasting organizations.)

8.56 The notion of neighboring rights is understood as meaning rights granted in an increasing number of countries to protect the interests of performers, producers of phonograms and broadcasting organizations in relation to their activities in connection with the public use of authors' works, all kinds of artists' presentations or the communication to the public of events, information, and any sounds or images. The most important categories are: the right of performers to prevent fixation and direct broadcasting or communication to the public of their performance without their consent; the right of producers of phonograms to authorize or prohibit reproduction of their phonograms and the import and distribution of unauthorized duplicates thereof; the right of broadcasting organizations to authorize or prohibit rebroadcasting, fixation and reproduction of their broadcasts. An increasing number of countries already protect some or all of these rights by appropriate rules, codified mainly within the framework of their copyright laws. Several countries also grant a sort of moral right to performers to protect them against distortion of their performances and grant them the right to claim the mention of their name in connection with their performances. Some countries are also prepared to protect the interests of broadcasting organizations to the extent of preventing the distribution on or from their territory of any programme-carrying signal by a distributor for whom the signal emitted to or passing through a satellite is not intended. No protection of any neighboring right can, however, be interpreted as limiting or prejudicing the protection secured to authors or beneficiaries of other neighboring rights under a national law or an international convention.

8.57 Protection of performers is provided in order to safeguard the interests of actors, singers, musicians, dancers, or other persons who act, sing, deliver, declaim, play in or otherwise perform literary or artistic works, including works of folklore, against certain unlawful uses of their performances. The term "producer of phonograms" denotes a person who, or a legal entity which, first fixes the sounds of a performance or other sounds. A phonogram is any exclusively aural fixation of sounds of a performance or of other sounds. A duplicate of a phonogram is any article containing sounds taken directly or indirectly from a phonogram and which embodies all or a substantial part of the sounds fixed in that phonogram. Gramophone records (discs), magnetophone cassettes and compact discs are duplicates of a phonogram. Broadcasting is usually understood as meaning telecommunication of sounds and/or images by means of radio waves for reception by the public at large. A broadcast is any program transmitted by broadcasting, in other words, transmitted by any wireless means (including laser, gamma rays, etc.) for public reception of sounds and of images and sounds.

8.58 Cable television is a facility developed from the community antenna system, receiving a program and distributing it by using coaxial cables not only for the purpose of simultaneously transmitting by wire programs broadcast by other stations, but also for deferred transmission of programs broadcast and for communicating own programs. It offers a better quality of reception than is often possible by wireless means. Cable television is a sort of communication to the public by wire which in the case of protected works is generally subject to authorization.

8.59 Communication to the public by wire is generally understood as meaning the transmission of a work, performance, phonogram or broadcast by sounds or images through a cable network to receivers not restricted to specific individuals belonging to a private group.

8.60 An ephemeral recording is an aural or audiovisual fixation of a performance or a broadcast made for a temporary period by a broadcasting organization by means of its own facilities and use for its own broadcasts. It is a matter for legislation to determine the legal status for such recordings. Their preservation in official archives, on the ground of their exceptional documentary character, may also be authorized by legislation.

8.61 By first fixation of sounds is meant the original embodiment of sounds of a live performance, or of any other sounds not taken from another existing fixation, in some enduring material form such as tapes, records or any other appropriate device permitting them to be perceived, reproduced or otherwise repeatedly communicated. First fixation of sounds is not to be confused with first publication of a phonogram.

8.62 Certain other notions include, for instance, that of playback and needle time. Playback in cinematographic or television production is understood as being the substitution for the voice of an actor of an audiovisual work by that of another performer, synchronizing the sound of the latter with the movements of the mouth and other actions of the actor shown. Such playback is mainly adopted when producing musical cinematographic works to combine the performance of a film star with the art of a singer. It is usually regarded as being conditional on the consent of both performers involved. Playback is sometimes also understood as meaning synchronization of a performer's actions with his own voice previously recorded.

8.63 Needle time is understood in some countries as meaning the amount of use that may be made of commercial records for broadcasting purposes, usually fixed in hours for definite periods, usually per week. Limitation of "needle time" in favor of transmitting live performances is motivated by the desire to safeguard the conditions for the interests of the musical profession; it is usually agreed upon between broadcasting organizations and musical performers' organizations.

8.64 Another notion, that of rebroadcasting, is either simultaneous transmission of a broadcast of a program being received from another source, or a new, deferred broadcast of a former recorded program transmitted or received earlier. The authorization to broadcast a work does not necessarily cover rebroadcasting of the works.

8.65 A satellite broadcast is generally understood as the transmission by satellite of works or other programs for public reception by electronically generated programme-carrying signals. In the case of "direct broadcast satellites" the transmission of the programme-carrying signals coming from space is already modified for direct reception by the general public. Direct reception from a satellite by the general public is reception of programme-carrying signals from a satellite without the intermediary of an earth station transforming the emitted signals into conventional radio waves; transformation is made in such cases by the direct broadcast satellite itself.

8.66 By distribution satellite is usually meant a satellite transmitting programme-carrying signals to be modified for public reception by a suitable earth station.

8.67 A programme-carrying signal is an electronically generated carrier transmitting programs of broadcasting organizations through space. "Emitted signal" is understood to be any programme-carrying signal that goes to or passes through a satellite; "derived signal" is a signal obtained by modifying the technical characteristics of the emitted signal mainly for purposes of transmission to the general public. Program in this context means a body of live or recorded material consisting of images, sounds, or both, embodied in signals emitted for the purpose of ultimate distribution.

8.68 Direct reception from a satellite by the general public is reception of programme-carrying signals from a satellite without the intermediary of an earth station transforming the emitted signals into conventional radio waves; transformation is made in such cases by the direct broadcast satellite itself. (The Satellites Convention of 1974 does not apply to cases of direct reception from space by the general public.)

8.69 Piracy is commonly understood in the field of neighboring rights as reproducing phonograms by any appropriate means for public distribution and also rebroadcasting another's broadcast, including satellite broadcasts, without authorization. Unlawful fixation of live performances at a concert or from a broadcast or television program and reproduction and sale of such fixation is usually referred to as "bootlegging."

8.70 Remedies for infringement or violation of neighboring rights or means of redress or sanctions include various measures afforded by law to performers, producers of phonograms and broadcasting organizations to protect them against trespass on their rights or lawful interests. Remedies for infringement consist first of all of civil redress, such as the case where infringers are obliged by court to cease the infringement and to undertake reparatory action by any appropriate means, for example, rectification in the press, liability for damages. Some laws also provide for penal remedies in the form of fines and/or imprisonment. Infringing copies, receipts resulting from infringement and any implement used for the same are usually subject to seizure.

8.71 Finally, it must be stated that since in the cultural life of countries, including the developing countries, due importance is attached to the artistic heritage, the protection of neighboring rights affords rights to those who contribute to the interpretation and dissemination of that heritage. It is particularly interesting for some developing countries whose tradition is largely oral and where the author is often the performer as well. In this context, the place occupied by works of folklore must be borne in mind and the interests of the artists performing and thus perpetuating them, must be safeguarded when use is made of their performances. By also protecting the producers of phonograms, particularly in developing countries, the basis for setting up of an industry in the tertiary sector of the economy is ensured. Such an industry, while guaranteeing the dissemination of national culture, both within the country and throughout the world, can additionally constitute a substantial source of revenue for the country's economy and, in those cases where its activities extend beyond the country's frontiers, can represent an inflow of foreign currency. The part played by the broadcasting organizations in developing countries should also not be forgotten nor that such organizations have a natural interest in the protection of their programs against rebroadcasting, reproduction and communication to the public.

8.72 The recognition and protection of neighboring rights in addition to copyright could be an important factor in the cultural, economic and social development of developing countries. By means of protection of neighboring rights and adherence to conventions granting international protection of these rights, the developing countries could balance their need for importation of books through the controlled utilization, for instance, of the performances, fixations and broadcasts of their folklore abroad.

References for Section E
International Bureau of WIPO, *Basic Notions of Neighboring Rights—International Conventions in the Field of Neighboring Rights*, WIPO/CR/GE/93/3

F. OWNERSHIP OF COPYRIGHT

8.73 The owner of copyright in a work is generally, at least in the first instance, the person who created the work—that is to say, the author of the work.

8.74 There can be exceptions to this general principle. Such exceptions are regulated by the national law. For example, the national law may provide that, when a work is created by an author who is employed for the purpose of creating that work, then the employer, not the author, is the owner of the copyright in the work.

8.75 It is to be noted, however, that the "moral rights" always belong to the author of the work, whoever may be the owner of the copyright.

8.76 In many countries, copyright (with the exception of moral rights) may be assigned. This means that the owner of the copyright transfers it to another person or entity, who becomes the owner of the copyright.

8.77 In some other countries, an assignment of copyright is not legally possible. However, very nearly the same practical effect as the effect of assignment can be achieved by licensing. Licensing means that the owner of the copyright remains the owner but authorizes someone else to exercise all or some of his rights subject to possible limitations. When such authorization or license extends to the full period of copyright and when such authorization or license extends to all the rights (except, of course, the moral rights) protected by copyright, the licensee is, vis-à-vis third parties and for all practical purposes, in the same position as an owner of copyright.

G. LIMITATIONS ON COPYRIGHT PROTECTION

(a) Temporal

8.78 Copyright does not continue indefinitely. The law provides for a period of time, a duration, during which the rights of the copyright owner exist.

8.79 The period or duration of copyright begins with the creation of the work. The period or duration continues until some time after the death of the author. The purpose of this provision in the law is to enable the author's successors to have economic benefits after the author's death.

8.80 In countries which are party to the Berne Convention, and in many other countries, the duration of copyright provided for by national law is the life of the author and not less than fifty years after the death of the author. In recent years, a tendency has emerged toward lengthening the term of protection.

(b) Geographic

8.81 The second limitation or exception to be examined is a geographical limitation. The owner of the copyright in a work is protected by the law of a

References for Section F
International Bureau of WIPO, *Introduction to Copyright: Basic Notions of Copyright*, WIPO/GIC/CNR/GE/86/1

country against acts restricted by copyright which are done in that country. For protection against such acts done in another country, he must refer to the law of that other country. If both countries are members of one of the international conventions on copyright, the practical problems arising from this geographical limitation are very much eased.

(c) Permitted Use

8.82 Certain acts normally restricted by copyright may, in circumstances specified in the law, be done without the authorization of the copyright owner. Some examples of such exceptions are described as "fair use." Such examples include reproduction of a work exclusively for the personal and private use of the person who makes the reproduction; another example is the making of quotations from a protected work, provided that the source of the quotation, including the name of the author, is mentioned and that the extent of the quotation is compatible with fair practice.

(d) Non-Material Works

8.83 In some countries, works are excluded from protection if they are not fixed in some material form. In some countries, the texts of laws and of decisions of courts and administrative bodies are excluded from copyright protection (it is to be noted that in some other countries such official texts are not excluded from copyright protection; the government is the owner of copyright in such works, and exercises the rights in accordance with the public interest).

(e) Miscellaneous

8.84 In addition to exceptions based on the principle of "fair use" other exceptions are to be found in national laws and in the Berne Convention. For example, when the broadcasting of a work has been authorized, many national laws permit the broadcasting organization to make a temporary recording of the work for the purposes of broadcasting, even if no specific authorization of the act of recording has been given. The laws of some countries permit the broadcasting of protected works without authorization, provided that fair remuneration is paid to the owner of copyright. This system, under which a right to remuneration can be substituted for the exclusive right to authorize a particular act, is frequently called a system of "compulsory licenses". Such licenses are called "compulsory" because they result from the operation of law and not from the exercise of the exclusive right of the copyright owner to authorize particular acts.

H. PIRACY AND INFRINGEMENT

8.85 The rights of an owner of copyright are infringed when one of the acts requiring authorization of the owner is done by someone else without his or its

References for Section G
International Bureau of WIPO, *Introduction to Copyright: Basic Notions of Copyright*, WIPO/GIC/ CNR/GE/86/1

consent. The unauthorized copying of copyright materials for commercial purposes and the unauthorized commercial dealing in copied materials is known as "piracy."

(a) Incidence of Piracy

8.86 An essential part of piracy is that the unauthorized activity is carried on for commercial gain. This element of commercial gain implies that piracy will often be carried out on an organized basis, since not only is the unauthorized reproduction of a work involved, but also the subsequent sale or distribution of the illegally reproduced work, which will require some form of organized distribution network or contact with potential purchasers. To the consumer, often only the end of the chain of such a distribution network will be visible in the form of one sales outlet selling a pirated product. It is important to bear in mind, however, particularly when addressing the question of the means of dealing effectively with piracy, that behind one such outlet will often lie a systematically organized illicit enterprise, which illegally reproduces a copyrighted work and distributes it to the public via a number of such sales outlets.

8.87 While piracy is not a recent phenomenon, two developments have occurred which have caused piracy to assume alarming proportions, and to threaten the basis of the copyright system.

8.88 The first of these developments has been the advances in the means by which intellectual works may be communicated. The medium of the printed word has been supplemented progressively by media for communicating audio and visual recordings in the form of phonograms, music cassettes, films and videograms. Similarly, widespread commercialization of the computer has added a further means of recording and communicating information. Most recently, the advent of digital technology has had a tremendous impact on the creation, dissemination and use of works.

8.89 The copyright system has responded to these developments by progressively enlarging the subjects over which the creators of intellectual works are granted rights. Copyright protection now, of course, extends not only to books, but also to musical and artistic works, visual recordings in films and videograms, broadcasts and, in certain systems, computer programs. The results of these advances in the means of communicating intellectual works are undeniably socially beneficial, and have enriched the nature of the relationship which an author may create with the public. One by-product of these advances, however, is the increase in scope for pirates to interfere in the control which an author exercises over the dissemination and use of his works by the public.

8.90 Simultaneously with the advances which have occurred in the means of communicating intellectual works have been significant advances in the means of reproducing tangible records of those works. Foremost amongst these latter developments have been:

(1) the development of the offset technique of printing and of duplicating and photocopying machines;

(2) the invention of the magnetic tape, the advent of the compact disc, and the development of higher quality and cheaper cassette recorders which enable

not only the playing of pre-recorded cassettes, but also the recording of music from live performances, radio or gramophone records; and

(3) the invention of the video recorder, which has extensively enlarged the means by which films and other, principally visual, works may be received.

8.91 One consequence of these advances in the means of reproducing a tangible record of an intellectual work is the difference in cost between, on the one hand, the making of the original recording by an author and his business partners and, on the other hand, the reproduction of such a recording by others. In the case of a film, a producer must, through his own and his partners investment, finance the script writer and any other literary author involved, the musical composer, the actors, the support cast, the cost of location and site facilities, and the use of sophisticated visual and sound recording equipment. Once a tangible record has been made of the film, however, particularly if the record is contained in a videogram recording, further records of the work can be reproduced with considerable ease and at little cost. Thus, advances in recording technology have produced the means whereby pirates can easily produce illegal versions of the original work. Since the pirate has not made, and therefore does not need to recover the cost of, any investment in the production of the original work, the pirated copies are usually sold at reduced prices, thereby undermining the original author's and investor's possibility of obtaining a just moral and economic reward for their work and investment.

(b) Effects of Piracy

8.92 Piracy affects all of the elements involved in the creation, production and distribution of intellectual works which together constitute the copyright system. These various elements, and the damage inflicted on them by piracy, are as follows:

(i) Authors and Performers

8.93 In illegally reproducing and distributing printed works and audio and visual recordings, and in illegally taping live performances and distributing for profit the illicit recordings of such performances, pirates pay no remuneration to authors and performers. Authors and performers, of course, are dependent on such remuneration in order to derive their living. Performers, in particular, lose control over the public exposure of their performances when piracy of the performances takes place, with the result that their employment prospects may be substantially diminished. In so depriving authors and performers of the proper economic reward for their creativity, piracy constitutes a substantial detriment to cultural development and, in particular, to the development of indigenous creativity.

(ii) Publishers and Producers

8.94 The investment of publishers in the design, printing and publication of books and other printed works, and the investment of producers in the arrangement and recording of sound and visual works is necessary to enable authors and performers to achieve a wide audience for their work. This investment requires not only financial resources, but also skill and judgment in the selection and presentation of works to the public. The possibility of market failure is a risk which must be assumed by publishers and producers and set off against the rewards of the market successes which they have promoted. No similar degree of investment, skill, judgment and risk is assumed by pirates, who are often able to select the works which they will illegally reproduce after the work has been on the market, and success has been established. In consequence, publishers and producers are often deprived of many of the benefits of their successes, with resultant financial consequences for the risks that they are able to assume in bringing new works on to the market.

(iii) Distributors

8.95 A further necessary element in the copyright system is distribution outlets for books, and music and sound recordings. Since pirates are able to distribute their works more cheaply owing to a lack of financial investment in the production of the works, legitimate distributors can often not compete against the prices charged by the distributors of pirated works. Again, the result is that the system of legitimate distribution of works to the public is prejudiced, with consequential detriment to authors, publishers and producers alike in obtaining legitimate market coverage for their works.

(iv) Consumers

8.96 While consumers may sometimes see short-term benefits in the availability of cheaper works as a result of piracy, the quality of reproductions made by pirates is often very inferior. Consumers are also disadvantaged in the long-term by piracy as a result of the absence of remuneration given to authors and performers by pirates, and of the misappropriation of the economic returns to publishers and producers. This diversion of economic rewards from authors and their business partners to pirates removes the incentive to the investment of time, effort, skill and resources in the creation of new works.

(v) Governmental Authorities

8.97 Since piracy is a clandestine activity, the profits derived by pirates are not subject to tax collection. Amongst the adverse consequences of this diminution in governmental revenue may be a reduction in the amount of government sponsorship available for the arts, as the level of such sponsorship may in part be determined by reference to the contribution which is made to the government budget by taxation derived from the distribution or sale of works subject to copyright protection.

8.98 Piracy can be seen to have detrimental effects, therefore, on each of the elements that make up the copyright system. In consequence, piracy threatens to stultify the evolution and development of national cultural identity which the copyright system is designed to promote.

References for Section H
P. Brazil, *Infringement of Copyright and the Problem of Piracy*, WIPO/IP/ISB/86/12
International Bureau of WIPO, *Piracy of Copyrighted Works and the Development of Legal Remedies*, WIPO/CR/KL/86/8

I. REMEDIES

(a) Introduction

8.99 Remedies for infringement of copyright or for violation of neighboring rights consist of civil redress, as where infringers are obliged by court to cease the infringement and to undertake reparatory action by any appropriate means, for example, rectification in the press or liability for damages. Some laws also provide for penal remedies in the form of fines and/or imprisonment. Infringing copies, receipts resulting from infringement and any implement used for the same are usually subject to seizure.

8.100 The main remedies which are available to a copyright owner in respect of infringement in common-law jurisdictions are an injunction to restrain the continuation of the infringement, and damages to compensate the copyright owner for the depreciation caused by the infringement to the value of his copyright. In the context of piracy, because it is often carried out as an organized activity, the effectiveness of these remedies may be jeopardized for a number of reasons.

8.101 In the first place, the organizer of the making and distribution of illegal reproductions may be using a large number of sales outlets of an impermanent nature. The copyright owner may be confronted with a situation in which it is possible to locate only a small proportion of these outlets, without being able to prove any linkage between the outlets, or any common source of supply for the outlets. Furthermore, the service of a writ commencing an action for infringement, by giving notice to the pirate or to those distributing the works which he has illegally reproduced, may precipitate the destruction of vital evidence required to indicate the source of supply and the extent of sales which have taken place. In addition, since piracy often involves an international dimension, there is a risk that the financial resources and other assets of a pirate may be removed from the jurisdiction in which legal proceedings are commenced against him, thereby depriving the copyright owner of the possibility of recovering damages.

8.102 These difficulties which piracy presents have accentuated the need for preliminary remedies which may be obtained speedily, which will assist in the collection of evidence against a pirate, and which will prevent the destruction of evidence and the removal of financial resources against which damages may be claimed. In many common-law jurisdictions a number of developments have occurred in recent years in response to this need.

(b) Anton Piller Orders

8.103 Foremost among the new developments which have occurred in preliminary remedies has been the so-called Anton Piller order. The Anton Piller order, named after the case in which the English Court of Appeal sanctioned its use (*Anton Piller K.G.* v. *Manufacturing Processes Ltd.* [1976] RPC 719), is an order granted by the court permitting the inspection of premises on which it is believed some activity is being carried on which infringes the copyright of the plaintiff. The order has a number of features which make it a particularly appropriate remedy in the context of piracy:

(1)   the order will be granted *ex parte*, that is, on the application and in the presence alone of the copyright owner, without prior warning being given to the defendant. The essence of the order is thus that it takes the defendant by surprise, and precludes the defendant from destroying or removing vital evidence;

(2)   the terms on which the order is granted enable the copyright owner to inspect the premises of the defendant, and all documents (including business information, such as bills, invoices, sources of supply and customer lists) relating to the alleged infringement. By virtue of these terms, the copyright owner is given the means whereby he may be able to establish the source of supply of pirated works, and the extent of sales which have taken place, which will assist in turn in establishing the amount of damages to which he may be entitled;

(3)   the order for inspection will often be accompanied by an injunction restraining the defendant from altering or removing in any way articles or documents referred to in the order for inspection.

8.104 The Anton Piller order can undoubtedly constitute an important weapon in the armory against piracy. Since it is granted on an *ex parte* basis, however, care needs to be exercised to ensure that the rights of persons against whom it is granted, and whose actions have not yet been judged, are adequately protected. Two safeguards, in particular, which have been required by courts in jurisdictions where it is available, should be noted. First, it will only be granted where it is essential that the plaintiff should have inspection so that justice can be done between the parties. In order to meet this criterion, usually a copyright owner will have to prove that there is clear evidence that the defendants have in their possession incriminating documents or material; that the circumstances are such that there is a real possibility or grave danger that the incriminating materials will be destroyed or hidden if the defendant is forewarned; and that the potential or actual damage to the plaintiff as a result of the defendant's alleged wrongdoings is very serious.

8.105 The second safeguard which is often required is proper respect for the defendant's rights in the execution of the order. In this respect, it may be required that, in executing the order, a copyright owner be attended by his lawyer, give the defendant adequate opportunity of considering the order, and not force entry into the defendant's premises against his will. Of course, if a defendant were to refuse entry into his premises, this would cause extremely adverse inferences to be drawn against him at the subsequent trial.

8.106 In relation to Anton Piller orders, it may finally be noted that the effectiveness of the orders was brought into question in one case when a defendant, pleading the privilege against self-incrimination, successfully applied to discharge orders on the ground that they would expose him to a real risk of prosecution for a criminal offense (*Rank Film Distributors Ltd.* v. *Video Information Centre* [1981] 2 All E.R. 76). In order to overcome the effects of this decision, it may be necessary to pass legislation revoking the privilege against self-incrimination as a basis for refusing to comply with an Anton Piller order, as was done in the Supreme Court Act of 1981 in the United Kingdom.

(c) Discovery against Third Parties

8.107 In certain common-law jurisdictions it has been decided that an innocent third party, who becomes caught up in the wrongdoings of another, is liable to furnish a plaintiff with evidence in his possession relevant to the prosecution of an action by the plaintiff against the wrongdoer. This decision arose in the English case of *Norwich Pharmacal Co.* v. *Commissioners of Customs and Excise* ([1972] RPC 743, [1974] AC 133]) where the plaintiffs, the proprietors of a patent covering a chemical compound, discovered that various persons were importing the compound into the country in contravention of their patent, but were unable to establish the identity of these persons. This information was in the possession of the Commissioners of Customs and Excise, since the importers were required under the customs regulations to fill in a form of entry specifying the name of the importer and a description of the goods. The customs authorities refused to disclose the identity of the importers on the ground that the information had been given to them in confidence. Nevertheless, it was decided that an innocent third party, such as the customs authorities, who inadvertently becomes involved in the wrongdoing of another, will be liable to furnish information concerning the wrongdoer to a plaintiff. While this case was concerned with patents, it also has an application to copyright and could be of particular use to copyright owners who are unable to establish the identity of persons importing pirated works into a country.

8.108 A related but more effective procedure is to be found in Section 53 of the Indian Copyright Act 1957. This provision enables the Registrar of Copyrights to order that copies made out of India of a work which, if made in India, would infringe copyright, shall not be imported. The section also authorizes the Registrar to enter any ship, dock or premises for the purpose of examining allegedly infringing works. The use of the section in a case involving the transportation of pirated audio cassettes over Indian territory was approved by the Indian Supreme Court in *Gramophone Company of India Ltd* v. *Panday* ([1984] 2 SCC 534).

(d) Interlocutory Injunctions

8.109 In order to minimize the damage being inflicted by piracy, it will be important for a copyright owner to take swift action in seeking to prevent the continuation of the piracy. For as long as piracy continues, he will be deprived of a portion of his potential market, and thus of the capacity to recover the economic reward for his creativity or investment. The aim of the interlocutory injunction is to meet this need by granting speedy and temporary relief during the period before a full trial of an infringement action takes place, thus preventing irreparable damage from occurring to the plaintiff's rights.

8.110 One of the difficulties which has been experienced with interlocutory proceedings is that they have tended to become themselves lengthy inquiries involving rather full consideration of the facts of the case, with the result that their effectiveness as a means of obtaining temporary relief is prejudiced. In many common-law jurisdictions, this has caused a reassessment of the principles on which interlocutory relief is granted and, in particular, of the standard of proof which a plaintiff is required to establish in order to obtain interlocutory relief.

8.111 Previously, a plaintiff was required to establish a *prima facie* case that his copyright was being infringed, that is, to establish on the balance of probabilities that his case for infringement had been made out. In order to overcome the delays and the length of proceedings which this standard of proof was involving, many jurisdictions have now required that a plaintiff establish only that there is a "serious question" to be tried. In other words, the merits of the legal issues involved in the case need only be considered at the interlocutory stage to the point where the court is satisfied that the plaintiff's claim for infringement is not frivolous. Thereafter, the decision as to whether an injunction should be granted is taken on the basis of the factual circumstances of the case, and whether, in particular, each party could be adequately compensated in damages for the temporary impairment of his right were he to be unsuccessful at the interlocutory stage, and later prove to be successful at the trial.

8.112 The adoption of this approach to interlocutory proceedings assists in avoiding excessive delays in obtaining relief during the period which is most important for the copyright owner, namely, the period immediately following the initial publication and marketing of his work.

(e) Final Remedies

8.113 The two usual remedies which are available for copyright owners in common-law jurisdictions following the final trial of an infringement action are a perpetual injunction and damages. The perpetual injunction is granted in order to prevent any further repetition of the infringing action. In order to make the injunction effective, it is often coupled with an order for the delivery by the infringer of all infringing copies of the copyright work, which are then subject to destruction so as to ensure that they cannot be re-used or sold.

8.114 The object of an award of damages to a copyright owner is to restore the copyright owner to the position he would have been in had his copyright not been infringed. A difficulty often encountered in obtaining a satisfactory judgment in damages is the production of evidence as to the extent of sales which have taken place and thus as to the extent of damage which has been caused to the plaintiff's copyright. It is for this reason that the recent developments in preliminary remedies, such as the Anton Piller order, which are aimed at enabling a plaintiff to acquire evidence of infringement, are particularly important.

8.115 Of particular relevance to piracy, is the provision in some jurisdictions for additional damages in the case of a flagrant infringement of copyright. Before an award of additional damages can be made in such jurisdictions, however, it is necessary to establish that the infringer's conduct has been deliberate and calculated, and that he has obtained a pecuniary advantage in excess of the damages that he would otherwise have to pay.

References for Section I
International Bureau of WIPO, *Piracy of Copyrighted Works and the Development of Legal Remedies*, WIPO/CR/KL/86/8

J. PROTECTION OF EXPRESSIONS OF FOLKLORE

(a) Introduction

8.116 Folklore is an important cultural heritage of every nation and is still developing—frequently in contemporary forms—even in modern communities all over the world. It is of particular importance to developing countries where folklore is often a basis of their cultural identity and an important means of self-expression both within their own communities and in their relationship with other parts of the world. Folklore is increasingly important from the point of view of their social identity as well. Particularly in developing countries, folklore is a living, functional tradition, rather than a mere souvenir of the past.

8.117 The accelerating development of technology, especially in the fields of sound and audiovisual recording, broadcasting, cable television and cinematography may lead to improper exploitation of this cultural heritage. Expressions of folklore are being commercialized by such means on a worldwide scale without due respect for the cultural or economic interests of the communities in which they originate. In connection with their commercialization, expressions of folklore are often distorted in order to correspond to what is believed to be better for marketing them. And generally no share whatsoever is conceded of the returns from the exploitation of expressions of folklore to the peoples who developed and maintained them.

8.118 In the industrialized countries, expressions of folklore are generally considered to belong to the public domain. This approach explains why, at least so far, industrialized countries generally did not establish a legal protection of the manifold national or other community interest related to the utilization of folklore.

8.119 During the last decade or two, however, it became obvious that—in order to foster folklore as a source of creative expression—proper legal solutions must be found both nationally and at the international level for the protection of folklore. Such protection should be against any improper utilization of expressions of folklore, including the general practice of making profit by commercially exploiting such expressions outside their originating communities without any recompense to such communities.

(b) Attempts to Protect Expressions of Folklore under Copyright Law

8.120 The first attempts to explicitly regulate the use of creations of folklore were made in the framework of certain copyright laws (Tunisia, 1967; Bolivia, 1968 (in respect of musical folklore only); Chile, 1970; Morocco, 1970; Algeria, 1973; Senegal, 1973; Kenya, 1975; Mali, 1977; Burundi, 1978; Ivory Coast, 1978; Guinea, 1980; Tunis Model Law on Copyright for Developing Countries, 1976) and in an international Treaty (the Bangui text of 1977 of the Convention concerning the African Intellectual Property Organization, hereinafter referred to as "the OAPI Convention"). All these texts consider works of folklore as part of the cultural heritage of the nation ("traditional heritage," "cultural patrimony"; in Chile, "cultural public domain", the use of which is subject to payment).

8.121 An attempt to protect expressions of folklore by means of copyright law was also undertaken at the international level in the Diplomatic Conference of Stockholm in 1967 for the revision of the Berne Convention. As a result, Article 15(4) of the Stockholm (1967) and Paris (1971) Acts of the Berne Convention contains the following provision: "(a) In the case of unpublished works where the identity of the author is unknown, but where there is every ground to presume that he is a national of a country of the Union, it shall be a matter for legislation in that country to designate the competent authority which shall represent the author and shall be entitled to protect and enforce his rights in the countries of the Union. (b) Countries of the Union which make such designation under the terms of this provision shall notify the Director General [of WIPO] by means of a written declaration giving full information concerning the authority thus designated. The Director General shall at once communicate this declaration to all other countries of the Union." This article of the Berne Convention implies the possibility of requesting, in certain cases, also protection of expressions of folklore.

8.122 Finally, neighboring rights cannot fully satisfy the need for legal protection against improper use of creations of folklore since they cannot prevent the copying of expressions of folklore which are not performed, broadcast or contained in phonograms. Furthermore, the limited duration of the protection of neighboring rights does not fit folklore for the same reasons as the limited duration of copyright does not fit it.

8.123 For these reasons, it was thought advisable to establish, as regards intellectual property aspects of expressions of folklore, a special *sui generis*, type of law for an adequate protection against unauthorized exploitation.

(c)   Special Model Provisions for National Laws on the Protection of Expressions of Folklore against Illicit Exploitation and other Prejudicial Actions

(i)   Evolution

8.124 At the meeting of WIPO's Governing Bodies in 1978 it was felt that despite concern among developing countries as to the need to protect folklore, few concrete steps had so far been taken to formulate legal norms. Following that meeting, the International Bureau of WIPO prepared a first draft of *sui generis* model provisions for an intellectual-property-type national protection of folklore against certain unauthorized uses and against distortion.

8.125 The first draft of WIPO's model provisions on intellectual-property-type protection of folklore was submitted in Dakar in March 1979 to WIPO's Permanent Committee on Copyright and Neighboring Rights, which recommended that a joint WIPO/UNESCO working group should be convened as soon as possible, and should preferably deal not only with domestic aspects, but also with the international aspects of the legal protection of folklore creations.

8.126 In accordance with the decisions of their respective Governing Bodies, WIPO and Unesco convened a Working Group in 1980 at Geneva, to study the draft of model provisions intended for national legislation prepared by WIPO, as well as international measures for the protection of works of folklore. The said Working Group recommended, in respect of the model provisions for national laws on the protection of creations of folklore, that the Secretariats of WIPO and Unesco should prepare a revised draft and commentary thereon, taking into consideration all the interventions made in the Working Group.

8.127 Accordingly, the Secretariats prepared a revised draft, and a Commentary, which were submitted to the Working Group convened by WIPO and Unesco for a second meeting at Paris in 1981. The outcome of the meeting was submitted a year later, in June-July 1982, to a Committee of Governmental Experts, convened by WIPO and Unesco at WIPO headquarters in Geneva, which adopted what is called "Model Provisions for National Laws on the Protection of Expressions of Folklore Against Illicit Exploitation and Other Prejudicial Actions" (hereinafter referred to as "the Model Provisions").

(ii)   Basic Principles

8.128 The basic requirement in providing for legal protection of expressions of folklore, is the necessity of maintaining a proper balance between protection against abuses of expressions of folklore, on the one hand, and the freedom and encouragement of their further development, dissemination as well as adaptation for creating original authors' works inspired by folklore, on the other. A major part of expressions of folklore forms a living body of human culture which should not be restricted in its unfolding and/or influence on creativity, by too tight a net of protection.

8.129 In this context the proposed protection has to be practicable and effective, rather than remaining a system of imaginative requirements removed from reality.

8.130 The Model Provisions were designed with the intention of leaving room for national legislation to adopt the system of protection best suiting the conditions existing in a given country.

(iii)   The Subject of Protection

8.131 No generally accepted definition of folklore has yet been found, in spite of countless proposals which have been made to this effect. Consequently, the Model Provisions do not offer any definition of folklore. However, for the purpose of the Model Provisions, Section 2 defines the term "expression of folklore" in line with the findings of the Committee of Governmental Experts on the Safeguarding of Folklore, which met in Paris in February 1982, and provides that "expressions of folklore" are understood as productions consisting of characteristic elements of the traditional artistic heritage developed and maintained by a community in the country or by individuals reflecting the traditional artistic expectations of such a community.

8.132 This definition of the expressions of folklore embraces the concepts of both collective and individual development of the traditional artistic heritage, since the generally applied criterion of "impersonal" creativity does not always correspond to realities of the evolution of folklore. The personality of the artist is often an important factor in folkloric expression, and individual contributions to the development and maintenance of such expressions may represent a creative source of enrichment of inherited folklore, if they are recognized and adopted by the community as expressions corresponding to its traditional artistic expectations.

8.133 The use of the words "expressions" and "productions" rather than "works" is intended to underline the fact that the provisions are *sui generis*, rather than of copyright, since "works" are the subject matter of copyright. Naturally, the expressions of folklore may, and—in fact—most of the time do, have the same artistic form as "works."

8.134 The fact that only "artistic" heritage is being considered, means that, among other things, traditional beliefs, scientific views (e.g. traditional cosmogony), substance of legends or merely practical traditions as such, separated from possible traditional artistic forms of their expression, do not fall within the scope of the proposed definition of "expressions of folklore." On the other hand, "artistic" heritage is understood in the widest sense of the term and covers any traditional heritage appealing to the aesthetic sense of man. Verbal expressions, which would qualify as literature if created individually by an author, musical expressions, expressions by action and tangible expressions may all consist of characteristic elements of the traditional artistic heritage and qualify as protected expressions of folklore.

8.135 In addition to the definition, for the purposes of the Model Provisions, an illustrative enumeration of the most typical kinds of expression of folklore is offered therein. Such expressions are subdivided into four groups depending on the form of the "expression," namely, expression by words ("verbal"), expressions by musical sounds ("musical"), expressions "by action" (of the human body) and expressions incorporated in a material object ("tangible expressions"). Each must consist of characteristic elements taken from the totality of the traditional artistic heritage. The first three kinds of expression need not be "reduced to material form," that is to say, the words need not be written down, the music need not exist in the form of musical notation and the bodily action—for example, dance—need not exist in a written choreographic notation. On the other hand, tangible expressions must be incorporated in a permanent material, such as stone, wood, textile, gold, etc. The provision also gives examples of each of the various forms of expression. They are, firstly, "folk tales, folk poetry and riddles"; secondly, "folk songs and instrumental music"; thirdly, "folk dances, plays and artistic forms of rituals"; and fourthly, "drawings, paintings, carvings, sculptures, pottery, terracotta, mosaic, woodwork, metalware, jewellery, basket weaving, needlework, textiles, carpets, costumes, musical instruments, architectural forms." The last-named appears in the Model Provisions in square brackets to show the hesitation which accompanied its inclusion, and to leave it to each country to decide whether or not to include it in the realm of protected expressions of folklore.

8.136 Identification of expressions of folklore originating in and developed by a community could be achieved by keeping an inventory of them. However, such an inventory being related mainly to conservation of folklore, its regulation does not fall within the scope of the Model Provisions.

(iv) Prejudicial Acts

8.137 As reflected in the Model Provisions, there are two main categories of acts against which expressions of folklore need to be protected. They are "illicit exploitation" and "other prejudicial actions" (Section 1).

8.138 *"Illicit Exploitation"* of an expression of folklore is understood in the Model Provisions (Section 3) as any utilization thereof if made both with gainful intent and outside its traditional or customary context, without authorization by a competent authority or the community concerned itself. This means, among other things, that a utilization—even with gainful intent—within the traditional or customary context should not be subject to authorization. On the other hand, a utilization, even by members of the community where the expression has been developed and maintained, requires authorization if it is made outside that context and with gainful intent.

8.139 *"Traditional Context"* is understood as the way of using an expression of folklore in its proper artistic framework based on continuous usage by the community. For instance, to use a ritual dance in its traditional context means to perform it in the actual framework of the respective rite. On the other hand, the term "customary context" refers rather to the utilization of expressions of folklore in accordance with the practices of everyday life of the community, such as for instance usual ways of selling copies of tangible expressions of folklore by local craftsmen. A customary context may develop and change more rapidly than the traditional ones.

8.140 The section under consideration then specifies the acts of utilization which require authorization where such circumstances exist. In doing so, it distinguishes between the case in which copies of the expressions are involved and the case in which copies of such expressions are not necessarily involved. In the first case, the acts requiring authorization are publication (in the broadest sense of the word, so as to cover any form of making available to the public the original, a copy or copies of an expression of folklore embodied in any material form, including recordings), reproduction and distribution; in the second case, the acts requiring authorization are public recitation, public performance, transmission by wireless means or by wire and "any other form of communication to the public."

8.141 *Permitted Use.* The Model Provisions would not prevent indigenous communities from using their traditional cultural heritage in traditional and customary ways and in developing it by continuous imitation. Keeping alive traditional popular art is closely linked with the reproduction, recitation or performance, in a stylistically varying presentation, of traditional expressions in the originating community. An unrestricted requirement for authorization to adapt, arrange, reproduce, recite or perform such creations could place a barrier in the way of the natural evolution of folklore and could not be enforced in societies in which folklore is a part of everyday life. Thus, the Model Provisions allow any member of a community of the country to freely reproduce or perform expressions of the folklore of his own community in their traditional or customary context, irrespective of whether he does it with or without gainful intent and even if done by means of modern technology, if such technology has been accepted by the community as one of the means of the evolution of its living folklore.

8.142 Section 4 sets out four special cases, in which there is no need to obtain authorization, even if the utilization of the expression of folklore was made against payment and outside its traditional or customary context. The four special cases are:

(1) use or utilization for purposes of education;
(2) utilization made "by way of illustration" in any original work of an author, provided that such utilization is compatible with fair practice as it is understood in the country concerned;
(3) where expressions of folklore are "borrowed" for creating an original work of an author. This important exception serves the purpose of allowing the free development of individual creativity inspired by folklore;
(4) "incidental utilization" which typically includes utilization in connection with reporting on current events and utilization of images where the expression of folklore is an object permanently located in a public place.

8.143 *Other Prejudicial Actions*, detrimental to interests related to the use of expressions of folklore are, according to the Model Provisions, four distinct offenses, subject to penal sanctions (Section 6).

8.144 Section 5 requires, as a rule, that in all printed publications, and in connection with any communication to the public, of any *identifiable* expression of folklore, its source shall be indicated in an appropriate manner, by mentioning the community and/or geographic place from where the expression utilized has been derived. In Section 6 non-compliance with the requirement of acknowledgment of the source is made subject to punishment.

8.145 Unauthorized utilization of an expression of folklore where authorization is required, constitutes an offense. It is understood that the offense of using an expression without authorization is also constituted by uses going beyond the limits or that which are contrary to the conditions of an authorization obtained. Deception of the public, by creating the impression that what is involved is an expression of folklore derived from a given community when, in fact, such is not the case, is likewise punishable.

8.146 Public utilization distorting the expression of folklore, in any direct or indirect manner "prejudicial to the cultural interests of the community concerned", is an offense. The term "distorting" covers any act of distortion or mutilation or other derogatory action in relation to the expression of folklore published, reproduced, distributed, performed or otherwise communicated to the public by the culprit.

8.147 All four kinds of offenses are conditional on willful action. However, as regards non-compliance with the requirement of acknowledgment of source and the need to obtain authorization to use the expression of folklore, the Model Provisions also allow for punishment of acts committed negligently. This takes account of the nature of the offenses concerned and the difficulties involved in proving willfulness in cases of omission.

(v) Implementing the Protection of Expressions of Folklore

8.148 *Authorizing Utilization of Expressions of Folklore.* Concerning the entity entitled to authorize the utilization of expressions of folklore, the Model Provisions alternatively refer to "competent authority" and "community concerned," avoiding the term "owner" of the expression involved. They do not deal with questions of ownership of expressions of folklore since this aspect of the problem may be regulated in different ways from one country to another. In some countries, expressions of folklore may be regarded as the property of the nation, in other countries, the sense of ownership of the traditional artistic heritage may have been more strongly developed in the communities concerned themselves. Who should be entitled to authorize the utilization of expressions of folklore depends very much on the situation as regards ownership of them and necessarily varies according to different legislation on the subject. In countries where aboriginal or other traditional communities are recognized as owners fully entitled to dispose of their folklore and where such communities are sufficiently organized to administer the utilization of the expressions of their folklore, such uses may be subject to authorization by the community itself, which would grant permission to prospective users in a manner similar to authorization given by authors, as a rule, at full discretion. In other countries, where the traditional artistic heritage of a community is basically considered as a part of the cultural heritage of the nation, or where the communities concerned are not prepared to adequately administer the use of their expressions of folklore themselves, "competent authorities" may be designated, to give the necessary authorizations in the form of decisions under public law.

8.149 *Supervisory Authorities*. Section 9 of the Model Provisions provides for the designation of the competent authority, if that alternative was preferred by the legislator. The same section also provides for designation of a "supervisory authority," if this should become necessary owing to the adoption of certain subsequent provisions suggested alternatively as regards activities to be carried out by such an authority.

8.150 According to the Model Provisions, the tasks of the *competent* authority are (provided such an authority has been designated) to grant authorizations for certain kinds of utilization of expressions of folklore, to receive applications for authorization of such utilizations, decide on them and, where authorization is granted, to fix and collect a fee—where required by law.

8.151 As far as the *supervisory* authority is concerned, the Model Provisions offer the possibility of providing in the law that the supervisory authority shall establish a tariff of the fees payable for authorizations of utilizations, or shall approve such tariff (without indication in the Model Provisions as to who will, in such case, propose the tariff, although it was understood by the experts adopting the Model Provisions that, in such a case, the competent authority would propose the tariff) (Section 10), and that the supervisory authority's decision may be appealed to a court (Section 11, paragraph 1).

8.152 Which authority or authorities will be designated in a given country, will largely depend on the legal system existing in that country. A possible solution would be to set up a special authority for the purpose of dealing with the tasks laid down in the Model Provisions and to designate a ministry, for example, the Ministry of Culture, as the supervisory authority. As far as the competent authority is concerned it could be the Ministry of Culture, any public institution for matters related to folklore, authors' society or similar institution. A representative body of the community concerned could likewise be designated, even where, for whatever reason, the legislator had preferred not to recognize the community itself, in its capacity of owner of its expressions of folklore, as being entitled to directly authorize utilizations of such expressions.

8.153 It would seem eminently useful and logical if representatives of the various folklore communities of the country were to be associated and given an important role in the work of any competent authority or authorities. Furthermore, representatives of cultural and ethnological institutions, including museums, having experience in certain aspects of the protection of folklore, could likewise be associated in the work of the competent authority or authorities.

8.154 If the legislator decided that the community as such was entitled to permit or prevent utilizations of its expressions of folklore subject to authorization, the community would act in its capacity of owner of the expressions concerned and would be free to decide how to proceed. There would be no supervisory authority to control how the community exercises its relevant rights. However, the experts were of the opinion that if it was not the community as such, but a designated representative body thereof, which was entitled by legislation to give the necessary authorization, such a body would qualify as a competent authority, subject to the relevant procedural rules laid down in the Model Provisions.

8.155 *Process of Authorization.* As regards the process of authorization it follows from Section 10 (1) of the Model Provisions that an authorization must be preceded by an "application" submitted to the competent authority. The authorization to be applied for may be "individual" or "blanket," the first meaning an *ad hoc* authorization, the second intended for customary utilizers such as cultural institutions, theaters, ballet groups and broadcasting and television organizations. In this latter context, national legislators may also consider the applicability of systems of non-voluntary licensing possibly existing in the country concerning utilization of works protected by copyright, with special regard to certain kinds of uses by broadcasting organizations and cable systems.

8.156 *Remuneration.* The Model Provisions (Section 10, paragraph 2) allow, but do not make mandatory, the collecting of fees for authorizations. Presumably, where a fee is fixed, the authorization will be effective only on condition of payment. Authorizations may be granted free of the obligation of paying a fee. Even in such cases, the system of authorization is justified since it may prevent such utilizations as would distort the expressions of folklore or otherwise be unworthy of their dignity. Where fees are charged, they must be fixed according to a tariff established or approved—as already mentioned—by the supervisory authority.

8.157 The Model Provisions deal, in the same paragraph, also with the purpose for which the collected fees must be used. They offer a choice between the promoting or safeguarding of national culture or of national folklore. Naturally, national folklore is part of national culture, but national culture concerns a greater number of potential beneficiaries than national folklore. It is advisable, in any case, to secure by decree that a certain percentage of any fee collected by the competent authority is to go to that community from which the expression of folklore for the utilization of which the fee was paid originates. The relevant decree may allow the competent authority to retain part of the collected fees to cover the costs of administering the authorization system. Where there is no competent authority designated and both authorization and collection of relevant fees is carried out directly by the community as such, it seems obvious that the employment of the collected fees should also be decided by the community. The

State should secure its share of such revenues, if at all, by imposing on them taxes or by providing for other appropriate measures.

(vi) Sanctions

8.158 The two main types of possible punishments appear to be fine and imprisonment. Which of these sanctions should apply, what kinds of other punishments could be provided for and whether the sanctions should be applicable separately or also in conjunction, depends on the nature of the offense, the importance of the interests to be protected and the solutions already adopted in a given country for similar offenses. The minimum and maximum amounts of fines or terms of imprisonment would likewise depend on the actual practice of each country. Consequently, the Model Provisions do not suggest any specific punishment; they are confined to the requirement of penal remedy, leaving it to national legislation to specify its form and measure.

8.159 As regards seizure and other actions, however, the Model Provisions are somewhat more explicit. The relevant Section 7 applies in the case of any violation of the law to both objects and receipts.

(d) Regional and International Protection of Folklore

8.160 The Model Provisions should pave the way for subregional, regional and international protection. It is of paramount importance to protect expressions of folklore against illicit commercialization and distortion beyond the frontiers of the country in which they originate. Regional and international protection of expressions of folklore serves to protect expressions of folklore against illicit use that takes place abroad. On the other hand, national legislation on the protection of expressions of folklore also provides the necessary basis for protecting the expressions of folklore of communities. By appropriate extension of their applicability under the principle of national treatment, national provisions may provide the substance of regional or international protection.

8.161 In order to further such a process, the Model Provisions provide for their application as regards expressions of folklore of foreign origin either subject to reciprocity or on the basis of international treaties (Section 14). Actual reciprocity in the relations of two or more countries already protecting their national folklore may sometimes be established and declared more easily than mutual protection by means of concluding and ratifying international treaties. However, a number of experts stressed that international measures are an indispensable means of extending the protection of expressions of folklore of a given country beyond the borders of the country concerned. Consequently, it is advisable to endeavor to conclude multilateral treaties based on national laws protecting expressions of folklore, in order to secure such protection in a greater number of countries. In this context, the possibility of developing existing intergovernmental cultural or other appropriate agreements, so as to cover also reciprocal protection of expressions of folklore, should likewise be considered.

References for Section J
International Bureau of WIPO, *Protection of Expressions of Folklore*, GIC/UK/CNR/VI/12

CHAPTER 9

Trademarks

A. INTRODUCTION

9.1 Trademarks already existed in the ancient world. Even at times when people either prepared what they needed themselves or, more usually, acquired it from local craftsmen, there were already creative entrepreneurs who marketed their goods beyond their localities and sometimes over considerable distances. As long as 3,000 years ago, Indian craftsmen used to engrave their signatures on their artistic creations before sending them to Iran. Manufacturers from China sold goods bearing their marks in the Mediterranean area over 2,000 years ago and at one time about a thousand different Roman pottery marks were in use, including the FORTIS brand, which became so famous that it was copied and counterfeited. With the flourishing trade of the Middle Ages, the use of signs to distinguish the goods of merchants and manufacturers likewise expanded several hundred years ago. Their economic importance was still limited, however.

9.2 Trademarks started to play an important role with industrialization, and they have since become a key factor in the modern world of international trade and market-oriented economies. Industrialization and the growth of the system of the market-oriented economy allow competing manufacturers and traders to offer consumers a variety of goods in the same category. Often without any apparent differences for the consumer they do generally differ in quality, price and other characteristics. Clearly consumers need to be given the guidance that will allow them to consider the alternatives and make their choice between the competing goods. Consequently, the goods must be named. The medium for naming goods on the market is precisely the trademark.

9.3 Businesses also need trademarks to individualize their products, however, in order to reach out to consumers and communicate with them. So, trademarks serve their owners in the advertising and selling of goods, and they serve the economy in a general sense by helping to rationalize the commercialization of goods.

9.4 By enabling consumers to make their choice between the various goods available on the market, trademarks encourage their owners to maintain and improve the quality of the products sold under the trademark, in order to meet consumer expectations. In a market that offers a choice, a consumer who is disappointed will not buy the same product again. One who is satisfied will tend to rely on the trademark for his future purchase decisions. Thus trademarks reward the manufacturer who constantly produces high-quality goods, and as a result they stimulate economic progress.

B. DEFINITIONS

(a) Trademarks

9.5 "A trademark is any sign that individualizes the goods of a given enterprise and distinguishes them from the goods of its competitors." This definition comprises two aspects, which are sometimes referred to as the different functions of the trademark, but which are, however, interdependent and for all practical purposes should always be looked at together:

9.6 In order to individualize a product for the consumer, the trademark must indicate its source. This does not mean that it must inform the consumer of the actual person who has manufactured the product or even the one who is trading in it: the consumer in fact often does not know the name of the manufacturer, still less the geographical location of the factory in which the product was made. This is not necessary for the trademark to fulfil its purpose of indicating origin. It is sufficient that the consumer can trust in a given enterprise, not necessarily known to him, being responsible for the product sold under the trademark.

9.7 The origin function as described above presupposes that the trademark distinguishes the goods of the given enterprise from those of other enterprises; only if it allows the consumer to distinguish a product sold under it from the goods of other enterprises offered on the market can the trademark fulfil its origin function. This shows that the distinguishing function and the origin function cannot really be separated. For practical purposes one can even simply rely on the distinguishing function of the trademark, and define it as "A sign which serves to distinguish the goods of one enterprise from those of other enterprises."

9.8 This is the approach chosen by Section 1(1)(a) of the WIPO Model Law for Developing Countries on Marks, Trade Names and Acts of Unfair Competition of 1967 ("the Model Law").

(b) Service Marks

9.9 In modern trade consumers are confronted not only with a vast choice of goods of all kinds, but also with an increasing variety of services which tend more and more to be offered on a national and even international scale. There is therefore also a need for signs that enable the consumers to distinguish between the different services such as insurance companies, car rental firms, airlines, etc. These signs are called service marks, and fulfil essentially the same origin-indicating and distinguishing function for services as trademarks do for goods. It is widely recognized that there is a need for protection of service marks as there is for trademarks, and modern trademark laws give protection to the marks for services in the same way as to the marks that identify goods.

9.10 Since service marks are signs that are very similar in nature to trademarks, basically the same criteria can be applied, so service mark protection has sometimes been introduced by a very short amendment to the existing trademark law, simply providing for the application to service marks, *mutatis mutandis*, of the provisions on the protection of trademarks.

9.11 It follows from the above principle that service marks can be registered, renewed and cancelled in the same way as trademarks; they can moreover be assigned and licensed under the same conditions. Rules devised for trademarks therefore apply equally, in principle, to service marks.

(c) Collective Marks and Certification Marks

9.12 Trademarks typically identify individual enterprises as the origin of marked goods or services. Some countries provide for the registration of collective and certification marks, which are used to indicate the affiliation of enterprises using the mark or which refer to identifiable standards met by the products with which a mark is used.

9.13 The following are the common features in the relevant provisions of national law on this topic:

(i) Collective Marks

9.14 A collective mark may be owned by an association which itself does not use the collective mark but whose members may use the collective mark; typically, the association has been founded in order to ensure the compliance with certain quality standards by its members; the members may use the collective mark if they comply with the requirements fixed in the regulations concerning the use of the collective mark. Thus, the function of the collective mark is to inform the public about certain particular features of the product for which the collective mark is used. An enterprise entitled to use the collective mark may in addition also use its own trademark.

9.15 The regulations concerning the use of the collective mark normally have to be included in an application for the registration of the collective mark and any modifications to the regulations have to be notified to the Trademark Office. In several countries (for example, the Federal Republic of Germany, Finland, Norway and Sweden and Switzerland), the registration of a collective mark may be cancelled if that mark is used contrary to the provisions of the regulations or in a manner which misleads the public. Collective marks, therefore, play an important role in the protection of consumers against misleading practices.

9.16 The Paris Convention contains provisions on collective marks in its Article 7*bis*. Those provisions, in particular, ensure that collective marks are to be admitted for registration and protection in countries other than the country where the association owning the collective mark has been established. This means that the fact that the said association has not been established in accordance with the law of the country where protection is sought is no reason for refusing such protection. On the other hand, the Convention expressly states the right of each member State to apply its own conditions of protection and to refuse protection if the collective mark is contrary to the public interest.

(ii) Certification Marks

9.17 The certification mark may only be used in accordance with the defined standards. The main difference between collective marks and certification marks is that the former may be used only by particular enterprises, for example, members of the association which owns the collective mark, while the latter may be used by anybody who complies with the defined standards. Thus, the users of a collective mark form a "club" while, in respect of certification marks, the "open shop" principle applies.

9.18 An important requirement for the registration of a certification mark is that the entity which applies for registration is "competent to certify" the products concerned. Thus, the owner of a certification mark must be the representative for the products to which the certification mark applies. This is an important safeguard for the protection of the public against misleading practices.

9.19 The definition of "certification mark" is not the same in all countries. In the United States of America, for instance, a certification mark may not be used by anybody who complies with the defined standards, but only by enterprises which have been authorized by the owner of the certification mark to use that mark. Thus, in the United States of America, the difference between a certification mark and a collective mark is smaller than in other countries; it only relates to the purpose of those two kinds of marks: the certification mark refers to certain standards of products or services, while the collective mark refers to the membership of its users in a particular organization.

C. SIGNS WHICH MAY SERVE AS TRADEMARKS

9.20 It follows from the purpose of the trademark that virtually any sign that can serve to distinguish goods from other goods is capable of constituting a trademark. Trademark laws should not therefore attempt to draw up an exhaustive list of signs admitted for registration. If examples are given, they should be a practical illustration of what can be registered, without being exhaustive. If there are to be limitations, they should be based on practical considerations only, such as the need for a workable register and the need for publication of the registered trademark.

9.21 If we adhere strictly to the principle that the sign must serve to distinguish the goods of a given enterprise from those of others, the following types and categories of signs can be imagined:

(1) Words
     This category includes company names, surnames, forenames, geographical names and any other words or sets of words, whether invented or not, and slogans.
(2) Letters and Numerals
     Examples are one or more letters, one or more numerals or any combination thereof.
(3) Devices
     This category includes fancy devices, drawings and symbols and also two-dimensional representations of goods or containers.
(4) Combinations of Any of those Listed Under (i), (ii) and (iii), Including Logotypes and Labels

References for Section B
International Bureau of WIPO, *Introduction to Trademark Law & Practice* (second edition), WIPO Pub. No. 653(E) (1993)
International Bureau of WIPO, *Comparative Trademark Law*, BTMC/1, BTMC/4 Rev., BMTC/6

(5) Colored Marks
     This category includes words, devices and any combinations thereof in
     color, as well as color combinations and color as such.
(6) Three-Dimensional Signs
     A typical category of three-dimensional signs is the shape of the goods or
     their packaging. However, other three-dimensional signs such as the
     three-pointed Mercedes star can serve as a trademark.
(7) Audible Signs (Sounds Marks)
     Two typical categories of sound marks can be distinguished, namely those
     that can be transcribed in musical notes or other symbols and others (e.g. the
     cry of an animal).
(8) Olfactory Marks (Smell Marks)
     Imagine that a company sells its goods (e.g. writing paper) with a certain
     fragrance and the consumer becomes accustomed to recognizing the goods
     by their smell.
(9) Other (Invisible) Signs
     Examples of these are signs recognized by touch.

9.22 As mentioned before, countries may set limits on registrability for practical
purposes. The majority of countries allow the registration only of signs that can
be represented graphically, since only they can be physically registered and
published in a trademark journal to inform the public of the registration of the
trademark.

9.23 A number of countries allow the registration of three-dimensional trademarks,
obliging the applicant either to submit a two-dimensional representation of the
three-dimensional sign (drawing, picture or any other representation capable of
being printed) or a description (or both). In practice, however, it is not always
clear what is protected by the registration of a three-dimensional sign.

9.24 A similar problem exists for audible signs. A sequence of notes can of
course be registered as a device mark, but that registration does not normally give
protection to the actual musical phrases so expressed. What is protected is the
sequence of notes, as registered, against the use of similar devices. Sound marks
clearly can serve as trademarks, however, and the United States of America, for
example, allows the registration of sound marks. In practical terms, this means
that the sound must be recorded and the cassette submitted to the U.S. Patent and
Trademark Office for registration.

9.25 The United States of America is the only country to have recognized,
in a recent decision, the registrability of a smell mark (fresh floral fragrance
reminiscent of Plumeria blossoms for sewing thread and embroidery yarn—
TTAB(1990)).

References for Section C
International Bureau of WIPO, *Introduction to Trademark Law & Practice* (second edition), WIPO
Pub. No. 653(E) (1993)

D. CRITERIA OF PROTECTABILITY

9.26 The requirements which a sign must fulfil in order to be capable of serving as a trademark are reasonably standard throughout the world.

9.27 Generally speaking, two different kinds of requirement are to be distinguished.

9.28 The first kind of requirement relates to the basic function of a trademark, namely, its function to distinguish the products or services of one enterprise from the products or services of other enterprises. From that function it follows that a trademark must be distinctive or capable of distinguishing different products.

9.29 The second kind of requirement relates to the possible harmful effects of a trademark if it has a misleading character or if it violates public order or morality.

9.30 These two kinds of requirement exist in practically all national trademark laws. They also appear in Article 6*quinquies* B of the Paris Convention where it is stated that trademarks enjoying protection under Article 6*quinquies* A may be denied registration only if "they are devoid of any distinctive character" or if "they are contrary to morality or public order and, in particular, of such a nature as to deceive the public."

(a) Requirement of Distinctiveness

9.31 We have seen that the trademark serves to distinguish the goods of one enterprise from those of others, so, in order to function as a trademark, it must be distinctive. A sign that is not distinctive cannot help the consumer to identify the goods of his choice. The word "apple" or an apple device cannot be registered for apples, but it is highly distinctive for computers. This shows that distinctive character must be evaluated in relation to the goods to which the trademark is applied.

9.32 The test of whether a trademark is distinctive is bound to depend on the understanding of the consumers, or at least the persons to whom the sign is addressed. Very often, however, a sign has not been used before it is filed for registration, and so the question can only be whether it is capable of distinguishing the goods to which it is to be applied.

9.33 In conclusion, a sign is distinctive for the goods to which it is to be applied when it is recognized by those to whom it is addressed as identifying goods from a particular trade source, or is capable of being so recognized.

9.34 The distinctiveness of a sign is not an absolute and unchangeable factor. It is a purely circumstantial matter. Depending on the steps taken by the user of the sign or third parties, it can be acquired or increased or even lost. Circumstances such as (possibly long and intensive) use of the sign have to be taken into account when the registrar is of the opinion that the sign lacks the necessary distinctiveness, that is, if it is regarded as being not inherently distinctive.

9.35 There are, of course, different degrees of distinctiveness, and the question is how distinctive a sign must be in order to be registrable, regardless of its possible use. In that connection a distinction is generally made between certain typical categories of marks:

9.36 So-called fanciful or coined trademarks, which are meaningless. A celebrated example of this highly distinctive category is the KODAK trademark.

9.37 These trademarks may not be the favorites of the marketing people, since they require heavy advertising investment to become known to consumers. They inherently enjoy very strong legal protection, however.

9.38 Common words from everyday language can also be highly distinctive if they communicate a meaning that is arbitrary in relation to the products on which they are used. The same is true of the corresponding devices. Examples are the famous CAMEL trademark for cigarettes (and the equally-famous device mark) and the previously-mentioned APPLE mark (both the word and the device) for computers.

9.39 CAMEL and APPLE are clearly not invented words, and yet they are highly distinctive for the goods concerned.

9.40 Marketing people are generally fond of brand names that somehow generate a positive association with the product in the mind of the consumer. They tend therefore to choose more or less descriptive terms. If the sign is exclusively descriptive, it lacks distinctiveness and cannot be registered as such as a trademark. However, not all signs that are neither meaningless nor arbitrarily used necessarily lack distinctiveness: there is an intermediate category of signs that are suggestive, by association, of the goods for which they are to be used, and of the nature, quality, origin or any other characteristic, of those goods, without being actually descriptive. Those signs are registrable. The crucial question in practice is whether a trademark is suggestive or descriptive of the goods applied for. This question has to be judged according to the local law and jurisprudence of the country and all the circumstances of the specific case. If the registrar has a doubt, or is convinced that the term is descriptive rather than suggestive, he has to consider whether and to what extent the term is descriptive rather than suggestive, he has to consider whether and to what extent the term has already been used by the applicant. As a general rule, it can be said that a descriptive term is distinctive for the goods concerned if it has acquired a secondary meaning, that is, if those to whom it is addressed have come to recognize it as indicating that the goods for which it is used are from a particular trade source.

9.41 In case of doubt as to whether a term is descriptive or suggestive, the very fact that the mark has been used in the course of trade for a certain period of time may be sufficient for accepting it for registration.

9.42 However, the more descriptive the term is, the more difficult it will be to prove secondary meaning, and a higher percentage of consumer awareness will be necessary.

(i) Lack of Distinctiveness

9.43 If a sign is not distinctive, it cannot function as a trademark and its registration should be refused. Since this is a ground for refusal of registration, the applicant normally need not prove distinctiveness. It is up to the registrar to prove lack of distinctiveness, and in the case of doubt the trademark should be registered. Some trademark laws, such as the British Trade Marks Act 1938 (and laws in countries which have followed the British approach) put the onus on the applicant to show that his mark ought to be registered. This practice may be considered strict, however, and sometimes prevents the registration of marks that are demonstrably capable of distinguishing their proprietor's goods. And yet the modern trend, as reflected in Article 3 of the EC Harmonization Directive and also in the Model Law, is clearly to treat lack of distinctiveness as a ground for refusing an application for registration of a trademark.

9.44 What are the criteria governing the refusal of registration for lack of distinctiveness?

(ii)   Generic Terms

9.45 A sign is generic when it defines a category or type to which the goods belong. It is essential to the trade and also to consumers that nobody should be allowed to monopolize such a generic term.

9.46 Examples of generic terms are "furniture" (for furniture in general, and also for tables, chairs, etc.) and "chair" (for chairs). Other examples would be "drinks," "coffee" and "instant coffee," which shows that there are larger and narrower categories and groups of goods, all having in common that the broad term consistently used to describe them is generic.

9.47 These signs are totally lacking in distinctiveness, and some jurisdictions hold that, even if they are used intensively and may have acquired a secondary meaning, they cannot be registered since, in view of the absolute need of the trade to be able to use them, they must not be monopolized. For these reasons the High Court of Delhi, India, in 1972 refused registration of the JANTA trademark as in Hindi the word means cheap in price.

(iii)   Descriptive Signs

9.48 Descriptive signs are those that serve in trade to designate the kind, quality, intended purpose, value, place of origin, time of production or any other characteristic of the goods for which the sign is intended to be used or is being used.

9.49 In line with the definition of the distinctive sign given earlier, the test to be applied must establish whether consumers are likely to regard a sign as a reference to the origin of the product (distinctive sign) or whether they will rather look on it as a reference to the characteristics of the goods or their geographical origin (descriptive sign). The term "consumer" is used here as an abbreviation denoting the relevant circles to be considered in a specific case, namely those to whom the sign is addressed (and in certain cases also those who are otherwise reached by the sign).

9.50 The fact of other traders having a legitimate interest in the fair use of a term can therefore be used as a kind of additional ground when making the decisive test of whether consumers are likely to regard the sign as a reference to origin or as a reference to characteristics of the goods. It should not, however, be used on its own as a basis for a decision to refuse the registration of a term when it is not clear that consumers are also likely to regard the term as descriptive.

(iv) Other Signs Lacking Distinctiveness

9.51 Signs may lack distinctiveness for other reasons. This is true of a device which, owing to its simplicity or pure illustrative or ornamental character, may not capture the consumer's attention at all as a sign referring to the origin of the product, but rather as a mere illustrative part of the packaging of the goods offered to him.

9.52 An example (with regard to words) would be a relatively long advertising slogan recommending the goods to the consumer which, even when reproduced on the packaging, would be much too complex to be understood by consumers as a reference to the origin of the product.

9.53 In practice the authorities have to deal with certain other typical categories of cases which in many laws are expressly listed as grounds for refusal, and which are dealt with below.

(v) Reference to Geographical Origin

9.54 References to geographical origin (as opposed to the origin of the goods in the sense of the origin-indicating function) are basically not distinctive. They convey to the consumer an association with the geographical name, indicated either as the place of manufacture of the goods in question or of ingredients used in their production, or—depending on factual circumstances—with certain characteristics of the goods attributable to their origin.

9.55 For such an association to be conveyed to the consumer, the geographical location referred to must of course—at least to a certain extent—be first known to him. Signs referring to practically unknown localities are therefore distinctive. References to areas where nobody would expect the goods concerned to be manufactured are also distinctive.

9.56 Even if a geographical area is known to the consumer, a sign that makes a reference to it can either be or become distinctive if there is no other manufacturer or trader in the same field of activity, and no potential for competitors to settle there in the future.

9.57 A geographical denomination may also, through long and intensive use, be associated with a certain enterprise to such an extent that it becomes distinctive as a trademark for it, even if competitors already exist or establish themselves in the future.

(vi) Letters, Numerals and Basic Geometrical Shapes

9.58 These signs are normally regarded as being indistinctive and therefore unregistrable. Some trademark laws (such as the German one) even expressly exclude them from registration or accept them only if at least three letters and/or numerals are combined, or in the case of letters, if the sequence is pronounceable.

9.59 It is certainly true that consumers will not normally regard letters, numerals or simple geometrical shapes as indications of the origin of the goods. Nevertheless, letters, numerals and their combinations can become distinctive through use and—as said before—the so-called legitimate interest of other traders in making fair use of them should be no reason for refusal.

9.60 Furthermore, even without any use, letters and numerals can be registrable if they are applied for in a fanciful device.

(vii) Foreign Script and Transliterations

9.61 Imagine the use of a Thai script mark in India or Sri Lanka, the use of Chinese characters in Switzerland, Singhala characters in the United States of America or Japanese characters (Katakana, Kandi) anywhere but in Japan. For the great majority of ordinary consumers these marks are purely fanciful devices. Consequently, they are in principle distinctive, except where the sign has no more than an ornamental effect, depending on its graphic presentation.

9.62 Since these marks are distinctive, they are basically registrable. The registrar may, however, ask for a translation (a description of its meaning) in local script.

(viii) Colors

9.63 The use of words and/or devices in colors or combined with colors generally increases their distinctiveness. Consequently, applications for such signs claiming the colors shown or described in the application are easier to register. The first trademark registered in the United Kingdom in 1876 (and still on the register) was a triangle (a basic geometrical shape) in red. However, protection is then in principle restricted to the actual colors in which the mark is registered. Signs that might have been regarded as confusingly similar to the registered mark, had it been in black and white may therefore fall outside the scope of protection in view of the use of different colors. Since signs registered in black and white are protected against the registration and use of confusingly similar signs regardless of color, and since the registered owners of such signs can normally use them in any color they may wish to use, the usual practice is not to register signs in color. However, a given color or combination of colors may be an important element of a trademark, constantly used by its owner, and therefore liable to be imitated by competitors. This shows that a trademark owner may have a real interest in registering his mark in the distinctive colors in which it is used, even where the mark was distinctive enough to be registrable in black and white. In order to eliminate the previously-mentioned risk of restricting the scope of protection of such a mark, its owner may register the mark both in black and white and in the colors actually used.

9.64 Signs consisting exclusively of color combinations can be registrable trademarks. They are listed in Section 1(2) of the Model Law as examples of registrable signs. It is a matter for practice in the various countries to determine whether they are considered inherently distinctive or—more probably—basically descriptive with the possibility of becoming distinctive through use.

(ix) Names, Surnames

9.65 Company names and trade names are registrable, except where they are deceptive or not distinctive.

9.66 Common surnames are not normally registrable, since they are not distinctive. As for less common surnames, it is important to establish whether another meaning in everyday language will be overwhelmingly recognized by consumers. If there is such a dominant meaning, the sign is registrable on the condition that the meaning in question is not descriptive of the goods for which the mark is to be used.

(b) Exclusions from Registration on other Grounds—Public Interest

(i) Deceptiveness

9.67 Trademarks that are likely to deceive the public as to the nature, quality or any other characteristics of the goods or their geographical origin do not, in the interest of the public, qualify for registration.

9.68 The test here is for intrinsic deception, inherent in the trademark itself when associated with the goods for which it is proposed. This test should be clearly distinguished from the test for the risk of confusing customers by the use of identical or similar trademarks for identical or similar goods.

9.69 It is true that fanciful trademarks or marks with an arbitrary meaning for the goods proposed cannot be deceptive. And yet trademarks that have a descriptive meaning, even if they are only evocative or suggestive and therefore distinctive, may still be deceptive. Such trademarks have therefore to be examined from two angles: first they must be distinctive, and secondly they must not be deceptive.

9.70 As a rule, it can be said that the more descriptive a trademark is, the more easily it will deceive if it is not used for the goods with the characteristics described.

(ii) Reference to Geographical Origin

9.71 Signs that are descriptive or indicative of geographical origin are false for products that do not come from the region described or indicated. In such cases the consumer will be deceived if the reference to the geographical origin has the wrong connotations for him.

9.72 This is particularly true if the region or locality has a reputation. Famous examples of such signs are "Champagne" and "Swiss Chocolate."

9.73 In practice, such cases of direct reference to geographical origin are relatively rare. More often indirect references are made, and these cases are more problematic. A reference to a famous Swiss mountain for chocolate would still deceive consumers, as would a device mark consisting of a typical alpine landscape.

9.74 Indeed even the use of foreign words can, under certain circumstances, be deceptive without any reference to a specific geographical origin. The very fact that a word comes obviously from a particular foreign language may give consumers the impression that the product comes from the country where that language is spoken. Consumers will therefore be deceived if the country concerned has a reputation for the goods concerned.

9.75 However, it should be realized that, in addition to being spoken in many different countries all over the world, English is also the modern international marketing language, with the result that many trademarks have an English-language connotation quite independent of the geographical origin of the goods marked with it, and that consumers are generally aware of the fact.

(iii) Partial Deceptiveness

9.76 We have seen that the question whether or not a trademark is inherently deceptive must be examined in relation to the goods in respect of which the application is made. Depending on the list of goods, therefore, an application may be distinctive for some, descriptive for others and/or deceptive for still others. In such cases the examiner has to require a limitation of the list of goods. Should the applicant not agree to such limitation, the examiner refuses the whole application in some countries. In others, he accepts the application only for the goods for which, in his opinion, the mark is not deceptive and refuses it for the others.

(iv) Signs Contrary to Morality or Public Policy

9.77 Trademark laws generally deny registration to signs that are contrary to morality or public policy. The Model Law also lists this ground for refusal under Section 5(1)(e), and mentions obscene pictures and emblems of public authorities or of forbidden political parties as examples.

(v) Signs Reserved for Use by the State, Public Institutions or International Organizations

9.78 A country generally protects its national flag, its official name and the names of official institutions in its own interest. Furthermore, countries are obliged by Article 6ter of the Paris Convention also to protect the notified signs of other member States and international intergovernmental organizations (such as the United Nations Organization).

E. PROTECTION OF TRADEMARK RIGHTS

9.79 A trademark can be protected on the basis of either use or registration. Both approaches have developed historically, but today trademark protection systems generally combine both elements. The Paris Convention places contracting countries under the obligation to provide for a trademark register. Over one hundred States have adhered to the Paris Convention. Nearly all countries today provide for a trademark register, and full trademark protection is properly secured only by registration.

9.80 Use does still play an important role, however: first of all, in countries that have traditionally based trademark protection on use, the registration of a trademark merely confirms the trademark right that has been acquired by use.

References for Section D
International Bureau of WIPO, *Introduction to Trademark Law & Practice* (second edition), WIPO Pub. No. 653(E) (1993)
International Bureau of WIPO, *Comparative Trademark Law I*, BTMC/4

Consequently, the first user has priority in a trademark dispute, not the one who first registered the trademark.

9.81 This approach has been chosen by the United States of America, the Philippines, Indonesia and all countries with systems of law on the traditional British model. Furthermore, use has an important bearing on many other aspects of the registration procedure and also on the defense of a registered trademark.

F. USE REQUIREMENTS

(a) Need for an Obligation to Use

9.82 Trademark protection is not an end in itself. Even though trademark laws generally do not require use as a condition for the application for trademark registration, or even the actual registration, the ultimate reason for trademark protection is the function of distinguishing the goods on which the trademark is used from others. It makes no economic sense, therefore, to protect trademarks by registration without imposing the obligation to use them. Unused trademarks are an artificial barrier to the registration of new marks. In this connection it is interesting to take a glance at WIPO statistics. According to the statistics from 83 countries that reported to WIPO in 1990, there were about 1.2 million trademarks filed for registration, while the total of registered trademarks in 63 countries (out of about 170 offices where trademarks can be registered with protection in nearly 200 countries) amounts to more than 6.5 million. There is therefore an absolute need to provide for a use obligation in trademark law.

9.83 At the same time trademark owners need a grace period after registration before the use obligation comes into effect. This is especially true of the many companies that are active in international trade. They cannot normally introduce a new product in the market in numerous countries at the same time. In order to avoid loopholes in the protection of their new trademarks of which competitors could take advantage, they must from the very beginning apply for the registration of their new trademarks in all countries of potential future use. Without a reasonable grace period for the use obligation written into the law, internationally active companies would obviously have enormous difficulties. Indeed even in their own countries companies often need several years before they can properly launch a newly-developed product on the market. This is especially true of pharmaceutical companies, which have to make clinical tests and have to apply for approval of their product by the health authorities.

9.84 The grace period granted in trademark laws that provide for a use obligation is sometimes three years, but more often five years.

(b) Practical Use Requirements

9.85 In principle, the trademark must be used in the country of registration. The use must be made in relation to the goods. Normally, the trademark will be

References for Section E
International Bureau of WIPO, *Introduction to Trademark Law & Practice* (second edition), WIPO Pub. No. 653(E) (1993)

affixed to the goods or to their packaging. In the case of certain goods (gasoline, etc.) use on accompanying documents or in advertising may be sufficient.

9.86 The use must be made publicly, that is, the goods must be offered for sale through normal trade channels. This does not mean that they must be available everywhere. It is sufficient if the goods are sold in certain specialty shops, from a restricted number of outlets or through some special trade channels (for instance to restaurants in the food service business). It is not sufficient, however, to use a trademark exclusively on goods offered in the shop or restaurant of the company that is the owner of the trademark, and available to its employees alone.

9.87 Use solely in advertising should be sufficient only if it the advertising is for a future sale and the process of launching the goods on the market has started.

9.88 The use must be genuine; token use is not sufficient. Market tests, if made in order to determine the acceptance of the product by consumers (and not with the sole intention of safeguarding the protection of the trademark), should be recognized as genuine use, as should clinical trials of pharmaceutical products.

9.89 In order to safeguard the protection of a registered trademark, it must be used for at least one of the goods for which it is registered. Use for one of the goods for which the trademark is registered should safeguard protection for all goods on the list of registered goods that are similar to the one used. In order to avoid unnecessarily weakening the effect of the use obligation, however, it may be going too far to provide that use for one product safeguards the registration for the whole class (Model Law, Section 30(4)), or for all goods for which the trademark is registered, and which may cover several classes.

9.90 The trademark must in principle be used as registered. However, the Paris Convention provides in its Article 5C(2) that the "use of a trademark by the proprietor in a form differing in elements which do not alter the distinctive character of the mark in the form in which it was registered (...) shall not entail invalidation of the registration and shall not diminish the protection granted to the mark." The same is provided for in Section 30(3) of the Model Law.

9.91 Word marks can be used in any form, type face or colors and in combination with additional elements (trade names, descriptive terms), provided that the registered mark maintains its distinctive character. If a word mark and a device mark are registered separately but always used together, that use is sufficient for the purpose of protection of the registered trademarks.

9.92 The majority of national laws allow the use to be made by the trademark owner himself or by a third party with his consent. Sometimes such use by third parties is formalized. If trademark law requires a formalized agreement, and if the agreement is legally invalid under unfair competition law or other rules such as food and drug regulations, it should be sufficient that the third party is effectively and genuinely entitled to use the mark on behalf of the trademark owner, irrespective of whether or not the agreement is legally valid.

(c) Consequences of Non-Use

9.93 The principal consequence of unjustified non-use is that the registration is open to cancellation at the request of a person with a legitimate interest. There is moreover a tendency to require of the registered owner that he prove use, since it is very difficult for the interested third party to prove non-use. In the interest of removing "deadwood" from the register, such reversal of the burden of proof is justified.

9.94 The burden of proof should be on the trademark owner not only in cancellation proceedings but also in any other proceedings where the owner is alleged to have taken advantage of his unused trademark right (opposition procedure, infringement action).

9.95 No evidence of use should be required for the renewal of a trademark registration, however. This is an administrative complication which is unnecessary in view of the fact that an interested person can at any time at all take appropriate action against an unused trademark registration.

9.96 Non-use does not always lead to invalidation of the trademark right. Non-use can be justified in the case of force majeure, and any other circumstance that is not due to fault or negligence on the part of the proprietor of the mark, such as import restrictions or special legal requirements within the country.

(d) Proper Use of Trademarks

9.97 Non-use can lead to the loss of trademark rights. Improper use can have the same result, however. A mark may become liable for removal from the Register if the registered owner has provoked or tolerated its transformation into a generic name for one or more of the goods or services in respect of which the mark is registered, so that, in trade circles and in the eyes of the public, its significance as a mark has been lost.

9.98 Basically, two things can cause genericness: namely, improper use by the owner, provoking transformation of the mark into a generic term, and improper use by third parties that is tolerated by the owner.

9.99 In order to avoid improper use, everyone in the company owning the trademark who is involved in advertising or publicizing the brand must follow some rules.

9.100 The basic rule is that the trademark should not be used as, or instead of, the product designation. By systematically using a product designation in addition to the trademark, the proprietor clearly informs the public that his mark identifies a specific product as one in a certain category. This is especially important if the trademark proprietor has invented a totally new product which at the outset is the only one in the category. Trademarks such as FRIGIDAIRE, CELLOPHANE and LINOLEUM became generic terms because they were the only product in their category, and no additional name was given to the category by its proprietors. When instant coffee, also called soluble coffee, was invented in 1938, the first product marketed by the company that invented it was called NESCAFE. However, from the start the company systematically used a product designation such as "instant coffee" or "soluble coffee" on its labels.

9.101 A second important rule is that trademarks should always be used as true adjectives and never as nouns, in other words the trademark should not be used with an article, and the possessive "s" and the plural form should be avoided. It would be wrong to talk about NESCAFE's flavor or about three NESCAFES instead of three varieties of NESCAFE.

9.102 Furthermore, it is advisable always to highlight the trademark, that is, to make it stand out from its surroundings.

9.103 Finally, a trademark should be identified as such by a trademark notice. Only a few laws provide for such notices, and making their use on goods compulsory is prohibited by Article 5D of the Paris Convention. Trademark law in the United States of America allows the use of a long statement (such as "Registered with the United States Patent and Trademark Office") to be replaced by a short symbol, namely, the circled R. Over the years this symbol has spread throughout the world and become a widely recognized symbol for a registered trademark. Its use is recommended for registered trademarks as a warning to competitors not to engage in any act that would infringe the mark.

9.104 However, it is not enough just to follow these rules: the trademark owner must also ensure that third parties and the public do not misuse his mark. It is specifically important that the trademark should not be used as or instead of the product description in dictionaries, official publications, journals, etc.

9.105 Consumers tend to use well-known marks as product designations. Many consumers all over the world refer to instant coffee as NESCAFE. Basically, the trademark owner can be proud of such use as it shows the strength of his mark. However, the more famous a mark is, the more it is in danger of turning into a generic term. This is why it is so important, in such cases, that companies should apply a very strict policy of proper use on their own part, and intervene against third parties (other than consumers) in the event of abuse. According to generally accepted rules of law and practice, the transformation of a trademark into a generic term occurs only if all the trade circles involved and the general public have become used to using the sign as a generic term. The proprietors of the trademark NESCAFE, for instance, have traditionally applied such a strict policy and this trademark, which is one of the best-known in the world, has consequently remained a protected trademark which enjoys strong protection, despite the habit of many consumers to refer to instant coffee in general as NESCAFE. Another example of this kind of trademark that continues to enjoy strong protection is COCA-COLA, probably the best-known trademark in the world.

G. TRADEMARK REGISTRATION

(a) Introduction

9.106 Applications for registration of a trademark are to be filed with the competent government authority which in most countries is the same as the authority competent for processing patent applications. Usually, it is called "Industrial Property Office" or "Patent and Trademark Office" or "Trademark Office."

References for Section F
International Bureau of WIPO, *Introduction to Trademark Law & Practice* (second edition), WIPO Pub. No. 653(E) (1993)

9.107 The tasks of the Office are defined by the applicable law, which is supplemented by regulations and administrative instructions. Usually, that law contains detailed provisions on the requirements of an application, on the processing of the application until the decision by the Office whether the trademark can be registered or not, and on any further procedures relating to trademark registrations.

(b) Application for Registration

9.108 In general, countries provide for an application form, the use of which is mandatory in certain countries. The application form has to be completed with the name and address of the applicant. Foreigners have either to give an address for service in the country or to use an agent holding a power of attorney to be signed by the applicant. Often further formalities are imposed, such as authentication by a notary public and legalization.

9.109 The sign filed for registration must appear in the application form or in an annex to it. If it is intended that the sign should be registered in color, the colors must be claimed and a specimen in color or the description of the color(s) must be submitted.

9.110 If a three-dimensional sign is filed for registration, it is necessary to claim protection of the sign in its three-dimensional form. The sign must moreover be graphically represented in a manner that allows it to be reproduced for a twofold purpose: it must be possible to register it (regardless of the form in which the register is established, that is, whether the marks are entered in a book, collected in a card index or integrated in a computerized system). Owners of prior rights must be able to take note of the trademark application (which normally is ensured by its publication in a trademark journal).

9.111 The applicant has also to list the goods for which the sign is to be registered. Trademark laws provide generally for a classification of goods for the purposes of registration. In some countries a separate application has to be made for each class, while in others one application is sufficient for several classes.

9.112 An important treaty for international trade is the Nice Agreement Concerning the International Classification of Goods and Services for the Purposes of the Registration of Marks which establishes an international classification of goods and services for the purpose of registration of trademarks. On October 1, 1996, this treaty had 47 Contracting States, including the United States of America.

9.113 Finally, one or more fees have to be paid for the registration of a trademark. A country may provide for a single, all-embracing fee or several (application fee, class fee, examination fee, registration fee, etc.). Both systems have advantages and disadvantages. On the one hand, it is simpler and more cost-efficient to charge a single fee. On the other hand, this may lead to unjust consequences for applicants who decide to withdraw the application totally or partially during the registration procedure (for example, because of an objection from the owner of a prior right, or because of insurmountable objections from the registrar). In such cases at least partial reimbursement of the fee paid should be provided for.

(c) Examination

(i) Examination as to Form

9.114 Countries generally accept an application for registration of a trademark only if the formal requirements are fulfilled.

(ii) Examination as to Substance

9.115 Most countries examine trademark applications as to substance in the interest of both the public and competitors.

9.116 One has to make a clear distinction between two types of grounds for refusal:

9.117 Trademarks may be examined for absolute, objective grounds for refusal, that is, whether they are sufficiently distinctive, not deceptive, not immoral, etc. Such an examination is highly desirable in the interest of consumer protection, but for competitors too, and the trade in general, it is important that nobody should be able to monopolize a descriptive or even a generic term by a simple administrative act.

9.118 The laws of many countries provide also for examination on relative grounds, that is, whether the rights applied for are identical or similar to prior rights that have been applied for or granted for identical or similar goods. Such examination may either made *ex officio* and/or on the basis of an opposition procedure.

9.119 In general, three typical approaches can be observed internationally:

9.120 The British system, providing for examination by the office for absolute and relative grounds, and also for an opposition procedure. This system is also applied, in Europe, by countries such as Portugal, Spain and the Northern European countries.

9.121 Under a second approach the office examines only for absolute grounds, the law provides for no opposition procedure and it is left to the owner of the prior rights to bring a cancellation or infringement action against the registration or use of a more recent sign. This system has been used under the old trademark laws of France and Switzerland (both countries introduced in their new laws opposition procedures).

9.122 The third system is the German one, which provides for examination by the office for absolute grounds and also for an administrative opposition procedure, in which the owner of prior rights can oppose the infringing trademark application by means of a simplified and not too costly procedure. This system is a compromise between the more extreme systems mentioned before, and follows a modern trend which is reflected in the proposed European Community Trade Mark system.

9.123 Industry in general prefers such a system, since it is less time-consuming and much more flexible. In view of the many trademarks on the registers of countries all over the world, it is in any case advisable to carry out a search for prior rights before applying for registration of a trademark, and even more so before beginning to use it. Most applicants do such searches regularly, while companies have at least their more important registered trademarks watched, either by their trademark agents or by one of the international watching services, in order to keep themselves informed of applications for registration of potentially conflicting similar marks.

9.124 The standards to be applied by the registrar when examining whether a trademark application is to be refused because of a prior right are the same, in principle, as those to be applied in an opposition procedure or by a judge in an infringement action (even though in the latter case the factual circumstances of the infringement will play an additional role).

9.125 Since one of the basic rights of the owner of a registered mark is to prevent others from using his mark or a confusingly similar one, it is more adequate to deal with all aspects of trademark similarity in Chapter 6, which deals with the rights deriving from trademark registration.

(d) Refusal of Registration

9.126 Before issuing a total or partial refusal of the application, the office should give the applicant an opportunity to make observations.

9.127 The decision refusing an application either partly or totally must be open to appeal. Depending on the legal system of the country, the appeal may be lodged with the registrar, with an administrative appeal board or with the court.

(e) Date of Registration

9.128 If the application leads to registration, the office issues a certificate to the owner. The owner's exclusive right exists from the date of registration. However, the priority of the right should date back to the date of filing for registration. While it is true that the application is not normally a sufficient basis for bringing an infringement action against a later right, it must be a valid basis for an opposition procedure. And, even more importantly, the date of the application for registration will be decisive in a later court case. The time that passes before an application leads to registration varies a great deal, and in certain cases can be very long. A later application can for various reasons lead to registration sooner (for instance where the earlier application was refused by the examiner and finally granted on appeal). Clearly, the owner of the earlier application must have the prior right in relation to the owner of a later application.

9.129 Furthermore, the applicant can claim the priority of his national registration under Article 4 of the Paris Convention if the application in the foreign country is made within six months of the filing date of the first application.

(f) Duration and Renewal

9.130 Since trademarks do not grant a monopoly right that could be exploited, there is no need to limit their validity. For administrative reasons, a time limit is generally provided for in trademark laws, but it is possible to renew registrations when the time limit expires.

9.131 One of the reasons for imposing such time limits is that the office can charge a fee for renewal, and this is a welcome source of revenue. Furthermore, the registration of trademarks without a time limit would lead to an undesirable amount of trademark registrations that are no longer of any interest to their owners. Even if unused marks may be removed from the register, such a procedure would be costly and time-consuming for the interested party, and not always successful.

9.132 Consequently, the requirement of renewal and the payment of a renewal fee is a welcome opportunity for a trademark owner to consider whether it is still worth having his registration renewed, as the trademark may have been superseded in its graphic form, or may even be no longer in use. For this reason, the renewal fee should be not too low, indeed probably even higher than the original registration fee. Excessive fees should also be avoided, however. In any case, renewals should be made simply on payment of the fee, without any new examination of the mark for absolute or relative grounds for refusal. Of course, it should be possible for the owner to make a voluntary restriction of the list of goods of the original registration, especially if he can save fees by doing so.

(g) Publication and Access to the Register

9.133 It is important for owners of prior rights and the public that all relevant data contained in the register, concerning applications, registrations, renewals and changes of name, address and ownership, should be published in an official gazette. This enables owners of prior rights to take the necessary steps, including opposition (if provided for) or an action for cancellation. The publication of applications and registrations should contain all the important data, such as the name and address of the applicant, a representation of the mark, the goods grouped according to the classification system, the colors claimed, where the mark is three-dimensional a statement to that effect, and where the priority of any other mark is claimed (Paris Convention, Article 4) a statement to that effect.

9.134 The register of marks should, moreover, be accessible to the public. To ensure that owners of prior rights are properly informed it is indispensable that the register contain up-to-date information, namely all recorded data not only on registrations, but also on the contents of pending applications, regardless of the medium on which the data are stored.

H. REMOVAL OF THE TRADEMARK FROM THE REGISTER

9.135 The cancellation of a trademark registration is a serious matter for its owner, as it leads to a loss of his rights under the registration. Nevertheless, there are a number of grounds on which a trademark can be removed from the register.

(a) Removal for Failure to Renew

9.136 It has been shown that, for administrative reasons, a trademark is registered for a certain period of time only. When that period expires, the trademark can be

References for Section G
International Bureau of WIPO, *Introduction to Trademark Law & Practice* (second edition), WIPO Pub. No. 653(E) (1993)

renewed and a renewal fee has to be paid. If the owner fails to renew his trademark registration and more specifically fails to pay the renewal fee, this leads to the removal of the trademark from the register. Registries generally allow a period of grace for payment of the renewal fee (usually with a surcharge).

9.137 If the law permits renewal of the trademark registration for just some of the registered goods (to be encouraged as a means of removing "deadwood" from the register), this leads to a partial cancellation of the trademark registration for all the goods in respect of which it is not renewed.

(b) Removal at the Request of the Registered Owner

9.138 The registered owner can himself, at any time, renounce his registration for either all or some of the goods for which the mark is registered. At the request of the registered owner, therefore, the authorities will in principle remove the mark from the register either wholly or in part.

(c) Removal for Failure to Use

9.139 If the owner of a trademark fails to use his mark within the grace period provided for in the law, any interested party can, in principle, ask for its cancellation. If the owner cannot justify the non-use, removal of the registration is ordered by the court. If the owner can prove use or justify the non-use, but only for some of the registered goods, the court orders partial cancellation. Partial cancellation extends either to all registered goods for which use cannot be proved or at least to all those not similar to the goods that the registered owner has used.

9.140 This does not mean that the registered owner's rights would be strictly limited to the goods used, or even to a single product on which his trademark has been used. Even if his registration is cancelled for all but the one product for which he can prove use, he can still defend his exclusive right to his registered trademark against the registration and use of an identical or confusingly similar trademark by a competitor for all goods that are identical or similar to the product for which his trademark is registered and used.

(d) Cancellation on Account of Nullity

9.141 If a trademark consists of a sign that should not have been registered, it can be declared null and void by the court at the request of any interested party. Sometimes trademark laws also provide an *ex officio* procedure for that purpose. As a consequence of the declaration, the trademark is removed from the register.

9.142 If the grounds for invalidity exist only with respect to some of the registered goods, the registration is removed for those goods only.

9.143 Normally, removal from the register is ordered only if the grounds for invalidity already existed when the trademark was registered. Moreover, even if the trademark should not have been registered owing to lack of distinctiveness, its cancellation is excluded if in the meantime it has become distinctive by use.

9.144 Such acquired distinctiveness cannot, however, prevent the removal from the register of trademarks that consist of generic or deceptive terms. And yet there can be exceptional cases in which the deceptive meaning that would have prevented trademark registration at the outset has been lost in the meantime.

(e) Removal of a Mark that has Lost its Distinctiveness

9.145 If the registered owner has provoked or tolerated the transformation of a mark into a generic name for one or more of the goods or services in respect of which the mark is registered, the mark becomes liable for removal from the register. Removal of the mark on these grounds has the effect of expropriation, so it can only be ordered if all the trade circles involved, the relevant consumers and the public in general have become accustomed to using the sign as a generic name for the product originally identified by it. Under these conditions the sign has totally lost its original significance as a trademark, and can therefore be removed from the register.

I. RIGHTS ARISING FROM TRADEMARK REGISTRATION

9.146 The registered owner has the exclusive right to use the trademark. This short definition of the specific subject matter of trademark rights encompasses two things: the right to use the trademark and the right to exclude others from using it.

(a) The Right to Use the Trademark

9.147 This positive right of use belonging to the trademark owner is recognized in most trademark laws. It would indeed be contradictory not to grant such a positive right of use while imposing an obligation to use. Of course, the right of use is subject to other laws and rights, as is any other right provided by law. What is allowed under trademark law may be prohibited under competition law or by public enactment.

9.148 What does the right of use mean? It means first the right of the owner of the mark to affix it on goods, containers, packaging, labels, etc. or to use it in any other way in relation to the goods for which it is registered.

9.149 It means also the right to introduce the goods to the market under the trademark.

9.150 It is important to make a distinction between these two rights, both derived from the right to use a trademark.

9.151 When the trademark owner has launched a product on the market under his mark, he cannot object to further sales of the product in the course of trade. This is the essence of the so-called principle of exhaustion of the trademark right. Some countries do not allow objections to parallel imports of products marketed in a foreign country by the trademark owner or by a third party with his consent. Other countries do allow such parallel imports to be objected to, namely by

References for Section H
International Bureau of WIPO, *Introduction to Trademark Law & Practice* (second edition), WIPO Pub. No. 653(E) (1993)

applying the principle of territoriality of rights. Still other countries, such as the United Kingdom and Switzerland, make the decision on whether the trademark owner can object to parallel imports dependent on whether consumers are likely to be mistaken as to the characteristics or quality of the imported goods.

9.152 Apart from this special aspect of parallel imports of goods marketed for the first time in a foreign country, the principle of exhaustion of trademark rights clearly applies within the country. However, it is a principle that applies only to the right to launch the product bearing the trademark on the market for the first time. The owner's exclusive right to affix the trademark on the goods and their packaging, containers, labels, etc. continues to exist. Consequently, he can object to acts that infringe that right, such as the repacking of goods bearing his mark, the destruction of his mark on the goods, or the alteration and subsequent sale of his products under his mark. Altering the product and selling it under the same mark has the same effect as affixing the mark to goods, that is, it gives the consumer the impression that the genuine product has been marketed by the trademark owner under his mark. If that is not true, the trademark owner has a right to intervene.

9.153 Finally, a third right out of the bundle of rights incorporated in the right to use a trademark is the trademark owner's right to use his mark in advertising, on business papers, documents, etc.

(b) The Right to Exclude Others from Using the Mark

9.154 It follows from the mark's basic function of distinguishing the goods of its owner from those of others that he must be able to object to the use of confusingly similar marks in order to prevent consumers and the public in general from being misled. This is the essence of the exclusive right afforded to the trademark owner by registration. He must be able to object to any use of his trademark by a third party for goods for which it is protected, to the affixing of the mark on such goods, to its use in relation to the goods and to the offering of the goods for sale under the mark, or the use of the mark in advertising, business papers or any other kind of document. Furthermore, since consumers are to be protected against confusion, protection generally extends to the use of similar trademarks for similar goods, if such use is likely to confuse the consumer.

9.155 It must be underlined, however, that the trademark owner cannot unconditionally object to the use of his trademark or a similar mark for the goods for which his trademark is registered or for similar goods. His trademark must be protected for the goods specified in the registration. Such protection operates automatically for all registered goods during the user's grace period, which is generally laid down by law. When that period has expired, protection has to be reduced to the goods on which the mark is actually used and goods similar to them. Any goods for which the trademark was registered but which are not in use should no longer be a valid basis for asserting exclusive trademark rights. Depending on the procedural system in the country, the trademark owner may be able to rely on those formal rights for goods for which the mark is registered but not used, but he could face a counterattack leading to partial cancellation of his trademark for non-use.

9.156 The exclusive rights of the trademark owner can be exercised by means of an infringement action. The trademark is infringed if, owing to the use of an identical or similar sign for identical or similar goods, there is a risk or a likelihood of the public being misled. The test to be applied in an infringement action is narrower than in an administrative procedure (examination *ex officio*, opposition procedure). The test is not a hypothetical one, but has to deal with the reality of infringement in the marketplace. Consequently, the court has to consider how the infringer is actually using the trademark, and the extent of use of the infringed mark may also be significant.

9.157 Many laws not only provide for an infringement action, but also offer an administrative opposition procedure against an application for the registration of a confusingly similar trademark. In that case, the test is much broader, because allowance has to be made for the risk of confusion that could arise from any use that the applicant might possibly make of his trademark if it were registered. The test is in fact the same as is applied by the office in its examination for prior third-party rights. However, there is more justification for applying such a broad test in opposition procedures, since it is the owner of the right who opposes the application and therefore demonstrates his interest in defending his right against the registration of a confusingly similar trademark.

9.158 Together with the question whether a trademark is distinctive, the question whether a trademark is confusingly similar to an earlier right is one of the cornerstones of practical trademark protection.

(i) Similarity of Goods

9.159 Trademarks are registered for goods in certain classes which have been established for purely administrative purposes. The classification of goods cannot therefore be decisive for the question of similarity. Sometimes totally different goods are listed in the same class (for instance computers, eyeglasses, fire extinguishers and telephones in class 9), while similar goods can clearly be listed in different classes (adhesives may fall into classes 1, 3, 5 and 16).

9.160 The test of whether goods are similar is based on the assumption that identical marks are used. Even identical marks are unlikely to create confusion as to the origin of the goods if the goods are very different. As a general rule goods are similar if, when offered for sale under an identical mark, the consuming public would be likely to believe that they came from the same source. All the circumstances of the case must be taken into account, including the nature of the goods, the purpose for which they are used and the trade channels through which they are marketed, but especially the usual origin of the goods, and the usual point of sale.

9.161 As far as the latter criterion is concerned, the problem is that in modern supermarkets, drugstores and department stores, goods of all kinds are sold together, so the usual point of sale is less relevant to whether consumers regard goods as coming from the same source as their usual origin. Still, the criterion does remain valid in many cases where goods are exclusively or at least commonly sold in specialty shops. In such cases, consumers may tend to believe the origin of goods to be the same if they are both sold in the same specialty shops, and may tend to deny that sameness of origin if they are not usually sold in the same shops.

9.162 If different goods are all manufactured by the same type of enterprise, or if consumers expect them to be typically manufactured by the same enterprise, they will generally be regarded as having a common origin.

9.163 A further aspect is the nature and composition of goods. If they are largely made of the same substance, they will generally be held to be similar, even if they are used for different purposes. Raw materials and finished goods manufactured out of the raw materials are not normally similar, however, since they are generally not marketed by the same enterprise.

9.164 Depending on the circumstances of the specific case, one or more of the aspects mentioned may determine the decision on whether goods are similar or not. Generally, however, they will all have to be taken into account.

(ii) Similarity of Trademarks

9.165 Trademarks can be more or less similar to each other. The test, of course, is whether they are confusingly similar. A trademark is confusingly similar to a prior mark if it is used for similar goods and so closely resembles the prior mark that there is a likelihood of consumers being misled as to the origin of the goods. If the consumer is confused, the distinguishing role of the trademark is not functioning, and the consumer may fail to buy the product that he wants. This is bad for the consumer, but also for the trademark owner who loses the sale.

9.166 No intention to confuse on the part of the infringer is necessary, nor is actual confusion. The likelihood of confusion is the test. That is the only way for the system to function.

9.167 Of course, phrases such as "likelihood of confusion of the consumer" (or "of the public") have to be interpreted. "The consumer" does not exist, and the public as such cannot be confused. Confusion arises, or is likely to arise, always in a section of the public. It has to be determined in the specific case what the relevant part of the public is that has to be considered, in other words who are actually addressed or reached by the trademark.

9.168 Since it is very difficult to work in practice with the broad definition of confusing similarity, some rules have been developed which help to define in specific cases whether, in view of the similarity of the two marks, confusion is likely to arise.

9.169 The most important point is that the consumer does not compare trademarks side by side; he is generally confronted with the infringing mark in the shop without seeing the product bearing the mark that he knows and remembers more or less accurately. He mistakes the products offered under the infringing mark for the genuine product that he actually wants to buy. In this context it must be taken into account that the average consumer also has an average memory, and that it must be sufficient for him to doubt whether the trademark with which he is confronted is the one he knows.

9.170 Since the average consumer generally does not at first glance recognize differences between the marks that he might spot if he took his time to study the mark and the product offered under it more carefully, the first impression that he gains must be decisive. This is especially true for mass-consumption goods offered in self-service stores.

9.171 Furthermore, unsophisticated, poorly-educated consumers and also children are more liable to be confused. The purchaser of a sophisticated and costly machine, car or aircraft will no doubt be more attentive than the consumer in the self-service store. In those fields, therefore, very similar trademarks do coexist, which would probably be easily confused if applied to mass-consumption goods.

9.172 Another interesting example of how the category of goods can influence the testing of confusing similarity is to be found in the field of pharmaceuticals. Prescription drugs are normally sold to the consumer (on prescription by doctors) by educated pharmacists, who are less likely to be misled by relatively similar brand names used for medicines for different indications, so the testing of similarity can be more generous. For drugs sold over the counter, the contrary is true. In view of the potentially serious consequences for the uneducated consumer if he buys a wrong product, the testing of similarity must be particularly strict.

9.173 The second important point when testing the similarity of trademarks is that they should be compared as a whole, and that more weight should be given to common elements which may lead to confusion, while differences overlooked by the average consumer should not be emphasized. Notwithstanding this basic rule of comparing trademarks as a whole and not dividing them into parts, the structure of the signs is important. Common prefixes are normally more important than common suffixes; if two signs are very similar or identical at the beginning, they are more likely to be confused than if the similarity is in their endings. Long words with common or similar beginnings are more likely to be confused than short words with different initial letters.

9.174 The third important point is that highly distinctive marks (coined or arbitrarily used marks) are more likely to be confused than marks with associative meanings in relation to the goods for which they are registered.

9.175 The same is true if a mark contains a highly distinctive part (part of the word mark or one of several words forming the mark), and that highly distinctive element is exactly or almost exactly duplicated by the infringing mark. If, on the other hand, the common element of the two signs is descriptive, the consumer's attention tends to focus on the rest of the mark.

9.176 When trademarks with a common element are compared, it also has to be established whether there are other trademarks on the register and used by different owners that have the same common element. If so the consumer will have become accustomed to the use of this element by different proprietors, and will no longer pay special attention to it as a distinctive element of the mark.

9.177 The situation is different, however, if all marks having such a common element (normally a prefix or suffix) are registered and used by the same proprietor (or with his consent). This is the special case of the series mark, where the consumers may have become accustomed to associate the series with a common source, and will tend to make the same assumption about any new trademark containing the same element. However, the mere fact of somebody using a series of trademarks that have a common element is not, as such, sufficient to exclude the use of the same element by a competitor as a component of a mark which on the whole is very different. The use of such a common element can only constitute infringement if consumers really have come to recognize the common element of the series of marks used by the registered owner as indicating the source of the goods offered by him under the different marks containing that element.

9.178 The fourth important point is that confusion can arise from similarity in the writing, the pronunciation and in the meaning of the sign, and that similarity in one of those areas is sufficient for infringement if it misleads the public.

9.179 With regard to similarity in writing, the graphic presentation of the trademark plays an important part. Similarity in pronunciation is important because trademarks that are written differently may be pronounced in the same way, and pronunciation counts in oral communication: even if similarity in writing is avoided by the use of very different graphic presentations, this does not make any difference when the two trademarks are compared orally.

9.180 Similarity in meaning may lead to confusion if the same idea is conveyed by both trademarks (DREAMLAND and SLUMBERLAND for mattresses). Conversely, a totally different meaning can preclude confusion between two marks that would normally be regarded as confusingly similar.

9.181 Independently of the above rules, some special aspects have to be taken into account for figurative marks (devices).

9.182 For purely fanciful marks the graphical impression conveyed by the two marks is decisive.

9.183 For composite marks the similarity of the word part is normally sufficient, as similarity in pronunciation constitutes trademark infringement. Similarity in the figurative part can only lead to confusion if that figurative part is a distinctive element of the mark. Furthermore, in the case of composite marks any similarity in the word parts of the two marks is likely to be emphasized if the figurative parts of the marks are also similar. Even though the words might not be confused in writing or pronunciation, the marks as a whole can be confusingly similar in view of the similarity of their figurative elements.

9.184 A special case is the device that can be named by a word. A star device will normally be designated by the word "star," and will therefore be confusingly similar to a word mark STAR. Also lion or tiger devices would be confusingly similar to the word marks LION and TIGER. The situation is different when two device marks are compared which both feature an animal. Case law generally hesitates to grant a monopoly on an animal device as such. Consequently, two such devices, for instance two tiger or lion or cow devices (there are numerous cow devices registered for milk products) must be sufficiently similar for there to be confusion. So should the use of the corresponding word as a trademark nevertheless be prohibited, and should the owner of a word mark TIGER really be able to object to all possible graphic presentations of a tiger in a device mark? To avoid any possible problem of restricted protection, the owner of a device mark should also secure trademark protection for the name of the animal shown in the device.

(iii) Influence of Use and Non-Use

9.185 Confusion in the marketplace can only arise from actual use on similar goods. To prevent confusion, however, it is still necessary that the trademark protection system allow the trademark owner to object to an application for registration of a trademark which is based on mere intention to use the mark.

9.186 For the same preventive purpose, many trademark laws allow the owner of a registered trademark to object in opposition procedures to the filing, and in infringement actions to the use, of similar marks for goods identical or even similar to all goods covered by the existing registration, regardless of the use of the latter. The defendant who is aware of the total or partial non-use must therefore counterattack by introducing an invalidation action seeking partial or total cancellation of the existing trademark registration for non-use.

9.187 More modern conceptions allow the trademark owner, after the five-year grace period has expired, to object by opposition or court action to an application for registration, or to the use, of an identical or similar mark for goods identical or similar only to those on which the owner is actually using his. If the owner is not using his trademark, the opposition is refused, and if he is using it on one or several of the goods for which it is registered, only those on which it is used are taken into consideration for the test of confusing similarity. The burden of proof of use in an opposition procedure is on the owner of the right.

9.188 Many laws also allow the defendant in trademark infringement actions to claim non-use of the trademark on which the action is based, and the owner can then only succeed in his infringement action if he can prove use of his mark.

9.189 If the infringed trademark is being used, the extent of the use can influence the test of confusing similarity. Intensive use increases the distinctiveness of the mark, and confusion with well-known marks is more likely even if the goods on which the infringing mark is used are less similar or if the similarity of the marks is less apparent.

(iv) Protection Beyond the Scope of Confusing Similarity

9.190 Well-known or famous marks, which are highly reputed, are in some countries given protection that goes beyond the scope of similarity of the goods. Such far-reaching protection should only be given if the use of the same mark or a nearly identical mark for other, dissimilar goods would be prejudicial to its distinctiveness or its reputation. This extended protection does not necessarily cover all possible goods. It could well be that the use of a mark identical to the well-known mark would do unjustified harm in relation to a certain category of goods, whereas the same use on totally dissimilar goods might not be against the interests of the registered owner of the well-known mark. The decision has to be determined by all the circumstances of the specific case, including the extent of reputation of the mark, the type of goods for which it is used by the infringer, the manner in which he presents his goods, and so on.

9.191 At present, the practice in most countries is to grant protection that goes beyond the scope of similarity of goods only in exceptional cases of famous or highly-reputed marks. Yet reputation is not sufficient on its own, of course; broader protection is justified only where the use of a sign without due cause would take unfair advantage of, or be detrimental to, the distinctive character or the reputation of the trademark.

(c) Restriction of the Exclusive Right in the Public Interest

9.192 In the same way as the owner's right to use his trademark can be restricted by other rights, his right to prevent third parties from using his mark can be restricted by the legitimate interests of others. The Model Law provides in Section 19 that "Registration of the mark shall not confer on its registered owner the right to preclude third parties from using bona fide their names, addresses, pseudonyms, a geographical name, or exact indications concerning the kind, quality, quantity, destination, value, place of origin, or time of production or of supply, of their goods and services, in so far as such use is confined to the purposes of mere identification or information and cannot mislead the public as to the source of the goods or services." A similar provision is contained in many trademark laws.

9.193 The trademark owner also cannot prevent third parties who are not his competitors from referring to his trademark by acts such as the listing of the mark in a compendium of trademarks or in dictionaries, or to use it in newspaper articles or in books or other publications.

9.194 Since the trademark owner has a justified interest in preventing his mark from becoming generic, he can, in certain cases, demand that it be properly used. Some legislations recognize a right of the trademark owner to have his trademark identified as such in dictionaries; if a dictionary lists a trademark without stating that it is one, its owner has the right to ask for a correction in the next edition of the dictionary.

(d) Remedies for Trademark Infringement

9.195 A successful infringement action leads to prohibition of the use of the confusingly similar mark. If the infringing mark is registered, cancellation of the registration is ordered.

9.196 The trademark owner can also, in principle, ask for compensation for damages. Damages are difficult to prove in trademark infringement cases, however, so this remedy is not very important in practice.

9.197 The situation is of course different in cases of counterfeiting, which will be dealt with in the following.

J. TRADEMARK PIRACY, COUNTERFEITING AND IMITATION OF LABELS AND PACKAGING

(a) Trademark Piracy

9.198 Trademark piracy means the registration or use of a generally well-known foreign trademark that is not registered in the country (or is invalid as a result of non-use).

References for Section I
International Bureau of WIPO, *Introduction to Trademark Law & Practice* (second edition), WIPO Pub. No. 653(E) (1993)

9.199 The Paris Convention provides in its Article 6*bis* that a well-known trademark must be protected even if it is not registered in the country. This is an important basis for the protection of well-known brands against piracy. Article 6*bis* is restricted to identical and similar goods, however. Often well-known trademarks are used by pirates on totally different goods, or for services. Furthermore, courts sometimes require a trademark to be well known in the country and deny protection, even if the true owner of the trademark can prove that it is internationally well-known in a considerable number of countries. Improved protection against trademark piracy is therefore needed.

(b) Counterfeiting

(i) What is Counterfeiting?

9.200 Counterfeiting is first of all the imitation of a product. The counterfeit is not only identical in the generic sense of the term, as a bag might be. It also gives the impression of being the genuine product (for instance a LOUIS VUITTON bag), originating from the genuine manufacturer or trader.

9.201 The offering of such a counterfeit product is only meaningful, of course, if the genuine product is known to the consumer. Consequently, counterfeit goods often belong to the category of luxury goods and bear a well-known trademark. In fact, however, this is only a coincidence: counterfeit goods can just as well be mass-consumption goods, or goods not sold under a trademark but protected by other intellectual property rights such as copyright or design protection. They can also be known to a small group of specialized consumers only, such as brakes to be used for cars, or aircraft, or pesticides known to clients in agriculture. These examples show at the same time how dangerous the use of counterfeit goods can be (a whole year's crop in a large part of Africa was once destroyed by the use of a counterfeit pesticide).

9.202 The most typical and widely-known examples of counterfeit goods are, however, the false LOUIS VUITTON bags, the false ROLEX, CARTIER and other luxury watches, the false PUMA and REEBOK sports shoes, the false LACOSTE sports shirts and so on. Worldwide sales of counterfeit LOUIS VUITTON bags and ROLEX watches exceed those of the genuine products. This shows that counterfeiting is an economic phenomenon of worldwide importance. In fact, worldwide sales of counterfeits are estimated at about 5% of world trade, and the figure is on the increase. Indeed, it is important to recognize that counterfeiting is an economic crime, comparable to theft. Counterfeiters not only deceive the consumer but also damage the reputation of the genuine manufacturer, apart from which they do not pay taxes and other duties to the State.

(ii) Legal Protection against Counterfeiting

9.203 Although it is not a condition and not always the case, counterfeit goods generally bear a trademark. This has the advantage of making counterfeiting actionable as trademark infringement, which is generally easier than fighting against infringement of other intellectual property rights, which may also be involved. More often than not, counterfeiting can be regarded as a specific serious instance of trademark infringement, apart from which, under trademark law, the cases are legally simple ones, as the trademark and the goods are usually identical or at least nearly identical. However, since counterfeiting is an economically serious and important problem, the remedies specified in trademark laws are often not sufficient to serve as an effective deterrent. This is a problem that concerns three areas of law enforcement, all of which are essential if counterfeiting is to be successfully combatted:

9.204 Laws must provide for severe criminal sanctions, including imprisonment. Most trademark laws provide for criminal sanctions for trademark infringement, but they were often enacted long ago and are no longer realistic, even for "normal" trademark infringement cases. Counterfeiters pay such fines from their pockets, and imprisonment is rarely ordered.

9.205 Rapid, far-reaching remedies are necessary. Counterfeiters do not conduct their business from a normal business address; in the event of prosecution they tend to disappear. Often they can only be found after a long and thorough investigation. There is therefore a pressing need for provisional measures such as interim injunctions (in the United Kingdom the so-called Anton Piller order is a very useful measure). By virtue of such provisional measures the counterfeit goods may be confiscated and the person who has them in his possession is obliged to inform the genuine trademark owner of their source.

9.206 Since counterfeiting is a phenomenon that occurs in international trade, it is also necessary to empower the customs authorities to check goods at the border of their country and confiscate counterfeit goods at the request of the owner of the trademark affixed to them.

(c) Imitation of Labels and Packaging

9.207 The cases discussed in this section lie between normal trademark infringement and counterfeiting (sometimes coming very close to counterfeiting). As in the case of counterfeiting, the label or packaging of the competing product is imitated, but in this case the imitation does not give the impression of being the genuine one. If one compares the genuine product and the imitation side by side, although consumers seldom proceed in this way, one can distinguish them and the imitator does not usually hide behind the manufacturer of the genuine product; he trades under his own name. He is not a criminal, but rather a competitor who uses unfair methods of competition.

9.208 Instead of developing at his own expense a label and packaging with an image of his own for his product, the imitator tries to take advantage of the reputation of the competing product by giving his product an appearance so similar to it that confusion arises in the marketplace.

9.209 Often the imitator uses a trademark (in the sense of a product name) which is confusingly similar to that of his competitor. If he does that he is committing trademark infringement.

9.210 In a number of cases the word mark used by the imitator is somewhat, but not confusingly, similar to the one used by his competitor, but may even be totally different from it. In such situations the confusion in the marketplace arises only, or mainly, from the use of colors and graphic elements that are identical or very similar to those of the competitor's label or packaging. Labels and packaging are rarely registered as trademarks, which means that trademark law mostly offers no basis for intervention in such cases. They have to be dealt with under the rules of unfair competition.

9.211 In principle, it is generally recognized as being unlawful (unfair competition) to pass off one's own goods as being those of a competitor. If a label or the packaging of a product is confusingly similar to that of a competitor's product, this requirement is normally fulfilled.

K. CHANGE OF OWNERSHIP

(a) Reasons for Change of Ownership

9.212 The ownership of a trademark can change for different reasons and in different ways.

9.213 Trademark rights may, on a natural person's death, pass to his heir. Such a change of ownership is only possible where trademark laws allow the private ownership of trademarks. Similarly, a trademark may pass to a new owner in the case of bankruptcy. Another automatic change of ownership may result from the merging of two companies. No automatic change takes place, however, in the case of a company takeover effected by the acquisition of shares, or when certain assets of a company, including the intellectual property rights, are acquired.

(b) Voluntary Change of Ownership: Assignment

9.214 Assignments are the most common form of change of ownership. They are normally, but not necessarily, part of a purchase contract, whereby trademarks are sold against payment of a certain amount of money.

9.215 The law of some countries allows trademark assignment only together with the goodwill related to the mark. It is argued that consumers are accustomed to the product sold under the trademark, so that an assignment without transfer of the enterprise, or part of the enterprise, using the mark would deceive consumers. Nevertheless, there is a clear tendency towards allowing free assignments of trademarks. Trademarks that are assigned without goodwill have often been unused for many years. Apart from that, companies often have a complicated legal structure and, when one company is taken over by another, it may well be that the trademarks are transferred to the new parent company while the factories in which the products sold under those trademarks are manufactured remain the property of the company taken over. As long as the new parent and trademark owner ensures that the consistent quality of the products sold under the assigned trademarks continues, consumers will then not be deceived.

9.216 There is therefore no absolute need to link the assignment of trademarks to the goodwill related to them. It is sufficient, and at the same time necessary, to ensure that consumers are protected against deception. This is the approach of

References for Section J
International Bureau of WIPO, *Introduction to Trademark Law & Practice* (second edition), WIPO Pub. No. 653(E) (1993)

Section 21 of the Model Law, whose paragraph (1) allows the assignment of trademark registrations or applications independently of the transfer of all or part of the enterprise using the mark, but which provides in its paragraph (2) that such assignment is null and void if its purpose or effect is liable to mislead the public. It should be added that such cases are very rare in real life, especially where trademark registrations are assigned as a whole.

9.217 Partial assignments are more problematic. In order to avoid confusion of the public in such cases, trademark laws sometimes allow transfers only where the goods involved are not similar to those remaining with the former owner. Confusion of the consumer is thus clearly avoided, as the two trademarks could have been registered by different owners from the very beginning.

(c) Recordal of Change of Ownership

9.218 In principle, a change of trademark ownership takes effect without any recording. This is clear in the case of the foreign owner's death or bankruptcy or a merger. Even a voluntary change of ownership by means of assignment does not, in principle, need to be recorded to become effective, at least *inter partes*. Nevertheless, trademark laws generally provide for the recording of changes of ownership for two reasons:

(1) the new owner cannot normally exercise his trademark rights if he is not the recorded owner;
(2) in principle, the transfer is not binding on third parties as long as it is not recorded.

9.219 This principle cannot be applied without restriction: if the new owner has completed all the necessary formalities, that is, if he has submitted the necessary documents to the office for registration of the change of ownership, he must be able to take action to defend his trademark against infringement. The recording procedure is sometimes very long and drawn-out, and some jurisdictions do not permit recordal of pending applications. In such cases, the new owner would often be totally blocked, as the former owner might no longer exist, or at least might no longer be interested in proceeding against infringements of his former trademark rights.

9.220 Trademark laws generally provide that the registrar refuses to record an assignment that in his opinion is liable to deceive consumers.

9.221 If the assignment really does deceive the consumer, it is usually automatically null and void and therefore cannot be validly recorded. However, the registrar should not refuse to record assignments if in his opinion there is only a risk of confusion for the public. Such cases obviously depend on factual circumstances that go beyond what he knows from the file, such as how the new owner will use the trademark, whether consumers will really be deceived, and so on, which establish that the deception of consumers is not inherent in the assignment.

9.222 Different from a partial transfer is the situation where the registered owner of several trademarks assigns some of them which, if the test of trademark similarity is applied, could be regarded as confusingly similar.

9.223 In such a case, deception of the consumer is not really inherent in the assignment. Whether or not the consumer will be deceived depends not only on how the new owner will make use of the trademark assigned to him, but also on how the former owner will make use of the trademark of which he is still the proprietor. The parties to the assignment will usually, in their own interest, include provisions in the contract of assignment that regulate the future use of both trademarks in such a manner as to avoid confusion of the consumers involved. In such cases the registrar should not have the power to refuse to record an assignment, and the matter should be left to the discretion of the courts.

9.224 If a trademark assignment is null and void because it inherently deceives the public, or for any other legal reason outside trademark law, but has been recorded, the question that arises is what the consequences of such recording are.

9.225 Nullity of the assignment does not lead to nullity of the trademark rights as such. The trademark rights do, however, remain with the assignor, the former owner. This means that any use of the trademark by the newly registered owner is not actually a use, and, after the grace period for use of the trademark has expired, the trademark is open for cancellation. Of course, the assignor and former registered owner of the trademark, who has remained the owner, could in fact use it, but he is unlikely to do so as the parties are usually unaware of the invalidity of the assignment.

(d) Formalities

9.226 In the interest of legal security, assignments should be evidenced in writing. The application for recording of the assignment must also be made in writing, either by the assignor or by the assignee. If it is the assignor who applies, a simple written request signed by himself or his legal representative should be sufficient. If on the other hand it is the assignee or any other new trademark owner who asks for the change of ownership to be recorded, the request generally needs to be accompanied by supporting documents (the contract of assignment signed by the assignor, or any other proof of the change of ownership). However, in such cases the mere signature of the demand for change of ownership by the new trademark owner or his legal representative should also be sufficient, without any need for authentication, legalization or other certification.

L. TRADEMARK LICENSING

(a) Importance of Licensing

9.227 It is common practice for trademark owners to license third parties to use their trademarks locally in the country where they exercise their own business. However, the main importance of the possibility of licensing the use of trademarks lies in its usefulness in international business relations. Licensing is indeed the principal means whereby the trademarks of foreign companies are used by local businesses. Such license agreements are very common between partners from different developed countries, and they do exist between partners who both

References for Section K
International Bureau of WIPO, *Introduction to Trademark Law & Practice* (second edition), WIPO Pub. No. 653(E) (1993)

originate in developing countries, or even between a licensor in a developing country and a licensee in a developed country.

9.228 The most important role they play, however, is in the relations between licensors in developed countries and licensees in developing countries. In these situations they are not normally simple trademark licenses, but general agreements including the licensing of patents, trademarks, know-how and possibly other intellectual property rights, as well as technical assistance to be given to the licensee. These agreements are a key factor in the economic development of developing countries and are usually characterized by the transfer of technology, the creation of jobs and the use of local raw materials. They are often regulated by special provisions of local laws which provide for the control or approval of the agreement by a local authority, such as a ministry responsible for technology transfer.

9.229 To the extent that such general agreements confer the right to use the licensor's trademarks, they have to comply with the relevant licensing provisions of the trademark law of the licensee's country (even though the above-mentioned special provisions may also apply). The trademark laws of many countries contain provisions on trademark licensing. The general guiding principles of trademark licensing are dealt with hereunder, independently of its foreign ownership and technology transfer aspects.

(b) Basic Concept: Control by the Owner

9.230 In terms of trademark law, the possibility of granting a trademark license seems to contradict the trademark's basic function of indicating the origin of goods, since the goods offered under the trademark then originate with the licensee and not with the registered owner. To safeguard the origin-indicating function of the trademark, it is therefore necessary and sufficient for the owner to exercise control over the use of the mark by the licensee, particularly with respect to the quality of the goods (compliance with quality standards set by the licensor) and the conditions under which they are marketed. If that control is effective, the registered owner of a trademark need not use it himself. Use of the mark by his licensee can be deemed to be use by himself for all trademark protection purposes. This means more particularly that the trademark cannot be attacked for alleged non-use, and the licensee cannot himself claim ownership rights in relation to the mark.

9.231 The Model Law also contains provisions on certain types of restrictive clauses that should not be allowed in license agreements. No doubt it is important that such clauses should be dealt with in the general context of license agreements, whether they concern the relations between partners located in developed countries or technology transfer agreements with licensees in developing countries. At the local level, however, such provisions should not be in the trademark law, the purpose of which is to secure protection for marks in order to give their owners and the consuming public a means of distinguishing their goods from those of competitors. Any other purpose, such as antitrust considerations, the control of foreign investment or the like should be regulated in other laws applicable to all license agreements, regardless of whether or not they contain provisions on the licensing of marks. As it happens, the trademark laws of the overwhelming majority of countries contain no such provisions.

(c) Formal Requirements

9.232 Basically, the trademark protection system does not impose any formalities on trademark licensing. The only important point, which is inherent in the system, is that the owner exercises effective control over the licensee. The importance of this principle is generally recognized, although only a few trademark laws provide for quality control in their provisions on trademark licensing (those of the United States of America and Sri Lanka, for instance). Indeed no purpose is served by the existence of a written agreement, which may even be recorded in the trademark register and which may contain all sorts of control provision, if the law does not provide for the legal consequences of failure to exercise control. Many trademark laws do nevertheless provide for obligatory recording of the license, and often the registrar carefully studies the conditions imposed on the licensee by the licensor.

9.233 Many laws, more particularly in Europe, provide that it is sufficient for a license agreement to be concluded orally, but a provision according to which a trademark license must be in writing, is reasonable in the light of legal security considerations. And it is acceptable to trademark owners that a license should be registered in order to be binding on third parties. What would not be acceptable would be to make registration of the license a condition of use by the licensee being considered use by the licensor in terms of the use obligations.

9.234 A special variety of trademark licensing formality that could be considered is the British system of registered user agreements. If such an agreement is recorded, use by the trademark by the registered user is deemed to be use by the trademark owner. However, it is not the actual license agreement between the parties, governing their commercial relations, that has to be registered; the law provides for a kind of simplified form, with certain conditions to be fulfilled before the registrar recognizes the registered user agreement. Since the register is open to inspection, the parties to a license agreement do not normally register the agreement but rather the simplified form.

(d) Restrictions on the Licensee

9.235 Licensees are not usually allowed to assign the license or grant sub-licenses, but such rights can of course be expressly granted in the agreement.

9.236 Licenses can be exclusive or non-exclusive.

9.237 In the case of an exclusive license the trademark owner is not allowed to license the mark to any other person in the territory and cannot even use the mark himself.

9.238 In the case of a non-exclusive license, of course, the owner may use the mark himself and even allow others to use it. In the case of multiple licenses, very strict quality control is necessary in the interest of the consuming public.

9.239 Exclusive as well as non-exclusive licenses can be concluded for the whole territory of a country or part of it, and they can cover all or some only of the goods

References for Section L
International Bureau of WIPO, *Introduction to Trademark Law & Practice* (second edition), WIPO Pub. No. 653(E) (1993)

for which the trademark is registered. Unlike in the case of assignments, there is no risk of confusion of the public to be considered, on condition that the trademark owner exercises efficient quality control.

M. TRADE NAMES

9.240 Enterprises may own and use one, several or many different trademarks to distinguish their goods and services from those of their competitors. However, they also need to distinguish themselves from other enterprises. For that purpose they will adopt a trade name.

9.241 Trade names have in common with trademarks and service marks that they exercise a distinguishing function. Unlike trademarks and service marks, however, trade names distinguish one enterprise from others, quite independently of the goods or services that the enterprise markets or renders.

(a) Legal Requirements

9.242 Countries in generally lay down certain requirements to be met for a trade name to be permissible and accepted for registration in the register of company names (which may exist on a national level, but in fact is often kept on a regional or even local level). The character of the enterprise must be mentioned (for instance with the abbreviation Ltd for limited company), and often the purpose of the business has also to be given. Trade names are generally quite lengthy, and are therefore not a very practical tool for use in daily business life as reference to the company.

9.243 Enterprises therefore tend to use a shorter business name or some other kind of corporate identifier in addition to the full, duly-registered trade name.

9.244 The trade name is not normally required to be distinctive as a condition of registration and subsequent use.

(b) Legal Protection

9.245 If a trade name or business name is distinctive it is protected by use, whether registered or not. If it is not distinctive, it can be protected after distinctiveness has been acquired by use. Distinctiveness in this context means that the consuming public recognizes the name as being a reference to a particular trade source.

9.246 A trade name or a business name can also be afforded protection by registration as a trademark. Usually, both the full corporate name and the short business name can be registered. To safeguard such a registration, it is of course necessary actually to use the trade name as a trademark. This requirement is normally not met by making a reference, somewhere on the label or packaging of a product, to the manufacturing or trading company with its full address in small print, as is often required by labelling regulations. It is therefore more adequate and commoner in practice to register the shorter business name as a trademark, the more so as that name is often at the same time an important trademark (such as the so-called "house mark") of the company.

9.247 In the same way as enterprises can register trade names and business names as trademarks, they can and often do use them not only to distinquish t hemselves but also to distinguish the goods or services that they offer (and, as mentioned before, this is even necessary in connection with the obligation to use if the name has been registered as a trademark).

9.248 It is therefore inevitable that conflicts between trade names, business names and trademarks arise. If a trade name or business name is used as a trademark (whether registered or not), the general rules of priority and the protection of consumers against confusion as to the origin of the goods or services offered under the signs concerned will determine the outcome of any conflict with a similar trademark.

9.249 Even if an enterprise uses a business name or trade name as such, in other words not as a trademark for the goods or services it offers, it is nevertheless widely recognized that a prior trademark is infringed if the use of the business name or trade name likely to create confusion as to the origin of the goods or services that the enterprise offers under its name. Conversely, the use of a trademark, service mark of collective mark can in the same way infringe a prior (registered or unregistered) business name or trade name.

References for Section M
International Bureau of WIPO, *Introduction to Trademark Law & Practice* (second edition), WIPO Pub. No. 653(e) (1993)

CHAPTER 10

Industrial Designs

A. INTRODUCTION

10.1 Industrial design, in a lay or general sense, refers to the creative activity of achieving a formal or ornamental appearance for mass-produced items that, within the available cost constraints, satisfies both the need for the item to appeal visually to potential consumers, and the need for the item to perform efficiently its intended function. In a legal sense, industrial design refers to the right granted in many countries, pursuant to a registration system, to protect the original ornamental and non-functional features of an industrial article or product that result from design activity.

10.2 Visual appeal is one of the considerations that influence the decision of consumers to prefer one product over another, particularly in areas where a range of products performing the same function is available in the market. In these latter situations, if the technical performance of the various products offered by different manufacturers is relatively equal, aesthetic appeal, along with, of course, cost, will determine the consumer's choice. The legal protection of industrial designs, thus, serves the important function of protecting one of the distinctive elements by which manufacturers achieve market success. In so doing, by rewarding the creator for the effort which has produced the industrial design, legal protection serves as an incentive to the investment of resources in fostering the design element of production.

B. EVOLUTION OF DESIGN PROTECTION

10.3 Historically, the emergence of protection for industrial designs is intimately connected with the growth of industrialization and methods of mass production. In the United Kingdom, the first law giving protection to industrial designs was the Designing and Printing of Linens, Cotton, Calicoes and Muslins Act of 1787, which gave protection for a period of two months to "every person who shall invent, design and print, or cause to be invented, designed and printed, and become the Proprietor of any new and original pattern or patterns for printing

References for Section A
International Bureau of WIPO, *The Main Objects of Industrial Property: Inventions, Industrial Designs, Marks*, WIPO/LIC/WL6/91/1

Linens, Cottons, Calicoes or Muslins." The contribution and importance of design in the growing textile industries was thereby recognized.

10.4 The small area of industry covered by this first law in the United Kingdom was extended soon after, in 1798, by the Sculpture Copyright Act, which gave protection to new models, copies or casts of "human and animal figures." The importance of the pottery and porcelain industries, and the integral role of design in these industries, was further recognized by the extension of the protection under this Act in 1840 to new models, copies or casts of "any subject being matter of invention in sculpture."

10.5 Growing recognition of the expansion of industrialization and of the possible application of methods of mass production to most areas of manufacture lead to the gradual extension of design protection to other fields of endeavor up until the consolidation achieved in the Designs Act of 1842, which extended protection to "any new and original design whether such design be applicable to the ornamenting of any article of manufacture, or of any substance, artificial or natural, or partly artificial and partly natural, and that whether such design be so applicable for the pattern, or for the shape or configuration, or for the ornament thereof, or for any two or more of such purposes and by whatever means such design may be so applicable, whether by printing, or by painting, or by embroidery, or by weaving, or by sewing, or by modelling, or by casting, or by embossing, or by engraving, or by staining, or by any other means whatsoever, manual, mechanical, or chemical, separate or combined." Design was thereby recognized as a fundamental element of all production and manufacture.

10.6 A somewhat similar evolution of design protection took place in France. The Law on Literary and Artistic Property of 1793 was applied in certain cases to the protection of designs. The growth of the textile industries, in particular, soon led to the enactment in 1806 of a special law dealing with industrial designs. The Law of March 18, 1806 established a special council (Conciliation Board or *Conseil de Prud'hommes*) in Lyon responsible for receiving deposits of designs and for regulating disputes between manufacturers concerning designs. While initially destined for industries in Lyon, particularly those manufacturing silk, the system of deposit and regulation by special council was extended to other cities and, through judicial interpretation, to two- and three-dimensional designs in all areas of industrial activity.

C. THE LEGAL PROTECTION OF INDUSTRIAL DESIGNS

10.7 The formulation of a legal system for the protection of industrial designs, like the provision of legal protection for all forms of intellectual property, requires the establishment of a balance of interests. On the one hand, there is the need to provide efficient and effective protection, in order that the law may fulfill its function of promoting the design element in production. On the other hand, there is the need to ensure that the law does not unnecessarily extend protection

References for Section B
International Bureau of WIPO, *The Main Objects of Industrial Property: Inventions, Industrial Designs, Marks*, WIPO/LIC/WL6/91/1

beyond what is necessary to create the required incentive for design activity, so that the least number of impediments are introduced to the free use of available designs. The establishment of this balance requires careful consideration of a number of matters, of which the most important are:

(1) the definition of the subject matter of protection;
(2) the rights which apply to the proprietor of the subject matter;
(3) the duration of such rights;
(4) the entitlement to such rights; and
(5) the method of acquisition of such rights;

(a) Definition of Subject Matter of Protection

(i) Design as Conception or Idea

10.8 The subject matter of the legal protection of industrial designs is not articles or products, but rather the design which is applied to or embodied in such articles or products. Thus, it was stated in the early British case *Dover* v. *Nurnberger Celluloid Waren Fabrik Gebruder Wolff*, 27 RPC 498, 503 per Buckley LJ:

"Design means ... a conception or suggestion or idea of a shape or of a picture or of a device or of some arrangement which can be applied to an article by some manual, mechanical, or chemical means. It is a conception, suggestion, or idea, and not an article, which is the thing capable of being registered ... It is a suggestion of form and ornament to be applied to physical body."

10.9 The emphasis on an abstract conception or idea as the subject matter of design protection may seem, at first, to be a somewhat academic point. It underlines, however, the very important and deliberate limitation of the scope of design protection. Design protection does not apply to articles or products in such a way as to grant the proprietor of the design exclusive rights over the commercial exploitation of those articles or products. Rather, design protection only applies to such articles or products as embody or reproduce the protected design. Protection does not, therefore, prevent other manufacturers from producing or dealing in similar articles fulfilling the same utilitarian function, provided that such substitute articles do not embody or reproduce the protected design.

10.10 The conception or idea that constitutes the design may be something which can be expressed either two-dimensionally or three-dimensionally. The definition of "design" which is used in the Registered Designs Act 1949 of the United Kingdom, for instance, refers to "features of shape, configuration, pattern or ornament" (Section 1). It has been generally considered that, in this definition, the words "shape" and "configuration" are synonymous, and that both signify the form in which an article is made or, in other words, something three-dimensional. Likewise, it has also been considered that the words "pattern" and "ornament" are synonymous, and that both refer to something embossed, engraved or placed upon an article for the purpose of its decoration or, in other words, to something essentially two-dimensional.

10.11 The Copyright, Designs and Patents Act 1988, of the United Kingdom, also provides for a "design right." Design is defined as referring to "any aspect of the shape or configuration (whether internal or external) of the whole or part of an article" (Section 213(2)).

10.12 A similar approach, emphasizing the inclusion of both two-dimensional and three-dimensional designs, is to be found in the laws of other countries. Thus, the Design Law of Japan (Law No. 125 of April 13, 1959, as amended) refers to "design" as meaning "the shape, pattern or color or a combination of these in an article," and laws of France and Italy refer to both drawings or sketches (*dessins*—two-dimensional) and models (*modèles*—three-dimensional).

(ii) Application to or Embodiment in an Article

10.13 While the subject matter of design protection is an essentially abstract conception, one of the basic purposes of industrial design protection is the stimulation of the design element of *production*. It is, accordingly, a usual feature of industrial design laws that a design can be protected only if the design is capable of being used in industry, or in respect of articles produced on a large scale.

10.14 The requirement that a design must be applied to utilitarian articles in order to be protected is one of the principal matters which distinguishes the objectives of industrial design protection from copyright protection, since the latter is purely concerned with aesthetic creations. The requirement is variously expressed in different laws. The WIPO Model Law for Developing Countries on Industrial Designs (hereinafter referred to as "the WIPO Model Law") protects designs in so far as they "can serve as a pattern for a product of industry or handicraft." The Design Law of Japan similarly extends protection to designs "capable of being used in industrial manufacture" (Article 3(1)).

10.15 In the Registered Designs Act of 1949 of the United Kingdom, the utilitarian requirement is expressed in the condition that a design must be "applied to an article by any industrial process or means" (Section 1(3)). These words have been criticized as insufficient for the case of three-dimensional designs, which are not, strictly speaking, "applied to" an article, but which are, rather, embodied in, or constitute the form or shape of, an article.

10.16 The Italian Law (Royal Decree No. 1411 of 1940), requires that the design be capable of giving a special ornamental aspect to an industrial product (Section 5). The Swedish Law (Design Protection Act of 1970), defines "design" as the prototype embodying the appearance of an article (Section 1).

(iii) Judgement of the Design by its Appearance

10.17 It is usually a condition of the protection of industrial designs that the design that is applied to or embodied in an article must have an appearance which is capable of visual judgement. Thus, the WIPO Model Law refers to designs which give "a special appearance to a product of industry or handicraft" (Section 2(1)); the Design Law of Japan refers to designs "which produce an aesthetic impression on the sense of sight" (Article 2(1)); and the Registered Designs Act of 1949 of the United Kingdom refers to "features which in the finished article appeal to and are judged solely by the eye" (Section 1(3)). The Laws of Italy and Sweden refer, respectively, to "aspect" and "appearance" of articles or products (see above). The purpose of this requirement is to emphasis that industrial design protection is concerned solely with *appearance* or aspect of articles, and not with their function.

(iv) Exclusion of Designs Dictated by Function

10.18 The concern of industrial design protection with appearance only is also apparent from the requirement, commonly found in industrial design laws, that designs which are dictated solely by the function which the article is to perform shall be excluded from protection. In this respect, the WIPO Model Law provides that protection shall not extend to "anything in an industrial design which serves solely to obtain a technical result" (Section 2(2)). The Swiss Law (Law on Industrial Designs, 1990), provides that the protection of an industrial design does not extend to the manufacturing processes, the use or the technical effect of the article produced to the design (Article 3).

10.19 The Registered Designs Act 1949 of the United Kingdom provides that the expression "design" shall not "include a method or principle of construction or features of shape or configuration which are dictated solely by the function which the article to be made in that shape or configuration has to perform" (Section 1(3)). The Laws of France (Section 2) and Italy (Section 8) exclude from protection any shape or configuration which would constitute a patentable invention, protectable under the applicable patent law.

10.20 A fundamental purpose is served by the exclusion from protection of designs dictated solely by the function which the article is to perform. Many articles to which designs are applied are not themselves novel, and are produced by a large number of different manufacturers. Belts, shoes, screws and piston rings, for example, may be produced by hundreds of different manufacturers, and all articles within each class are intended to perform the same function. If a design for one such article, for example, screws, is dictated purely by the function which the screw is intended to perform, protection for that design would have the effect of excluding all other manufacturers from producing items intended to perform the same function. Such an exclusion is not warranted, unless the design is sufficiently novel and inventive to qualify under the rigorous standards for patent protection. Designs which are dictated exclusively by function are, therefore, the proper province of patent law, and not industrial design law, which is concerned only with visual effect and appearance.

10.21 Since, under certain theories of design, form should follow function, it is often said that the exclusion from protection of designs which are dictated purely by function may have the effect of excluding too broad a range of designs from protection. Such a fear is in practice, however, unwarranted, since the exclusion relates only to those designs which are *indispensable* for achieving the desired function. In reality, many ways of achieving a given function will be possible. Thus, only if the given function could not be achieved after a design is altered would the design be excluded from protection. The question is thus whether the design for which protection is sought constitutes the sole solution for an intended function.

(b) Novelty or Originality

10.22 It is a requirement of all industrial design laws that protection through registration shall be granted only to designs which are novel or, as it is sometimes expressed, original. The novelty of the design constitutes the fundamental reason for the grant of a reward to the originator through protection by registration of the industrial design.

10.23 While the requirement of novelty is to be found in all laws, the nature of the novelty that is required as a condition of protection differs amongst the laws of various countries. The novelty required is sometimes absolute or universal, meaning that the design for which registration is sought must be new as against all other designs produced in all other parts of the world at any previous time and disclosed by any tangible or oral means. On the other hand, a qualified standard of novelty is sometimes required. In this latter situation, the qualification may relate to time, meaning that novelty is judged by reference to designs published within a limited preceding period of time; or may relate to territory, meaning that novelty is judged by reference to all designs published within the relevant jurisdiction, as opposed to anywhere in the world; or may relate to means of expression, meaning that novelty is assessed by reference to written or tangible disclosures anywhere in the world and to oral disclosures only within the relevant jurisdiction.

10.24 The broad policy argument in favor of a standard of unqualified universal novelty is that exclusive rights by registration should be granted only where the originator of the design has produced something which is truly novel, and which therefore justifies the reward of exclusive rights. The broad policy argument in favor of a qualified standard of novelty is that one purpose of design registration is to encourage new design within the relevant jurisdiction, so that a novel design registered within that jurisdiction should not be deprived of protection by the publication elsewhere of a design which its originator did not introduce into the jurisdiction to add to the designs available to industry. It should be noted, however, that it would not necessarily follow from a qualified standard of novelty that a person could obtain valid rights within the jurisdiction simply by registering a design which he had seen overseas and copied, since it is often also a requirement of design law that the applicant be the author of the design.

D.   RIGHTS IN INDUSTRIAL DESIGNS

10.25 The rights which are accorded to the proprietor of a validly registered industrial design again emphasize the essential purpose of design law in promoting and protecting the design element of industrial production. Thus, whereas copyright accords to an author the right to prevent the copying of a work, industrial design law accords to the proprietor the exclusive right to prevent the unauthorized exploitation of the design in industrial articles.

(a)   Entitlement to Rights

10.26 The right to legal protection in respect of an industrial design belongs to the creator (or author or originator) of the industrial design. Two questions concerning the operation of this principle arise and are often the subject of particular legislative provisions.

10.27 First, there is the question of the entitlement to legal protection in respect of an industrial design that has been created by an employee, or by a contractor

References for Section C
International Bureau of WIPO, *The Main Objects of Industrial Property: Inventions, Industrial Designs, Marks*, WIPO/LIC/WL6/91/1

pursuant to a commission. In these situations, the law usually provides that the entitlement to legal protection of the design shall belong the employer, or to the person who has commissioned the design. The basis for this rule is that the creation of the design falls within the duties which the employee is paid to perform, so that the employee should seek the reward for his creative activity in an appropriate level of remuneration, responsibility and other conditions of employment. Likewise, in the case of the contractor, the thing for which the contractor is being paid is the production of the design for the use of the person commissioning the design.

10.28 Much contemporary design is produced with the assistance of computers. The question arises whether it can be said that there is an author or creator who is entitled to legal protection in respect of designs generated with the assistance of a computer. One approach to this question is to treat the computer like any other tool which may be used by a designer to assist in the process of generating a design. On this basis, the person who is responsible for manipulating the computer's capacity to produce a design would be considered to be the author of the design. A provision to this effect is to be found in Section 214(2) of the Copyright, Designs and Patents Act 1988, of the United Kingdom which provides:

"In the case of a computer-generated design the person by whom the arrangements necessary for the creation of the design are undertaken shall be taken to be the designer."

(b) Acquisition of Rights

(i) Registration

10.29 Industrial design protection is usually granted pursuant to a procedure for the registration of such designs. The most commonly adopted examination system provides for a formal examination only of an application for a registered design. Pursuant to this system, an application is examined to ensure that it meets with each of the formal requirements for an application which are imposed by the relevant law (for example, whether the requisite number of representations or specimens of the design are filed with the application), but no search is made of the prior art to determine whether the substantive criterion of novelty or originality is satisfied by the design for which registration is sought.

10.30 A system requiring only formal examination has the effect of shifting the burden of assessing novelty to those interested persons in the market who may wish to use, or who may have used, the design or a substantially similar design. Any person interested in using such a design will have the opportunity either to oppose the registration of the design for which application has been made, if the relevant law provides for an opposition procedure, or of bringing proceedings for the cancellation of a registration which it is alleged is invalid. The system thus offers a means of reducing the administrative burden of the maintenance of a system of registration of industrial designs. It also offers a solution to the problem of maintaining an adequate search file to undertake a substantive examination of the novelty of designs. Such a search file can very often be almost impossible to maintain, since, on the basis of a condition of unqualified universal novelty, it would need to include all designs made at any time in any part of the world since the commencement of recorded history.

10.31 The alternative system of examination provides for a search of past designs and an examination of the design for which registration is sought to ascertain whether it satisfies the required condition of novelty. It necessitates the maintenance of a search file and sufficient skilled manpower to undertake the substantive examination.

(ii) Creation and Fixation

10.32 Rights in designs may, under certain laws, also be acquired by the act of creation and fixation of the design, in a document or by embodying the design in an article. These systems do not require any formal registration procedure for the acquisition of exclusive rights in the design. Examples of this system are provided by the Law of France, and the "design law" under the Copyright, Designs and Patents Act 1988, of the United Kingdom.

(c) Nature of the Rights

10.33 The right to prevent others from exploiting an industrial design usually encompasses the exclusive right to do any of the following things for industrial or commercial purposes:

(1) make articles to which the design is applied or in which the design is embodied;
(2) import articles to which the design is applied or in which it is embodied;
(3) sell, hire or offer for sale any such articles.

10.34 In some laws, the exclusive rights of the proprietor also extend to preventing another from stocking any articles to which the design has been applied or in which it is embodied (see, for example, Section 21(1)(c) of the WIPO Model Law). While this right is sometimes considered as excessive in that it deals only with preparatory acts, it is on the other hand often included in order to facilitate the enforcement of a proprietor's rights, since it may often be easier to locate a stock of infringing articles than to apprehend a person in the act of selling or offering for sale such articles.

10.35 As opposed to copyright, where the subject matter of the right is the work which is created by the author and which is thus defined by the author, the subject matter of the rights of the proprietor of an industrial design are defined by the design which has been registered. However, it is usual to provide that the proprietor's rights extend not only to the unauthorized exploitation of the exact design which has been registered, but also to the unauthorized exploitation of any imitations of such a design which differ from the registered design only in immaterial respects.

(d) Duration of Rights

10.36 The term for an industrial design right varies from country to country. The usual maximum term goes from 10 to 25 years, often divided into terms requiring the proprietor to renew the registration in order to obtain an extension of the term.

References for Section D
International Bureau of WIPO, *The Main Objects of Industrial Property: Inventions, Industrial Designs, Marks*, WIPO/LIC/WL6/91/1

The relatively short period of protection may be related to the association of designs with more general styles of fashions, which tend to enjoy somewhat transient acceptance or success, particularly in highly fashion conscious areas, such as clothing or footwear.

E. RELATION TO COPYRIGHT

10.37 Objects qualifying for protection under the law of industrial designs might equally well receive protection from the law of copyright. Thus, industrial designs law has relations both with copyright law and with industrial property law. Suppose a particular design embodies elements or features which are protected both by the copyright law and the industrial design law, may a creator of an industrial design claim cumulatively or simultaneously the protection of both laws? The Model Law provides in Section 1, paragraph (2), that protection by this law does not exclude protection by another branch of law, especially the law of copyright. This means that protection may be cumulative. Cumulation of protection means that the design is protected simultaneously and concurrently by both laws in the sense that the creator can invoke the protection of either or both, the copyright law or the industrial design law, at his choice. It also means that if he has failed to obtain the protection of the industrial design law by failing to register his design, he can claim the protection of copyright law, which is available without compliance with any formality. Finally, it means that after the term of protection of the registered design expires, the creator may still have the protection of the copyright law.

10.38 But it is to be noted that cumulation must be distinguished from "co-existence". Co-existence of protection means that the creator may choose to be protected either by the industrial design law or by the copyright law. If he has chosen the one, he can no longer invoke the other. If he has registered the industrial design, at the expiration of such registration he can no longer claim protection under the copyright law, at least for the particular application of the industrial design.

10.39 The system of cumulation of protection by the industrial design law and the copyright law exists in France and the Federal Republic of Germany. And the system of co-existence of protection by both laws prevails in most other countries.

10.40 The difference between protection by the copyright law and protection by the industrial design law is as follows:

(1) under the industrial design law, protection is lost unless the industrial design is registered by the applicant before publication or public use anywhere, or at least in the country where protection is claimed. Copyright in most countries subsists without formalities. Registration is not necessary;

(2) industrial design protection endures generally for a short period of three, five, ten or fifteen years. Copyright endures in most countries for the life of the author and fifty years after his death;

(3) the right conferred by registration of an industrial design is an absolute right in the sense that there is infringement whether or not there has been deliberate copying. There is infringement even though the infringer acted

independently and without knowledge of the registered design. Under copyright law, there is infringement only in the reproduction of the work in which copyright subsists.

Infringement no matter known or unknown

v.

Infringement only when reproduced

References for Section E
T. Zongshun, "Industrial Designs," 10 *Intellectual Property in Asia and the Pacific*

CHAPTER 11

Geographical Indications

A. INTRODUCTION

11.1 "Champagne," "Cognac," "Roquefort," "Chianti," "Pilsen," "Porto," "Sheffield," "Havana," "Tequila," "Darjeeling"—some well-known examples for names which are associated throughout the world with products of a certain nature and quality. One common feature of all those names is their geographical connotation, that is to say, their function of designating existing places, towns, regions or countries. However, when we hear "Champagne" today, we rather think of sparkling wine than of a French region, "Cognac" we associate with *eau de vie* aged in oak barrels rather than with a small French town, "Chianti" makes us think of a red Italian wine rather than of a region in the south of Florence, "Pilsen" reminds us of beer but not of a town in the Czech Republic and "Tequila" of a liquor distilled from a cactus rather than of a town in Jalisco State, Mexico.

11.2 Those examples show that geographical indications can acquire high reputation and thus may be valuable commercial assets. For this very reason, they are often exposed to misappropriation, counterfeiting or forgery and their protection—national as well as international—is highly desirable.

11.3 With the exception of design law, there is probably no category of intellectual property law where there exists such a variety of concepts of protection as in the field of geographical indications. This is maybe best demonstrated by the term "geographical indication" itself, which is relatively new and appeared only recently in international negotiations.

11.4 The Paris Convention for the Protection of Industrial Property does not contain the notion of geographical indication. Article 1 paragraph (2) defines as subjects of industrial property, *inter alia*, indications of source and appellations of origin. This is the terminology traditionally applied and still officially used in the conventions and agreements administered by WIPO. According to this terminology, the following distinction is made between indications of source and appellations of origin: "indication of source" means any expression or sign used to indicate that a product or service originates in a country, a region or a specific place, whereas "appellation of origin" means the geographical name of a country, region or specific place which serves to designate a product originating therein the characteristic qualities of which are due exclusively or essentially to the geographical environment, including natural or human factors or both natural and human factors.

11.5 It is important to highlight the difference between indications of source and appellations of origin, namely the requirement that a product designated by an appellation of origin must have certain characteristic qualities which are due to the geographical environment, including human or natural factors. In other words, the use of an appellation of origin requires a quality link between the product and its area of production. This qualitative link consists of certain characteristics of the product which are exclusively or essentially attributable to its geographical origin such as, for example, climate, soil or traditional methods of production. On the other hand, the use of an indication of source on a given product is merely subject to the condition that this product originates from the place designated by the indication of source. Appellations of origin can be understood as a special kind of indication of source. According to the terminology traditionally applied, the term "indication of source" comprises all appellations of origin, but, in its general use, it has become rather a designation for those indications of source which are not considered to be appellations of origin.

11.6 The term "geographical indication" has been chosen by WIPO to describe the subject matter of a new treaty for the international protection of names and symbols which indicate a certain geographical origin of a given product. In this connection, the term is intended to be used in its widest possible meaning. It embraces all existing means of protection of such names and symbols, regardless whether they indicate that the qualities of a given product are due to its geographical origin (such as appellations of origin), or they merely indicate the place of origin of a product (such as indications of source). This definition also covers symbols, because geographical indications are not only constituted by names, such as the name of a town, a region or a country ("direct geographical indications"), but may also consist of symbols. Such symbols may be capable of indicating the origin of goods without literally naming its place of origin. Examples for such indirect geographical indications are the Eiffel Tower for Paris, the Matterhorn for Switzerland or the Tower Bridge for London.

11.7 On the other hand, the term "geographical indication" is also used in the EC Council Regulation No. 2081/92 of July 14, 1992, on the Protection of Geographical Indications and Designations of Origin for Agricultural Products and Foodstuffs and in the Agreement on TRIPS. In both texts, this term is applied to products whose quality and characteristics are attributable to their geographical origin, an approach that closely resembles the appellation of origin-kind of protection. In other words, "mere" indications of source are not covered by the specific notion of geographical indication used in those two legal texts. However, this presentation, in trying to take into account all existing forms of protection of geographical indications, uses the term in its widest meaning.

11.8 When considering geographical indications as a special kind of distinctive signs used in commerce and thus as a particular category of intellectual property, it is important to distinguish them from trademarks: whereas a trademark identifies the enterprise which offers certain products or services on the market, a geographical indication identifies a geographical area in which one or several enterprises are located which produce the kind of product for which the geographical indication is used. Thus, there is no "owner" of a geographical indication in the sense that one person or enterprise can exclude other persons or enterprises from the use of a geographical indication, but each and every enterprise which is located in the area to which the geographical indication refers has the right to use the said indication for the products originating in the said area. However, the right to apply a geographical indication to a product may well be subject to compliance with certain quality requirements such as prescribed, for example, in administrative decrees governing the use of appellations of origin.

11.9 Before looking at the various forms of protection of geographical indications, it seems to be useful to briefly explain what is meant by "protection" of geographical indications. First of all, protection means the right to prevent unauthorized persons from using geographical indications, either for products which do not originate from the geographical place indicated, or not complying with the prescribed quality standards. Furthermore, there is a second aspect related to the issue of protection, namely the question of protecting geographical indications against becoming generic expressions. Once a geographical indication has turned into a generic expression, it has lost all its distinctiveness and, consequently, will loose its protection. The question whether a geographical indication is a generic term and void of any protection is, in the absence of an international agreement, to be determined by national law. It might well be that a geographical name is regarded in one country as a geographical indication and is protected accordingly, whereas it is considered to be a generic or semi-generic term in another country. Notorious examples for such diverging treatment of geographical names are the French names "Champagne" and "Chablis" which, in France, are only allowed to be used for products originating from a certain geographical area and produced according to certain quality standards, whereas, in the United States of America for example, they are regarded as being semi-generic names, and therefore may be also used for wines not originating from the French area of production. This aspect of protection is especially important in the context of international protection of geographical indications and is dealt with, for example, by the Lisbon Agreement for the Protection of Appellations of Origin and their International Registration.

B.   PROTECTION OF GEOGRAPHICAL INDICATIONS
ON THE NATIONAL LEVEL

11.10 As regards the various forms of protection of geographical indications on the national level, three main categories can be distinguished. The first category comprises all possibilities of protection which are not based on a decision taken by the competent authority establishing protection with respect to a particular geographical indication, but which result from the direct application of legislative provisions or principles established by jurisprudence. The second category covers the protection of geographical indications through registration of collective marks (including agricultural labels) or certification marks (or guarantee marks). The third category includes all special titles of protection of geographical indications which result from a decision made by the competent government authority establishing the protection. This category, in particular, comprises the protection of appellations of origin—whether they result from a registration with the industrial property office, as under the new Russian law, or from the adoption of decrees, as is the practice in France since the adoption, in 1919, of a special law for the protection of appellations of origin. This category also comprises titles of protection established under the EC Council Regulations on wine (for example, "quality wines produced in specified regions" (EC Regulation 823/87 as amended by EC Council Regulation 2043/89) and "vins de pays" (EC Regulation 2393/89)) and under EC Council Regulation 2081/92 on the Protection of Geographical Indications and Designations of Origin for Agricultural Products and Foodstuffs.

(a) Special Titles of Protection

11.11 Already early in this century it was felt that the protection of indications of source against false or deceptive use was insufficient. In addition, the need for the protection and the encouragement of local, traditional methods of production emerged. It was in France where the first statute was enacted which provided for the protection of geographical indications through a special title of industrial property, namely appellations of origin.

11.12 The French Law of May 6, 1919, recognized the existence of appellations of origin and laid down conditions for their protection. According to this law, an appellation of origin consists of the name of a country, region or locality that serves to designate a product originating therein, the quality and characteristics of which are due to the geographical environment, including both natural and human factors. This means that only such products are protected under this special title which originate from a specific area and which owe their specific quality to their place of origin. In other words, a special link between the goods and their place of origin, i.e., natural and human factors which are to be found exclusively in the respective area, must be established. In order to ensure that the products possess the specified qualities, a control mechanism has been set up by the competent authorities, and quality controls are carried out regularly. Only products which comply with the quality standards are protected by an appellation of origin. Initially, appellations of origin only concerned wines and spirits, but later the concept of appellation of origin was extended to include other products (such as dairy products (mainly cheese and butter), poultry and plant products).

11.13 Because of the success of the French appellations of origin, the same or a similar system was introduced also in other countries, mainly in the sector of wines and spirits. It is recalled that appellations of origin—contrary to the impression given by the word "or" in Article 1(2) of the Paris Convention—are a special kind of indications of source. In other words, all appellations of origin are indications of source, but not all indications of source are appellations of origin.

(b) Registration of Collective Marks or Certification Marks

11.14 The protection of a given geographical indication may not only be based on a public or administrative act, but may also result from a private initiative. With regard to the latter approach, collective marks or certification marks provide a means for the protection of geographical indications independent from statutory or judicial measures. The concepts of collective mark and certification mark (or, in some countries, guarantee mark) differ from country to country. Depending on the applicable national law, a collective mark or certification mark may serve to indicate, *inter alia*, the origin of goods or services, and therefore may to some extent be suitable for the protection of a geographical indication.

11.15 A collective mark is a mark the use of which is only allowed to the members of a collective body. Such a body can be an association or cooperative of manufacturers, producers or traders. The collective mark is owned by the association which exclusively grants its members the right to use it. The association may be a domestic one or a foreign one. A collective mark indicates that the person who uses it for his goods or services is a member of the association which owns the collective mark. Normally, the use of the collective mark is governed by regulations which have to be submitted to the industrial property office together with the application for registration. The question whether a geographical indication is registrable as a collective mark depends entirely on a given national law. Some national trademark laws exclude the registration of geographical indications as collective marks, although, more recently, that exclusion has been abolished by some countries.

11.16 Once a geographical indication has been registered as collective mark, the association that owns it has the right to prohibit its use by persons who are not members of the association. However, in case of conflict with a senior right, the members of the association may be excluded from using the collective mark. Moreover, the registration of a geographical indication as collective mark may not, *per se*, prevent the mark from becoming a generic term. Furthermore, the law of some countries contain strict use requirements which may result in the cancellation of the registration of the collective mark in case it is not continuously used.

11.17 In contrast to collective marks, certification marks and guarantee marks are not owned by a collective body such as an association of producers, but by a certification authority. Such authority may be a local council or an association which is not engaged in the production or the trade of the products concerned. The latter is of particular importance because it is the owner of the certification mark who must ensure that the goods bearing the certification mark possess the certified qualities. A certification mark may be used to certify, *inter alia*, the origin of products or services. The application for the registration of a certification mark has to be accompanied by regulations which govern the use of the certification mark. Regarding the registrability of geographical indications as certification marks and guarantee marks, the same principles as for the registration of collective marks apply.

11.18 Where a geographical indication has been registered as a certification mark or guarantee mark, it may normally be used by everybody whose products comply with the requirements set out in the regulation. Such right to use, however, may not exist in case of conflict with a senior right. The institution which owns the registered certification mark or guarantee mark has the right to prohibit the use of that mark by persons whose products do not comply with the requirements set out in the regulations. In general, the protection of a geographical indication through registration as certification mark or guarantee mark is equivalent to that conferred by registration as a collective mark.

11.19 A special form of protected geographical indication resembling the concept of collective marks is the French "agricultural label" (in French "label agricole"). It is regulated by the Decree Relating to Agricultural Labels of June 1983 as last amended in 1990 and may be applied for in respect of agricultural products. An agricultural label is a collective mark that certifies that a foodstuff or a non-nutritious and non-transformed agricultural product (such as cereal seeds) possesses a combination of specific characteristics and a level of quality which is higher than that of similar products. An agricultural label can be a national label (known as "red label") or a regional label, the latter referring to characteristics which are specific, traditional or representative of a region. Products in respect of which an appellation of origin has been established and some categories of wines (even if not benefitting from an appellation of origin) may not be the subject of protection by way of an agricultural label. The agricultural label is registered in the name of the entity that controls its use. The application of the Decree is not limited to French products, but so far only little use has been made of the possibility of applying the Decree to foreign products (an example of a foreign product is the label for "Scottish salmon").

(c) The Law of Unfair Competition

11.20 The use of a certain geographical indication for goods or services not originating from the respective area may be misleading and thus may result in a deception of consumers. Furthermore, such use may constitute a misappropriation of the goodwill of the person who is truly entitled to use the geographical indication. An action for unfair competition—which, depending on the national law, is either based on statutory provisions, as interpreted by court decisions, or on common law—can be instituted in order to prevent competitors from resorting, in the course of trade, to such misleading practices.

11.21 Although the conditions for a successful action for unfair competition vary from country to country, the following basic principles appear to be generally recognized. In order to be protectable, a given geographical indication must have acquired a certain reputation or goodwill. In other words, the potential buyers of the product must associate the geographical indication with the place of origin of the goods or services. Such an action further requires that the use of the geographical indication on goods or services not originating from the respective geographical area is misleading, so that consumers are deceived as to the true place of origin of the products or services. Under some national laws, proof of damages or the likelihood of damages caused by such misleading practices is required.

11.22 Whereas the principle that misleading use of a geographical indication may give rise to an action for unfair competition is generally recognized, the outcome of such an action may be uncertain. In particular, the extent to which the geographical indication in question must have acquired a reputation may vary from country to country. It may be required that the geographical indication must have been used in the course of trade for a certain time and that an association between the geographical indication and the place of origin of the products and services must have been created amongst the relevant circles. Therefore, a geographical indication the reputation of which is not yet established on the market, may not be protectable against misleading use by competitors through an action for unfair competition. Furthermore, a geographical indication which has not been used for a certain time may loose its reputation and therefore may no longer be protectable by an action for unfair competition. Moreover, the availability of protection against acts of unfair competition does not prevent geographical indications from becoming generic terms. Geographical indications which become generic terms in a particular country lose their distinctive character and are no longer protectable in that country.

C. PROTECTION OF GEOGRAPHICAL INDICATIONS ON THE INTERNATIONAL LEVEL THROUGH MULTILATERAL TREATIES

11.23 Three multilateral treaties administered by WIPO contain provisions for the protection of geographical indications: the Paris Convention for the Protection of Industrial Property, the Madrid Agreement for the Repression of False or Deceptive Indications of Source on Goods of 1891, as last revised in 1967 (hereinafter referred to as the "Madrid Agreement"), and the Lisbon Agreement for the Protection of Appellations of Origin and their International Registration (hereinafter referred to as the Lisbon Agreement).

(a) The Paris Convention for the Protection of Industrial Property

11.24 Several provisions of the Paris Convention deal specifically with indications of source or appellations of origin: Article 1(2) contains a reference to "indications of source" and "appellations of origin" in the list of objects of industrial property; Article 10 deals with the protection of indications of source; Article 9 provides for certain sanctions which are applicable, *inter alia*, in cases of direct or indirect use of false indications of source; and Article 10*ter* reinforces the provisions of Articles 9 and 10.

11.25 *Article 1(2)* provides that the protection of industrial property has as its object, among others, "indications of source" or "appellations of origin." The obligation to protect indications of source is specifically provided for in Article 10, but there are no special provisions in the Paris Convention for the protection of appellations of origin. Nevertheless, Articles 9, 10 and 10*ter* are applicable to appellations of origin since each appellation of origin by definition constitutes an indication of source.

11.26 *Article 10(1)* is the basic provision of the Paris Convention on indications of source. It provides that the sanctions prescribed by Article 9 in respect of goods unlawfully bearing a trademark or trade name apply to any use of a "false indication of the source" of a product. This means that no indications of source may be used that refers to a geographical area from which the products in question do not originate. For the provision to be applicable, there is no need for the false indication to appear on the product, since any direct or indirect use, for example in advertising, is sanctionable. However, Article 10(1) does not apply to indications which, without being false, may mislead the public, or at least the public of a certain country (for example, where certain geographical areas in different countries have the same name but only one of those areas is internationally known for particular products, the use of that name in connection with products originating from another area may be misleading).

11.27 As regards the sanctions in the case of the use of a false indication of source, *Article 9* establishes the principle that seizure upon importation must be provided for, or at least prohibition of importation or seizure inside the country but, if those sanctions do not exist in a particular country, the actions and remedies available in such cases are to be applied.

11.28 Article 9(3) and Article 10(2) determine who may request seizure on importation or the imposition of other sanctions: the public prosecutor, any other competent authority, any interested party. *Article 10(2)* defines what is meant by "interested party," stipulating that "any producer, manufacturer, or merchant, whether a natural person or a legal entity, engaged in the production or manufacture of or trade in such goods and established either in the locality falsely indicated as the source, or in the region where such locality is situated, or in the country falsely indicated, or in the country where the false indication of source is used, shall in any case be deemed an interested party."

11.29 *Article 10bis* concerns the protection against unfair competition and as such provides a basis for protection against the use of confusing, false or misleading geographical indications. Article 10*bis* obliges countries, of the Paris Union to assure effective protection against unfair competition, sets a general definition of what constitutes an act of unfair competition and contains a non-exhaustive list of three types of acts which, in particular, must be prohibited.

11.30 *Article 10ter* is also relevant inasmuch as it obliges countries of the Union to provide, on the one hand, appropriate legal remedies and to permit, on the other, federations and associations representing interested industrialists, producers or traders to take action, under certain conditions, with a view to the repression of false indications of source.

11.31 The main advantage of the protection afforded by the Paris Convention to indications of source lies in the extent of the territorial area covered by the Paris Union, which on October 1, 1996, comprised 140 member States. On the other hand, the question of indications which, in countries other than the country of origin, are generic names of a product in other countries is not dealt with in the Paris Convention, so that member States of the Paris Union seem to be entirely free in that respect. Finally, sanctions, although specifically mentioned in the Paris Convention, are not in all cases mandatory and apply only to false but not to misleading indications of source.

(b) The Madrid Agreement for the Repression of False and Deceptive Indications of Source on Goods

11.32 The Madrid Agreement for the Repression of False and Deceptive Indications of Source on Goods is a special agreement within the framework of the Paris Union. The Agreement aims at the repression not only of false but also of deceptive indications of source.

11.33 Article 1(1) of the Madrid Agreement provides that any product bearing a false or deceptive indication by which one of the States party to the Madrid Agreement or a place situated therein is directly or indirectly indicated as being the country or place of origin must be seized on importation into any of the States party to the Madrid Agreement.

11.34 The other paragraphs of Articles 1 and 2 specify the cases and the manner in which seizure or similar measures may be requested and carried out. There is no express provision to the effect that private individuals may request seizure directly. Thus, member States are free to provide that such persons have to apply through the public prosecutor or any other competent authority.

11.35 Article 3 authorizes a vendor to indicate his name or address on goods coming from a country other than that in which the sale takes place, but obliges him, if he does so, to have his name or address accompanied by an exact indication in clear characters of the country or place of manufacture or production, or by some other indication sufficient to avoid any error as to the true source of the wares.

11.36 Article 3*bis* obliges the States party to the Madrid Agreement to prohibit the use, in connection with the sale or display or offering for sale of any goods, of all indications capable of deceiving the public as to the source of the goods.

11.37 Article 4 provides that the courts of each country have to decide what appellations, on account of their generic character, do not fall within the provisions of the Madrid Agreement. Only regional appellations concerning the source of products of the vine are excluded from the reservation inherent in the provision. The reservation substantially limits the scope of the Madrid Agreement, in spite of the important exception constituted by the case of regional appellations concerning the source of products of the vine, for which protection is absolute.

11.38 As of October 1, 1996, 31 States were party to the Madrid Agreement for the Repression of False and Deceptive Indications of Source on Goods: Algeria, Brazil, Bulgaria, Cuba, Czech Republic, Dominican Republic, Egypt, France, Germany, Hungary, Ireland, Israel, Italy, Japan, Lebanon, Liechtenstein, Monaco, Morocco, New Zealand, Poland, Portugal, San Marino, Slovakia, Spain, Sri Lanka, Sweden, Switzerland, Syria, Tunisia, Turkey and United Kingdom.

(c) The Lisbon Agreement for the Protection of Appellations of Origin and their International Registration

11.39 The limited geographical scope of the Lisbon Agreement for the Protection of Appellations of Origin and their International Registration is due to particular characteristics of the substantive provisions of the Agreement.

11.40 Article 2(1) contains a definition according to which appellation of origin means "the geographical name of a country, region or locality which serves to designate a product originating therein, the quality and characteristics of which are due exclusively or essentially to the geographical environment, including natural and human factors." It follows that only names conforming to the definition may be protected by virtue of the Lisbon Agreement. Simple indications of source (which can be used for products whose characteristics do not result from the geographical environment) are excluded from its purview. This limitation has prevented the accession of countries which do not know the concept of appellation of origin.

11.41 The first element of the definition is that the appellation must be the geographical name of a country, region or locality. The second element of the definition is that the appellation of origin must serve to designate a product originating in the country, region or locality referred to. The third element of the definition is that there must be a qualitative link between the product and the geographical area: the "quality and characteristics" must be due exclusively or essentially to the geographical environment; if the qualitative link is insufficient, that is, if the characteristic qualities are not due essentially, but only to a small extent, to the geographical environment, the name is not an appellation of origin but merely an indication of source; as for the geographical environment, it includes natural factors, such as soil or climate, and human factors, such as the special professional traditions of the producers established in the geographical area concerned.

11.42 Even if interpreted broadly, the definition of appellation of origin in Article 2(1) has a serious drawback for countries whose denominations typically do not apply to agricultural products or products of handicraft but to products of industry. The difficulty arises from the fact that Article 2(1) requires the existence of a qualitative link between the geographical environment and the product, even though the presence of purely human factors would be considered sufficient. This link, which may have existed at the start of the manufacture of an industrial product, may subsequently have been stretched to the point that its existence is difficult to prove. Moreover, traditions in manufacture and skilled staff can be shifted from one geographical area to another, in particular in view of the increasing mobility of human resources in all parts of the world.

11.43 Article 1(2) provides that the countries party to the Lisbon Agreement undertake to protect on their territories, in accordance with the terms of the Agreement, the appellations of origin of products of the other countries party to the Lisbon Agreement, recognized and protected as such in the country of origin and registered at the International Bureau of WIPO. Therefore, in order to be protected under the Lisbon Agreement, the appellation of origin must fulfill two conditions. The first condition is that the appellation of origin must be recognized and protected as such in the country of origin (the latter being defined in Article 2(2)). This condition means that it is not sufficient for the country in question to protect its appellations in a general way. Each appellation still has to benefit from distinct and express protection, deriving from a specific official act (a legislative or administrative provision, or a judicial decision, or a registration). Such an official act is required because the specific elements of the object of protection (the geographical area, the lawful users of the appellation of origin, the nature of the product) must be determined. Those elements must be indicated in the application for international registration in accordance with Rule 1 of the Regulations under the Lisbon Agreement.

11.44 The second condition laid down by Article 1(2) is that the appellation of origin must be registered with the International Bureau of WIPO. Article 5 and 7 of the Agreement itself and the Regulations set forth the procedure for international registration.

11.45 Article 2(2) defines the country of origin as being "the country whose name, or the country in which is situated the region or locality whose name, constitutes the appellation of origin which has given the product its reputation."

11.46 Article 5(1) and the corresponding provisions of the Regulations issued under the Lisbon Agreement define the procedure for international registration. International registration must be applied for by the competent Office of the country of origin, and therefore may not be requested by interested parties. The national Office, however, does not apply in its own name for international registration, but in that of "any natural persons or legal entities, public or private, having a right to use (*titulaire du droit d'user*)" the appellation, according to the applicable national legislation. The International Bureau of WIPO has no competence to examine the application with respect to substance; it may only make an examination as to form. Under Article 5(2) of the Lisbon Agreement, the International Bureau notifies the registration without delay to the Offices of the countries party to the Lisbon Agreement and publishes it in its periodical *Les Appellations d'origine* (Rule 7 of the Regulations). Up to January 1995, 730 appellations of origin have been so registered under the Lisbon Agreement, 717 of which were still in force on that date.

11.47 In accordance with Article 5(3) to (5), the Office of any State party to the Lisbon Agreement may, within a period of one year from the receipt of the notification of registration, declare that it cannot ensure the protection of a given appellation. Apart from the time limit mentioned, the right of refusal is subject to only one condition: the grounds for refusal must be indicated. The grounds which may be so indicated are not restricted by the Lisbon Agreement; this in fact gives each country the discretionary power to protect or refuse to protect a registered appellation of origin. In all countries not having made a declaration of refusal, the registered appellation enjoys protection. However, if third parties have been using the appellation in a given country prior to the notification of the registration, the Office of that country may, under Article 5(6) of the Lisbon Agreement, grant them a maximum of two years in which to terminate such use.

11.48 The protection conferred by international registration is unlimited in time. *Article 6* provides that an appellation which has been granted protection cannot be deemed to have become generic, as long as it is protected as an appellation of origin in the country of origin. Article 7 provides that the registration need not be renewed and is subject to payment of a single fee which, at present, is 500 Swiss francs. An international registration ceases to have effect only in two cases: either the registered appellation has become a generic name in the country of origin, or the international registration has been cancelled by the International Bureau at the request of the Office of the country of origin.

11.49 The content of the protection afforded to an appellation of origin registered under the Lisbon Agreement, according to Article 3 of the Agreement, is very extensive. Any usurpation or imitation of the appellation is prohibited, even if the true origin of the product is indicated or if the appellation is used in translated form or qualified by terms such as "kind," "type," "make," "imitation," or the like.

11.50 With regard to the enforcement of the protection of an appellation of origin registered under the Lisbon Agreement, Article 8 refers to national legislation. It specifies that the right to take action belongs to the competent Office and the public prosecutor, on one hand, and to any interested party, whether a natural person or a legal entity, whether public or private, on the other. In addition to any sanctions applicable pursuant to the Paris Convention and the Madrid Agreement (Article 4), all the sanctions provided for in national legislation, whether civil (injunctions restraining or prohibiting unlawful acts, actions for damages, etc.), penal or administrative, are to be applied. However, the Lisbon Agreement does not establish a standard with respect to the sanctions to be provided for by the States party to it.

11.51 On October 1, 1996, 17 countries were party to the Lisbon Agreement: Algeria, Bulgaria, Burkina Faso, Congo, Cuba, Czech Republic, France, Gabon, Haiti, Hungary, Israel, Italy, Mexico, Portugal, Slovakia, Togo and Tunisia.

D.   PROTECTION OF GEOGRAPHICAL INDICATIONS ON THE INTERNATIONAL LEVEL THROUGH THE PROVISIONS OF BILATERAL AGREEMENTS

11.52 A further possibility of international protection of geographical indications is the conclusion of bilateral agreements between two states. A number of countries have entered into such agreements, and the Agreement between Germany and France on the Protection of Indications of Source, Appellations of Origin and Other Geographical Denominations, of March 8, 1960 (see "Industrial Property" of September 1974, p. 373) can be cited as example. In general, such bilateral agreements consist of lists of geographical indications which were drawn up by the contracting parties and an undertaking to protect the geographical indications of the respective contracting party. The agreement usually also specifies the kind of protection that is to be granted. A number of countries have concluded agreements which follow the same pattern. Although in general useful, bilateral agreements cannot constitute an entirely sufficient solution to the problem of the lack of international protection because of the multiplicity of negotiations required and, resulting therefrom, an inevitable diversity of standards.

References for Section D
International Bureau of WIPO, *Protection and Registration of Geographical Indications (including Appellations of Origin) on the National and International Level; The Lisbon Agreement for the Protection of Appellations of Origin and their International Registration,* OMPI/ACAD/S/94/8 (Spanish only)

CHAPTER 12

Protection Against Unfair Competition

A. INTRODUCTION

12.1 Protection against unfair competition has been recognized as forming part of industrial property protection for almost a century. It was in 1900, at the Brussels Diplomatic Conference for the Revision of the Paris Convention for the Protection of Industrial Property (hereinafter referred to as "the Paris Convention"), that this recognition was first manifested by the insertion of Article 10*bis* in the Convention. In its original version, as adopted at the Brussels Diplomatic Conference, the Article read as follows: "Nationals of the Convention (Articles 2 and 3) shall enjoy, in all the States of the Union, the protection granted to nationals against unfair competition." As a result of the subsequent revision conferences, the Article now reads as follows (in the Stockholm Act (1967) of the Paris Convention):

"(1) The countries of the Union are bound to assure to nationals of such countries effective protection against unfair competition.
(2) Any act of competition contrary to honest practices in industrial or commercial matters constitutes an act of unfair competition.
(3) The following in particular shall be prohibited:
   1. all acts of such a nature as to create confusion by any means whatever with the establishment, the goods, or the industrial or commercial activities, of a competitor;
   2. false allegations in the course of trade of such a nature as to discredit the establishment, the goods, or the industrial or commercial activities, of a competitor;
   3. indications or allegations the use of which in the course of trade is liable to mislead the public as to the nature, the manufacturing process, the characteristics, the suitability for their purpose, or the quantity, of the goods."

12.2 At first glance, there seem to be basic differences between the protection of industrial property rights, such as patents, registered industrial designs, registered trademarks, etc., on the one hand, and protection against acts of unfair competition on the other. Whereas industrial property rights, such as patents, are granted on application by industrial property offices and confer exclusive rights with respect to the subject matter concerned, protection against unfair competition is based not on such grants of rights but on the consideration—either stated in legislative provisions or recognized as a general principle of law—that acts contrary to honest business practice are to be prohibited. Nevertheless, the link between the two kinds of protection is clear when certain cases of unfair competition are considered. For example, in many countries unauthorized use of a trademark that has not been registered is considered illegal on the basis of general principles that belong to the field of protection against unfair competition (in a number of

243

countries such unauthorized use is called "passing-off"). There is another example of this kind in the field of inventions: if an invention is not disclosed to the public and is considered to constitute a trade secret, the unauthorized performance by third parties of certain acts in relation to that trade secret may be illegal. Indeed the performance of certain acts in relation to an invention that has been disclosed to the public and is not patented or in respect of which the patent has expired, may under very special circumstances also be illegal (as an act of "slavish imitation").

12.3 The above examples show that protection against unfair competition effectively supplements the protection of industrial property rights, such as patents and registered trademarks, in cases where an invention or a sign is not protected by such a right. There are, of course, other cases of unfair competition, for example the case referred to in Article 10*bis*(3)2 of the Paris Convention, namely that of a false allegation in the course of trade of such a nature as to discredit a competitor, in which protection against unfair competition does not perform such a supplementary function. This is due to the fact that the notion of unfair competition covers a great variety of acts, as will be discussed in the analysis below.

B. THE NEED FOR PROTECTION

12.4 In the wake of recent political developments, a number of countries are currently in the process of adopting market economy systems, which allow free competition between industrial and commercial enterprises within certain limits defined by law. These developments are taking place not only in Central and Eastern European countries, but also in a number of developing countries. Free competition between enterprises is considered the best means of satisfying supply and demand in the economy and of serving the interests of consumers and the economy as a whole. However, where there is competition, acts of unfair competition are liable to occur. This phenomenon has been discernible in all countries and at all times, regardless of prevailing political or social systems.

12.5 Sometimes economic competition has been compared to competition in sport, because in both the best should win. In economic competition, that should be the enterprise providing the most useful and effective product or service on the most economical and (to the consumer) satisfying terms. This result can only be achieved, however, if all participants play according to a certain set of basic rules; and also as in sport, it may be tempting to disregard the rules. Violations of the basic rules of economic competition can take various forms, ranging from illegal but harmless acts (which can be committed by the most honest and careful entrepreneur) to malicious fouls, intended to harm competitors or mislead consumers. They may consist in a direct attack on an individual competitor or in a surreptitious deception of the "referee," who in economic competition typically is the consumer. Whatever form such violations may take, it is in the interest of

References for Section A
International Bureau of WIPO, *Protection Against Unfair Competition*, WIPO Pub. No. 725(E) (1994)

the honest entrepreneur, the consumer and the public at large that they should be prevented as early and as effectively as possible.

12.6 Experience has shown that there is little hope of fairness in competition being achieved solely by the free play of market forces. In theory consumers, in their role as referees of economic play, could deter dishonest entrepreneurs by disregarding their goods or services and favoring those of honest competitors. Reality, however, is different. As an economic situation becomes more complex, consumers become less able to act as referees. Often they are not even in a position to detect by themselves acts of unfair competition, let alone react accordingly. Indeed it is the consumer who—along with the honest competitor—has to be protected against unfair competition.

12.7 Self-regulation has sometimes been referred to as a remedy but it has not proved to be a sufficient safeguard against unfair competition. Without doubt, self-regulation by associations of enterprises can play an important role in ensuring honest business conduct: if self-regulation is well developed and generally observed, it can even be faster, less expensive and more efficient than any court system. Yet it stands or falls on continuing observance by all participants.

12.8 In order to prevent unfair competition effectively, self-regulation must, at least in certain areas, be supplemented by a system of legal enforcement. Only such a system can assure honest entrepreneurs that their chances of success will be determined by their own efforts, and assure consumers that they can make optimum buying choices, thus avoiding the waste of scarce resources, and ensuring improved market transparency and maximum economic welfare.

12.9 The rules on the prevention of unfair competition and those on the prevention of restrictive business practices (antitrust law) are interrelated: both aim at ensuring the efficient operation of a market economy. They do so in different ways, however: antitrust law is concerned with the preservation of the freedom of competition by combating restraints on trade and abuses of economic power, while unfair competition law is concerned with ensuring fairness in competition by forcing all participants to play according to the same rules. Yet both laws are equally important, although in different respects, and supplement each other. Countries setting up a system of market economy need an antitrust law, but one cannot rely on antitrust law alone to ensure fairness of competition as a side effect: that can be achieved only by distinct rules providing for protection against unfair competition.

12.10 Industrial property laws protecting inventions, industrial designs, marks, trade names, geographical indications, etc., are insufficiently comprehensive on their own to ensure honest practice in the marketplace. It is true that the protection of industrial property rights is in the interest not only of their owners, but also of consumers and of the public at large, and thus also serves the objective of ensuring fairness in competition. In particular, the unauthorized use of a trademark for a competing product not only constitutes undue exploitation of the trademark owner's goodwill, but also deceives the public as to the commercial origin of the product (and hence its characteristics). It can therefore be argued that trademark law is a specific part of the larger field of unfair competition law and that the enforcement of trademark protection serves to prevent acts of unfair competition, in particular, passing-off and dilution of distinctive quality or advertising value. The same is true, to a lesser extent, of other industrial property rights, such as patents, which protect inventors against undue exploitation of their efforts.

12.11 However, in spite of these common objectives, fair play in the marketplace cannot be ensured only by the protection of industrial property rights. A wide range of unfair acts, such as misleading advertising and the violation of trade secrets, are usually not dealt with by the specific laws on industrial property. Unfair competition law is therefore necessary either to supplement the laws on industrial property or to grant a type of protection that no such law can provide. In order to fulfill this function, unfair competition law must be flexible, and protection thereunder must be independent of any formality such as registration. In particular, unfair competition law must be able to adapt to all new forms of market behavior. Such flexibility does not necessarily entail a lack of predictability. Of course, unfair competition law can never be as specific as patent law or trademark law; yet experience in many countries has shown that it is possible to develop an efficient and flexible system of unfair competition law and at the same time to ensure sufficient predictability.

C. THE LEGAL BASIS FOR PROTECTION

(a) Development of Unfair Competition Law

12.12 All countries that have established market economy systems have devised some kind of safeguard against unfair business practices. In doing so, however, they have chosen quite different approaches. While in other areas of industrial property law, such as those dealing with patents, designs or marks, it is generally agreed that protection is best afforded by a specific, comprehensive statute, the legal basis for the repression of unfair competition can range from a succinct general tort provision to detailed regulation in a special statute. The reason for this diversity of approaches is often purely historical.

12.13 The concept of unfair competition law emerged first in France around 1850. Although at that time there was no specific prohibition of dishonest business practices, the French courts were able to develop a comprehensive and effective system of unfair competition law on the basis of the general provision contained in Article 1382 of the French Civil Code, according to which unlawful acts entail an obligation to pay damages. As far as the protection of competitors is concerned, the principles developed by court decisions on the basis of Article 1382 of the French Civil Code are still the main bases for relief against unfair competition in France. For the protection of consumers, a law on fraud in connection with products was enacted as early as 1905, and has since been complemented by numerous statutes and decrees, including the so-called "Loi Royer" of 1973, which prohibits misleading advertising, and the Consumer Information Laws of 1978 and 1989.

References for Section B
International Bureau of WIPO, *Protection Against Unfair Competition*, WIPO Pub. No. 725(E) (1994)

12.14 In Germany, the situation evolved differently. Since the courts refused to extend the tort provisions of the Civil Code to unfair business practices, it was necessary to enact specific legislation on the subject. Thus the "Law Against Unfair Competition" of 1909 became, and has remained, the main basis for the repression of acts of unfair competition. The Law contains two general provisions on dishonest and deceptive trade practices, around which special provisions, for example, on the protection of trade secrets, are grouped. Furthermore, it relies almost exclusively on private party complaints, granting capacity to sue to competitors, consumers and business organizations. The German courts, relying especially on the two general provisions contained in Articles 1 and 3 of the Law, have developed a comprehensive system for the repression of unfair trade practices, which aims at protecting not only competitors but also consumers and the public at large.

12.15 The law of the various jurisdictions that make up the United Kingdom (England, Scotland, Wales and Northern Ireland) has taken a different approach, based on common law and equity, and has not developed a separate legal regime for protection against unfair competition. A traditionally liberal approach makes for reluctance to enact general rules that allow subjective opinions to be held on what is "fair" or not. The tort of passing-off, which has been recognized since 1824, is regarded as sufficient protection for competitors. Consequently, civil remedies for competitors are still restricted to isolated cases under uncodified tort principles, in particular the protection against passing-off, claims of injurious falsehood or breach of confidence. On the other hand, provisions on consumer protection against misleading acts were already introduced in 1862 and have in the meantime been supplemented by an autonomous set of consumer protection statutes, such as the Trade Descriptions Act of 1968, the Fair Trading Act of 1973, the Unsolicited Goods and Services Acts of 1971 and 1975 and the Consumer Protection Act of 1987. In 1988, the Control of Misleading Advertisements Regulations were enacted pursuant to the EC Directive of 1984. Additionally, a number of self-disciplinary advertising codes are fully recognized.

12.16 As in the United Kingdom, unfair competition law in the United States of America developed from judicial decisions, especially from the common law tort of passing-off. And, again as in the United Kingdom, there was—and is—no comprehensive common law tort of unfair competition. However, limited statutory relief against false claims about one's own product in interstate commerce has been granted since 1946 under the trademark protection provision of Section 43(a) of the trademark law (Lanham Act). In 1988 that provision was extended to cover also false or misleading representations about another's product or service. In addition, a federal agency, the Federal Trade Commission (FTC), was created in 1914, which has broad jurisdiction to pursue any unfair or deceptive act or practice in or affecting interstate commerce. However, Section 5(a) of the FTC Act gives no right of action to injured competitors or consumers, whereas the statutes against unfair business practices which all States enacted in the latter half of this century (typically modelled on the FTC Act) often allow legal action to be brought by interested parties.

12.17 The above examples show how unfair competition law has developed differently in different countries. In the meantime many countries have passed special legislation on the subject or have replaced earlier laws on unfair competition. As regards recent legislative activity in this area, Switzerland adopted a Law Against Unfair Competition in 1986 which contains a broad general provision and a detailed regulation of specific market behavior, for example slavish imitation; Hungary adopted a Law on the Prohibition of Unfair Market Practice in 1990 which regulates unfair competition and antitrust law; Spain's Unfair Competition Law of 1991 contains a detailed regulation on practices harmful to consumers and competitors; and in 1991 Belgium adopted a Trade Practices and Consumer Protection Law which emphasizes the idea of consumer protection.

(b)   International Protection: Article 10*bis* of the Paris Convention for the Protection of Industrial Property

12.18 Article 1(2) of the Paris Convention mentions the repression of unfair competition along with patents, utility models, industrial designs, trademarks, trade names, indications of source and appellations of origin among the objects of industrial property protection, and Article 10*bis* contains an express provision on the repression of unfair competition. In the more than one hundred States party to the Paris Convention the legal basis for the protection against unfair competition may thus be found not only in national legislation but also at the international level.

12.19 Under Article 10*bis*(1) of the Paris Convention, the countries of the Paris Union are bound to ensure effective protection against unfair competition. Article 10*ter*(1) of the Convention further provides for the obligation to ensure "appropriate legal remedies." In particular, measures must be taken to permit federations and associations representing interested industrialists, producers or merchants to take action, provided that this is not contrary to the laws of the country concerned and does not exceed the rights normally granted to national associations.

12.20 Article 10*bis*(2) of the Paris Convention defines unfair competition as any act of competition contrary to honest practices in industrial or commercial matters. This definition leaves the determination of the notion of "commercial honesty" to the national courts and administrative authorities. Member States of the Paris Union are also free to grant protection against certain acts even if the parties involved are not competing against each other.

12.21 Article 10*bis*(3) of the Paris Convention gives three examples of cases that "in particular" have to be prohibited. These examples must not be seen as exhaustive, but rather as the minimum protection that has to be granted by all member States. The first two—creating confusion and discrediting—can be regarded as belonging to the "traditional" field of competition law, namely that of competitor protection. The third one—misleading—was added by the 1958 Revision Conference in Lisbon, and takes into account the interests of both competitors and consumers.

12.22 Apart from Articles 10*bis* and 10*ter*, the Paris Convention contains several provisions relevant to protection against acts of unfair competition in a broader sense, especially those concerning trademarks and trade names. For example, Articles 6*sexies* and 8 provide for the protection of service marks and trade names, respectively. The protection of indications of geographical origin, to the extent that it is not provided by Article 10*bis*(3), results from Article 10 and Article 9, to which Article 10 refers. Special agreements concluded within the Paris Convention, namely, the Madrid Agreement for the Repression of False or Deceptive Indications of Source on Goods and the Lisbon Agreement for the Protection of Appellations of Origin and their International Registration, along with bilateral treaties, specifically provide for the international protection of geographical indications.

(c) National Protection: Three Main Approaches to Unfair Competition Law

12.23 According to Article 10*bis*(1) of the Paris Convention, the member States of the Paris Union have to provide effective protection against unfair competition. Although they are not obliged to introduce special legislation for the purpose, they must provide—at least on the basis of existing general legislation—effective safeguards against all acts "contrary to honest trade practices" and specifically against the practices referred to in Article 10*bis*(3). In the implementation of these treaty obligations, three main approaches can be distinguished.

"Article 9

(1) All goods unlawfully bearing a trademark or trade name shall be seized on importation into those countries of the Union where such mark or trade name is entitled to legal protection.

(2) Seizure shall likewise be effected in the country where the unlawful affixation occurred or in the country into which the goods were imported.

(3) Seizure shall take place at the request of the public prosecutor, or any other competent authority, or any interested party, whether a natural person or a legal entity, in conformity with the domestic legislation of each country.

(4) The authorities shall not be bound to effect seizure of goods in transit.

(5) If the legislation of a country does not permit seizure on importation, seizure shall be replaced by prohibition of importation or by seizure inside the country.

(6) If the legislation of a country permits neither seizure on importation nor prohibition of importation nor seizure inside the country, then, until such time as the legislation is modified accordingly, these measures shall be replaced by the actions and remedies available in such cases to nationals under the law of such country.

Article 10

(1) The provisions of the preceding Article shall apply in cases of direct or indirect use of a false indication of the source of the goods or the identity of the producer, manufacturer, or merchant.

(2) Any producer, manufacturer, or merchant, whether a natural person or a legal entity, engaged in the production or manufacture of or trade in such goods and established either in the locality falsely indicated as the source, or in the region where such locality is situated, or in the country falsely indicated, or in the country where the false indication of source is used, shall in any case be deemed an interested party."

(i) Protection Based on Specific Legislation

12.24 Several countries have enacted special statutes or specific provisions within broader statutes, which, sometimes combined with provisions in general statutes such as the Civil Code, deal with protection against unfair competition. These statutes provide for civil or criminal sanctions and contain a broad general provision (often modelled on Article 10*bis*(2) of the Paris Convention) which is supplemented by detailed provisions on specific forms of unfair trade practice; they usually provide for civil sanctions and, in respect of specific cases, also for criminal sanctions. Although many of these countries have also enacted additional legislation concerning acts relating to certain products (food, drugs, etc.), the media (television) or marketing practices (gifts, bonuses), the statute against unfair competition remains the main basis for protection. Often the scope of that statute has been made even broader by the assumption that the violation of any other law can be an unfair trade practice because it gives an undue advantage in competition over the law-abiding competitor. In some countries the concept of a special law on competition has evolved towards the adoption of a more general law on market behavior, or the link with antitrust law is stressed by the enactment of statutes that deal with the institution of competition itself as well as with fairness in competition.

(ii) Protection Based on General Tort Law and/or on the Law Concerning "Passing-Off" and Trade Secrets

12.25 In a group of countries with a civil-law tradition, which follow the approach consisting in the protection of the honest businessman, such protection is usually to be found in the general tort law. In another group of countries which follow common law traditions, the actions for passing-off and for violation of trade secrets developed by the courts (at least originally) remain the main basis for the protection of competitors. As for the protection of consumers, a number of the same two groups of countries have, in addition, enacted separate sets of laws regulating specific cases of undesirable market behavior, such as misleading advertising, price comparisons, lotteries, games and bonuses; those laws are essentially independent of the protection of competitors under civil law or common law principles.

(iii) Combination of the Above Two Approaches

12.26 Most countries party to the Paris Convention—even those that at first attempted to regulate unfair competition by means of general tort law—provide for a combination of general civil code principles, case law and special laws. In many countries with a federal structure, the division of legislative competence between the federal legislature and the legislatures of the federated States has led to an even more complex combination of the various forms of protection. In some of those countries, the federal legislator even has no jurisdiction over unfair competition to the extent that it is considered a State common law tort. Where, in such countries, protection is granted by the States, it is in general better developed than that granted at the federal level. In the United States of America, in particular, the limited availability of common law remedies against unfair competition was first dealt with in federal law through the establishment of an administrative authority (the Federal Trade Commission), and more recently through the extension of a federal law provision on trademarks (Article 43(a) of the trademark law (Lanham Act)) to a wide variety of misleading representations. Yet the most progressive regulation is to be found in the "business laws," "little FTC Acts," "Consumer Protection Laws" and other legislation adopted by States within the United States of America.

(d) The Role of Jurisprudence

12.27 In spite of the different approaches mentioned above, all countries that have introduced effective safeguards against unfair competition take particular care over the enforcement of the law, and usually allow their courts considerable discretion. The success of an unfair competition law depends largely on what the courts make of it. A few words in a general tort provision may be a sufficient basis on which to develop an efficient system of unfair competition law, while a most impressively drafted statute may give disappointing results. This does not mean, however, that an explicit and detailed regulation of unfair trade practices is not useful: it will at least have some preventive effect on market behavior; but it will remain ineffectual if it is not activated by the courts. In the ever-changing world of competition, even the most perceptive legislator cannot possibly anticipate all future forms of unfair market behavior and must rely on interpretation of the law by the courts. Many countries have therefore supplemented their explicit provisions against certain market practices with a general provision, which allows the courts to include new forms of unfair market practice in the general system.

D. THE ACTS OF UNFAIR COMPETITION

(a) General Definition

12.28 According to Article 10bis(2) of the Paris Convention, unfair competition consists in "any act of competition contrary to honest practices." Most countries with special laws on unfair competition have adopted the same or similar definitions for their general provision—using such terms as "honest trade practices" (Belgium and Luxembourg), "the principle of good faith" (Spain and Switzerland), "professional correctness" (Italy) and "good morals" (Germany, Greece and Poland). In the absence of specific legislation, the courts have defined fair competition with phrases like "the principles of honesty and fair dealing" or "the morals of the marketplace" (United States of America).

12.29 It is true that describing unfair competition as acts contrary to "honest trade practices," "good faith" and so on does not make for clear-cut, universally accepted standards of behavior, since the meaning of the terms used is rather fluid. The standard of "fairness" or "honesty" in competition is no more than a reflection of the sociological, economic, moral and ethical concepts of a society, and may therefore differ from country to country (and sometimes even within a country). That standard is also liable to change with time. Furthermore, there are always new acts of unfair competition, since there is ostensibly no limit to inventiveness in the field of competition. Any attempt to encompass all existing and future acts of competition in one sweeping definition—which at the same time defines all prohibited behavior *and* is flexible enough to adapt to new market practices—has so far failed.

12.30 This does not mean, however, that unfair competition is incapable of any general definition, and that the best one can do is label concrete examples of market behavior as being unfair. On the contrary, there are some aspects that clearly indicate which practices are to be considered "fair" and which "unfair."

12.31 It has been generally recognized that certain acts of commercial behavior are always (or, as Article 10*bis*(3) of the Paris Convention puts it, "in particular") considered to constitute unfair competition. The most notable of those acts are the causing of confusion, discrediting and the use of misleading indications. The common aspect of these most important, but by no means exhaustive, examples of unfair market behavior is the attempt (by an entrepreneur) to succeed in competition without relying on his own achievements in terms of quality and price of his products and services, but rather by taking undue advantage of the work of another or by influencing consumer demand with false or misleading statements. Practices that involve such methods are therefore doubtful at the outset as to their fairness in competition.

12.32 Another reference point could be the subjective element in the unfair act. At first sight, the notion of "honesty" seems to refer to a moral standard, and some sort of legal/ethical standard is indeed involved. This, however, has to be distinguished from the question whether an act of unfair competition can be established in the absence of any fault, bad faith or negligence. Where unfair competition law has been developed on the basis of general tort provisions, the "tort of unfair competition" requires some kind of subjective element such as "fault" or "bad faith." In practice, however, the element of fault or bad faith is often assumed by the courts. Such subjective elements are therefore not essential to the notion of fairness in competition. Indeed, with certain exceptions, rather objective standards are applied for the purposes of establishing an act of unfair competition; of course, subjective conditions may be relevant for the purpose of determining the sanction applicable. Sometimes this objective approach to unfair competition law is expressly stated in the legislation, as in the Spanish law of 1991, which uses the expression "any act against good faith in an objective sense."

12.33 The most important factor for determining "unfairness" in the marketplace, however, is derived from the purpose of unfair competition law. In this respect, unfair competition law was initially designed to protect the honest businessman. In the meantime, consumer protection has been recognized as equally important. Moreover, some countries put special emphasis on the protection of the public at large, and especially its interest in the freedom of competition. Modern unfair competition law therefore serves a threefold purpose, namely: the protection of competitors, the protection of consumers and the safeguarding of competition in the interest of the public at large. As stated in the Swiss law of 1986 and the Spanish law of 1991, the purpose of unfair competition law is to ensure fair and undistorted competition in the interest of all concerned. In practice, this means that unfair competition has also to be defined functionally, taking into account particularly the interests of those "concerned" by it, namely the parties involved in the operation of the marketplace.

12.34 One party who is always "concerned" is the honest businessman. Since unfair competition law started as a special law for the protection of the honest businessman, a businessman's standard of behavior logically serves as a starting point. A practice that is condemned as improper by all businessmen can, therefore, hardly qualify as a "fair" act of competition.

12.35 On the other hand, certain practices may be generally accepted within a branch of business but nevertheless considered "improper" by other market participants. In such cases, there has to be some ethical correction of the actual standards of behavior. Ethical standards dictate in particular that the interests of consumers must not be unnecessarily impaired, for example, by disregard for the principle of truthfulness (on which the consumer relies in his transactions), by enticement of the consumer into unsocial or even harmful behavior or by invasion of his privacy.

12.36 Furthermore, there may be practices that at first sight are not prejudicial either to other businessmen or to consumers, but nevertheless may have unwanted effects on the economy at large. For example, selling at dumping prices may in the long run destroy small and medium-sized businesses, and thus have adverse effects on free competition. Where these economic aspects are incorporated in unfair competition law, such behavior will often be expressly labelled as "unfair."

12.37 When determining "honesty" in business dealings, all these factors have to be taken into account. In practice, the concept of unfair competition has increasingly become a balancing of interests. Differences in the evaluation of what is "fair" or "unfair" can generally be explained by the different emphasis placed on the aspects referred to above. For example, a particular kind of market behavior may well be seen differently in countries where the traditional law of unfair competition still focuses on the protection of the honest competitor, as opposed to countries that put special emphasis on the protection of consumers or the public at large.

12.38 On the other hand, there is broad agreement that at least some acts and practices are always irreconcilable with the notion of fairness in competition. These are discussed in detail below.

(b) Categories of Acts of Unfair Competition

12.39 Acts of unfair competition may be categorized in a variety of ways, depending on the criteria applied or the emphasis given to certain aspects of a given act or form of behavior. An act which is found to be "unfair" will often have taken place in circumstances which are complex, and which require scrutiny and judgment on the basis of established or prevailing standards. An act may be found to be unfair on more than one count, depending on the approach adopted to characterize the act. Therefore, one and the same act may fall into two or more categories. Likewise, no systematic categorization or classification of the acts of unfair competition can avoid some degree of overlap among the concepts and categories used.

12.40 For the purposes of establishing categories of acts of unfair competition and facilitating their analysis in this study, two broad groups of acts of unfair competition are distinguished, namely acts of the types expressly mentioned in Article 10*bis* of the Paris Convention and acts not expressly mentioned in Article 10*bis*.

12.41 Article 10*bis*(3) contains a non-exhaustive list of three types of acts of unfair competition, namely, acts likely to cause confusion, acts that discredit a competitor, and acts that may mislead the public. Because the acts that are likely to cause confusion and those that may mislead the public are akin to one another and sometimes overlap, they are dealt with before the act of discrediting a competitor.

12.42 There are a number of acts not mentioned in Article 10*bis* which have been recognized by the courts as unfair practices and which, increasingly, have become the subject of legislative provisions.   Of particular interest in this connection is the trend towards explicit protection of trade secrets by express provisions in unfair competition laws, and the continuing evolution of provisions governing the practice of comparative advertising. Moreover, there has been an increasing recognition of the need to grant protection against undue "misappropriation" of, or "free riding" on, the achievements of competitors, regardless of the availability of specific industrial property rights, provided that, under the circumstances of the case, such acts are found to be unfair.

(c) Causing Confusion

(i) General Circumstances under which Confusion is Established

12.43 Article 10*bis*(3)1 of the Paris Convention obliges member States to prohibit all acts that are of such a nature as to create confusion, by any means, with the establishment, the goods or the industrial or commercial activities of a competitor. The scope of Article 10*bis*(3)1 is very broad, as it covers any act in the course of trade involving a mark, sign, label, slogan, packaging, shape or color of goods, or any other distinctive indication used by a businessman.   Thus not only indications used to distinguish goods, services or businesses but also the appearance of goods and the presentation of services are considered relevant for the prohibition of confusion. For example, Article 2598(1) of the Italian Civil Code expressly provides that anyone who uses names or distinctive signs likely to cause confusion with those of another person, or slavishly imitates the product of a competitor, or by whatever other means creates confusion with the names, signs, products or activities of competitors, commits an act of unfair competition. Similarly, under Article 6 of the Spanish Law on Unfair Competition, any acts that are capable of creating confusion with the activities, achievements or business of another, including the likelihood of association by consumers with respect to the commercial source, is deemed unfair.   In the countries with a common law tradition, the concept of "passing-off" is broad enough to provide all types of indication, product and other subject matter with protection against confusion.

12.44 Under Article 10*bis*(3)1 of the Paris Convention, the "intent" to confuse is immaterial for the purposes of determining whether such an act constitutes an act of unfair competition. However, bad faith on the part of the imitator may have a bearing on the sanctions to be applied. Also, it is not usually necessary for confusion actually to have occurred, as the likelihood of confusion is often sufficient for an action based on unfair competition. Finally, protection against confusion is provided without any limitation in time. Protection is available as long as confusion is likely, but sufficient latitude is allowed for the use of non-confusing indications in respect of products, services and businesses, so that competition in the relevant market is not stifled. However, as soon as the marketable creation becomes generic or commonplace, it loses its original or distinctive character, and likelihood of confusion may no longer be assumed to the same degree.

12.45 There are two main areas in which confusion frequently occurs. These are indications of commercial origin on the one hand, and the appearance of goods on the other. However, this does not preclude or limit the protection of other attributes or achievements against confusion.

(ii) Types of Confusion

12.46 Confusion can be established in different ways. The test for the basic type of confusion is whether the similar mark so resembles the protected mark that it is liable to confuse a substantial number of average consumers as to the commercial source of the goods or services. Factors frequently considered in determining confusion are the degree of distinctiveness of the protected mark, the size and reputation of its owner, the sophistication of the consumers concerned and, of course, the similarity of the marks and the goods or services involved. In many countries, confusion is not restricted to basic confusion as to the commercial source, but also includes that which gives the impression of a strong business connection between the two users of the same trademark or similar trademarks, i.e., confusion as to affiliation. However, the use of an identical or similar mark on clearly unrelated or completely different goods usually falls outside the scope of protection, as a large degree of dissimilarity of the goods or services involved will lead consumers to assume that the source of the goods or services is not the same and also that there is no particular business connection between the users.

12.47 A third form of confusion that has been referred to, for example, under Section 43(a) of the Lanham Act of the United States of America and under Section 53 of the Australian Trade Practices Act, is called confusion as to sponsorship. Under this test for confusion, consumers will assume both that the goods or services do not originate from the same source and that the two enterprises do not entertain business relations so intensive and continuous as to cause confusion as to affiliation. Nevertheless, the consumer will expect, from the similarity of the marks, from the types of product or service that the mark is used for and from the manner of use by the second user, that the use of the protected mark by the second user has been authorized by agreement for a certain period of time. This type of confusion can be relevant, for example, in cases where the third party uses the mark (without authorization) for ornamental purposes on goods. However, unlike confusion as to source or affiliation, this third type of confusion has not the same status as other fully established grounds for relief under statutory trademark laws, as its exact boundaries are still developing.

12.48 This concept of confusion may be relevant to so-called "publicity" rights, relating to well-known artists and media or sports personalities, and to "merchandising" rights, relating to fictional characters in literary or artistic works. These rights concern relatively new marketing techniques whereby enterprises are "licensed," for a certain period of time, to make use of the popularity or fame symbolized by the names or likenesses of certain personalities or characters, as this use is expected to stimulate consumer demand for the product or service of the "licensee." Consumers would generally be misled by the use of the name or likeness of the personality or character in connection with the product or service into believing that the personality or the owner of rights in the character, which could also be a registered mark, had expressly authorized the use of their personality or character.

(iii) Confusion with Respect to Indications

12.49 An indication can be any sign, symbol or device that conveys to the consumer the message that a product or service on the market comes from a particular commercial source, even if this source is not known by its name. Indications may therefore consist of two-dimensional or three-dimensional signs, labels, slogans, packaging, colors or tunes, but are not limited to these. Protection against confusion with respect to indications is already available under specific legislation on trademarks, service marks and trade names. However, this protection is often limited in several ways. The limitations may concern the applicability of the specific law to certain types of indication, or the exact scope of protection. Thus protection against confusion under unfair competition law may still be relevant where the specific legislation does not afford overall protection against confusion. This aspect is also relevant to the protection of well-known marks against confusion, as required by Article 6bis of the Paris Convention.

12.50 The general applicability of trademark law is usually confined to particular indications. Some countries do not, for example, recognize titles of single literary works or films, get-up (product appearances), shop interiors, colors or color combinations, or trade dress under statutory trademark law. As regards service marks, although most countries have a system for the registration of such marks in the same way as trademarks, in those that do not, protection under the rules of prevention of unfair competition is needed. Also, even in countries where three-dimensional trademarks are recognized and registrable, particular shapes may nevertheless be excluded. For example, shapes determined solely by the nature of the goods, appearances resulting from some technical or industrial function of the goods and product configurations determining the essential value of the goods are expressly excluded by the EC Directive to Approximate the Laws Relating to Trade Marks. The "functionality" doctrine, particularly developed in the United States of America, produces similar results.

12.51 Apart from this, protection under trademark law can sometimes be invoked only for marks that have been properly registered in the country where protection is sought. In this respect Article 6bis of the Paris Convention constitutes an exception in favor of a well-known mark, which does not need to be registered in order to be protected against the potentially confusing use of a mark that is a reproduction or an imitation of the well-known mark and is used for identical or similar articles. It is to be noted that a trademark may be well known in a country before it is registered or even used in that country, as a result of the advertising or reputation of the mark in other countries.

12.52 Unfair competition law may provide protection against confusion for indications or signs that are not protectable under trademark law. However, the availability of protection for a sign under unfair competition law will depend partly on the reasons for the lack of protection for unregistered signs under the special laws. If a sign can in principle be covered by the specific legislation but does not meet the substantive requirements of that legislation, it would not seem consistent with a balanced system of protection to grant that sign the same protection under unfair competition law as would be granted to it under the special law. It is therefore argued that protection against confusion should only be available under unfair competition law if the indication or sign to be protected has sufficient distinctiveness to distinguish the products, services or other business activities concerned from the same or similar activities of other traders. Nevertheless, in order to promote the registration of marks, some unfair competition laws require more than just a minimum degree of distinctiveness for the protection of unregistered indications. For example, Article 2(1) of the Unfair Competition Prevention Law of the Republic of Korea requires the indication to be "widely known," which could in some cases restrict actual protection to one particular region.

12.53 The degree of distinctiveness of an indication that is not protected under statutory trademark law is assessed in relation to the same factors as apply to registered marks, including the meaning and the appearance of the indication, and its uniqueness compared with other indications for the same or a similar activity. Even if distinctiveness is inherently lacking, for example, owing to the descriptive nature of the indication for particular goods or services, the indication can be protected if it has acquired "distinctiveness by use," or secondary meaning, in the country where protection is sought. Secondary meaning implies that, as a result of continuous and exclusive use of the mark on the market, a substantial number of consumers have become aware of it and will associate the activity carried on under it with a particular commercial source. In Germany, for example, the trademark "4711" for perfume has been considered sufficiently distinctive as a result of public awareness that the goods under that mark come from a particular source. In fact the degree of secondary meaning depends on the market for the goods or services involved and the degree of descriptiveness of the indication in relation to those goods or services. The degree of secondary meaning (or percentage of consumers) necessary to achieve sufficient distinctiveness varies according to the practices of the court concerned. In some countries, opinion polls or market surveys on consumer reactions often provide empirical data with which to determine the degree of secondary meaning, whereas in other countries the courts themselves will judge whether an indication has acquired sufficient distinctiveness.

12.54 Secondary meaning analysis also applies to indications that have been expressly excluded from statutory trademark protection. For example, the configurations or shapes of goods that are deemed to be excluded from statutory protection under trademark law by the EC Directive to Approximate Laws Relating to Trade Marks may still acquire secondary meaning among consumers in a particular market. Under those circumstances, protection against confusion is justified if consumers could be led to believe mistakenly that other goods using the configuration come from the first user. It may not always be easy, however, to establish the necessary degree of secondary meaning, since the particular configuration of the goods must be recognized by the relevant consumers as indicating a particular source. If the exclusion in the specific legislation is clearly intended to dismiss the indication as not worth protecting at all, for example, in the case of purely descriptive words, protection is likely to be denied also under unfair competition law.

12.55 Limitations on the scope of protection afforded by trademark law may also have the effect of allowing indications to be protected against confusion under unfair competition law. Although trademark laws usually grant protection against any potentially confusing use of a registered trademark, there may still be differences with respect to the exact scope of the protection against confusion. For example, protection against the use of the same or a similar mark might be restricted to those goods or services for which the mark is registered. If a mark identical or similar to the registered trademark is used for other goods or services and that use is likely to cause confusion, such protection might only be available under unfair competition law or passing-off principles. Generally, trademarks are protected against the use of identical or similar signs not only in respect of identical goods or services but also in respect of similar goods or services. This type of protection derives from what is sometimes called the "principle of speciality," as the protection is related to the trademark's primary function of distinguishing the goods of one enterprise from those of competitors and other market participants. Thus if trademark protection is not available because the goods or services involved are held to be dissimilar (although confusion as to source may in fact be possible), protection against confusion can be sought under unfair competition law. However, there are also trademark laws that consider the likelihood of confusion to be the sole criterion for protection, regarding the similarity of the goods or services involved as not decisive in itself, but only as one of several determining factors. This kind of statutory protection would encompass all types of confusion.

12.56 The criteria used to judge the similarity of indications are, with some minor differences, the same throughout the world. The determining factors include the common elements of appearance, pronunciation and meaning or verbal translation of the marks involved, but the decisive factor is the overall impression on the average consumer of the goods or services involved. Particularly if the goods are for mass consumption, the individual elements of the marks involved are less carefully examined by the average consumer. Since the two marks are as a rule not closely examined side by side, in practice the similarities between the indications are more important than the differences. The similarity of the goods or services depends largely on the question whether consumers would generally expect the goods or services to originate from the same source. However, they do not need to be either functionally interchangeable or competitive.

12.57 Protection against confusion may be too limited for so-called "well-known" marks and, in particular, for marks with an even higher reputation. Article 6*bis* of the Paris Convention requires member States to protect trademarks that are well known in their country against any potentially confusing use of similar trademarks, but that obligation is only relevant for identical or similar goods. In certain cases, the unauthorized use of well-known marks for different goods or services may nevertheless cause confusion among consumers. For example, if the mark has been used for a broad range of products and has been extensively advertised or is well known for the particular "image" of its proprietor, consumers might associate such a mark with a certain origin and quality consistency rather than with goods or services of a specific kind. Such associations can also cause confusion. The member States are not obliged under Article 6*bis* to grant this extended protection, but unfair competition law may be relevant. The question whether a trademark is "well known" in a given country for the purposes of Article 6*bis* of the Paris Convention has to be decided in each case on the basis of the facts. Usually, the factual determination of the notoriety of a trademark is based on its reputation and image in the mind of the trade circles and consumer groups concerned at the place and time relevant in the particular case. Factors such as the mark's inherent distinguishing power, the length of time that it has been used in the given country, the amount of advertising and other publicity given to it in various media and its established association with particular goods or services are often taken into consideration.

12.58 Statutory trademark law frequently requires that the use of a similar mark must be a form of trademark use, that is, use as an indication of the commercial source of the products or services. Thus ornamental use, such as use on advertising material or as a mere decoration on goods, for instance on ballpoint pens or ashtrays, or even as the configuration of an actual product such as an earring in the shape of the mark, is not always regarded as falling within the scope of statutory trademark protection. Protection against this type of use could, however, be sought under unfair competition law. One example of a trademark law that is very extensive in the above respects is the Uniform Benelux Trademark Law of 1971, which provides a broad definition of registrable marks and protection against any use of an identical or similar trademark by others without proper justification that is likely to cause prejudice to the trademark proprietor.

12.59 Similar limitations on protection against the unauthorized use of traders' or businesses' indications are to be found in the protection of trade names. Trade names serve to identify and to distinguish an enterprise and its business activities from those of other enterprises. Article 8 of the Paris Convention imposes the obligation to protect trade names in all countries of the Paris Union, without specifying what kind of protection should be granted or how it should be given. Nevertheless, trade names must be protected without any obligation of filing or registration. Most countries already protect trade names against the risk of confusion. This protection applies not only where trade names are covered by a special law, but also where they are protected under special provisions of unfair competition law, civil law, company law or commercial law. As a general rule, a direct competitive relationship between the enterprises concerned is not decisive, but remains relevant in determining whether the use of the same or similar trade names might confuse consumers regarding the identity of enterprises or the relationship between them. The protection may extend beyond the particular field in which the prior trade name is used, as trade practice or the likelihood of expansion and diversification of the activities of the enterprise is frequently taken into account by the courts. Thus the scope of protection of trade names against confusion may sometimes be a little wider than the scope of protection of trademarks under trademark law.

(iv) Confusion with Respect to Product Shapes

12.60 The actual shape of a product could also lead to confusion among consumers. If the shape is so well known that consumers will relate the product with a particular commercial source (as in the case of the "Coca-Cola" bottle), then the shape can be regarded as a protectable indication.

12.61 It must also be noted that specific legislation is available in many countries for the protection of industrial designs, either to complement or to replace copyright protection for works of so-called "applied art." Such legislation usually prohibits the use of identical or similar product appearances for identical or similar goods. However, as with trademark legislation, protection under special laws on industrial designs is also limited in several ways, which vary significantly from country to country. In a manner similar to the specific protection under trademark laws, such limitations may concern the general applicability of the designs law to certain product appearances and also the exact scope of the protection granted by the specific legislation. For example, if the design protection of a surface decoration is limited to the use of the decoration on products for which the design is registered, protection against copying of the design for the decoration of other products may be obtained under unfair competition law, if the copied design is misleading or causes confusion as to the commercial source.

12.62 For protection against confusion concerning the products only, most requirements under unfair competition law are established by case law, frequently with reference to the practice of "slavish imitation." Within this particular field of unfair competition law, it has often been stated that, as a principle inherent in the free market system, market participants are free to imitate designs or other shapes, appearances or visual characteristics of products that are not protected by specific laws such as patent, copyright, design or possibly trademark laws. Some of those specific laws even expressly preclude protection under unfair competition law for acts that are covered by the specific legislation if the design involved could be protected under that legislation. For example, Article 14(5) of the Uniform Benelux Designs Law of 1975 precludes actions to protect registrable designs under unfair competition law if protection could have been granted had the design been properly registered. Therefore, the mere risk of confusion as to the shape of the products will be insufficient to constitute unfair competition if the design would have been protectable under a specific law and product imitation would have been covered by that specific legislation. On the other hand, the risk of confusion as to the products may be sufficient to obtain protection under unfair competition if the design involved reveals a certain degree of originality but cannot be registered as a design owing to other requirements of the specific legislation, or if registration has been applied for but not yet secured.

12.63 If the design, shape or other characteristic non-functional features of the product are associated to a substantial degree by consumers with a certain source or origin, potential confusion as to the source of the product will usually constitute an act of unfair competition. Whether such potential confusion occurs in cases of imitation will be determined by the same factors as outlined above with respect to indications, that is, after examination of the question whether the characteristic features of a product have acquired a sufficient degree of secondary meaning, and the product designs involved will be judged on their similarities. In some countries it is accepted that the risk of confusion as to source can be reduced by the use of disclaimers, like a clearly visible statement ruling out the possible assumption that the product or service comes from a particular source. However, such disclaimers are only seldom recognized as sufficiently reducing the risk of confusion.

12.64 Protection against confusion as to the commercial source of a product may also be available under specific trademark law if the applicable trademark legislation provides for the protection of three-dimensional marks or the "get-up" of products. However, if the product's appearance is not registered as a trademark, or if particular forms are possibly excluded from statutory trademark protection, the same principles as outlined above will apply to the protection against confusion between product shapes under unfair competition law.

(d) Misleading

(i) General

12.65 Misleading can roughly be defined as creating a false impression of a competitor's own products or services. It may well be the single most prevalent form of unfair competition, and it is by no means harmless. On the contrary, misleading can have quite serious consequences: the consumer, relying on incorrect information, may suffer financial (or more harmful) prejudice. The honest competitor loses clients. The transparency of the market diminishes, with adverse consequences for the economy as a whole and economic welfare.

12.66 Since truthfulness is rightly considered to be one of the main principles of honest trade practice, it is generally agreed that the prohibition of deception is essential to the concept of fairness in competition. Or, as Article 10*bis*(3) of the Paris Convention states, any indication or allegation that is likely to mislead, has "in particular" to be regarded as being contrary to honest practice.

12.67 Consequently, most member States of the Paris Union have included the prohibition of misleading acts or practices in their legal systems (or have even passed specific laws on the subject). In addition, the courts have developed a particularly abundant case law on misleading. Even in countries where in the past protection against deception has been less strong than in others, recent developments indicate a move towards greater strictness. In the search for effective legal solutions, however, countries have chosen quite divergent methods. A significant factor of this divergence is that misleading acts are primarily directed to the consumer and not directly to competitors. Where consumer protection is primarily looked upon as a matter of criminal law, enforcement is left to the State enforcement authorities. However, most of the countries that have specific legislation on unfair competition have included a provision against deception into the relevant laws, thus adopting a civil law approach.

12.68 While, on the whole, the regulation of misleading makes a many-faceted picture, most countries share the distinction between "normal" misleading, which may be done in good faith, and special cases of misleading, which may have particularly severe consequences. For the most serious cases of misleading, such as malicious misleading or deception in the health and drug field, several countries have introduced criminal sanctions in addition to civil law remedies. Moreover, special cases of potential deception such as bonuses, gifts, clearance sales and travelling sales are often regulated in detail. Even tighter restrictions are frequently imposed by self-regulatory institutions, which in some countries have reached a particularly advanced state of development as regards protection against misleading.

12.69 In some countries the existing protection against misleading practices is to some extent a result of international harmonization. Because of the internationalization of commerce and communication media such as television, misleading acts and practices, especially in advertising, seldom stop at the border of a given country. Different national laws not only result in different and thus at least to some extent inadequate levels of consumer protection, but also affect the free circulation of goods and services. Countries that are economically bound in a common market have a particular need for harmonization of diverging national laws on misleading. Thus the European Community issued a Directive on Misleading Advertising in 1984 in order to set up a minimum objective criterion for determining whether advertising is misleading. A certain degree of harmonization has also been reached among the Nordic and the African countries.

(ii)   The Concept of Misleading

12.70 There is a consensus according to which the concept of misleading is restricted neither to inherently false statements nor to statements that have actually led to a false impression on the part of the consumer. Instead it is considered sufficient (as it is by Article 10*bis*(3)3 of the Paris Convention) that the indications in question are likely to have a misleading effect. Even statements that are literally correct can be deceptive. If, for example, chemical ingredients are generally forbidden in bread, the courts of most countries would consider an advertising claim that a certain bread "was without chemical ingredients" to be deceptive, because, though literally true, it gives the misleading impression that the advertised fact is something out of the ordinary.

12.71 It is likewise not necessary for the product in question to be inferior, in an objective sense, so long as the indication or allegation has some enticing effect on the consumer. For example, if the public prefers domestic goods to foreign goods, a false declaration to the effect that imported goods are domestic is misleading even if the imported goods are of superior quality.

12.72 It is generally agreed that the question whether or not there is deception must be determined by the reaction of the addressee to the statement and not by the intention of its maker. However, the actual determination and evaluation of this reaction may differ from country to country and may also depend on the kind of addressee (consumers or traders) and the type of goods or services. The Paris Convention leaves this question to member States (as does the EC Directive on Misleading Advertising). The different opinions as to what standards have to be applied are the result of different answers to the following questions:

(1) Is the prohibition of misleading meant to protect the average or (also) the less educated, less critical consumer?
(2) How is the public reaction determined?   Empirically or by an overall estimation by the judge himself?
(3) How many of the addressees must be likely to be misled for a statement to be considered misleading?

12.73 In a number of countries the relevant standards are set on the basis of the notion of the average consumer. Where the courts base their assessments on the judges' own experience, there is a tendency to assume that the average consumer is generally well informed and intelligent enough to be immunized against most of the dangers of deception. In those countries the threshold is also considerably higher. Although it is frequently stressed that it is sufficient if a "not unsubstantial proportion of the addressees" are likely to be misled, the tendency is to favor an average deception rate.

12.74 However, in Germany the emphasis is clearly on the less educated, less critically prepared consumer, who is easily influenced by false statements. Misleading is frequently proven by empirical methods, mainly consumer surveys, and the interference threshold is set very low, at 10 to 15 percent of the consumers.

(iii)   The Communication of Misleading Statements

12.75 Since the main area of misleading in commerce is to be found in advertising, most countries with special legislation have focused on misleading advertising. Other countries have chosen, as Article 10*bis*(3) of the Paris Convention has, the broader notion of "indication or allegation." In countries that have a general provision on unfair competition this difference is minimal, however, since there is basic agreement that deceptions other than those in advertising are irreconcilable with "honest trade practice" and can therefore be judged under the general provision.

12.76 It is further agreed that the exact way in which the allegation, indication or presentation is made is immaterial. So is the form of the message. All methods of communication—written, oral or even symbolic—have to be taken into account. Communications may be in the form of trademarks, labels, brochures, radio commercials, television publicity spots, posters and so on. In general, misleading is concerned only with the effect a statement has on the addressee and not with the way in which the statement is communicated.

12.77 The communication need not contain "information" in a neutral, objective sense in order to be considered under the heading of misleading practices. On the other hand, the concept of misleading is restricted to those indications that might cause misconceptions on the part of the consumer. The allegation, indication or presentation must therefore be able to create some sort of concrete impression which can be shown to be true or untrue. "Unobjective" or suggestive advertising which does no more than create vague positive feelings about a product is therefore outside the scope of misleading. If in some countries certain kinds of suggestion are forbidden, this is not done under the provisions on misleading, but rather under the general provision concerning honest trade practices.

12.78 A misleading communication does not necessarily have to be a positive one: a half-truth is always also a half-lie. For example, if it is claimed that a particular slice of bread has fewer calories than others, while this is solely due to the fact that it is thinner, the omission of this information can create as strong an incorrect impression as an express statement would have done. Consequently, some countries have expressly mentioned the omission of relevant facts in their lists of misleading practices, or alternatively the courts have recognized that such omission can be a misleading practice. An omission cannot always be equated with a positive statement, however. Since no businessman has the general duty to reveal adverse features of the product that he is offering, there can only be deception if the public, in the absence of express information, expects a certain characteristic to be present.

(iv) Exaggerations

12.79 The consequences of the different concepts of misleading can best be seen in the treatment of exaggerations. Although in all countries obvious exaggerations (even if literally inaccurate) are not considered deceptive because they can easily be recognized as "sales talk," the question of what is mere "hot air" or "puffing" and what is to be taken seriously is answered differently in different countries. In some countries (such as Germany), it is assumed that the public basically believes all advertising statements, and especially those that claim uniqueness ("the best, the first," etc.); consequently a specially strict standard is applied. Other countries (such as Italy and the United States of America) take the exact opposite position and tolerate generally formulated indications, in particular those in the form of claims of uniqueness. Thus in the United States of America the courts have generally only intervened if the product advertised as the best is in reality inferior.

(v) The Subject Matter of Misleading

12.80 Deceptive statements can be made on all relevant aspects of business matters. However, in principle, the prohibition of deception should be broad enough to cover those new forms of misleading that the legislator has not thought of. On the other hand, a statutory provision must give guidance to the courts. In countries with a predominantly civil law approach, this is often achieved by expressly naming those forms that "in particular" must be regarded as misleading, leaving the courts free to take other forms of deception into account. Usually at least the examples given in Article 10bis(3)3 of the Paris Convention are included, namely, "the nature, the manufacturing process, the characteristics, the suitability for their purpose, or the quantity, of the goods." Often services and indications of geographical origin are also included. Recent legislation on unfair competition also mentions some "modern" examples of misleading. The Greek Decree on Misleading Advertising, for example, expressly refers to misleading statements in the endorsement of products or the passing-off of an advertisement as a press article. The same applies in Belgium. In Hungary, any misleading references to the environment, among other things, are expressly forbidden. Still other countries (and the EC Directive on Misleading Advertising) prohibit any deception with respect to the identity of the advertiser. This is interesting inasmuch as there seems to be basic agreement that these specific errors of identity (while they do, of course, involve deception) are rather dealt with under the heading of confusion (or passing-off), which is largely covered by specific laws on trademarks and trade names. However, the express inclusion of errors as to commercial origin under the heading of deception is significant in that the special procedure provisions of unfair competition law may be applied. For example, consumer associations may bring an action in a case of misleading involving trademarks, whereas trademark law itself would restrict the right of action to the trademark owner.

12.81 A list of examples of misleading practices supplemented with a general provision is only possible, however, if the sanctions against misleading are predominantly those of civil law. Criminal law usually requires a relatively narrowly worded, enumerative prohibition, although in practice this difference is mitigated by the fact that usually the list of expressly named practices is fairly comprehensive.

(vi)   Subjective Requirements

12.82 Even the most careful businessman can issue a statement that the public misunderstands in a way not foreseen by him. Misleading statements, especially in advertising, are therefore not always made in bad faith. On the other hand, even in the absence of any fault on the part of the advertiser, deception in competition has to be stopped in the interest of the consumer and of other competitors. The EC Directive on Misleading Advertising, for example, obliges member States to ensure the cessation of misleading "even without proof of actual loss or damage or of intention or negligence on the part of the advertiser." Countries that favor a civil law approach in the repression of unfair competition usually have few problems in doing so, but where the law against misleading conduct is essentially part of criminal law, at least in theory some subjective element is required. Because of the difficulty of furnishing such evidence, this "subjective" concept has proved a hindrance. Thus, in practice, the courts have gradually reduced the requirement of intent. This can best be seen in France, where the (criminal) prohibition of misleading advertising in Article 44 of the Loi Royer in theory still requires "bad faith," but where the courts have first reduced this requirement to mere knowledge of facts, and have later even assumed such knowledge.

12.83 This primarily objective approach to the repression of misleading statements is, of course, restricted to a cease-and-desist action (and possibly to the remedy of publication). In all countries, an action for damages will only be successful if there is at least negligence. Intent, or even malicious behavior, is required in cases that can be described as real criminal offenses, for example in the food and drug field.

(vii)   Burden of Proof

12.84 The question of who has to furnish evidence of the accuracy of a statement or the likelihood of deception can be of paramount importance in misleading advertising cases. According to general principles of procedural law in most countries, it is the plaintiff (or the public prosecutor or administrative authority) who bears the burden of proof. In the field of misleading, especially misleading advertising, however, some exceptions to this rule are made. The EC Directive on Misleading Advertising, for example, obliges member States to require the advertiser to furnish evidence of the accuracy of factual claims if "such a requirement appears appropriate on the basis of the circumstances of the particular case." Some countries have gone even further by implementing a general reversal of the burden of proof or by placing the advertiser under the obligation to "reasonably substantiate" all advertising claims.

(e)   Discrediting Competitors

(i)   General

12.85 Discrediting (or disparagement) is usually defined as any false allegation concerning a competitor that is likely to harm his commercial goodwill. Like misleading, discrediting tries to entice customers with incorrect information. Unlike misleading, however, this is not done by false or deceptive statements about one's own product, but rather by casting untruthful aspersions on a competitor, his products or his services. Discrediting, therefore, always involves a direct attach on a particular businessman or a particular category of businessmen, but its consequences go beyond that aim: since the information on the competitor or his products is incorrect, the consumer is liable to suffer also.

12.86 Article 10*bis*(3)2 of the Paris Convention obliges member States to prohibit all "false allegations in the course of trade of such a nature as to discredit the establishment, the goods, or the industrial or commercial activities, of a competitor." A similar provision can be found in most national laws on unfair competition. But even without such an express prohibition, it is generally agreed that discrediting is irreconcilable with the notion of "fairness" in competition. Where unfair competition law has been developed on the basis of general tort provisions, it is considered one of the "classical" forms of unfair competition. In all common law countries a (common law) tort of disparagement or discrediting is recognized; additionally some of those countries have recently granted statutory relief. Since it is primarily the individual businessman who suffers from disparaging remarks, civil law sanctions (injunctive relief or damages) are preferred. However, in the most serious cases, especially those involving intentional or malicious defamation, criminal sanctions are also provided, often under the general criminal code.

(ii) Reference to an Individual Competitor

12.87 As mentioned above, it is in the very nature of discrediting to be directed against a particular businessman or a particular category of businessmen. The target need not necessarily be named, however: easy identification by the addressee of the statement is sufficient. This can be achieved by references like "a certain enterprise in X" or may even be the result of a special market situation, for example if there is only one relevant competitor.

12.88 Frequently, the person attacked will be a competitor. As in Article 10*bis*(3)2 of the Paris Convention, most countries restrict unfair competition law protection against disparagement to cases where there is at least some sort of competitive relationship between the plaintiff and the defendant. In some countries, however, the requirement of a competitive relationship has been totally abandoned, and this has led to a considerably broader concept of discrediting: not only competitors but also consumer associations or the media can be held liable under unfair competition law if they make derogatory statements about an individual businessman.

(iii) The Subject Matter of the Attack

12.89 As to the subject matter of the attack, Article 10*bis*(3)2 of the Paris Convention names the establishment, the goods and the industrial or commercial activities (of a competitor). However, any kind of disparaging remark that is likely to harm the goodwill of an entrepreneur should be forbidden. The way in which the harm is done should be irrelevant. Harm to a business reputation can be caused by all forms of reference to the enterprise or to its goods, prices, employees, credit rating, qualifications and so on. It can also be caused by references to an entrepreneur's personal status, for example, his race, his nationality, his religion or his political position. These so-called "personal references" which have nothing to do with commercial activities are in some countries expressly forbidden as disparaging; in others they are considered illegal under the general provisions on protection against unfair competition.

(iv) Intent or Actual Damage

12.90 References to a competitor that affect his commercial goodwill can be made in good faith, for example if the maker of the statement believes it to be true. Effective protection against discrediting is therefore typically independent of any proof of actual damage or intent. In some countries (such as the United States of America), however, the common law tort of disparagement in theory requires proof of malice and damage. Although the courts in the United States of America have gradually eased that requirement, the concept still has proved to be too narrow, and that has led to the enactment of legislative provisions for the grant of statutory relief against disparagement without any evidence of damage or intent (see Section 43(a) of the Lanham Act).

(v) Statements of Fact

12.91 Opinions differ on whether discrediting should be restricted to statements of fact. In some countries, the statutory notion of discrediting is broad enough to cover also statements of opinion. In other countries, it has at least been recognized by the courts that such statements are within the scope of the general provision against dishonest trade practices. In still other countries, disparagement is concerned mainly with statements of fact.

(vi) False Statements

12.92 The question whether statements of opinion can be discrediting has to be considered in connection with another question, namely, whether protection should be extended to the case of accurate statements. Article 10*bis*(3)2 of the Paris Convention speaks of false allegations. Many countries go further, however, recognizing that true, but nevertheless discrediting remarks are either directly within the scope of the express prohibition of discrediting, or at least a violation of the general provisions on honest trade practices. Thus, a literally truthful remark about a competitor may be considered unfair competition if the "attack" is blown up out of proportion, or if the words used are needlessly injurious. On the other hand, some countries expressly restrict the notion of discrediting to inaccurate or at least misleading statements. In the United States of America, for example, true but nevertheless disparaging statements are neither within the scope of the common law tort of disparagement nor within that of the statutory relief granted by Section 43(a) of the Lanham Act or—at State level—the statutes on business practices.

12.93 An explanation of this difference in attitudes can be found in the diverging assessment of "commercial honor." Where unfair competition law has its roots in the protection of the commercial reputation of the individual businessman— as it does in the continental European countries—a "special tort of business disparagement" has emerged, to which, in principle, much stricter rules apply than to defamatory statements outside the bounds of competition, where constitutional considerations such as freedom of speech have to be taken into account.   In other countries, especially those that have not developed a comprehensive system of protection against unfair competition, the attitude is exactly the opposite: it is assumed that, in the interest of competition, attacks on individual competitors are unavoidable, that they must be widely tolerated and that a line should only be drawn where the attack is based on false facts. In those countries, the plaintiff usually also bears the burden of proof as to the falseness of the statement (which can sometimes make an action impossible).

(f) Violation of Trade Secrets

(i) General

12.94 Competitive strength usually depends on innovative techniques and accompanying know-how in the industrial and/or commercial field. However, such techniques and know-how are not always protectable by patent law. Firstly, patents are available only for inventions in the field of technology and not for innovative achievements concerning the conduct of business, etc. Moreover, some technical discoveries or information, while providing a valuable commercial advantage for a particular trader, may lack the novelty or inventive step required to make them patentable. Furthermore, during the pendency of a patent application, as long as the information has not been disclosed to the public, the owner of the information to be patented ought to be protected against any wrongful disclosure of the information by others, regardless of whether or not the application eventually leads to the grant of a patent. Although the Paris Convention does not mention trade secrets, the need for their protection against wrongful disclosure is generally recognized. The unauthorized use of valuable secret information by persons other than the holder of the secret is regarded as a misappropriation of business values that have been developed by the holder, who loses his competitive and economic advantage over competitors as soon as the information is used or disclosed by another.

12.95 Trade secrets are protected against unauthorized use and disclosure by various statutory means. Some countries have special provisions for the protection of trade secrets either under specific legislation on unfair competition or as part of another law. Other countries treat trade secrets as an aspect of tort law. Still other countries have enacted criminal, administrative, commercial or civil law provisions prohibiting the unauthorized use or disclosure of business secrets. The criminal provisions are less important in practice, however, since normally knowledge of the secrecy, as well as malicious or fraudulent intent, have to be proved. Yet if the disclosure of a trade secret constitutes a criminal offense, it will normally constitute an act of unfair competition as well. Furthermore, since employees, consultants, independent contractors and joint venturers are often privy to trade secrets, several aspects of civil law concerning employment contracts and general contract law are also relevant, depending on the circumstances of the case. Finally, it is not unusual to have combinations of the above means available. For example, violation of trade secrets could result in unfair competition or tort liability, as well as in criminal sanctions. On the other hand, in situations where non-competitors have intimidated or influenced agents or employees, or have otherwise induced them or other persons bound to secrecy to disclose the secret information, only civil tort law might be applicable.

(ii) What Information can be a Trade Secret?

12.96 Although a legal definition of a trade secret rarely exists, several countries (following the example of France) differentiate between manufacturing (or industrial) secrets and commercial secrets, which could have consequences for the applicability of criminal law. The first category of trade secrets is related to information of purely technical character, like production methods, chemical formulae, blueprints or prototypes. Such information could constitute a patentable invention but, generally, patentability of the information in question, in particular, novelty in a patent law sense, is not required for the secret to be protectable. Commercial secrets include sales methods, distribution methods, contract forms, business schedules, details of price agreements, consumer profiles, advertising strategies and lists of suppliers or clients. Usually, the subject matter of trade secrets is rather broadly defined, and the final determination of what information can be a trade secret will depend on the specific circumstances of each individual case. For example, in the Unfair Competition Prevention Act of Japan, a trade secret is defined as any information relating to a production method, a sales method or any other information on technology or business that is unknown to the public. A similar definition is contained in the Uniform Trade Secrets Act of the United States of America, which has been adopted by about 20 States.

12.97 There are several lines of inquiry that serve to determine what information constitutes a trade secret: the extent to which the information is known to the public or within a particular trade or industry, the amount of effort and money expended by the trader in developing the secret information, the value of that information to the trader and to his competitors, the extent of measures taken by the trader to guard the secrecy of the information and the ease or difficulty with which the information could be properly acquired by others. From a subjective point of view, the trader involved must have a considerable interest in keeping certain information as a trade secret. Although contractual obligations are not necessary, the trader must have shown the intention to have the information treated as a secret. Frequently, specific measures to maintain the secrecy of the particular information are also required. The fact that the information has been supplied confidentially will not always be sufficient. In some countries (for example, the United States of America and Japan), the efforts made by the owner of the information to keep it secret are considered by courts to be of primary importance in determining whether the information constitutes a trade secret at all.

12.98 From an objective point of view, the information must, in order to qualify as a trade secret, be known to a limited group of persons only, that is, it must not be generally known to experts or to competitors in the field. Even patent applications may be regarded as trade secrets as long as they are not published by the patent office. Therefore, external publications or other information that is readily available will not be considered secret. For example, the use or disclosure of a trade secret by a person who has acquired it in a legitimate business transaction and without any negligence is not deemed unfair. On the other hand, absolute secrecy is not a requirement, for the information might also be discovered independently by others. Also, business partners can be informed without loss of secrecy if it is obvious that the information has to remain secret. Factors that indicate whether the information has the necessary degree of confidentiality to constitute a protectable trade secret are whether it contains material that is not confidential if looked at in isolation, whether it has necessarily to be acquired by employees if they are to work efficiently and whether it is restricted to senior management or is also known at the junior level. Still, the most solid proof is the strict confidentiality of the information and the contractual duty to keep it secret.

(iii)   Use and Disclosure by (Former) Employees

12.99 Even in countries where specific provisions on wrongful or unfair disclosure apply, employment contracts may serve to reinforce and supplement the protection afforded to trade secrets under the law of unfair competition or tort law. It is generally accepted that employees have a basic right to use and exploit, for the purpose of earning their living, all skills, experience and knowledge that they may have acquired in the course of previous periods of employment, even with the help of trade secrets. Yet, an employee does have the duty, during the period of employment, to act with good faith towards his employer and, after the employment has come to an end, not to use or disclose any confidential information about his employer's affairs that may have come to his notice during his employment. For example, Article 85 of the Mexican Law on the Promotion and Protection of Industrial Property of 1991 provides that any person who, by reason of his work, employment, function or post, the practice of his profession or the conduct of business relations, has access to a trade secret and he has been warned that this information must be kept secret, shall abstain from revealing it without just cause and without the consent of the person keeping the secret or of its authorized user. Thus in many cases the use or disclosure of information will constitute a breach of the employment contract by the (former) employee if the information in question must remain secret. However, the distinction between using the skills, knowledge and experience legitimately acquired during employment and the prohibition on the use or disclosure of the former employer's industrial or commercial secrets is often difficult to make. Clearly, in cases where the behavior of the employee is equivalent to theft, embezzlement, industrial espionage or conspiracy with a competitor, a willful breach of confidence will be presumed.

12.100 Frequently, employment contracts incorporate specific provisions prohibiting the disclosure of business or trade secrets, but such provisions, like undertakings not to compete, must not be so restrictive of the professional abilities of the employee in the future that they constitute an undue restraint of trade. Criminal law, as well as civil and labor law, could create relevant duties in employment relations. For example, according to Article 237 of the Criminal Code of the Netherlands, the disclosure of trade secrets by a person employed by a trader is an offense, and Article 2622 of the Italian Civil Code forbids the disclosure of secret business information by directors, general managers and legal auditors of any type of company. Such provisions may be very important in situations where the employee is not bound by contractual clauses, or where the use of such information by former employees is not related to a competitive action. If the former employee can be regarded as a competitor of the former employer, for example if he has set up a company on his own in the same sector, a breach of confidence by the former employee will normally be an act of unfair competition. For example, the inducement of customers of the former employer to become clients of the employee in his new position will probably be deemed unfair, particularly if the employee misuses lists of customers or internal business details in order to make better offers. However, there can also be wrongful misuse of confidential information if special knowledge of the employer's activities in relation to clients' affairs is made use of to persuade those clients to transfer their business to another.

(iv) Use and Disclosure by Competitors

12.101 Competitors are usually very interested in acquiring the trade secrets of others. However, as trade secrets themselves are not fully equivalent to exclusive rights under industrial property law, the determination of the unfairness of competitors who use or disclose the trade secrets of others is based on the means of acquiring the information. For example, it is expressly stated in the Unfair Competition Prevention Law of Japan that the rules concerning the protection of trade secrets will not apply where a trade secret is obtained in the course of a legitimate trade activity, provided that the person obtaining the secret did not use dishonest means to do so, or did not negligently disregard the dishonesty of such means. Thus competitors who have not used any influence to bring about the disclosure of the secret information, but have merely taken advantage of the breach of contract of a former employee or partner of the competitor, will seldom be held liable. The competitor's awareness that the disclosure of the trade secret by the former employee or partner would be a breach of contract is regarded as a minimum level of intent for determining liability. The Mexican law, for example, makes it an offense to use a trade secret which has been disclosed by a third party where the person to whom the secret was disclosed knew that the third party was not authorized to disclose the secret. In any case, competitors are not allowed to interfere recklessly with the contractual relations of others. For example, if a competitor has bribed or otherwise unlawfully persuaded a (former) employee to disclose a competitor's trade secret, he will be liable for unfair competition.

12.102 There are many situations that will depend on the specific circumstances of the case. For example, where the use of trade secrets was part of a former business relationship between the competitors, the fact that the know-how was to be kept secret does not in itself imply that use by the competitor would always be deemed unfair. On the other hand, the possible lack of a contractual clause concerning the use of trade secrets does not preclude unfairness. If the disclosure of trade secrets by a (former) employee is willfully induced by a competitor, the competitor is committing an actionable offense, provided he should reasonably have known or suspected that disclosure of the information was a breach of contract at the time of receiving the information. Frequently, the inducement of employees to disclose trade secrets is combined with a (separate) act of unduly enticing employees away, which is consistently deemed to be a violation of unfair competition law.

(g) Taking Undue Advantage of Another's Achievement ("Free Riding")

(i) General

12.103 In addition to the likelihood of confusion, there are other circumstances that may be held relevant under various doctrines with respect to the imitation of indications, products or other marketable creations. Such circumstances involve the act of taking undue advantage of, or free riding on, another person's achievement recognized by consumers and other market participants like dealers, traders and suppliers. Frequently such achievements concern a certain indication or product but they could also be of purely technical character.

12.104 Protection in such cases depends on a number of requirements which vary from country to country. The unfairness of the competitive act is regarded as resulting not only from the obvious exploitation of the notoriety of the indication, commercial success of the product or technical achievement of the competitor without any proper effort being made to depart substantially from the characteristic features of that particular achievement, but also from the risk of damage to the reputation of the existing business. As a minimum prerequisite, the indication or the product must have a certain distinctiveness (which may be of a level not sufficient for protection under specific legislation). As the scope of protection may depend on the degree of distinctiveness, completely banal indications or products will not usually qualify for protection against mere imitation.

12.105 From a purely systematic point of view, the notion of "free riding" has a number of common features with the notions of causing confusion and misleading. Free riding on another person's market achievements can be defined as any act that a competitor or another market participant undertakes with the intention of directly exploiting another person's industrial or commercial achievement for his own business purposes without substantially departing from the original achievement. In that sense, free riding is the broadest form of competition by imitation. Under the principles of a free market, however, the exploitation or "appropriation" of another person's achievements is unfair only under specific circumstances. On the other hand, acts that cause confusion or mislead normally imply free riding on another person's achievements, but are generally recognized as forms of free riding that are always unfair.

12.106 When assessing the availability of protection against unfair competition for market achievements of others in the absence of confusion, it has often been stated that the mere exploitation of another's achievement is consistent with the principles of a free market system. Thus protection under the rules concerning unfair competition cannot simply be regarded as an alternative route to the securing of protection which would be available without the obligation to comply with the various requirements of protection imposed by specific industrial property legislation. As a certain balance of interests on the relevant market has been achieved by adopting specific legislation on patents, industrial designs, trademarks and so on, that balance must also be taken into consideration in the application of unfair competition law. As a general rule, protection under unfair competition law will be denied if the achievement that has been copied or appropriated is covered by specific industrial property legislation and the type of protection sought by resorting to unfair competition law could have been obtained, at least for a certain period of time, under that specific legislation (principle of "preemption").

12.107 As indicated above, protection as such may be invoked if the subject matter of specific legislation does not cover the achievement involved, for example, if the law is not applicable to achievements made before a certain date, or if the protection granted by the special law is not broad enough to give the relief sought in the specific case. Some industrial property laws expressly provide that protection under unfair competition provisions may be invoked for achievements that are not protectable under the specific law. Some industrial property laws expressly exclude additional protection under unfair competition law for inventions, indications, signs or product shapes that are protectable under those laws. Still, it is not always clear what interests the legislation has in fact balanced by adopting the special law. Even legislative commentaries do not comprehensively clarify that question. Thus a common approach to the grant of protection against free riding under unfair competition law is to make such protection available only under specific circumstances, which must differ in some respects from the circumstances under which protection is granted by the specific legislation. The definition of those circumstances is often possible only under some sort of "catch-all" provision, and thus usually is established by case law. For the following types of free riding, specific circumstances resulting in an act of unfair competition are already recognized in many countries: dilution of the distinctive quality or advertising value of a mark, misappropriation of a reputation, slavish imitation and so-called "parasitic acts." These are dealt with in the following paragraphs.

(ii)   Dilution of the Distinctive Quality or Advertising Value of a Mark

12.108 Generally, where the unauthorized use of a mark for different goods or services is not likely to cause confusion, there is neither trademark or service mark infringement nor an act of unfair competition. This follows from the "speciality principle" in trademark law, which is a consequence of the distinguishing function of trademarks and service marks. In some countries, however, such as Canada, the EC member States under the EC Directive to Approximate National Laws on Trade Marks and several States of the United States of America, marks that have acquired a certain renown are given additional protection against the so-called dilution of their distinctive quality or advertising value. The concept of "dilution" is understood as the watering down or gradual lessening of the ability of a mark to be immediately associated by consumers or the general public with a particular source. As some dilution can be regarded as being an inherent result of the use of identical or similar marks for totally different goods or services, the main rationale behind the notion of dilution is that marks that have acquired a certain renown should be protected against the obvious desire of other market participants to take advantage of the essential "uniqueness" of a mark. The likelihood of substantial damage to the proprietor of the mark is assumed from the fact that the mark may lose its established association with certain products. The required degree of renown of the mark involved is determined by the relevant public or consumer groups. If it is a trademark for goods that appeal only to a selected group of consumers, it will have a better chance of reaching the required degree of renown than if it is one for mass-consumption goods. However, the required degree may still vary considerably from country to country.

(iii)   Exploitation of Another's Reputation

12.109 Another type of misappropriation that has been recognized in recent years as being contrary to honest business practice is that of unfairly taking advantage of the reputation or "prestige" of the market achievements of other industrial or commercial enterprises. This doctrine has been particularly relevant in the appropriation of well-known indications. For example, if the quality of the genuinely marked product or service has led consumers to associate the mark with a certain origin or consistency of product quality, its unauthorized use for other goods or services, while not causing confusion as to their source, might still be considered unfair appropriation of a reputation. The doctrine may equally apply to product appearances, but in such a case the appearance must be recognized as indicating a certain degree of quality, image or prestige. Countries have different approaches to this kind of misappropriation, however. For example, whereas in France the appropriation of the prestige of another's mark or product is usually assumed to be unfair, in Spain that type of misappropriation is expressly prohibited without any further prerequisites in Article 12 of the Law Against Unfair Competition of 1991. In Germany it is required, for the appropriation by a third person to be allowed, that a secondary exploitation of the mark could not reasonably be expected. In the United States of America there is in principle no objection to appropriation unless a likelihood of confusion, for example as to "sponsorship," is established, for which purpose the prestige of the mark is taken into account.

12.110 Taking advantage of another's trademark or service mark may occur as a more or less veiled form of appropriation. For example, a competitor may use a generally similar, but noticeably different mark, nevertheless consciously drawing closely on the characteristic and well-known features of another's mark. Alternatively, he may use the mark in advertising his own trademarked goods with the aim of transferring the image of the well-known mark to his own goods, or again he may use another's mark with qualifying terms like "model," "type," "style," and so on (however, in some countries the term "suitable for" or other similar terms may be permissible in connection with spare parts and accessories). In this respect, it is not necessary that the market participant be a direct competitor of the proprietor of the mark, as long as there is a likelihood of damage to the exclusive image or reputation of the mark or the business involved.

(iv) Slavish Imitation

12.111 The concept of slavish imitation as a separate act of unfair competition has been developed in several countries of Europe. This kind of unfair free riding is usually regarded as an exception to the general rule of free appropriation in the area of products or indications that are not protectable or for which protection has lapsed under specific legislation, or where there is no likelihood of confusion as to the source of the products. In the absence of likelihood of confusion, the specific circumstances of the case must reveal some exceptional character for the act to be deemed unfair. Usually the unfairness is seen in the lack of research, investment, creativeness and expense on the part of the imitator, who has merely copied the achievement of another, despite the fact that alternative ways of competing effectively were available. The imitated products or indications would still have to possess a particular distinctiveness, which must not merely derive from technical features necessary for the product to function properly, but must concern aesthetic or decorative features that leave sufficient room for alternative shapes and designs.

12.112 Not all prerequisites of slavish imitation are equivalent in all countries, however. Apart from that, the qualifying circumstances may sometimes be combined with the concepts of dilution, misappropriation of reputation or "parasitic competition." Frequently, there has to be a marked contrast between the efforts made by the competitor to develop his achievement, to introduce it on the market and to win some success or recognition and the efforts made by the imitator to copy and exploit that achievement for the act to be deemed unfair. One statutory example of a provision against this kind of unfair misappropriation is to be found in Article 5(c) of the Swiss Law Against Unfair Competition, which specifically treats as unfair any act which, by means of technical reproduction processes and without any corresponding effort, takes the marketable results of the work of another person and exploits them as such. There is a similar provision in Article 11(2) of the Spanish Law on Unfair Competition, which considers imitation of the achievements of another to be unfair if undue advantage is taken of the other's goodwill or efforts.

12.113 Acts of slavish imitation should be distinguished from acts of so-called "reverse engineering." The latter is generally understood to consist in examining or analyzing, by taking apart or decomposing, a product or substance in order to understand its structure, composition or operation and find out how it was made or constructed, and subsequently producing an improved version of the product or substance. The practice of reverse engineering is commonly practiced in industry in connection with the products of competitors, with the purpose of learning the technology they embody, and eventually producing a competing (improved or different but equivalent) product. In fact, it is part of the normal exercise of competition in a free market environment which, in turn, is based on broader public policy considerations. The practice of reverse engineering is, therefore, not in and of itself unfair; nevertheless, the product or other result obtained through reverse engineering may, under certain circumstances, constitute an infringement of an industrial property right. For example, if a product made after reverse engineering of a competitor's product falls under the claims of a valid patent (where appropriate, taking into account the doctrine of equivalence), that would constitute patent infringement. If a patent is not infringed, but the manner in which the original product was copied is found to be dishonest or unfair (regardless of whether reverse engineering took place), the relevant acts might still be actionable on grounds of unfair competition.

(v) Parasitic Acts

12.114 Another variety of unfair free riding recognized in some countries is the concept of "parasitic acts." This concept has many features in common with the concept of slavish imitation. Here the mere imitation of the achievements of others is still considered inherent in a free market system, but exceptional circumstances may make the imitation unfair. For example, the imitation of one product which is not particularly new or original could possibly be allowed, but, as soon as the achievement involved is recognized as innovative or strongly appealing to consumers, the imitator has less reason to claim the fairness of his action. What tips the balance definitely against the imitator is his systematic and methodical appropriation of the characteristic achievements of one particular competitor in a routine manner. Moreover, circumstances relating to the modus operandi of a competitor may denote unfairness: for example, ordering samples from a competitor for the purpose of imitating his products more easily and systematically may be found to be unfair parasitic behavior. Some countries adopt a flexible approach in these cases, in particular, by adapting the scope of injunctions and also the time limits of protection to the particular circumstances. For example, the amortization of the innovation costs could be considered a relevant factor in determining whether or not a particular imitation is fair. As a result, protection could be restricted to identical imitations, and only for a period of time that is much shorter than under specific industrial property legislation. It is to be noted, however, that in some countries (for example, the United States of America) just copying the product of another person (even if done systematically, or in respect of one particular competitor) will not be recognized as unfair competition unless there is copying of non-functional features which are distinctive or have acquired secondary meaning.

(h) Comparative Advertising

(i) Definition

12.115 The different attitudes towards true but nevertheless discrediting statements can best be seen in the examination of comparative advertising. Comparative advertising may take two forms: a positive reference to another's product (claiming that one's own product is as good as the other) or a negative reference (claiming that one's own product is better than the other). In the first instance, where the competitor's product is usually well known, the crucial question relates to the possibility of misappropriation of another's goodwill. In the second case, where the competitor's product is criticized, it is the question of disparagement that arises. However, both forms of comparison involve an (unauthorized) reference to a competitor, who is either mentioned by name or implicitly identifiable as such by the public.

(ii) The General Restrictions: "Misleading" and "Discrediting" Comparisons

12.116 It goes without saying that comparative advertising has to respect the restrictions applicable to all advertisements. In particular, it must not be misleading or disparaging. Comparison based on false or misleading statements about one's own product or involving false statements about the competitor's product is forbidden in all countries.

12.117 It must be remembered, however, that there are differences in the evaluation of the notion of "misleading" and especially in that of "discrediting." As mentioned above, some countries, consider statements claiming superiority or uniqueness (like "the best," etc.) misleading unless they can be proved correct, while others consider them harmless exaggerations. Different assessments of the notions of "discrediting" and "misappropriation" are of even greater importance. In countries with a rather permissive attitude towards true but nevertheless disparaging statements, comparative advertising is generally tolerated. As long as what is said is true, the courts will not interfere, even if the reference to the competitor or his product is clearly disparaging or exploits his goodwill. In countries that traditionally put special emphasis on the protection of the "honest" businessman and his reputation, comparative advertising is either forbidden or at least severely restricted. Sometimes the mere fact that a competitor is named against his will is considered discrediting and therefore unfair competition. According to the rule that "the honest businessman has a right not to be spoken of, even if the truth is spoken," the legislation of some countries has even expressly forbidden all comparisons that needlessly identify a competitor. The same argument has led the courts of other countries to find comparative advertising more or less automatically against honest trade practice (and therefore against the general provision on unfair competition law). Although it has sometimes been stressed that true comparisons might be in the interest of consumers, doctrine and case law have in practice allowed comparisons only under very special circumstances, for example, if they have been expressly required by a customer, if they have been made to counter an illegal attack on the advertiser, or if the comparison is necessary to explain a certain system or new technical developments in general.

(iii)   The Trend towards Admission of True Comparisons

12.118 In recent years, however, this negative attitude towards comparative advertising has changed. It has been increasingly recognized that true comparisons of relevant facts can not only reduce the consumer's information search costs, but also have positive effects on the economy by improving market transparency. The courts of those countries that traditionally view comparative advertising as disparaging have gradually relaxed the strict prohibition on all statements identifying a competitor. In France, for example, price comparisons, if based on true, relevant and ample material, are allowed. More important, recent statutes on unfair competition at least indirectly allow comparative advertising. At the European Community (EC) level, a new Directive has been proposed that would oblige member States of the EC to allow truthful comparative advertising. On the whole, there seems to be a clear trend towards the admission of truthful comparative advertising.

(iv)   Special Dangers of Comparative Advertising

12.119 On the other hand, it cannot be denied that comparative advertising can more easily be misleading or disparaging than most other forms of advertising, for example if the comparison is based on irrelevant (or not really comparable) aspects, or if the overall impression is misleading. These potential dangers require special safeguards against abuse. Countries that allow comparisons place special emphasis on the fact that even true statements must not be unnecessarily disparaging or that irrelevant facts must not be compared. The 1991 EC proposal for a Directive on Comparative Advertising goes even further by expressly requiring that only relevant, objective and verifiable characteristics be compared, that the overall impression be not misleading, that there be no risk of confusion between the products compared and that the competitor and his product be in no way disparaged or discredited. Furthermore, the advertiser can be required to prove any claims made in surveys used to support the comparison.

(v)   Comparative Advertising and Trademark Law

12.120 Comparison is often impossible without reference to a certain mark which refers to a particular product, service or business. In these cases, not only unfair competition law, but also trademark law has to be taken into account.

12.121 In countries where trademarks are protected solely as indications of the source of a product or service, the use of a trademark in comparative advertising may not be within the scope of trademark law. However, there are countries where the use of another's trademark in comparative advertising may be considered trademark infringement. Article 13A of the Uniform Benelux Trademark Law, for example, protects the "advertising value" of trademarks against any use in potentially adverse circumstances (which can also take the form of an unwanted reference in comparative advertising). Canadian trademark law generally protects the goodwill of a trademark, while the current United Kingdom trademark law in principle forbids any reference to another's trademark. Even in the United States of America, where comparative advertising is generally allowed, the so-called "antidilution statutes" enacted by many States are in theory applicable to the use of another person's marks in comparative advertising, since they grant—regardless of confusion—trademark protection against all acts that are liable to injure the business reputation or that dilute the distinctive quality of a mark. However, the statutes so far have not been applied in cases of truthful comparative advertising, and there may be constitutional reasons for such an exception in cases of comparative advertising. It is noteworthy that the proposal for a EC Directive on Comparative Advertising would allow such advertising provided, in particular, that it does not cause confusion between the marks of the advertiser and those of a competitor, and that it does not discredit, denigrate or indicate contempt for a competitor's marks.

(vi) Comparisons Made by Third Parties

12.122 In many countries product testing is done by consumer organizations and/or private or public institutions like the press, television and other media. Usually two questions will arise here: are the organizations liable under unfair competition law, and may the results of their testing be used in advertising?

12.123 In those countries that have given up the requirement of a competitive link between plaintiff and defendant, unfair competition law is applicable to these organizations too. In other countries, "unfair" product tests, which have an adverse effect on a business reputation, are primarily dealt with under general civil law tort provisions.

12.124 There seems to be no general agreement on the question whether and under what conditions such test results may be used by advertisers. In some countries (such as Germany) that in general do not accept comparative advertising, this kind of indirect comparison is basically considered legal. In other countries (such as Belgium), it is expressly forbidden for a competitor to refer to tests conducted by consumer organizations, and in still others (such as Switzerland), such references are severely restricted. In the proposal for an EC Directive on Comparative Advertising, tests by third parties may be used only with the express consent of the person who conducted them, apart from which the advertiser would be held responsible for any advertising claim based on such surveys.

(i) Other Acts of Unfair Competition

(i) General

12.125 As mentioned earlier, unfair competition law particularly reflects the sociological, economic and ethical conceptions of a society. Apart from the specific categories of acts already discussed which are generally considered unfair competition, there is a wide range of acts and practices that may be dealt with under unfair competition law in one country but not necessarily in another. The discussion that follows is therefore restricted to those aspects that most countries appear to consider (although perhaps with different emphasis) contrary to "honest trade practice," either in the form of an express prohibition in the specific law or, more frequently, under the general provisions on unfair competition, or in specific other laws, decrees and the like. It is to be noted that the following explanations only give examples, not an exhaustive list of these other unfair practices.

(ii) Nuisance Advertising, Exploitation of Fear, Undue Psychological Pressure, etc.

12.126 Modern competition law aims to protect all those concerned by unfair market practices. Consequently, practices that "unduly" influence the consumer (or try to do so) may be considered contrary to honesty in competition. In practice, however, it is difficult to determine what requirements have to be met before a practice is deemed to be "undue" in relation to the consumer. Since the very purpose of all marketing or advertising practice is to influence consumers favorably, a certain borderline of influence has to be crossed. This is often asserted in cases where the privacy of the consumer has been invaded or where he has been manipulated by means of advertising techniques.

12.127 For example, in many countries the delivery of unsolicited goods to a person who is required to pay for them unless he expressly refuses or returns them is considered unfair competition, because it plays on the fact that many consumers either tend to forget to return the goods or even feel under an obligation to keep them. On the other hand, many countries tolerate unsolicited home visits ("door-to-door sales") as long as they do not involve any deception or impose undue psychological pressure on the consumer. Opinions may vary on the question of unsolicited telephone calls: while some countries consider them per se an intrusion into the privacy of the consumer, most other countries tolerate them as long as the consumer's lack of experience and his privacy are not exploited. The same is true of the unsolicited sending of advertising material.

12.128 It is further considered unfair in many countries to abuse the consumer's superstitions, credulity, fears or feelings of charity. For example, an advertisement that exploits elderly people's fears of ending up in a nursing home, or causes unnecessary anxiety over death or health problems can be considered contrary to "honest" trade practice. The same is true if a special situation in which the consumer is especially vulnerable is exploited for commercial purposes, for example, if victims of car accidents are pestered with offers of towing services, or if the recently bereaved are offered funeral services. Most countries, moreover, take special precautions against any abuse of children's lack of experience.

12.129 Apart from these special cases, often regulated in specific laws, the courts of some countries have identified a group of cases under the general clause against unfair competition which can be described as "psychological pressure to purchase" or "exaggerated enticement." These cases are mainly seen in connection with special marketing practices, however, like the offering of free goods or discounts and lotteries.

(iii) Sales Promotion: Bonuses, Gifts, Lotteries, etc.

12.130 A frequent marketing technique to attract new customers consists in the offering of bonuses, gifts and other inducements, and in the organization of competitions, lotteries or games. Such sales promotion can be a new and efficient channel of distribution and may thus stimulate competition. On the other hand, it may distract consumers from the merits of the principal goods or services and thereby entice them to buy something that is either not worth its price or not really needed. This is particularly true of marketing techniques like games, lotteries and other competitions, which exploit for advertising purposes a consumer's predisposition to gambling. Most of these are therefore regulated in one way or another, and sometimes even expressly forbidden. Additionally, they are subject to self-regulation measures. There is, however, little agreement (and little consistency) on the question of what specific practices should be considered unfair competition. For example, bonuses, or any discount or other advantage dependent on the purchase of a product, are forbidden in principle in some countries, allowed in principle in others and more or less strictly regulated in others. Lotteries, where the winning of prizes is a matter of pure chance, are generally forbidden if they are linked to the purchase of a product, and otherwise are severely restricted. Contests in which the outcome can be influenced to a certain extent by the participant's own skill are generally viewed more favorably, provided that no deception is involved and that the consumer is not put under any pressure to buy. On the other hand, "pyramid" ("snowball") sales and other such methods are often considered potentially misleading and consequently forbidden (sometimes even on pain of criminal sanctions), or are at least severely restricted, whereas sweepstakes are often considered legal.

12.131 On the whole, the courts of most countries, even those that allow the sales promotion techniques mentioned above, pay special attention to the actual conditions under which these sales practices take place: if the consumer is put under any psychological or other pressure to buy, if the prizes are extremely valuable and so all the more enticing, an otherwise accepted marketing practice may well be considered contrary to "honest trade practice."

(iv) Impeding of Market Activities

12.132 Finally, there are several acts which may hinder or obstruct a competitor in his business activities, either directly or indirectly. An example of a direct obstruction would be the actual obstruction of trading on a particular market location, which would normally be considered unfair. Another example would be the deliberate destruction of bottles destined to be recycled and refilled by a producer of soft drinks in order to lessen his ability to supply the market. Other (indirect) impediments are often controlled by antitrust law but, under certain circumstances, unfair competition law may offer some additional protection.

Impediments that are traditionally covered by antitrust law are discrimination, boycotting and dumping, but that does not preclude the application of unfair competition law, at least if the acts are perpetrated on an individual scale. For example, unreasonable interference with the business activities of competitors, sales at unreasonably low prices, like below-cost prices, or the imposition of fixed retail prices are practices that have been designated by the Fair Trade Commission of Japan as being prohibited by the Japanese Anti-Monopoly Act, but which might also be regarded, in theory, as forms of unfair competition. In some countries, selling below cost or at an "exceptionally low profit margin" is expressly prohibited under unfair competition law. In the United Kingdom, the United States of America and other countries, "predatory pricing" with a view to damaging a competitor may be prohibited under competition law.

12.133 Other such unfair practices consist in enticing away from competitors, or in inducing the personnel or agents of competitors to terminate their employment or agency contracts. As indicated earlier, these acts of unfair competition are frequently accompanied by the violation of trade secrets but may, nevertheless, constitute separate unfair acts. Merely inducing the clients or employees of competitors to change suppliers or employers by offering better conditions is inherent in free competition and cannot therefore be regarded as unfair. However, means such as bribery or deception of clients, agents or employees, or inducement to breach a valid undertaking not to compete, will be deemed unfair, as will the systematic enticing away of personnel with a view to damaging one particular competitor.

References for Section D
International Bureau of WIPO, *Protection Against Unfair Competition*, WIPO Pub. No. 725(E) (1994)

CHAPTER 13

Franchising

A. INTRODUCTION

(a) A Brief Explanation of Franchising

13.1 Even if the term "franchising" is unfamiliar to most consumers, they are familiar with the results of franchising. The most widely known results of franchising appear to be fast-food restaurants such as McDONALD'S, hotels such as HOLIDAY INN or cosmetics retail shops such as YVES ROCHER. Franchising extends, however, to industries as diverse as the hiring of formal wear, car tuning, the preparation of taxation statements or returns, lawn care, day-care schools and dentistry. In short, it may apply to any economic activity for which a system can be developed for the manufacture, processing and/or distribution of goods or the rendering of services. It is this "system" that is the subject matter of franchising.

13.2 In developed market economy countries, the sale of goods and services through franchising has grown remarkably since the 1950s. Indeed it has been estimated that, in the United States of America, franchising accounts for more than a third of all retail sales in terms of dollars. In Australia, it is estimated that franchised fast-foods account for 90% or more of total sales in that market. It has been reported that franchising is practiced in altogether more than 70 countries around the world.

13.3 This rapid growth and success of franchising has been attributed to a number of factors, the most basic one being perhaps that franchising combines the depth of knowledge and the strength of one entity, the franchisor, with the entrepreneurial spirit of a businessman, the franchisee, and that it is possible to increase the number of franchisees according to market conditions. In this way, a large and stable organization is able to grow and develop, motivated or indeed driven by the spirit of small business.

13.4 From a legal standpoint, franchising relies on contract law and, therefore, does not necessarily require any special regulatory or legislative structure in order to function and develop. It is, therefore, appropriate to stress at the outset that no specific regulation of franchising has been or would be necessary for franchises to thrive in any economy.   However, some governments have nevertheless chosen to adopt legislation to regulate franchising. Overregulation could, however, have the effect of discouraging investment in this area.

13.5 Whether such government-mandated regulation is provided or not as in all commercial activities, the best protection against the possibility of abuse is knowledge—knowledge held by potential franchisees and their professional advisers as to what franchising is and how it works. Accordingly, the purpose of this chapter is to give a brief general survey of the structure and nature of a franchising arrangement and, in particular, to help prospective franchisees understand franchising and better defend their interests, thereby allowing franchising to fulfill a positive role in the economy.

13.6 Franchising is a complex subject, and informed advice on the business, financial and legal aspects of franchising should be sought from professionals with extensive franchising experience before any particular franchise agreement is entered into. This chapter should not be viewed as a substitute for such advice.

(b) An Example of a Franchising Agreement

13.7 In order to illustrate better the discussion on franchising, this chapter uses a fictional franchise from time to time as an example. That fictional franchise relates to a restaurant selling Italian food and operating under the name of VESPUCCI. While VESPUCCI is the mark (both for goods and services) and the trade name under which the franchisees operate the restaurants, the company offering the franchise (the franchisor) is referred to as Vespucci, Inc.

13.8 Vespucci, Inc. has developed a system for preparing and selling its food products, which are sold in large volume and in a uniform manner. The system includes various factors that contribute to the success of VESPUCCI restaurants, including recipes and methods of preparing food that produce a product of consistent quality, good sitting of the restaurant, the design of employees' uniforms, the design of the buildings and billboards, quality sources for supplies, the design of packaging, an inventory of ingredients used in the preparation of the food, and management and accounting systems.

13.9 Vespucci, Inc. has developed this system over a period of years, and its development has not been easy, since it had many failed experiments before arriving at the system that it is willing to share with franchisees.

13.10 Vespucci, Inc. imparts its knowledge to its franchisees to assist them in developing a new business. Thus the franchisee opening a VESPUCCI restaurant has the benefit of Vespucci, Inc.'s experience. Even if the local franchisee has no previous experience of running a restaurant, he will, by following Vespucci, Inc.'s system, stand a better chance of operating a successful business. Without the franchisor's guidance, the local restaurant owner is liable to make serious mistakes which could cause the business to fail. Moreover, Vespucci, Inc. retains the right to supervise and control the way in which the local franchisee is operating the local VESPUCCI restaurant. By retaining that right, Vespucci, Inc. can be sure that the local VESPUCCI restaurant is operated in a proper manner, so that the goodwill of the VESPUCCI mark and trade name is maintained and the value of the local restaurant, indeed of the whole system under which VESPUCCI restaurants are operated, is not reduced.

13.11 Vespucci, Inc. trains the local franchisee to operate a restaurant in exchange for a financial benefit (to Vespucci, Inc.). The benefit is received in the form of a payment by the local franchisee to Vespucci, Inc. That payment may include an advance payment or "up-front fee" and some form of continuing payment based, for example, on a percentage of the franchisee's total sales. Payment in kind might also be envisaged. In addition, depending on the nature of the agreement, the franchisee may have a number of other payments to make for items such as special food spices, rental of equipment (e.g. ovens, cutting machines, etc.), purchase of consumable goods and miscellaneous articles necessary for his business.

B. COMPARISON OF RETAIL SALES, STANDARD LICENSING AND FRANCHISING ARRANGEMENTS

13.12 Business transactions can take a variety of forms; franchising arrangements are only one of them. In order to understand what a franchising arrangement is, it may be useful to discuss first two other types of business arrangement which, while different from franchising, share with it certain important features: retail sales arrangements and standard license arrangements.

(a) Retail Sales Arrangements

13.13 Retail sales arrangements are governed by the traditional principles of civil and commercial law, such as contract law. The manufacturer or distributor makes a profit by selling his products to the retailer at a sufficiently high price.

13.14 A retail sales arrangement involves one party that manufactures and/or distributes a product and a second party that sells it. The seller may be an agent of the manufacturer or may be an independent merchant, purchasing the goods for resale. If the seller is a independent merchant, he may have concluded a "distributorship" agreement with the manufacturer or distributor of the goods. If the distributorship is exclusive the merchant is assured that the manufacturer or distributor will deal only with him for the purposes of distributing those goods within the territory (e.g. a province, a region or a whole country) defined in the contract. The exclusive distributor would normally be entitled to announce his special relationship with, and use the marks and trade names of, the manufacturer or distributor for the purposes of advertising and selling the goods.

13.15 Although exclusive distributorships exist, distributorships are typically non-exclusive. From this viewpoint, a franchising arrangement may be more attractive.

(b) Standard License Arrangements

13.16 In its simplest terms, a standard license arrangement is one under which one person (the licensor), who is the owner of a right to prevent other persons from commercially exploiting or using certain intellectual creations (e.g. inventions, designs) or distinctive signs (e.g. marks, trade names), agrees not to exercise that right against a given person (the licensee) in exchange for a fee, and perhaps also subject to the licensor's control of such commercial exploitation or use. In the case of license agreements involving marks or other distinctive signs, the licensor will not normally exercise any more control over the licensee than is necessary to ensure that the goods being sold, or services provided, under his sign are of a certain quality, and/or that they possess certain specified characteristics.

13.17 For example, a company called Desk Gear, Inc. (another fictional example) may own the rights in a trademark affixed to certain goods, such as the mark FLUME for writing instruments. Another company is given permission by Desk Gear, Inc. to manufacture and sell pens having the mark FLUME affixed to them in exchange for a fee paid to Desk Gear, Inc. for each such pen manufactured and sold. Desk Gear, Inc. will normally have retained the right to check that the pens meet the quality standards necessary to maintain the goodwill of its FLUME trademark. It may also have retained a right to control the manner in which the mark itself is actually applied to the pens, and to their labels or containers, and the manner in which the goods are presented to the public by the licensee.

(c) Franchising Arrangements

13.18 Although different definitions could be proposed, franchising may be described as an arrangement whereby one person (the franchisor), who has developed a system for conducting a particular business, allows another person (the franchisee) to use that system in accordance with the prescriptions of the franchisor, in exchange for consideration. The relationship is a continuing one, as the franchisee operates in accordance with standards and practices established and monitored by the franchisor and with his continuing assistance and support.

13.19 The franchising arrangement therefore relates to a *system*, which the franchisor allows—or licenses—the franchisee to exploit. This may be referred to as the franchised system, or simply "the system." The franchised system is a package comprising intellectual property rights relating to one or more marks, trade names, industrial designs, inventions and works protected by copyright, together with relevant know-how and trade secrets, to be exploited for the sale of goods or the provision of services to end users.

13.20 The factors that typically characterize a franchise relationship include:

13.21 *A license to use the system:* In return for an agreed payment, the franchisee is allowed to use the franchised system. He is in effect given a license to use the franchisor's system to carry out his business. Where the franchised system is to be exploited at a particular location, such as at a franchised restaurant or shop, that location is usually referred to as the "franchised unit."

13.22 *An ongoing interactive relationship:* The relationship is ongoing, involving multiple sales of the franchised product (or offering of franchised services) over a period of time, with the franchisor giving continuous assistance to the franchisee in establishing, maintaining and promoting the franchised unit. This includes updating the relevant information as the franchisor develops new or better techniques for operating a franchised unit. The franchisee for his part has a continuing obligation to pay fees to the franchisor for the use of the franchised system or to compensate the franchisor for providing ongoing management services.

13.23 *The franchisor's right to prescribe the manner of operating the business:* The franchisee agrees to abide by directives issued by the franchisor which set out the manner of operation of the system. Such directives may include quality control, protection of the system, territorial restrictions, operational details and a host of other regulations governing the conduct of the franchisee in relation to the franchise.

(d) Comparison of Types of Arrangement

13.24 The preceding discussion identified three distinguishing characteristics of a typical franchise arrangement: the license to use the uniform system, the ongoing interactive relationship and the following of a prescribed manner of operation. These characteristics may be used to compare a franchise arrangement with a retail sales arrangement and a standard license arrangement. In practice, franchise arrangements may also take a "hybrid" form, borrowing features from two or more types of contract. Moreover, businessmen prepared to engage in franchise arrangements are generally less concerned with the precise legal form of the agreement than with the business aspects of the deal.

(i) Grant of a License to Use the Franchised System

13.25 The heart of a franchising arrangement is a license, granted by the franchisor to the franchisee, to use the franchised system. This is essential to allow the franchisee to conduct his business in the manner developed by the franchisor. In contrast, a retail sales arrangement involves the simple sale of goods and does not necessarily require the grant of a license.

13.26 In this regard the distinction between a franchise arrangement and a standard license arrangement is a more subtle one. It has been stated that franchising is merely a sophisticated form of a standard license arrangement and that a franchising arrangement goes beyond the mere licensing of one or more specific intellectual property rights, such as trademarks, because it is a license to use a system that includes, but is not limited to, intellectual property rights. Indeed, under a franchise arrangement, the franchisee does more than merely selling goods or providing services under another's mark, although he might not himself do any manufacturing at all. Franchising goes further by allowing the franchisee to manufacture and sell goods or provide services as part of a larger system.

13.27 For example, the licensing by Desk Gear, Inc. of the manufacture and sale of pens bearing the FLUME mark can be considered a standard license agreement. If, however, Desk Gear, Inc. decides to establish a system including store design and marketing techniques for the sale of its pens and to allow someone to make use of that system to sell FLUME pens, that would be franchising.

13.28 In a retail sales relationship, the first party manufactures the goods and transfers them to the second party at a price which includes its profit and the second party resells the goods at a higher price, thereby making its own profit. In a typical, straightforward franchising relationship, the franchisor explains to each franchisee how to make use of the system and, in return, acquires income by receiving a portion of the franchisees' income, for instance a percentage of sales. In addition, the franchisor may ensure income by selling goods to the franchisee, who becomes a permanent "customer" of the franchisor by agreeing to acquire from him certain goods needed for the operation of the franchise.

(ii) Ongoing Interactive Relationship

13.29 In a retail sales arrangement, the manufacturer and the distributor are usually independent of each other. In a standard licensing arrangement and in a franchising arrangement, the parties are independent but have a close working relationship defined by the terms of the license agreement and franchise agreement, respectively. The income of each party is dependent on the combined efforts of both parties. The more successful the licensee's or franchisee's business becomes, the greater the income for both parties.

13.30 In contrast to a standard license arrangement, however, the franchisee's success is also dependent on the franchisor's ability to develop a profitable system, to train the franchisee in the proper operation of the system, to improve and promote the system, to supervise or monitor the franchisee and to assist him during the term of the franchise agreement in order to enhance the likelihood of success. In a franchise arrangement, at least part of the ongoing nature of the relationship presupposes the franchisor continuing to develop the franchised system and communicating the new developments to the franchisee.

(iii) Following the Prescribed Method

13.31 In a retail sales arrangement, the seller does not exercise control over the manner in which the goods are sold by the buyer to the end user. In a license arrangement that gives the licensee consent to use the licensor's mark, the owner of the mark will normally exercise some sort of control over the quality of the goods or services produced or offered under the license. This will, in particular, assure the licensor that he can prevent any damage to his mark's goodwill due to diminishing or inconsistent quality of the goods or services produced or offered by the licensee. With respect to marks, the legal systems of some countries require license contracts to contain provisions requiring quality control by the licensor and such provisions are essential under the legal systems of many countries to enforce and avoid the loss of rights in licensed marks.

13.32 Specifically with respect to a franchise arrangement, the franchisor will supervise not only the manner in which specific rights, such as trademark rights, are used by the franchisee, but also prescribe the manner in which the fundamental aspects of the franchised system are implemented and managed. Therefore, the extent of the franchisor's influence over the franchisee is greater than that of a licensor over a licensee.

C. TYPES OF FRANCHISE

13.33 This chapter deals with only one general category of franchises, which may be referred to as *business format* franchises. This broad category, of course, comprises a number of variations. Such variations may consist of changes in the nature of the franchised system, the scope and content of the license granted, the nature or object of the ongoing relationship and the scope and degree of supervision exercised by the franchisor over the manner in which the franchise is exercised.

13.34 A business format type of franchise has been described as being characterized by an ongoing business relationship between franchisor and franchisee that includes not only the product, service and trademark, but the entire business format itself—a marketing strategy and plan, operating manuals and standards, quality control, and continued two-way communications.

13.35 In order to perceive more clearly the potential of franchising, a brief description of certain basic types of business format franchises is useful. Categorizing franchises on the basis of their function yields three principal types: processing franchises, distribution franchises and service franchises. Franchises could also be categorized in terms of the possible relationship existing between franchisor and franchisee. These include relationships like those between manufacturer and wholesaler, manufacturer and retailer, wholesaler and retailer and service industry and retailer.

13.36 In a processing franchise, sometimes called a "manufacturing" franchise, the franchisor supplies an essential ingredient or technical knowledge to a processor or manufacturer. The franchisor will grant the franchisee authorization to manufacture and sell products under the marks of the franchisor. In certain instances the franchisee may further be licensed to use trade secret information or patented technology held by the franchisor, apart from which he may be provided with training and/or information relating to the marketing, distribution and servicing of the product. Such franchises are common, for example, in the restaurant and fast-food industry.

13.37 In a service franchise, the franchisor develops a certain service which is to be rendered by the franchisee, under the terms of the franchise agreement, to his customers. An example of a service franchise would be one involving the provision of automobile tuning or repair services, or the provision of credit card services.

13.38 In a distribution franchise, the franchisor (or someone else on his behalf) manufactures the product and sells it to the franchisees. The franchisees then sell the products to customers, under the franchisor's trademark, in their own geographical areas. For example, the distribution of automobile fuel, cosmetics or consumer electronics can be carried out under franchises.

D. STRUCTURES FOR CARRYING OUT FRANCHISING

13.39 Before dealing with the provisions that are typically found in a franchise agreement, the ways in which franchising may be structured have to be considered. Those structures are only examples and are not intended to be an exhaustive enumeration of the ways in which franchising can be organized.

13.40 A franchisor may wish to set up a franchising program in a number of ways. He may, for example, conclude franchise agreements directly with one or more franchisees. A franchise agreement may also consist of, or include, a franchise development agreement, whereby the franchisee (franchise developer) agrees to open a number of outlets or trading units. A franchisor may wish to enter into what is called a "master franchise agreement," whereby the other party to the agreement, the "master franchisee," will grant franchises to a number of franchisees.

13.41 Making a choice between the different possible structures depends very much on the particular circumstances of the franchisor and the franchisee and the nature of the franchise. Several factors should be taken into consideration, including:

(1) the franchisor's reasons for franchising;
(2) the resources of the franchisor;
(3) the size and resources of the master franchisee or franchise developer; and
(4) the nature of the market to be served (including its location, foreign or domestic, and its relative importance to the franchisor).

(a) Unit Franchising

13.42 Unit franchising is the most straightforward way in which franchising can be carried out, because it involves direct relations between the franchisor and the franchisee, whereby the franchisor enters into a franchise agreement directly with the franchisee.

13.43 In domestic situations—where the franchisor and franchisee are in the same country—unit franchising is the most commonly used structure. It allows the franchisor to replicate his business as efficiently as possible without having to establish new structures, such as subsidiaries or joint ventures.

13.44 Unit franchising is less common, however, in international dealings— where the franchisor and franchisee are located in different countries. Linguistic, cultural, commercial, political and economic differences between the countries in which the franchisor and franchisee are located generally dictate different approaches to the implementation of the franchise in those countries. The franchisor may find that, because a different approach is necessary in the franchisee's country, it may be necessary to establish a local presence there in the form of a master franchisor, or engage in multiple-unit franchising through a local subsidiary or a joint venture.

13.45 The alternative to establishing such a local presence is for the franchisor to establish within his own organization the expertise that will enable him to adapt his franchise to the needs of each of the local markets in which he wishes to operate. While this approach maximizes the franchisor's supervision of the way in which the franchise is implemented, it significantly increases the administrative burden, and hence the cost, of operating in other countries and would detract from one of the major advantages of franchising, which is not to divert resources to establishing business operations abroad.

(b) Territorial Franchises

13.46 Franchise agreements which aim at covering a substantial territory or geographical area by setting up, simultaneously or successively, a number of units, shops or outlets, over an agreed period of time, may be referred to as "territorial franchising." Two forms of setting-up territorial franchises are the "franchise developer agreement" and the "master franchise agreement," which may be combined. These two forms are discussed below.

13.47 The type of structure chosen for a franchise agreement may have a bearing on the manner in which a franchisee or a master franchisee is legally organized. Two organizational forms should be mentioned, particularly in connection with the establishment of international or cross-border franchise agreements: subsidiaries and joint ventures. It should be noted, however, that in a franchise agreement any manner of legal organization or corporate form may be used, depending on business considerations and the applicable legislation (in particular, tax, labor, foreign investment and competition law).

13.48 In international franchising, where the local master franchisor is a *subsidiary* of the franchisor, the latter will have direct control over the network of franchisees, while still securing the necessary local input. This would require the existence of a subsidiary entity, possibly constituted as a local company, in the country in which the franchisor wishes to operate. The subsidiary would then act as the franchisor, granting franchises to one or more local franchisees.

13.49 Unlike a subsidiary, a *joint venture* is a form of alliance of two separate companies. The companies agree to act together, typically forming a separate legal entity, for a particular purpose. The exact form of the joint venture, in other words the type of legal entity that it is, depends on the wishes of the parties to the joint venture and on national law. The franchisor will actively participate in the joint venture entity to carry out the franchise. The formation of a joint venture can sometimes provide security for the owner of the intellectual property rights because, with the franchisor involved in the management of the joint venture entity, the use of the franchised system by franchisees can be controlled.

13.50 A problem that is unique to joint ventures is the relationship with the franchisor's joint venture partner. Typically, the joint venture partner is a local individual or enterprise chosen by the franchisor as a partner for his experience in local customs and business. Such experience will be valuable in tailoring the franchise to local needs and tastes, not to mention dealing with local business and legal matters, although the franchisor would have to share the management of the joint venture with his partner.

(i) Franchise Developer Agreement

13.51 A franchise developer agreement links the franchisor directly with the franchisee, who is expected to open and operate several units. This franchise will include a "development agreement" whereby the franchisee is required to develop the assigned territory by establishing a number of franchise units or outlets which he will usually own directly. In this case the franchisee will not sub-franchise out to third parties.

13.52 Generally this agreement will include a schedule setting out the time frame for establishing the franchise units and developing the assigned territory. The individual units opened by the franchisee under this type of structure would not have independent legal standing, and could be divisions or branches of the franchisee's enterprise.

(ii) Master Franchising

13.53 In a master franchise agreement the franchisor grants another party, usually called the "master franchisee," rights (which may be exclusive) for a given geographical area. The master franchisee is given the right, by the franchisor, to grant franchises to third parties, usually called "sub-franchisees," to exploit fully the potential business opportunities in the larger geographical area. It may be agreed that some of those sub-franchisees will run more than one franchise unit, in which case the sub-franchise agreement is called a "multi-unit franchise."

13.54 A master franchise agreement allows a franchisor to delegate the exploitation of a geographical area to another person, the master franchisee, in situations where that geographical area is remote from or little known to the franchisor, or where it is found to be convenient for business strategy purposes.

13.55 This approach to franchising is particularly important in international franchising, because a franchisor may wish to establish franchise operations in a given country, in which he may have no business experience. Accordingly, a candidate is found who has such business experience and who can establish one or more sub-franchisees to take advantage of business opportunities in the country. A master franchise agreement may, however, be a business strategy choice in any case, regardless of whether the franchisor has had prior experience in a given market.

13.56 One possible disadvantage of master franchising for a franchisor is that he has to share some degree of control over the manner in which the franchise is implemented in the country in which a master franchisee is established. This is often mitigated, however, by provisions in the master franchise agreement specifying the latitude that the master franchisee has for making alterations to the franchised system in order to accommodate local needs.

(iii)   Combined Structures

13.57 A franchise agreement may be based on a combination of the structures mentioned above. It may, for example, combine a master franchise, under which a number of independent sub-franchisees will be established, with a franchise developer agreement under which the same master franchisee, or one of his sub-franchisees, is additionally committed to open a number of his own units in the same territory. A master franchisor could also be mandated to conclude franchise development agreements with one or more of the independent franchisees under the master franchise.

E.   TYPICAL PROVISIONS IN A FRANCHISE AGREEMENT

13.58 Provisions typically found in a business format type of franchise agreement will vary depending on its particular object and purpose. Competent professional advice should be sought where required to understand the objects and purposes of a given franchise agreement and to determine whether its provisions are appropriate and balanced.

13.59 The typical provisions of a franchise agreement are discussed below in three sections: section A details the rights and obligations of the franchisor and section B the rights and obligations of the franchisee, while section C refers to miscellaneous provisions and deals with the possibility of the agreement being breached or terminated, as well as its term and the means of renewal.

13.60 When speaking of the obligations of the franchisor, it should be borne in mind that one of the legal structures discussed in part IV other than direct franchising may be used. In such cases, the obligations of the franchisor may actually be assumed by a master franchisee. It is of critical importance to review the franchise agreement carefully to determine which entity owes obligations to the franchisee under the agreement. Similarly, it is important to the franchisee to know to which entity obligations are owed.

(a) Rights and Obligations of the Franchisor

13.61 The obligations of a franchisor towards the franchisee can be divided into two principal areas. The first includes the obligation of the franchisor to license intellectual property rights and other relevant rights to a franchisee to allow the franchisee to use the franchised system. The second includes the obligation to communicate the franchised system to the franchisee to allow the grant of the franchise to have practical effect. In other words, the franchisor must not only grant a right to the franchisee to use the franchised system, but also tell him how it is done.

13.62 The heart of the franchise agreement—the license given by the franchisor to a franchisee to use the franchised system. For example, Vespucci, Inc. agrees to allow the franchisee to do business under the franchised system using its trademarks, trade name, trade dress, industrial designs, inventions, copyrighted works and trade secrets. All specific intellectual property titles, such as trademark registrations, design registrations and patents are enumerated. Trade secrets, technical know-how, manufacturing data and business information are described in general terms or incorporated in the agreement by reference to other documents, such as an operating manual or a set of guidelines.

13.63 The franchisor is required to identify precisely these various intellectual property rights and the manner of their use by the franchisee. This can be done in the franchise agreement, including appendices and supporting documents.

13.64 Intellectual property rights are established and maintained in accordance with national laws. Since successful franchising depends on establishing, maintaining and, where necessary, enforcing strong intellectual property rights, the agreement should specify that it is the franchisor's obligation to keep those rights in force. The agreement should also specify whose obligation it is to take care of or follow up the administrative procedures that have to be pursued to that end before the local authorities, and to take action in defense of intellectual property rights which have been infringed. It may be agreed, for example, that the franchisor must prosecute any infringer, but the franchisee must provide cooperation and assistance for that purpose.

13.65 The strong protection of intellectual property rights held by the franchisor benefits the franchisee since these are the rights under which the franchisee is licensed to operate the franchised system and which give him a competitive advantage over those who cannot use the system. So, any weakening of those intellectual property rights will accordingly weaken the competitive advantage of the franchisee.

13.66 However, it is not sufficient for a franchisor to have developed a franchised system and to grant a franchisee a license to use the system. To allow the franchisee to make effective use of the system, it must be communicated to him. The franchised system will be communicated to the franchisee in one or more of several possible ways, which include the provision of a manual of operations and training courses.

(i)   Operating Manual

13.67 The operating manual is certainly one of the most important means of communicating the franchised system for many franchises. It should include the information necessary for actually carrying out the franchised system.

13.68 For example, Vespucci, Inc. has developed an Operating Manual which contains a specific description of all aspects of the operation of a franchised unit, including information on site selection for the unit, employee recruitment and training, accounting, supplies and stock control, recipes, food preparation, cleaning schedules, sales routines and business policy. In short, it contains a comprehensive enumeration of all the specific details that have made VESPUCCI restaurants successful in the past in other locations.

(ii)   Training

13.69 A franchisor can be expected to provide a franchisee and, where appropriate, his employees with sufficient training to operate the franchised system, and also with further training, as necessary, after the franchised unit is opened.

13.70 The training provided by the franchisor may include the following elements:

(1) Marketing Training: The franchisor will generally train the franchisee in marketing, selling and promotional techniques in relation to his products, their advantages over products distributed by others and the recommended use of the franchisor's products to enhance the franchisee's ability to sell them.

(2) Processing Training: In respect of franchises where goods are to be prepared and sold, for example, fast food, the franchisor will provide training in the manner in which the goods are to be prepared or processed, and in the manner of dispensing them to the public.

(3) Repair Training: The franchisor will probably train the franchisee in product repair, as well as ensure that he has the proper stock of replacement parts and diagnostic and service equipment. It is imperative for the success of a distribution franchise that the franchisee should be capable of repairing and servicing the product. Where services are provided, the franchisee should be capable of correcting insufficient or improper servicing.

(4) General Business Training: The franchisor may teach the franchisee how to keep proper accounting records, inventory, credit sales records, personnel records, tax records and all the other financial and administrative details that are necessary for the operation of a successful business. The franchisor may even develop computer programs designed to assist the franchisee in maintaining proper records.

13.71 Whatever the extent of the training program, it should be clearly revealed to the prospective franchisee, including any expenses that the franchisee may incur (such as fees, travel, accommodation or meals) in connection with his participation in the training. The franchise agreement should specify who bears the costs associated with such training. The agreement should also mention the consequences of not completing the initial training provided by the franchisor, including the possible forfeiture of fees which may have been paid in that connection.

13.72 The training program may take place in several phases, depending on the circumstances of the franchise. For example, the first phase of training by Vespucci, Inc. may involve bringing the new franchisee to its head office to conduct an initial training program. The second phase may involve sending instructors to the franchisee's restaurant just prior to its first opening. The instructors train the franchisee's employees and work with them in establishing the new franchise. The third phase may involve subsequent retraining, after the franchise has started operating. This may be particularly important if new products, equipment or procedures are adopted by Vespucci, Inc. to make the franchised system more efficient or profitable.

(iii)   Opening Assistance

13.73 If the franchisor is responsible for selecting or approving the site of the franchised unit, constructing a building on the site, setting up and stocking the building and eventually opening the franchised unit, he should provide a reasonable schedule up to the date when the building will be ready for occupancy. It is important to have this information because, if the franchisee has paid an initial fee and made commitments to purchase equipment or hire workers, he should be advised as to how soon the franchised unit will be ready to operate, so that the commitments can be met on time.

(iv)   Continued Support

13.74 The franchisee will interact with the franchisor and provide him with feedback on a continuous basis during the operation of the franchise. The franchisee may ask for specific assistance from the franchisor when he needs it, and the agreement should prescribe the fashion in which such help should be requested by the franchisee and provided by, or on behalf of, the franchisor.

13.75 The franchise system will undoubtedly undergo changes to take into account changes in the tastes or wishes of consumers and in the conditions under which franchisees operate. Accordingly, for franchisees to remain competitive, the franchisor must continue to develop and improve the franchised system to align it with such changes.

13.76 Such improvements to the franchised system must be communicated to the franchisee, for example, by additional training or the operating manual. If these improvements are protected by the franchisor in the form of additional intellectual property rights, the original franchise agreement should be so drafted that it automatically accords a license to the franchisee to use them and thereby take advantage of the improvements.

13.77 The franchisee will normally be required to accept and follow the instructions of the franchisor in respect of such changes and improvements. The changes should not, however, be such that they fundamentally alter the essential elements of the system which was agreed upon initially. On the other hand, an agreement in an international franchising set-up should contemplate some leeway for the franchisee, allowing him to make certain adjustments to the changes or improvements communicated by the franchisor, in the light of prevalent local conditions.

(b) Rights and Obligations of the Franchisee

13.78 The franchisee's obligations can be divided into four basic areas: compliance with a development schedule, payment of the various fees required under the franchise agreement, compliance with certain requirements imposed by the franchisor to allow quality control to be exercised, and respect for the confidentiality of certain information.

(i) Development Schedule

13.79 In the case of development franchises, and sometimes also in the case of master franchises, a development schedule will be included in the agreement. The development schedule will specify the number of franchise units, shops or other outlets which have to be opened by the franchisee, or by the sub-franchisees under a master franchise, within an agreed period of time. Compliance with the development schedule is an important factor in taking the best advantage of the commercial opportunities existing in a given territory or market. Not only will the income of both parties to the franchise agreement depend on the timely opening of the franchise units, but the creation of clientele and the extent of market share will also be contingent on the timely establishment of such units in the appropriate locations.

13.80 The franchise agreement may stipulate that untimely compliance with an agreed development schedule may produce certain consequences, such as limitation or forfeiture of the franchisee's exclusivity status. Serious cases of non-compliance with the development schedule could be grounds for termination of the franchise agreement between the franchisor and the developer franchisee. That would not, however, necessarily affect the sub-franchises or individual unit agreements which may have been concluded by the master franchisee.

(ii) Payment of Fees

13.81 One of the most important provisions in the franchise agreement is the identification of the various fees to be paid by the franchisee to the franchisor, and the method of their calculation. The franchise agreement should specify all payments to be made by the franchisee to the franchisor, including any initial payment, also called an "entrance fee," for granting the franchise, and ongoing royalty payments, payment for advertising and promotion, security deposits and any other payments. More specialized fees that are unique to a particular type of franchised system may also be required. These may, for example, include charges for the use of a computerized reservation network in the case of hotel franchises. The basis for computing ongoing fees, such as royalties and advertising payments, should be specified in the agreement, together with a schedule of due dates and an indication of the reports that are required to show the correctness of such payments.

13.82 It should be noted that, in some countries, the types of fee that afford the franchisor his income may have implications as to the level of the taxes payable. In some countries, transfer of technology agreements and service agreements may be subjected to different treatment for taxation purposes. Countries seeking foreign investment will generally grant favorable taxation treatment to transfer of technology and licensing agreements. To the extent that franchising agreements can be considered as transfer of technology agreements (not merely service agreements), they may benefit from that favorable treatment. This fact should be borne in mind particularly by parties entering into an international franchise agreement.

13.83 Information on the fees to be paid is important to the franchisee because one of the major areas of consideration will be the franchisee's ability to raise sufficient funds to enter the franchise relationship and eventually open one or more franchised units. Thus, a particular concern of franchisees is whether the franchisor has not understated the amount of money necessary for a franchisee to start a franchised unit. Some franchisees have eventually failed because they have been under-capitalized owing to the franchisor's lack of candor in explaining the amount of money that the franchisee would need in order to start.

13.84 Fees may be levied in a number of different ways. They may, for example, take the form of a monetary payment, or entail the purchase of products by the franchisee at an agreed marked-up price which includes the franchisor's profit "fee." It should, however, be noted that in some countries the franchisor cannot insist on setting the price at which the franchisee should sell the product.

13.85 The initial or entrance fee is typically a lump-sum payment, although it may be paid in installments (for example, 25% on signing the contract; 25% on completion of training; 25% on opening of first franchised unit; etc). The franchisor may regard this fee as a payment for the license to use his intellectual property rights, for the initial training he offers and for the administrative expenses associated with establishing the new franchised unit, or a combination of two or more of these.

13.86 Ongoing fees may be presented as royalty fees or as service fees, depending on the applicable legislation, in particular, tax law. Royalties paid by the franchisee may be regarded by the franchisor as his basic source of income, representing payment for the continued use of the system already developed. They should, moreover, at least in part, represent payments to the franchisor for the conduct of research and development efforts to improve the franchised system and communicate the improvements to the franchisee. Service fees, considered as earned fees, might be more favorably treated under tax law.

13.87 National laws may require that agreed ongoing fees be broken down and attributed to different elements of the franchise package. In such cases, if one of the elements, for example, a patent or design right ceases to exist during the operation of the franchisee, the ongoing fees may be adjusted accordingly.

13.88 In most franchising relationships, it is of critical importance for the success of individual franchised units, and for the franchised system as a whole, to advertise and promote both the units and the system. This ensures a continuing demand for the products or services of the franchised units. The franchisor will therefore normally require the franchisee to spend a specified amount on advertising and promotion.

13.89 Payments made for advertising or promotion are therefore not properly "fees" which go to the franchisor. They rather constitute an obligation to spend specified amounts of money to ensure continuing demand for the franchise's products or services. Depending on the type of franchise and the specific franchise agreement, the specified amounts can be divided among local, regional, national or even international promotion efforts.

13.90 In most franchises, the franchisor has an ongoing responsibility to render services to the franchisee, in the form of advice on the management of franchised units, advice on the form and content of advertising and the updating of the franchise. Often the franchise agreement will provide that fees for these services are to be separately calculated and paid.

(iii)   Compliance with Quality Control Requirements

13.91 The franchisor's control over the manner in which the franchisee operates the franchised system is essential to ensure that the operation is properly carried out and that intellectual property rights owned by the franchisor, in particular his distinctive signs, are protected. This is necessary because in a franchise operation the public will directly associate the franchisor with the franchisee. Therefore, sustaining the reputation and goodwill of the franchisor's distinctive signs is in the interest of both parties. As regards the control of the quality of the goods produced or the services provided by the franchisee, the franchisor will usually insist on the instructions and recommendations in the operating manual being complied with, on having the right to inspect the franchisee's operation and on supplies being ordered from him or from a recommended or approved source.

13.92 While it seems clear that the franchisor must impose quality control requirements on the franchisee to protect both parties' interests in the franchised system, care should be taken to ensure that the requirements do not violate national competition laws. On the other hand, national trademark laws often require licensors to exercise control over the use of their licensed marks in order to enforce their rights and preserve the validity of the license contract. As franchise agreements normally include the licensing of rights in marks and other distinctive signs, these control requirements should be borne in mind.

13.93 Provision is made in the franchise agreement for requiring the franchisee to comply with the recommendations made by the franchisor on the operation of the franchise, and especially those set forth in the operating manual. As mentioned above, the franchisee would be required to comply also with any changes, improvements or updates incorporated in the operating manual.

13.94 The requirement that a franchisee devote his best efforts to the proper operation of the franchised unit is common. Vespucci, Inc., for example, relies on the franchisee, within his exclusive territory, in order to benefit from the franchise to the fullest extent possible. To that end Vespucci, Inc. would seek to prevent the franchisee from entering into any business relationship that is in direct or indirect competition with Vespucci, Inc. during the period of the franchise.

13.95 Moreover, in the case of owner-operated franchise units, it may be reasonable for a franchisor to require a franchisee not to be involved in the same or a similar business during the term of the franchise agreement. If such a condition forms part of the franchise agreement, the prospective franchisee should be clearly informed.

13.96 In order to ensure that the requirements laid down by the franchisor are being adhered to, the franchise agreement will provide for the franchisor's right to conduct periodical inspections of the franchised unit. It may also be provided that the franchisor will be allowed to speak to customers and staff members of the franchisee.

13.97 As noted above, the franchisor has a strong interest in ensuring that the franchisee meets a minimum level of quality of the finished product. One way of controlling the quality of the finished product is to control the quality of the raw materials used by the franchisee, to the extent that those materials constitute an essential factor of the franchised system. For example, the requirement that a restaurant such as a VESPUCCI franchisee purchase flour or beef only from the franchisor or from an approved supplier prevents the franchisee from lowering the quality of the finished product through the use of inferior materials, which may be less expensive. Therefore, the requirement that the franchisee use only flour or beef purchased from Vespucci, Inc. or from a supplier approved by it, in the preparation of the food sold under the franchise helps, where that requirement is justified, to ensure that the standard of quality established by Vespucci, Inc. is met.

13.98 The franchisee should also be informed of any benefit that the franchisor may derive from such an arrangement, so as to be in a position to determine whether the price of the products is excessive in the light of prices for similar goods or services on the open market. This information should also include benefits accruing to the franchisor from any requirement to purchase, rent or lease of real estate, services, signs or equipment, if the purchase, rent or lease must be made from specific persons (or companies), including the franchisor.

13.99 It should be noted that such provisions may run counter to national or regional laws protecting free competition. In some countries or regions this issue has been resolved by allowing such obligations only where necessary to protect the intellectual property rights of the franchisor or to maintain the reputation of the franchised system. Moreover, it may be required by competition laws that such restrictions apply only where it is impractical to lay down objective quality specifications so that the franchisee can buy the goods from any person subject to compliance with those specifications.

13.100 A franchise agreement may require the franchisee not to sell products other than those approved by the franchisor. The franchisor does not want the franchisee to sell any line of goods which he considers will reflect adversely on the franchised system or compete with his own product line.

13.101 Again, such a restriction may raise problems with national or regional competition laws but is generally accepted as reasonable where the sale of the product or provision of the service in question by the franchisee would compete with the sale of the franchisor's line of products, reflect adversely on the reputation of the franchised system or expose the franchisor to additional liability.

(iv) Confidentiality Requirement

13.102 An undertaking to preserve confidentiality over certain elements of the franchised system will operate to the benefit of both franchisor and franchisee. Any franchisor will have spent a great deal of time and energy on developing the franchised system, which is to a large extent contained, or described, in the operating manual. Accordingly, it is essential to the maintenance of the trade secrets of the franchisor that the operating manual and any other information of a confidential nature be kept in confidence by the franchisee. Naturally, such information may be disclosed to the franchisee's employees in order that the business of the franchised unit may be carried out. The franchisee may therefore be required by the franchise agreement to oblige his employees to keep that information confidential.

(c) Miscellaneous Provisions

13.103 There are a number of provisions which can be found in most business contracts, including franchise agreements, such as those pertaining to exclusivity, term and renewal of the agreement, the implications of breach, transfer and termination. These provisions are discussed below, with particular reference to their implications for a franchise agreement.

(i) Exclusivity

13.104 A franchisor may decide that if each franchisee is limited in some fashion to a specific geographical area the income of the individual franchised units, and hence the overall income of the franchisor, could be maximized. In such cases, "exclusivity" clauses may be included in the franchise agreement.

13.105 Exclusivity in respect of a territory or geographical area will generally require commitments by both the franchisor and the franchisee. The franchisor will protect a franchisee from competition by other franchisees within the exclusive territory by undertaking not to grant other franchises for that territory. Such obligation may be absolute or limited to certain types of sales, sectors of consumers or period of time.

13.106 In turn, the franchisee would have to accept limitations aimed at preventing him from interfering with other franchisees outside the assigned territory. Those other franchisees would have undertaken equivalent obligations. The limitation on the franchisee's activities could include one or more of the following:

(1) prohibition to establish a franchise unit other than at a specified location or within a specified territory;
(2) prohibition to sell other than from a specified franchised unit or within a specified territory;
(3) prohibition to advertise, solicit or accept sales other than at a specified location or within a specified territory.

13.107 Different degrees and sorts of exclusivity may be considered for the purposes of franchising. A franchisee (or master franchisee) may be accorded exclusivity to sell goods (or provide services) to the general public, but the franchisor may have reserved for himself or for other franchisees the sale to, for example, hospitals or armed forces establishments in the specified area, or in the entire territory or country. A franchisee may have exclusivity to sell through agreed outlets open to the public, but sales through other means, for example, by correspondence or door-to-door sales, might be expressly reserved.

13.108 Of particular concern to a franchisee is whether a franchisor will be entitled to locate a store owned and operated by him (known as a "company store") in the area assigned to an exclusive franchisee. Such a company store may have a competitive advantage over a franchised unit. Unless the agreement specifically forbids the franchisor to establish a store in the designated area, he may have the right to do so.

13.109 Exclusivity may also be linked to a time factor. A franchisee may be given the first franchise in an area where a franchisor intends to establish further franchises at a later date. Exclusivity might be agreed for a number of years so as to give the franchisee lead time over future franchisees. The franchisor may grant the franchisee an exclusive territory, with a provision that no further franchised units will be established within, for example, a period of two years. After that, the franchisor may have the right to open a limited number of new franchised units in the area, but it may be agreed that none of them will be located within a limited distance (for example, three kilometers) from the original franchisee. The franchisor may agree to give the original franchisee a right of first refusal to operate all or some of those new franchises.

13.110 The length of the period of exclusivity could be made to depend on the achievement of a minimum volume of sales or on compliance with a development schedule in case of a multiple-unit or master franchise.

13.111 Whatever exclusivity arrangements are made, their scope and effect, should be explained to the franchisee before the franchise agreement is concluded. Additionally, care should be taken to ensure that provisions dealing with the grant of exclusive geographical areas do not conflict with national or regional laws protecting free competition.

(ii)   Term of Agreement

13.112 The parties to a franchise agreement normally decide to set a definite term on the agreement, subject to premature termination, as discussed below. The term should be long enough for both parties to derive some benefit from the agreement if it is not renewed, mainly owing to the high initial training and starting costs of a franchised unit. In particular, if the franchisee is required to make a significant investment, such as in land, building, assets and inventory, this justifies giving the franchise agreement quite a long term. But the term should still be short enough for the parties to sever the relationship in a reasonable period of time for personal or business reasons without being in breach of the agreement.

13.113 It should be noted that, under the laws of certain countries, certain particular kinds of industrial property license or technology transfer agreement, of which a franchise agreement may be one, are subject to a fixed time limit or a time limit that must meet specified criteria. Certain laws may also prohibit an automatic renewal of the contract.

13.114 It should be further noted that the laws of some countries provide that an industrial property license such as a franchise agreement may not contain a provision prohibiting the free use of the technology or related technical information after the expiration of the licensed industrial property right. On the other hand, balanced grant-back clauses are generally acceptable under such laws.

13.115 Termination of the franchise agreement may, of course, take place at any time by mutual consent between the parties. The agreement may also provide for the possibility of termination at any time by one party giving the other advance notice to that effect.

(iii) Provisions on Breach of Agreement

13.116 If both parties are dissatisfied with the agreement and wish to terminate or modify it, that may be done. The terms of the franchise agreement should, however, provide for the case where one party unilaterally terminates the agreement, and for the consequences of such action.

13.117 It should be noted that in certain countries, under the laws governing the transfer of technology (which may include franchise agreements), if the parties to an industrial property license or technology transfer agreement terminate it before the end of its normal term, notice to that effect must be given to the government authorities within a fixed time limit after the date of termination.

13.118 The parties may wish to include in the contract a provision to the effect that, if the franchisor breaches an essential provision of the agreement, the franchisee should have the option of terminating it and claiming redress.

13.119 The franchise agreement may contain a definition of "material breach." For example, any action that invalidates the franchisor's trademark, or the supply of substandard products by the franchisor to the franchisee, where high-quality products are essential to the franchisee's operation, may be considered material breaches and provide grounds for termination of the agreement. If the franchisor promises the franchisee continuing support in the form of new product line development, advertising and promotion, celebrity participation or the opening of new territories, and unjustifiably fails to fulfill its promises, such a failure may constitute a material breach of the franchise agreement.

13.120 A breach on the part of the franchisor may amount to a material breach, but may be susceptible of cure or correction. For such cases the franchise agreement will normally provide that the franchisor is to be called upon and given the opportunity to make the necessary corrections within a specified period, for example, 30 days, before the franchisee can terminate the agreement.

13.121 In order to protect his interest in the franchised system, as well as his interest in ensuring a steady income, the franchisor will probably wish, in turn, to secure the right to terminate the franchise for any major breach of the agreement. Therefore it is normally required that the breach be a "material" one.

13.122 The failure of the franchisee to operate the franchise properly may constitute a material breach which may make the agreement liable to termination.

For example, if the franchisee is not meeting a reasonable sales quota which has been discussed and agreed upon, the franchisor may want to terminate the agreement. Also, if the franchisee becomes insolvent, has breached the confidentiality requirement, is under-reporting royalties, is failing to pay royalties when due or is otherwise operating in a manner that falls short of the franchisor's standards of quality and service, with resulting poor quality of the product or poor service, termination may be justified. Moreover, where allowed under national law, any challenge by the franchisee to the intellectual property rights that form part of the franchise may provide a basis for termination of the contract. If a breach of the aforementioned kind does occur, and it is possible to correct it, the franchisee should be given an opportunity to do so.

13.123 In addition, the persistent breaching of certain minor obligations over a period of time, or a series of minor breaches occurring at the same time, may amount to a material breach justifying termination of the agreement.

13.124 Where a franchisee declares himself bankrupt, commits fraud or is found guilty of criminal acts, the franchisor could terminate the franchise without having to give advance notice to the franchisee, since this type of situation would not normally be capable of "correction."

(iv) Rights and Duties of the Parties on Termination

13.125 Termination occurs when the term of the franchise agreement comes to an end and the agreement is not renewed, or if the agreement is terminated before its normal expiration because a material breach has been committed by the franchisee or franchisor. The agreement can also be terminated prior to expiry by mutual consent between the parties. In any case, the question arises what are the rights and duties of the franchisor and franchisee upon termination. Accordingly, the franchise agreement should indicate what the parties are to do upon termination of the agreement.

13.126 On termination of the agreement, the former franchisee is no longer entitled to use the intellectual property rights that were licensed under the franchise. This is because they are rights that have been granted to, or registered by, the franchisor and to which the franchisee has no claim. In particular, the franchisee must be aware that the moneys paid by him (in fees or otherwise) for the advertising and promotion of the marks and trade names used under the franchise agreement would not afford him any right of continued use of those proprietary signs after the termination of the agreement. When the franchise agreement ends so too does the franchisee's entitlement to use the subject matter of any intellectual property included in the franchised system, in particular, the franchisor's distinctive signs (marks, trade name, trade dress, etc.)

13.127 With respect to technology not covered by registered industrial property rights, the laws of certain countries governing the transfer of technology provide that, after the expiration of some types of agreement, such as those conveying trade secrets or "proprietary" know-how, the technology recipient will be free to use the technology. It may, however, be permissible to oblige the technology recipient not to communicate the confidential information to others for a specified period of time or until the information is disclosed or otherwise becomes public.

13.128 The reason for including in the franchise agreement a so-called "post-termination restriction" is that the franchisor, having taught the franchisee how to operate a successful business, does not want the franchisee to compete with him in the same area after the franchise is terminated. Also relevant is the interest of the franchisor to be left in a position to offer something to new franchisees who may wish to step in. On the other hand, the former franchisee will have spent a period of his life running the franchised business, and as a result will have learned to do it well, and might not be interested in moving. Thus the former franchisee may not want to be prohibited from practicing that business in the same area. A fair balance has to be struck between these two competing interests.

13.129 The laws of some countries recognize that there are grounds for restricting the franchisee from operating the same type of franchise in the same geographical marketing area for a reasonable period of time after termination. The franchisor should have the opportunity to train a new franchisee and be permitted a reasonable period of time to set up the new franchisee in the business. After the new franchise is established, the former franchisee may compete with the new one on equal terms, but using his own distinctive signs.

13.130 These post-termination restrictions and the reasonableness of their scope will generally concern three questions: the length of time, the geographical area and the types of business activity prohibited. The question of the length of time during which a former franchisee can reasonably be prohibited from competing generally depends on the particular circumstances of each situation, but may be subject to a specific limitation imposed by national or supranational competition laws.

13.131 As for the size of the geographical area in which a former franchisee can be precluded from competing, it should generally match the market area in which the franchised unit operates. Certain national or supranational competition laws may allow such restrictions to extend to all areas in which the former franchisee would be in competition with other franchisees or with the franchisor.

13.132 Another restriction that will have to be assessed for its reasonableness is that relating to the type of business that the former franchisee is precluded from operating. For example, a restaurant franchisee could be restricted from operating the same type of restaurant in the same area after the franchise is terminated, such as, in the case of VESPUCCI, an Italian-food restaurant where food is served on the premises. A former VESPUCCI franchisee should not, however, be prohibited from operating a restaurant that specializes in fast food, for example, which is a different type of operation aimed at a different segment of consumers.

13.133 Finally, any money owed by the franchisee to the franchisor, or vice versa, should be paid. Inventories and other assets purchased by the franchisee that have no significant value outside the franchise operation should be transferred to the franchisor, and the franchisee should be paid a fair market price for them.

13.134 It should be borne in mind that, even if the goodwill value of the franchised system has increased during the operation of the franchise agreement, the franchisee will not be entitled to any payment in that connection upon termination of the agreement.

(v) Transfer of Agreement

13.135 Provisions on the transfer of the agreement usually relate to two situations. First, the situation where a franchisee wishes to sell the franchised unit, in its entirety or only in part, or to transfer all or part of his rights under the franchise agreement, or both; and, secondly, the situation where a franchisee dies or is incapacitated.

13.136 It would seem that, if the franchisee has developed a successful franchise and wishes to sell it to a willing buyer at a price that includes a profit, he should have the right to do so; he may wish to pursue some other business or retire from business altogether.   The increased value of the business, achieved by the franchisee's efforts, should give him the right to profit by the sale of the franchise to a buyer capable of paying the contract price. If the franchisee is not permitted to sell the franchise to such a buyer, he loses the benefit of the effort he has expended in developing a successful franchise.

13.137 The franchise relationship is a very personal one, however. The franchisor relies heavily on the ability of his franchisees to operate their franchised units in the prescribed manner. The franchise agreement establishes a sort of partnership based on the conviction that the other party is trustworthy and capable of fulfilling his obligations. This is all the more true where know-how and trade secrets are to be communicated by one party to the other. If the franchisor does not have the right to approve a purchaser, he may find himself bound to accept a franchisee whom he believes will be unable to operate the franchise properly, or with whom he will not be able to develop a bona fide business relationship.

13.138 One solution is to require the consent of the franchisor prior to sale by the franchisee of the franchised unit or rights under the agreement. Such consent should not be withheld unreasonably. Furthermore, the franchising agreement may provide that the franchisor may himself purchase a franchised unit that is offered for sale.

13.139 Another solution is to give a franchisor a right of first refusal in the event of any bona fide offer made by a third party. Under such an arrangement, if the franchisee receives, from a qualified purchaser, a bona fide offer in writing to purchase the franchise, the franchisee may notify the franchisor of the terms of the offer and the identity of the prospective purchaser. The franchisor should be allowed a reasonable period of time to investigate and match the offer if he wishes. If he fails to do so, then the sale to the new franchisee is deemed to have been approved by him.

13.140 Where the franchisee is a company or a limited liability entity, change in share ownership may entail a change in the ownership of the franchised units. It may also bring about a change in the management of the franchisee's enterprise. The franchise contract should provide for those cases. In international franchising, the commercial legislation of the country where the franchisee is to be set up should be taken into account.

13.141 The same situation as in the case of a sale by a franchisee arises when the franchisee dies and the ownership of the franchise passes to his heirs. If the franchisor can establish that the heirs are incapable of operating the business properly, then he should have a right to repurchase the franchise at a fair market price.

(vi)   Renewal of Agreement

13.142 The renewal of a franchise agreement is not necessarily automatic. Renewal is therefore an issue which the agreement must deal with in some detail. Moreover, renewal should not be expected in franchising agreements, especially in the case of development or multi-unit franchises. These agreements will generally not be extended beyond their term once the development objective has been attained.

13.143 The question of renewing the franchise, on terms that will be fair to both parties, presents certain difficulties. If the franchisee is successful, he would like to continue the arrangement under the original conditions. At the end of the first term of the franchise agreement, the franchisor may be offering new franchises for a higher royalty than was agreed many years earlier, when the original franchise was negotiated, and he would like the renewed franchisee to pay the same royalty rate as the new ones.

13.144 The franchisor would therefore usually grant a renewal on the same terms as are being offered to new franchisees, but the renewing franchisee would not be required to pay another initial fee on renewal because the franchisor would not have to incur the investigation and training costs again. On renewal it is not usual for the franchisee to be required to pay another advance or "up-front" franchise fee.

13.145 It may have been stipulated that renewal of the agreement may be contingent on meeting certain requirements, or that certain conditions are to be agreed upon prior to the extension of the franchise. The franchisee might, for example, be required to upgrade or refurbish the franchised unit, or adjust to new features or technical requirements contained in an updated operating manual.

References for Section E
International Bureau of WIPO, *Franchising Guide*, WIPO Pub. No.480, 1994

CHAPTER 14

Character Merchandising

A. THE NOTION OF CHARACTER

(a) Definition

14.1 Broadly speaking, the term "character" covers both fictional humans (for example, Tarzan or James Bond) or non-humans (for example, Donald Duck or Bugs Bunny) and real persons (for example, famous personalities in the film or music business, sportsmen).

14.2 In the context of the merchandising of characters, it is mainly the essential personality features easily recognized by the public at large which will be relevant. Those personality features are, for example, the name, image, appearance or voice of a character or symbols permitting the recognition of such characters.

(b) Sources and Primary Use of Characters

14.3 The main sources of fictional characters are:

(1) literary works (such as Pinocchio by Collodi or Tarzan by E.R. Burroughs);
(2) strip cartoons (such as Tintin by Hergé or Astérix by Uderzo and Goscinny);
(3) artistic works (such as paintings (Mona Lisa by Leonardo da Vinci)) or drawings (the panda of the World Wide Fund for Nature (WWF) or the young boy Fido Dido by Joanna Ferrone and Susan Rose);
(4) cinematographic works (such as Crocodile Dundee, King Kong, Rambo or E.T. with respect to movies, McGyver or Columbo with respect to television series or Bambi with respect to motion picture cartoons).

14.4 It should be noted that, in the case of cinematographic works, the character may, and in fact often does originate in a literary work (such as the character Oliver Twist by Charles Dickens) or in a strip cartoon (such as the character Batman).

14.5 As regards the primary use of a fictional character, it can in most cases be referred to as an "entertainment function." Such a character may appear in a novel, a tale or a strip cartoon (for example, the character Tarzan in the novel entitled "Tarzan, the Lord of the Jungle", the character Mr. Brown in the tale entitled "Squirrel Nutkin" or the characters named James Bond or Tintin), and the success gained by the work depicting the character generally leads to new stories. Such primary use will be made by the creator of the character, although, where a character has reached a high degree of reputation and the creator has died, the heirs if any, or the holders of the publishing rights, may organize by means of contracts the "survival" of the character in new stories (for example the books featuring James Bond after the death of Ian Fleming). Other creators, on the contrary, may wish that the characters they have created should not be the subject of new stories after their death (for example, Hergé, the creator of Tintin). The situation is somewhat different in the case of cinematographic works, where it is seldom the creator of a character (the maker of the original drawings or scripts) who makes the primary use (but exceptions do exist, such as the "little man" character created by Charlie Chaplin).

14.6 In other cases, the primary uses of a fictional character can sometimes be referred to as "promotional, advertising and recognition functions." This will concern, for example, characters which are closely linked to a certain company (such as the "Michelin Man," the Exxon (Esso) tiger or the Peugeot lion), to a certain product (such as the character Johnnie Walker to a Scotch whisky) or to a given event (such as the mascots used to personalize Olympic Games or World Cup football). Those characters are created with a view to popularizing legal entities, products or services, and activities. Generally, the primary use will not originate from the creator of the character, i.e. the person entrusted with the task of creating the character.

14.7 The main sources, where the character is a real person, are the movie and show businesses and sporting activities. In the case of real persons, one should speak of "primary activity" in preference to "primary use." The difficulty with real persons is that actors, for example, may enjoy a reputation both as persons and as the character they may have portrayed in a movie or television series. In some cases, the real person is only referred to under the name of the character portrayed (see developments below on the types of character merchandising).

B. THE CONCEPT OF CHARACTER MERCHANDISING

(a) Definition

14.8 Character merchandising can be defined as the adaptation or secondary exploitation, by the creator of a fictional character or by a real person or by one or several authorized third parties, of the essential personality features (such as the name, image or appearance) of a character in relation to various goods and/ or services with a view to creating in prospective customers a desire to acquire those goods and/or to use those services because of the customers' affinity with that character.

14.9 It should already be emphasized that the person or legal entity which will organize the merchandising activity (the merchandiser) will very seldom be the creator of the fictional character or the real person concerned. The various property or personality rights vesting in the character will be the subject of contracts (such as transfer or license agreements or product or service endorsement agreements) enabling one or several interested third parties to be regarded as authorized users of the character.

14.10 The following examples of character merchandising can be given:

(1) a toy is the three-dimensional reproduction of the fictional character Mickey Mouse;

(2) a T-shirt bears the name or image of the fictional characters Ninja Turtles;

(3) the label attached to a perfume bottle bears the name "Alain Delon";

(4) tennis shoes bear the name "André Agassi";

(5) an advertising movie campaign for the drink Coca Cola Light shows the pop star Elton John drinking Coca Cola Light.

(b) A Brief History of Character Merchandising

14.11 As an organized system, character merchandising originated and was initiated in the United States of America in the 1930s in the Walt Disney Studios in Burbank (California). When this company created its cartoon characters (Mickey, Minnie, Donald), one of its employees, Kay Kamen, established a department specialized in the secondary commercial exploitation of those characters and, to the surprise of most, succeeded in granting an important number of licenses for the manufacture and distribution of low-priced mass market merchandise (posters, T-shirts, toys, buttons, badges, drinks).

14.12 Of course, the idea of secondary exploitation of the reputation of a character existed before the twentieth century, but the reasons were not directly commercial. In South East Asia, for example, the religious characters of "Ramayana," such as Prince Rama, Vishnu and Sita, have for centuries been represented in the form of sculptures, puppets or toys. Furthermore, in more recent times (late 19th century), some industrialists, with a view to popularizing the goods they manufactured, decided to create fictional characters which would be represented on the goods, the packaging or any documents and would be used to generate secondary exploitation for functional or ornamental goods such as decorative plates, articles of clothing, clocks, puppets, etc. (for example in France, the character Pierrot Gourmand (a famous mark for lollipops) or the Michelin Man of the tire manufacturer). Furthermore, the exploitation of literary characters probably started with the works of Beatrix Potter (the books Peter Rabbit and Squirrel Nutkin with the animal characters which became and still are represented in the form of soft toys or other articles for children) or with the work of Lewis Carroll (Alice in Wonderland), the characters of which also became soft toys and were later adapted into a motion picture cartoon.

14.13 This phenomenon developed rapidly during the 20th century. In the 1950s, political, movie and show-business personalities authorized, for example, the reproduction of their names or images on articles of clothing (so-called "tie-in advertising"). In the 1970s and the 1980s, "merchandising" programs were set up on the basis of famous characters from films (for example, Star Wars, E.T. or Rambo). The financial consequences are very significant since, for example, the Walt Disney Merchandising Division in 1978 sold over $27 million in merchandised goods bearing the names or images of the famous characters created in their studios, and in 1979 Kenner Products sold over $100 million in merchandised goods relating to the characters depicted in the movie "Star Wars."

14.14 Furthermore, the range of goods or services covered by "merchandising" expanded considerably since, for example in the United States of America, it concerns at least 29 of the 42 classes of the International Classification of Goods and Services established by the Nice Agreement.

14.15 Today, "merchandising" programs (whether or not they include the use of the essential personality features of a character) may concern:

(1) universities (in the United States of America, merchandising of the University of California in Los Angeles with its symbol U.C.L.A.);
(2) organizations (advertising campaign for Amnesty International in France with the participation of famous film actors, or merchandising of the representation of a panda by the World Wide Fund for Nature (WWF));
(3) sports events (merchandising of the mascots of the 1992 Olympic Games in Albertville (France) and Barcelona (Spain));
(4) social events (wedding of Prince Charles and Lady Diana in the United Kingdom);
(5) art exhibitions (merchandising of the images of Van Gogh or Toulouse-Lautrec);
(6) natural events (merchandising in connection with Halley's Comet), scientific events (the comic strip character Snoopy was the mascot of the first American astronauts);
(7) personalities in many fields of activity (actors, pop stars, sportsmen, etc., whose names and images are reproduced on various goods, packaging, documents or other material).

14.16 This historical introduction can be concluded with four examples showing the impact and importance of character merchandising. Firstly, in the United States of America, after the wide advertising campaign made by the IBM Company for its computers, using a look-alike of Charlie Chaplin, the character who appeared was sometimes referred to no longer as Charlie Chaplin but as "the IBM Guy." Secondly, in the case of the Euro Disney Park which was inaugurated in April 1992 near Paris, a company obtained, for the whole of Europe, the exclusive right to reproduce the Walt Disney characters. Thirdly, the profits made in France from the recent Toulouse-Lautrec retrospective exhibition (mainly by the sales of merchandised products relating to the image of the painter) enabled the Louvre Museum to purchase an important painting for its collection. Finally, the Sony Corporation has recently formed a character merchandising unit that will sell products based on its music, film and video businesses.

(c) Types of Character Merchandising

14.17 From a commercial or marketing point of view, character merchandising can probably be dealt with in a single category. However, from the legal point of view it is important to differentiate between the various subjects of merchandising, since the scope and duration of legal protection may vary according to the subject involved.

14.18 Two main categories exist depending on whether the merchandising involves the use of fictional characters or of real personalities (generally referred to as "personality merchandising"). Between those two categories, a third hybrid category exists which is generally referred to as "image merchandising."

(i) Merchandising of Fictional Characters

14.19 This is the oldest and the best known form of merchandising. It involves the use of the essential personality features (name, image, etc.) of fictional characters in the marketing and/or advertising of goods or services.

14.20 Originally, the practice of character merchandising, as an organized system of promotion, developed as a means of exploiting the popularity of cartoon characters, drawings of attractive figures and the like. Such cartoon characters originated:

(1) in a literary work being adapted to the cartoon form (for the purpose of a movie or a comic strip) such as the characters Pinocchio or Alice in Wonderland;

(2) in a work created as a cartoon character, originally for films (Mickey Mouse, Donald Duck, Pluto) or for comic strips (Tintin, Snoopy, Astérix, Batman);

(3) in a film character, later reproduced or adapted as a cartoon for advertising and merchandising purposes (the character Zorro or even a real creature such as the shark in the film "Jaws");

(4) in a cartoon character created mainly for the purpose of merchandising and not, originally, intended for a movie or comic strip (for example, the character Fido Dido, exploited by Fido Dido, Inc. for a number of goods including the drink "Seven-Up" which was the subject of a worldwide advertising campaign, or the numerous mascots created and used in respect of various events, such as sports competitions);

(5) in a puppet or doll character designed for a film or a television show (for example, the character E.T., the Gremlins or the Muppets).

14.21 Character merchandising with cartoon characters involves mainly the use of the name, image and appearance of the character. The appearance may involve two-dimensional reproduction (drawings, stickers, etc.) or three-dimensional reproduction (dolls, key rings, etc.).

(ii) Personality Merchandising

14.22 This more recent form of merchandising involves the use of the essential attributes (name, image, voice and other personality features) of real persons (in other words, the true identity of an individual) in the marketing and/or advertising of goods and services. In general, the real person whose attributes are "commercialized" is well known to the public at large; this is the reason why this form of merchandising has sometimes been referred to as "reputation merchandising." In fact, from a commercial point of view, merchandisers believe that the main reason for a person to buy low-priced mass goods (mugs, scarves, badges, T-shirts, etc.) is not because of the product itself but because the name or image of a celebrity appealing to that person is reproduced on the product.

14.23 This category can be subdivided into two forms. The first form consists in the use of the name, image (in two or three dimensions) or symbol of a real person. This form relates mainly to famous persons in the film or music industries. However, persons connected with other fields of activity may be concerned (for example, members of a royal family). As indicated above, it is not so much the product which is of principal importance to the consumer, but rather the name or image that it bears is the main marketing and advertising vehicle. The second form occurs where specialists in certain fields, such as famous sports or music personalities, appear in advertising campaigns in relation to goods or services. The appeal for the potential consumer is that the personality represented endorses the product or service concerned and is regarded as an expert. Of course, the more the product or service advertised is linked with the activity of the personality, the more the potential consumer will consider that the said product or service is endorsed and approved by that personality (advertising for tennis shoes or rackets by a tennis champion, advertising for an energy drink by a cross-country runner or advertising for high-fidelity equipment or musical instruments by a pop star).

(iii)   Image Merchandising

14.24 This is the most recent form of merchandising. It involves the use of fictional film or television characters, played by real actors, in the marketing and advertising of goods or services. In those cases, the public sometimes finds it difficult to differentiate the actor (real person) from the role he plays (character portrayed). Sometimes, however, there is a complete association and the real person is referred to and known by the name of the character. The following examples can be given to illustrate this notion: from the film industries, Laurel and Hardy, the Marx Brothers, Crocodile Dundee, James Bond 007 played by Sean Connery and Roger Moore, Frankenstein's monster by Boris Karloff and Tarzan by Johnny Weissmuller; from television series, Columbo played by Peter Falk, the character J.R. in "Dallas," played by Larry Hagman, or the character McGyver played by Richard Dean Anderson. In the case of the latter, a T-shirt bearing the image of R.D. Anderson would be referred to as a "McGyver T-shirt," while packs of dairy products reproducing the image of R.D. Anderson would mention the name McGyver, the purchasing of such product giving the possibility of winning secondary "McGyver" products such as T-shirts or travel bags.

14.25 In the case of image merchandising, goods or services will be marketed with the merchandising of distinctive elements of a film or series (appearance and dress of the actor when playing the character coupled with memorable aspects of a scene (for example, introductory scenes of the James Bond films, the appearance and weapons of Rambo or the "knife scene" in Crocodile Dundee)).

C.   FORMS OF LEGAL PROTECTION

(a)   Copyright

14.26 In the context of copyright, the most relevant aspects of the merchandising of fictional characters and of image merchandising are books, pamphlets and other writings, cinematographic works, works of drawing and photographic works. As regards personality merchandising, the relevance of copyright is primarily in the sphere of photographic works.

14.27 Furthermore, the notion of adaptation is very important. Article 2(3) of the Berne Convention reads as follows:

14.28 "Translations, adaptations, arrangements of music and other alterations of a literary or artistic work shall be protected as original works without prejudice to the copyright in the original work."

14.29 The multiplicity of communication media offer, at the present time, a great number of possibilities for the creation of adaptations (derivative works). Many film adaptations are probably more well known than the novel or short story on which they were based (for example, the Pinocchio and Cinderella cartoons by the Walt Disney Studios are probably better known to children than the original stories, written by Collodi and Charles Perrault respectively). Some famous artistic figures have been widely merchandised once they have fallen into the public domain. For some goods or services a fictional character may be the subject of a monopoly (through trademark protection), but generally it may be exploited by anybody. For example, the famous Mona Lisa (La Gioconda) by Leonardo da Vinci has been, and still is, used on various goods or their packaging (postcards, card games, dolls, alcoholic beverages, chocolate or fruit boxes, mineral water, diaries); it has also been the subject of multiple transformations (cartoons, caricatures, fancy photographs, etc.).

14.30 Drawings or cartoons (two-dimensional works) may be protected independently if they meet the substantive requirements of copyright protection. In that respect, it should be emphasized that a work which is original is not necessarily new, since a graphic adaptation of an already existing literary character (whether or not he has fallen in the public domain) may qualify for copyright protection (for example, the literary characters Pinocchio or Cinderella adapted to the cartoon form by the Walt Disney Company). The same will apply to the drawing of a common creature (for example, the cartoon character Donald Duck). Furthermore, it should be noted that, mainly in the case of cartoon strips and animated cartoons, copyright protects each different original pose adopted by the character.

14.31 Three-dimensional works (mainly sculptures, dolls, puppets or robots), which may be original works or original adaptations of two-dimensional or audiovisual fictional characters, will generally enjoy copyright protection independently of the work in which they appear if they meet the required criteria.

14.32 Audiovisual works including fictional characters (films, video games, photographs, film frames or stills) will, as a whole (image and soundtrack), generally enjoy copyright protection if they meet the required criteria. This will be all the more probable since audiovisual fictional characters will often have "started life" as drawings (storyboards or strip cartoons) or been described in a literary work. Copyright protection may extend to the individual visual attributes or to the physical or pictorial appearances (costumes, disguises or masks) of a fictional character.

14.33 The relevance of copyright protection in the case of personality merchandising is limited, because copyright does not vest in the real person concerned but in the person who created the work in which the essential personality features of a real person appear (for example, in the case of a biography, copyright belongs to the author; in the case of a sculpture, drawing or painting representing a real person, the copyright belongs to the artist; in the case of a film or television series, the copyright in the work belongs to the person who made it possible for the work to be made and who supervised and directed the work of the actors (author or film producer)). However, in the latter example, as a performer, an actor has some rights if the law of the country of which he is a national provides for performers' rights, or if that country is party to the Rome Convention of October 26, 1961, for the Protection of Performers, Producers of Phonograms and Broadcasting Organizations.

14.34 The question is probably more debatable in respect of photographic works. The reply will depend on who owns the copyright. In most cases the author of the photographs (or more accurately of the negatives) will own the copyright. If a photograph is commissioned for private and domestic purposes, the commissioning party has usually a right to prevent the making of copies of the photograph or its being shown in public. A final problem relates to the case where the party commissioning the work is not the person who is the subject of the photograph. In any case, forms of protection other than copyright are available for the control of the commercial use of photographic works.

(b) Trademarks and Service Marks (Marks)

14.35 The essential personality features of a fictional character may, under certain conditions (mainly of a substantive nature) be registered as marks. As regards the essential personality features of a real person, the question seems more debatable, mainly with respect to the image (portrait). In the context of merchandising, the trend has been to adopt stage names and personalized logos which may be more easily registrable (for example, in the pop music area, such stage names as the Beatles and the Rolling Stones with their respective "Apple" and "Tongue and Lip" logos). Another way for a real person to protect his name is to obtain registration of the nickname by which he is known (for example, in the United States of America, the famous football player Elroy Hirsch, known as "Crazy Legs").

14.36 In countries where rights only result from registration, the main impediment however is the time needed to obtain registration because, in the context of merchandising, delays should be as short as possible since the public's recognition of many characters (such as E.T., Dick Tracy or Batman) and their popularity are of limited duration. However, there are some exceptions such as the cartoon characters of Walt Disney or the literary characters of Beatrix Potter.

14.37 Some of the conditions of form to be met by a mark which is the subject of an application will have an important impact in the context of merchandising. One of those conditions which exists in a few countries concerns the relation which should exist between the goods or services to which the mark applies and the business of the owner of the mark. Generally, neither a merchandising agency nor the creator of a character will themselves be engaged in the manufacture or marketing of secondary products, and it will therefore be difficult for them to acquire trademark rights in a fictional character because they will not themselves be dealing with the goods or services. Furthermore, the activity carried out by a licensee will not be considered as business generated by the licensor, unless the latter becomes joint owner of the licensee's business.

14.38 The modern trend is more favorable however, since it is more and more widely recognized that a mark can be applied to an unlimited number of goods or services, independently of the true activity of the applicant but notwithstanding the provisions which may exist with respect to the non-use of a registered mark.

14.39 In view of the "aesthetic functionality" doctrine (mainly in the toy or doll area) or the "primarily functional" external appearance of goods, three-dimensional configurations of goods (applied for in the form of two-dimensional graphic representations) are in principle not accepted for registration as trademarks in many countries, except where the trademark has acquired secondary meaning in connection with the goods.

14.40 Further conditions are of a substantive nature. One of the main conditions is that a mark should be distinctive, in other words, neither generic nor descriptive in respect of the goods or services covered. Furthermore, a mark should not be misleading (capable of deceiving the public) or contrary to public order or morality.

14.41 In some countries, however, distinctiveness alone is not sufficient and the personality features of a fictional character will be registrable as marks only if they have acquired a secondary meaning. In other countries the acquisition of a secondary meaning can remedy the inherent lack of distinctiveness of the essential features of a fictional character.

14.42 A number of countries have a more favorable approach, and most names and appearances of fictional characters are considered fanciful and therefore sufficiently distinctive.

14.43 As regards the essential features of a real person, the latter, or the person or entity entitled to act in his name, may obtain the registration of his name or appearance as a mark in some countries. However, where a surname (which can also be a trade name) is registered as a mark, the exclusive right of the holder may be limited, since other persons bearing the same name may, under certain conditions, continue to use their names, unless the registered mark concerns a well-known personality and/or trade name and the other persons intend to take advantage of the reputation of the registered mark by parasitic means.

14.44 In countries where proof of use is required in order to obtain protection, the use made by authorized users such as licensees or merchandisers is considered as use of the mark made by its holder. This provision which is most relevant to holders engaged in merchandising programs.

(c) Industrial Designs

14.45 Industrial design protection is mainly relevant for cartoon characters represented in the form of aesthetic designs for three-dimensional articles which mainly belong to the toy or costume jewellery areas (dolls, robots, puppets, action figures, brooches, "pins") which generally originate in cartoons, but which may sometimes represent real persons. The relevance of design protection will be of importance notably when copyright protection is excluded or reduced, mainly when a character has been created with the intention of being industrially exploited. Furthermore, since design protection is often subject to registration, a design application will be helpful to establish prima facie evidence of ownership as from the date of the application, although effective protection will only commence on the date of registration of the design.

(d) Other Forms of Protection

14.46 Many countries have enacted provisions, either under general law (Constitution, Civil Code, etc.) or under specific statutes, which enable a real person as such to be protected against the unauthorized commercial or advertising use of the essential features of his or her personality (name, pseudonym or nickname, image, symbols, etc.) or a real recognizable person portraying a character against the unauthorized commercial or advertising use of the essential features of the character portrayed. Those rights will, in general, supplement the protection which may be available within the scope of intellectual property in its broadest sense (including marks, industrial designs, copyright, unfair competition). Such protection may be achieved through the notions of defamation or libel, privacy rights and personality or publicity rights.

References for Section C
International Bureau of WIPO, *Character Merchandising*, WO/INF/108

PART IV

Enforcement of Intellectual Property Rights

CHAPTER 15

Enforcement of Industrial Property Rights, Copyright and Neighboring Rights

A. INTRODUCTION

(a) General

15.1 A particularly important part of any intellectual property law consists of provisions which aim at securing respect for the rights provided for in the law. Those provisions on *enforcement* have become of increasing importance due to the formidable expansion of technologies which have made possible infringing uses of protected rights to an extent which was unthinkable some decades ago.

15.2 Accessible, sufficient and adequately funded arrangements for the protection of rights are crucial in any worthwhile industrial property system. There is no point in establishing a detailed and comprehensive system for granting rights and disseminating information concerning them if it is not possible for the rights owners to enforce their rights in a satisfactory way. They must be able to take action against infringers in order to prevent further infringement and recover the losses incurred from any actual infringement. They must also be able to call on the state authorities to deal with counterfeits.

15.3 Small companies in particular might often be reluctant to use the intellectual property system for acquiring and enforcing patents, trademarks and registered designs, or to enforce copyright, because of the perceived costs and complexities of litigation. But this is a relatively negative view: litigation should be seen as a last resort. It is probable that 99% of patents and other rights do not get litigated. Because the need for litigation does not often arise, rights owners may be unaware of the positive value of the rights in marking out a protected field which others must avoid. Most competitors do not wish to risk injunctions which would stop their business, and therefore try to avoid existing rights.

15.4 All intellectual property systems need to be underpinned by a strong judicial system for dealing with both civil and criminal offenses, staffed by an adequate number of judges with suitable background and experience. Intellectual property disputes are in the main matters to be decided under civil law and the judicial system should make every effort to deal with them not only fairly but also expeditiously. Without a proper system for both enforcing rights and also enabling the grant of rights to others to be resisted, an intellectual property system will have no value.

(b) Avoiding Litigation

15.5 A competitor whose operations are obstructed by earlier rights will usually seek to avoid or overcome the problem in a legitimate way, e.g. by inventing around the protected area in the case of an earlier patent. Another approach is to seek a license or to negotiate some other agreement in a friendly way. In coming to agreements with competitors, of course, companies must be careful not to contravene competition policy rules aimed at avoiding distortion of competition. This normally means that the terms of any license must not contain anticompetitive or unreasonable provisions.

15.6 Of course, a company affected by another's right will carefully assess what its scope is and whether or not it is valid. This highlights a point of particular importance to the owners of patents, that claims must be well drafted and properly supported by the disclosure of the invention. They must clearly distinguish the protected subject matter from the prior art and must neither be over-covetous nor too modest. A well drafted patent will often be enough in itself to deter potential infringers. Similar arguments can apply to other rights such as trademarks and designs.

15.7 It is up to a right owner to act as his own policeman. He must keep an eye on the industrial and commercial markets in which he sells his products, or provides his services, or in which his processes might be used. He must keep abreast of his competitor's activities. If he becomes aware of an apparent infringement he should not necessarily assume that the infringement is deliberate (though if the infringing item is an exact copy or counterfeit, infringement will almost certainly have been deliberate). He should first contact the competitor to point out the existence of his right. Laws in a number of countries concerning patents, designs and trademarks, provide that a right owner may not make groundless threats against competitors or their distributors, for example threatening a court action when there is no ground for alleging infringement or when the right relied upon has expired, but he can send a simple letter drawing attention to the right so that the infringer cannot subsequently argue ignorance.

15.8 If the manufacturer of goods or the provider of services becomes aware of an earlier right, e.g. from the presence of goods in the market place carrying notice of the right, or from searching the literature, he should examine its scope carefully. He may be able to invent or design round it, or may consider that its scope is such that it does not really affect his position.

15.9 Negotiation is an important aspect of protecting and enforcing rights. In negotiation, an infringer might well be persuaded to change what he is doing. Alternatively, unless a right owner is very concerned to preserve the whole of a market to himself (and for that he must have adequate production capacity, because it is an implicit or explicit requirement in many laws that the market, especially in relation to patented products, must be adequately supplied at reasonable cost) it might well be in the interest of all concerned to propose a license. Negotiation and compromise are in most cases better than litigation.

15.10 During the attempts to negotiate, the supposed infringer may claim that he is not infringing; or he may allege that the right is of little value and does not justify significant royalties; or he may argue against the proposed license terms.

It may well be worth suggesting that the services of a mediator be used or that the issue should be decided by arbitration. Of course, both sides need to agree to accept an arbitrator's decision and a contract to this effect may be needed.

B.   ENFORCEMENT OF INDUSTRIAL PROPERTY RIGHTS IN GENERAL

(a)   Action before an Industrial Property Office

15.11 Industrial property offices frequently have quasi judicial functions in the administration of industrial property systems and provide a forum for procedures for contesting rights under consideration or granted by the office.   These procedures are often referred to as opposition procedures.

15.12 The expression "opposition" may be construed widely, as referring to all possibilities open to third parties to intervene before the industrial property office both in proceedings leading to the grant of a right and in proceedings for contesting the grant after it has occurred.   The possibilities for opposition arise particularly in relation to registrable rights such as patents and trademarks, because the registration can be disputed.   The possibility of opposition rarely arises in relation to copyright and neighbouring rights, since these rights in the great majority of jurisdictions arise automatically on the creation of the protected work.

15.13 Why do States provide for opposition?   With even the most rigorous examination system, the State cannot guarantee that the rights which it grants are valid—there is always the possibility that a prior right has been overlooked or a specification misunderstood.   Many systems are not particularly rigorous, which makes it all the more likely that rights might be granted in conflict with earlier rights. Thus the owners of earlier rights must be able to object at some stage. This could of course be before a court. However, in everyone's interests, opposition should be a relatively straightforward, speedy and inexpensive matter, handled as early as possible in the life of the right.   Thus many systems provide that opposition can be considered by the national industrial property office acting in a quasi-judicial role, as well as by courts.   Pre-grant opposition is invariably before the office.

15.14 The first opportunity that others, for example competitor enterprises producing goods of the same character as those covered by the patent application, have to become aware that a patent which could affect their business is being applied for is at the first publication stage, 18 months after the priority date. Enterprises, particularly those which own patents, should keep their eye on the activities of competitors and what is happening in the market place. In particular, they should keep an eye on patent applications made in their areas of interest, e.g. by scrutinizing patent office journals and published applications.   Not only is it

References for Section A
H. Olsson, *Enforcement of Rights in Phonograms and Audiovisual Works*, WIPO/SEM/BKK/94/8
A. Sugden, *The Role of Judiciary and Law Enforcement Agencies for Effective Protection of Industrial Property Rights*, WIPO/IP/JKT/95/8

important to know if competitors are seeking to protect developments which come within the scope of one's own patents, but it is also important to be warned if they are seeking to protect known technology or technology patented by others. One can also learn from the search report, published with the application, of the prior art which will be considered at the examination stage.

15.15 Some systems allow for formal opposition before the grant of the patent or an opportunity for third parties to become a party in arguments about whether or not the patent should or should not be granted. The problem with such pre-grant opposition is that very considerable delay in achieving grant often occurs. Delay means that a patentee who needs a granted patent in order to pursue an infringement could not settle an action against the infringer quickly.

15.16 It can be important to bring post-grant opposition proceedings in good time. If too long a delay occurs, the user of the later patent might argue that the owner of the earlier one has acquiesced in the grant of the later one and as a result should not be allowed to take action. This might make it difficult to enforce the earlier patent against products or processes covered by the later one.

15.17 In some major countries, such as the United States, there is no provision for opposition. However, third parties concerned about a granted patent can ask for it to be re-examined by the patent office. Such parties do not become direct parties to the procedure, but may draw prior art which may have been overlooked in the first examination to the attention of the examiner. Re-examination may result in refusal or in a more tightly drafted patent.

15.18 In many countries there is no provision at all for opposition because the industrial property office lacks the expertise. This can be the case in those countries, such as France, where no substantive examination is carried out. In such situations, revocation before the courts is the only possibility for securing cancellation or amendment of a competitor's patent.

15.19 Many countries provide for pre-registration opposition to trademark registration. Trademarks are published in the form in which they are to be registered and a short period allowed for opposition. Proceedings can be quite involved but in general, considerations are much more straightforward than those for patents and procedures can be much more rapid. In the United Kingdom, there are very few oppositions of trademarks, probably because there is a rigorous examination involving search of earlier rights. In other countries, for example Germany, there are many oppositions because there is no official search during examination; so opposition is the only way in which the owner of an earlier trademark can get the industrial property office to take account of this earlier right. Procedures in countries with large numbers of oppositions are often very quick and informal.

15.20 After registration of a trademark in many countries it is possible for an aggrieved party to apply to the office for removal of the mark from the register, or to seek its modification. One of the main grounds for this would be non use of the mark. Many who might have grounds for opposing a registration might wait to see what effect it has, or what use is to be made of it, before seeking cancellation after registration.

15.21 As for registered designs, where there is no provision for pre-registration opposition, interested parties may seek cancellation of registrations by the office.

(b) Civil Court Procedures

15.22 Despite efforts to achieve friendly settlement, circumstances can and do arise where the owner of a right feels that he must take action against an infringer in order to protect his markets (present or future). In most jurisdictions this will be handled in the civil courts. In most situations, there will be considerable dispute as to whether for example the claims in a patent to be enforced are entitled to be of the scope claimed and as to whether the alleged infringement actually falls within the valid scope. With trademarks, arguments also concern the scope of the registration and whether the alleged infringement is sufficiently similar. Most infringers genuinely believe that they have an arguable case on such aspects. Most patent infringements are not slavish imitations but, arguably, take advantage of the protected inventive concepts of the patent. In view of the fact that most patent cases involve subjective arguments which will have to be resolved on the basis of expert opinion rather than absolute fact, patent infringement is not treated as a criminal matter in many countries.

15.23 In an action for patent infringement, the patent owner, acting through his immediate lawyers (solicitors), arranges for a writ or complaint to be served on the alleged infringer. In the writ the patent owner, as plaintiff, will specify the nature of the alleged infringement and the remedy sought. Almost always, an injunction restraining the alleged infringer, the defendant, from continuing with what he has been doing, will be requested, as well as damages. The defendant will usually acknowledge the writ and give notice that he intends to defend. If he does not, the plaintiff may be entitled to a final or interlocutory ruling (one which decides the issue but leaves open the question of damages, etc.) forthwith. If the defendant does defend, and the issue is not settled out of court or dealt with summarily, pleadings will be exchanged, on the one hand stating the material facts of the claim and on the other, the defenses or counterclaims. The purpose of pleadings is to define precisely the issues in dispute and eliminate agreed or irrelevant matters. They go back and forth and can take several months. A counterclaim may be an allegation that the patent is invalid; this will have to be defended by the patent owner. Once the pleadings have been completed the plaintiff will issue a summons for directions. Such directions, given by the judge will deal with discovery and inspection of documents and in general with the trial preparations. Notice to inspect documents may be served on the other side by leave of the court. So may interrogatories, which take the form of written questions which the other side must answer under oath, e.g. by sworn affidavit, before the trial.

15.24 It is noteworthy that perhaps only 10% of cases actually get to the trial stage, the rest are settled along the way. As you will appreciate, the procedure is demanding of the time of highly paid lawyers and can be extremely expensive.

15.25 Cases involving complex technology can take a very long time in court with expert witnesses being called and subjected to examination and cross-examination by both sides. In issuing his decision, which will be fully reasoned and often lengthy, the judge can make various awards. In addition to injunctions, the court may also award damages in respect of the infringement, i.e. compensation for lost sales and markets as a result of the infringing activity. As an alternative to damages, the owner of the patent can be awarded an account of profits. All the profits derived by the defendant as a result of the infringement should be surrendered to the patent owner. An order requiring the defendant to deliver up to the patent owner, or to destroy, any products or articles incorporating the patented invention can also be made. Finally, the patent owner can secure a declaration that the patent is valid and infringed.

(c) Criminal Actions—Counterfeiting

15.26 As already mentioned, patent actions are essentially civil actions for infringement. In the case of trademarks and copyright, much of what has been explained about procedures in relation to civil actions applies to ordinary actions for infringement. But with trademarks and copyright, the serious criminal offense of counterfeiting can also arise. A trader may knowingly manufacture, distribute or sell goods marked with a trademark where the marking has been done without the permission of the owner or where the goods have been illicitly copied.

15.27 There are several ways that counterfeits can come to the attention of the authorities. Rights owners themselves may become aware of distributors or retailers trading in counterfeit goods and bring the trade to the attention of the police. Also counterfeits may be detected by law enforcement officers which are specifically empowered under trademark legislation to take action against traders in counterfeit goods and regularly do so with good effect. Their powers may be extended to enable them to deal with copyright offenses. On conviction, traders in counterfeit goods can face stiff penalties, and seizure of all offending products is normal. In respect of items protected by copyright, such as sound recordings on tape or compact disk, the police are the normal enforcement authority and will take action on the basis of a complaint by the lawful rights owner. They often need little more than 24 hours warning in order to secure warrants and make checks.

15.28 Another way in which action against counterfeit goods can be taken occurs at ports of entry of imports. If a mark owner becomes aware that consignments of counterfeit goods are on their way to the country, he can alert the customs authorities, who will keep watch for the goods and impound them when they arrive. Action can then be taken against the importer. Again, as much information as possible has to be given to the customs authorities.

C. ENFORCEMENT OF PATENT RIGHTS

15.29 In most systems, a patent is the right enforceable in a court to stop someone from doing something. It is not, as many people think, a permission to practice the patented invention. What can be prevented by patent enforcement is usually the manufacture, the sale and the use of the patented invention. The procedure seems very straightforward. You have a patent for an invention. Someone else

References for Section B

A. Sugden, *The Role of Judiciary and Law Enforcement Agencies for Effective Protection of Industrial Property Rights*, WIPO/IP/JKT/95/8

is making, or selling, or using the invention. Application is made to the court to stop the unauthorized manufacture, sale or use of the invention; the court grants the appropriate order and the infringement stops. How simple it sounds. But real life may bear little relationship to this ideal scenario.

(a) Assessing the Scope of Patent Rights

15.30 When thinking about patent enforcement, the very first task that a patentee must set himself is the assessment of what he has patented. In the early days of patents in the United Kingdom, that is in the 17th and 18th centuries, there was very little in the way of a patent specification describing the invention or claims defining the exclusive right that the patentee staked out as belonging to him. But it is now a feature of just about all patent systems that a patent must include either a specification containing claims or a description, claims or any required drawings (depending on the terminology of the particular law). In most systems, the claims are decisive, as they define the scope of protection sought and eventually granted on the patent. The specification, or the description and drawings, may be used to interpret the claims which must be fully supported by these.

15.31 Most inventors use the services of a patent attorney to write the specification for them. Frequently an inventor does not understand the specification, and particularly does not understand the claims. Usually he looks at the drawings, and, if he sees his invention illustrated there, he is satisfied. Patent attorneys try to explain the significance of the claims and the terminology used in them during the preparation and prosecution of a patent application, but many inventors still do not fully comprehend how infringement is assessed; very often they get this confused with considerations of patentability. Even where the patentee has some idea of the exclusive right granted to him in his own country, it is very rare for him to know with any precision what rights he may have in corresponding patents in other jurisdictions. The patentee's first real understanding of the extent of his patent rights often only comes to him when he is considering enforcement.

15.32 So it is clear that the seeds of enforcements of patent rights are sown right at the start of the patenting process when the patent specification is written by the inventor or the inventor's patent attorney. The examination process in the Patent Office can modify the original wording. But the inventor will normally try to resist any modification which will result in a limitation of the scope of protection— with good reason. Any reduction in the scope of protection makes it easier for a competitor to avoid infringement. If a competitor can easily supply the market with something that is equivalent to the invention, but does not infringe the patent, then the patent may be of limited commercial value. Patent Office examiners should try to remember this when an applicant for a patent steadfastly resists amending his claims in order to overcome an objection, but instead tries to deal with the objection by argument. While acceding to an amendment might lead to the early grant of a patent on the application, it may also lead to a patent right of doubtful commercial utility.

(b) Evaluating Validity and Infringement of a Patent

15.33 Having assessed what is the scope of the patent right, the next task is to attempt to decide if there is infringement. You may well ask why the patentee needs to bother with this step, since the assessment of infringement is for the court. Why not just hand everything to the court and let them decide? That would be ideal if a decision could be reached quickly and cheaply. But patent cases are amongst the most time-consuming and expensive of all forms of litigation. Before committing himself to the financial risk of a patent case, a patentee, unless he is very wealthy and careless about money, must make some attempt to forecast what will happen in court. This is not by any means easy, but it should at the least prevent the patentee from bringing a hopeless case.

15.34 The issue of infringement is very rarely considered on its own. Patents, like other forms of intellectual property, do not only affect the parties to a dispute; they have an effect on the public at large. This being the case, it is normally thought to be wrong that a patent which can be shown to be invalid should be enforceable. In spite of the examination of patent applications during prosecution, no patent system guarantees the validity of a granted patent. In a patent enforcement action, therefore, a defendant will usually add to any defense of non-infringement a further defense, often in the form of a counterclaim, that the patent is invalid and hence not enforceable even if infringed. In some jurisdictions, the issues of infringement and validity are heard together. In others, the question of validity is heard separately by a different court or it may be referred to the Patent Office.

15.35 Because of the principle that no invalid patent should be enforceable, the defendant in a patent action is usually allowed to bring in evidence of invalidity at any stage of the proceedings, in some jurisdiction even during the trial itself. As a result, the position of the patentee during patent enforcement proceedings tend to deteriorate as a defendant makes searches and usually finds evidence which is relevant to validity.

15.36 As already stated, the task of the court in the determination of infringement is the assessment of the scope of protection defined by the patent and whether the alleged infringement falls within that assessed scope. In the determination of validity, the court (or whatever tribunal is considering validity) should take the same scope of protection as has been defined for the purposes of infringement and consider whether the evidence produced by the defendant renders the patent invalid with respect and to the extent of the scope of protection claimed by the patentee. Different issues will almost always arise in these two assessments. The starting point for both, however, is almost always the wording of the claims.

15.37 Frequently, there will be a problem as to whether the actual wording of the claims, if necessary, with the assistance of the specification (or the description and any drawings), defines an invention which includes the allegedly infringing subject matter. For example, the claim may include as a feature "a spring." If the allegedly infringing device does not include a spring, but instead has a solid rubber tube which in some respects acts like a spring, can that be infringement? Different jurisdictions will handle this kind of question differently, depending on the way in which their law has developed the procedure for the definition of an invention. In addition, many courts require or expect the assistance of an expert to give guidance as to the technical merit of an argument, such as, based on the example above, that a rubber tube can be considered to fall within the term, "spring."

15.38 The technical content in many patent cases can be very complex indeed, and the resolution of the technical points of dispute may not only involve one or more expert witnesses, but may need experimental evidence as well. For instance, in a case concerning the alleged infringement of a patent granted for an invention consisting of an air plasma cutting torch, the claim included a feature which defined what was happening within the torch when it was operated. To prove infringement, an experiment was necessary to define the temperature gradient of the plasmagenic air within the torch itself. This is not as simple as it sounds. A probe inserted into the torch has the effect of modifying the air flow through the torch, which in turn will affect the temperature gradient. A better means of evaluation is thermal imaging, but it is expensive to set up. No sooner has one side carried out experiments, then the other side may feel obliged to carry out experiments themselves to check the worth of the first set of experiments or with the aim of disproving the first experiments.

15.39 Assisted by argument which in turn is supported by expert evidence and experimental evidence, the court will reach a conclusion about whether or not an infringement has occurred. But you may have noticed that most patents contain more than one claim. The inclusion of a number of claims is to give the patentee extra chances of preventing an infringement. If one claim is held invalid, the patentee may still succeed in restraining infringement if it is held that the claim is valid and an infringement has occurred with respect thereto. Where the patent in suit has a number of claims with respect to which the patentee alleges an infringement, the court will have to consider each claim separately to see if it is infringed.

15.40 Similar expert evidence and experiments may be needed in order to deal with validity. Using the "spring" example given above, it may be that the defendant can show that it was known before the date of the patent to use a member having elastic properties in some respects similar to a spring. As with the determination of infringement, the court will need to decide whether the known information invalidates the claims. And that exercise needs to be carried out for all the claims.

(c) The Cost of Patent Litigation

15.41 Whether the submission and evidence concerning infringement and validity are made in writing or given orally at a hearing, or a combination of both, the parties to a patent dispute will find themselves involved in lengthy consideration of the issues and preparation of material for the court. As already pointed out, it is mainly the borderline cases that go to trial. This has the effect of extending the arguments by which each side hopes to secure a decision in its favor. Where the patent dispute is in a field of high commercial value, and most disputes are because of their high cost, the parties may be inclined to drag any point into the dispute, however peripheral, if it appears to help their case. The costs arising from all of this can range from very high to outrageous.

15.42 This is really the key point about patent enforcement. Of all the kinds of intellectual property cases, patent infringement litigation tends to be the most expensive. However carefully one makes an estimate of the costs at the start of

References for Section C
P. Low, *Enforcement of Patent Rights*, WIPO/SEM/BKK/94/6

the litigation, they almost invariably have to be revised upwards as new issues come to light during the development of the case. Patent enforcement, or defense against enforcement, occurs because someone wishes to receive a commercial advantage, in other words, to make money. That advantage must constantly be reviewed against the cost of the litigation.

D. ENFORCEMENT OF COPYRIGHT AND NEIGHBORING RIGHTS

(a) Introduction

15.43 The evolution of new international standards for the enforcement of copyright and neighboring rights has been dramatic in recent years, and this evolution has been driven principally by two factors. The first is the advance of technological means for the creation and use (both authorized and unauthorized) of protected material, including, most recently, the advent of digital technology, which makes it possible to transmit and make perfect copies of any information existing in digital form, including works and productions protected by copyright and neighboring rights. The second factor is the increasing economic importance of goods and services protected by intellectual property rights in the realm of international trade; simply put, trade in products embodying intellectual property rights is now a booming, worldwide business.

(b) Provisions on Enforcement of Rights in International Copyright and Neighboring Rights Conventions

15.44 While the international copyright and neighboring rights conventions administered by WIPO do not contain extensive provisions dealing with enforcement of rights, the obligation of States to provide adequate means for enforcement of rights is clearly present in these conventions. The Berne Convention contains two specific provisions on the enforcement of rights, Article 16(1) and (2), which provide that infringing copies of a work are subject to seizure in any country of the Berne Union where the work enjoys protection, even when the copies come from a country where the work is not or no longer protected, and Article 13(3), which provides for seizure of copies of certain recordings of musical works imported without permission of the author or other owner of copyright in the country of importation.

15.45 The Berne, Rome and Phonograms Conventions also contain provisions indirectly requiring appropriate enforcement measures in any country party to the conventions. For example, Article 36(1) of the Berne Convention provides that "[a]ny country party to this Convention undertakes to adopt, in accordance with its constitution, the measures necessary to ensure the application of this Convention;" paragraph (2) of the same Article provides that "[i]t is understood that, at the time a country becomes bound by this Convention, it will be in a position under its domestic law to give effect to the provisions of this Convention." Similar provisions are found in Article 26(1) and (2) of the Rome Convention. Article 2 of the Phonograms Convention obligates each Contracting State to protect producers of phonograms against the making of duplicates (copies) without the consent of the producers and against the importation and distribution of such duplicates;   Article 3 of the Convention leaves the implementation to the Contracting States, which may choose one or more of the following: copyright or other specific ["neighboring"] rights, unfair competition, or penal sanctions.

(c) New International Standards for the Enforcement of Rights

15.46 It is obvious that the above provisions of the Berne, Rome and Phonograms Conventions cannot be respected without appropriate measures for the enforcement of rights provided under the national laws of their member States. Over the last two decades, it has become obvious that such provisions alone do not provide the necessary guidance to national governments concerning appropriate and modern standards for the enforcement of rights. Thus, evolution of new standards for enforcement of rights has taken place in a number of contexts, including the activities of WIPO.

15.47 Since the beginning of the 1980s, WIPO has devoted ever-greater attention to questions relating to the enforcement of rights. A short list is illustrative: two WIPO Worldwide Forums on Piracy were held in 1981 and 1983; extensive and detailed recommendations for measures to combat piracy of audiovisual works, phonograms and the printed word were developed in the series of meetings on categories of works (1986 to 1988); a committee of experts was convened in 1988 to elaborate measures against both piracy and counterfeiting, which were included by reference in the draft WIPO Model Law on Copyright prepared by the International Bureau and discussed by a Committee of Experts in 1989 and 1990; a detailed chapter on enforcement of rights was included in a draft WIPO Model Law on the Protection of Producers of Sound Recordings considered by a Committee of Experts in 1992, which, in addition to provisions on conservatory measures, civil remedies and criminal sanctions, contained proposed sanctions against the abuse of technical means applied for the protection of copyright.

15.48 The experience gained in all of the above activities during the 1980s and early 1990s has been reflected in the work of a Committee of Experts towards development of a Protocol to the Berne Convention, which began in 1991, and on the development of a possible international instrument on the protection of the rights of performers and producers of phonograms, which began in 1993. Naturally, provisions on enforcement of rights have figured prominently in the discussions of both Committees.

(d) National Legislation Concerning Enforcement of Rights

15.49 The availability of appropriate provisional (conservatory) measures is an indispensable element of any efficient mechanism for the enforcement of copyright. The most important objectives of such measures are the prevention of acts of infringement and the seizure of infringing copies, reproducing equipment and other implements that could be used for (further) infringements and that constitute essential evidence and could disappear if not brought under the control of the court. These measures must be available on an *ex parte* basis where giving the defendant prior notice would be counterproductive.

15.50 In particular, it should be possible for right owners to be granted temporary preliminary injunctions to prohibit the committing, or the continuation of the committing, of infringements. Also, courts must be able to order the search, temporary seizure and temporary impounding of suspected unauthorized copies of works and other protected subject matter, of packaging materials, of implements for the making of such copies, and of documents, accounts or business papers relating to such copies.

15.51 The purposes of civil remedies are (i) to provide compensation for the prejudice caused by infringements, (ii) to dispose appropriately of the infringing copies (typically through destruction or other disposal outside the normal channels of commerce), (iii) to dispose appropriately of implements used for infringing activities and (iv) to grant injunctions to prohibit further infringements. Such remedies should always be available irrespective of whether the infringement has been committed willfully and/or for profit-making purposes.

15.52 Civil remedies are not always sufficient deterrents. Where infringement becomes a business, the closing down of one plant with the assistance of courts and law enforcement authorities may only mean that the plant will re-open somewhere else. Infringements committed willfully and with profit-making purposes should be punished by criminal sanctions, and the level of such sanctions must make it clear that such infringements of copyright are serious offenses. It is normally preferable that criminal sanctions are also applicable in case of infringements committed through gross negligence, for profit-making purposes, because it may be difficult to prove that infringements are committed willfully. Increased punishments in cases of recidivism are also justified. The criminal sanctions available should comprise both fines and imprisonment, and, where merited by the case, courts should be able to impose both these sanctions on the infringer.

15.53 In certain cases, the only practical means of preventing copying is through so-called "copy-protection" or "copy-management systems," that is, systems containing technical devices that either entirely prevent the making of copies or make the quality of the copies made so poor that they are unusable. Technical devices are also used to prevent the reception of encrypted commercial television programs except with the help of decoders (and the would-be viewers have to buy or rent such decoders). However, it is technically possible to make devices by means of which copy-protection and copy-management systems as well as encryption systems may—although illegally—be circumvented. Where such devices are manufactured or imported and distributed illicitly, the normal exploitation of the works is undermined and may cause serious prejudice to the authors of, or other owners of copyright in, those works. Such activities are violations of the protected rights and should be sanctioned in a way similar to that of other kinds of infringements.

(e) Border Measures

15.54 Piracy is by no means an exclusively national activity, i.e., the production in a country of infringing copies for sale in that country; but it is very much an international operation, with vast quantities of infringing copies being manufactured in one country and shipped to others, often on the other side of the world; quantities of infringing copies which are shipped to other countries substantially undermine the legitimate business to the extent that international companies often withdraw from the market and investment in recording and producing local talent virtually dries up. For this reason, the power to stop infringing copies entering a market is of vital importance, and provisions which enable this to be done are an essential feature of modern copyright legislation. Much attention has been given to this subject in recent years and the Customs Co-operation Council (now the World Customs Organization) has developed a model law which would give customs authorities the power to impound imports of pirated and counterfeit articles.

15.55 Border measures are intended to prevent infringing copies—or lawful copies in violation of the right of importation—from being brought into the country concerned. They constitute an effective way to counter acts of infringement, because it is frequently easier to prevent the distribution of infringing copies at the border than after the copies have already been brought into the country and put into circulation. Border measures are usually carried out by administrative authorities (customs authorities) and not by judicial authorities. In national legislation on this issue, a number of safeguards and appropriate procedural rules are normally found which ensure the fairness and effectiveness of measures applied by such authorities.

15.56 Providing for the availability of various enforcement measures, may not be entirely sufficient. It is, of course, necessary that national legislation also provide general safeguards to ensure due procedures for the application of those measures in keeping with the principles of justice and fairness and with the need for efficiency. For example, national legislation must ensure that procedures for the enforcement of copyright are fair, equitable, transparent, expeditious, not unnecessarily complicated, costly or burdensome, and do not impose unreasonable time-limits, and both plaintiffs and defendants must have equal access to information and equal possibilities to present their case. Such demands, of course, are not only related to infringements of copyright and neighboring rights, and rules to this respect are normally found in other legislation, such as laws on civil and criminal procedure.

(f) Anti-Piracy Measures for Phonograms, Audiovisual Works and Computer Programs

15.57 The notion of piracy covers a number of different phenomena. For example, in the field of music, three expressions are used in common parlance which are all covered by the wider notion of piracy as used here. Those expressions are "counterfeits", "bootlegs" and "pirate copies". "Counterfeits" are usually exact copies of a sound or video disk or tape, with, for instance, exactly the same packaging as the original, including usually also the trade mark. The copies could be either tapes or—more sophisticated—industrially manufactured CDs. "Bootlegs" are copies of recordings of a live performance or a broadcast, if the recording was made without the authorization of the right-owner concerned. "Pirate copies", finally, are unauthorized copies of a sound or video recording which do not attempt to imitate the original but are generally of low quality, with hand-written labels, etc. Those are nowadays becoming more rare because in general people prefer recordings of higher quality. The use of the notion "piracy" in the following covers all three kinds of infringements now mentioned.

15.58 Generally speaking, five categories of works, performances or productions are the most exposed victims of piracy, namely:

(1) sound recordings;
(2) video recordings;
(3) computer programs;
(4) broadcasts;
(5) books.

15.59 Particularly the first three categories of works or productions have been hit by piracy in recent decades because they are, with modern digital reproduction technology, very easy to copy. It takes, for instance, no great effort to make copies, by means of a personal computer, of computer programs of the same quality as the original and with high speed and efficiency; as computer programs are very costly to develop, uncontrolled copying hurts considerably the interests of the right-owners.

15.60 As regards the extent of piracy, it is generally estimated that piracy of sound recordings causes losses for the phonographic industry in the order of more than one billion US$ per year. As regards the other categories now mentioned the losses are less easy to quantify; it suffices to mention that the harm caused to the legitimate industry and to the right-owners are considerable. The annual losses for the computer software industry due to piracy of programs have, by some sources, been estimated to around 14 billion dollars.

(i) Reasons for Taking Action against Piracy

15.61 There are several reasons for a State to take efficient measures against piracy activities.

15.62 The first and perhaps most important reason is that the rights under copyright law are violated, which means that the authors, performers and phonogram and videogram producers, publishers, broadcasters and others suffer a considerable economic damage. This is detrimental not only to the personal economic interests of the beneficiaries but also to the society as a whole because it hampers the creativity and is contrary to the interests which copyright law is there to serve, including that of establishing domestic cultural industries. For example, it is hardly feasible to establish a domestic phonographic industry if piracy activities are allowed to go on unhindered. In addition, the individual authors and performers, etc., lose a considerable share of their income.

15.63 It should be noted that piracy generally hurts the most those productions which are successful; they are the only ones which are of interest for pirates. In the phonographic industry only a small share of the productions are economic successes and it is the income from this share that makes it possible for the industry to engage in the production of less successful but perhaps more valuable productions. If this incentive is lost, the industry may not be able to continue those productions and the output will be qualitatively less important, something which is, in the long run, detrimental to the interests of the consumers and of the society as a whole.

15.64 The reasons for fighting piracy should be seen both in a short and a long-term perspective. It is sometimes said that piracy is not a bad phenomenon because it supplies the market with popular products at low prices. Occasionally it is added that the pirates employ a considerable work force and thus give increased job opportunities. Also, it is said that there are more urgent priorities in society than combating piracy. These arguments are, naturally, not valid if a State wants to maintain its international reputation and participate in the international exchange of culture, information and entertainment.

(ii) Anti-piracy Measures

15.65 Various practical measures can be undertaken in order to combat piracy. To some extent protection can be obtained through various types of copy-protection systems, that is, that mechanisms ("spoiler signals" in sound or video recordings) are built in which prevent unauthorized copying. Another measure is to have an efficient collective administration in respect of musical works; if it is easy for users to contact and obtain authorization from the right-owners through such an organization the temptation to engage in piracy activities may be less.

15.66 The system of copyright and neighboring rights is a branch of private law in that it grants personal exclusive rights to the individual beneficiaries. Therefore, the basic approach in most countries, is, or has been, that it is for the injured party himself to take action. Consequently, the basic possibility for the him is to take civil action.

15.67 Recent years have, however, seen a change in the attitude in many countries, mainly in view of the alarming growth of the piracy activities. Therefore a number of countries have introduced heavy *penal sanctions* for at least certain kinds of infringement of copyright, in particular such which would be considered as piracy.

15.68 As concerns penal sanctions, those should—and in most countries do—include both fines and imprisonment (the maximum of which usually may be up to several years). In order for penal sanctions to work in a satisfactory way, the objective criteria for the infringement must be clearly defined. This means, in particular, that the rights should be framed and described in a clear and unequivocal way so that it is obvious which the act or acts are which must not be undertaken without the authorization of the author or other right-owner. Also, the so-called subjective criteria must be determined in a clear way. At least in some national laws the penal provisions for copyright violations apply not only to acts which are committed willfully but also to those committed with gross negligence. The sanctions should be applicable not only to the person who directly committed the violation but also to those who contributed to it, for instance by providing equipment used for unauthorized reproduction with full knowledge of the intended use of that equipment.

15.69 Penal sanctions have mainly a repressive function. While such a function is very important in the interest of the society and also for the authors in order to ensure respect for the law (and this is of course particularly obvious in cases of piracy) at least equally important from the individual author's point of view is the compensatory aspect. The law has to provide the beneficiaries with real and effective possibilities to obtain compensation for the injury caused to them by the violation of their rights. That compensation should not be limited to a mere reparation of the direct losses inflicted on the specific right-owner. He should also be compensated for, for example, loss of market shares for the work, possible violation of his moral rights and also other relevant elements; in short, account has to be taken of the material and moral prejudice caused. It may sometimes be difficult to establish the exact size of the remuneration. In many national laws there are, however, special provisions aiming at making an equity assessment of the amount to be paid; otherwise, it has to be left to the judges' discretion.

15.70 If copies exist which have been produced through the unlawful acts, it is important that action is taken so as to avoid that those copies, and their packaging, be brought on the market without the consent of the copyright owner. This is particularly important in case of pirate copies. The desirable principle should be that such copies should be destroyed unless the injured party requests otherwise. Alternatively, they should be surrendered to the injured party. Also, equipment used for the manufacture of unauthorized copies should, by court order, be either destroyed or surrendered to the injured party, at least if there is a real risk that they may be used for continued acts of infringement. In this latter case, that is, if there is a risk for continuation of the infringing acts, there should exist possibilities for the courts to issue orders expressly prohibiting the continuation of the acts, with mention of the fine to be paid in case the order is not respected.

15.71 Another important aspect in this context are the conservatory measures which should be available particularly in cases of piracy, where the existence on the market of the unlawful copies can cause considerable damage. Such measures are intended to freeze or conserve the situation as it is when the measure is ordered or taken. More specifically the purpose of such measures is twofold: to prevent the committing, or the continuation of the committing, of acts of piracy; and to secure evidence as to the nature, quantity, location, source and destination of the piracy copies or to the identity of the person who is suspected to have committed or to be likely to commit acts of copyright violations.

15.72 Usually such measures have to be taken only at the request of the person or legal entity who claims to be injured or to be threatened to be injured by an act of piracy. Under most laws the requesting party will be liable for damages caused by the measure, and, where necessary, he should be ordered to post a bond The measures should include the following:

(1) seizure of the goods suspected to be unauthorized copies;
(2) sealing the premises where the unauthorized copies are being manufactured, packaged, stored or offered for sale, rental, lending or other distribution;
(3) seizure of the tools that could be used to manufacture or package the unauthorized copies and of business documents referring to the said copies;
(4) ordering the termination of the manufacture or distribution of the unauthorized copies; and
(5) ordering the disclosure of the source of the copies suspected to be unauthorized copies.

15.73 It is, generally speaking, not enough that proper provisions on sanctions for violations of copyright law exist in the country. They also have to be implemented properly by enforcement authorities. This is particularly important in cases of piracy and it is so for several reasons. One is that lack of an efficient enforcement of at least more severe violations of copyright law hurts not only the right-owners but also the international reputation of the country concerned; with today's economic significance of copyright and its role in international trade this is an important aspect. Another reason is that any law which is not enforced in a proper way does not fulfill the aims for which it was adopted; in the case of copyright law the development process in various sectors and the creation of a cultural identity suffers.

15.74 Because of the recognized need to take efficient action against copyright piracy, some countries have set up special enforcement units either in the Ministry responsible for copyright law matters or within the police or customs forces. Also, in some countries, special State bodies, have particular responsibilities in the field of enforcement. They can act on behalf of their members, they can initiate investigations and they can bring matters to court. In most countries the enforcement is, however, entrusted to the ordinary enforcement authorities, that is, the courts, the police, the public prosecutors and the customs authorities.

E. ACTIVITIES WITHIN WIPO CONCERNING ENFORCEMENT

15.75 The repression of activities such as piracy and counterfeiting, which are factors of major economic importance, is at the very center of the task of the World Intellectual Property Organization (WIPO), a task that comprises three main fields of activity.

15.76 Firstly, WIPO administers twenty-three international conventions and treaties relating to intellectual property. This aspect of WIPO's work consists basically in ensuring the proper operation of the bodies that govern these various international agreements and to obtain the accession of the largest possible number of States to them. This latter objective, that is to say the universality of the international intellectual property conventions, is a basic aim since it represents one of the keys to the success of any operation aimed at stemming piracy. For any repression to have proper effect it is, indeed, necessary that the most uniform legal framework possible be established, comprising high-level provisions well adapted to new circumstances and the new technological facilities available to "pirates."

15.77 The second aspect of WIPO's task is to develop new legislative provisions, both to adapt existing provisions to the new technologies and to reflect the progressively emerging consensus in favor of increasing the level of these provisions. For example, the impact of digital technology on copyright and neighboring rights, that is to say the rights of performers, phonogram producers and broadcasting organizations, will be gigantic. Once it is possible to transmit

References for Section D
Basic Notions of the Exercise, Administration and Enforcement of Rights, WIPO/CR/GE/94/8
Enforcement of Copyright and Neighboring Rights in WIPO's Activities, WIPO/CR/PRG/94/1
H. Olsson, *Enforcement of Rights in Phonograms and Audiovisual Works*, WIPO/SEM/BKK/94/8
D. de Freitas, *Recent Developments and Issues Pertaining to Enforcement of Intellectual Property Rights, with Emphasis on Protection of Producers of Sound Recording*, WIPO-ASEAN/SEM/JKT/93/8

by electromagnetic waves, by cable or by satellite, musical works that are incorporated in sound or audiovisual recordings, the problem will arise of unlawful reproduction and also of private copying, since works stored in digital form can be reproduced any number of times without loss of quality when compared with the original from which the copies are made.

15.78 The final basic aspect of WIPO's activities, but not the least important, is the transfer of know-how required to administer the international conventions. Indeed, it is of prime importance that the provisions drawn up at international level be applied at national level, since promotion of creativeness first requires suitable management and the implementation of provisions adopted in favor of creators. WIPO's development cooperation activities are particularly important in this respect.

F. ENFORCEMENT PROVISIONS OF THE TRIPS AGREEMENT

15.79 It is worth recalling that the Agreement on Trade-Related Aspects of Intellectual Property Rights (TRIPS) which forms part of the overall Agreement to set up the World Trade Organization (WTO), resulting from the recently completed GATT Uruguay Round, requires the members of the WTO to ensure that effective enforcement procedures are available. The procedures are expected to be expeditious, fair and equitable, and not unnecessarily complicated or costly. The TRIPS Agreement also includes provisions requiring action by customs authorities against suspected counterfeit or pirated goods. These provisions of the TRIPS Agreement are set out in Chapter 28 of the present work.

References for Section E
Enforcement of Rights Under Copyright and Neighboring Rights Law, WIPO/CNR/S/94/8

References for Section F
A. Sugden, *The Role of Judiciary and Law Enforcement Agencies for Effective Protection of Industrial Property Rights*, WIPO/IP/JKT/95/8

CHAPTER 16

Intellectual Property Litigation

A. INTRODUCTION

16.1 In most intellectual property systems, it is common to have some form of internal appeal against a patent or trademark examiner's decision. Boards of Appeal exist, for instance, in the European Patent Office and the United States Patent and Trademark Office. While in the United Kingdom Patent and Trademark Office there is no formal internal appeal, a dispute between the applicant and examiner can be taken to a hearing before a senior officer.

16.2 Whatever the arrangement for internal appeal may be, in most intellectual property systems the courts play an important role in hearing appeals from decisions of the Industrial Property Offices and in adjudicating infringement actions.

B. REVIEW OF INDUSTRIAL PROPERTY OFFICE DECISIONS

(a) Introduction

16.3 The functions of Patent Offices in most countries are administrative in character rather than judicial. However, because Commissioners and Registrars are obliged to interpret the law in order to carry out their functions properly, and because third parties' rights and the public interest must be taken into account, there is at times a tendency to treat office decisions as sacrosanct. In a number of countries, the Commissioner or Registrar is able to summon witnesses, administer oaths, require the production of documents or articles, and award costs. His functions are therefore often referred to as "quasi-judicial". It must not be forgotten, however, that a Patent Office decision is administrative in character, notwithstanding that certain functions of the Commissioner or Registrar have quasi-judicial features.

16.4 Generally speaking the decisions against which one may appeal can be divided into decisions taken during or at the end of the procedure relating to an application for a patent for invention and decisions taken after the grant of a patent for invention. The appeals can also be divided into two kinds, namely, "pre-grant appeals," which are lodged against the first kind of decision, and "post-grant appeals," which are lodged against the second kind of decision. "Pre-grant appeals" only involve a third party, in addition to the owner of the patent for invention and the Patent Office. Similar appeals exist in relation to decisions of the Trademarks Office.

(b) Pre-Grant Appeals

16.5 Chronologically, the first decision of the Patent Office is the decision by which it does or doesn't accord a filing date. The applicant may disagree with the date accorded and may wish to appeal against a decision. As an example, suppose the payment of the application fee in a particular country is one of the requirements for according a filing date, and the Patent Office and the applicant disagree as to when the application fee was actually paid. The Patent Office alleges that the application fee was paid two days after the date on which the documents constituting the application were filed, whereas the applicant claims that it was paid on the same day the application itself was filed. If the invention claimed in the application was published the day after the application itself was filed, the decision of the Patent Office according a filing date is crucial. If the applicant is not able to convince the Patent Office that the application fee was paid before the publication of the invention, the application will eventually be rejected for lack of novelty of the invention. Therefore, it is important for the applicant to have the right to appeal against the decision according a filing date.

16.6 Another decision against which the applicant may appeal to the court is the decision, taken during the preliminary (or formal) examination, by which the Patent Office declares that the application is deemed to be withdrawn. Such a decision may be taken, for example, on the ground that a formal defect in the application has not been eliminated in due time or that the invention claimed in the application is contrary to public order or morality.

16.7 The most frequent decision against which the applicant may appeal to the court is the decision, taken as a result of the examination of the application as to substance, by which the Patent Office rejects the application. Such a decision may be taken, for example, on the ground that the invention claimed in the application is not new, does not involve an inventive step or is not industrially applicable. Another possible ground for rejection of the application might be that the claims or the description contain substantive defects which have not been eliminated by the applicant.

(c) Post-Grant Appeals

16.8 After the grant of the patent for invention, there may also be cases where an appeal may be lodged against a decision of the Patent Office. For example, the Patent Office may have declared that the patent for invention has lapsed because an annual fee has not been paid in due time. On the other hand, the owner of the patent for invention may allege that the annual fee was paid in due time and, as a consequence, the said owner may wish to appeal to the court against the declaration of lapse. In such a case, the appeal only involves the owner of the patent for invention and the Patent Office.

16.9 Another example of a "post-grant appeal" would be against a decision by the Patent Office to grant a compulsory license. Where the law so provides, a similar appeal would also be possible against a decision by the Patent Office to refuse to grant a compulsory license. In both cases, the appeal would involve three parties, namely, the owner of the patent for invention, the party requesting the grant of a compulsory license and the Patent Office.

(d) Appeal Procedure

(i) Introduction

16.10 Appeal procedures are usually determined by regulations or rules which may be provided for in the patent law, in the rules of the specific court, or in the general rules of procedure of the country.

16.11 In Japan, the Federal Republic of Germany and France, the codes of civil procedure govern; in common law countries such as the United Kingdom and Canada, the rules of procedure of the appropriate courts apply.

16.12 Normally, the industrial property law sets out the time limit within which an appeal should be filed.

16.13 The rules of procedure determine when and how each step should be taken. These rules usually give the court wide discretion so that the parties can put forth their best case. For example, if amendment to refused claims is permitted, it is frequently possible to resolve the dispute without a hearing.

16.14 Usually, the rules of procedure will establish the time periods for the completion of each step of the procedure. For example, the evidence may be required to be filed with the court one month after the "notice of appeal," and the memorandum (or brief) on appeal may be required to be filed within a further month.

16.15 At common law the rules of procedure will require each party—the appellant (the one who is appealing) and the respondent (the one whose decision is being appealed)—to give the other notice of each step it takes and to give the court proof that notice has been given. If a third party is involved in an appeal, the same rule should apply with respect to that third party.

16.16 The rules of procedure will also usually provide for the possibility to deviate from the rules to permit the parties to present their cases properly. For example, extensions of time may be required if the appellant cannot give proper instructions on time.

16.17 Usually, there are also rules which compel the parties to proceed under penalty of dismissal of their case.

16.18 Whether or not deviation is permitted in each case is within the discretion of the court. Under the common law practice, a request for the court to permit deviation is made in writing with supporting evidence, and notice is given to the other side. The other side may consent or may appear in court and oppose the request. A similar process exists in the continental system.

(ii) Pre-Hearing Conference

16.19 Often, under common law, provision is made for the convening of a pre-hearing conference to resolve any question as to the procedure which is to be followed at the hearing; the question may then be settled by the court. At the pre-hearing conference there may be questions as to who will have the opportunity to speak, the order, the material which is to be considered, and what facts will be admitted by either side.

16.20 In this regard the court may perform a useful function which is sometimes unofficially called "banging heads together." The intervention of a third party with authority, the court, may resolve differences between obstinate parties.

(e) Evidence

16.21 The word "evidence" as used in judicial proceedings usually means that which may be placed before the court to enable it to determine the issues of fact.

16.22 For example, a document executed by an inventor transferring a patent for invention to another entity or person duly registered by the Patent Office is the best evidence that the other entity or person is the owner of the patent for invention. This is also called "direct" evidence. If the document is lost, then a statement by a witness that he or she saw the inventor sign such a transfer may be sufficient. This is secondary evidence.

16.23 If the document is available, then it should be submitted. If it is not, then there is no option but to follow the second course.

16.24 The evidence put forward in pre-grant appeals will in most cases be quite different from the evidence presented in post-grant appeals.

16.25 In a pre-grant appeal where the appealed decision was to reject the application, the main issue is usually whether what is claimed in the application is or is not a patentable invention. The evidence on that issue will be highly technical.

16.26 In a post-grant appeal where the appealed decision was to grant or to refuse a compulsory license, the evidence will tend to be almost exclusively commercial, relating to competition in the marketplace, market demand or need, costs of production, research, selling or marketing, profits and royalty rates. The requesting party will also probably submit evidence as to its or his technical personnel, facilities, market costs, proposed market, and selling price.

16.27 Three forms of evidence may be distinguished: "documentary evidence"—namely, evidence supplied by writings and documents of all kinds—"real evidence"—namely, evidence supplied by things themselves rather than by a description of them—and "expert evidence"—namely, oral evidence supplied by an expert.

16.28 To the extent possible, all evidence should be introduced in writing. Oral testimony, if any is given, is usually taken down verbatim and recorded in print for review by the authority; however, if a hearing of oral testimony is requested, it will normally be granted.

16.29 As a general rule, statements made by parties are usually accepted as true unless they are uncorroborated or contested. If this is the case, the court may call for further evidence. A requirement may be made for money to be deposited to cover the costs of these proceedings prior to their commencement. These proceedings may include hearing the parties, requests for information, production of documents, hearing witnesses, opinions by experts, inspection and sworn statements in writing.

16.30 In the case of oral evidence, the party or witness testifying will have to be prepared to be subjected to questioning by the adversary or the court.

(i) Documentary Evidence

16.31 Documentary evidence can be subdivided into three elements, namely, the file history, statements and other documentary evidence.

16.32 The file history usually comprises the patent application, including the description, drawings and claims, the objections or observations made by the Patent Office, and the observations made by the applicant.

16.33 If the Patent Office had rejected the application because there is in the state of the art a publication which destroys the novelty of the invention, the observations by the Patent Office will normally include that publication, together with the Patent Office comment on its significance, and, of course, the decision of the Patent Office and its reasons.

16.34 The observations made by the applicant will normally include observations on the said publication, that is, comments on the structure, the mode of operation and result of the solution disclosed in the publication, together with comments on how the applicant's invention differs on each of these points from that solution.

16.35 Sometimes the "supposed" evidence may also include statements by the inventor. The word "supposed" is used intentionally because frequently this "evidence" is not proof but rather is argument. Statements which indicate nothing other than that the subject matter of the application is a patentable invention are merely self-serving and are consequently not persuasive. Such statements are no more than mere unsubstantiated opinions.

16.36 There may be other documentary evidence, for example, experimental reports, market surveys, photographs, sales figures, unsolicited testimonials. Again, all these materials should be introduced by showing the source, what they show, why they are presented and an explanation as to their technical significance.

(ii) Real Evidence

16.37 Real evidence such as models, actual machines described in the state of the art and the subject matter of the patent application, may also be shown.

(iii) Expert Evidence

16.38 In relation to the issue of validity in patent proceedings, general evidence is often received from expert witnesses as to prior use; the commercial success of the invention; the intelligibility and sufficiency of the patent specification to a competent technician; the utility or usefulness of the invention; the state of common general knowledge at material dates; the meaning of technical terms, and the novel or surprising nature of the invention claimed when considered in the light of prior art and knowledge.

16.39 A classic statement of the proper role of an expert at the trial and the proper nature of his evidence is found in the speech of Lord Tomlin in *British Celanese* v. *Courtaulds* (1935) 52 RPC 171 at 196:

16.40 "The area of the territory in which in cases of this kind an expert witness may legitimately move is not doubtful. He is entitled to give evidence as to the state of the art at any given time. He is entitled to explain the meaning of any technical terms used in the art. He is entitled to say whether in his opinion that which is described in the specification on a given hypothesis as to its meaning is capable of being carried into effect by a skilled worker. He is entitled to say what at a given time to him as skilled in the art a given piece of apparatus or a given sentence on any given hypothesis as to its meaning would have taught or suggested to him. He is entitled to say whether in his opinion a particular operation in connection with the art could be carried out and generally to give an explanation required as to facts of a scientific kind. He is not entitled to say nor is Counsel entitled to ask him what the Specification means, nor does the question become any more admissible if it takes the form of asking him what it means to him as an engineer or as a chemist. Nor is he entitled to say whether any given step or alteration is obvious, that being a question for the Court."

(iv) Market Survey Evidence

16.41 In trademark cases in particular, evidence of the "public mind" or the state of public opinion in relation to a particular trade name, mark or get-up is both relevant and admissible. In recent times there have been endeavors to put into evidence the results of market surveys and market research as evidence of the "public mind." There is some dispute as to the effect of such evidence. Evidence of a market survey may prove no more than that certain opinions were expressed by individual persons interviewed. It cannot show, in the absence of direct evidence to the court, that such opinions were genuinely held by them or how they arrived at them.

(v) Presentation of Evidence

16.42 In common law, and some civil law, countries evidence is presented in the form of sworn statements, or "affidavits," on the most important points. These statements or affidavits are written documents which are signed by the person making them before either an officer of the State or an officer of the court who ensures that the person signing knows the consequences and penalties for making false statements. The general law makes provision for penalties where false statements have been made.

16.43 In the absence of a third party to any proceedings, these sworn statements are normally accepted as evidence of the facts to which they attest. One, therefore, has to be sure that they are relevant and true.

16.44 In some countries, when a third party is involved—for example, in the case of a compulsory license—the third party may be given the opportunity to "cross-examine" the party who gave the statement to test the validity of the facts set out. "Cross-examination" is a procedure in which an adverse party questions the person who gave the statement. The questions may be directed to any matter raised in the statement and are generally directed to the accuracy and basis for the statement.

(f) Final Disposition

16.45 When disposing of the appeal, the court normally has the following courses of action available: it may refuse the appeal; it may grant the appeal; it may refer the case back to the Patent Office for reconsideration; or, if the decision appealed against was a decision to reject the application, it may amend the claims and give directions to the Patent Office to grant the patent for invention. If the court refers the case back to the Patent Office, it may make recommendations for amendment of the claims, description or drawings to overcome positions one or both parties have taken unjustifiably. The basis for the court's authority to act is usually in the patent law or it may be found in other general legislative provisions.

C. INFRINGEMENT ACTIONS

(a) Patent Infringement

16.46 The first task in any patent infringement action is to accurately assess the limit of the monopoly. This will require the court to construe the patent specification. In general it is not permitted to adduce expert evidence to construe words which are capable of an ordinary meaning in English. The only exception is when technical words are used for which the court may require a technical explanation. Similarly, considering the claims, it is not permissible to look into the body of the specification so as to try and twist or strain the meaning of ordinary English words so that they can "catch" the infringement. In fact, the court's first task in construing the specification is to have no regard to either the alleged infringement or what is called the "prior art".

16.47 The next task facing the court is the practical one: to take the alleged infringement and decide whether it falls within the scope of the claims which it has construed. This is often not easy, particularly when the defendant has been well advised. It is in this area that expert evidence is frequently called. Moreover, in patent infringement actions, the use of experiments is often resorted to in order to prove infringement, the burden of which always remains with the plaintiff.

16.48 The usual defense in an infringement action is that the alleged infringement simply does not fall within the scope of the patent in suit. But far more important than the defense will often be a counterclaim for revocation of the patent. As in trademark infringement, there are a number of statutory grounds by which a defendant can seek to impugn the validity of the patent: to mention some, he may rely upon anticipation, that is lack of novelty, that the invention is obvious, that the patentee has not sufficiently or fairly set out the manner in which the invention is to be worked, that the invention is not useful, that it has been obtained on a false

References for Section B
P.A. Smith, *Appeals, Infringement, Invalidation from the Patent Office's Point of View*, MY/PDA/ 84/15
M.S. Johnston, *Appeals*, BLTC/28
J. Garnsey, *Evidence with Special Reference to Scientific Evidence*

suggestion or misrepresentation or that it has wrongfully been obtained from another. Some or all of these grounds are available in most patent statutes in the Commonwealth. Again, this is an area where expert evidence is important and it is not unusual for the counterclaim in a patent infringement action to take more time than the claim itself. Naturally, the onus here is on the defendant seeking revocation of the patent.

(b) Copyright Infringement

16.49 The first of the acts restricted by copyright is "reproduction". By reproduction is generally meant the right to multiply copies of the work, the production of even one copy being an infringement. Reproduction is not defined in any of the acts but its meaning is probably very similar to "copy". What is a copy will be a question of fact and degree. When the copy is not exact, the court must examine the degree of resemblance with this in mind: that for infringement to arise, there must be such a degree of similarity as would lead one to say that the alleged infringement is a copy or reproduction of the original—having in other words adopted its essential features and substance.

16.50 A causal connection between the copyright work or the alleged infringement is essential and is a major distinction between the protection afforded by patents and registered designs—both of which are full monopolies. The plaintiff must prove that directly and indirectly the defendant has copied from the work matter in which he claims copyright. He must show that this causal connection is the explanation of the similarity between the two. If, for example, they both copied from a common source or they arrived at their results truly independently, there will be no infringement.

16.51 Many statutes qualify "reproduction" with some such phrase as "or substantial reproduction". The question of what is "substantial" will again depend upon the facts and circumstances of each case and will be for the court to assess. It has been said in a leading case that "the question whether the defendant has copied a substantial part depends much more on the quality than the quantity of what he has taken". And in another case "what is worth copying is *prima facie* worth protecting".

16.52 It is submitted that what the court must do is to assess whether, assuming a causal connection, the defendant has helped himself to too liberal a portion of another's labor or work. On the other hand, bearing in mind particularly that copyright does not protect ideas (which may or may not be the proper subject of a patent) but rather the way in which ideas are expressed and articulated, the court will by way of balance always be mindful not in effect to give a plaintiff the benefit of a "50 year patent" under the guise of copyright. The two species of protection are very different.

16.53 In view of the foregoing it is clear that the most obvious defense is that the impugned work was independently arrived at. Other defenses may be:

(1) that, although there has been some degree of copying, a substantial part of the work in issue has not been taken or;
(2) that the work is no longer in copyright or;
(3) certain other statutory defenses such as fair dealing and use for educational purposes.

(c) Trademark Infringement and Passing-Off

16.54 These two topics are closely related. If infringement of a registered trademark exists in a particular case the plaintiff will usually also plead passing off. Historically, the action to restrain a defendant from passing off his goods as the goods of the Plaintiff was a generalized form of an action to restrain the infringement of a trademark. When the possibility of registration of trademarks first became available at the end of the last century, the distinction between the two types of action arose. In spite of the co-existence of these two forms of action, passing off has never been abolished or allowed to slip into disuse.

(i) Trademark Infringement

16.55 This is a statutory tort arising by virtue of registration of the trademark in issue at a national Trademarks Registry. Trademarks may of course only be registered after satisfying specific conditions imposed by statute and enforced by the Registry. Registration involves consideration of such topics as distinctiveness of the proposed mark, whether it is an invented word, whether it has any direct reference to the character or quality of the goods in respect of which registration is sought, whether it has a geographical signification, whether it has signification as a surname etc. In several countries trademark registration is available in respect of both goods and services. In many Commonwealth countries, there exist two categories of trademark—those in so called Part A and Part B of the Register, in respect of which different considerations arise. The concept of Part B marks was introduced so as to satisfy a somewhat lower standard of distinctiveness for registration and as a consequence, to give a somewhat lower level of protection in litigation.

16.56 Evidence of ownership of a trademark will generally be adduced by a duly certified copy of the entry in the national Trademark Register. The copy certificate should, however, be scrutinized with care for at least the following information:

(1) the mark itself and the exact manner in which it is represented, particularly if it is a device mark;
(2) the goods in respect of which registration has been secured;
(3) the name and details of its proprietor;
(4) the date of the registration;
(5) whether it has been registered in Part A or Part B of the Register.

16.57 An important distinction between the action for trademark infringement and passing off is that whereas in passing off it is essential that the plaintiff should by evidence prove his reputation, this is not necessary for the purposes of proving trademark infringement. Registration may take place before any reputation has been acquired in the mark through actual use; to secure registration, it is enough that the mark is inherently distinctive, and the plaintiff has a bona fide intention to use it as a trademark for the goods in question. Once registered, the registered proprietor may proceed against infringers without the uncertainty and expense of having each time to prove his actual trading reputation. This is the main respect in which protection of goodwill has been made easier and more efficacious by registration.

16.58 In trademark infringement actions, the court is often faced with the likelihood of a counterclaim for rectification of the Register of Trademarks by expunging therefrom the trademark in issue. The various national trademark laws establish grounds on which a trademark may be so removed and these involve in part the grounds available to an opponent at the registration stage. In addition, further grounds are available such as the non-use of the mark.

(ii)   Passing-Off

16.59 Passing off can arise in respect of a common law trademark, a trading name or style for either goods or services or through "get-up", that is, by the addition to an article of something that gives it a distinctive appearance—be it color, shape or packaging. In essence passing off concerns the wrongful appropriation of the benefit of the reputation or goodwill of another.

16.60 Any misrepresentation calculated to injure another in his trade or business may provide the basis for a passing off action. But in each case the plaintiff must establish two propositions before he can succeed: the first is that he has a legal right, in the nature of a monopoly; in other words, he must show that he has an exclusive right to a particular name for his goods or a particular trade description or particular "get-up"; secondly, the plaintiff must demonstrate that the defendant has infringed that right by selling goods under a name or description or with a "get-up" which is likely to lead to confusion, such that consumers are likely to buy the defendant's goods in the belief that they are the plaintiff's goods.   It should be noted that the second proposition does not arise unless and until the plaintiff has established the first.

(d)   Registered Designs Infringement

16.61 Registered designs have a close analogy with patents. They consist of a pure monopoly of limited duration.

16.62 The United Kingdom, for instance, has the following definition of design:

> "the expression design means features of shape, configuration, pattern or ornament applied to an article by any industrial process or means, being features which in the finished article appeal to and are judged solely by the eye, but does not include a method or principle of construction or features of shape or configuration which are dictated solely by the function which the article to be made in that shape or configuration has to perform" (Section 1(3) of the United Kingdom Registered Designs Act, 1949).

16.63 In other words the proper subject of a registered design consists of what the eye can appreciate in its application to an article, except such features as are functional. Like a patent the design has to be construed by the court prior to considering issues of infringement and validity. By its nature the entire exercise here is done by the eye, that is the eye of the court. It will seldom be appropriate to adduce evidence to assist the eye in this respect.

16.64 Apart from the obvious defense that the product in issue does not fall within the scope of the design, the defendant will invariably counterclaim for rectification of the register of designs. As with patents, he may choose to rely on lack of novelty, which is a fundamental requirement for a valid design, in the light of prior art. Unlike a patent, he may also wish to impugn the design by showing it to be or consist of features or shapes or configuration which are dictated by the function above.

D. REMEDIES

16.65 The remedies typically available in intellectual property infringement actions are injunctions, damages and account of profits. Most actions start with an application for some form of preliminary or interlocutory relief and in most cases do not get beyond this preliminary stage.

(a) Preliminary Relief—The Interlocutory Injunction

16.66 Preliminary remedies are of the utmost importance to the protection of all these intellectual property rights. The period from the time of commencement of proceedings to the final determination of an issue can allow significant damage in the form of lost sales and profits, to reputation, and through other exploitation of material and/or information. Furthermore, the nature of the infringement or other unlawful conduct may be such as to make damages or an account of profits an inadequate remedy. One of the reasons for this is that the defendant may be impecunious or may disappear. But these will not be the only reasons why, in a particular case, damages may not be an adequate remedy. More often, this is because of the nature of the industrial or intellectual property right in question and the difficulty of reaching a precise estimate of the loss suffered as the result of an infringement. If, in such a case, the defendant's unlawful conduct is restrained at the outset, the problem of damages may either disappear from the case altogether or be very much less difficult than otherwise would be the case.

16.67 The most useful and used preliminary remedy is the interlocutory or interim injunction, the main purpose of which is usually described as being to preserve the *status quo* until the hearing of the main action. Although preserving the *status quo* as at the time of making an application is usually the most appropriate order, this is not as such the main concern of the interlocutory injunction. The primary matter with which the court is concerned in granting an interlocutory injunction is the maintenance of a position that will most easily enable justice to be done when the final determination is made. Thus, a court will sometimes order that an earlier position be restored, or that the parties arrange their affairs in some other way that is more in accordance with the requirements of justice.

16.68 In an increasing number of cases interlocutory injunctions are not sufficient to protect intellectual property rights against the threat of continuing infringement. This is often because the evidence needed to sustain an application for both interim and final relief is not readily available and will not become available through the usual processes of discovery. In such a case the plaintiff will be unlikely to obtain an interim injunction because he will not have the necessary

References for Section C
M. Fysh, *The Action for Infringement of Intellectual Property Rights*, WIPO/IP/ISB/86/9

evidence. Sometimes the defendant will remove or destroy the infringing material. In recent years a speedy and effective means of obtaining and preserving such evidence has been developed by courts in the United Kingdom. The relief granted is an *ex parte* order for entry and inspection of premises and removal of evidence. These orders are known as Anton Piller orders. An Anton Piller order may be a necessary step before an interlocutory injunction can be obtained.

16.69 Similarly, the collection of evidence and even a final judgment in favor of a plaintiff may be to no avail if the defendant has no assets which can be used to fund any damages ordered. This is a serious problem given the increasing resourcefulness of those attempting to avoid their obligations, the ease with which money can be moved from one country to another, and advances in technology. In order to address this problem the courts of common law countries have formulated and developed the Mareva injunction which operates to prevent defendants from removing assets from the jurisdiction or from disposing or dealing with them within the jurisdiction in such a way as to frustrate any judgment that may be entered against them.

(b) Final Injunction

16.70 In the normal course, a successful plaintiff in an industrial property action will be entitled to a final injunction. The grant of injunctions is discretionary and only in unusual situations (for example, where the defendant is the sole source of a life giving drug, or in a copyright case, where there has been extreme delay) will a permanent injunction be refused. If an injunction were not granted, for example, to a successful patent proprietor, the result would be tantamount to enabling the defendant to take a compulsory license under the patent without having to go through the statutory provisions relating to compulsory licenses. Should the injunction be breached, the plaintiff can, of course, move for contempt of court, and in the field of industrial property experience shows that such action on the part of a plaintiff is not at all infrequent.

(c) Damages or Account of Profits

16.71 The assessment of damages in industrial property cases invariably demands as a first step an election by the successful plaintiff as to whether he will take an inquiry as to damages on the one hand, or an account of profits on the other. These alternatives are of course mutually exclusive since by electing to go for an account, the plaintiff has adopted the defendant's acts as his own. The choice in each case will depend upon the facts. Sometimes, for instance, time may be of the essence and the trial as to liability may have itself generated enough material evidence to enable a plaintiff to move speedily for an account. Sometimes a defendant may have been able to secure more sales of the product in issue during the infringing period than the plaintiff could possibly have done. In such cases, the plaintiff will again be likely to choose an account rather than an inquiry— which will incidentally be for net profits.

16.72 Usually, however, a successful plaintiff will ask for an order that an inquiry as to damages be taken. When this is done, in a difficult case, the plaintiff may have to endure a fresh trial almost as substantial as the trial as to liability. For this reason, fully litigated industrial property cases seldom go as far as a full inquiry as to damages; they tend to settle when liability has been established.

16.73 The assessment of appropriate damages in industrial property cases vary somewhat between the several causes of action. Passing off and trademark infringement may be considered together as may patents and registered designs. Judicial views on the correct approach to damages for breach of confidence have been divergent and in copyright cases special statutory provisions exist. There is however no universally appropriate test or formula for assessing damages. Damages in any of these fields are notoriously difficult to assess with any degree of accuracy and the courts have sensibly taken this into account by declining to lay down general rules.

16.74 A common approach has been to assess damages on the basis of a notional arm's length license: this will arise for example when the parties are competitors and is usually appropriate to patent and registered design cases. Damages for past infringement are then based upon a payment of a royalty in respect of, for example, each infringing article. But problems do arise here—particularly when in reality the plaintiff would never have granted a licence. This approach has also been used in breach of confidence and copyright infringement cases. Another approach which is more difficult to prove is through consideration of sales lost to the Plaintiff; in this case the plaintiff is entitled to the entire lost profit.

References for Section D
I.F. Sheppard, "Preliminary Remedies in Intellectual Property Law", (1986) 15 *Intellectual Property in Asia and the Pacific*
M. Fysh, *The Action for Infringement of Intellectual Property Rights—Part II*, WIPO/IP/ISB/86/10

CHAPTER 17

Arbitration of Intellectual Property Disputes

A. ALTERNATIVE DISPUTE RESOLUTION

17.1 Alternative Dispute Resolution, or ADR, refers to methods of arriving at solutions between parties in intellectual property disputes without having to resort to bringing a lawsuit in the courts. There are many forms of alternative dispute resolution. The most common are arbitration, conciliation and expert determination.

(a) Arbitration

17.2 Perhaps the most common form of alternative dispute resolution is arbitration. Arbitration has a long history and in certain areas of business has been much used as a means of resolving disputes.

17.3 Arbitration is consensual in nature in that the parties must agree to have their dispute referred to an arbitrator. In many cases the parties will do this in advance by including in their agreement a clause providing for the submission of disputes (or certain disputes) to arbitration. The parties have considerable flexibility in the powers that they permit the arbitrator to exercise and may provide in great detail the procedures to be adopted in resolving disputes. In the absence of such provisions the legislation of the country the laws of which govern the contract or the rules of the arbitration body to which the dispute is referred will provide the relevant procedures to be adopted.

17.4 The advantages of arbitration are generally regarded to be the speed with which a decision can be handed down and the comparatively lower cost at which this can be done. However, this may not always be the case and some arbitration proceedings can take long periods of time to be completed and cost substantial amounts of money. One factor which should be borne in mind in considering arbitration over litigation as a means of resolving disputes is that the state provides the forum and the judge at low cost in the case of litigation whereas the parties must provide the forum and the arbitrator at their own cost in the case of arbitration.

17.5 Whilst arbitration will be a less formal procedure to litigation it is still likely to bring with it some of the formality of a Court. Although the rules or evidence need not be applied there will generally be some regard paid to them. Moreover, an arbitrator would normally want to hear evidence from witnesses and receive both argument and written submissions.

17.6 Reacting to the need for speed in the resolution of some disputes the Institute of Arbitrators Australia promulgated its "Expedited Commercial Arbitration Rules" in 1988 to provide for expedited arbitrations. These rules give the arbitrator broad powers to bring about a speedy and cost effective resolution. Other bodies which provide rules and resources for arbitration include the International Chamber of Commerce and the American Arbitration Association. Attached to this paper are sample arbitration causes as suggested by those bodies for inclusion in agreements where disputes are to be resolved by arbitration according to the rules of that body.

(b) Conciliation

17.7 Another form of alternative dispute resolution is conciliation. A conciliator will be a person who will be given the task of assisting the parties to resolve their dispute. Again the agreement of the parties to submit their dispute to conciliation will need to be obtained.

17.8 Conciliation is particularly attractive where both parties wish to build an on-going relationship and resolve a matter privately.

(c) Expert Determination

17.9 In technology transfer agreements is not unusual to find that the parties have agreed in advance that they will refer any technical disputes to a technical expert. In doing so the parties hope that disputes on these issues will be resolved speedily and cheaply.

17.10 Generally, an expert will be an independent third party and will have the necessary expertise in the relevant technology field to be able to quickly grasp the nub of the dispute and determine the matter accordingly. In general terms an expert will not act as an arbitrator and will not be required to follow the rules of natural justice.

17.11 An expert is particularly well suited to determine technical factual matters and should not be used to determine the rights and obligations of the parties to an agreement.

B.   ENFORCEMENT IN THE INTERNATIONAL CONTEXT

17.12 Many technology transfer agreements are international by their very nature. In the context of dispute resolution this raises an extremely important difficulty which should be addressed by the parties at the outset.

17.13 The recognition and enforcement in one jurisdiction of a judgment obtained in another jurisdiction is often an extremely difficult and expensive undertaking and is generally not guaranteed of success. In general terms these problems can be overcome by initiating proceedings in the defendant's jurisdiction. However for a variety of reasons this may not be an acceptable option to the would be plaintiff.

17.14 One of the critical questions in any dispute resolution procedure is the manner in which the decision or agreement can be enforced. If parties to a technology transfer agreement are relying on the courts of the particular country to resolve disputes between them they must ensure that a judgment obtained will be enforceable in any jurisdiction in which it is sought to enforce that judgment.

17.15 Many agreements confer exclusive jurisdiction to decide disputes to specific courts. However a judgment of a court is only useful to a party if it is enforceable in a jurisdiction in which the party to whom it is directed has assets.

17.16 The New York Convention on the Recognition and Enforcement of Foreign Arbitral Awards has been widely accepted and in excess of 80 countries are now a party to it. The signatories to the Convention are obliged under the Convention to pass implementing legislation. Under the terms of the Convention the signatories are required to enforce arbitral awards in accordance with procedural rules of the territory where the award is relied upon.

C. THE WIPO ARBITRATION CENTER

17.17 At its meeting in September 1993, the WIPO General Assembly unanimously approved the establishment of the WIPO Arbitration Center. The Center will offer services for the resolution of intellectual property disputes between private parties through arbitration and mediation.

17.18 The Center was established to establish a bridge between two spheres of activity and two communities of professionals, both of which have been subject in recent years to somewhat radical processes of change that have taken place in parallel to, rather than in conjunction with, each other. The two spheres of activity are, of course, arbitration or, more generally, alternative dispute resolution, on the one hand, and intellectual property, on the other hand, and the two community of professionals are those that service the participants, principally business and industry, in those two activities.

17.19 Both spheres of activity have undergone quantitative and qualitative changes over the past two decades, in particular. In the field of arbitration, the number of institutions administering arbitration throughout the world has grown considerably and a large number of those institutions have reported significant increases in the numbers of proceedings initiated. At the same time, particularly in the United States of America, the types of procedure available for the resolution of disputes have evolved well beyond traditional arbitration and mediation to include new forms of arbitration adapted from the classical model of arbitration, mini-trials or executive trials and various combinations of procedures in the context of complex disputes.

17.20 The developments that have occurred in the sphere of arbitration have not been fully absorbed into the intellectual property community. The incomplete statistical evidence that is available does show a marked increase in resort to arbitration in intellectual property disputes, but the increase does not seem to be proportionate to the increase in the resort to arbitration in commercial disputes in general. There are however, good reasons, resulting both from recent developments in intellectual property and from the traditional advantages offered by arbitration, why arbitration and other forms of alternative dispute resolution should hold particular appeal in the context of intellectual property disputes.

17.21 As to the recent developments that are pertinent, it is apparent that the increasingly technological basis of production, the emphasis on image and marketing as key factors in the successful distribution of goods and services, and the proliferation and variety of media of communication and telecommunication have all contributed to the attainment of a position of unprecedented prominence on the part intellectual property. The new prominence of intellectual property is reflected in the rapidly increasing number of intellectual property rights sought throughout the world. For example, over the five-year period from 1986 to 1990, the aggregate number of patent applications received by the European Patent Office, the Japanese Patent Office and the United States Patent and Trademark Office rose for 459,393 to 576,889, an increase of 25.6 %. Similarly, in the case of trademarks and service marks, the aggregate number of applications received by France, Japan and the United States of America over the same five-year period rose from 180,576 to 357,491, an increase of 97.97 %. There has been some slow-down in the rate of increase in the years since 1990, reflecting the prevailing adverse economic conditions, but the general trend remains consistently upward.

17.22 The major factor accounting for the increase in the number of intellectual property titles sought has been the increase in foreign-origin applications. This trend is borne out by the statistics, which show that, in the OECD countries, the proportion of all applications constituted by foreign applications has steadily increased since 1960 in all countries, with the exception of Japan. For example, from 1965 to 1985, the proportion of total patent applications constituted by foreign-origin applications increased in France 63.4 % to 77.8 %, in Germany from 42.6 % to 56.6 %, in the United Kingdom from 56.3 % to 70.8 % and in the United States of America from 23.6 % to 47.3 %. This development is a reflection of the internationalization of markets, which has meant that, as enterprises seek to penetrate markets covering a wider geographical area, they have similarly sought protection for their intellectual property throughout that extended geographical area.

17.23 The increased resort to intellectual property protection and the international character of the protection sought open several new possibilities for the application of alternative dispute resolution in the context of intellectual property. In the first place, the existence of more rights raises the potential for a larger number of conflicts between those rights. Those rights are, moreover, the subject of a growing volume of trade in the transfer of technology, carried out through licensing and other contractual arrangements in which dispute-settlement clauses feature as a matter of course. Those negotiating the contractual arrangements have their attention directed more to the successful conclusion of a potential business arrangement, rather than to the consequences of a breakdown in that arrangement. The developments that have occurred in the area of arbitration have not necessarily found expression in contractual provisions directed at the efficient resolution of disputes in such a way as to facilitate the continued productive exploitation of the subject matter of the intellectual property rights covered by the business arrangement between the parties.

17.24 In addition, the existence of a multiplicity of national and regional rights covering the same subject matter suggests the desirability of procedures for resolving disputes in relation to that subject matter which avoid recourse to a multiplicity of national court actions. Even if a multiplicity of separate national claims is not involved, the opposition of two foreign parties, which is a more frequent occurrence as a result of the large proportion of foreign-origin intellectual property titles in each country, suggests the desirability of dispute-resolution procedures that do not involve actions in the court system of one of the parties, which may cause the foreign party at least to feel disadvantaged by an alien legal culture.

17.25 Besides the potential for the application of alternative dispute resolution that is suggested by recent developments in intellectual property protection, many of the traditional advantages in favor of alternative dispute resolution in general apply with particular acuity to intellectual property. In particular, the possibility that alternative dispute resolution offers of choosing arbitrators or other neutrals with specialized expertise is of great importance in the context of the highly technical and scientifically sophisticated subject matter covered patents, trade secrets and plant variety rights. While specialized courts exist in a number of countries, and the possibility for courts to call on expert assistance is also increasingly common, it may be more efficient and cost-effective to commit a dispute to an arbitral tribunal whose composition includes at least one expert chosen for his or her specialized knowledge of the field to which the dispute belongs. In addition, the confidentiality under which arbitration and other procedures may be conducted offers special advantages where know how or other confidential information must be exposed in the course of a dispute in order to achieve a satisfactory resolution.

17.26 The WIPO Arbitration Center services will be available in relation to four dispute-settlement procedures:

(1) *Mediation*: a procedure in which a neutral intermediary, the mediator, endeavors, at the request of the parties to a dispute, to assist them in understanding their respective positions in relation to the dispute, and in which, while not having the power to impose a settlement, the mediator endeavors to aid the parties in reaching a mutually satisfactory settlement.
(2) *Arbitration*: a procedure involving the submission of a dispute, pursuant to an agreement of the parties, to an arbitrator or a tribunal of arbitrators, chosen or approved by the parties, for resolution, in accordance with the law and procedure adopted by the parties, through a binding decision given by the arbitrator or the tribunal.
(3) *Mediation and Default Arbitration*: a combined procedure in which the parties to a dispute agree to endeavor first to resolve the dispute through mediation. If a settlement is not reached through mediation, either party may require that the dispute be submitted to arbitration for a binding decision.
(4) *Expedited Arbitration*: a procedure which is the same as arbitration, except that the rules pursuant to which the arbitration is conducted are drafted so as to limit the choices that both the arbitrator and the parties might otherwise make with respect to the arbitration process, in order to obtain a quick result at a relatively low cost. It is thus a procedure which might be expected to appeal particularly to those involved in small-scale disputes concerning intellectual property rights, which do not justify, either in terms of personnel or financial costs, resort to court litigation or to conventional arbitration.

17.27 The services that WIPO will provide in relation to the four above-mentioned procedures are essentially of two types. The first type involves making available to parties that so desire the instruments needed to submit a dispute for resolution pursuant to one of the above-mentioned procedures administered by WIPO. Two such instruments are necessary: model contract clauses and submission agreements for initiating recourse to one of the four procedures, and rules for the conduct of each of the four procedures.

17.28 The second sort of service that will be provided derives from the rules for the conduct of the four procedures. Those rules envisage that certain functions will be performed by the International Bureau with respect to the conduct of the dispute-settlement procedure. Those functions include the following:

(1) whenever the parties to a given dispute cannot agree on the person of the mediator or arbitrator, the appointment, by the Director General of WIPO, in consultation with the parties and in accordance with the procedures set out in the rules, of the mediator or arbitrator;

(2) the determination, by the International Bureau of WIPO, in consultation with the mediator or the arbitrator and the parties, of the fees of the mediator or arbitrator, in accordance with the procedures set out in the rules, as well as the establishment of the modalities for the payment of those fees;

(3) the processing of notifications initiating any given mediation or arbitration;

(4) the administration of the deposit of fees and costs of any given mediation or arbitration and the rendering of an account of such administration to the parties to the dispute during and after the conclusion of the mediation or arbitration proceedings;

(5) on the request of the parties to a given dispute, and where the place of mediation or arbitration is Geneva, the provision, against payment of a fee, of hearing rooms and secretarial and interpretation facilities.

References for Section C
International Bureau of WIPO, *Enforcement of Intellectual Property Rights and Dispute Settlement,*
WIPO/ACAD/E/93/15

PART V

International Treaties and Conventions on Intellectual Property

CHAPTER 18

The Paris Convention for the Protection of Industrial Property

A. HISTORY

18.1 During the last century, before the existence of any international convention in the field of industrial property, it was rather difficult to obtain protection for industrial property rights in the various countries of the world because the laws were very different. Moreover, patent applications had to be made roughly at the same time in all countries in order to avoid a publication in one country destroying the novelty of the invention in the other countries. These practical problems created a strong desire to overcome such difficulties.

18.2 In addition to those practical considerations, there was, as more and more countries developed a system for the protection of inventions during the second half of the last century, a general desire, as in other fields of law, for the harmonization of the laws of industrial property on an international, and even worldwide, basis. This was due to the development of a more internationally oriented flow of technology and to the increase of international trade, which made such harmonization urgent in both the patent and the trademark field.

18.3 The lack of adequate protection of foreign inventions became particularly apparent when the Government of the Empire of Austria-Hungary invited the other countries to participate in an international exhibition of inventions held in 1873 at Vienna. Participation was hampered by the fact that many foreign visitors were not willing to exhibit their inventions at that exhibition in view of the inadequate legal protection offered to exhibited inventions.

18.4 This led to two developments: firstly, a special Austrian law secured temporary protection to all foreigners participating in the exhibition for their inventions, trademarks and industrial designs. Secondly, the Congress of Vienna for Patent Reform was convened during the same year 1873. The Congress for Patent Reform passed several resolutions, setting forth a number of principles on which an effective and useful patent system should be based, and urging governments "to bring about an international understanding upon patent protection as soon as possible."

18.5 As a follow-up to the Vienna Congress, an International Congress on Industrial Property was convened at Paris in 1878. The main result of that second Congress was a decision that one of the governments should be asked to convene an international (diplomatic) conference "with the task of determining the basis of uniform legislation" in the field of industrial property.

18.6 Following that Congress, a final draft proposing an international "union" for the protection of industrial property was prepared in France. That draft was sent by the French Government to a number of other countries, together with an invitation to attend the International Conference in Paris of 1880. That Conference adopted a draft convention which contained in essence those substantive provisions which are still today the main features of the Paris Convention.

18.7 A new Diplomatic Conference was convened in Paris in 1883, which ended with final approval and signature of the Paris Convention for the Protection of Industrial Property. The Paris Convention was signed by 11 States: Belgium, Brazil, El Salvador, France, Guatemala, Italy, the Netherlands, Portugal, Serbia, Spain and Switzerland. When the Paris Convention came into effect on July 7, 1884, Great Britain, Tunis and Ecuador had adhered as well, bringing the initial number of member countries to 14. At the end of the nineteenth century, the number of member countries had risen to 19. It was only during the first quarter of this century and then in particular after World War II that the Paris Convention increased its membership more significantly.

18.8 The Paris Convention has been revised from time to time after its signature in 1883. Revision Conferences were held in Rome in 1886, in Madrid in 1890 and 1891, in Brussels in 1897 and 1900, in Washington in 1911, in The Hague in 1925, in London in 1934, in Lisbon in 1958 and in Stockholm in 1967. The last Revision Conference held its first session in Geneva in 1980, its second session in Nairobi in 1981, its third session in Geneva in 1982 and its fourth session in Geneva in February-March 1984.

18.9 Each of the revision conferences, starting with the Brussels Conference in 1900, ended with the adoption of a revised Act of the Paris Convention. With the exception of the Acts concluded at the revision conferences of Brussels and Washington, which are no longer in force, all those earlier Acts are still of significance, although the great majority of the countries are now party to the latest Act, that of Stockholm of 1967.

B. PRINCIPAL PROVISIONS

18.10 The provisions of the Paris Convention may be sub-divided into four main categories.

18.11 A first category of provisions contains rules of substantive law which guarantee a basic right known as the right to national treatment in each of the member countries.

18.12 A second category of provisions establishes another basic right known as the right of priority.

18.13 A third category of provisions defines a certain number of common rules in the field of substantive law which contain either rules establishing rights and obligations of natural persons and legal entities or rules requiring or permitting the member countries to enact legislation following those rules.

18.14 A fourth category of provisions deals with the administrative framework, which has been set up to implement the Convention, and includes the final clauses of the Convention.

(a) National Treatment Principle

18.15 The provisions concerning national treatment are contained in Articles 2 and 3 of the Convention.

18.16 National treatment means that, as regards the protection of industrial property, each country party to the Paris Convention must grant the same protection to nationals of the other member countries as it grants to its own nationals.

18.17 The same national treatment must be granted to nationals of countries which are not party to the Paris Convention if they are domiciled in a member country or if they have a "real and effective" industrial or commercial establishment in such a country. However, no requirement as to domicile or establishment in the country where protection is claimed may be imposed upon nationals of member countries as a condition for benefitting from an industrial property right.

18.18 This national treatment rule is one of the cornerstones of the system of international protection established under the Paris Convention. It guarantees not only that foreigners will be protected, but also that they will not be discriminated against in any way. Without that rule, it would frequently be very difficult and sometimes even impossible to obtain adequate protection in foreign countries for inventions, trademarks and other subjects of industrial property.

18.19 The national treatment rule applies first of all to the "nationals" of the member countries. The term "national" includes both natural persons and legal entities. With respect to legal entities, the quality of being a national of a particular country may be difficult to determine. Generally, no nationality as such is granted to legal entities by the various national laws. There is of course no doubt that State owned enterprises of a member country or other entities created under the public law of such country are to be considered as nationals of the member country concerned. Legal entities created under the private law of a member country will usually be considered a national of that country. If they have their actual headquarters in another member country, they may also be considered a national of the headquarters country.

18.20 According to Article 2(1), the national treatment rule applies to all advantages that the various national laws grant to nationals. This means that the national law, as it is applied to the nationals of a particular member country, must also be applied to the nationals of other member countries. In this respect, the national treatment rule excludes any possibility of discrimination to the detriment of nationals of other member countries.

18.21 This means furthermore, that any requirement of reciprocity of protection is excluded. Suppose that a given member country has a longer term of patent protection than another member country: the former country will not have the right to provide that nationals of the latter country will enjoy a term of protection of the same length as the term of protection is in the law of the latter country. This principle applies not only to codified law, but also to the practice of the courts (jurisprudence) and to the practice of the Patent Office or other administrative governmental institutions, as it is applied to the nationals of the country.

18.22 The application of the national law to the national of another member country does not, however, prevent him from invoking more beneficial rights specially provided in the Paris Convention. These rights are expressly reserved. The national treatment principle must be applied without prejudice to such rights.

18.23 Article 2(3) states an exception to the national treatment rule. The national law relating to judicial and administrative procedure, to jurisdiction and to requirements of representation is expressly "reserved." This means that certain requirements of a mere procedural nature which impose special conditions on foreigners for purposes of judicial and administrative procedure, may also validly be invoked against foreigners who are nationals of member countries. An example is a requirement for foreigners to deposit a certain sum as security or bail for the costs of litigation. Another example is expressly stated: the requirement on foreigners to either designate an address for service or to appoint an agent in the country in which protection is requested. This latter is perhaps the most common special requirement imposed on foreigners, and is a permitted exception from the national treatment rule.

18.24 As indicated initially, the application of the national treatment rule extends also to nationals of non-member countries, provided they are *domiciled* or have an industrial or commercial establishment in a member country. This provision is contained in Article 3.

18.25 The term "domiciled" is generally interpreted not to require a domicile in the strict legal sense of the term. A person is also "domiciled" in the sense of Article 3 if he lives more or less permanently in a particular place, without having his legal residence there. In other words, a mere residence, as distinct from a legal domicile, is sufficient. Legal entities are domiciled at the place of their actual headquarters.

18.26 If there is no domicile, there may still be an industrial or commercial establishment which gives a person the right to national treatment. The notion of the industrial or commercial establishment in a member country of a national of a non-member country is further qualified by the text of the Convention itself. It requires that the establishment be real and effective. This means that there must be actual industrial or commercial activity. A mere letter box or the renting of a small office with no real activity is not sufficient.

(b)   The Right of Priority

18.27 The provisions concerning the right of priority are contained in Article 4 of the Convention.

> The right of priority means that, on the basis of a regular application for an industrial property right filed by a given applicant in one of the member countries, the same applicant (or its or his successor in title) may, within a specified period of time (six or 12 months), apply for protection in all the other member countries. These later applications will then be regarded as if they had been filed on the same day as the first (or earlier) application. In other words, these later applications enjoy a priority status with respect to all applications relating to the same invention filed after the date of

the first application. They also enjoy a priority status with respect to all acts accomplished after that date which would normally be apt to destroy the rights of the applicant or the patentability of his invention.

18.28 The right of priority offers great practical advantages to the applicant desiring protection in several countries. The applicant is not required to present all applications at home and in foreign countries at the same time, since he has six or 12 months at his disposal to decide in which countries to request protection. The applicant can use that period to organize with due care the steps to be taken to secure protection in the various countries of interest in this case.

18.29 The beneficiary of the right of priority is any person entitled to benefit from the national treatment rule who has duly filed an application for a patent for invention or another industrial property right in one of the member countries.

18.30 The right of priority can be based only on the *first* application for the same industrial property right which must have been filed in a member country. It is therefore not possible to follow a first application by a second, possibly improved application and then to use that second application as a basis of priority. The reason for this rule is obvious: one cannot permit an endless chain of successive claims of priority for the same subject, as this could, in fact, considerably prolong the term of protection for that subject.

18.31 Article 4A(1) of the Paris Convention recognizes expressly that the right of priority may also be invoked by the successor in title of the first applicant. The right of priority may be transferred to a successor in title without transferring at the same time the first application itself. This allows in particular also the transfer of the right of priority to different persons for different countries, a practice which is quite common.

18.32 The later application must concern the same subject as the first application the priority of which is claimed. In other words, the same invention, utility model, trademark or industrial design must be the subject of both applications. It is, however, possible to use a first application for a patent for invention as priority basis for a registration of a utility model and vice versa. The same change of form of protection in both directions is also possible between utility models and industrial designs.

18.33 The first application must be "duly filed" in order to give rise to the right of priority. Any filing, which is equivalent to a regular national filing, is a valid basis for the right of priority. A regular national filing means any filing that is adequate to establish the date on which the application was filed in the country concerned. The notion of "national" filing is qualified by including also applications filed under bilateral or multilateral treaties concluded between member countries.

18.34 Withdrawal, abandonment or rejection of the first application does not destroy its capacity to serve as a priority basis. The right of priority subsists even where the first application generating that right is no longer existent.

18.35 The effect of the right of priority is regulated in Article 4B. One can summarize this effect by saying that, as a consequence of the priority claim, the later application must be treated as if it had been filed already at the time of the filing, in another member country, of the first application the priority of which is claimed. By virtue of the right of priority, all the acts accomplished during the time between the filing dates of the first and the later applications, the so-called priority period, cannot destroy the rights which are the subject of the later application.

18.36 In terms of concrete examples, this means that a patent application for the same invention filed by a third party during the priority period will not give a prior right, although it was filed before the later application. Likewise, a publication or public use of the invention, which is the subject of the later application, during the priority period would not destroy the novelty or inventive character of that invention. It is insignificant for that purpose whether that publication is made by the applicant or the inventor himself or by a third party.

18.37 The length of the priority period is different according to the various kinds of industrial property rights. For patents for invention and utility models the priority period is 12 months, for industrial designs and trademarks it is six months. In determining the length of the priority period, the Paris Convention had to take into account the conflicting interests of the applicant and of third parties. The priority periods now prescribed by the Paris Convention seem to strike an adequate balance between these conflicting interests.

18.38 The right of priority as recognized by the Convention permits the claiming of "multiple priorities" and of "partial priorities." Therefore, the later application may not only claim the priority of one earlier application, but it may also combine the priority of several earlier applications, each of which pertaining to different features of the subject matter of the later application. Furthermore, in the later application, elements for which priority is claimed may be combined with elements for which no priority is claimed. In all these cases, the later application must of course comply with the requirement of unity of invention.

18.39 These possibilities correspond to a practical need. Frequently after a first filing further improvements and additions to the invention are the subject of further applications in the country of origin. In such cases, it is very practical to be able to combine these various earlier applications into one later application, when filing before the end of the priority year in another member country. This combination is even possible if the multiple priorities come from different member countries.

(c) Provisions Concerning Patents

(i) Independence of Patents

18.40 The rule concerning the "independence" of patents for invention is contained in Article 4bis. This rule means that patents for invention granted in member countries to nationals or residents of member countries must be treated as independent of patents for invention obtained for the same invention in other countries, including non-member countries.

18.41 This principle is to be understood in its broadest sense. It means that the grant of a patent for invention in one country for a given invention does not oblige any other member country to grant a patent for invention for the same invention. Furthermore, the principle means that a patent for invention cannot be refused, invalidated or otherwise terminated in any member country on the ground that a patent for invention for the same invention has been refused or invalidated, or that it is no longer maintained or has terminated, in any other country. In this respect, the fate of a particular patent for invention in any given country has no influence whatsoever on the fate of a patent for the same invention in any of the other countries.

18.42 The underlying reason and main argument in favor of the principle of independence of patents for invention is that the national laws and administrative practices are usually quite different from country to country. A decision not to grant or to invalidate a patent for invention in a particular country on the basis of its law will frequently not have any bearing on the different legal situation in the other countries. It would not be justified to make the owner lose the patent for invention in other countries on the ground that it or he lost a patent in a given country as a consequence of not having paid an annual fee in that country or as a consequence of the patent's invalidation in that country on a ground which does not exist in the laws of the other countries. Moreover, a system where patents are dependent from foreign patents would not be in conformity with the national treatment rule.

18.43 A special feature of the principle of independence of patents for invention is contained in Article 4bis(5). This provision requires that a patent granted on an application which claimed the priority of one or more foreign applications must be given the same duration which it would have according to the national law if no priority had been claimed. In other words, it is not permitted to deduct the priority period from the term of a patent invoking the priority of a first application. For instance, a provision in a national law starting the term of the patent for invention from the (foreign) priority date, and not from the filing date of the application in the country, would be in violation of this rule.

(ii)   The Right of the Inventor to be Mentioned

18.44 Another important common rule is Article 4ter which deals with the mentioning of the inventor. The Paris Convention provides for this question only a general rule. It states that the inventor must have the right to be mentioned as such in the patent for invention.

18.45 National laws have implemented this provision in several ways. Some give the inventor only the right for civil action against the applicant or owner in order to obtain the inclusion of his name in the patent for invention. Others—and that tendency seems to be increasing—enforce the naming of the inventor during the procedure for the grant of a patent for invention on an *ex officio* basis. In some countries, for instance the United States of America, it is even required that the applicant for a patent be the inventor himself.

(iii)   Importation; Failure to Work and Compulsory Licenses

18.46 The Convention deals in Article 5A with the questions of failure to work the patented invention, of importation of articles covered by patents, and of compulsory licenses.

18.47 With respect to importation the provision states that importation by the patentee, into the country where the patent has been granted, of articles covered by the patent and manufactured in any of the countries of the Union will not entail forfeiture of the patent. This provision is quite narrowly worded, and hence only applies when several conditions are met. Consequently the countries of the Union have considerable leeway to legislate with respect to importation of patented goods under any of the circumstances which are different to those foreseen in this provision.

18.48 This Article applies to patentees which are entitled to benefit from the Paris Convention and who, having a patent in one of the countries of the Paris Union, import to this country goods (covered by the patent) which were manufactured in another country of the Union. In such a case, the patent granted in the country of importation may not be forfeited as a sanction for such importation.

18.49 In this context, the term "patentee" would also cover the representative of the patentee, or any person who effects the importation in the name of such patentee.

18.50 With respect to the goods that are imported, it suffices that they be manufactured in a country of the Union. The fact that the goods, having been manufactured in a country of the Union, are thereafter circulated through other countries and eventually imported from a country which is not a member of the Union, would not prevent this Article from being applicable.

18.51 Finally, it may be mentioned that the term "forfeiture" in Article 5A(1) includes any measure which has the effect of definitively terminating the patent. Therefore it would cover the concepts of invalidation, revocation, annulment, repeal, etc. Whether "forfeiture" may, in the light of the purpose of this Article or the spirit of the Paris Convention, be construed as covering also other measures that would have the effect of preventing importation (fines, suspension of rights, etc.) is left for the national legislation and courts to decide.

18.52 With respect to the working of patents and compulsory licenses, the essence of the provisions contained in Article 5A is that each country may take legislative measures providing for the grant of compulsory licenses. These compulsory licenses are intended to prevent the abuses which might result from the exclusive rights conferred by a patent for invention, for example failure to work or insufficient working.

18.53 Compulsory licenses on the ground of failure to work or insufficient working are the most common kind of coercive measure against the patent owner to prevent abuses of the rights conferred by the patent for invention. They are expressly dealt with by Article 5A.

18.54 The main argument for enforcing working of the invention in a particular country is the consideration that, in order to promote the industrialization of the country, patents for invention should not be used merely to block the working of the invention in the country or to monopolize importation of the patented article by the patent owner. They should rather be used to introduce the use of the new technology into the country. Whether the patent owner can really be expected to do so, is first of all an economic consideration and then also a question of time. Working in all countries is generally not economical. Moreover, it is generally recognized that immediate working in all countries is impossible. Article 5A therefore tries to strike a balance between these conflicting interests.

18.55 Compulsory licenses for failure to work or insufficient working of the invention may not be requested before a certain period of time of non-working or insufficient working has elapsed. This time limit expires either four years from the date of filing of the patent application or three years from the date of the grant of the patent for invention. The applicable time is the one which, in the individual case, expires last.

18.56 The time limit of three or four years is a minimum time limit. The patent owner must be given a longer time limit, if he can give legitimate reasons for his inaction. In other words, the patent owner can produce evidence that legal, economic or technical obstacles prevent working, or working more intensively, the invention in the country. If that is proven, the request for a compulsory license must be rejected, at least for the time being. The time limit of three or four years is a minimum time limit also in that sense that national law can provide for a longer time limit.

18.57 The compulsory license for non-working or insufficient working must be a non-exclusive license and can only be transferred together with the part of the enterprise benefitting from the compulsory license. The patent owner must retain the right to grant other non-exclusive licenses and to work the invention himself. Moreover, as the compulsory license has been granted to a particular enterprise on the basis of its known capacities, it is bound to that enterprise and cannot be transferred separately from that enterprise. These limitations are intended to prevent that a compulsory licensee obtains a stronger position on the market than is warranted by the purpose of the compulsory license, namely, to ensure sufficient working of the invention in the country.

18.58 All these special provisions for compulsory licenses in Article 5A(4) are only applicable to compulsory licenses for non-working or insufficient working. They are not applicable to the other types of compulsory licenses which the national law is free to provide for. Such other types of compulsory licenses may be granted to prevent abuses other than non-working or insufficient working. Such abuses may be, for example, excessive prices or unreasonable terms for contractual licenses or other restrictive measures which hamper industrial development.

18.59 Compulsory licenses may also be granted, by considerations of public interest, in cases where there is no abuse by the patent owner of his rights. These are in particular cases where a patent for invention affects a vital public interest, for example, in the fields of military security or public health.

18.60 There are also cases where a compulsory license is provided for to protect the public interest in unhampered technological progress. This is the case of the compulsory license in favor of the so-called *dependent patents*. If a patented invention cannot be worked without using an earlier patent for invention granted to another person, then the owner of the dependent patent, under certain circumstances, may have the right to request a compulsory license to enable the use of that invention. If the owner of the dependent patent for invention obtains the compulsory license, he may in turn be obliged to grant a license to the owner of the earlier patent for invention.

18.61 All these other types of compulsory licenses can be grouped together under the general heading of compulsory licenses *in the public interest*. The national laws are not prevented by the Paris Convention to provide for such compulsory licenses, and they are not subject to the restrictions provided for in Article 5A. This means in particular that compulsory licenses in the public interest can be granted without waiting for the expiration of the time limits provided for compulsory licenses that relate to failure to work or insufficient working.

(iv) Grace Period for the Payment of Maintenance Fees

18.62 Article 5*bis* provides for a grace period for the payment of maintenance fees for industrial property rights and deals with the restoration of patents for invention in case of non-payment of fees.

18.63 In most countries the maintenance of certain industrial property rights, mainly the rights in patents for invention and trademarks, is subject to the periodic payment of fees. For patents, the maintenance fees must generally be paid annually, and in that case are also called annuities. Immediate loss of the patent for invention in the event that one annuity is not paid at the due date would be too harsh a sanction. Therefore, the Paris Convention provides for a period of grace, during which the payment can still be made after the due date with the effect to maintain the patent. That period is six months, and is established as a minimum period so that countries are free to accord a longer period.

18.64 The delayed payment of the annuity may be subjected to the payment of a surcharge. In that case, both the delayed fee and the surcharge must be paid within the grace period. During the grace period, the patent for invention remains provisionally in force. If the payment is not made during the grace period, the patent for invention will lapse retroactively, that is, as of the original due date of the annuity.

(v) Patents in International Traffic

18.65 Another common rule of substantive importance, containing a limitation of the rights of the patent owner under special circumstances, is contained in Article 5*ter*. It deals with the transit of devices on ships, aircraft or land vehicles through a member country in which such device is patented.

18.66 The effect of this provision is essentially the following. Where ships, aircraft or land vehicles of other member countries enter temporarily or accidentally a given member country and have on board devices patented in that country, the owner of the means of transportation is not required to obtain prior approval or a license from the patent owner. Temporary or accidental entry of the patented device into the country in such cases constitutes no infringement of the patent for invention.

18.67 The device on board the ship, aircraft or vehicle must be in the body, in the machinery, tackle, gear or other accessories of the conveyance, and must be used exclusively for operational needs.

18.68 The provision covers only the use of patented devices. It does not allow the making of patented devices on board a means of transportation, nor the sale to the public of patented products or of products obtained under a patented process.

(vi)   Inventions Shown at International Exhibitions

18.69 A further common rule of a substantive nature is the provision concerning the temporary protection in respect of goods exhibited at international exhibitions, contained in Article 11 of the Convention.

18.70 The principle stated in Article 11 is that the member countries are obliged to grant, in conformity with their domestic legislation, temporary protection to patentable inventions, utility models, industrial designs and trademarks in respect of goods exhibited at official or officially recognized international exhibitions held in the territory of any member country.

18.71 The temporary protection may be provided by various means. One is to grant a special right of priority, similar to that provided for in Article 4. This priority right would start from the date of the opening of the exhibition or from the date of the introduction of the object at the exhibition. It would be maintained for a certain period, say twelve months, from that date, and would expire if the application for protection does not follow the exhibition within that period.

18.72 Another means of temporary protection, which is found in a number of national laws, in particular with respect to patents for invention, is that of prescribing that, during a certain period of, say, twelve months before the filing or priority date of a patent application, a display of the invention at an international exhibition will not destroy the novelty of the invention. When choosing that solution, it is important to protect the inventor or other owner of the invention during the same period also against abusive acts of third parties. This means in particular that the person exhibiting the invention must be protected against any copying or usurpation of the invention for purposes of a patent application by a third party. The owner of the invention must also be protected against disclosure by third parties based on the exhibition.

18.73 Article 11 applies only to official or officially recognized exhibitions. The interpretation of that term is left to the member country where protection is sought. An interpretation corresponding to the spirit of Article 11 is to consider an exhibition as "official," if it is organized by a State or other public authority, to consider it as "officially recognized," if it is not official but has at least been recognized as official by a State or other public authority, and to consider it as "international," if goods from various countries are exhibited.

(d)   Provisions Concerning Trademarks

(i)   Use of Trademarks

18.74 The Convention touches on the issue of the use of marks in Article 5C(1), (2) and (3).

18.75 Article 5C(1) relates to the compulsory use of registered trademarks. Some of the countries which provide for the registration of trademarks also require that the trademark, once registered, be used within a certain period. If this use is not complied with, the trademark may be expunged from the register. For this purpose, "use" is generally understood as meaning the sale of goods bearing the trademark, although national legislation may regulate more broadly the manner in which use of the trademark is to be complied with. The said Article states that where compulsory use is required, the trademark's registration may be cancelled for failure to use the trademark only after a reasonable period has elapsed, and then only if the owner does not justify such failure.

18.76 The definition of what is meant by "reasonable period" is left to the national legislation of the countries concerned, or otherwise to the authorities competent for resolving such cases. This reasonable period is intended to permit the owner of the mark enough time and opportunity to arrange for its proper use, considering that in many cases the owner has to use his mark in several countries.

18.77 Cancellation of a mark's registration may only be decided if the owner does not justify the failure to use his trademark. Such justification would be acceptable if it were based on legal or economic circumstances beyond the owner's control, for example if importation of the marked goods had been prohibited or delayed by governmental regulations.

18.78 The Convention also establishes in Article 5C(2) that the use of a trademark by its proprietor in a form differing in elements which do not alter the distinctive character of the mark in the form in which it was registered in one of the countries of the Union shall not entail invalidation of the registration nor diminish the protection granted to the mark. The purpose of this provision is to allow for unessential differences between the form of the mark as it is registered and the form in which it is used, for example in cases of adaptation or translation of certain elements for such use. This rule applies also to similar differences in the form of the mark as used in the country of its original registration.

18.79 Whether in a given case the differences between the mark as registered and the mark as actually used alter the distinctive character is a matter to be decided by the competent national authorities.

(ii) Concurrent Use of the Same Trademark by Different Enterprises

18.80 Article 5C(3) of the Convention deals with the case where the same mark is used for identical or similar goods by two or more establishments considered as co-proprietors of the trademark. It is provided that such concurrent use will not impede the registration of the trademark nor diminish the protection in any country of the Union, except where the said use results in misleading the public or is contrary to the public interest. Such cases could occur if the concurrent use misleads the public as to the origin or source of the goods sold under the same trademark, or if the quality of such goods differs to the point where it may be contrary to the public interest to allow the continuation of such inconsistency.

18.81 This provision does not, however, cover the case of concurrent use of the mark by enterprises which are not co-proprietors of the mark, for instance when use is made concurrently by the owner and a licensee or a franchisee. These cases are left for the national legislation of the various countries to regulate.

(iii) Grace Period for the Payment of Renewal Fees

18.82 Article 5bis requires that a period of grace be allowed for the payment of fees due for the maintenance of industrial property rights. In the case of trademarks this provision concerns primarily the payment of renewal fees, since it is by renewal that trademark registrations (and hence the rights that depend on such registrations) may be maintained. A failure to renew the registration will normally entail the lapse of the registration, and in some cases the expiration of the right to the mark. The period of grace provided by the Convention is intended to diminish the risks of a mark being lost by an involuntary delay in the payment of the renewal fees.

18.83 The countries of the Paris Union are obliged to accord a period of grace of at least six months for the payment of the renewal fees, but are free to provide for the payment of a surcharge when such renewal fees are paid within the period of grace. Moreover, the countries are free to provide for a period of grace longer than the minimum six months prescribed by the Convention.

18.84 During the period of grace, the registration remains provisionally in force. If the payment of the renewal fees (and surcharge where appropriate) is not made during the period of grace, the registration will lapse retroactively as of the original date of expiration.

(iv) Independence of Trademarks

18.85 Article 6 of the Convention establishes the important principle of the independence of trademarks in the different countries of the Union, and in particular the independence of trademarks filed or registered in the country of origin from those filed or registered in other countries of the Union.

18.86 The first part of Article 6 states the application of the basic principle of national treatment to the filing and registration of marks in the countries of the Union. Regardless of the origin of the mark whose registration is sought, a country of the Union may apply only its domestic legislation when determining the conditions for the filing and registration of the mark. The application of the principle of national treatment asserts the rule of independence of marks, since their registration and maintenance will depend only on each domestic law.

18.87 This Article also provides that an application for the registration of a mark, filed in any country of the Union by a person who is entitled to the benefits of the Convention, may not be refused, nor may a registration be cancelled, on the ground that filing, registration or renewal of the mark has not been effected in the country of origin. This provision lays down the express rule that obtaining and maintaining a trademark registration in any country of the Union may not be made dependent on the application, registration or renewal of the same mark in the country of origin of the mark. Therefore no action with respect to the mark in the country of origin may be required as a prerequisite for obtaining a registration of the mark in that country.

18.88 Finally, Article 6 states that a mark duly registered in a country of the Union shall be regarded as independent of marks registered in the other countries of the Union, including the country of origin. This means that a mark once registered will not be automatically affected by any decision taken with respect to similar registrations for the same marks in other countries. In this respect, the fact that one or more such similar registrations are, for example, renounced, cancelled or abandoned, will not *eo ipso* affect the registrations of the mark in other countries. The validity of these registrations will depend only on the provisions applicable in accordance with the legislation of each of the countries concerned.

(v) Well-Known Trademarks

18.89 The Convention deals with well-known trademarks in Article 6*bis*. This Article obliges a member country to refuse or cancel the registration and to prohibit the use of a trademark that is liable to create confusion with another trademark already well-known in that member country. The effect of this Article is to extend protection to a trademark that is well-known in a member country even though it is not registered or used in that country. The protection of the well-known trademark results not from its registration, which prevents the registration or use of a conflicting trademark, but from the mere fact of its reputation.

18.90 The protection of well-known trademarks is deemed justified on the grounds that a trademark that has acquired goodwill and a reputation in a member country ought to give rise to a right for its owner and because the registration or use of a confusingly similar trademark would, in most cases, amount to an act of unfair competition and be prejudicial to the interests of the public who would be misled by the use of a conflicting trademark for the same or identical goods than those in connection with which the well-known trademark is registered.

18.91 The trademark that is protected by Article 6*bis* must be a "well-known" trademark. Whether a trademark is well known in a member country will be determined by its competent administrative or judicial authorities. A trademark may not have been used in a country, in the sense that goods bearing that trademark have not been sold there, yet that trademark may be well-known in the country because of publicity there or the repercussions in that country of advertising in other countries.

18.92 The protection of a well-known trademark under Article 6*bis* exists only where the conflicting trademark has been filed, registered or used for identical or similar goods. Whether the condition is fulfilled will be determined by the administrative or judicial authorities of the country in which protection is claimed.

18.93 The protection of a well-known trademark under Article 6*bis* results from the obligation of a member country to take *ex officio* where its legislation so permits, or at the request of an interested party, the following type of action:

(1) a member country must refuse the application for registration of the conflicting trademark;
(2) the member country must cancel the registration of a conflicting trademark. A member country is required to allow at least a period of five years from the date of registration within which a request for cancellation of the conflicting trademark may be made, unless that trademark was registered in bad faith, in which event no time limit may be fixed;
(3) the member country must prohibit the use of the conflicting trademark. A member country is free to prescribe a period within which that request must be made; however, no time limit may be fixed for such a request in the case of a conflicting trademark used in bad faith.

(vi) State Emblems, Official Hallmarks and Emblems of International Organizations

18.94 The Convention deals with distinctive signs of States and international intergovernmental organizations in Article 6*ter*. This Article obliges a member country, in certain circumstances, to refuse or invalidate the registration and to prohibit the use, either as trademarks or as elements of trademarks, of the distinctive signs specified in that Article of member countries and certain international intergovernmental organizations.

18.95 The purpose of Article 6*ter* is not to create an industrial property right in favor of the State or the intergovernmental organization in respect of the distinctive signs concerned, but simply to prevent the use of those signs as trademarks in industrial or commercial activities.

18.96 The provisions of Article 6*ter* do not apply if the competent authorities of the member country allow the use of its distinctive signs as trademarks. Similarly, the competent authorities of an intergovernmental organization may allow others to use its distinctive signs as trademarks. Moreover, in the case of the distinctive signs of a member country, nationals of any member country that are authorized to use the distinctive signs of their country may do so even if those signs are similar to those of another member country.

18.97 The distinctive signs of States that are referred to in Article 6*ter* are the following: armorial bearings, flags and other emblems, official signs and hallmarks indicating control and warranty and any imitation of those signs from a heraldic point of view.

18.98 The objective of the provisions of Article 6*ter*, insofar as the distinctive signs of States are concerned, is to exclude the registration and use of trademarks that are identical or present a certain similarity to the armorial bearings, flags or other emblems of *States*. The reasons for this are that such registration would violate the right of the State to control distinctive signs of its sovereignty and, further, might mislead the public with respect to the origin of the goods to which such marks would be applied.

18.99 To give effect to the provisions of Article 6*ter*, a procedure is established pursuant to that Article whereby the distinctive signs of the member countries and intergovernmental organizations concerned are communicated to the International Bureau of WIPO, which in turn transmits those communications to all the member countries.

(vii) Assignment of Trademarks

18.100 Article 6*quater* of the Convention deals with the assignment of trademarks. The rule of Article 6*quater* arises because of the situation where a trademark is used by an enterprise in various countries and it is desired to make a transfer of the right to the trademark in one or more of those countries.

18.101 Some national legislations allow an assignment without a simultaneous or corresponding transfer of the enterprise to which the trademark belongs. Others make the validity of the assignment depend on the simultaneous or corresponding transfer of the enterprise.

18.102 Article *6quater* states that it shall suffice for the recognition of the validity of the assignment of a trademark in a member country that the portion of the business or goodwill located in that country be transferred to the assignee, together with the exclusive right to manufacture in the said country, or to sell therein, the goods bearing the trademark assigned. Thus, a member country is free to require, for the validity of the assignment of the trademark, the simultaneous transfer of the enterprise to which the trademark belongs, but such a requirement must not extend to parts of the enterprise that are located in other countries.

18.103 It should be noted that Article *6quater* leaves a member country free not to regard as valid the assignment of a trademark with the relevant part of the enterprise, if the use of that trademark by the assignee would be of such a nature as to mislead the public, particularly as regards important features of the goods to which the trademark is applied. This freedom may be exercised, for example, if a trademark is assigned for part only of the goods to which it is applied, and if these goods are similar to other goods for which the trademark is not assigned. In such cases, the public may be misled as to the origin or essential qualities of similar goods to which the assignor and assignee will apply the same trademark independently.

(viii) Protection of Trademarks Registered in one Country of the Union in other Countries of the Union

18.104 Parallel to the principle of independence of marks which is embodied in the provisions of Article 6, the Convention establishes a special rule for the benefit of owners of trademarks registered in their country of origin. This exceptional rule is governed by Article *6quinquies* of the Convention.

18.105 The provisions of Article *6quinquies* come into operation in the case where a registration in the country of origin is invoked in the country where protection is sought. Whereas the principle of national treatment of applications calls for the normal rule of complete independence of trademarks (as recognized in Article 6), in the exceptional situation regulated by Article *6quinquies* the opposite rule prevails, providing for extraterritorial effects of the registration in the country of origin.

18.106 There are two main reasons for this special rule. On the one hand, it is in the interest of both owners of trademarks and the public to have the *same* trademark apply to the *same* goods in various countries. On the other hand, there are some important differences in the domestic legislation of the member countries regarding the registration of trademarks. As a consequence, the differences in domestic legislation could prevent this uniform use of the same trademark.

18.107 In order to diminish the impact of those differences on the registration of trademarks in respect of goods in international trade, Article *6quinquies* of the Paris Convention establishes certain effects where registration in the country of origin has taken place and is invoked in another member country where registration and protection is sought. This provision has the effect of bringing about certain uniformity of the law of the various countries as to the concept of trademarks.

18.108 For Article *6quinquies* to apply it is necessary that the trademark concerned should be duly registered in the country of origin. A mere filing or use of the trademark in that country is not sufficient. Moreover, the country of origin must be a country of the Union in which the applicant has a real and effective industrial or commercial establishment or, alternatively, in which he has his domicile, or otherwise, the country of the Union of which he is a national.

18.109 The rule established by Article 6*quinquies* provides that a trademark which fulfills the required conditions must be accepted for filing and protected— *as is* (to use the expression found in the English version) or *telle quelle* (to use the expression adopted in the authentic French text)—in the other member countries, subject to certain exceptions. This rule is often called the *"telle quelle"* principle.

18.110 It is to be noted that the rule only concerns the *form* of the trademark. In this respect, the rule in this Article does not affect the questions relating to the nature or the function of the trademarks as conceived in the countries where protection is sought. Thus a member country is not obliged to register and extend protection to a subject that does not fall within the meaning of a trademark as defined in the law of that country. If, for example, under the law of a member country, a three-dimensional object or musical notes indicating tunes is not considered a "trademark" in that country, it is not obliged to accept that subject matter for registration and protection.

18.111 Article 6*quinquies*, Section B, contains certain exceptions to the obligation of accepting a registered trademark "as is" for registration in the other countries of the Union. That list of exceptions is exhaustive so that no other grounds may be invoked to refuse or invalidate the registration of the trademark. However, the list does not exclude any ground for refusal of protection for which there is a need in national legislation.

18.112 The first permitted ground for refusal or invalidation of a trademark exists where the trademark infringes rights of third parties acquired in the country where protection is claimed. These rights can be either rights in trademarks already protected in the country concerned or other rights, such as the right to a trade name or a copyright.

18.113 The second permitted ground for refusal or invalidation is when the trademark is devoid of distinctive character, or is purely descriptive, or consists of a generic name.

18.114 The third permissible ground for refusal or invalidation exists where the trademark is contrary to morality or public order, as considered in the country where protection is claimed. This ground includes, as a special category, trademarks which are of such a nature as to deceive the public.

18.115 A fourth permissible ground for refusal or invalidation exists if the registration of the trademark would constitute an act of unfair competition.

18.116 A fifth and last permissible ground for refusal or invalidation exists where the trademark is used by the owner in a form which is essentially different from that in which it has been registered in the country of origin. Unessential differences may not be used as grounds for refusal or invalidation.

(ix) Service Marks

18.117 A service mark is a sign used by enterprises offering services, for example, hotels, restaurants, airlines, tourist agencies, car-rental agencies, employment agencies, laundries and cleaners, etc., in order to distinguish their services from those of other enterprises. Thus service marks have the same function as trademarks, the only difference being that they apply to services instead of products (or goods).

18.118 Article 6*sexies* was introduced into the Paris Convention in 1958 to deal specifically with service marks, but the revision Conference did not accept a more ambitious proposal to entirely assimilate service marks to trademarks. However, a member country is free to apply the same rules it applies for trademarks also to service marks in analogous situations or circumstances.

18.119 By virtue of Article 6*sexies*, member countries undertake to protect service marks, but are not required to provide for the registration of such marks. This provision does not oblige a member country to legislate expressly on the subject of service marks. A member country may comply with the provision not only by introducing special legislation for the protection of service marks , but also by granting such protection by other means, for example, in its laws against unfair competition.

(x) Registration in the Name of the Agent without the Proprietor's Authorization

18.120 Article 6*septies* of the Convention deals with the relationship between the owner of a trademark and his agent or representative regarding registration or use of the trademark by the latter.

18.121 This Article regulates those cases where the agent or representative of the person who is the owner of a trademark applies for or obtains the registration of a trademark in his own name or uses a trademark without the owner's authorization.

18.122 In such cases, Article 6*septies* confers upon the owner of the trademark the right to oppose the registration or to demand cancellation of the registration or, if the national law so allows, to demand an assignment of the registration in his favor. In addition, Article 6*septies* confers upon the owner of a trademark the right to oppose the unauthorized use of the trademark by his agent or representative, whether or not application for registration of the trademark has been made or its registration has been granted.

(xi) Nature of the Goods to which a Trademark is Applied

18.123 Article 7 of the Convention stipulates that the nature of the goods to which a trademark is to be applied shall in no case be an obstacle to the registration of the mark.

18.124 The purpose of this rule, and also the comparable rule in Article 4*quater* regarding patents for invention, is to make the protection of industrial property independent of the question whether goods in respect of which such protection would apply may or may not be sold in the country concerned.

18.125 It sometimes occurs that a trademark concerns goods which, for example, do not conform to the safety requirements of the law of a particular country. For instance, the food and drug laws of a country may prescribe requirements concerning the ingredients of a food product or the effects of a pharmaceutical product and allow its sale only after approval of the competent authorities on the basis of an examination of the food product or of clinical trials as to the effect of the use of the pharmaceutical product on human beings or animals.

18.126 In all such cases, it would be unjust to refuse registration of a trademark concerning such goods. The safety or quality regulations may change and the product may be permitted for sale later on. In those cases where no such change is contemplated but the approval of the competent authorities of the country concerned is still pending, such approval, if imposed as a condition to filing or registration in that country, may be prejudicial to an applicant who wishes to make a timely filing for protection in another member country.

(xii) Collective Marks

18.127 A collective mark may be defined as a sign which serves to distinguish the geographical origin, material, mode of manufacture, quality or other common characteristics of goods or services of different enterprises that simultaneously use the collective mark under the control of its owner. The owner may be either an association of which those enterprises are members or any other entity, including a public body.

18.128 Article 7bis of the Convention deals with collective marks. It obliges a member country to accept for filing and to protect, in accordance with the particular conditions set by that country, collective marks belonging to "associations." These will generally be associations of producers, manufacturers, distributors, sellers or other merchants, of goods that are produced or manufactured in a certain country, region or locality or that have other common characteristics. Collective marks of States or other public bodies are not covered by the provision.

18.129 In order that Article 7bis be applicable, the existence of the association to which the collective mark belongs must not be contrary to the law of the country of origin. The association does not have to prove that it conforms to the legislation of its country of origin, but registration and protection of its collective mark may be refused if the existence of that association is found to be contrary to that legislation.

18.130 Refusal of registration and protection of the collective mark is not possible on the ground that the association is not established in the country where protection is sought, or is not constituted according to the law of that country. Article 7bis adds a further stipulation that the association may not even be required to possess an industrial or commercial establishment anywhere. In other words, an association, without possessing any industrial or commercial establishment itself, may be one that simply controls the use of a collective mark by others.

(xiii) Trademarks Shown at International Exhibitions

18.131 The provision concerning marks shown at international exhibitions is contained in Article 11 of the Convention, which also applies to other titles of industrial property.

18.132 The principle stated in Article 11 is that the member countries are obliged to grant, in conformity with their domestic legislation, temporary protection to trademarks in respect of goods exhibited at official or officially recognized international exhibitions held in the territory of any member country.

18.133 The temporary protection may be provided by various means. One is to grant a special right of priority, similar to that provided for in Article 4. Another possibility for protection, which is found in certain national laws, consists in the recognition of a right of prior use in favor of the exhibitor of the goods bearing the trademark as against possible rights acquired by third parties.

18.134 In order to apply its national legislation regarding temporary protection, the competent authorities of the country may require proof, both as to the identity of the goods exhibited and as to the date of their introduction at the exhibition, in whatever form of documentary evidence they consider necessary.

(e) Provisions Concerning Industrial Designs, Trade Names, Appellations of Origin and Indications of Source, and Unfair Competition

(i) Industrial Designs

18.135 The Paris Convention deals with industrial designs in Article 5*quinquies*.

18.136 This provision merely states the obligation of all member countries to protect industrial designs. Nothing is said about the way in which this protection must be provided.

18.137 Member countries can therefore comply with this obligation through the enactment of special legislation for the protection of industrial designs. They can, however, also comply with this obligation through the grant of such protection under the law on copyright or the law against unfair competition.

18.138 The normal solution, chosen by a great number of countries for compliance with the obligations under Article 5*quinquies* is, however, to provide for a special system of protection of industrial designs by registration or by the grant of patents for industrial designs.

18.139 There is a special provision dealing with forfeiture in the case of industrial designs. It is contained in Article 5B, and states that the protection of industrial designs may not under any circumstance be subject to any measure of forfeiture as sanction in cases of failure to work or where articles corresponding to those protected are imported. "Forfeiture" in this provision includes equivalent measures, such as cancellation, invalidation or revocation. Member countries could, however, provide other sanctions for those cases, such as compulsory licenses in order to ensure working in case of non-working or insufficient working. "Working" means here the manufacture of products representing or incorporating the industrial design.

(ii) Trade Names

18.140 Trade names are dealt with by the Convention in Article 8. This Article states that trade names shall be protected in all the countries of the Union without the obligation of filing or of registration, whether or not they form part of a trademark.

18.141 The definition of a trade name for the purposes of protection, and the manner in which such protection is to be afforded, are both matters left to the national legislation of the countries concerned. Therefore, protection may result from special legislation on trade names or from more general legislation on unfair competition or the rights of personality.

18.142 In no case can protection be made conditional upon filing or registration of the trade name. However, if in a member country protection of trade names were dependent on the use of the name and to the extent that another trade name may cause confusion or prejudice with respect to the first trade name, such requirement and criterion could be applied by that member country.

(iii) Appellations of Origin and Indications of Source

18.143 Appellations of origin and indications of source are included among the various objects of protection of industrial property under the Paris Convention (Article 1(2)).

18.144 Both these objects can be referred to under the broader concept of geographical indications, although traditionally, and for the purposes of certain special treaties (e.g., the Madrid Agreement for the Repression of False or Deceptive Indications of Source on Goods, and the Lisbon Agreement for the Protection of Appellations of Origin and their International Registration), both concepts have been distinguished.

18.145 Indications of source include any name, designation, sign or other indication which refers to a given country or to a place located therein, which has the effect of conveying the notion that the goods bearing the indication originate in that country or place. Examples of indications of source are the names of countries (e.g., Germany, Japan, etc.) or of cities (e.g., Hong Kong, Paris, etc.) when used on or in connection with goods in order to indicate their place of manufacture or their provenance.

18.146 Appellations of origin have a more limited meaning, and may be considered a special type of indication of source. An appellation of origin is the geographical name of a country, region or locality which serves to designate a product originating therein, the quality and characteristics of which are due exclusively or essentially to the geographical environment, including natural and human factors.

18.147 The Paris Convention contains in Articles 10 and 10bis provisions on the protection of indications of source. These provisions cover in general any direct or indirect use of a false indication of the source (including, where applicable, the appellation of origin) of the goods or the identity of the producer, manufacturer or merchant, as well as any act of unfair competition by the use of indications or allegations which are liable to mislead the public as to the nature or the characteristics of the goods for which they are applied.

18.148 The Convention requires the countries to seize the goods bearing false indications or, to prohibit their importation, or otherwise to apply any other measures that may be available in order to prevent or stop the use of such indications. However, the obligation to seize goods on importation only applies to the extent that such a sanction is provided for under the national law.

18.149 The Convention provides that action may be taken not only by the public prosecutor but also by any interested party. In this connection, Article 10(2) states that any producer, manufacturer or merchant, whether a natural person or a legal entity, engaged in the production, manufacture or trade in such goods established in the locality, region or country falsely indicated as the source or in the country where such false indications used, is in any case deemed to be an interested party. Moreover, in accordance with Article 10*ter*, states that the countries are required to provide measures to permit federations and associations representing interested industrialists, producers and merchants to take action before the competent authorities with a view to the repression of the acts referred to above.

(iv) Unfair Competition

18.150 The Convention provides in Article 10*bis* that the countries of the Union are bound to assure to persons entitled to benefit from the Convention effective protection against unfair competition. The Convention does not specify the manner in which such protection should be granted, leaving this to the laws existing in each of the member countries.

18.151 Article 10*bis* defines acts of unfair competition as those acts of competition which are contrary to honest practices in industrial or commercial matters. Further, the Article gives some typical examples of acts of unfair competition which should be prohibited in particular.

18.152 The first example refers to all acts of such a nature as to create confusion by any means whatever with the establishment, the goods or the industrial or commercial activities of a competitor. These acts cover not only the use of identical or similar marks or names, which could be attacked as an infringement of proprietary rights, but also the use of other means which can create confusion. Such could be the form of packages, the getup or style used on products and on their corresponding outlets or points of distribution, titles of publicity, etc.

18.153 The second example relates to false allegations in the course of trade of such a nature as to discredit the establishment, the goods or the industrial or commercial activities, of a competitor. It has been left to the domestic legislation or case law of each country to decide whether, and under what circumstances, discrediting allegations which are not strictly untrue may also be considered acts of unfair competition.

18.154 The third example of acts of unfair competition concerns indications and allegations which are liable to mislead the public as to the nature, the manufacturing process, the characteristics, the suitability for their purpose or the quality of their goods. This provision may be distinguished from the previous cases to the extent that it is concerned with the interests and well-being of the public and is one of the provisions in the Convention that is more directly related to the consumer protection role of industrial property.

C. ADMINISTRATIVE AND FINANCIAL PROVISIONS

(a) Organs of the Paris Union

18.155 The countries party to the Paris Convention constitute a "Union" for the Protection of Industrial Property. In creating a Union, the Paris Convention goes beyond a mere treaty establishing rights and obligations. It also establishes a legal entity in international law with the necessary organs to carry out certain tasks. The Union forms a single administrative entity, and an administrative link among the various Acts of the Paris Convention.

18.156 Under this concept of the Union, a state which becomes a member of the Union by acceding to the most recent (the Stockholm) Act of the Paris Convention becomes bound with respect to all member countries, even those not yet party to the Stockholm Act. Article 27(3) of the Convention says that such a country must apply the Stockholm Act also to member countries of the Union not yet party to that Act, and must recognize that member countries not yet bound by the substantive provisions of the Stockholm Act may apply, in their relations with it, that earlier Act which is the most recent of the Acts to which they are party.

18.157 The Union has three administrative organs, the Assembly, the Executive Committee and the International Bureau of WIPO, headed by the Director General of the World Intellectual Property Organization (WIPO).

18.158 The Assembly is dealt with in Article 13. It consists of all member countries bound at least by the administrative provisions of the Stockholm Act. The Assembly is the chief governing body of the Union in which all policy-making and controlling powers are vested. It deals with all matters concerning the maintenance and development of the Union and the implementation of the Paris Convention. In particular, it gives directions for the preparation of conferences of revision of the Convention. It reviews and approves the reports and activities of the Director General of WIPO concerning the Union and gives him instructions concerning matters within the competence of the Union. It determines the program, adopts the biennial budget of the Union, and approves its final accounts. The Assembly meets once in every second calendar year in ordinary session, together with the General Assembly of WIPO.

18.159 The Assembly has an Executive Committee, which is dealt with in Article 14. It consists of one-fourth of the countries members of the Assembly, and is elected by the Assembly for the period between two ordinary sessions with due regard to an equitable geographical distribution. The Executive Committee meets once a year in ordinary session, together with the Coordination Committee of WIPO.

18.160 The Executive Committee is the smaller governing body of the Union. It deals with all the functions which have to be carried out during the period between the ordinary sessions of the Assembly and for which the Assembly is too big a body. It prepares the meetings of the Assembly and takes all necessary measures to ensure the execution of the program.

18.161 The provisions concerning the International Bureau are contained in Article 15. The International Bureau of WIPO is the administrative organ of the Union. It performs all administrative tasks concerning the Union. It provides the secretariat of the various organs of the Union. Its head, the Director General of WIPO, is the chief executive of the Union.

(b) Finances

18.162 The financial provisions are contained in Article 16. The Union has its own budget which is mainly financed by mandatory contributions from member countries. The contributions are calculated in applying a class and unit system to the total sum of contributions needed for a given budgetary year. The highest class I corresponds to a share of 25 units, the lowest class VII to a share of one unit. Each member country determines freely the class to which it wishes to belong, but it may also change class afterwards.

(c) Amendments and Revision

18.163 Article 18 contains the principle of periodic revision of the Paris Convention. The Convention must be submitted to revision with a view to the introduction of amendments designed to improve the system of the Union. These revisions are dealt with by diplomatic conferences of revision in which delegations appointed by the governments of the member countries participate. According to Article 18(2), such conferences must be held successively in one of the member countries.

18.164 The preparations for the conferences of revision of the Paris Convention are carried out by the International Bureau of WIPO in accordance with the directions of the Assembly and in cooperation with the Executive Committee. In performing it, the International Bureau of WIPO may also consult with other intergovernmental and with international non-governmental organizations.

(d) Special Agreements

18.165 An important provision among the administrative clauses of the Paris Convention is Article 19, dealing with special agreements.

18.166 According to that provision, the member countries have the right to make separately among themselves special agreements for the protection of industrial property. These agreements must, however, comply with the condition that they do not contravene the provisions of the Paris Convention.

18.167 Such special agreements may take the form of bilateral agreements or multilateral treaties. Special agreements in the form of multilateral treaties may be agreements prepared and administered by the International Bureau of WIPO, or agreements prepared and administered by other intergovernmental organizations.

(e) Becoming Party to the Convention

18.168 Accession to the Paris Convention is effected by the deposit of an instrument of accession with the Director General of WIPO, as provided in Article 21. The Convention enters into force, with respect to a country so adhering, three months after the accession has been notified by the Director General of WIPO to all Governments of the member countries. Accession therefore needs only unilateral action by the interested country and does not require any decision by the competent bodies of the Union.

18.169 Accession to the Convention automatically entails acceptance of all the clauses in the Convention, as well as admission to all the advantages thereof, as is indicated in Article 22.

18.170 Provisions concerning denunciation are contained in Article 26 of the Convention. Any member country may denounce the Convention by addressing a notification to the Director General of WIPO. In that case, the denunciation takes effect one year after the day on which the Director General receives the notification to that effect.

18.171 It is provided, however, that the right of denunciation may not be exercised by any country before the expiration of five years from the date on which it became a member of the Union.

(f) Disputes

18.172 The matter of disputes is dealt with in Article 28 of the Convention. Any dispute between two or more countries of the Union concerning the interpretation or application of the Convention, which has not been settled by negotiation, may be brought, by any of the countries concerned, before the International Court of Justice. However, the countries concerned may agree on any other method for settling their dispute, for example, by international arbitration. In any case, it should be noted that the International Bureau of WIPO may not take a position in controversies concerning the interpretation or application of the Paris Convention among member countries.

18.173 Any country acceding to the Convention may declare upon accession that it does not consider itself bound by the preceding provisions concerning the solving of disputes before the International Court of Justice.

18.174 The following 139 States were party to the Paris Convention for the Protection of Industrial Property as of October 1, 1996: Albania, Algeria, Argentina, Armenia, Australia, Austria, Azerbaijan, Bahamas, Bangladesh, Barbados, Belarus, Belgium, Benin, Bolivia, Bosnia and Herzegovina, Brazil, Bulgaria, Burkina Faso, Burundi, Cameroon, Canada, Central African Republic, Chad, Chile, China, Colombia, Congo, Costa Rica, Côte d'Ivoire, Croatia, Cuba, Cyprus, Czech Republic, Democratic People's Republic of Korea, Denmark, Dominican Republic, Egypt, El Salvador, Estonia, Finland, France, Gabon, Gambia, Georgia, Germany, Ghana, Greece, Guinea, Guinea-Bissau, Guyana, Haiti, Holy See, Honduras, Hungary, Iceland, Indonesia, Iran (Islamic Republic of), Iraq, Ireland, Israel, Italy, Japan, Jordan, Kazakstan, Kenya, Kyrgyzstan, Latvia, Lebanon, Lesotho, Liberia, Libya, Liechtenstein, Lithuania, Luxembourg, Madagascar, Malawi, Malaysia, Mali, Malta, Mauritania, Mauritius, Mexico, Monaco, Mongolia, Morocco, Netherlands, New Zealand, Nicaragua, Niger, Nigeria, Norway, Paraguay, Peru, Philippines, Poland, Portugal, Republic of Korea, Republic of Moldova, Romania, Russian Federation, Rwanda, Saint Kitts and Nevis, Saint Lucia, Saint Vincent and the Grenadines, San Marino, Senegal, Singapore, Slovakia, Slovenia, South Africa, Spain, Sri Lanka, Sudan, Suriname, Swaziland, Sweden, Switzerland, Syria, Tajikistan, The former Yugoslav Republic of Macedonia, Togo, Trinidad and Tobago, Tunisia, Turkey, Turkmenistan, Uganda, Ukraine, United Arab Emirates, United Kingdom, United Republic of Tanzania, United States of America, Uruguay, Uzbekistan, Venezuela, Viet Nam, Yugoslavia, Zaire, Zambia and Zimbabwe.

References for Section C
International Bureau of WIPO, *The Paris Convention for the Protection of Industrial Property*, WIPO-CEIPI/IP/SB/93/2

CHAPTER 19

The Berne Convention for the Protection of Literary and Artistic Works

A. HISTORY

19.1 Copyright protection on the international level began by about the middle of the nineteenth century on the basis of bilateral treaties. A number of such treaties providing for mutual recognition of rights were concluded but they were neither comprehensive enough nor of a uniform pattern.

19.2 The need for a uniform system led to the formulation and adoption on September 9, 1886, of the Berne Convention for the Protection of Literary and Artistic Works. The Berne Convention is the oldest international treaty in the field of copyright. It is open to all States. Instruments of accession or ratification are deposited with the Director General of the World Intellectual Property Organization (WIPO).

19.3 The original text of the Convention has undergone revision since. The Berne Convention has been revised several times in order to improve the international system of protection which the Convention provides. Changes have been effected in order to cope with the challenges of accelerating development of technologies in the field of utilization of authors' works; in order to recognize new rights as also to allow for appropriate revisions of established ones. The first major revision took place in Berlin in 1908, twenty two years after the initial formulation of the Berne Convention in 1886. This was followed by the revisions in Rome in 1928, in Brussels in 1948, in Stockholm in 1967 and in Paris in 1971.

19.4 The purpose of the Stockholm revision was to provide for rapid technological developments as well as the needs of several newly independent developing countries, and to introduce administrative and structural changes. As for the preferential provisions for developing countries worked out in Stockholm, these were further taken up at the Paris Revision Conference in 1971, where new compromises were worked out. The substantive provisions of the Stockholm Act which had also never entered into force were, however, adopted by the Paris Revision Conference in fact as they had been worked out and included in the Stockholm Act.

19.5 The aim of the Berne Convention as indicated in its preamble is "to protect, in as effective and uniform a manner as possible, the rights of authors in their literary and artistic works." Article 1 lays down that the countries to which the

Convention applies constitute a Union for the protection of the rights of authors in their literary and artistic works.

B. PRINCIPAL PROVISIONS

(a) Basic Principles

19.6 The Convention relies on three basic principles: Firstly, that of "national treatment," according to which works originating in one of the member States are to be given the same protection in each of the member States as the latter grant to works of their own nationals; secondly, that of automatic protection, according to which such national treatment is not dependent on any formality; in other words protection is granted automatically and is not subject to the formality of registration, deposit, or the like; and thirdly, that of independence of protection, according to which enjoyment and exercise of the rights granted is independent of the existence of protection in the country of origin of the work.

(b) Works Protected

19.7 Article 2 contains a non-limitative (illustrative and not exhaustive) list of such works, which include any original production in the literary, scientific and artistic domain, whatever may be the mode or form of its expression. Derivative works, that is those based on other pre-existing works, such as translations, adaptations, arrangements of music and other alterations of a literary or artistic work, receive the same protection as original works (Article 2(3)). The protection of some categories of works is optional; thus every State party to the Berne Convention may decide to what extent it wishes to protect official texts of a legislative, administrative and legal nature (Article 2(4)), works of applied art (Article 2(7)), lectures, addresses and other oral works (Article 2*bis*(2)) and works of folklore (Article 15(4)). Furthermore, Article 2(2) provides for the possibility of making the protection of works or any specified categories thereof subject to their being fixed in some material form. For instance, protection of choreographic works may be dependent on their being fixed in some form.

19.8 One of the important provisions is the one that covers works or expressions of what is called "folklore". Without mentioning the word, the Convention provides that any member country may give protection to unpublished works where the identity of the author is unknown, but where there is every ground to presume that the author is a national of that country, by designating, through the national legislation, the competent authority which should represent the author of unknown identity and protect and enforce his rights in the countries party to the Convention. By providing for the bringing of actions by authorities designated by the State, the Berne Convention offers to countries whose folklore is a part of their heritage, a possibility of protecting it.

(c) Owners of Rights

19.9 Article 2(6) lays down that protection under the Convention is to operate for the benefit of the author and his successors in title. For some categories of works, however, such as cinematographic works (Article 14*bis*), ownership of copyright is a matter for legislation in the country where protection is claimed.

(d) Persons Protected

19.10 Authors of works are protected, in respect of both their unpublished or published works if, according to Article 3, they are nationals or residents of a member country; alternatively, if, not being nationals or residents of a member country, they first publish their works in a member country or simultaneously in a non-member and a member country.

(e) Minimum Standards of Protection

19.11 Certain minimum standards of protection have been prescribed relating to the rights of authors and the duration of protection.

(f) Rights Protected

19.12 The exclusive rights granted to authors under the Convention include the right of translation (Article 8), the right of reproduction in any manner or form (which includes any sound or visual recording) (Article 9), the right to perform dramatic, dramatico-musical and musical works (Article 11), the right to broadcasting and communicating to the public by wire, by broadcasting or by loudspeaker or any other analogous instrument of the broadcast of the work (Article 11*bis*), the right of public recitation (Article 11*ter*), the right of making adaptations, arrangements or other alterations of a work (Article 12) and the right of making the cinematographic adaptation and reproduction of a work (Article 14). The so-called "droit de suite" provided for in Article 14*ter* (concerning original works of art and original manuscripts) is optional and applicable only if legislation in the country to which the author belongs so permits.

19.13 Independently of the author's economic rights, Article 6*bis* provides for the right of the author to claim authorship of his work and to object to any distortion, mutilation or other modification of, or other derogatory action in relation to, the work which would be prejudicial to his honor or reputation ("moral rights").

(g) Limitations

19.14 As a sort of counterbalance to the minimum standards of protection there are also other provisions in the Berne Convention limiting the strict application of the rules regarding exclusive right. It provides for the possibility of using protected works in particular cases without having to obtain the authorization of the owner of the copyright and without having to pay any remuneration for such use. Such exceptions which are commonly referred to as free use of protected works are included in Articles 9(2) (reproduction in certain special cases), 10 (quotations and use of works by way of illustration for teaching purposes), 10*bis* (reproduction of newspaper or similar articles and use or works for the purpose of reporting current events), 11*bis*(3) (ephemeral recordings).

19.15 There are two cases where the Berne Convention provides the possibility of compulsory licenses: in Articles 11*bis*(2) (for the right of broadcasting and communication to the public by wire by rebroadcasting or by loudspeaker or any other analogous instrument of the broadcast of the work) and 13(1) (for the right of recording musical works).

19.16 In so far as the exclusive right of translation is concerned, the Berne Convention offers a choice, in that a developing country may, when acceding to the Convention, make a reservation under the so-called "ten-year rule" (Article 30(2)(b)). This provides for the possibility of reducing the term of protection in respect of the exclusive right of translation; this right, according to the said rule, ceases to exist if the author has not availed himself of it within 10 years from the date of first publication of the original work, by publishing or causing to be published, in one of the member countries, a translation in the language for which protection is claimed.

(h)   Duration of Protection

19.17   The minimum standards of protection provided for in the Berne Convention also relate to the duration of protection. Article 7 lays down a minimum term of protection. According to this, the term shall be the life of the author and 50 years after his death.

19.18   There are, however, exceptions to this basic rule for certain categories of works. For cinematographic works, the term is 50 years after the work has been made available to the public, or, if not made available, then 50 years after the making of such a work. For photographic works and works of applied art, the minimum term of protection is 25 years from the making of the work (Article 7(4)).

19.19   A majority of countries in the world have legislated for life plus a 50-year term of protection since it is felt fair and right that the lifetime of the author and the lifetime of his children should be covered; this could also provide the incentive necessary to stimulate creativity, and constitute a fair balance between the interests of the authors and the needs of society.

19.20   The term of protection, insofar as moral rights are concerned, extends at least until the expiry of the economic rights.

C.   THE LATEST (PARIS) ACT OF THE CONVENTION

19.21   The Berne Convention was developed initially according to the standards and requirements of the industrialized countries in Europe. Later, when the system of the Berne Convention extended to other areas of the globe, it started acquiring new dimensions. Particularly in the wake of the Second World War, when the political map of the world changed considerably, the Berne Convention also had to face new problems of development. Several territories previously having colonial or similar status, and in that capacity being bound by the provisions of the Berne Convention, progressively became independent and other States were newly created. These countries had to face the question of possible accession to the international system of copyright protection as contained in the Convention. They were free to join or not to join it or, where they were already members, to withdraw from the Convention.

19.22 While it was almost universally recognized that authors and other creators should be afforded the necessary protection for their intellectual creations, there was also a consciousness that the newly independent developing countries had genuine problems in gaining greater and easier access to works protected by copyright, particularly for their technological and educational needs, from the developed countries, both in respect of formal as well as non-formal educational programs. Solutions had to be found for meeting the immense and urgent needs of educational material in developing countries. The necessity for setting up of an international arrangement for permitting developing countries a greater degree of access to protected works while respecting the rights of authors, seemed to gather momentum. Meanwhile, the advance of technology made the extension of the geographical scope of the international conventions and multilateral agreements to an increasingly larger number of countries, more attractive.

19.23 In view of these new facts and circumstances, it was felt by many that the systems of international protection of copyright required adaptation or modification to suit the new concepts and the new needs. Deliberations at the more recent revision conferences were, therefore, directed to adapting the systems of international protection of literary and artistic works to the needs of these newly independent countries.

19.24 The question of incorporating into the Convention special provisions for the newly independent developing countries was initially mooted at an African Copyright Meeting in Brazzaville in 1963. This matter was pursued at the Conference called in Stockholm in 1967 for revision of the Berne Convention where a "protocol regarding developing countries" known as the Stockholm Protocol was added to the Convention.

19.25 However, it soon became clear that the solution (the Stockholm Protocol) proposed was unlikely to gain much acceptance among Union countries, particularly those whose works were likely to be made use of under the provisions of the Protocol. If the needs of the developing countries were to be met without too much delay, it seemed necessary to take a second look at conditions under which translation and reproduction of the works of other countries might be made for purposes of education and scientific research.

19.26 The Revision Conference convened in Paris in 1971 was predominantly concerned with finding solutions in order to support the universal effect of the Convention and to establish an appropriate basis for its operation, particularly in relation to the increasing number of newly independent States which had to face serious problems in the nascent stage of their economic, social and cultural development as independent nations. After the Second World War, with the break-up of colonial structures, the lurking question was whether it was fair and workable to ask these newly developing countries to take on obligations under the Convention that were agreed upon by developed countries, without taking into consideration the special situations in the developing ones. There was certainly a challenge then posed to international copyright itself and this was, in a manner, sorted out through the give and take that culminated in the special provisions concerning developing countries that were incorporated in an Appendix which now forms an integral part of the Convention.

19.27 The Appendix to the Paris (1971) Act of the Berne Convention provides for special faculties open to developing countries concerning translation and reproduction of works of foreign origin. The Appendix augments the Convention's existing exceptions to the author's exclusive rights including those of reproduction and translation (Articles 2*bis*, 9(2), 10(2), 10*bis*) and the ten-year rule (Article 30(2)(b)).

19.28 According to this Appendix, countries which are regarded as developing countries in conformity with the established practice of the General Assembly of the United Nations may, under certain conditions, depart from the minimum standards of protection provided for in the Convention. This exceptional regime concerns two rights: the right of translation and the right of reproduction.

19.29. The Berne Convention provides, in respect of developing countries, for the possibility of granting non-exclusive and non-transferable compulsory licenses in respect of (i) translation for the purpose of teaching, scholarship or research, and (ii) reproduction for use in connection with systematic instructional activities, of works protected under the Convention; the term systematic instructional activities including systematic out-of-school or non-formal education. These licenses could be granted under certain conditions to any national of a developing country which has duly availed itself of one or both of the faculties provided for in the Appendix for grant of such compulsory licenses in respect of translation and/or reproduction of works of foreign origin.

19.30 These licenses may be granted, after the expiry of certain time limits and after compliance with certain procedural steps, by the competent authority of the developing country concerned. They have to be applied for from the authority designated in the developing country as being competent to grant such licenses. They must provide for just compensation in favor of the owner of the right. In other words, the payment to be made by the compulsory licensee must be consistent with standards of royalties normally operating in respect of licenses freely negotiated between persons in the two countries concerned.

19.31 Provision has also to be made in the legislation to ensure a correct translation or an accurate reproduction of the work, as the case may be, and to indicate the name of the author on all copies of such translations or reproductions. Copies of translations or reproductions made and publication under such licenses are not, however, allowed to be exported. In other words, such copies may be distributed only in the country in which the compulsory license was granted.

19.32 Since the license is non-exclusive, the copyright owner is entitled to bring out and place on the market his own equivalent copies upon which the power of the licensee to continue making copies under the license would cease. However, in that event, the compulsory licensee's stock can be disposed of.

19.33 Compulsory license for translations can be granted for languages generally spoken in the developing country concerned. There is a distinction between languages in general use also in one or more developed countries (particularly English, French and Spanish) and those not in general use there (largely local languages of developing countries). In the case of a language in general use in one or more developed countries, a period of three years, starting on the date of the first publication of the work, has to elapse before a license can be applied for, whereas for a language not in general use in a developed country, the period is one year.

19.34 In respect of reproduction, the period after which compulsory licenses may be obtained may vary according to the nature of the work to be reproduced. Generally, it is five years from the first publication. However, for works connected with the natural and physical sciences and with technology (and this includes mathematical works), the period is three years; and for works of fiction, poetry and drama, the period is seven years.

19.35 The possibility that the Appendix provides of granting a compulsory license, if authorization is desired, may favorably influence negotiation and may lead to increased scope for voluntary licensing.

D. ADMINISTRATION

(a) Administrative Provisions

19.36 The provisions of the Berne Convention fall into two categories viz. those of substance covering the material law and the administrative and final clauses covering matters of administration and structure. In the latest text of the Convention as revised at Paris in 1971, Articles 1 to 21 and the Appendix contain the substantive provisions and Articles 22 to 38 the administrative and final clauses.

19.37 The Berne Convention is administered by the World Intellectual Property Organization (WIPO). The administrative tasks performed by WIPO include assembling and publishing information concerning the protection of copyright. Each member country communicates to WIPO all new copyright laws. WIPO publishes a monthly periodical entitled "Industrial Property Copyright"; it conducts studies and provides services designed to facilitate protection of copyright; as the Secretariat, it participates in all meetings of the Assembly, the Executive Committee or any other Committee of Experts or Working Groups; in accordance with the directions of the Assembly and in cooperation with the Executive Committee, it shall also, when required, make preparations for the conferences to revise the Convention.

19.38 The administrative provisions provide for an Assembly in which the Government of each member State shall be represented by one delegate. The Assembly determines the program, adopts the budget and controls the finances of the Union. It also elects members of the Executive Committee of the Assembly. One fourth of the number of member countries are to be elected to the Executive Committee. The Executive Committee meets once every year in ordinary session and generally once in two years in extraordinary session.

19.39 The contributions payable by member States are based on a system of classes. There are seven classes (I to VII). Each State is free to choose the class in which it wishes to be placed. The rights of each State are the same, irrespective of the contribution class chosen. However, the amount of the contribution varies according to the class.

(b) Becoming Party to the Convention

19.40 In order to become a party to the Berne Convention, an instrument of accession has to be deposited with the Director General of WIPO (Article 29(1)). Accession to the Berne Convention and membership of the Berne Union becomes effective three months after the date on which the Director General of WIPO has notified the deposit of the above-mentioned instrument of accession (Article 29(2)(a)). In accordance with Article I of the Appendix, a developing country has to specifically declare, at the time of its ratification of or accession to the Paris Act, that it will avail itself of the provisions in the Appendix concerning the compulsory licenses for translation and/or reproduction.

19.41 In becoming party to the Berne Convention, the State concerned becomes a member of the Berne Union. It would therefore be entitled:

(1) to full membership (right to vote) in the Berne Union Assembly (Article 22(3)(a));

(2) to the right to vote in elections of or to be elected to the Executive Committee of the Berne Union (Article 23(2)(a));

(3) to automatic membership in the WIPO Coordination Committee during the period of its membership in the Executive Committee of the Berne Union (Convention establishing WIPO, Article 8(1)(a)).

19.42 To become a member of the Berne Union is in the interest of every country that wants to establish healthy conditions for the development of its culture and economy, and it is particularly in the interest of every developing country.

E. DEVELOPING COUNTRIES AND THE BERNE CONVENTION

19.43 The predominant concern at the last revision of the Berne Convention was to find solutions in order to support the universal effect of the Convention and to establish an appropriate basis for its operation, particularly in relation to the increasing number of newly independent States which had to face serious problems in the nascent stage of their economic, social and cultural development as independent nations. The lurking question was whether it was fair and workable to ask these newly developing countries to take on obligations under the Convention that were agreed upon by developed countries without taking into consideration the special situations in the developing ones. The latest (1971) Paris Act of the Berne Convention thus recognizes a special right in favor of developing countries. It provides that in case of unpublished works, where the identity of the author is unknown, but where there is every ground to presume that he is a national of a country of the Union, the rights in such a work are to be acknowledged in all countries of the Union. By this provision the Berne Convention has rendered it possible for the developing countries to get their folklore values protected also abroad. It was made a matter for legislation in the country of origin of such works to designate the competent authority which should represent the unknown author, and protect and enforce his rights in the countries of the Union. By providing for the bringing of actions by authorities designated by the State, the Berne Convention offers to developing countries whose folklore is a part of their heritage, a possibility of exploiting it.

19.44 In the Appendix which forms an integral part of the Paris Act, special provisions were included concerning developing countries. The Appendix provides for the possibility of granting non-exclusive and non-transferable compulsory licenses in respect of (i) translation for the purpose of teaching, scholarship or research, and (ii) reproduction for use in connection with systematic instructional activities, of works protected under the Convention. These licenses may be granted, after the expiry of certain time limits and after compliance with certain procedural steps, by the competent authority of the developing country concerned. They must provide for just compensation in favor of the owner of the right. In other words the payment to be made by the compulsory licensee must be consistent with standards of royalties normally in vogue in respect of licenses freely negotiated between persons in the two countries concerned. Provision has also to be made to ensure a correct translation or an accurate reproduction of the work, as the case may be, and to indicate the name of the author on all copies of such translations or reproductions. Copies of translations and reproductions made and publication under licenses are not, however, allowed to be exported. Since the license is non-exclusive, the copyright owner is entitled to bring out and place on the market his own equivalent copies upon which the power of the licensee to continue making copies under the license would cease. However, in that event, the compulsory licensee's stock-in-trade can be disposed of.

19.45 Compulsory licenses for translations can be granted for languages generally spoken in the developing country concerned. There is a distinction between languages in general use also in one or more developed countries (English, French and Spanish, for example) and those not in general use there (largely local languages of developing countries). In the case of a language in general use in one or more developed countries, a period of three years, starting on the date of the first publication of the work has to elapse before a license can be applied for, whereas for other languages the period has been reduced to one year. To this has to be added a period of six to nine months, as the case may be, for obtaining licenses according to the formalities provided for in the Convention. It would also be germane here to point out that the system of translation licenses includes licenses for broadcasting, and this is important when we take into account the part played in today's context by the radio and television for educational purposes. These licenses, however, are not for authorizing the broadcasting of a translated work; they relate only to translations made for broadcasting purposes.

19.46 In respect of reproduction, the period after which licenses could be obtained varies according to the nature of the work to be reproduced. Generally it is five years from the first publication. For works connected with the natural and physical sciences and with technology (and this includes mathematical works) the period is three years; while for works of fiction poetry and drama, the period is seven years.

19.47 In so far as compulsory licenses for translation are concerned, instead of availing itself of the facility offered by the system mentioned earlier, the Berne Convention offers a choice in that a developing country may, when ratifying or acceding to the Paris Act, make a reservation under the so-called "ten-year rule" (Article 30(ii) (b)), which provides for the possibility of reducing the term of protection as far as the exclusive right of translation is concerned; this right, according to the said rule, ceases to exist if the author has not availed himself of it within ten years from the date of first publication of the original work, by publishing or causing to be published, in one of the countries of the Berne Union, a translation in the language for which protection is claimed. The Appendix to the Paris Act of the Berne Convention thus allows a choice between a compulsory license system and the possibility of limiting the right of translation to ten years as provided for in this Convention. Any developing country may choose between those possibilities but cannot combine them. In other words this "ten-year" system, provides that for ten years from the publication of the work, the author's consent has to be sought before the right to translate is obtained; after this period the right of translation is in the public domain.

19.48 To become a party to the Berne Convention an instrument of accession has to be deposited with the Director General of WIPO (Article 29(1)). Accession to the Berne Convention and membership of the Berne Union becomes effective three months after the date on which the Director General of WIPO has notified the deposit of the above-mentioned instrument of accession (Article 29(2)(a)). In accordance with Article I of the Appendix, a developing country has to declare specifically, at the time of its ratification of or accession to the Paris Act, that it will avail itself of the provisions in the Appendix concerning the compulsory licenses for translation and/or reproduction.

19.49 The following 119 States were party to the Berne Convention for the Protection of Literary and Artistic Works as of October 1, 1996: Albania, Argentina, Australia, Austria, Bahamas, Barbados, Belgium, Benin, Bolivia, Bosnia and Herzegovina, Brazil, Bulgaria, Burkina Faso, Cameroon, Canada, Central African Republic, Chad, Chile, China, Colombia, Congo, Costa Rica, Côte d'Ivoire, Croatia, Cyprus, Czech Republic, Denmark, Ecuador, Egypt, El Salvador, Estonia, Fiji, Finland, France, Gabon, Gambia, Georgia, Germany, Ghana, Greece, Guinea, Guinea-Bissau, Guyana, Haiti, Holy See, Honduras, Hungary, Iceland, India, Ireland, Israel, Italy, Jamaica, Japan, Kenya, Latvia, Lebanon, Lesotho, Liberia, Libya, Liechtenstein, Lithuania, Luxembourg, Madagascar, Malawi, Malaysia, Mali, Malta, Mauritania, Mauritius, Mexico, Monaco, Morocco, Namibia, Netherlands, New Zealand, Niger, Nigeria, Norway, Pakistan, Panama, Paraguay, Peru, Philippines, Poland, Portugal, Republic of Korea, Republic of Moldova, Romania, Russian Federation, Rwanda, Saint Kitts and Nevis, Saint Lucia, Saint Vincent and the Grenadines, Senegal, Slovakia, Slovenia, South Africa, Spain, Sri Lanka, Suriname, Sweden, Switzerland, Thailand,   The former Yugoslav Republic of Macedonia,   Togo, Trinidad and Tobago, Tunisia, Turkey, Ukraine, United Kingdom, United Republic of Tanzania, United States of America, Uruguay, Venezuela, Yugoslavia, Zaire, Zambia and Zimbabwe.

References for Section E
International Bureau of WIPO, *Berne Convention for the Protection of Literary and Artistic Works: Basic Rules and Special Rules for Developing Countries*, WIPO/GIC/CNR/GE/86/4
International Bureau of WIPO, *The Berne Convention*, WIPO/IP/SUV/93/4(a)

CHAPTER 20

The Patent Cooperation Treaty

A. INTRODUCTION

(a) The Traditional Patent System

20.1 The traditional patent system requires the filing of individual patent applications for each country for which patent protection is sought, with the exception of the regional patent systems such as the African Intellectual Property Organization (OAPI) system, the Harare Protocol system established in the framework of the African Regional Industrial Property Organization (ARIPO) and the European patent system. Under the traditional Paris Convention route, the priority of an earlier application can be claimed for applications filed subsequently in foreign countries but such later applications must be filed within 12 months of the filing date of the earlier application. This involves for the applicant the preparation and filing of patent applications for all countries in which he is seeking protection for his invention within one year of the filing of the first application. This means expenses for translation, patent attorneys in the various countries and payment of fees to the patent Offices, all at a time at which the applicant often does not know whether he is likely to obtain a patent or whether his invention is really new compared with the state of the art.

20.2 Filing of patent applications under the traditional system means that every single patent Office with which an application is filed has to carry out a formal examination of every application filed with it. Where patent Offices examine patent applications as to substance, each Office has to make a search to determine the state of the art in the technical field of the invention and has to carry out an examination as to patentability.

20.3 The principal difference between the traditional national patent system and the regional patent systems such as those mentioned above is that a regional patent is granted by one patent Office for several States. Otherwise, the procedure is the same, and the explanations given in the preceding two paragraphs are equally valid.

(b) History of the PCT

20.4 In order to overcome some of the problems involved in the traditional system, the Executive Committee of the International (Paris) Union for the Protection of Industrial Property invited, in September 1966, BIRPI (the predecessor of WIPO) to undertake urgently a study of solutions to reduce the duplication of the effort both for applicants and national patent Offices. In 1967, a draft of an international treaty was prepared by BIRPI and presented to a Committee of Experts. In the following years, a number of meetings prepared revised drafts and a Diplomatic Conference held in Washington in June 1970 adopted a treaty called the Patent Cooperation Treaty. The Patent Cooperation Treaty or "PCT" entered into force on January 24, 1978, and became operational on June 1, 1978, with an initial eighteen Contracting States. As of October 1, 1996, 87 Contracting States had adhered to the PCT, a significant increase indicative of interest in the implementation of the Treaty.

20.5 The filing of international applications under the PCT commenced on June 1, 1978. Up to the end of 1995, a total of 246,622 international applications had been received by the International Bureau of WIPO. More than 38,906 international applications were received in 1995, replacing over 1,809,000 national filings.

20.6 These brief indications of the progress of the PCT merely demonstrate the certainty that many more countries, developing as well as developed, will become party to the PCT in the years ahead and that its use, evidenced by the number of applications filed, will continue to increase significantly.

(c) Objectives of the PCT

20.7 As its name suggests, the Patent Cooperation Treaty is an agreement for international cooperation in the field of patents. It is often spoken of as being the most significant advance in international cooperation in this field since the adoption of the Paris Convention itself. It is, however, largely a treaty for rationalization and cooperation with regard to the filing, searching and examination of patent applications and the dissemination of the technical information contained therein. The PCT does not provide for the grant of "international patents": the task of and responsibility for granting patents remains exclusively in the hands of the patent Offices of, or acting for, the countries where protection is sought (the "designated Offices"). The PCT does not compete with but, in fact, complements the Paris Convention. Indeed, it is a special agreement under the Paris Convention open only to States which are also party to the Paris Convention.

20.8 The principal objective of the PCT is to simplify and to render more effective and more economical—in the interests of the users of the patent system and the Offices which have responsibility for administering it—the previously established means of applying in several countries for patent protection for inventions.

20.9 Before the introduction of the PCT system, virtually the only means by which protection of an invention could be obtained in several countries was to file a separate application in each country; these applications, each being dealt with in isolation, involved a repetition of the work of filing and examination in each country. To achieve its objective, the PCT:

(1)   establishes an international system which enables the filing, with a single patent Office (the "receiving Office"), of a single application (the "international application") in one language having effect in each of the countries party to the PCT which the applicant names ("designates") in his application;

(2) provides for the formal examination of the international application by a single patent Office, the receiving Office;

(3) subjects each international application to an international search which results in a report citing the relevant prior art (mainly published patent documents relating to previous inventions) which may have to be taken into account in deciding whether the invention is patentable; that report is made available first to the applicant and is later published;

(4) provides for centralized international publication of international applications with the related international search reports, as well as their communication to the designated Offices; and

(5) provides an option for an international preliminary examination of the international application which gives to the Offices that have to decide whether or not to grant a patent, and to the applicant, a report containing an opinion as to whether the claimed invention meets certain international criteria for patentability.

20.10 The procedure described in the preceding paragraph is commonly called the "international phase" of the PCT procedure, whereas one speaks of the "national phase" to describe the last part of the patent granting procedure which, as explained in paragraph 7, above, is the task of the designated Offices, i.e., the national Offices of, or acting for, the countries which have been designated in the international application. In PCT terminology, a reference to "national" Office, "national" phase or "national" fees includes the reference to the procedure before a regional patent Office.

20.11 Even in the most developed countries, patent Offices have been struggling for years with heavy workloads (leading to delays) and with questions of how best to allocate resources so as to ensure that the patent system yields the greatest return from the available manpower. Under the PCT system, by the time the international application reaches the national Office, it has already been examined as to form by the receiving Office, been searched by the International Searching Authority and possibly examined by an International Preliminary Examining Authority, thus providing the national patent Offices with the important benefit of reducing their workloads since they have the benefit of these international phase centralized procedures and thus need not duplicate those efforts.

20.12 Further main objectives of the PCT are to ensure that only strong patents are granted by the patent Offices of the PCT Contracting States, to facilitate and accelerate access by industries and other interested sectors to technical information related to inventions and to assist developing countries in gaining access to technology.

B. THE FUNCTIONING OF THE PCT SYSTEM

(a) Filing an International Application

20.13 Any national or resident of a PCT Contracting State can file an international application. International applications can be filed in most cases with the national Office, which will act as a PCT receiving Office (or in Western Europe also with the European Patent Office). Nationals and residents of the OAPI countries and of some other developing countries can file international applications with the International Bureau of WIPO, which acts as receiving Office for them. In addition, the International Bureau acts as a receiving Office at the option of nationals and residents of all PCT Contracting States.

20.14 An international application has the effect, as of the international filing date, of a national application in those PCT Contracting States which the applicant designates in his application. It has the effect of an ARIPO patent application if the applicant desires an ARIPO patent with effect in a designated State which is party to the Harare Protocol, or of a European patent application if the applicant wants a European patent with effect in a designated State which is party to the European Patent Convention. If any designated State is a member of OAPI, the international application has the effect of an application for an OAPI patent.

20.15 States party to the regional patent systems established by the Harare Protocol and by the European Patent Convention have the possibility of "closing the national route" for obtaining patent protection, whereby an international application designating such a State will automatically be treated as an application for a regional (ARIPO or European) patent and will thus be handled by the respective regional Patent Office.

20.16 The PCT prescribes certain standards for international applications. An international application which is prepared in accordance with these standards will be acceptable, so far as the form and contents of the application are concerned, to all the PCT Contracting States, and no subsequent modifications because of varying national or regional requirements (and the cost associated therewith) will become necessary. No national law may require compliance with requirements relating to the form or contents of the international application different from or additional to those which are provided for by the PCT.

20.17 Only a single set of fees is incurred for the preparation and filing of the international application and they are payable in one currency and at one Office (the receiving Office). Payment of national fees to the designated Offices is delayed. The national fees become payable much later than for a filing by the traditional Paris Convention route.

20.18 The fees payable to the receiving Office for an international application consist of three main elements:

(1)   the transmittal fee—to cover the work of the receiving Office;
(2)   the search fee—to cover the work of the International Searching Authority; and
(3)   the international fee—to cover the work of the International Bureau.

20.19 The language in which an international application can be filed depends upon the requirements of the receiving Office with which the application is filed. It is usually the national language. The main languages in which international applications may be filed are Chinese, English, French, German, Japanese, Russian and Spanish; other languages also accepted, so far, are: Danish, Dutch, Finnish, Norwegian and Swedish.

(b) International Search

20.20 The receiving Office, after having made a formal check and accorded an international filing date, sends a copy of the international application to the International Bureau of WIPO (the "record copy") and another copy (the "search copy") to the International Searching Authority. It keeps a third copy (the "home copy"). The receiving Office also collects all the PCT fees and transfers the search fee to the International Searching Authority and the international fee to the International Bureau.

20.21 Every international application is subjected to an international search, that is, a high quality search of the patent documents and patent related literature in those languages in which most patent applications are filed (Chinese, English, French, German, Japanese, Russian and Spanish). The high quality of the international search is assured by the standards prescribed in the PCT for the documentation, staff qualifications and search methods of the International Searching Authorities, which are experienced patent Offices that have been specially appointed to carry out international searches by the Assembly of the PCT Union (the highest administrative body created under the PCT) on the basis of an agreement to observe PCT standards and time limits.

20.22 The following Offices have been appointed to act as International Searching Authorities: the Australian Patent Office, the Austrian Patent Office, the Chinese Patent Office, the European Patent Office, the Japanese Patent Office, the Russian Patent Office, the Spanish Patent and Trademark Office, the Swedish Patent Office and the United States Patent and Trademark Office.

20.23 Each International Searching Authority is required to have at least the prescribed PCT minimum documentation, properly arranged for search purposes, which can be described in general as comprising the patent documents, as from 1920, of the major industrialized countries, together with agreed items of non-patent literature. The International Searching Authority, in making the search, must make use of its full facilities, i.e., the minimum documentation and any additional documentation it may possess. The obligation to consult at least the PCT minimum documentation guarantees a high level of international searching.

20.24 The results of the international search are given in an international search report, which is made available to the applicant by the fourth or fifth month after the application is filed. The citations of relevant prior art in the international search report enable the applicant to calculate his chances of obtaining a patent in or for the countries designated in the international application.

20.25 A search report assists the applicant in the subsequent prosecution of the application before the designated Offices. The high quality of the international search assures the applicant that any patent granted is a "strong" patent, one which is unlikely to be successfully challenged, and thus provides a sound basis for investment or licensing actions.

20.26 The international search report assists designated Offices, in particular Offices which do not have technically qualified staff and an extensive collection of patent documents arranged in a manner suitable for search purposes, in examining applications and otherwise evaluating the inventions described.

20.27 The international search report enables the applicant to decide whether it is worthwhile, in the light of the state of the art evidenced by the documents cited in the search report, to continue to seek protection for his invention in the designated States or whether to continue only after the claims in his international application have been amended to better distinguish the invention from the state of the art.

20.28 For applications not filed under the PCT system, the PCT also provides a feature to strengthen national patent systems and to assist national Offices in the processing and granting of national patents. The national patent law can include provisions for an "international-type search" (provided for in Article 15(5) of the PCT) of purely national applications. This search is the same as an international search and is carried out by the International Searching Authority which the national Office specifies for carrying out international searches. Adoption of an international-type search mechanism has a two-fold benefit for the country. Firstly, it means that all patents would have been subjected to the same kind of search whether or not the corresponding applications took the PCT route. Secondly, national enterprises and inventors could have the benefits of an international-type search report even without filing an application under the PCT.

20.29 The International Searching Authority sends the international search report to the applicant and to the International Bureau. The International Bureau includes the search report in the international publication of the international application and sends a copy to the designated Offices.

(c) International Publication

20.30 International publication serves two main purposes: to disclose to the public the invention (i.e., in general, the technological advance made by the inventor) and to set out the scope of the protection which may ultimately be obtained.

20.31 The International Bureau publishes a (PCT) pamphlet which contains a front page setting out bibliographic data furnished by the applicant, together with data such as the International Patent Classification (IPC) symbol assigned by the International Searching Authority and the abstract and also contains the description, the claims, any drawings and the international search report. If the claims of the international application have been amended, the claims are published both as filed and as amended. International publication occurs, in general, 18 months after the priority date of the international application.

20.32 The pamphlet is published in the language of the international application as filed, if that language is Chinese, English, French, German, Japanese, Russian or Spanish. (If, however, the international application is published in Chinese, French, German, Japanese, Russian or Spanish, the title of the invention, the abstract and the international search report are also published in English.) If the international application has been filed in any other language, it is translated and published in English.

20.33 The publication of each pamphlet is announced in the PCT Gazette, which lists the published international applications in the form of entries reproducing the front pages of the pamphlets. Each issue of the PCT Gazette also contains a Classification Index, allowing the selection of the published international applications by technical fields.

20.34 These publications, the pamphlet and the PCT Gazette, are distributed free of charge by the International Bureau on a systematic basis to all PCT Contracting States. They are now also available in CD-ROM format in searchable form. To the public, they are supplied on request, against payment of a fee.

(d) International Preliminary Examination

20.35 Once the applicant has received the international search report, he has the possibility of requesting an international preliminary examination in order to obtain an opinion as to whether the claimed invention meets any or all of the following criteria: whether it appears to be novel, whether it appears to involve an inventive step and whether it appears to be industrially applicable. The international preliminary examination, which is provided for in Chapter II of the PCT, is of an optional nature for the PCT Contracting States. Only two of the PCT Contracting States exclude Chapter II, however, and both are considering a withdrawal of the reservation excluding that chapter in the near future. Chapter II is also optional for the applicant. The international application does not proceed automatically to an international preliminary examination but only upon a specific demand by the applicant for international preliminary examination in which he states his wish to use the results of such examination in specific States designated in the international application—in the procedure under Chapter II, these are called the "elected States" to distinguish them from other designated States. A fee for international preliminary examination is due when a demand is filed with the International Preliminary Examining Authority, together with a handling fee (to cover the work of the International Bureau).

20.36 As in the case of the International Searching Authorities, the International Preliminary Examining Authorities are appointed by the Assembly of the PCT Union. The Offices which have been appointed are the same as those appointed as International Searching Authorities, with the exception of the Spanish Patent and Trademark Office.

20.37 The results of the international preliminary examination are given in a report which is made available to the applicant and the "elected Offices" (which are the Offices of, or acting for, the elected States) through the International Bureau, which is also responsible for translating the report into English, if required by any elected Office. The opinion on the patentability of the invention, on the basis of the international criteria mentioned above, provides the applicant with an even stronger basis for calculating his chances of obtaining patents, and the elected Offices have an even better basis for their decision whether to grant a patent. In countries where patents are granted without examination as to substance, the international preliminary examination report will provide a solid basis for parties interested in the invention (e.g., for licensing purposes) to evaluate the validity of such patents.

20.38 Usually upon publication of the international application (but at the latest by the end of the 19th month after the priority date), the International Bureau communicates the international application to the designated Offices. The copy communicated will be used for the subsequent prosecution of the international application before those Offices since, as explained above, the PCT is only a system for filing and not for granting patents, the latter remaining the exclusive task and responsibility of the designated Offices. The designated Offices, and those Offices only, will each decide whether or not to grant a patent. The international search report and, if any, the international preliminary examination report, are only intended to facilitate that task.

20.39 The processing of an international application before the designated (or elected) Offices—the national phase—may not start prior to the expiration of 20 months (or 30 months if Chapter II is applicable) from the priority date of the international application, unless the applicant requests an earlier start.

(e) Prosecution before the Designated (or Elected) Offices (the "National Phase")

20.40 After having received an international search report and, where appropriate, an international preliminary examination report, and after having had the possibility of amending his application, the applicant is now in a good position to decide whether he has a chance of obtaining patents in the designated States. If he sees no likelihood, he can either withdraw his application or do nothing; in the latter case, the international application will lose the effect of a national application and the procedure will automatically come to an end. The applicant has in such a case saved himself great expense, namely, the costs involved in filing separate national applications under the traditional Paris Convention route. He has not paid for applications and translations for the national Offices, he has not paid fees to those Offices, and he has not appointed local agents, all of which are required under the traditional Paris Convention route within 12 months from the priority date and must be done without having the basis for evaluating the likelihood of obtaining a patent, which is afforded under the PCT by the international search report and, optionally, the international preliminary examination report.

20.41 Where the applicant decides to continue the procedure, and only in that event, he must pay the prescribed national fees to the designated (or elected) Offices and, if required, furnish to these Offices translations of his international application into their official language; a local agent may also have to be appointed. The furnishing of the translation and the payment of the national fees must be effected within 20 months (or 30 months, if Chapter II is applicable) from the priority date. Once national processing starts, the normal national procedures apply, subject to specific exceptions arising out of the PCT procedure (for example, matters of form and contents of the international application, and the provision of copies of the priority document).

20.42 WIPO has published a "PCT Applicant's Guide." Volume I of this Guide contains general information for users of the PCT (relating to the international phase); Volume II contains information on the procedure before the designated and elected Offices (national phase). Further information is regularly published in the PCT Gazette, Section IV, Notices and Information of a General Character.

C. ADVANTAGES OF THE PCT SYSTEM

(a) Advantages for Patent Offices

20.43 More and more patent Offices are having to consider how to employ their available manpower to greatest advantage. This is true not only because of the number of patent applications which they must handle (in a country in the process of development, the number must surely rise considerably in the future as a consequence of an increase in the country's industrial activity) but also because of the expanding role that patent Offices are being required to fulfill in providing technical advisory services to local industry (because of available patent documentation and technically trained staff), either in terms of advising on available technologies or in connection with national research and development activities. The PCT assists patent Offices in meeting these demands in various ways outlined in the following paragraphs.

20.44 Patent Offices can reduce their workload in connection with the handling of patent applications since the work of verification as to compliance with formal requirements becomes practically negligible.

20.45 Patent Offices can save part of the cost of publishing. If the international application has been published in an official language of the country, they can forego publication altogether. Countries having a different official language may limit themselves to publishing only a translation of the abstract which accompanies international applications. Copies of the full text of the international application could be supplied upon request to interested parties.

20.46 The PCT does not affect the revenue of designated Offices unless they decide voluntarily to give a rebate on national fees in view of the savings they make through the PCT and in order to make the use of the international application route more attractive to the applicant. In any case, the most profitable source of revenue for most Offices is from annual or renewal fees, which are not affected by the Treaty.

20.47 Examining patent Offices are able to cut costs since the system renders superfluous all or most of the work of searching for most applications filed by foreigners and also—when an international preliminary examination report is required—most of the work of examination.

20.48 Non-examining Offices receive an application which has already been examined as to form, which is accompanied by an international search report and possibly by an international preliminary examination report. This will put the Office, and the national industry affected by a patent and/or interested in licensing, in a much better position compared to the traditional system of filing national or regional applications. National authorities involved in approving licensing agreements likewise benefit from the greater value of a patent granted on the basis of an international application.

20.49 Patent Offices of States party to the Harare Protocol or to the European Patent Convention which opt to close the national route, as outlined above, are not involved in the processing of international applications designating such States. Choosing this option is therefore particularly advisable if the national Patent Office is less well equipped than the regional Office and is not prepared to receive and process increasing numbers of applications.

(b) Advantages for the Applicant

20.50 Applicants may file their application in their own country (or, where applicable, with the competent regional Office, or with the International Bureau as receiving Office) with effect in foreign countries and have more time to make up their minds as to those foreign countries in which they wish to seek protection, and in a typical case they have spent much less money in the stage prior to granting than otherwise.

20.51 If the applicant does not use the international procedure offered by the PCT, he must start preparations for filing abroad three to nine months before the expiration of the priority period. He must prepare translations of his application and must have them put into a different form for each country. Under the PCT, the applicant, within the priority year, makes only one application (the international application), which may be identical both as to language and form with his own national application.

20.52 The cost of further translation has to be met eventually, but not until eight (or 18) months later than under a procedure which does not use the PCT and only if the applicant, having evaluated the international search report and, where available, the international preliminary examination report also, is still interested in the countries concerned. These reports help the applicant to make up his mind whether it is worthwhile continuing his efforts. If he decides that it is not, he saves all subsequent costs.

(c) Advantages for the National Economy and for Industry

20.53 In most countries (even developed countries), the majority of patent applications are filed by foreigners. This is a consequence of the need of the owner of new technology to obtain patent protection separately in or for each of several countries in which he is economically interested. Foreign filings are a basis for the inflow of technology. By facilitating the filing of patent applications, the PCT contributes to a country's acquisition of new technology.

20.54 By being able to offer the PCT route to foreign entrepreneurs owning patentable technology, a country will find them more willing to transfer (sell or license) their technology and will, in general, attract more foreign investment. The industrialization of the country is thus further promoted.

20.55 Of course, care needs to be taken to ensure that the freedom of the market is not hampered by unjustified (weak) patents. The PCT system helps to prevent this. Although it facilitates the filing of patent applications, the PCT also contains mechanisms which assist the national and regional patent systems in avoiding the grant of patents where it is not justified. Applications filed under the PCT first pass through the central processing mechanism of the international phase of the PCT procedure. They are centrally examined as to form, centrally searched as to novelty, centrally published and, where applicable, centrally examined as to patentability. When the PCT application reaches the national phase of the procedure for the grant of a patent, it is formally in order, publicly available in one of the most important languages (with an English language abstract, when not in English) and accompanied by an international search report and possibly an international preliminary examination report.

20.56 By adding to the national law the requirement that each national patent application must be accompanied by an international-type search report (see paragraph 28, above), the advantages of the PCT can be extended to national applications. Such a requirement contributes to the elimination of worthless patents and wasteful duplication of effort in a developing country by providing a basis for assessing patentability, and thus results in a net gain for the national economy.

(d) Technical Information

20.57 A further important advantage of the PCT for developing countries lies in its information effect. It is now always very difficult to obtain a complete picture of all the patent documents published in many countries and many languages and of the most recent state of the art resulting therefrom. Since many important inventions are the subject of PCT applications, developing countries have, through the international publication of these applications, early and easier access to modern technological information. The access will be early, because international applications are published 18 months after the priority date of the application. It will be easier, because the application will be published in one of the most important languages and, where not in English, with an English language abstract, and because the international search report, published together with the application, will make it easier to evaluate the technology disclosed in the application. Patent Offices of PCT Contracting States are entitled to receive, free of charge, a copy of all published international applications, of the PCT Gazette, and of any other publication of general interest published by the International Bureau in connection with the PCT.

20.58 The PCT offers distinct advantages for developing countries participating in this new system of international patent cooperation and requires no payment of contributions. That there is sufficient awareness of these advantages is confirmed by the impressive number of developing countries already party to the Treaty—over one third of all PCT Contracting States.

20.59 The following 87 States were party to the Patent Cooperation Treaty as of October 1, 1996: Albania, Armenia, Australia, Austria, Azerbaijan, Barbados, Belarus, Belgium, Benin, Bosnia and Herzegovina, Brazil, Bulgaria, Burkina Faso, Cameroon, Canada, Central African Republic, Chad, China, Congo, Côte d'Ivoire, Cuba, Czech Republic, Democratic People's Republic of Korea, Denmark, Estonia, Finland, France, Gabon, Georgia, Germany, Greece, Guinea, Hungary, Iceland, Ireland, Israel, Italy, Japan, Kazakstan, Kenya, Kyrgyzstan, Latvia, Lesotho, Liberia, Liechtenstein, Lithuania, Luxembourg, Madagascar, Malawi, Mali, Mauritania, Mexico, Monaco, Mongolia, Netherlands, New Zealand, Niger, Norway, Poland, Portugal, Republic of Korea, Republic of Moldova, Romania, Russian Federation, Saint Lucia, Senegal, Singapore, Slovakia, Slovenia, Spain, Sri Lanka, Sudan, Swaziland, Sweden, Switzerland, Tajikistan, The former Yugoslav Republic of Macedonia, Togo, Trinidad and Tobago, Turkey, Turkmenistan, Uganda, Ukraine, United Kingdom, United States of America, Uzbekistan and Viet Nam.

References for Section C
International Bureau of WIPO, *The Patent Cooperation Treaty (PCT) and its Importance to Developing Countries*, PCT/GEN/7 Rev.14

CHAPTER 21

The Madrid Agreement Concerning the International Registration of Marks and the Protocol Relating to the Madrid Agreement

A. INTRODUCTION

21.1 The Madrid Agreement Concerning the International Registration of Marks (hereinafter referred to as "the Madrid Agreement") is an international treaty that was adopted in April 1891. It has since undergone a number of revisions. The last revision took place at Stockholm in 1967. A Protocol Relating to the Madrid Agreement Concerning the International Registration of Marks was adopted at Madrid on June 27, 1989. That Protocol, which modifies certain features of the Madrid Agreement in order to facilitate the accession of new countries entered into force on December 1, 1995 and into operation on April 1, 1996. It is discussed in a subsequent chapter of this book.

B. THE PRINCIPLE OF INTERNATIONAL REGISTRATION

21.2 The trader or manufacturer wishing to obtain protection for his trademark in a number of States must normally comply with the trademark registration formalities of the national Offices of each individual State (differing procedures, need to file the application in different languages, varying terms of protection resulting in different renewal dates, and the need, in some cases, to appoint a local agent). Moreover, the need to file national applications in each country leads to very considerable costs (national fees, fees of the various agents and the costs of translation to be paid in each country). The purpose of the Madrid Agreement is to avoid all these complications. To file an application for international registration having effect in the countries party to the Madrid Agreement, the applicant need only comply with one set of formalities with the International Bureau of WIPO. The application is submitted in one language, French, and fees are paid once only to the International Bureau; the term of protection is twenty years for all countries in which protection has effect.

21.3 Under Article 1(2) of the Madrid Agreement, nationals of the countries party to the Agreement are entitled to apply for international registration. In addition, Article 2 of the Madrid Agreement, which refers to Article 3 of the Paris Convention for the Protection of Industrial Property, places nationals of other countries (but party to the Paris Convention) who have their domicile or a real and effective industrial or commercial establishment in a country party to the Madrid Agreement on the same footing as nationals of the countries party to the Madrid Agreement.

C. REGISTRATION PROCEDURE

(a) National Registration in the Country of Origin

21.4 Prior to international registration, the trademark must be registered at the national level with the industrial property Office of the country of origin. The country of origin is not left to the discretion of the applicant, however, since Article 1(3) of the Madrid Agreement defines it as follows:

(1) the country of the Madrid Union where the applicant has a real and effective industrial or commercial establishment;
(2) if the applicant has no such establishment in a country of the Union, the country of the Union where he has his domicile;
(3) if the applicant has no domicile within the Union, the country of the Union of which he is a national.

(b) Submission of the Application for International Registration

21.5 It is to the Office of the country of origin that the application for international registration must be sent and not directly to the International Bureau of WIPO. Before forwarding the application to the International Bureau, the national Office checks and certifies that the mark as reproduced in the application for international registration is entered in the national trademark register in the name of the applicant and that the goods and/or services listed in the international application are covered by the national registration.

(c) Fees Accompanying the Application

21.6 The application must be accompanied by the required fees, namely:

(1) the basic fee;
(2) the complementary fee, for each country for which protection is requested; and
(3) the supplementary fee for each class after the third in cases where the list of goods and services comprises more than three classes of the International Classification set up under the Nice Agreement.

21.7 The basic fee, is intended to cover the costs of the International Bureau, while the proceeds of the other two fees are distributed each year to the countries party to the Madrid Agreement. Each country's share is proportional to the number of registrations for which extension of protection to its territory has been requested during the year and, in the case of countries carrying out a preliminary examination, is multiplied by a coefficient which varies from 2 to 4 depending on the extent of the examination carried out (Article 8(5) and (6) of the Madrid Agreement).

(d) Right of Priority

21.8 The owner of an international registration enjoys the right of priority provided for in Article 4 of the Paris Convention without having to comply with the formalities prescribed in the case of a national filing (Article 4(2)). This means that, if the international registration is effected not later than six months after the date of the first regular national filing made in one of the countries party to the Paris Convention, that international registration has priority not from the date of the said registration but from that of the first national filing.

(e) Examination by the International Bureau; Registration, Notification and Publication

21.9 On receipt of the application for international registration, the International Bureau checks whether it complies with the provisions of the Agreement and the Regulations.

21.10 When the International Bureau is in possession of a correct and complete application for registration (i.e., which complies with the Madrid Agreement and its Regulations), it proceeds with the registration of the mark, its notification to the States concerned and its publication in the periodical "WIPO Gazette of International Marks/Gazette OMPi des marques internationales" (replacing as of June 1996 "Les Marques internationales").

(i) Irregularities in General

21.11 When the International Bureau is not in possession of a correct and complete application for registration, it defers registration and notifies the Office of origin.

21.12 If the application is not put in order within three months from the date of the notification, the International Bureau allows a further period of three months for the application to be put in order; in addition to the Office of origin, it notifies the applicant or his agent. In this case too, the reply should be addressed to the International Bureau by the Office of origin.

21.13 If the application is not put in order within the second period of three months, it is considered abandoned and any fees already paid are reimbursed (Rule 11(3)).

(ii) Classification of Goods and Services

21.14 If, in the application, the goods and services are not classified or grouped in classes, or if the International Bureau considers the classification indicated to be incorrect, it submits its proposals for classification to the Office of origin (Rule 12(1)). If, as a result of the International Bureau's proposals, a supplementary fee must be paid, the International Bureau will inform the applicant or his agent, or the Office of origin if the required fees have been paid through the intermediary of that Office (Rule 12(1)).

21.15 The International Bureau allows a period of three months from the date of its classification proposals for the application to be put in order (Rule 12(3)). If, by the expiration of that period, the International Bureau has not received any contrary opinion with regard to its proposals, it will register the mark with the classification it has proposed (Rule 12(4)), provided that the required fees have been paid and that the application complies in other respects with the Agreement and the Regulations.

21.16 If a contrary opinion is received within three months, the International Bureau may either make further proposals, if that period permits, or register the mark with the classification it considers appropriate (Rule 12(5)), provided that the required fees have been paid and that the application complies in other respects with the Agreement and the Regulations.

21.17 If a supplementary fee has to be paid and is not paid within three months, the application is considered abandoned and any fees already paid are reimbursed (Rule 12(6)). If a classification fee has to be paid and is not paid within three months, the International Bureau allows a second period of three months; if the application is not put in order by the expiration of this second period, the application is considered abandoned and any fees already paid are reimbursed (Rule 12(7)).

(iii)   List of Goods and Services Containing too Vague, Incomprehensible or Linguistically Incorrect Terms

21.18 If the International Bureau considers that the goods and services are indicated in the application for international registration in too vague, incomprehensible or linguistically incorrect terms, it shall advise the Office of origin, and where appropriate shall submit amendment proposals to it, with the invitation that it put the application for international registration in order within a period of three months from the date of the advice. In the event of failure to put the application for international registration in order within the period of three months, the International Bureau shall allow a period of the same duration for the said application to be put in order; it shall advise the applicant as well as the Office of origin. If the application for international registration is not put in order within the second period of three months, the International Bureau shall register the mark with the too vague, incomprehensible or linguistically incorrect term, provided that the Office of origin, has specified the class in which the term should be classified, and shall indicate that, in its opinion, the said term is too vague, incomprehensible or linguistically incorrect. Where no class has been specified by the Office of origin, the International Bureau shall delete the said term *ex officio* and inform the Office of origin and the applicant accordingly.

D.   THE EFFECTS OF INTERNATIONAL REGISTRATION

(a)   Territorial Effect

21.19 The international registration has no effect, and cannot have any effect at any time, in the country of origin. The trademark is protected in that country under the national registration that constitutes the basis for the international registration.

21.20 As regards the other countries party to the Madrid Agreement, the international registration has effect only in those for which protection has been explicitly requested in accordance with Article 3*ter*(1) of the Agreement. All the countries party to the Madrid Agreement have in fact made use of the faculty offered by Article 3*bis* of the Madrid Agreement, which stipulates that any contracting country may notify the Director General of WIPO that the protection resulting from the international registration shall extend to that country only at the express request of the proprietor of the mark.

(b) Legal Effect

21.21 Under Article 4 of the Madrid Agreement, a trademark that has been covered by an international registration enjoys, as from the date of such registration, in each of the countries concerned, the same protection it would have enjoyed had it been filed directly in those countries. It is therefore not possible to speak under the Madrid Agreement of a true "international trademark" with the same status in all countries in which it has effect (that is the case, for example, in a more restricted framework, for the European Community trademark). International registration constitutes, in a way, a bundle of national marks and remains, in principle, subject to the legislation of each country in which it has effect, in the same way as marks entered in their national register. This is particularly true of the examination procedure required by the legislation of a number of countries.

(c) Term and Date of International Registration

21.22 Under Article 6(1) of the Madrid Agreement, the international registration has a uniform term of 20 years whatever the national provisions on the term of a registration. It is to be noted, however, that under Rule 10(1) of the Regulations it is possible to pay the basic fee at the time of registration for an initial period of ten years only. In this case, the balance of the fee is payable before the expiration of the initial period, failing which the international registration is cancelled *ex officio*.

(d) Link between the International Registration and the Basic National Registration

21.23 Under Article 6(3) of the Madrid Agreement, protection resulting from the international registration remains dependent, for a period of five years from the date of the international registration, on the protection afforded to the mark in the country of origin. If, during the above five-year period, the mark ceases to enjoy national protection in the country of origin, the protection resulting from the international registration may no longer be invoked in any of the countries concerned. The same applies if national protection in the country of origin comes to an end following legal proceedings instituted before the expiry of the five-year period counted from the date of international registration.

21.24 Where protection ceases to exist following voluntary or *ex officio* cancellation within the five-year period of the basic national registration, the Office of the country of origin requests the International Bureau to cancel the international registration. In such cases, the International Bureau does not act *ex officio* but solely at the request of the Office of the country of origin.

21.25 In the event of legal proceedings against the basic national registration instituted prior to the expiry of that same five-year period, the Office of the country of origin is required to communicate to the International Bureau (*ex officio* or at the request of the plaintiff) documentary evidence of the proceedings having been instituted and also a copy of the final decision. The International Bureau then makes a corresponding entry in the International Register (Article 6(4)) but does not cancel the international registration. On the expiration of the period of five years from the date of the international registration, the latter becomes independent of the national protection afforded to the mark in the country of origin (subject to the case of legal proceedings mentioned above); the protection resulting from the international registration is therefore no longer affected, in other Madrid Union countries, by loss of protection in the country of origin.

E. REFUSAL OF PROTECTION

21.26 In those countries where the legislation authorizes them to do so, the Offices to which the International Bureau notifies the international registration of a mark have the right to declare that protection cannot be afforded to the mark on their territory. The notification of refusal of protection must be sent to the International Bureau, together with a statement of all the grounds, at the latest, before the expiration of one year from the date on which the mark was actually recorded in the International Register. The owner of the international registration enjoys, in the country pronouncing refusal, the same remedies as are enjoyed by the owner of a national registration.

(a) Grounds for Refusal

21.27 The second sentence of Article 5(1) of the Madrid Agreement stipulates that a mark entered in the International Register may only be refused on grounds which would apply, under the Paris Convention, for a mark filed nationally. The grounds which the Office of the country concerned may advance to support its decision to refuse the international registration of a mark are, normally, the same as those it could invoke against the national filing of the same mark.

21.28 Article 6*quinquies* of the Paris Convention, however, stipulates that every trademark duly registered in the country of origin (and that is always the case of marks entered in the International Register) must be accepted for filing and protected "as is" in the other countries party to the Convention and that refusal may only concern the following cases:

(1) when it is of such a nature as to infringe rights acquired by third parties in the country where protection is claimed;

(2) when it is devoid of any distinctive character, or consists exclusively of signs or indications which may serve, in trade, to designate the kind, quality, quantity, intended purpose, value, place of origin, of the goods or the time of production, or has become customary in the current language or in the bona fide and established practices of the trade of the country where protection is claimed;

(3) when it is contrary to morality or public order and, in particular, of such a nature as to deceive the public.

(b) Time Limit for Notification to the International Bureau

21.29 Under Article 5(2) of the Madrid Agreement and Rule 17(1) of its Regulations, refusal of protection must be notified to the International Bureau, together with a statement of all grounds, within the period prescribed by domestic law and, at the latest, before expiry of one year from the date on which the mark was actually recorded in the International Register. This date is later than that of the registration of the mark to ensure that national Offices have a full one-year period to pronounce any refusal.

(c) Examination of Refusals

21.30 On receipt of a notification of refusal, the International Bureau carries out a formal examination of the notification. If it does not contain any of the irregularities listed in Rule 17(2) of the Regulations, the refusal is recorded in the International Register and a copy of the notification of refusal is transmitted to the Office of the country of origin and to the owner of the mark or his agent.

21.31 The owner of the international registration enjoys, in the country pronouncing refusal, the same remedies as are enjoyed by the owner of a national registration.

21.32 Where the notification of refusal is not communicated to the International Bureau within the required one-year period, or where it does not state the grounds for refusal or contains any other irregularity listed in Rule 17(2) of the Regulations, refusal is not recorded in the International Register. The notification or refusal is nevertheless transmitted, for information, to the owner of the international registration or his agent and to the Office of the country of origin, who are informed (along with the Office that has pronounced the refusal) that the refusal has not been recorded in the International Register (Rule 17(3) of the Regulations).

F. CHANGES AFFECTING THE INTERNATIONAL REGISTRATION

21.33 Various changes may be entered in the International Register during the validity of the registration.

(a) Territorial Extension after Registration

21.34 It is possible for an international registration not to have effect in a country party to the Agreement either because protection in that country had not been requested when the initial registration was made or as a result of a refusal of protection, invalidation or renunciation on the part of the owner of the mark. In such cases, the owner may subsequently ask for extension of protection to that country for all or a part only of the goods and services entered in the International Register.

21.35 Territorial extension after registration has the same effect as the international registration in those countries for which it is requested. Pursuant to Article 5 of the Madrid Agreement, a territorial extension can be refused by a national Office within one year from the date it was entered on the International Register. Grounds for refusal must be based on reasons that are valid on the date the territorial extension would take place.

(b) Other Changes

21.36 Other changes may be entered in the International Register during the validity of the registration: transfer or partial assignment of the registration, limitation of the list of goods and services for one or more countries, renunciation of protection in one or more countries, change of name or address of the owner of the registration, cancellation of the registration.

21.37 Some types of requests for entry of a change cannot be accepted. Such is the case, for example, of a request for a change in the reproduction of the mark as registered or for the addition of new goods or services to the list of goods and services entered in the International Register. In such cases, a new international registration has to be made (Article 9(5) of the Madrid Agreement).

21.38 As for the correction of errors affecting an international registration, this can be done at any time if the error is attributable to the International Bureau (Rule 23(1)). Where an error is attributable to a national Office, there are two separate cases. Correction can be made at any time if it does not adversely affect (in the view of the International Bureau) the rights deriving from the registration (Rule 23(3)). Where the error may adversely affect the rights deriving from the registration, on the other hand, the request for correction must reach the International Bureau, at the latest, within six months after the publication containing the error (Rule 23(2)).

G. RENEWAL

21.39 The international registration may be renewed an unlimited number of times for a full 20-year period counted from the expiry of the preceding period (Article 7(1) of the Madrid Agreement).

(a) Unofficial Reminders

21.40 Six months before the expiry date of the international registration, the International Bureau sends an unofficial reminder to the owner of the registration and to any representative recorded in the International Register.

(b) Fees

21.41 Under Article 7(1) of the Madrid Agreement, renewal is effected by simple payment of the required fees. The latter are the same as those for the international registration.

21.42 Under Rule 25(2) of the Regulations, the required fees may not be paid earlier than one year before the date of expiration of the current period of the registration to be renewed. They must be paid, at the latest, on the date of expiration of that period or within a period of grace of six months following that date, subject, in the latter case, to payment of a surcharge amounting to 50% of the required fees.

(c) Nature and Effects of Renewal

21.43 Renewal constitutes a simple prolongation of the registration. According to Article 7(2) of the Madrid Agreement, no change may be made to the registration in its latest form, that is to say, as entered in the International Register on expiry of the 20-year period. Rule 25(6) of the Regulations under the Madrid Agreement stipulates, however, that a limitation of the list of countries concerned does not constitute a change within the meaning of that Article 7(2).

21.44 Since renewal constitutes a simple prolongation of the registration and not a new registration which could include changes to the mark itself or new goods and services, the Offices of the countries concerned may not pronounce a refusal in respect of a renewal. If a refusal were nevertheless to be notified to the International Bureau, it could not, in any event, be recorded in the International Register since it would necessarily be sent more than one year after the date on which the mark was entered, 20 years earlier, in the International Register.

H. NOTIFICATIONS ADDRESSED TO NATIONAL OFFICES AND PUBLICATIONS

21.45 Registrations, renewals, changes, refusals of protection and invalidations recorded in the International Register are notified to the Offices of the countries concerned and published in the review "WIPO Gazette of International Marks/ Gazette OMPi des marques internationales."

21.46 Each Office receives free copies of that review. According to the last sentence of Article 3(5) of the Madrid Agreement, publication in the review is to be deemed in all the contracting countries to be sufficient publicity and no other publicity may be required of the applicant.

21.47 Since the entry into force of the Madrid Agreement in 1892, over 640,000 marks have been internationally registered. Of that number, some 300,000 are still in force. In 1994, 22,000 new registrations and renewals were made and some 72,000 changes entered in the International Register. In 1994, over 23 million Swiss francs, representing supplementary and complementary fees, have been collected by the International Bureau and distributed to the States party to the Madrid Agreement under Article 8(5) and (6) of that Agreement. These figures prove the interest shown by users in the Madrid Agreement and the advantages, both practical and financial, which the member States may derive.

I. THE PROTOCOL RELATING TO THE MADRID AGREEMENT CONCERNING THE INTERNATIONAL REGISTRATION OF MARKS ("MADRID PROTOCOL")

21.48 The absence from the Madrid Agreement of some of the major countries in the trademark field—including the United States of America, the United Kingdom and Japan—was a long standing problem that WIPO had been trying to solve. Different attempts had been made to create a new system concerning the

References for Section H
International Bureau of WIPO, *The Madrid Agreement Concerning the International Registration of Marks and the 1989 Protocol*, WIPO/IP/WDH/93/11

International Registration of Marks in the last decade. Finally, it was decided to try to amend the Madrid system to make it acceptable to more countries.

21.49 In June 1989, the Diplomatic Conference for the Conclusion of a Protocol Relating to the Madrid Agreement Concerning the International Registration of Marks, convened and organized by WIPO, was held at facilities offered by the Government of Spain, at the "Instituto Nacional de Industria (INI)", in Madrid. The Diplomatic Conference unanimously adopted on June 27, 1989, the "Protocol Relating to the Madrid Agreement Concerning the International Registration of Marks."

21.50 The main changes introduced by the Protocol to the Madrid system are as follows:

(1) the Protocol allows that, at the option of the applicant, international registrations be based on national applications (and not only on national registrations) (Article 2(1)(a));

(2) the Protocol allows, as option for the Contracting Parties, 18 months (instead of one year) for refusals and an even longer period in the case of oppositions (Article 5(2)(b) to (d));

(3) the Protocol provides that the office of a designated Contracting Party may, if it so desires, receive the amount of the fees that it charges for national (or regional) registration or renewal, the said amount being diminished by the savings resulting from the international procedure (Article 8(7));

(4) the Protocol allows the transformation of a failed international registration—failed, for example, because of central attack—into national (or regional) applications in each designated Contracting Party, and such applications will have the filing date and, where applicable, the priority date of the international registration (Article 9*quinquies*).

21.51 These changes are intended to remove certain impediments to a wider acceptance of the Madrid system. Another objective of the Protocol is usually referred to as "the establishment of a link" between the Madrid system and the future regional trademark system of the European Communities. The Community Trade Mark will be a mark registered in the Community Trade Mark Office, and each registration in that Office will have effect in all the member countries (presently 15) of the European Communities. The link would mean that a Madrid registration could be based on a Community application or registration and that the European Communities could be designated in a Madrid registration. This results from Article 2 of the Protocol. In order to make the participation of the European Communities in the Madrid system full and to put the Community Trade Mark Office in exactly the same position as the national offices of the member countries, the Protocol provides that not only States but also certain intergovernmental organizations can become party to the Protocol (Article 14(1)(b)). The European Communities is such an organization.

21.52 It has to be noted that the Protocol contains an Article entitled "Safeguard of the Madrid (Stockholm) Agreement". The reason for the safeguard clause resides in the often repeated statements of the governments of present member States of the Madrid Union, and the representatives of private associations using the present Madrid system, that the present system fully satisfies them as it is and that they wish that it continue, among themselves.

21.53 The safeguard clause provides that where the Office of origin of an international application or registration is the Office of a State that is party to both the Protocol and the Madrid Agreement, the provisions of the Protocol have no effect (i.e., the Protocol is not applicable and, consequently, only the Madrid Agreement—that represents the *status quo*—applies) as regards a State that is also party to both the Protocol and the Madrid Agreement. In other words, territorial extensions with respect to such States are governed by the Agreement and not by the Protocol. It is to be noted that, naturally, the Protocol does apply in the relations between a State that is party to both the Protocol and the Madrid Agreement and any State or Organization that is party to the Protocol but is not party to the Madrid Agreement (Organizations cannot become a party to the Madrid Agreement).

21.54 Among the consequences of such a maintaining of the *status quo* between parties to both the Madrid Agreement and the Protocol are the following: (i) an international application cannot be based on a national application (but only on a national registration) (see Article 2(1) of the Protocol), (ii) the time limit of the refusal cannot be longer than one year (see Article 5(2)(b) and (c) of the Protocol), (iii) the designated Office cannot receive an "individual fee" (but only a share in the revenue produced by supplementary and complementary fees) (see Article 8(2) of the Protocol) and (iv) one cannot "transform" an international registration into national applications (see Article 9*quinquies* of the Protocol).

21.55 It should finally be noted that the Assembly of the Madrid Union may, by a three-fourths majority, repeal the safeguard clause or restrict its scope, after the expiry of a period of ten years from the entry into force of the Protocol, but not before the expiry of a period of five years from the date on which the majority of the countries party to the Madrid Agreement have become party to this Protocol.

21.56 The following 46 States were party to the Madrid Agreement Concerning the International Registration of Marks as of October 1, 1996: Albania, Algeria, Armenia, Austria, Azerbaijan, Belarus, Belgium, Bosnia and Herzegovina, Bulgaria, China, Croatia, Cuba, Czech Republic, Democratic People's Republic of Korea, Egypt, France, Germany, Hungary, Italy, Kazakstan, Kyrgyzstan, Latvia, Liberia, Liechtenstein, Luxembourg, Monaco, Mongolia, Morocco, Netherlands, Poland, Portugal, Republic of Moldova, Romania, Russian Federation, San Marino, Slovakia, Slovenia, Spain, Sudan, Switzerland, Tajikistan, The former Yugoslav Republic of Macedonia, Ukraine, Uzbekistan, Viet Nam and Yugoslavia.

21.57 By the date until which it was open for signature (that is, December 31, 1989), the following 27 States had signed the Protocol Relating to the Madrid Agreement: Austria, Belgium, Democratic People's Republic of Korea, Denmark, Egypt, Finland, France, Germany, Greece, Hungary, Ireland, Italy, Liechtenstein, Luxembourg, Monaco, Mongolia, Morocco, Netherlands, Portugal, Romania, Russian Federation, Senegal, Spain, Sweden, Switzerland, United Kingdom and Yugoslavia. The following 12 States were party to the Madrid Protocol as of October 3, 1996: China, Cuba, Czech Republic, Democratic People's Republic of

Korea, Denmark, Finland, Germany, Monaco, Norway, Spain, Sweden and United Kingdom.

References for Section I
International Bureau of WIPO, *The Use of Marks in the Commercialization of Goods in Domestic and International Markets; National and International Systems of Legal Protection of Marks*, PC/IP/XVI/SYM/2

CHAPTER 22

The Hague Agreement Concerning the International Deposit of Industrial Designs

A. INTRODUCTION

22.1 The institution of an international registration of industrial designs had already been the subject matter of a wish expressed by the Washington Diplomatic Conference in 1911. However, it was not until November 6, 1925, that the Hague Agreement Concerning the International Deposit of Industrial Designs (hereinafter referred to as "the Hague Agreement") was adopted within the framework of the Paris Convention. The Agreement entered into force on June 1, 1928, and has been revised on a number of occasions: at London on June 2, 1934 (hereinafter referred to as "the 1934 Act") and at The Hague on November 28, 1960 (hereinafter referred to as "the 1960 Act") it has been supplemented by the Additional Act of Monaco, of November 18, 1961, and the Complementary Act of Stockholm, of July 14, 1967. A Protocol, signed in Geneva on August 29, 1975, permitting certain articles of the 1960 Act to be applied prior to entry into force of that Act, is no longer of application, since that 1960 Act entered into force on August 1, 1984.

B. THE PRINCIPLE OF INTERNATIONAL DEPOSIT

22.2 The international deposit of industrial designs arose from a need for simplicity and economy. Its main aim is to enable protection to be obtained for one or more industrial designs in a number of States through a single deposit filed with the International Bureau of WIPO. Under the provisions of the Hague Agreement, any person entitled to effect an international deposit has the possibility of obtaining by means of a single deposit protection for his industrial designs in a number of States with a minimum of formalities and of expense. The applicant is thus relieved of the need to make a separate national deposit in each of the States in which he requires protection, thus avoiding the inherent complication of procedures that vary from one State to another. He does not have to submit the required documents in various languages nor keep a watch on the deadlines for renewal of a whole series of national deposits. He also avoids the need to pay a series of national fees and agents' fees in varying currencies. Under the Hague Agreement the same results can be obtained through a single deposit made with a single office, in one language, on payment of a single set of fees and in one currency.

C. MAIN PROVISIONS OF THE HAGUE AGREEMENT

22.3 The Hague Agreement permits persons entitled to make an international deposit to obtain protection for their industrial designs in the contracting States for which they request protection by means of a single deposit made with the International Bureau of WIPO.

22.4 An international deposit may be made by any "national" of one of the contracting States, that is to say any natural or legal person having the nationality of one of those States or having his domicile or a real and effective industrial or commercial establishment in one of those States.

22.5 An international deposit does not require any prior national deposit. It is made directly with the International Bureau of WIPO by the depositor or his representative on a form provided free of charge by the International Bureau. It may, however, be made through the national Office of a contracting State if the law of such State so permits (Article 4(1)2). The law of a contracting State may also require, in cases where that State is the State of origin, that the international deposit be made through the national Office of that State. Non-compliance with this requirement does not prejudice the effects of the international deposit in the other contracting States (Article 4(2)).

22.6 The international deposit has the same effect in each of the States for which protection is requested as if the designs included in the deposit had been directly deposited in that State on the date of the international deposit, subject to the special rules established under the Hague Agreement, particularly as regards the term of protection.

22.7 Protection may also be requested and obtained, by means of an international deposit, in the State of origin, unless the domestic legislation of that country provides otherwise.

22.8 Any contracting State whose domestic legislation offers the possibility of refusing protection as the result of an administrative *ex officio* examination or of opposition by a third party may refuse protection for any industrial design not meeting the requirements of its domestic law. Refusal of protection may not, however, extend to the formalities and other administrative acts that must be considered by each contracting State as having been accomplished as of the time the international deposit is recorded at the International Bureau. No contracting State may require, in particular, publication of the international deposits other than that made by the International Bureau.

22.9 Refusal of protection has to be notified to the International Bureau, addressed to the depositor, within six months of the date on which the national Office received the periodical bulletin in which the international deposit to which refusal refers was published. The depositor has the same remedies against the decision to refuse as he would have had if he had deposited the design or designs concerned with the Office of the State that has taken the decision to refuse.

22.10 Where no refusal is notified within the period of time referred to above, the international deposit has the same status as a deposit entered in the national register of each of the States for which protection has been requested.

22.11 International deposits are published by the International Bureau in a monthly periodical with the title "International Designs Bulletin." Publication comprises, in particular, a reproduction of the article or articles in which the deposited designs are to be incorporated.

22.12 The depositor may ask for publication to be deferred for a period of his choice, which may not, however, exceed 12 months as from the date of the international deposit or, where appropriate, from the date of priority claimed.

22.13 The national Office of each contracting State is entitled to receive free of charge from the International Bureau a certain number of copies of the International Designs Bulletin.

22.14 The owner of an international deposit enjoys the priority right afforded under Article 4 of the Paris Convention for the Protection of Industrial Property if he claims this right and if the international deposit is made within six months of the first national, regional or international deposit made in one of the States party to the Paris Convention or having effect in one of those States.

22.15 An international deposit is made for an initial term of five years. It can be renewed at least once, for an additional period of five years, for all or part of the designs included in the deposit or for all or some only of the States in which it has effect. For those contracting States whose domestic legislation allows a term of protection of more than 10 years for national deposits, an international deposit may be renewed more than once, in each case for an additional period of five years, with effect in each such State up to expiry of the total allowed term of protection for national deposits under that State's domestic legislation.

22.16 International deposit is subject to the payment of fees, in Swiss francs, the amounts of which are decided by the Assembly of the Hague Union.

22.17 The working languages for the implementation of the Hague Agreement are English and French. International deposits and any amendment affecting them are entered in the international register and published in English and in French, and the correspondence between the International Bureau and the depositor is in English or in French, depending on the choice of the applicant in using either of those languages for the application for international deposit.

D. BENEFITS OF ACCESSION TO THE HAGUE AGREEMENT

22.18 Nationals of a member State of the Hague Union are able to obtain protection for their designs in a number of States with a minimum of formalities and expense. In particular, they are relieved of the need to make a separate national deposit in each of the States in which they require protection, thus avoiding the complications arising from procedures which differ from State to State. They do not have to submit the required documents in various languages nor keep a watch on the deadlines for renewal of a whole series of national deposits, varying from one State to the other. They also avoid the need to pay a series of national fees and agents' fees in various currencies. Under the Hague Agreement, the same results can be obtained by means of a single international deposit, made in one language, on payment of a single set of fees, in one currency and with one Office (i.e. the International Bureau).

22.19 The simplification of the formalities and the reduction of the cost of obtaining protection abroad will favorably influence the development of foreign trade. Domestic manufacturers and traders will be encouraged to apply for protection of their designs in the States party to the Hague Agreement and to export their products to those States. International deposits will therefore assist domestic manufacturers and traders which are export-oriented.

22.20 The manufacturers and traders in other States party to the Hague Agreement will, in turn, be able to protect more easily their designs in a State which has acceded to the Agreement and will thus have more incentive to export their products to that State. The result will be a growth in trade and an increased likelihood of new industrial and commercial activities being set up on the territory of the new member State, promoting its economic development.

22.21 A part of the fees paid by depositors is distributed each year, by the International Bureau, to the competent authorities of the States party to the Hague Agreement.

22.22 The Offices of the contracting States have no specific tasks in the implementation of the Hague Agreement except in those cases where the domestic or regional legislation of the State permits or requires the international deposit to be effected through them or lays down a novelty examination for deposited designs.

22.23 The following 25 States were party to the Hague Agreement Concerning the International Deposit of Industrial Designs as of October 1, 1996: Belgium, Benin, Côte d'Ivoire, Democratic People's Republic of Korea, Egypt, France, Germany, Holy See, Hungary, Indonesia, Italy, Liechtenstein, Luxembourg, Monaco, Morocco, Netherlands, Republic of Moldova, Romania, Senegal, Slovenia, Spain, Suriname, Switzerland, Tunisia and Yugoslavia.

References for Section D
International Bureau of WIPO, *The Hague Agreement Concerning the International Deposit of Industrial Designs*, WO/INF/14 Rev.2

CHAPTER 23

The Trademark Law Treaty

A. INTRODUCTION

23.1 The Trademark Law Treaty was adopted on October 27, 1994, at a Diplomatic Conference in Geneva. The purpose of the Trademark Law Treaty is to simplify and harmonize the administrative procedures in respect of national applications and the protection of marks. Individual countries may become party to the Treaty as well as intergovernmental organizations which maintain an office for the registration of trademarks with effects in the territory of its member states such as the European Union (EU) and the African Intellectual Property Organization (OAPI). The provisions of the Treaty are supplemented by the Regulations and Model International Forms. The Treaty does not deal with the substantive parts of trademark law covering the registration of marks. The Treaty will enter into force three months after five States have deposited their instruments of ratification or accession.[1]

B. PROVISIONS OF THE TREATY

(a) Marks to which the Treaty Applies

23.2 According to Article 2, the Treaty applies to marks for goods and services. Not all countries currently register service marks and an effect of accession by a country to the Treaty is, therefore, that the country will be obliged to register such marks. In addition, such a country is also obliged, according to Article 16, to apply the provisions of the Paris Convention which concern trademarks to service marks.

23.3 Collective marks, certification marks and guarantee marks are not covered by the Treaty, as the registration of these marks normally requires the fulfillment of special, vastly varying conditions in the different countries which would make harmonization particularly difficult. Holograms and non-visible signs, such as sound marks and olfactory marks are also excluded from the scope of application because they are not easily reproduced by graphic means and because only very few countries provide for the protection of these marks in their national law.

23.4 A registrable mark must consist of visible signs, and, as far as three-dimensional marks are concerned, only those countries which accept three-dimensional marks for registration are obliged to apply the Treaty to such marks.

---

1   Editor's note: the Treaty entered into force on August 1, 1996 (see 23.23 below).

(b) Applications

23.5 Article 3 of the Treaty contains an exhaustive list of information which may be required by an Office in respect of an application for the registration of a trademark. Such indications are, for example, the name and address of the applicant and of the representative, if any, a declaration of priority if priority of an earlier application is claimed, one or more reproductions of the mark depending on the colors or dimensions of the mark, names of the goods or services for which registration is sought grouped according to the classes of the Nice Classification, or a declaration of intention to use the mark or of actual use. No Office may require other information than that referred to in the Treaty, such as an extract from a Commercial Register, an indication that the applicant is carrying on an industrial or commercial activity or that the applicant is carrying on an activity corresponding to the goods or services listed in the application.

23.6 The same application may relate to several goods or services. According to Article 6 of Treaty, the Office must accept the application irrespective of whether the goods or services belong to several classes of the Nice Classification. In this case the application must lead to a single registration.

23.7 An Office can not refuse an application in writing on paper if it is on a form corresponding to the model application form contained in the Regulations or, where the transmittal of communications to the Office by telefacsimile is allowed, the paper copy resulting form such transmittal corresponds to the application form.

(c) Representation

23.8 Article 4 of the Treaty allows a Contracting Party to require that the representative of an applicant or a holder is a representative admitted to practice before its Office and that a person who has neither a domicile nor a real and effective industrial or commercial establishment on its territory be represented by a representative. According to this provision the power of attorney may relate to several existing or future applications or registrations.

(d) Filing Date

23.9 The according of a filing date is essential in view of the rights which come into existence on that date and in view of the possibility of claiming a right of priority effective from the said date in respect of successive applications in other countries. Article 5 of the Treaty provides for the maximum information that an Office may require for the according of a filing date. These include the identification of the applicant, information sufficient to contact the applicant or his representative, a reproduction of the mark, a list of the goods and services for which registration is sought, etc. In addition, for according a filing date, an Office may require the payment of a fee if the national trademark law applied this condition before the adhering to the Treaty by the country.

23.10 If registration of a trademark is refused in respect of certain goods or services, Article 7 of the Treaty provides that the applicant can divide the application in order to avoid any delay in obtaining registration for the trademark on the goods or services that have not been refused and still keep the filing date of the initial application or the priority date, if any. At the same time the applicant may proceed with an appeal regarding the application concerning the goods or services which have been refused.

(e) Signature

23.11 Article 8 of the Treaty contains provisions in respect of the signature and other means allowing the identification of the source of a communication such as the filing of an application to the Office, in particular where the transmission of the communication is by facsimile or electronic means. Instead of a handwritten signature, the Office may accept a printed or stamped signature or the use of a seal. Of special importance is the prohibition of requirements for the attestation, notarization, authentication, legalization or other certification of the signature, except where the signature concerns the surrender of a registration, if such an exception is prescribed in the national law.

(f) Changes and Corrections Concerning Applications and Registrations

23.12 The Treaty sets forth in Articles 10 and 11 the requirements that apply to a request for the recordal of change in names, addresses and ownership. Article 12 contains the maximum requirements that an Office may request for the correction of mistakes made by an applicant or holder in any communication to the Office, which is reflected in the register. The provisions in Articles 10 to 12 apply equally to changes or corrections in respect of applications and registrations. These provisions provide that a single request is sufficient even where the changes or corrections relate to several applications or registrations or to both. The request must clearly identify the present relevant information held by the Office and the changes or corrections requested. The Office may not ask for further information than that mentioned in the Treaty, except where the Office may reasonably doubt the veracity of the information received, for example if it suspects that a change in name and address is in fact a change in ownership. In particular, the Office is not allowed to require the furnishing of any certificate concerning the change of a name or address, evidence to the effect that the new owner carries on an activity corresponding to the goods or services affected by the change in ownership, or that the holder transferred his business to the new owner.

23.13 In case of a request of the recordal of change in ownership the Office may, according to Article 11, require a certified copy or extract of the contract, a certificate of transfer and a document of transfer. Where the change in ownership results from a merger or from an operation of law or a court decision, for example in case of inheritance or bankruptcy, the Office may require that the request be accompanied by a certified copy of a document evidencing the change in ownership.

23.14 A mistake made by the Office must be corrected *ex officio* or upon request.

(g) Duration and Renewal of Registration

23.15 Article 13 of the Treaty provides for a duration of ten years for the initial period of registration of the trademark with a possibility of renewal for further ten year periods. With respect to renewal, the provision enumerates the maximum requirements that an Office can impose. These correspond to those in respect of the filing of an application. In particular, the Office may not, for the purposes of effecting the renewal, examine the registration as to the substance or request a reproduction of the mark or the furnishing of evidence concerning use of the mark.

(h) Other Provisions in the Treaty

23.16 In case of the intention to refuse a request for the recordal of a change in names, addresses and ownership or a request for the correction of a mistake or for renewal, the Office must, according to Article 14, give the requesting part an opportunity to make observations on the intended refusal within a reasonable time limit.

23.17 In general, where the Treaty sets forth the maximum requirements that an Office may request in respect of applications, representation, renewal, etc., the Office is entitled to require further information if it may reasonably doubt the veracity of the information received.

23.18 The Treaty further allows an Office to request that any filing or communication to be registered must be submitted in the language, or in one of the languages, admitted by the Office.

(i) Compliance with other Conventions

23.19 The Trademark Law Treaty contains no obligations for a Contracting Party to be party to other international conventions. However, it provides in Article 15 that Contracting Parties must comply with the provisions in the Paris Convention which concern marks. It follows from Article 3 concerning the filing of an application that Contracting Parties must provide that the Nice Classification is applied in respect of the grouping of the names on goods and services in the application.

(j) Regulations and Model International Forms

23.20 The provisions of the Treaty are supplemented by the Regulations, which provide rules concerning details useful in the implementation of the provisions on administrative requirements and procedures according to the Treaty. The rules apply to the requirements in respect of applications, representation, filing date, signature, duration, renewal, the manner of indicating names and addresses, and the identification of an application without its application number. The rules prescribe, for example, the number of reproductions of the mark that should accompany the application, time limits concerning the payment of fees and other communications to the Office such as the filing of the power of attorney, invitation to make corrections in case of non-compliance, etc.

23.21 The Regulations also contain eight Model International Forms which concern the filing of an application, the requests for renewal, recordal of change in names, addresses and ownership, correction of mistakes, appointment of representative, certificates of transfer and transfer documents. In cases where the request of information is not required under national law but nevertheless permitted according to the Treaty, for example in respect of an application, the Office may prepare an "Individualized International Form." This form must not contain mandatory requirements additional to or contrary to the Treaty or the Regulations. By using the Model International Forms or the Individualized International Forms, applicants and other parties are assured that no Office of a Contracting Party can refuse an application or a request in accordance with the forms.

(k) Transitional Provisions

23.22 The transitional provisions of the Treaty allow a Contracting Party to postpone the conformity of its national trademark law with the Treaty at the latest by October 28, 2004, in respect of, for example, the multiple class application system, prohibition of requirements concerning certification of signature of an application and a power of attorney, furnishing of a declaration and/or evidence concerning use on the occasion of renewal of a trademark registration and substantive examination on the occasion of the renewal.

23.23 The following six States were party to the Treaty as of October 1, 1996: Czech Republic, Monaco, Republic of Moldova, Sri Lanka, Ukraine and United Kingdom.

References for Section B
International Bureau of WIPO, *Trademark Law Treaty and Regulations*, WIPO Pub. No. 225, 1994

CHAPTER 24

Conventions on Classification*

A. THE NICE AGREEMENT CONCERNING THE INTERNATIONAL CLASSIFICATION OF GOODS AND SERVICES FOR THE PURPOSES OF THE REGISTRATION OF MARKS

(a) Introduction

24.1 The Nice Agreement Concerning the International Classification of Goods and Services for the Purposes of the Registration of Marks is a multilateral international treaty signed on June 15, 1957. It entered into force on April 8, 1961, was revised in Stockholm on July 14, 1967, and in Geneva on May 13, 1977 (the text resulting from this latter revision is referred to hereinafter as "the Geneva Act"). This note is based on the provisions of the Geneva Act.

24.2 The International Classification Under the Nice Agreement Comprises:

(1) a List of Classes, accompanied, where appropriate, by explanatory notes; the list comprises 34 classes of goods and 8 classes of services;
(2) an Alphabetical List of Goods and Services (hereinafter referred to as "the Alphabetical List"), giving the class in which each product or service is classified.

24.3 The Nice Classification exists in both English and French authentic texts. Currently, there are also official texts or official translations of the Nice Classification in the following languages: Dutch, German, Italian, Norwegian, Portuguese, Russian and Spanish. Though they are not official translations, a Chinese and a Japanese version are also available.

(b) Legal Scope and Application of the Nice Classification

24.4 Under Article 2(3) of the Nice Agreement, the countries of the Nice Union are required to include in the official documents and publications concerning the registrations of marks the numbers of the classes of the Classification to which the goods or services for which the mark is registered belong.

24.5 The effect of the Nice Classification is that given to it by each Nice Union country. For example, the classification does not bind the Nice Union countries

---

*   The Strasbourg Agreement Concerning the International Patent Classification is discussed in the context of the International Patent Classification (IPC). See Chapter 6, Section F of this work.

either as regards evaluation of the extent of protection of a mark or the recognition of service marks (Article 2(1)).

24.6 Furthermore, Article 2(2) of the Nice Agreement provides that each of the Nice Union countries will reserve the right to use the Nice Classification either as a principal system or as a subsidiary system, meaning that the Nice Union countries are free to adopt the Nice Classification of Goods and Services as the sole classification to be used for the purposes of registration of marks or to keep an existing national system of classification of goods and services and to use the Nice Classification as a supplementary classification which will also be shown in the official publications of marks.

24.7 Finally, Article 2(4) of the Nice Agreement stipulates that the fact that a term is included in the Alphabetical List of Goods and Services of the Nice Classification in no way affects any rights which may subsist in that term.

(c) The Nice Union Assembly and the Committee of Experts

24.8 On becoming party to the Nice Agreement, a country automatically becomes a member of the Nice Union Assembly.

24.9 The Assembly meets in ordinary session once every two years; usually, such ordinary sessions are held during the same period and at the same place as the ordinary sessions of the Paris Union Assembly and the Conference and General Assembly of WIPO. The Assembly deals with all matters concerning the maintenance and development of the special Union and the implementation of the Nice Agreement. In particular, it determines the program and adopts the budget of the Union.

24.10 Each country party to the Nice Agreement is also represented in the Committee of Experts set up by the Agreement. The Committee of Experts:

(1) decides on any changes to be made to the Classification;
(2) addresses recommendations to the countries of the special Union for the purpose of facilitating use of the Classification and promoting its uniform application;
(3) takes any other measures which, without financial implication for the budget of the special Union or of the Organization, are such as to facilitate application of the Classification by the developing countries;
(4) is empowered to set up subcommittees and working groups.

24.11 In practice, the proposed changes to the Nice Classification are examined by such subcommittees or working groups and have then to be adopted by the Committee of Experts for incorporation in the Classification.

24.12 Membership of the Nice Union therefore enables countries to participate actively in the periodical reviews of the Nice Classification and to adapt it as far as possible to technical developments and to national interests.

(d) Utilization and Updating of the Nice Classification

24.13 Currently, in addition to the countries party to the Nice Agreement, over 80 other countries use the Nice Classification. In all, therefore, more than 100 countries use the Classification.

24.14 A Trademark Classification Service has been set up at the International Bureau of WIPO. Its aim is to give advice in classification to anyone so requesting. The requester may be just as well the national office of any country, an agent, an individual or a private undertaking. This service is particularly useful where it is necessary to classify new products or products that are not specifically named in the Alphabetical List and may, therefore, raise difficulties in classification. However, the national offices of the member countries of the Nice Agreement, and also those of the developing countries, enjoy a reduction in fees. The International Bureau of WIPO receives some 10 to 20 requests for classification each month from national offices and industrial property agents acting for the owners of marks.

24.15 The Nice Classification has to be kept constantly up to date. It must be borne in mind that the first full draft of the Alphabetical List was produced in 1935. An amended draft was adopted at the Nice Diplomatic Conference in 1957. This means that the Nice Classification has been in force for more than thirty years. During those thirty years, numerous products shown in the first Alphabetical List have disappeared from the market, whereas numerous other products have appeared. For instance, new goods of plastics have appeared, as have the laser, the computer and word-processing systems, that have completely revolutionized traditional ways of working. All these new products have to be incorporated in the Alphabetical List and the products that are no longer marketed must be removed. The updating of the Nice Classification is carried out by the Committee of Experts composed of representatives of the countries party to the Nice Agreement (see paragraph 12 above).

24.16 The Committee of Experts meets regularly every three to five years at the invitation of the Director General of WIPO. So far, the Committee of Experts has met fifteen times. The Committee of Experts decides on the amendments to be made to the Alphabetical List, on the wording of the class headings and the relevant explanatory notes and on the general remarks preceding the list of classes.

24.17 The amendments to the Alphabetical List may take the following forms:

(1) deletion of an item shown in the Alphabetical List. This is done particularly in those cases where the product can no longer be found on the market or where a more generic term covers the product in question. For example, it has been proposed to the next Committee of Experts that item G0288 grooving planes be deleted. A grooving plane is used in carpentry for making grooves. It is therefore a specific kind of plane already covered in fact by item P0386 planes, and the translation of its name may present problems in various languages;

(2) addition of a product to the Alphabetical List. Products added to the Alphabetical List are above all new articles that have appeared on the market between two sessions of the Committee of Experts. One may mention, for example, solar batteries (S0590) or solar collectors [heating] (S0591), which were added to the Alphabetical List after the possibilities for using solar energy had been discovered;

(3) amendment of the wording of an item in the Alphabetical List. It is sometimes necessary to detail the existing wording by adding the function

or purpose of a product, for example "electric" or "for medical purposes" or to distinguish between homonyms that are to be classified differently, for example beauty masks (Cl. 03) and toy masks (Cl. 28);

(4) transfer of a product from one class to another. Although such a change is quite rare, it is nevertheless necessary on occasion to carry out this operation. For example, tie pins and cuff links of common metal, originally classified in Class 26 as clothing accessories, are now held to be items of jewelry and are therefore classified in Class 14.

24.18 The wording of the class headings and of the explanatory notes is also constantly reviewed in order to improve the definition of the content of each class and to adapt it to changes in trade and industry.

24.19 Countries that are not party to the Nice Agreement, intergovernmental organizations that specialize in marks and also representatives of international non-governmental organizations may be invited by the Director General of WIPO to send observers to meetings of the Committee of Experts.

24.20 In practice, the updating of the Nice Classification takes place as follows: to begin with, the International Bureau invites the member countries of the Nice Union to send to it any proposed changes to the Classification that they would like the Committee of Experts to look at; subsequently, the International Bureau prepares a document, on the basis of the proposals received, which it sends to the member countries of the Preparatory Working Group for examination. When they meet, the members of the Preparatory Working Group submit their observations and decide on the recommendations to be made to the Committee of Experts, that is to say, which proposals they recommend accepting, which should be rejected or in what way they should be amended before acceptance. As a result of the fact that the number of countries represented in the Preparatory Working Group is relatively small, the work progresses more rapidly than would be the case in the Committee of Experts. The Committee of Experts is therefore able to work on proposals for amendments that have already been discussed and which should not lead to protracted debate. As a result of the work carried out by the Preparatory Working Group, that of the Committee of Experts can be carried out under optimum conditions and can lead to decisions more rapidly.

24.21 The following 47 States were party to the Nice Agreement Concerning the International Classification of Goods and Services for the Purposes of the Registration of Marks as of October 1, 1996: Algeria, Australia, Austria, Barbados, Belgium, Benin, Bosnia and Herzegovina, China, Croatia, Cuba, Czech Republic, Denmark, Estonia, Finland, France, Germany, Hungary, Iceland, Ireland, Israel, Italy, Japan, Latvia, Lebanon, Liechtenstein, Luxembourg, Malawi, Monaco, Morocco, Netherlands, Norway, Portugal, Russian Federation, Slovakia, Slovenia, Spain, Suriname, Sweden, Switzerland, Tajikistan, The former Yugoslav Republic of Macedonia, Trinidad and Tobago, Tunisia, Turkey, United Kingdom, United States of America and Yugoslavia.

References for Section A
International Bureau of WIPO, *The Nice Agreement Concerning the International Classification of Goods and Services for the Purposes of the Registration of Marks*, WIPO-CEIPI/IP/SB/93/16

B. THE VIENNA AGREEMENT ESTABLISHING AN INTERNATIONAL CLASSIFICATION OF THE FIGURATIVE ELEMENTS OF MARKS

(a) Introduction

24.22 The Vienna Agreement Establishing an International Classification of the Figurative Elements of Marks was adopted on June 12, 1973, by a Diplomatic Conference held in Vienna, Austria. The Agreement entered into force on August 9, 1985.

(b) Basic Features of the Agreement

24.23 The Agreement is closely aligned with other instruments, particularly the Nice Agreement concerning the International Classification of Goods and Services for the Purpose of the Registration of Marks, of June 15, 1957, and the Strasbourg Agreement Concerning the International Patent Classification, of March 24, 1971.

24.24 As with the above-mentioned Agreements, the Vienna Agreement has established, under the Paris Convention for the Protection of Industrial Property, a special union (hereinafter referred to as "the Union") which uses a common classification for the figurative elements of marks (hereinafter referred to as "the International Classification"). A large number of trademarks and service marks contain such figurative elements and the Classification makes it possible to identify marks composed of elements that are alike or similar.

24.25 The International Classification is defined in the Agreement as comprising "a list of categories, divisions and sections in which the figurative elements of marks are classified, together with, as the case may be, explanatory notes." The authentic copy, in English and French, of the International Classification is presently deposited with the Director General of WIPO. German and Spanish versions have been drawn up by the International Bureau.

24.26 The main aim of the International Classification being to facilitate anticipation searching, it has no effect, pursuant to the Agreement itself, on the scope of protection afforded to a mark. However, States are at liberty to give the Classification the legal scope they wish, beyond the simple administrative scope afforded to it by the Agreement.

24.27 The Union States may use the International Classification either as a principal or as a subsidiary system. In other words, they are free to consider the International Classification as the sole classification to be used or to use it at the same time as a national classification.

24.28 The responsible Offices of the Union countries are required, by the Agreement, to include in the official documents and publications relating to registrations and renewals of marks the numbers of the categories, divisions and sections in which the figurative elements of those marks have been placed. However, this requirement is not retroactive to the extent that the Offices of the countries party to the Agreement are not required to classify figurative marks registered prior to entry into force of the Agreement for their territory; on the other hand, they have to be classified as and when the registration of such marks is renewed.

24.29 The numbers of the categories, divisions and sections given in the official documents and publications relating to registrations must be proceeded by the words "Classification of Figurative Elements" or an abbreviation that has still to be determined by the Committee of Experts.

24.30 The Agreement permits the member countries to reserve the possibility of not applying the International Classification (or not applying it in whole) as far as the finest subdivisions are concerned, that is to say the sections. This provision is of importance particularly for those Offices that only register a small number of marks.

24.31 The International Classification contains not only the sections required to place all figurative elements. It also contains auxiliary sections intended for figurative elements that are already covered by (main) sections, but which it is considered useful to group according to a particular criterion in order to facilitate searching.

24.32 Otherwise, the countries party to the Agreement are required to apply the International Classification as it stands. They may not, for example, change the content or number of categories, divisions or sections, group together varying sections to form a single one or create new sections, whether main or auxiliary.

24.33 Since it is not possible to directly place obligations on intergovernmental organizations, the Agreement provides that, if a country party to the Agreement entrusts the registration of marks to an intergovernmental authority, it must take all possible measures to ensure that such authority uses the International Classification in accordance with the Agreement. Once it has done so, such an authority would be in the same situation, as far as application of the International Classification is concerned, as a national Office. In particular, it would have the same possibility of entering the reservation referred to above.

24.34 The Agreement has established a Committee of Experts to make amendments and additions, as required by changes in technology and trade or as dictated by experience, to the International Classification. This Committee of Experts is made up of representatives of the Union countries and, in addition to its revision work, described above, has the task of facilitating the use of the Classification—particularly by the developing countries—and of promoting its uniform application. The intergovenmental organizations specialized in the field of marks, as also other intergovernmental organizations or non-governmental organizations, may be represented as observers if so decided by the Committee of Experts or the Director General.

24.35 The amendments and additions made by the Committee of Experts, together with its recommendations, are notified by the International Bureau of WIPO to the competent Offices in the Union countries and enter into force six months after notification; they are contained in an authentic copy deposited with the Director General of WIPO. Additionally, the International Bureau of WIPO incorporates the amendments and additions in the Classification and publishes them in the periodicals designated by the Assembly of the Union.

(c) Advantages of the International Classification

24.36 The internationalization of industrial, technical and commercial relations demands the creation of uniform tools of work in the industrial property field. Such is the case of the international classifications produced by cooperation between States and by means of which the national Offices are provided with tools which each of them would otherwise have been obliged to establish and maintain. When documents are exchanged, there is no need to reclassify them.

24.37 These advantages are particularly telling for the developing countries that do not always have the necessary staff to undertake such tasks and which permit them to make noticeable savings in means and time so that they can devote themselves to other priorities.

24.38 In the specific field of marks, there already exists an International Classification of Goods and Services established by the Nice Agreement of June 15, 1957. That Classification constitutes for the Offices responsible for anticipation searching a working tool whose usefulness and effectiveness have long since been proved.

24.39 However, in carrying out those searches, it is also necessary to classify the figurative elements of marks. Thus, a uniform classification facilitates the anticipation searching work of the national Offices. For its part, the International Bureau of WIPO uses the International Classification of the Figurative Elements of Marks for coding the figurative marks that are internationally registered under the Madrid Agreement.

24.40 The following 7 States were party to the Vienna Agreement Establishing an International Classification of the Figurative Elements of Marks as of October 1, 1996: France, Luxembourg, Netherlands, Sweden, Trinidad and Tobago, Tunisia and Turkey.

C. THE LOCARNO AGREEMENT ESTABLISHING AN INTERNATIONAL CLASSIFICATION FOR INDUSTRIAL DESIGNS

(a) Introduction

24.41 The Locarno Agreement Establishing an International Classification for Industrial Designs is a multilateral international treaty, which was signed on October 8, 1968. It entered into force on April 27, 1971.

24.42 The Locarno Classification comprises three parts:

(1) a list of Classes and Subclasses; in total, there are 31 classes and 211 subclasses;
(2) an Alphabetical List of Goods in which industrial designs are incorporated; this List contains in total approximately 6,000 entries;
(3) explanatory Notes.

References for Section B
International Bureau of WIPO, *The Vienna Agreement Establishing an International Classification of the Figurative Elements of Marks*, WIPO-CEIPI/IP/SB/93/17

24.43 The Locarno Classification has been established in the English and French languages, both texts being equally authentic. Official texts of the Locarno Classification, in such languages as the Assembly referred to in paragraphs 7 and 8 of this Note may designate, are established after consultation with the interested Governments by the International Bureau of the World Intellectual Property Organization (WIPO).

24.44 At present, a translation of the Locarno Classification into German and Spanish has been established. A translation of said Classification into Italian and Portuguese is under way.

(b) Legal Effect and Use of the Locarno Classification

24.45 According to Article 2(3) of the Locarno Agreement, the industrial property offices of the countries of the Locarno Union must include in the official documents for the deposit or registration of designs, and if they are officially published, in the publications in question, the numbers of the classes and subclasses of the Locarno Classification into which the goods incorporating the designs belong.

24.46 Each country may attribute to such classification the legal consequences, if any, which it considers appropriate. In particular, the Locarno Classification does not bind the countries of the Locarno Union as regards the nature and the scope of protection afforded to the design in those countries (Article 2(1)).

24.47 Further, Article 2(2) of the Locarno Agreement provides that each of the countries of the Locarno Union reserves the right to use the Locarno Classification, either as a principal or as a subsidiary system, which means that the countries of the Locarno Union are free to adopt the Locarno Classification as the only classification to be used for industrial designs, or to maintain an existing national classification system for industrial designs and to use the Locarno Classification as a supplementary classification, also to be included in official documents and publications concerning the deposit or registration of designs.

24.48 Finally, Article 2(4) of the Locarno Agreement provides that the inclusion of any word in the Alphabetical List of Goods is not an expression of opinion of the Committee of Experts on whether or not such a word is subject to exclusive rights.

24.49 The following 26 States were party to the Locarno Agreement Establishing an International Classification for Industrial Designs as of October 1, 1996: Austria, Bosnia and Herzegovina, China, Croatia, Czech Republic, Denmark, Finland, France, Germany, Hungary, Iceland, Ireland, Italy, Malawi, Netherlands, Norway, Russian Federation, Slovakia, Slovenia, Spain, Sweden, Switzerland, Tajikistan, The former Yugoslav Republic of Macedonia, Trinidad and Tobago and Yugoslavia.

References for Section C
International Bureau of WIPO, *The Locarno Agreement Establishing an International Classification for Industrial Designs*, WIPO-CEIPI/IP/SB/93/18

CHAPTER 25

The International Convention for the Protection of Performers, Producers of Phonograms and Broadcasting Organizations (The "Rome Convention")

25.1 Several international conventions on neighboring rights are administered by WIPO. The following sections will describe the important aspects of the International Convention for the Protection of Performers, Producers of Phonograms and Broadcasting Organizations, generally referred to as the "Rome Convention." Other Special Conventions in the field of neighboring rights will be dealt with in the following chapter.

A. GENESIS OF THE ROME CONVENTION

25.2 Neighboring rights are primarily an offshoot of technological development. At the national level, it was first the phonogram industry that looked for protection against unauthorized duplication of sound recordings of musical performances. In the United Kingdom, the Copyright Act recognized in 1911 a copyright for the benefit of the producers of sound recordings, and this copyright approach has been followed in several countries which have adopted the Anglo-Saxon concept of copyright, despite the different implications of the protection of authors' works, on the one hand, and phonogram products, on the other. It was in that context also that the question of protecting performers emerged in some countries. At the international level, it was likewise the development of the phonogram industry that promoted the establishment of special protection for the so-called neighboring rights.

25.3 As in the case of some national laws, the first proposals aiming at the protection of producers of phonograms and performers at the international level were also based on copyright protection. The rights involved were discussed by the Berne Union for the Protection of Literary and Artistic Works at its Diplomatic Conference in Rome in 1928, where it was proposed that "when a musical work has been adapted to a mechanical instrument by the contribution of performing artists these latter should also benefit from the protection granted to that adaptation." Corresponding to this approach, a resolution was passed asking governments to consider the possibility of adopting measures to safeguard the interests of performers.

25.4 Later on, in 1934, CISAC, the International Confederation of Societies of Authors and Composers, signed an agreement in Stresa with the International Federation of the Gramophone Industry according to which during the forthcoming revision of the Berne Convention (i) the protection of phonograms against unauthorized duplication and (ii) the right of producers of phonograms to equitable remuneration for communication to the public of their phonograms by broadcasting or cinematography should be proposed by means of an annex to be added to the Berne Convention. On the other hand, the International Labour Organisation (ILO) had maintained since 1926 a continuing interest in the protection of performers and the problem was considered at a meeting in Samaden, Switzerland, in 1939. Drafts were prepared in cooperation with the Bureau of the Berne Union but all progress was stopped for several years by the outbreak of World War II.

25.5 After the war, the matter was taken up again, on the occasion of the revision of the Berne Convention in Brussels in 1948, but the attempts to secure at the international level a kind of copyright for performers and producers of phonograms were of no avail. However, wishes were expressed that governments should continue their efforts towards providing some sort of adequate protection. Different committees of experts prepared drafts of conventions also including protection of the interests of broadcasting organizations: the so-called Rome Draft (1951), a draft produced under the sponsorship of the International Labour Office (1957) and the Monaco Draft (1957) prepared by experts convened by the International Bureau of the Berne Union and by Unesco. Finally, in 1960, a committee of experts convened jointly by WIPO, Unesco and the International Labour Office, met at The Hague and drew up the draft convention which served as a basis for the deliberations in Rome, where a Diplomatic Conference agreed upon the final text of the International Convention for the Protection of Performers, Producers of Phonograms and Broadcasting Organizations, the so-called Rome Convention of October 26, 1961.

B. RELATION BETWEEN THE PROTECTION OF NEIGHBORING RIGHTS AND COPYRIGHT

25.6 Considering that the use of literary and artistic works was usually implied in the work of performers, recorders and broadcasters, the Diplomatic Conference at Rome established a link with copyright protection. The first article of the Rome Convention provides that the protection granted under the Convention shall leave intact and shall in no way affect the protection of copyright in literary and artistic works. Consequently, no provision of the Rome Convention may be interpreted as prejudicing such protection. Under the text of Article 1 it is clear that whenever, by virtue of the copyright law, the authorization of the author is necessary for the use of his work, the need for this authorization is not affected by the Rome Convention.

25.7 The majority of the Conference at Rome decided to go even further. They considered the possibility that the performers, producers of phonograms and broadcasting organizations of a country would enjoy international protection even when the literary and artistic works they used might be denied protection in that country because it was not a party to at least one of the major international copyright conventions. The Rome Convention therefore provides that in order to become a party to the Convention a State must not only be a member of the United Nations, but also a member of the Berne Union or a party to the Universal Copyright Convention (Article 24(2)). Accordingly, a Contracting State shall cease to be a party to the Rome Convention as from that time when it is not party to either the Berne or the Universal Copyright Convention (Article 28(4)). Because of this link with the copyright conventions, the Rome Convention is sometimes referred to as a "closed" convention from the point of view of the circle of States which may adhere to it.

C. THE BASIC PRINCIPLE OF PROTECTION UNDER THE ROME CONVENTION: NATIONAL TREATMENT

25.8 Similar to the Berne Convention, the protection accorded by the Rome Convention consists basically of the national treatment that a State grants under its domestic law to domestic performances, phonograms and broadcasts (Article 2(1)). National treatment is, however, subject to the minimum of protection specifically guaranteed by the Convention, and also to the limitations specifically provided for in the Convention (Article 2(2)). That means that, apart from the rights guaranteed by the Convention itself as constituting that minimum of protection, and subject to specific exceptions or reservations allowed for by the Convention, performers, producers of phonograms and broadcasting organizations to which the Convention applies, enjoy in Contracting States the same rights as those countries grant to their nationals.

D. ELIGIBILITY FOR PROTECTION

25.9 One of the most important questions to be answered unequivocally by each international convention is to whom and in what cases does it apply? The Rome Convention provides for its application by determining criteria of eligibility for national treatment.

25.10 National treatment should be granted to performers, if the performance takes place in another Contracting State (irrespective of the country to which the performer belongs) or if it is incorporated in a phonogram protected under the Convention (irrespective of the country to which the performer belongs or where the performance actually took place) or if it is transmitted "live" (not from a phonogram) in a broadcast protected by the Convention (irrespective again of the country to which the performer belongs) (Article 4). These alternative criteria of eligibility for protection allow for the application of the Rome Convention to the widest possible circle of performances.

25.11 National treatment should be granted to producers of phonograms if the producer is a national of another Contracting State (criterion of nationality) or the first fixation was made in another Contracting State (criterion of fixation) or the phonogram was first or simultaneously published in another Contracting State (criterion of publication) (Article 5).

25.12 The Convention allows reservations in respect of these alternative criteria. By means of a notification deposited with the Secretary-General of the United Nations, any Contracting State may at any time declare that it will not apply the criterion of publication or, alternatively, the criterion of fixation. Any State which, on the day the Convention was signed at Rome, granted protection to producers of phonograms solely on the basis of the criterion of fixation, can exclude both the criteria of nationality and publication. This possibility has been provided for mainly in view of the contemporary Nordic legislation. Thus the implementation of the Rome Convention can easily be adapted to conditions of protection already existing under different national laws.

25.13 National treatment has to be granted to broadcasting organizations if their headquarters is situated in another Contracting State, (principle of nationality) or the broadcast was transmitted from a transmitter situated in another Contracting State, irrespective of whether the initiating broadcasting organization was situated in a Contracting State (principle of territoriality). Contracting States may declare that they will protect broadcasts only if both the condition of nationality and of territoriality are met in respect of the same Contracting State (Article 6).

E. THE MINIMUM PROTECTION REQUIRED BY THE CONVENTION

25.14 The minimum protection guaranteed by the Convention to performers is provided by "the possibility of preventing certain acts" done without their consent. Instead of enumerating the minimum rights of performers, this expression was used in order to allow countries like the United Kingdom to continue to protect performers by virtue of penal statutes, determining offenses and penal sanctions under public law. It was agreed, however, that the enumerated acts which may be prevented by the performer, require his consent in advance. In fact, the possibility of preventing certain acts as defined in the Convention amounts to a distinct bundle of rights granted to performers.

25.15 The restricted acts comprise (i) broadcasting or communication to the public of a "live" performance; (ii) recording an unfixed performance; (iii) reproducing a fixation of the performance, provided that the original fixation was made without the consent of the performer or the reproduction is made for purposes not permitted by the Convention or the performer (Article 7).

25.16 Producers of phonograms have the right to authorize or prohibit the direct or indirect reproduction of their phonograms (Article 10). The Rome Convention does not provide for any right to authorize performances of the phonogram and does not explicitly prohibit distribution or importation of unauthorized duplicates of phonograms.

25.17 Broadcasting organizations have the right to authorize or prohibit (i) the simultaneous rebroadcasting of their broadcasts, (ii) the fixation of their broadcasts, (iii) the reproduction of unauthorized fixations of their broadcasts or reproduction of lawful fixations for illicit purposes, and (iv) the communication to the public of their television broadcasts by means of receivers in places accessible to the public against payment. It should be noted, however, that this last-mentioned right does not extend to communication to the public of merely sound broadcasts, and that it is a matter for domestic legislation to determine the conditions under which such a right may be exercised. It should also be observed that the Rome Convention does not protect against distribution by cable of broadcasts.

F. PROVISIONS FOR DISCRETIONARY REGULATION OF THE EXERCISE OF RIGHTS

25.18 The Rome Convention, over and above the minimum requirements of protection, also contains provisions allowing national laws to regulate certain aspects of the protection at their discretion.

25.19 As regards the protection of performers, it is a matter for domestic legislation to regulate the protection against rebroadcasting of the performance and fixation thereof for broadcasting purposes, where the broadcasting of the performance was consented to by the performer. The principle of preeminence of contractual arrangements was embodied in a provision requiring that domestic laws shall not operate to deprive performers of the ability to control by contract their relations with broadcasting organizations (Article 7(2)) whereas it was understood that the meaning of contract in this context includes collective agreements and also decisions of an arbitration board if involved.

25.20 If several performers participate in the same performance, the manner in which they should be represented in connection with the exercise of their rights may be specified by each Contracting State (Article 8).

25.21 Concerning both the protection of performers and producers of phonograms, Article 12 (perhaps the most controversial part of the Convention) provides that if a phonogram published for commercial purposes is used directly for broadcasting or any communication to the public, an equitable remuneration shall be paid by the user to the performers, or to the producers of the phonogram, or to both. This Article does not grant any right to either the performers or producers of phonograms to authorize or to prohibit the secondary use of a phonogram. By guaranteeing a single remuneration for the use of the phonogram it seems to establish a sort of non-voluntary license. It does not, however, obligatorily specify the beneficiary or beneficiaries of the remuneration for the secondary use of the performance and the phonogram embodying it. Article 12 only says that at least one of the interested parties should be paid for the use; nevertheless it provides that in the absence of agreement between these parties, domestic law may (if considered appropriate) lay down the conditions for the sharing of this remuneration.

25.22 The implementation of these provisions, however, can be excluded or restricted by the Contracting States at any time by an appropriate notification (Article 16(1)(a)). A State may declare that it will not apply the provisions of Article 12 at all. A Contracting State may declare that it will not apply this article in respect of certain uses, for instance as regards communications to the public other than broadcasting; or broadcasting of phonograms acquired before the date of the Convention, etc. It is also possible to apply this Article only as regards phonograms of which the producer is a national of another Contracting State.

Furthermore, as regards phonograms, of which the producer is a national of another Contracting State, the extent and term of protection can be limited so as to correspond to the protection granted by the other State concerned. The fact, however, that the protection in both countries concerned is not granted to the same beneficiary, cannot be considered as justifying the restriction of the protection provided for in Article 12.

G. LIMITATIONS

25.23 The Rome Convention allows for certain limitations of the rights granted and, as regards the performers, also imposes limitations on rights itself.

25.24 Any Contracting State may provide for exceptions as regards private use, use of short excerpts in connection with reporting current events, ephemeral fixation by a broadcasting organization by means of its own facilities and for its own broadcasts, and for all kinds of uses solely for the purpose of teaching or scientific research (Article 15(1)). This latter possibility of introducing exceptions may be of special benefit to developing countries.

25.25 Besides the exceptions specified by the Convention, any Contracting State may also provide for the same kind of limitations with regard to the protection of performers, producers of phonograms and broadcasting organizations as it provides for in connection with copyright protection. There is, however, an important difference: compulsory licenses may be provided for only to the extent to which they are compatible with the Rome Convention (Article 15(2)).

25.26 In view of the cinematographic industry's interest in exclusively exploiting the contributions made to their productions, Article 19 of the Rome Convention provides that once a performer has consented to the incorporation of his performance in a visual or audiovisual fixation, he shall have no further rights under the Rome Convention as regards the performance concerned.

H. DURATION OF PROTECTION

25.27 The minimum term of protection under the Rome Convention is a period of twenty years to be computed from the end of the year in which (i) the fixation was made, as far as phonograms and performances incorporated therein are concerned, or (ii) the performance took place, as regards performances not incorporated in phonograms, or (iii) the broadcast took place, for broadcasts (Article 14).

I. RESTRICTION OF FORMALITIES

25.28 If a country requires compliance with formalities as a condition of protecting neighboring rights in relation to phonograms, these should be considered as fulfilled if all copies in commerce of the published phonogram or their containers bear a notice consisting of the symbol P , accompanied by the year date of the first publication. If the copies of their containers do not identify the producer or his licensee, the notice shall also include the name of the owner of the rights of the producer and, if the copies or their containers do not identify the principal performers, the notice shall also include the name of the person who owns the rights of such performers (Article 11). It should be emphasized that this provision is *not* a formality requirement; it is a restriction of formalities, which may be required by some national laws.

J. THE IMPLEMENTATION OF THE ROME CONVENTION

25.29 The Rome Convention has been referred to as a kind of "pioneer convention." Whereas the conventions concluded towards the end of the nineteenth century for the protection of copyright resulted from developments in national laws, this Convention defined standards of protection of neighboring rights at a time when very few countries had any rules enacted to protect performing artists, producers of phonograms and broadcasting organizations. Thus it was only natural that the impetus of the Convention in the field of the protection of neighboring rights during the first years following its adoption could not be measured so much by the number of ratifications or accessions as by the impact the Convention had on national laws.

25.30 Since 1961, more than 60 countries have legislated on the protection of neighboring rights, increasing the number of national laws protecting producers of phonograms or broadcasting organizations to about 90 in both fields mentioned. More than 40 States have granted specific protection to performing artists by law, the majority of them as a result of the coming into existence of the Rome Convention. The disproportion between the number of national laws protecting performers' rights and those granting protection to producers of phonograms and broadcasting organizations is still unduly great. There are, however, further draft laws under preparation in several countries, which continue to demonstrate the tendency to pay more attention to the protection of performers' rights.

25.31 Since 1974, additional assistance is available to national laws in the form of a Model Law Concerning the Protection of Performers, Producers of Phonograms and Broadcasting Organizations, with a commentary on it, prepared by WIPO, Unesco and the International Labour Organisation, the international organizations which jointly administer the Rome Convention. This Model Law has proved an efficient aid, especially to developing countries.

25.32 In spite of the comparatively slow progress of national laws in the field of neighboring rights, and in particular the unequal development of protection as regards different beneficiaries of these rights, which even today hinders accession to the Rome Convention since it requires at the same time protection of performers, producers of phonograms and broadcasting organizations, the number of countries party to this Convention has grown so far to 46. It is to be expected that the development of national laws will result in further accessions to the Rome Convention.

K. THE ROME CONVENTION AND DEVELOPING COUNTRIES

25.33 More than half of the States party to the Rome Convention are developing countries. This is quite natural since most developing countries attach great importance to music, dance and other creations, in their national heritage. The value of the Rome Convention to such countries stems from the fact that it affords the protection of those who contribute to the dissemination of that heritage abroad.

25.34 The Convention is particularly interesting for those countries whose civilization and tradition are oral and where the author is often the performer as well. In this context, the place occupied by expressions of folklore must be borne in mind and the interests of the artists constantly performing, and thus perpetuating them, must be safeguarded when use is made of their performances. Whilst the possibilities of protecting creations of folklore by copyright seem to be limited, and the establishment of a more adequate kind of protection *sui generis* appears to still require some time, expressions of folklore can efficiently be protected indirectly by protecting performances, fixations, and broadcasts of them.

25.35 By also protecting the producers of phonograms, the Rome Convention promotes, particularly in developing countries, the setting-up of an industry in the tertiary sector of the economy whose dynamic activity needs no proving. Such an industry, while guaranteeing the dissemination of national culture, both within the country and throughout the world, can additionally constitute a substantial source of revenue for the country's economy and, in those cases where its activities extend beyond the frontiers, can represent an inflow of foreign currency.

25.36 By giving performers and phonogram producers the possibility of benefiting from their performances and productions, the Rome Convention is instrumental in promoting the artistic heritage and represents an important incentive to creativity. It is also certain that, where the interests of performers and producers of phonograms are safeguarded by law, works will enjoy greater development and that those works will suffer less from the competition of unprotected performances of foreign works. Where performances and phonograms are exported, there is one reason more to protect them internationally, that is to say, by accepting the relevant international conventions.

25.37 Finally, the part played by the broadcasting organizations in the developing countries should not be forgotten either, since they also have an interest in the protection of their costly program against rebroadcasting, reproduction and communication to the public of their broadcasts. The rebroadcasting or reception of television broadcasts in public places can be very profitable, especially when the subject of the original broadcast is an exceptional event. Frequently, the organizers of such events only allow broadcasting for certain territories or on the condition that no public reception close to the place of the event drains away potential spectators. The broadcasting organization must therefore be able to prohibit rebroadcasting and public reception. The same refers to broadcasting of performances or recordings of expressions of national folklore: the broadcasting organization should be entitled internationally to prevent rebroadcasting or fixation for reproduction of its own broadcast of works of national heritage.

25.38 The following 51 States were party to the International Convention for the Protection of Performers, Producers of Phonograms and Broadcasting Organizations as of October 1, 1996: Argentina, Australia, Austria, Barbados, Bolivia, Brazil, Bulgaria, Burkina Faso, Chile, Colombia, Congo, Costa Rica, Czech Republic, Denmark, Dominican Republic, Ecuador, El Salvador, Fiji, Finland, France, Germany, Greece, Guatemala, Honduras, Hungary, Iceland, Ireland, Italy, Jamaica, Japan, Lesotho, Luxembourg, Mexico, Monaco, Netherlands, Niger, Nigeria, Norway, Panama, Paraguay, Peru, Philippines, Republic of Moldova, Saint Lucia, Slovakia, Spain, Sweden, Switzerland, United Kingdom, Uruguay and Venezuela.

References for Section K
International Bureau of WIPO, *Basic Notions of Neighboring Rights—International Conventions in the Field of Neighboring Rights*, WIPO/CR/GE/93/3

CHAPTER 26

Other Special Conventions in the Field of Neighboring Rights

A. THE SPECIAL CONVENTIONS

26.1 The Rome Convention of 1961, discussed in the previous chapter, protects at the international level all the three categories of beneficiaries of neighboring rights: the performers, the producers of phonograms and the broadcasting organizations. Besides this basic convention, two other international instruments have been drawn up with regard to certain neighboring rights. These are the Convention for the Protection of Producers of Phonograms Against Unauthorized Duplication of Their Phonograms, concluded in Geneva in October 1971 and generally referred to as "the Phonograms Convention," and the Convention Relating to the Distribution of Programme-Carrying Signals Transmitted by Satellite; concluded in Brussels in May 1974 and known briefly as "the Satellites Convention." These two Conventions are also within the area of neighboring rights, and their purpose is to protect producers of phonograms and broadcasting organizations, respectively, against certain prejudicial acts that have been widely recognized as infringements or acts of piracy.

26.2 From the point of view of the Rome Convention, the Phonograms Convention and the Satellites Convention may be regarded as special agreements, the conclusion of which is reserved for Contracting States insofar as the agreements grant to performers, producers of phonograms or broadcasting organizations more extensive rights than those granted by the Rome Convention or contain other provisions not contrary to the Convention (Article 22 of the Rome Convention).

B. REASONS FOR AND PURPOSES OF THE SPECIAL CONVENTIONS

26.3 The Phonograms Convention already has 53 ratifications or accessions to its credit, which is quite an impressive rate of acceptance. The secret of the rapid acceptance of this Convention is due, on one hand, to the accelerating increase in international piracy during the last two decades, and, on the other hand, to the legal characteristics of the Convention itself.

26.4 While a number of countries were preparing new legislation in the field of neighboring rights in view of the standards set by the Rome Convention, international record piracy was growing. The total value of pirated records sold worldwide has been increasing steadily. This dramatic development of record piracy made it necessary, already in the early seventies, to establish without delay a special convention intended solely for the international protection of the basic interests of producers of phonograms and taking into consideration all measures already available under various national laws. The subject was raised in May 1970 in the Preparatory Committee for the revision of the two major copyright conventions, and the new Convention was signed in less than 18 months in Geneva.

26.5 As far as the legal characteristics of the Phonograms Convention are concerned, it takes into account all the measures that had already been adopted in various national laws, and allows for the application of all of them instead of requiring uniform solution for the same purpose, as is the case under the Rome Convention, which provides for the granting to producers of phonograms the right to authorize or prohibit the reproduction of their phonograms. Thus, amendments of existing national laws became largely unnecessary to States which already protected producers of phonograms by some other means and wanted to extend this kind of protection also at the international level.

26.6 The adoption of the Satellites Convention is due to the fact that the use of satellites in international telecommunications has, since about 1965, been presenting a new problem for the protection of broadcasting organizations.

26.7 Nowadays the transmission of programs by satellite still takes place mainly indirectly. Electronic signals carrying broadcast programs pass through a satellite to reach remote parts of the globe that cannot be reached by traditional broadcasting; but the programme-carrying signals passed on by the satellite cannot be picked up directly by conventional receivers generally used by the public at large. They have first to be picked up by ground stations, which make them accessible and so distribute them to the public.

26.8 In the case of direct broadcasting, which is in the process of becoming an everyday occurrence, the signals sent to the satellite are demodulated by the satellite itself; as a result, the signals transmitted down to earth can be received directly from space by ordinary receivers, without the intervention of ground receiving stations. However, the signals transmitted upwards to the satellite remain inaccessible to the public even with this mode of transmission.

26.9 The legal problem stems from the wording of Article 3 of the Rome Convention, under which broadcasting means the transmission by wireless means for public reception of sounds or of images and sounds. The difficulties with regard to satellite transmission are twofold: on one hand, the signals emitted by the originating organization are not suitable for public reception; on the other hand, the derived signals, generally obtained by means of ground stations, are frequently transmitted to the public by wire and not by wireless means.

26.10 The Satellites Convention provides a solution by requiring Contracting States to take adequate measures to prevent the distribution of any programme-carrying signals by any distributor for whom the signal emitted to or passing through the satellite is not intended. "Distribution" is defined by the

Convention as the operation by which a distributor transmits derived signals to the public, and therefore also encompasses cable distribution.

C. MAIN FEATURES OF THE SPECIAL CONVENTIONS

26.11 While it can be said that the Phonograms Convention and the Satellites Convention supplement the Rome Convention to a certain extent, it should nevertheless be mentioned that their philosophy is different, in three main respects.

26.12 First, the Rome Convention gives the beneficiaries of neighboring rights essentially a right to authorization or prohibition, without of course overlooking the safeguarding of the rights of authors. The Phonograms and Satellites Conventions, on the other hand, do not introduce piracy rights but rather leave the Contracting States free to choose the legal means of preventing or repressing acts of piracy in that area.

26.13 Second, the Rome Convention is based on the "national treatment" principle. That means that the protection prescribed by the Rome Convention is only minimum protection and that, apart from the rights guaranteed by that Convention itself as constituting that minimum of protection, and within the limits of reservations conceded by it, performers, producers of phonograms and broadcasting organizations enjoy the same rights in countries party to the Convention as those countries grant their nationals. The Phonograms Convention does not speak of the system of "national treatment," but defines expressly the unlawful acts against which Contracting States have to provide effective protection; consequently, the States are not bound to grant foreigners protection against all acts prohibited by their national legislation for the protection of their own nationals. For instance, countries whose national legislation provides protection against the public performance of phonograms are not obliged to make this form of protection available to the producers of phonograms of other Contracting States, because the Phonograms Convention does not itself guarantee any protection against the use in public of lawfully reproduced and distributed phonograms. It should be mentioned, however, that even the Phonograms Convention is in no way to be interpreted as limiting the protection available to foreigners under any domestic law or international agreement (Article 7(1)). The question of national treatment does not arise, as a general rule in the Satellites Convention either. This Convention places Contracting States under the obligation to take the necessary steps to prevent just one type of activity, namely the distribution of programme-carrying signals by any distributor for whom the signals emitted to or passing through the satellite are not intended.

26.14 Third, it was in the interests of combating piracy over the widest possible area that the new international agreements were made open to all States members of the United Nations or any of the specialized organizations brought into relationship with the United Nations, or parties to the Statute of the International Court of Justice (virtually all States of the world); whereas the Rome Convention is a so-called "closed" Convention, its acceptance being reserved for States party to at least one of the two major international copyright conventions.

D. SUBSTANTIVE PROVISIONS OF THE
PHONOGRAMS CONVENTION

26.15 As far as the substantive provisions are concerned, the Phonograms Convention differs from the Rome Convention mainly as regards (i) the criteria of eligibility for protection, (ii) the scope of protection, and (iii) the means of ensuring the protection provided for.

26.16 The Phonograms Convention requires only the criterion of nationality as a condition of granting protection. Any Contracting State, however, which on October 29, 1971, afforded protection solely on the basis of the place of first fixation may, by a declaration deposited with the Director General of WIPO, declare that it will apply this criterion.

26.17 Protection is granted not only against making duplicates of the phonogram, but also against the distribution of illicit duplicates and importation of such duplicates for distribution (Article 2). On the other hand, the scope of protection does not extend to claiming remuneration for secondary uses of the phonogram.

26.18 The means by which the Phonograms Convention is to be implemented are a matter for domestic legislation. They may include protection by granting copyright in the phonogram, by granting other specific (neighboring) rights, by the law relating to unfair competition, or by penal sanctions (Article 3).

26.19 The Phonograms Convention permits the same limitations as those accepted in relation to the protection of authors. The Convention also permits compulsory licenses if reproduction is intended exclusively for teaching or scientific research, limited to the territory of the State whose authorities give the license, and in return for equitable remuneration.

26.20 Regarding the term of protection, the same minimum duration is required by the Phonograms Convention as by the Rome Convention: if the domestic law prescribes a specific duration for the protection, that duration shall not be less than 20 years from the end either of the year in which the sounds embodied in the phonogram were first fixed or of the year in which the phonogram was first published.

26.21 It should be noted that the Phonograms Convention also contains a provision concerning performers. Under its Article 7, the national legislation of each Contracting State may lay down, where necessary, the scope of protection afforded to performers whose performance is fixed on a phonogram and the conditions of enjoying such protection.

E. SUBSTANTIVE PROVISIONS OF THE
SATELLITES CONVENTION

26.22 The Satellites Convention enlarges the scope of the protection of broadcasting organizations by suppressing the unlawful distribution of programme-carrying signals transmitted by satellite irrespective of the fact that such signals are not suited to reception by the public, and, consequently, their emission does not constitute broadcasting according to the definition of this notion under the Rome Convention. Furthermore, the protection provided for by the Satellites Convention also applies when the derived signals are distributed by cable and not by wireless means, a kind of communication to the public of broadcasts not covered by the Rome Convention. Formally, however, the Convention gives no new right to the broadcasting organizations. It obliges the Contracting States to prevent the distribution of programme-carrying signals by any distributor from whom the signals passing through the satellite are not intended.

26.23 It should be noted that the Satellites Convention does not protect the transmitted program since the subject of the protection is the signals emitted by the originating organization. As regards the rights related to the programs, the Convention simply lays down that it may not be interpreted in any way as limiting or prejudicing the protection afforded to authors, to performers, to phonogram producers and to broadcasting organizations.

26.24 The Satellites Convention permits the distribution of programme-carrying signals by non-authorized persons if those signals carry short excerpts containing reports of current events or, as quotations, short excerpts of the program carried by the emitted signals, or, in the case of developing countries, if the program carried by the emitted signals is distributed solely for the purposes of teaching, including adult teaching or scientific research.

26.25 With regard to the duration of the protection, the Satellites Convention refers to national legislation in this special context. In any State in which the application of the above measures is limited in time, the duration is to be fixed by its domestic law.

26.26 The Satellites Convention is not of application when the signals emitted by the originating organization are intended for direct reception from a satellite by the public (Article 3). In such cases the signals emitted are not intended for any intervening distributor of derived signals; they are directly accessible to the public at large.

F. THE PHONOGRAMS AND SATELLITES CONVENTIONS AND DEVELOPING COUNTRIES

26.27 It is particularly significant that the States that have joined the Phonograms and Satellites Conventions, similar to the countries party to the Rome Convention, are not necessarily highly industrialized market economy States. Quite the contrary, of the 53 States bound by the Phonograms Convention, 24 are developing countries. Six of the 20 States party to the Satellites Convention are also developing countries. This may be explained by the role that protection of neighboring rights is capable of playing in the development of those countries.

26.28 By protecting the phonogram producers, the Phonograms Convention promotes the creation, particularly in the developing countries, of an industry in the tertiary sector of the economy whose vitality needs no demonstrating. Such an industry, while ensuring that the national culture is propagated both throughout the country itself and throughout the world, can also constitute a source of substantial revenue for the national economy and, where its activities extend beyond the frontiers, lead to an inflow of foreign currency. The international protection of phonogram producers also promotes the protection of expressions of folklore incorporated in phonograms against unlawful reproduction abroad.

26.29 By giving the phonogram producers the possibility of deriving profit from their productions internationally, the Phonograms Convention becomes an instrument serving to promote the artistic heritage and an indisputable encouragement to creativity. It is also a certain fact that if the interests of foreign performers and phonogram producers are equally safeguarded, national productions will enjoy greater dissemination and it will therefore be national works, and not above all foreign works, which will be increasingly used by the mass media and the public. Further, if the results of this type of activity are exported, it becomes necessary for these interests concerned to be protected on an international scale also, and that can be done by acceding to the relevant international conventions.

26.30 Finally, the broadcasting organizations play a part in developing countries since they also have an interest in protecting their costly programs against rebroadcast, reproduction and other communication to the public of their broadcasts, including broadcasting via satellites. Frequently, the broadcasting of a particular program, concert or other event is permitted only for given territories and on condition that no televised presentation is made outside that territory. The broadcasting organization therefore needs to be able to prohibit the rebroadcasting and presentation to the public of television shows. The same principle applies to the broadcasting of performances and recordings of expressions of national folklore. The broadcasting organization should have the possibility at the international level to prevent illicit distribution or fixation for the purpose of reproduction of its own broadcast programs in respect of creations belonging to the national heritage.

26.31 The recognition and international protection of the rights of performers, producers of phonograms and broadcasting organizations, in conjunction with copyright, quite definitely contribute to the development of nations, as does protection of intellectual property as a whole. Thus it is desirable that more and more developing countries recognize the necessity of establishing legal protection of authors, performers, producers of phonograms and broadcasting organizations as an interdependent system, both at the national and international levels.

26.32 The following 53 States were party to the Convention for the Protection of Producers and Phonograms Against Unauthorized Duplication of Their Phonograms as of October 1, 1996: Argentina, Australia, Austria, Barbados, Brazil, Bulgaria, Burkina Faso, Chile, China, Colombia, Costa Rica, Cyprus, Czech Republic, Denmark, Ecuador, Egypt, El Salvador, Fiji, Finland, France, Germany, Greece, Guatemala, Holy See, Honduras, Hungary, India, Israel, Italy, Jamaica, Japan, Kenya, Luxembourg, Mexico, Monaco, Netherlands, New Zealand, Norway, Panama, Paraguay, Peru, Republic of Korea, Russian Federation, Slovakia, Spain, Sweden, Switzerland, Trinidad and Tobago, United Kingdom, United States of America, Uruguay, Venezuela and Zaire.

26.33 The following 20 States were party to the Convention Relating to the Distribution of Programme-Carrying Signals Transmitted by Satellite as of October 1, 1996: Armenia, Australia, Austria, Bosnia and Herzegovina, Croatia, Germany, Greece, Italy, Kenya, Mexico, Morocco, Nicaragua, Panama, Peru, Portugal, Russian Federation, Slovenia, Switzerland, United States of America and Yugoslavia.

References for Section F
International Bureau of WIPO, *Basic Notions of Neighboring Rights—International Conventions in the Field of Neighboring Rights*, WIPO/CR/GE/93/3

CHAPTER 27

The International Convention for the Protection of New Varieties of Plants

A. INTRODUCTION

27.1 The availability to growers of improved plant breeding and new plant varieties is critically important to the agricultural and horticultural industries of all countries. Improved disease resistance, higher yields and improvements in a host of other features of plants can dramatically affect the economics of the production of a crop and its acceptability to its final consumers. The speed of events in international agricultural and horticultural developments today is such that improved varieties must be available to growers at the earliest possible moment if their competitiveness is to be assured.

27.2 However, the breeders of new varieties of plants have a particular vulnerability, since their new varieties, developed after many years of patient work and heavy investment, are frequently capable of self-reproduction with the result that the release of a small quantity of reproductive material of a plant variety can mean that it is thenceforth available to all. Experience has shown that the plant breeder cannot secure a sufficient economic return from his initial release of material of his variety to secure a reasonable return upon his investment and efforts. Accordingly, the granting to breeders of rights of exclusive exploitation of their varieties has proved to be essential to provide an incentive for private investment in plant breeding in many species.

B. THE INTERNATIONAL UNION FOR THE PROTECTION OF NEW VARIETIES OF PLANTS (UPOV)

(a) Background

27.3 The need for exclusive rights for plant breeders was recognized by the United States of America as early as 1930 when it introduced a special form of exclusive right called a plant patent which was available however only for asexually reproduced varieties and by a group of European states which came together in 1961 to establish the International Convention for the Protection of New Varieties of Plants which was subsequently revised in 1972 and 1978 and in its 1978 revised form is hereafter referred to as "the 1978 Act." The 1978 Act potentially protects all plant varieties irrespective of their mode of reproduction or of the technology used in their development.

27.4 The 1978 Act is, in effect, an agreement between States under which States adhering to the Convention undertake to create a system for the grant of plant breeders' rights, within their domestic laws, in accordance with internationally agreed and uniform principles. Each UPOV member State must entrust the granting of breeders' rights to an appropriate administrative unit. Under the 1978 Act, plant breeders' rights are granted in each member State for its own territory. They are not granted on an international basis.

27.5 The 1978 Act also establishes the International Union for the Protection of New Varieties of Plants which is known as UPOV (the name "UPOV" is an acronym derived from the French translation of these words).

27.6 UPOV is an international intergovernmental organization. This means that its members are States and not private associations or private individuals. UPOV is an independent organization with international legal personality. Its headquarters are in Geneva where it employs its own staff.

27.7 UPOV cooperates very closely in administrative matters with the World Intellectual Property Organization (WIPO), a specialized agency of the United Nations. The Secretary-General of UPOV is the Director General of WIPO, the UPOV headquarters is in the same building as WIPO, and UPOV receives a range of support services from WIPO.

27.8 The 1978 Act is the Act of the Convention that is in force. However, in March 1991, a Diplomatic Conference was held in Geneva which resulted in the unanimous adoption by the member States of UPOV of a new revised 1991 Act of the UPOV Convention ("the 1991 Act"). This new 1991 Act will not come into force until five States have acceded to it and even when it comes into force it will only bind States which have chosen to accede to it. Existing member States only become bound by the 1991 Act when they have modified their existing laws and deposited an instrument of accession to the new Act. The United States of America and Canada have changed their laws to conform with the new Act, while the European Union has introduced a form of protection based on the 1991 Act under which a breeder's right is granted which has effect throughout the European Union

27.9 The next section will consider the 1978 Act of the Convention. This is the Act which binds all existing member States of UPOV, and is the basis of the existing UPOV system of plant variety protection. The subsequent section will outline the 1991 Act.

(b) The Criteria for Protection

27.10 The 1978 Act provides a system for the protection of a new plant variety, that is to say, the physical unit of plant material selected by the plant breeder with its set of morphological and physiological characteristics. If a legal right is to be granted in respect of the unit of plant material that constitutes a plant variety and if that right is subsequently to be effectively enforced, the identity of the plant material must be established beyond doubt. When seeking to conclude whether particular plant material constitutes or belongs to a "variety" the classifier must exercise judgment but inevitable elements in making a judgment will always include the extent of its distinctness from other material, its uniformity in the sense that variations from a standard description are within reasonable limits and its stability in the sense that it will retain its distinguishing features from one generation to the next. The 1978 Act accordingly requires in Article 6 that member States adopt the three criteria of distinctness, uniformity (the 1978 Act uses the word "homogeneity") and stability as the technical basis for the protection of plant varieties and adds the further two requirements of commercial novelty and the submission of an acceptable denomination for the variety, a total of five criteria for protection.

27.11 A variety must be commercially novel to secure protection. Article 6(1)(b) of the 1978 Act provides that the variety must not, prior to the date of application, have been offered for sale or marketed with the agreement of the breeder in the territory of the State where the application in question has been filed. States are, however, given a choice in relation to this provision and are permitted, if they wish, to permit varieties to be offered for sale or market in their own territories for a maximum of one year prior to the date of application. In addition, the variety must not have been offered for sale or marketed with the agreement of the breeder in the territory of any other state for longer than six years, in the case of certain woody species, or for four years in the case of all other *species*. These periods of grace relating to commercialization in other countries, recognize the lengthy nature of trials to ascertain the agronomic value of varieties and enable the breeder to carry out necessary trials before making an application for protection without prejudicing his right to protection.

27.12 The novel variety must be given a denomination in accordance with the provisions of Article 13 of the 1978 Act. Article 13 provides that the variety must be designated by a denomination which is destined to be its generic designation and it establishes rules designed to ensure that, in the interests of growers and consumers, this denomination does indeed provide a clear-cut generic designation. Thus the denomination may not consist solely of figures, except where this is an established practice for designating varieties of a particular species. It must not be liable to mislead or cause confusion concerning the characteristics of the variety or its value or identity and it must, of course, be different from every designation which designates in any UPOV member State another variety of the same species or of a closely related species.

27.13 The technical criteria of distinctness, uniformity and stability, and the further criteria of commercial novelty and the establishment of a denomination accordingly represent the standard conditions that must be fulfilled to secure protection for a new plant variety under the laws of UPOV member States. The 1978 Act provides in Article 6(2) that, provided the breeder complies with its necessary formalities, a UPOV member State may not make the grant of protection subject to conditions other than the five conditions described above.

(c) The Scope of Protection

27.14 Article 5 of the 1978 Act establishes the nature of the rights that member States must as a minimum undertake to grant to breeders. Breeders must as a minimum be given the exclusive right to produce reproductive or vegetative propagating material of their varieties for the purposes of commercial marketing and the exclusive right to offer for sale and market such material of their varieties.

The breeder's right is limited to the production and sale of reproductive or vegetative propagating material of his variety. The breeder does not, for instance, in the case of a cereal variety, have the exclusive right to sell grain of that variety, but only seed. It is a question of fact to be established by evidence whether a sale is of seed or grain. A further very important aspect to note here is that under the 1978 Act the breeder's exclusive right relates only to production for the purposes of commercial marketing. If production of reproductive material is not for the purpose of the commercial marketing of the material or if such material is not marketed, it is not covered by the breeders' rights so that a farmer, for instance, who produces seed on his own farm for the purposes of resowing on his own farm, can do so freely without obligation to the breeder.

27.15 The 1978 Act only establishes the minimum scope of the right that States must grant. Member States are expressly permitted, under their own laws, if they so wish, to grant to breeders of a particular genera or species, a more extensive right than that described above, even extending to the marketed product of the variety. In practice, however, few states have availed themselves of this right.

27.16 Article 5 further provides that any authorization given by the breeder in relation to the production or marketing of his variety may be made subject to such conditions as he may specify. The breeder is thus to be free to decide whether he will exploit his exclusive right by producing and selling all the reproductive or propagating material of his variety that is needed by the market or whether he will grant licenses to others, perhaps in exchange for a royalty. The practice in individual states varies. In many countries, in relation to species where very large volumes of seed must be produced and sold, and where the ease of keeping their own seed influences the price which farmers will be prepared to pay, the practice of plant breeders is to select the least-cost method of production and distribution. For example, in the case of small grain cereals, in most European countries, licenses are granted very widely to organizations such as local cooperatives and grain merchants, who provide a wide range of services and supplies to farmers. Organizations of this kind produce seed locally under contract and sell it back to local farmers thus minimizing the cost of transportation. The breeder is content to receive a royalty on each ton of seed which is sold. In the case of more specialized seed production such as the production of some cross-pollinating species, of hybrid varieties, of high-quality vegetable seed or of new varieties of trees or vines, the practice of the breeder will probably be to control very tightly the production of seed or plants in order to maintain the quality and reputation of his variety. In these cases he may seek his reward directly in the price of the seed. Many different situations exist, however, depending upon the commercial structure of seed and nursery plant distribution in each country and the logistical aspects of the production and distribution of a particular species. The 1978 Act is silent on all these marketing questions. It simply requires of UPOV member States that they permit breeders to specify conditions of licenses for their varieties.

27.17 Article 5(3) of the 1978 Act contains a truly fundamental principle. It states that the authorization of the breeder shall not be required for the utilization of the variety as an initial source of variation for the purpose of creating other varieties. The only permitted exception to this rule arises when the repeated use of the variety is necessary for the commercial production of another variety. This limited exception relates to the use of an inbred line in the commercial production of seed of a hybrid. The free availability of protected varieties as a germ plasm source for other breeders is a fundamental tenet of the 1978 Act and demonstrates that its authors were agriculturalists who were totally aware of the nature of plant breeding and of the manner in which incremental progress is achieved by building upon the progress embodied in existing varieties.

27.18 The 1978 Act requires States to grant a minimum period of protection of 18 years in the case of vines, forest trees, fruit trees, and ornamental trees and 15 years in the case of all other species.

27.19 The 1978 Act does not immediately impose upon its member States the obligation to protect all botanical genera and species. The 1978 Act states that its provisions may be applied to all botanical genera and species, but it does not require member States to protect all botanical genera and species. What it does require is that member States apply the Convention to a minimum of five genera when first acceding to the UPOV Convention and that, over a period of years, they progressively apply the Convention to a greater number of protected species. Most member States protect all species of economic importance in their countries and, in an increasing number of cases, protect the entire plant kingdom.

27.20 Article 10 of the 1978 Act includes amongst its provisions one to the effect that the breeder of a protected variety shall forfeit his right if he is no longer in a position to provide the authorities with reproductive or propagating material capable of reproducing the protected variety with its morphological and physiological characteristics as defined when the right was granted. In other words, the breeder must competently maintain his variety if he wishes to retain the benefit of protection.

27.21 Article 2 of the 1978 Act provides that a state may provide protection for plant varieties in the form of plant variety protection or of a patent but once it has opted to protect varieties of a species by plant breeders' rights it may not subsequently protect varieties of that same species by patent. This is the so-called prohibition on "double protection."

27.22 Article 3 of the 1978 Act states that each member State must accord to nationals and residents of other member States the same treatment as far as the recognition and protection of their varieties are concerned as that which it accords to its own nationals.

27.23 Article 7 of the 1978 Act provides that member States shall only grant protection after the examination of the variety in the light of the criteria of distinctness, uniformity, stability and commercial novelty referred to above. This provision has been interpreted to mean that member States should require a growing test which should be conducted either by the State or by the breeder provided that the test follows relevant guidelines and that the breeder is required to supply a sample of the variety at the time of application and to permit persons authorized by the State to visit the trials.

27.24 Article 9 of the 1978 Act provides that UPOV member States may not restrict the exercise of the exclusive right accorded to the breeder otherwise than for reasons of public interest and that, where any such restriction is imposed, the member State involved shall take all necessary measures to ensure that the breeder receives equitable remuneration.

27.25 Article 10 of the 1978 Act provides that the right of the breeder should not be annulled unless it is shown that the variety did not fulfill the commercial novelty and distinctness requirements when the rights were granted, or be cancelled unless the breeder fails to maintain the variety or pay the necessary fees.

27.26 Article 12 of the 1978 Act requires member States to establish rules giving priority for a period of 12 months to an application for a variety where an application has already been filed for that variety in another country. This means that an application in a member State must be treated as if filed on the date of an earlier application in another member State for which priority is claimed.

27.27 Article 14 of the 1978 Act provides that the grant or refusal of breeders' rights for a variety must be independent from the regulation in any UPOV member State which are concerned with the production, certification and marketing of seeds.

27.28 Articles 1 to 14 of the 1978 Act are the Articles which establish the main legal rules which the member States of UPOV undertake to incorporate into their national laws. The remaining provisions of the 1978 Act are for the most part concerned with the establishment of UPOV and its management.

27.29 The question immediately arises: "Why should it be necessary to revise such an excellent Convention and what changes have been incorporated into the new 1991 Act of the Convention?"

C. THE 1991 ACT OF THE UPOV CONVENTION

27.30 Advances in technology and the experience of operating the Convention since 1961 led to a number of suggestions for improvements to the Convention. Accordingly, in 1987, the Council of UPOV decided to put in hand the work necessary to effect a revision of the 1978 Act. A meeting of UPOV with international non-governmental organizations (in effect a hearing at which the Council of UPOV listens to the views of international non-governmental organizations on a particular topic) had already been held in 1987 on possible changes to the Convention and influenced the decision of the Council to commence work on a revision. There followed two further meetings with international non-governmental organizations in 1989 and 1990 and seven working sessions in 1988, 1989 and 1990 of the Administrative and Legal Committee of UPOV which was charged by the Council with the task of preparing a draft of a revised Convention. The Council adopted in October 1990 a draft revised Convention ("the Basic Proposal") and decided to hold a Diplomatic Conference in March 1991 to revise the Convention.

27.31 In addition to the, then 20, member States of UPOV, some 30 observer States participated in the Conference, as well as 24 intergovernmental and non-governmental observer organizations. In excess of 130 proposals for amendments to the Basic Proposal were considered by the Conference which finally adopted unanimously on March 19, 1991, a revised 1991 Act of the UPOV Convention ("the 1991 Act"). Fifteen member States of UPOV signed the 1991 Act either at the conclusion of the Conference or during the period when it remained open for signature. The effect of signature is not, of course, to bind the signatory State but simply represents an acknowledgment of its intention to enact a law based on the Convention and, in due course, to ratify the Convention. It is only the ratification of the Convention by an existing member State which has signed the Convention, or accession to the Convention by a new member State, which creates an international legal obligation.

27.32 Article 37 of the 1991 Act provides that it will come into force one month after five States have deposited their instruments of adherence, provided that at least three of such instruments are deposited by existing member States of UPOV. After the entry into force of the 1991 Act, the 1978 Act will, in principle, be closed to further accessions.

27.33 However, two "periods of grace" were incorporated into the 1991 Act. The 1978 Act was to remain open for accession by developing countries until December 31, 1995, and by any other country until December 31, 1993. The period of grace in favor of developing countries recognized the fact that there is a sea change in attitude amongst developing countries in relation to the protection of plant varieties, but that it would take some time for those countries then expressing interest to actually introduce legislation. It was thought that whilst the 1978 Act was of great interest to many developing countries as a basis for national legislation, the 1991 Act might in some cases require further study prior to its incorporation into the national laws of some developing countries. The period of grace in favor of developing countries in no way implied that the new Act was not suitable for developing countries. On the contrary, the provisions relating to essentially derived varieties, for example, are of fundamental importance for developing countries. The period of grace for other countries took account of the fact that a number of States had already initiated proposals for legislation upon the basis of the 1978 Act, and the grace period until December 31, 1993, was to enable them to finalize their legislative activity and accede to the Convention on the basis of the 1978 Act.

27.34 Article 34(1)(b) of the 1991 Act provides for possible membership of UPOV by an intergovernmental organization. This provision was designed to open the possibility of membership by the European Economic Community if and when the proposal for the Council Regulation (EEC) on Community Plant Variety Rights was adopted by the Community. It was in fact adopted by the Community and came into force on 27 April, 1995. Article 26(6)(b) which concerns voting in the Council, and Article 6(3) and 16(3) concerning novelty and exhaustion also contain provisions which reflect the interests of the Community.

27.35 The structure of the 1978 Act was fundamentally revised in the new Act. In the 1991 Act, the articles are grouped together in ten chapters and the chapters follow a chronological order dealing first with the "General Obligations of the Contracting Parties," followed by "Conditions for the Grant of the Breeder's Right," provisions concerning the "Application for the Grant of the Breeder's Right," "The Rights of the Breeder," "Variety Denomination" and "Nullity and Cancellation of the Breeder's Right." The administrative and final provisions of the Convention are contained in the last three chapters.

27.36 The remainder of this chapter examines the text of the 1991 Act in the numerical order of the articles, mentioning the corresponding articles in the old text and the nature of the changes. No attempt is made to deal with every article or with every paragraph of every article. Only those which are of major importance from the substantive standpoint are addressed.

(a) Definitions

27.37 Article 1 contains "definitions" which are, for the most part, self-explanatory. Item (vi) contains a definition of "variety." The 1978 Act contains no definition of "variety" while the 1961 Act of the Convention provides that "For the purposes of this Convention, the word "variety" applies to any cultivator, clone, line, stock or hybrid which is capable of cultivation and which satisfies the provisions of subparagraph (1)(c) and (d) of Article 6." The provisions of these subparagraphs specify the conditions of homogeneity and stability which must be satisfied by a plant variety prior to a grant of breeders' rights. Whether a definition was necessary in the Convention at all was much discussed during preparations for the revision; patent circles, having earlier favored the introduction of a definition which would be the same for the purposes of patenting as for the purposes of plant variety protection, had more recently begun to suggest that a definition was unnecessary. It seems that patent circles were concerned that the definition of "variety" might embrace a plant cell line and that the exclusion provisions of Article 53(b) of the European Patent Convention, which exclude plant varieties from patenting, might be interpreted in the light of the new definition so as to exclude a plant cell line from patenting.

27.38 The definition of "variety" incorporated into the 1961 Act of the Convention is almost, but not quite, synonymous with "variety which is protectable under the Convention." In framing a definition in 1991, it was thought that there should be a clear distinction between the definition of "variety" and a variety which meets the technical criteria of Articles 7, 8 and 9 of the 1991 Act of the Convention so as to be a protectable variety. This is to ensure that a variety with a level of uniformity which is unacceptable for the purposes of a grant of rights may still exist as a "variety" and be taken into account, for example, for the purposes of common knowledge and distinctness under Article 7. The fact that the definition of "variety" is wider than "protectable variety" is made clear by the use of the words "irrespective of whether the conditions for the grant of a breeder's right are fully met" in the introductory phrase.

27.39 In order to establish an identity for any variety, protectable or otherwise, it must be distinct from other varieties, certain characteristics must be displayed with reasonable uniformity by its component individuals, and it must retain its identity from one generation to the next. The conditions of distinctness, uniformity and stability which are necessary for the purposes of establishing an identity for a unit of plant material to which breeders' rights are to attach, are thus also necessary, but possibly to a more limited extent, when deciding that particular plant material constitutes a variety. The three indents in the definition correspond respectively to the requirements for uniformity, distinctness and stability but were considered to set these requirements at a lower level than that necessary for protection.

27.40 The expression "plant grouping" used within the definition corresponds to the French "ensemble végétal" and leaves open the question whether a variety must invariably be constituted by more than one whole plant.

(b) The Basic Obligation of Contracting Parties

27.41 The basic obligation of States party to the Convention that "each Contracting Party shall grant and protect breeders' rights" is imposed by Article 2. "Breeder's right" is defined in Article 1 as "the right of the breeder provided for in this Convention." Accordingly, each State party to the Convention must grant protection on the conditions specified in Chapter III (and subject to no further and different conditions), with the minimum scope of protection required by Chapter V, and in accordance with all other relevant provisions of the Convention. The provisions of Article 2 correspond to the provisions of Articles 1 and 30(3) of the 1978 Act.

27.42 Unlike the first sentence of Article 2(1) of the 1978 Act, the 1991 Act is silent on the form of the breeder's right. It may take the form of a special *sui generis* breeder's right, or it may be called a "patent" or given any other designation provided it has the minimum substance provided for in the Convention. The 1991 Act equally contains no provision corresponding to the second sentence of Article 2(1) of the 1978 Act (the so-called "ban on double protection") so that a Contracting Party is, so far as the 1991 Act is concerned, free to protect varieties, in addition to the grant of a breeder's right, by the grant of other titles, particularly patents. A member State exercising this freedom to grant patents in addition to the breeder's right is free to decide whether an applicant must choose between a breeder's right and a patent, that is, if he applies for one, he cannot apply for the other, or whether he can apply for and be granted both the breeder's right and the patent. If, for any given variety, cumulative protection of this kind is obtained, the resolution of any conflict between the two kinds of protection is left to the legislation and courts of the member State where the titles were obtained and is not regulated by the Convention.

(c) Genera and Species to be Protected

27.43 Article 3 corresponds to Article 4 of the 1978 Act and is concerned with the genera and species to be protected. The system of the 1978 Act is to require member States to protect a minimum of five genera or species on accession to the Convention, and to require that thereafter member States protect genera or species on a progressive basis, leading to a minimum of 24 genera or species after eight years. Article 4 of the 1978 Act does contain a provision that member States should undertake to adopt all measures necessary for the progressive application of the Convention to the largest possible number of botanical genera and species, but in no way imposes on member States a clear commitment to protect the whole plant kingdom. Article 3 of the 1991 Act, however, requires existing member States to protect all plant genera and species five years after becoming bound by the new text and requires new member States to protect all plant genera and species ten years after they become bound by the 1991 Act, so that over time a worldwide UPOV system of plant variety protection will emerge which requires all member States to protect all plant genera or species.

27.44 The emergence of such a system has some interesting implications for the future, particularly in view of the increased scope of protection which is now provided in Article 14 of the new text. If Sweden, for example, decides to modify its national law and to ratify the 1991 Act, it should in due course become possible to protect a new banana variety in Sweden, notwithstanding the fact that the variety will never be grown there, but with a view to taking action against imports derived from the unlicensed propagation of the variety in countries where plant variety protection is not available. Thus far, Sweden, as an importing country, has probably been uninterested in the protection of bananas. The absence of any protection of the harvested material of a plant variety in importing countries has meant that it has also been a matter of no concern to exporting countries without breeders' rights if varieties were piratically exploited in their territories with no reward to the breeders of the varieties. This situation may well change in the future in relation to species where the harvested material of the variety moves in international trade.

(d) Conditions for the Grant of the Breeder's Right

27.45 These articles contain the conditions for the grant of a breeder's right and correspond to Article 6 of the 1978 Act of the Convention. There have been extensive changes in language but, except where some express reference is made below, there is no specific intention to change the substance.

27.46 Article 6 of the new text deals with the novelty-destroying prior commercialization of a variety. In the existing text, a variety must not have been offered for sale or marketed with the agreement of the breeder prior to the filing of an application for protection in the territory where the application is filed or, where the law of the relevant State so provides, for one year prior to such filing. The new text requires all member States to make provision in their laws for this one-year grace period; it is no longer optional.

27.47 The provisions of Article 6(1)(b) of the 1978 Act state that the variety must not have been offered for sale or marketed with the agreement of the breeder prior to the date of application. The provisions of Article 6 of the 1991 Act state that propagating or harvested material of the variety must not have been sold or otherwise disposed of to others by or with the consent of the breeder for the purposes of exploitation of the variety. The language of the 1991 Act is very different from that of Article 6(1)(b) of the 1978 Act and may have the effect of catching certain commercial activities with varieties that fall outside the corresponding provisions in the existing laws of some UPOV member States. An example might be the use of an inbred line as the parent of a hybrid where the inbred line was not itself sold or marketed. It has been claimed that the use of an inbred in this way, perhaps protected by trade secrecy, would not debar its breeder from applying for protection for the inbred line many years after it was first used for commercial purposes.

27.48 Paragraph (3) of Article 6 of the 1991 Act makes reference to special rules that may be adopted where sales are effected in the member States of an intergovernmental organization. This provision relates to the possible future UPOV membership of the EEC, and enables the EEC and its member States to enact provisions which will make a sale in one EEC member State a novelty-destroying event for all EEC member States so as to conform with the concept of the single market.

27.49 Article 7 of the 1991 Act deals with distinctness and requires simply that a variety must be clearly distinguishable from any other variety whose existence is a matter of common knowledge at the time of the filing of the application. The language of the existing text, by which a variety must be clearly distinguishable by one or more important characteristics from any other variety, has been abandoned since it was thought to be needlessly ambiguous. The word "important" has frequently suggested to persons reading the text of the 1978 Act for the first time that a variety must, to be protectable, be distinct from existing varieties by some feature related to merit. This has never been the case. The UPOV Convention affords protection to any variety which is clearly distinguishable from other varieties irrespective of any judgment concerning its worth. The view has been consistently taken over the years in UPOV circles that the worth or merit of a variety varies too greatly with time and environment to be used as a criterion for the grant of protection in an international intellectual property rights' system. The simplified new text avoids the ambiguity of the word "important."

27.50 The 1978 Act provided a non-exhaustive list of examples of common knowledge which included "an entry in an official register of varieties already made or in the course of being made," which plainly does not constitute common knowledge in the normal sense since the relevant information may not necessarily be publicly available. Accordingly, Article 7 in the new text leaves the notion of common knowledge undefined and refers only to the specific instances of applications for protection or entry in an official register where, for the purposes of the Convention, common knowledge is deemed to exist notwithstanding that the information may not be generally available.

27.51 An application for the grant of a breeder's right or for the entering of a variety in an official register of varieties does not, however, make the variety in question a matter of common knowledge unless the application leads to the granting of a breeder's right or the entering of the variety in an official register of varieties. This is to avoid a situation where the system becomes cluttered with large numbers of "varieties" which were the subject of applications which have been refused or withdrawn and which no longer exist since they have been discarded by their breeders.

27.52 The language of Articles 8 and 9 of the 1991 Act, dealing with uniformity and stability respectively, is different from that in the corresponding provisions of the 1978 Act but there is no intended change in substance.

(e) Examination of the Application

27.53 Article 12 of the 1991 Act deals with the examination of the application and corresponds to Article 7 of the 1978 Act. There is some change of emphasis in the new text in that it expressly makes reference to the authority responsible for the test "taking into account the results of growing tests or other trials which have already been carried out." The eventual extension of protection to the whole plant kingdom under Article 3 of the 1991 Act will mean that examining authorities may be called upon to examine plant varieties of any species for distinctness, uniformity and stability, including species which are rare or unknown or in relation to which the authority has little or no knowledge or experience. Clearly in these circumstances, the authority may not itself be in a position to conduct the necessary tests and may find it necessary to ask the breeder to conduct tests or to take into account data which has been generated by the breeder. In cases of this kind, tests conducted by the breeder may well be acceptable provided that the data in question is presented in a common format and is generated by tests which follow the principles established in the General Introduction to the UPOV Guidelines for the Conduct of Tests for Distinctness, Uniformity and Stability, and that a sample of the variety is made available to the authority at the date of application.

(f) Provisional Protection

27.54 Provisional protection is dealt with in Article 7(3) of the 1978 Act which does not, however, make it obligatory for member States to provide provisional protection. Article 13 of the 1991 Act, however, obligates member States to make provision for protecting the interests of the breeder during the period between the filing or the publication of an application and the subsequent grant. The Article requires Contracting Parties to ensure that, as a minimum, the holder of the breeder's right should be entitled to equitable remuneration in respect of acts which will require the breeder's authorization once the right has been granted. The Article reflects the present practice of some countries by permitting Contracting Parties to provide that the provision of protection shall only take effect in relation to persons whom the breeder had notified of the filing of the application.

(g) Scope of the Breeder's Right

27.55 Article 5 of the 1978 Act provides that the prior authorization of the breeder "shall be required for:

(1)   the production for purposes of commercial marketing;
(2)   the offering for sale;
(3)   the marketing.

of the reproductive or vegetative propagating material, as such, of the variety." The article further provides that "vegetative propagating material shall be deemed to include whole plants" and that "the right of the breeder shall extend to ornamental plants or parts thereof, normally marketed for purposes other than propagation, when they are used commercially as propagating material in the production of ornamental plants or cut flowers."

27.56 The fact that the breeder's authorization is only required for the production of propagating material "for purposes of commercial marketing" means that production of propagating material that is not intended for marketing, but only for use on the farm where it was produced, falls outside the scope of protection. This has the effect of creating implicitly the so-called "farmer's privilege" whereby farmers may replant on their farms propagating material from the previous year's harvest.

27.57 Article 14(1) of the 1991 Act provides that, in respect of the propagating material of a protected variety, any production, reproduction (multiplication), conditioning for the purpose of propagation, offering for sale, selling or other marketing, exporting, importing, or stocking for any of these purposes, shall require the authorization of the breeder. Accordingly, the basic scope of the protection extends to all production or reproduction (multiplication) without a reference to its purpose and, unlike the 1978 Act, does not have the effect of creating, by implication, a "farmer's privilege."

27.58 The very widely differing natures of the agricultural industries of UPOV member States and the varying political situations in these States have nonetheless made it essential to include in the new Act a provision entitling States on an optional basis to except the planting of farm-saved seed from the requirement for the breeder's authorization. The provision in question is contained in Article 15(2). It provides that "each Contracting Party may, within reasonable limits and subject to the safeguarding of the legitimate interests of the breeder, restrict the breeder's right in relation to any variety in order to permit farmers to use for propagating purposes, on their own holdings, the product of the harvest which they have obtained by planting, on their own holdings, the protected variety." The structure of the provision should ensure that countries give careful thought to the interests of plant breeders when exercising this option. It is hoped that States will examine the issues involved on a species by species basis. The Diplomatic Conference formally recommended that the provision of Article 15(2) "should not be read so as to be intended to open the possibility of extending the practice commonly called "farmer's privilege" to sections of agricultural or horticultural production in which such a privilege is not a common practice."

27.59 Apart from the special provision relating to the production of ornamental plants or cut flowers, the mandatory minimum scope of protection under Article 5 of the 1978 Act is limited to the reproductive or vegetative propagating material, as such, of the variety. Paragraph (4) of Article 5 does provide that member States may grant to breeders, in respect of certain botanical genera or species, a more extensive right than that otherwise provided in Article 5, extending, in particular, to the marketed product. Few States have taken advantage of this optional provision. A major question debated in the course of the revision process was whether the scope of the breeder's right should be extended in a more general way to the harvested material of the protected variety or to products produced by processing the harvested material.

27.60 The Diplomatic Conference decided the above question positively. Article 14(2) of the 1991 Act does make provision for the scope of the breeder's right to extend to harvested material including entire plants and parts of plants where these have been obtained through the unauthorized use of propagating material of a protected variety, but qualifies the scope by providing that this scope of protection exists, "unless the breeder has had reasonable opportunity to exercise his right in relation to the propagating material of the variety."

27.61 The majority of the member States of UPOV who voted in the Diplomatic Conference on the text of Article 14(2) were not prepared to extend to the breeder an untrammeled choice between the exercise of his right in relation to the propagating material and its exercise in relation to the harvested material. They were not, for example, prepared to permit the breeder to be totally free to exercise his intellectual property right over the grain instead of the seed. There was, however, general agreement in the Diplomatic Conference that a breeder needed to have a right exercisable over the harvested material of his variety when he had had no opportunity to exercise a right in relation to the propagating material. The most commonly quoted example of the breeder being unable to exercise his right was that of the piratical use of a breeder's variety in another country, perhaps a country which makes no provision for plant variety protection, followed by a subsequent import of harvested material of the variety into a country where the variety is protected. A further example would be the exercise by the breeder of his right in relation to any harvested material which arises from an infringement, of which he was unaware, of his rights in respect of propagating material.

27.62 Article 14(2) provides that the breeder has a right to protection in relation to harvested material "unless he has reasonable opportunity to exercise his right in relation to the propagating material." Accordingly, it is the alleged infringer who will usually bear the burden of establishing that the breeder has indeed had reasonable opportunity to exercise his right in relation to the propagating material of the variety.

27.63 Article 14(3) of the 1991 Act provides for the further extension of the right of the breeder to products made directly from harvested material. This provision is not, however, part of the mandatory minimum scope of protection under the 1991 Act. States adhering to the 1991 Act may choose whether they wish to extend the breeder's right in accordance with Article 14(3). Under the Article, the authorization of the breeder is required to produce, sell, market, etc. any product made directly from harvested material, provided that the harvested material itself results from infringement. Once again, the exercise by the breeder of any right under the Article in relation to products made directly from harvested material exists "unless the breeder has had reasonable opportunity to exercise his right in relation to the harvested material." The provisos attached to Article 14(2) and (3) together constitute what has been called a "cascade." The idea of those who promote the notion of a cascade is that the breeder should only exercise his right in relation to harvested material if he has not been able to exercise it in relation to the propagating material and that he should only exercise his right in relation to a product made directly from harvested material if he has been unable to exercise his right in relation to the harvested material.

27.64 As already mentioned, interesting future consequences arising from the extended scope of protection in the 1991 Act can be envisaged once protection extends to the whole plant kingdom.

(h) Essentially Derived Varieties

27.65 Under the provisions of Article 6(1)(a) of the 1978 Act, any variety is protectable which, *inter alia*, is clearly distinguishable, at the time of application, by one or more important characteristics from other commonly known varieties and which is sufficiently uniform and stable. Article 5(3) of the 1978 Act provides that a protected variety may be used as an initial source of variation for the purpose of creating other varieties. The two provisions taken together create a situation in which an existing protected variety may be used as a source of initial variation and a variety selected therefrom may be freely exploited by the selector free of any obligation to the breeder of the protected variety, provided that the selection is clearly distinguishable by one or more important characteristics from the protected variety. Since the word "important" in this context has been construed to mean "important for the purposes of making a distinction" and not "important in the sense of having value," this has meant that a person selecting a mutant or a minor variant from an existing variety or inserting an additional gene into it by back-crossing or some other procedure can protect the resulting variety without rewarding the original breeder for his contribution to the final result. Typical examples are the selection of a color mutant from an ornamental variety, the insertion of a single gene into a maize line by back-crossing (under the favorable conditions of the tropics, multiple back-crosses can be effected in one year) and more recently, the insertion of a single gene by genetic engineering. The fact that the 1978 Act does not enable the breeder to prevent breeding approaches of this kind has been criticized as unjust by industrial circles and the 1991 Act remedies this situation by introducing the principle of "essential derivation." Article 14(5) of the 1991 Act provides that a variety which is essentially derived from a protected variety cannot be exploited without the authorization of the breeder of the protected variety. A variety is deemed to be essentially derived from another variety ("the initial variety") for this purpose when

"(a) it is predominantly derived from the initial variety or from a variety that is itself predominantly derived from the initial variety while retaining the expression of the essential characteristics that result from the genotype or combination of genotypes of the initial variety;
(b) it is clearly distinguishable from the initial variety;
(c) except for the differences which result from the act of derivation, it conforms to the initial variety in the expression of the essential characteristics that result from the genotype or combination of genotypes of the initial variety."

27.66 Article 14(5) provides a non-exhaustive list of examples of acts that may result in essential derivation including the selection of a natural or induced mutant, or of a somaclonal variant, the selection of a variant individual from plants of an initial variety, back-crossing, or transformation by genetic engineering.

27.67 It is not envisaged that a determination concerning the essential derivation of a variety will be made by an examining office as part of the grant procedure, but rather that the question will be resolved between plant breeders by agreement or in the last resort through litigation.

27.68 The existence of the new principle should ensure in future that those working as innovators in the field of plants will reach agreement before they undertake a program of activity which could result in varieties that are essentially derived from protected varieties. It is hoped that in the vast majority of cases amicable arrangements will be made between plant breeders and/or biotechnologists. If a plant breeder inserts a gene falling within the claims of an invention relating to genetic information (a "patented gene") into his variety, the resulting variety could fall within the scope of the patent enabling the patentee, in effect, to prohibit the exploitation of the variety. If, on the other hand, the patentee inserts the patented gene into the same variety, the breeder of the variety has no possibility at present to forbid the exploitation of the modified variety. In future, if a patentee of a gene inserts his patented gene into a protected variety, there will exist the possibility that the modified variety will be essentially derived and fall within the scope of protection of the protected variety. It is thought that the new balance established between the two systems in this way will facilitate the exchange of technology between plant breeders and biotechnologists. Plant breeders and biotechnologists are described here as if they pursue fundamentally separate activities. UPOV is well aware that their activities may be pursued in one and the same organization or by one person but it does still help, occasionally, for present purposes to talk of the two activities separately. It should be noted that there is no suggestion in the essential derivation provision that the breeder of an essentially derived variety should be able to force the breeder of the initial variety to grant a license through some compulsory license procedure. This possibility was considered and rejected in the course of the revision process.

(i) Exceptions to the Breeder's Right

27.69 A description has already been given, in connection with the scope of protection, of the provisions of Article 15(2) relating to an optional exception from the scope of protection in favor of certain farmers in certain circumstances. Article 15(1)(iii) provides that "acts done for the purpose of breeding other varieties" are compulsorily excepted from the breeder's right. This provision reproduces the substance of Article 5(3) of the 1978 Act whereby the authorization of the breeder is not required for the utilization of a protected variety as an initial source of variation for the purpose of creating other varieties, thus creating the so-called "breeder's exemption." This is a very important feature of the Convention and is strongly supported by plant breeders and by interested circles generally. The breeder's exemption principle was strongly reaffirmed by the Diplomatic Conference. Some parties have sought to suggest that the introduction of the principle of essential derivation represents a fundamental departure from the breeder's exemption. Essential derivation is not seen in this light in UPOV. A variety will be essentially derived from another only when it retains the expression of the essential characteristics that result from the genotype or combination of genotypes of the initial variety. Accordingly, a variety will only be caught by the essential derivation provision when it resembles the initial variety very closely and uses virtually the whole genetic structure of the initial variety apart from specific limited modifications. Any variety may still be used under the 1991 Act of the Convention for the purpose of breeding other varieties and, unless they fall within the limited category of varieties which are essentially derived, such newly bred varieties may be freely exploited. The nature of the essential derivation principle is such that any breeder who embarks upon a program which will result in a variety which is essentially derived, will know what he is doing and why he is doing it and will either reach agreement with the breeder of the initial variety or will take the risk that the time and effort of his program will be wasted if the breeder of the initial variety declines to grant a license.

27.70 The new principle is seen in UPOV circles as an important extension of the zone of protection around a protected variety. This zone will in future comprise the minimum distance that results from the existing distinctness rule together with an additional zone created by the essential derivation principle.

(j) Exhaustion of the Breeder's Right

27.71 The breeder's right (Article 16) does not extend to acts concerning any material of the protected variety which has been sold or otherwise marketed by the breeder or with his consent, unless such acts

(1) involve further propagation of the variety; or
(2) involve an export of material of the variety, which enables the propagation of the variety, into a country which does not protect varieties of the plant genus or species to which the variety belongs, except where the exported material is for final consumption purposes.

The breeder's right to prohibit propagation of the variety is thus never exhausted.

(k) Duration of the Breeder's Right

27.72 Article 19 adjusts the minimum period of the breeder's right from 18 years for trees and vines and 15 years for all other species to periods of 25 years and 20 years respectively for these same categories. In large measure, these adjustments reflect the existing practice of member States. The substitution of the 20-year period for the 18-year period of protection will have the effect that the period of protection available for the majority of applicants in the plant breeders' rights system will be the same as that available in the patent system.

(l) Administrative and Final Provisions

27.73 For the most part, the administrative and final provisions of the 1991 Act, which are contained in Articles 21 to 42, reproduce the substance of the 1978 Act.

27.74 Article 35 of the 1991 Act is worthy of comment. It provides that any State which, at the time of becoming a party to the 1991 Act, is a party to the Act of 1978 and which, as far as varieties reproduced asexually are concerned, provides for protection by an industrial property title other than a breeder's right shall have the right to continue to do so without applying this Convention to those varieties. This provision is designed, as was Article 37 of the 1978 Act, specifically for the situation of the United States of America, which protects asexually reproduced plant varieties, other than potatoes and Jerusalem artichokes, by a special form of plant patent (which does not strictly accord with the provisions of the UPOV Convention) and which protects sexually reproduced varieties (other than hybrids) by the Plant Variety Protection Act (which does accord with the provision of the UPOV Convention). Accordingly, unless the United States of America changes its law rather fundamentally, it will not be in a position to meet the requirements of Articles 2 and 3 which will ultimately require it to grant and protect breeders' rights (that is rights which accord with the UPOV Convention) for all plant genera and species. Article 35 of the 1991 Act, which can only apply to the United States of America, enables it in large measure to continue with its present system, unless or until, of course, it decides to rationalize the present provisions of its law.

D. RECENT DEVELOPMENTS

27.75 In Europe, Portugal, the Russian Federation and Ukraine have laws which accord with the UPOV Convention and have taken the first steps towards accession to the 1978 Act, and in the case of the Russian Federation, also to the 1991 Act. Belarus, Bulgaria, Estonia, Moldova, Kazakhstan, Romania and Uzbekistan also have plant variety protection laws or drafts at an advanced stage.

27.76 In Latin America, Chile, Colombia and Paraguay have laws which conform with the UPOV Convention and have taken the first steps towards accession to the 1978 Act. A "consensus draft" has been prepared in Brazil which has not so far been presented to the Congress. On October 21, 1993, the Commission of the Cartagena Agreement adopted Decision 345 which brought into existence a system of plant variety protection within the domestic laws of Bolivia, Colombia, Ecuador, Peru and Venezuela. The provisions of Decision 345 are such that member States may, optionally, adjust their laws so as to conform with either the 1978 or the 1991 Acts. The law of Colombia is based upon Decision 345 and a national implementing Decree, Number 533. It incorporates virtually all the improvements in protection of the 1991 Act. Mexico is required by the terms of the North American Free Trade Agreement (NAFTA) to introduce a law which will conform with the 1978 or 1991 Act. Costa Rica, Cuba, Panama, Guatemala and Honduras have recently expressed interest in legislating in this field. It would seem that well before the end of the century virtually all Latin-American countries will have laws for the protection of new plant varieties which accord with the UPOV Convention and many of them will have become member States of UPOV.

27.77 In Asia, China, India, Indonesia, Malaysia, Pakistan, the Philippines, the Republic of Korea and Thailand have draft laws at an advanced stage.

27.78 In Africa, Kenya and Zimbabwe have laws which largely accord with the UPOV Convention, while Morocco, Tanzania and Zambia have draft laws at an advanced stage. Interest in legislation has been expressed by Côte d'Ivoire, Malawi, Morocco, Senegal and Uganda.

27.79 Protection of plant varieties is addressed in the TRIPS Agreement under the GATT Uruguay Round. Article 27 of that Agreement, which relates to patents, provides that States may exclude from patentability "plants and animals other than microorganisms and essentially biological processes for the production of plants and animals other than non-biological and microbiological processes. However, Members shall provide for the protection of plant varieties either by patents or by an effective *sui generis* system or by any combination thereof." A model of an "effective *sui generis* system" is provided by the UPOV Convention.

27.80 The following 31 States were party to the International Convention for the Protection of New Varieties of Plants (UPOV) as of October 1, 1996: Argentina, Australia, Austria, Belgium, Canada, Chile, Colombia, Czech Republic, Denmark, Finland, France, Germany, Hungary, Ireland, Israel, Italy, Japan, Netherlands, New Zealand, Norway, Poland, Portugal, Slovakia, South Africa, Spain, Sweden, Switzerland, Ukraine, United Kingdom, United States of America and Uruguay. The 1991 Act, which is not yet in force, has been signed by 16 States as of October 1, 1996: Belgium, Canada, Denmark, France, Germany, Ireland, Israel,

Italy, Netherlands, New Zealand, South Africa, Spain, Sweden, Switzerland, United Kingdom and United States of America. Numerous other States have either introduced laws which accord with the UPOV Conventions or are studying the possibility of doing so.

References for Section D
The International Union for the Protection of New Varieties of Plants and the Basic Principles of
the International Convention for the Protection of New Varieties of Plants, WIPO/ACAD/E/94/26

CHAPTER 28

The Agreement on Trade-Related Aspects of Intellectual Property Rights ("TRIPS")

A. INTRODUCTION

(a) GATT, the WTO and the TRIPS Agreement

28.1 The Uruguay Round of multilateral trade negotiations held under the framework of the General Agreement on Tariffs and Trade ("GATT") was concluded on December 15, 1993. The agreement embodying the results of those negotiations, the Agreement Establishing the World Trade Organization ("WTO Agreement"), was adopted on April 15, 1994, in Marrakesh.

28.2 Those negotiations included, for the first time within the GATT, discussions on aspects of intellectual property rights which impacted on international trade. The result of those negotiations, contained in an Annex to the WTO Agreement, was the Agreement on Trade-Related Aspects of Intellectual Property Rights (the "TRIPS Agreement").

28.3 The WTO Agreement, including the TRIPS Agreement (which is binding on all WTO Members), entered into force on January 1, 1995. The former agreement established a new organization, the World Trade Organization ("WTO"), which began its work on January 1, 1995.

(b) Transitional Arrangements and Technical Cooperation (Part VI)

28.4 No Member of WTO shall be obliged to apply the provisions of the TRIPS Agreement before the expiry of a general period of one year following the date of entry into force of the Agreement Establishing the WTO (that is, before January 1, 1996). (Article 65.1) However, additional transitional periods are available for certain countries. The date on which the relevant transitional period expires for a Member is referred to as the date of application of the Agreement for that Member.

28.5 Developing countries which are members of WTO, and also countries which are in the process of transformation into a market, free-enterprise economy and which are undertaking structural reform of their intellectual property systems and facing special problems in the preparation and implementation of intellectual property laws and regulations, are entitled to delay for a further period of four years (that is, until January 1, 2000) the date of application of the Agreement, except for obligations concerning national treatment and most-favored-nation treatment. (Article 65.2 and 65.3)

28.6 Developing countries which are obliged by the Agreement to extend product patent protection to types of products not previously patentable in that country may avail themselves of an additional five years (that is, until January 1, 2005) before applying the provisions of the agreement to such products. (Article 65.4)

28.7 Least-developed country Members are not required to apply the provisions of the Agreement, other than those concerning national treatment and most-favoured-nation treatment, for a period of 10 years from the general date of application of the Agreement (that is, until January 1, 2006). That period will be extended upon duly motivated request. (Article 66.1)

28.8 The TRIPS Agreement also requires developed country Members to provide, on request and on mutually agreed terms and conditions, technical and financial cooperation in favor of developing and least-developed country Members, including assistance in preparation of laws and support regarding establishment or reinforcement of domestic offices and agencies, including training of personnel. (Article 67)

(c) Institutional Arrangements (Part VII)

28.9 The WTO Agreement creates a three-tiered organizational structure for the WTO. The highest tier is the Ministerial Conference, which meets at least once every two years. (Article IV.1) It has the authority to take decisions on all matters under the WTO Agreement. The second tier is the General Council, consisting of representatives of all the Members, which is to meet "as appropriate" to carry out its own duties as well as those of the Ministerial Conference in the intervals between meetings of the latter body. (Article IV.2) The General Council also serves as the Dispute Settlement Body and the Trade Policy Review Body. (Article IV.3 and IV.4)

28.10 The WTO Agreement (Article IV.5) also establishes a Council for Trade-Related Aspects of Intellectual Property Rights (the "TRIPS Council") which, under the general guidance of the General Council, is to oversee the functioning of the TRIPS Agreement. (Article IV.5) Membership in the TRIPS Council is open to representatives of all Members. Under the provisions of the TRIPS Agreement (Part VII, Article 68), the TRIPS Council is charged with monitoring the operation of the TRIPS Agreement and Members' compliance with the obligations under that Agreement. The TRIPS Council shall also review the implementation of the TRIPS Agreement after the expiration of the transitional period for developing countries (that is, after January 1, 2000), and every two years thereafter (or when amendment or modification is warranted by new developments). (Article 71.1)) The first meeting of the TRIPS Council was held on March 9, 1995.

(d) Arrangements for Cooperation with WIPO

28.11 Consultations to establish arrangements for cooperation and a mutually supportive relationship between the WTO and WIPO concerning intellectual property are required by the TRIPS Agreement. The Preamble of the Agreement contains the following statement: "Desiring to establish a mutually supportive relationship between the WTO and the World Intellectual Property Organization as well as other relevant international organizations..."

28.12 The TRIPS Agreement further states that the TRIPS Council, in carrying out its functions, may consult with and seek information from any source it deems appropriate and that, in consultation with WIPO, the Council is to seek to establish, within one year of its first meeting, appropriate arrangements for cooperation with bodies of WIPO. (Article 68).

28.13 Consultations for specific areas of cooperation between WIPO and WTO are also required by the Agreement. In particular, Article 63.2, which concerns notification of laws and regulations by Members to the TRIPS Council, states that "The Council shall attempt to minimize the burden on Members in carrying out this obligation and may decide to waive the obligation to notify such laws and regulations directly to the Council if consultations with WIPO on the establishment of a common register containing these laws and regulations are successful. The Council shall also consider in this connection any action required regarding notifications pursuant to the obligations under this Agreement stemming from the provisions of Article 6ter of the Paris Convention (1967)."

B. GENERAL PROVISIONS, BASIC PRINCIPLES AND FINAL PROVISIONS (PARTS I AND VII)

28.14 A basic principle concerning the nature and scope of obligations under the TRIPS Agreement is that Members must give effect to the provisions of the Agreement and accord the treatment provided for in the Agreement to the nationals of other Members. A "national" is understood as meaning those natural or legal persons who would be eligible for protection if all Members of WTO were also bound by the Paris, Berne and Rome Conventions and by the Washington Treaty on Intellectual Property in Respect of Integrated Circuits (the "IPIC Treaty").

28.15 Members are free to determine the appropriate method of implementing the provisions of the TRIPS Agreement within their own legal system and practice, and may implement more extensive protection than is required, provided that such additional protection does not contravene other provisions of the Agreement. (Article 1.1 and 1.3)

(a) Definition of Intellectual Property

28.16 The TRIPS Agreement states that, for the purposes of the Agreement, the term "intellectual property" refers to all categories of intellectual property that are the subject of Sections 1 through 7 of Part II of the TRIPS Agreement, namely, copyright and neighboring rights, trademarks, geographical indications, industrial designs, patents, layout-designs (topographies) of integrated circuits, and undisclosed information. (Article 1.2)

(b) Incorporation-by-Reference of the Paris and Berne Conventions

28.17 The TRIPS Agreement is built on the century-old principles embodied in the Paris Convention for the Protection of Industrial Property and the Berne Convention for the Protection of Literary and Artistic Works. In fact, almost all the substantive provisions of these two Conventions are incorporated by reference directly into the TRIPS Agreement.

28.18 Concerning industrial property, the TRIPS Agreement requires that Members comply with Articles 1 through 12, and Article 19, of the Paris Convention, in respect of Parts II, III and IV of the Agreement. (Article 2.1) This includes all of the substantive provisions of the Paris Convention.

28.19 In the field of copyright, Members are required to comply with Articles 1 through 21 of the Berne Convention and its Appendix. However, Members do not have rights or obligations in respect of Article 6bis of the Berne Convention concerning moral rights, or of the rights derived therefrom. (Article 9.1)

28.20 The TRIPS Agreement, however, stipulates that nothing in Parts I to IV of the Agreement shall derogate from existing obligations that Members may have to each other under the Paris or Berne Conventions. (Article 2.2)

(c) The Principle of National Treatment

28.21 TRIPS provides for the principle of national treatment, requiring that Members accord the treatment provided for in the Agreement to the nationals of other Members, the latter defined in terms, for the corresponding rights, of the relevant provisions of the Paris, Berne and Rome Conventions, and the IPIC Treaty. Exceptions provided for under the relevant conventions are respected within the context of the TRIPS Agreement. As regards industrial property and copyright, this principle applies to all rights. As regards rights in respect of performers, producers of phonograms and broadcasting organizations, the obligation only applies in respect of the rights provided under the Agreement. (Article 3) Also exempted from this principle are procedures provided in multilateral agreements concluded under the auspices of WIPO relating to the acquisition or maintenance of intellectual property rights. (Article 5)

(d) The Most-Favored-Nation Principle (MFN)

28.22 The TRIPS Agreement contains a principle, the most-favoured-nation principle, which has not traditionally been provided for in the context of intellectual property rights, at least on the multilateral level. This principle provides that any advantage, favor, privilege or immunity granted by a Member to the nationals of any other country (whether a Member or not) shall be accorded immediately and unconditionally to the nationals of all other Members, with certain specified exemptions. (Article 4) As is the case for national treatment, procedures provided in multilateral agreements concluded under the auspices of WIPO relating to the acquisition or maintenance of intellectual property rights are exempted from this principle. (Article 5)

(e) Protection of Existing Subject Matter

28.23 The TRIPS Agreement contains specific provisions regarding the effect of the Agreement on the subject matter of intellectual property rights that exists on the date of application of the Agreement in a Member. While the Agreement does not give rise to obligations in respect of acts which occurred before the date of application of the Agreement for the Member in question (Article 70.1), the Agreement does give rise to obligations in respect of all subject matter existing and protected at the date of application of the Agreement, or which meets or comes subsequently to meet the criteria for protection under the terms of the Agreement (Article 70.2). However, copyright obligations with respect to existing works and obligations with respect to the rights of producers of phonograms and performers in existing phonograms are determined solely under Article 18 of the Berne Convention. (Article 70.2)

28.24 A member may provide for limited remedies for acts which become infringing as a result of the implementation of the Agreement and which were commenced, or in respect of which a significant investment was made, before the date of acceptance of the Agreement. These must include at least the payment of equitable remuneration. (Article 70.4)

28.25 There are certain exceptions to these general rules. In particular, there is no obligation to restore protection to subject matter which has fallen into the public domain. (Article 70.3) In addition, certain obligations concerning computer programs, cinematographic works and phonograms (Articles 11 and 14(4)) need not be applied with respect to originals or copies purchased prior to the date of application of this Agreement. (Article 70.5) Further, provisions concerning guidelines for use without authorization (Article 31) and non-discrimination as to the field of technology (Article 27.1) need not be applied to use without the authorization of the right holder where authorization for such use had been granted by the government before the date the Agreement became known. (Article 70.6)

28.26 Applications for protection of intellectual property rights which are pending on the date of application of the Agreement may be amended to claim any enhanced protection provided under the Agreement, but such amendments may not include new matter. (Article 70.7)

(f) Reservations

28.27 Reservations may not be entered in respect of any of the provisions of the Agreement without the consent of the other Members. (Article 72)

(g) Security Exceptions

28.28 The Agreement provides a general exception for matters which are deemed to be essential to national security interests. In particular, a Member is not required to furnish any information if it considers disclosure to be contrary to its essential security interests. In addition, it may take any action which it considers necessary for the protection of its essential security interests relating to fissionable materials or the materials from which they are derived, relating to traffic in arms, ammunition and implements of war and to such traffic in other goods and materials as is carried on directly or indirectly for the purpose of supplying a military establishment, or taken in time of war or other emergency in international relations. It may also take any action in pursuance of its obligations under the United Nations Charter for the maintenance of international peace and security. (Article 73)

C. STANDARDS CONCERNING THE AVAILABILITY, SCOPE AND USE OF INTELLECTUAL PROPERTY RIGHTS (PART II)

28.29 Part II of the TRIPS Agreement provides minimum standards concerning the availability, scope and use of intellectual property rights. This Part contains eight sections relating, respectively, to copyright and related rights, trademarks, geographical indications, industrial designs, patents, layout-designs (topographies) of integrated circuits, protection of undisclosed information and control of anti-competitive practices in contractual licenses (the latter subject is not contained in the definition of intellectual property of Article 1.2).

(a) Copyright and Related Rights (Section 1)

28.30 The essential elements of the standards concerning the availability, scope and use of copyright and related rights include the following:

(1) members must comply with Articles 1-21 of the 1971 Paris Act of the Berne Convention and, where applicable, with the Appendix to that Act (containing special provisions for developing countries). However, Members do not have rights or obligations under the Agreement concerning the subject matter of Article 6*bis* of the Berne Convention (concerning moral rights), or of the rights derived therefrom (Article 9.1);

(2) copyright protection shall extend to the expression and not to ideas, procedures, methods of operation or mathematical concepts as such (Article 9.2);

(3) computer programs, whether in source or object code, must be protected as literary works under the Berne Convention (Article 10.1);

(4) compilations of data or other material, whether in machine readable or other form, which by reason of the selection or arrangement of their contents constitute intellectual creations shall be protected "as such." The protection does not extend to, but is without prejudice to any copyright subsisting in, the data or material itself (Article 10.2);

(5) a commercial rental right is provided in respect of at least computer programs except where the program itself is not the essential object of the rental, and to cinematographic works; however, Members are excepted from the latter obligation unless such rental has led to widespread copying which materially impairs the exclusive right of reproduction in a Member (Article 11);

(6) the term of protection for works other than photographic works or works of applied art, where the term is calculated on a basis other than the life of a natural person, shall be no less than 50 years from the end of the calendar year of authorized publication or, if publication has not taken place within 50 years from the making of the work, 50 years from the end of the calendar year of the making of the work (Article 12);

(7) limitations or exceptions to exclusive rights are confined to cases which do not conflict with normal exploitation of the work and do not unreasonably prejudice the legitimate interests of the right holder (Article 13);

(8) with respect to related rights, performing artists shall have the right to prevent the fixation and reproduction of their unfixed performances on phonograms, and the wireless broadcasting and communication to the public of their live performances (Article 14.1);

(9) producers of phonograms shall have the right to authorize or prohibit the direct or indirect reproduction of their phonograms (Article 14.2);

(10) broadcasting organizations (or, if such rights are not granted to broadcasting organizations, the owners of copyright in the subject matter of broadcasts) shall have the right to prohibit the fixation, reproduction, wireless rebroadcasting and communication to the public by television broadcast (Article 14.3);

(11) a rental right is provided for producers of, and certain other right holders in, phonograms; Members may maintain systems, in existence on April 15, 1994, of equitable remuneration in respect of the rental of phonograms, provided such system does not materially impair exclusive rights of reproduction (Article 14.4);

(12) the term of protection for performers and producers of phonograms is at least 50 years from the end of the calendar year of fixation or performance, and for broadcasters at least 20 years from the end of the calendar year of broadcast (Article 14.5);

(13) the conditions, limitations, exceptions and reservations permitted by the Rome Convention may be applied to certain related rights (under paragraphs 14.1 to 14.3) granted in the Agreement; however, the provisions of Article 18 of the Berne Convention apply, *mutatis mutandis*, to the rights of performers and producers of phonograms in phonograms (Article 14.6).

(b) Trademarks (Section 2)

28.31 The essential elements of the standards concerning the availability, scope and use of trademark rights include the following:

(1) any sign capable of distinguishing the goods or services of one undertaking from those of other undertakings (thus including service marks) shall be eligible for registration as a trademark (Article 15.1);

(2) registrability may be conditional upon visual perceptibility and, for signs which are not inherently distinctive, on distinctiveness acquired through use (Article 15.1);

(3) registrability may be conditional upon use (Article 15.2), but use may not be a condition for filing and an application may not be refused solely on the ground that intended use has not taken place within three years of the filing date (Article 15.3);

(4) the nature of the goods or services to which a trademark is to be applied may not be an obstacle to the registration of the mark (Article 15.4);

(5) members shall publish each trademark and afford a reasonable opportunity for petitions to cancel the registration, and may afford an opportunity to oppose the registration (Article 15.5);

(6) the rights conferred by registration shall include the exclusive right to prevent third parties from using identical or similar signs for identical or similar goods or services, where such use would result in a likelihood of confusion, the latter to be presumed where the goods or services are identical (Article 16.1), subject to certain allowable exceptions such as the fair use of descriptive terms (Article 17);

(7) certain rights are provided for the owners of well-known trademarks and service marks (Article 16.2 and 16.3);

(8) the term of initial registration and renewals shall be no less than seven years, renewable indefinitely (Article 18);

(9) if a showing of use is required for the maintenance of a registration, the registration may be cancelled only after an uninterrupted period of at least three years of non-use, unless valid reasons for non-use are shown (Article 19.1);

(10) certain restrictions on use are not permitted (Article 20);

(11) compulsory licensing of trademarks is not permitted (Article 21);

(12) trademarks may be assigned with or without the transfer of the business to which the trademark belongs (Article 21).

(c) Geographical Indications (Section 3)

28.32 The essential elements of the standards concerning the availability, scope and use of rights involving geographical indications include the following:

(1) "geographical indications" are defined as indications which identify a good as originating in the territory of a Member, or a region or locality in that territory, where a given quality, reputation or other characteristic of the good is essentially attributable to its geographical origin (Article 22.1);

(2) Members must provide the legal means for interested parties to prevent the use of indications that misleadingly indicate or suggest that a good originates in a geographical area other than the true place of origin (Article 22.2(a));

(3) Members shall refuse or invalidate the registration of a trademark which consists of a misleading indication (Article 22.3), and provide means to prevent any use which constitutes an act of unfair competition within the meaning of Article 10*bis* of the Paris Convention (Article 22.2(b));

(4) protection shall be applicable against a geographical indication which is literally true but misleading (Article 22.4) and, in the case of wines or spirits, even where the true origin of the goods is indicated or the geographical indication is used in translation or accompanied by expressions such as 'kind', 'type', or 'style', 'imitation' or the like (Article 23.1);

(5) protection is not required in respect of a geographical indication of another Member which is identical with the common name for goods or services, or, for products of the vine, which is identical with the customary name of a grape variety existing in the territory of that Member as of the date of entry into force of the WTO Agreement (Article 24.6);

(6) there is no obligation to protect geographical indications which are not or cease to be protected in their country of origin, or which have fallen into disuse in that country (Article 24.9);

(7) guidelines are provided for additional protection for geographical indications for wines and spirits (Article 23), including concurrent protection of homonymous geographical indications for wines (Article 23.3), certain exceptions to substantive rights such as prior rights (Article 24.4) and the right to use personal names (Article 24.8), and time limits for registration in certain cases (Article 24.7);

(8) in order to facilitate the protection of geographical indications for wines, negotiations are to be undertaken in the TRIPS Council concerning the establishment of a multilateral system of notification and registration of geographical indications for wines which would be effective for those Members participating in the system (Article 23.4).

(d) Industrial Designs (Section 4)

28.33 The essential elements of the standards concerning the availability, scope and use of industrial design rights include the following:

(1) Members shall provide protection for independently created industrial designs that are original or new, certain standards for determining protectability being allowed (Article 25.1);
(2) requirements for protection of textile designs, which may be provided through industrial design or copyright law, shall not unreasonably impair the opportunity to obtain protection, particularly in regard to any cost, examination or publication (Article 25.2);
(3) exclusive rights shall include the right to prevent third parties from making, selling or importing, for commercial purposes, articles bearing or embodying a protected industrial design (Article 26.1), subject to certain allowable exceptions (Article 26.2);
(4) the duration of protection shall amount to at least 10 years (Article 26.3).

(e) Patents (Section 5)

28.34 The essential elements of the standards concerning the availability, scope and use of patent rights include the following:

(1) patents shall be available for products and processes in all fields of technology, provided they are new, involve an inventive step and are capable of industrial application (Article 27.1), except that Members may exclude inventions, the prevention within their territory of the commercial exploitation of which is necessary to protect *ordre public* or morality, including to protect human, animal or plant life or health or to avoid serious prejudice to the environment, provided that such exclusion is not made merely because the exploitation is prohibited by their law (Article 27.2); and Members may further exclude diagnostic, therapeutic and surgical methods for the treatment of humans or animals, plants and animals other than micro-organisms, and essentially biological processes for the production of plants or animals other than non-biological and microbiological processes (Article 27.3); however, Members shall provide for the protection of plant varieties either by patents or by an effective *sui generis* system or by any combination thereof (Article 27.3);
(2) patents shall be available and patent rights enjoyable without discrimination as to the place of invention, the field of technology and whether products are imported or locally produced (Article 27.1);
(3) exclusive rights shall include, for products, the right to prevent third parties from making, using, offering for sale, selling or importing the patented product, and for processes, the right to prevent third parties from using the process and from using, offering for sale, selling or importing for those purposes the product obtained directly by that process (Article 28.1), subject to certain allowable exceptions (Article 30);
(4) patents shall be assignable, transferable and shall be available for licensing (Article 28.2);
(5) certain conditions are imposed concerning the disclosure of the invention in a patent application (Article 29);
(6) any use allowed without the authorization of the right-owner (commonly known as a compulsory license), and such use by the government, is made subject to certain enumerated conditions (Article 31); such use in the case of semi-conductor technology is limited to certain enumerated purposes (Article 31(c));

(7) judicial review shall be available for any decision to revoke or forfeit a patent (Article 32);

(8) the term of protection shall be at least 20 years from the date of the filing of the application (Article 33);

(9) the burden of proof concerning whether a product was made by a patented process shall in certain cases be placed on the alleged infringer (Article 34).

28.35 In addition to the foregoing obligations, where a Member had not made available, as of the date of entry into force of the WTO Agreement (that is, January 1, 1995), patent protection for pharmaceutical and agricultural chemical products commensurate with its obligations under Article 27, that Member must provide as from that date a means by which applications for patents for such inventions can be filed. The Member must, as of the date of application of the Agreement, apply to such applications the criteria for patentability as if those criteria were being applied on the filing date or priority date of the application. If the subject matter of the application meets the criteria for protection, the Member must provide patent protection for the remainder of the patent term counted from the filing date. (Article 70.8)

28.36 Where such an application is filed, exclusive marketing rights must be granted for a period of five years after the obtaining of marketing approval or until a product patent is granted or rejected in that Member, whichever period is shorter, provided that, subsequent to the entry into force of the WTO Agreement, a patent application has been filed and a patent granted for that product in another Member and marketing approval obtained in that other Member. (Article 70.9)

(f) Layout-Designs (Topographies) of Integrated Circuits (Section 6)

28.37 The TRIPS Agreement incorporates nearly all of the substantive provisions, with a few exceptions, of the IPIC Treaty. The IPIC Treaty provides for a regime of legal protection for layout-designs (topographies) of integrated circuits, and includes provisions on, *inter alia*, protectable subject matter, the legal form of protection, national treatment, scope of protection, exploitation, registration, disclosure and duration of protection. The requirements of the TRIPS Agreement are as follows:

(1) Members must provide protection for the layout-designs (topographies) of integrated circuits in accordance with Articles 2 through 7 (other than Article 6(3), which contains provisions on compulsory licenses), Article 12 and Article 16(3) of the IPIC Treaty (Article 35);

(2) the TRIPS Agreement substitutes a minimum term of ten to 15 years for the minimum term of eight years provided in Article 8 of the IPIC Treaty (Article 38);

(3) the TRIPS Agreement contains an additional prohibited act to those listed in the IPIC Treaty, namely any act relating to an article incorporating an integrated circuit, but only in so far as it continues to contain an unlawfully reproduced layout-design (Article 36);

(4) the TRIPS Agreement provides that certain acts engaged in unknowingly will not constitute infringement (Article 6(4) of the IPIC Treaty explicitly allows such exclusions), but that a reasonable royalty shall be payable with respect to stock on hand after notice is given (Article 37.1).

(g) Protection of Undisclosed Information (Section 7)

28.38 The TRIPS Agreement provides that, in the course of ensuring effective protection against unfair competition as provided in Article 10*bis* of the Paris Convention, Members shall protect undisclosed information and data submitted to governments or governmental agencies in accordance with the following provisions (Article 39.1):

(1) natural and legal persons shall have the possibility of preventing information lawfully within their control from being disclosed to, acquired by, or used by others without their consent in a manner contrary to honest commercial practices (Article 39.2);

(2) such protection is required for information which is secret (that is, not generally known among or readily accessible within the circles that normally deal with such information), which has commercial value because it is secret, and which has been subject to reasonable steps to keep it secret (Article 39.2);

(3) certain undisclosed test or other data submitted as a condition of approving the marketing of pharmaceutical or agricultural chemical products which utilize new chemical entities, shall be protected against unfair commercial use and, under certain circumstances, against disclosure (Article 39.3).

(h) Control of Anti-Competitive Practices in Contractual Licenses (Section 8)

28.39 Recognizing that some licensing practices or conditions pertaining to intellectual property rights which restrain competition may have adverse effects on trade and may impede the transfer and dissemination of technology (Article 39.1), the TRIPS Agreement provides that Members may specify in their national laws licensing practices or conditions which may, in particular cases, constitute an abuse of intellectual property rights having an adverse effect on the competition in the relevant market, and that they may adopt appropriate measures to control or prevent such practices. (Article 40.2)

28.40 Members agree to enter into consultations with each other, upon request, to secure compliance with laws in this regard (Article 40.3) or where their nationals are subject to such proceedings in other Members (Article 40.4).

D. ENFORCEMENT OF INTELLECTUAL PROPERTY RIGHTS (PART III)

(a) General Obligations (Section 1)

28.41 The TRIPS Agreement requires that specified enforcement procedures be available to permit effective action against any act of infringement of intellectual property rights covered by the Agreement, including expeditious remedies to prevent infringements and remedies which constitute a deterrent to further infringements. The procedures must be applied in such a manner as to avoid the creation of barriers to legitimate trade and to provide for safeguards against their abuse. (Article 41.1)

28.42 Enforcement procedures are to be fair and equitable, not be unnecessarily complicated or costly, nor entail unreasonable time-limits or unwarranted delays. (Article 41.2) Decisions on the merits of a case shall preferably be in writing and reasoned, shall be made available at least to the parties to the proceeding without undue delay, and shall be based only on evidence in respect of which parties were offered the opportunity to be heard. (Article 41.3) Parties to a proceeding shall have an opportunity for review of final administrative decisions and of at least the legal aspects of initial judicial decisions on the merits of a case (except for acquittals in criminal cases). (Article 41.4)

28.43 However, Members have no obligation to put in place a judicial system for intellectual property enforcement distinct from that for the enforcement of law in general, nor with respect to the distribution of resources as between enforcement of intellectual property rights and the enforcement of law in general. (Article 41.5)

(b) Civil and Administrative Procedures and Remedies (Section 2)

28.44 The TRIPS Agreement establishes guidelines concerning civil and administrative procedures which must be followed with respect to enforcement of intellectual property rights, including provisions on fair and equitable procedures (Article 42), evidence (Article 43), injunctions (Article 44), damages (Article 45), other remedies such as the authority to order that infringing goods or that materials and implements used in the creation of infringing goods be disposed of (Article 46), right of information, for example the authority to order that the infringer inform the right owner of the identity of third persons involved in the production and distribution of infringing goods or services and of their channels of distribution (Article 47), indemnification of the defendant (Article 48), and application of the above guidelines to administrative procedures (Article 49).

(c) Provisional Measures (Section 3)

28.45 The TRIPS Agreement establishes guidelines concerning provisional measures to prevent an infringement of any intellectual property right from occurring, and in particular to prevent the entry into the channels of commerce in their jurisdiction of goods, including imported goods immediately after customs clearance, and to preserve relevant evidence in regard to the alleged infringement, and to adopt provisional measures *inaudita altera parte* where delay is likely to cause irreparable harm or where there is a risk of evidence being destroyed. (Article 50)

(d) Special Requirements Related to Border Measures (Section 4)

28.46 The TRIPS Agreement provides for certain procedures concerning enforcement related to border measures to enable a right holder who has valid grounds for suspecting that the importation of counterfeit trademark or pirated copyright goods may take place to lodge an application for the suspension by the customs authorities of the release into free circulation of such goods. Guidelines are established with respect to suspension of release by customs authorities (Article 51), application for such procedures (Article 42), security or equivalent assurance (Article 53), notice of suspension (Article 54), duration of suspension (Article 55), indemnification of the importer and of the owner of the goods

(Article 56), right of inspection and information (Article 57), *ex officio* action (Article 58), remedies (Article 59) and *de minimis* imports (Article 60).

(e) Criminal Procedures (Section 5)

28.47 The TRIPS Agreement requires that Member provide for criminal procedures and penalties to be applied at least in cases of willful trademark counterfeiting or copyright piracy on a commercial scale, and that they make available remedies such as imprisonment, monetary fines, and seizure, forfeiture and destruction of the infringing goods and of any materials and implements the predominant use of which has been in the commission of the offense.

E.   ACQUISITION AND MAINTENANCE OF INTELLECTUAL PROPERTY RIGHTS AND RELATED PROCEDURES (PART IV)

28.48 The TRIPS Agreement provides general language relating to principles concerning procedures for acquisition and maintenance of industrial property rights. Members may require, as a condition of the acquisition or maintenance of the industrial property rights covered by the Agreement (except protection of undisclosed information), compliance with reasonable procedures and formalities consistent with the Agreement. (Article 62.1) Any procedures for grant or registration must permit the granting or registration of the right within a reasonable period of time so as to avoid unwarranted curtailment of the period of protection. (Article 62.2) Procedures concerning acquisition, maintenance, administrative revocation and *inter partes* procedures are to be governed by the guidelines applicable to enforcement (Article 62.4, referring to Article 41.2 and 41.3), and most final administrative decisions are subject to judicial or quasi-judicial review (Article 62.5).

28.49 The Agreement also stipulates that Article 4 of the Paris Convention concerning the right of priority shall apply, *mutatis mutandis*, to service marks.

F.   DISPUTE PREVENTION AND SETTLEMENT (PART V)

(a) Transparency

28.50 The TRIPS Agreement requires that laws and regulations, final judicial decisions, administrative rulings of general application and bilateral agreements pertaining to the subject matter of the Agreement be published or made publicly available by Members. (Article 63.1)

28.51 Members are further required to notify such laws and regulations to the TRIPS Council. The Council, in turn, is to attempt to minimize this burden on Members by engaging in consultations with WIPO on the possible establishment of a common register containing these laws and regulations. (Article 63.2)

28.52 The TRIPS Council will also consider, in this connection, any action required regarding notifications pursuant to the obligations under the Agreement stemming from the provisions of Article 6*ter* of the Paris Convention.

(b) Dispute Settlement

28.53 A particularly important element of the TRIPS Agreement is the system of dispute settlement established under the WTO Agreement. The TRIPS Agreement itself invokes the provisions of Article XXII and XXIII of GATT 1994 (the WTO Agreement), as elaborated by the WTO Understanding on Rules and Procedures Governing the Settlement of Disputes (included as an Annex to the WTO Agreement), which applies to consultations and the settlement of disputes under the TRIPS Agreement. (Article 64.1)

28.54 However, subparagraphs 1(b) and 1(c) of Article XXIII of GATT 1994, which refer to so-called "non-violation" dispute settlement cases, are not to apply to the settlement of disputes under the TRIPS Agreement for at least five years from the date of entry into force of the WTO Agreement (i.e., at least until January 1, 2000). Any extensions of that period are to be decided in the Ministerial Conference by consensus. (Article 64.2 and 64.3)

References for Section F
The Agreement on Trade-Related Aspects of Intellectual Property Rights (TRIPS), Annex 1C to the Agreement Establishing the World Trade Organization adopted April 15, 1994, in Marrakesh, which entered into force on January 1, 1995.

PART VI

Administration and Teaching of Intellectual Property

CHAPTER 29

Administration of Industrial Property

A. INTRODUCTION

29.1 The organizational structures which need to be established by the government of a country in order to enable industrial property laws to operate effectively, fall into three categories:

(1) bodies which are operated directly as part of the government machinery— i.e. an Industrial Property Office and a Policy Unit;

(2) bodies which are outside the government machinery but which may call for government supervision—i.e. patent and trademark agents;

(3) special arrangements in the courts.

29.2 The Industrial Property Office is often called, for short, the "Patent Office" because that indicates its major function, even though it handles trade marks and designs as well as patents. In some countries the three functions are, for historical or other reasons, operated independently by separate offices, but it is usually more efficient to combine the functions in one office.

29.3 The Industrial Property Office is essentially a government institution. Its precise position in the government organization as a whole can vary according to the administrative structure of the government of the country in question. In the United Kingdom, for example, it has always been part of the Department of Trade. This is because industrial property has been seen as existing in order to further the development of trade and industry. However, the function of the Office is to grant and regulate property rights and the Office, therefore, needs to be linked with the judicial system. Some countries have, therefore, associated the Industrial Property Office with the Ministry of Justice. The Federal Republic of Germany is a case in point. On the other hand, France and the United States of America follow much the same course as the United Kingdom.

29.4 The Office may be integrated completely into the Ministry concerned, being staffed by civil servants who can be transferred into and out of the Office from other parts of the Ministry. This has been the solution adopted in the United Kingdom, apart from the patent examining staff who are specialist staff remaining permanently in the Office. The advantage of frequent transfers is that the Office receives a regular intake of staff with wider experience and perhaps fresh ideas. The disadvantage is that experienced officials are lost as they move elsewhere.

29.5 The Office may be organized as a semi-autonomous body, able to recruit and train its own staff on its own terms, to control its own fees and other charges and to manage its own finances.   It may then have a management board representing both the government and the people who use the Office's services. The advantages are freedom from general government restrictions on manpower and spending; more freedom to finance investment in new developments; greater ease in responding to user and consumer interests;   and more retention of experienced staff. The disadvantage, particularly for a small Office, is that the staff's career is more restricted and that might affect the quality of the recruits to the Office.

29.6 Whatever administrative structure is adopted the Office must be judicially autonomous. The decisions of the Office to grant, refuse or revoke an industrial property right, or to resolve disputes between parties, are quasi-judicial decisions, not administrative ones. The Office must, therefore, be free from any interferences in particular decisions, being answerable only to the court in so far as there is a right of appeal from an Office decision to the court.

29.7 The Office must be subject to administrative supervision by the Ministry in charge of its general performance, on the level of its fees and on the appointment of the head of the Office or members of any management board. In addition, it is highly desirable to establish an advisory committee of representatives of user organizations (such as patent and trademark agents' institutes, chambers of commerce, industrial federations and consumer groups).

B. ADMINISTRATIVE STRUCTURE IN THE INDUSTRIAL PROPERTY OFFICE

29.8 The managers of many of today's Industrial Property Offices are increasingly called upon to plan and organize their operations with optimum efficiency in mind. In recent years, Industrial Property Offices have become much more active in the promotion and delivery of services related to the role of industrial property information as important factors for technological development in addition to the carrying out of the traditional functions of search and examination related to the granting of industrial property rights.

29.9 Most Industrial Property Offices have also experienced, in recent years, substantial increases in workloads because of rises in filing rates. Often and for a variety of reasons, these increased workloads have not been accompanied by corresponding increases in human resources. Consequently, managers have been looking at various ways and means including automation to increase the efficiency of their operations and deliver more with the same or fewer resources. In this context, managers have been studying different organizational set-ups in order to promote the most efficient use of their human resources.

29.10 The current trend is to group all of the industrial property activities under one authority, since this results in the more efficient use of management skills and the interchangeability of a certain number of employees particularly in the support areas. Such an organizational structure allows having managers with

References for Section A
E. Armitage, *Administrative Structures in the Field of Industrial Property*, IP/G/3 Add.

specific technical and operational knowledge and experience at certain levels but liberates others to concentrate on primarily management issues. The structure also reduces the number of managers requiring in-depth knowledge of industrial property. Other advantages are:

(1) providing a variety of advancement paths for employees;
(2) possibility of amalgamation of certain functions and avoidance of duplication of certain others;
(3) management teams with a variety of experience and background;
(4) making optimum use of management skills by having these skills applied over wider areas;
(5) presents the possibility of shared services, often reducing the amount of equipment and office space requirements;
(6) makes certain services affordable by having their costs shared by different centers.

29.11 This structure also has some disadvantages. The primary disadvantages are inherent in the fact that certain employees have to become generalists rather than acquiring in-depth experience in any one field. As well, certain managers are called upon to deal with a multitude of areas which are quite different in nature. Others are:

(1) because the educational requirements are different in the different sectors, the employees of one sector can tend to dominate the managerial levels;
(2) because of fewer management positions at certain levels, there are fewer advancement possibilities to these levels.

(a) Directorate General

29.12 The Directorate General is the authority to which all the organizational centers report. The actual title of this position may vary as, for instance, Commissioner of Patents, Registrar of Trademarks, etc., as well as that of Director General. The officer holding this position is responsible for the management of all operations related to industrial property.

29.13 In practically every Industrial Property Office, this responsibility would be too vast for only one manager. The situation may be handled by the appointment of Deputy Directors General who are responsible for specific operations, or by dividing the Directorate General into legal and administrative areas of responsibility.

(b) Industrial Property Operations

29.14 Industrial property operations are managed by the various centers under the Directorate General. These centers are the ones which are involved with the activities leading to the grant of property rights. Both for these operations as well as the auxiliary operations, the functions listed are illustrative and are not necessarily exhaustive.

(i) Patent Examination

29.15 This center is responsible for functions related to the search and examination of patent applications for the grant of patents. In most Industrial Property

Offices, this center is often the largest, generating the majority of revenues. In countries having petty patent legislation, this responsibility center would also handle this type of industrial property.

(ii) Trademark Examination

29.16 This center is responsible for functions related to the search and examination of trade-mark applications for the registration of trade-marks. This part of the Directorate has experienced substantial efficiencies through automation, particularly in the search function.

(iii) Industrial Design Examination

29.17 This center is responsible for functions related to the search, examination and grant of industrial design applications. In countries having utility model systems, this center could be made responsible for functions related to this type of industrial property.

29.18 It is to be noted that for each of the examination centers, the searches are performed within the center itself and not by a central search unit. Depending on the availability of resources, the size and the specific role of the Office, the patent search function could, of course, effectively be performed by a central unit. This arrangement would be suitable, for example, to Offices having Patent Information and Documentation Centers (PIDC).

(iv) Support Services

29.19 This center is responsible for providing the full range of support services to the three examination centers. Examples of these services are:

(1) receiving of applications and formality verification to ensure that the applications meet physical and content requirements, that fees are timely paid, etc.;
(2) publication of patent applications and grants, of trade-mark advertisings and registrations, of industrial design grants, of industrial property journals, of statistical or other reports, etc.;
(3) maintenance of registers of assignments, licenses, bibliographical information, etc.;
(4) maintenance of search files and search rooms, of reference libraries, etc.;
(5) clerical support for examination functions;
(6) document supply services for sales, exchanges;
(7) collection of maintenance fees, etc.

29.20 A variant of this arrangement might be to have clerical support units directly under the specific examination activity, i.e. a support unit for patent examination, trade-mark examination or industrial design examination. The nature of prosecution of these types of industrial property applications is such that a clerical support unit for each could be appropriate.

(v) Appeals/Oppositions

29.21 This center, made up of specialists in each area of industrial property, deals with appeals related to the prosecution of applications or with opposition procedures where such procedures exist. While the organizational chart shows these activities under one responsibility center, experts with experience in each specific area of industrial property are usually required because of the complex nature of the work carried out by this center.

(vi) PCT

29.22 Where the Industrial Property Office is a national office of a member state of the Patent Cooperation Treaty, this responsibility center looks after the national responsibilities under the Treaty. These include the functions of Receiving Office for international patent applications filed by nationals or residents of the member state as well as the functions of designated office under Chapter I of the Treaty or elected office under Chapter II of the Treaty.

(vii) Documentation and Information

29.23 This center is responsible for a wide range of activities related to documentation services and various activities related to the exploitation of the information contained in industrial property documents. In recent years, offices have become much more aware of the benefits of these activities for industrial development particularly at the small and medium sized enterprise level. This center could also be responsible for the management of entities such as Patent Information and Documentation Centers (PIDC) and other industrial property information centers. Other examples of activities carried out by this center are:

(1) maintenance and upkeep of classification systems whether they be national or more likely international such as the International Patent Classification system (IPC);
(2) providing advisory services for the determination of search patterns;
(3) maintenance of a general inquiries unit;
(4) adaptation and packaging of industrial property information;
(5) establishment of networks of intermediaries or regional representatives;
(6) responsibility for public education and awareness, for conducting seminars and lectures, for establishing working relations with industrial property professional groups, etc.;
(7) performance of state-of-the-art searches;
(8) maintenance of working relations with R&D institutions, universities and other research organizations.

(viii) Automation

29.24 This center is responsible for various activities related to the computerization and automation of all industrial property activities. This would include automation planning, research and development, testing of systems, contacts with firms, contracting, purchase and maintenance of equipment, design of systems, user consultation, etc.

(ix) Programs and Research

29.25 This responsibility center looks after a wide range of programs and activities. In many respects, it is the hub of an industrial property office. Many of the activities enumerated below are often handled by central agencies of departments to which the Office belongs. Examples of these are:

(1)   internal training for both professional and other employees;
(2)   planning and policy making;
(3)   statutory and regulatory revisions;
(4)   international affairs;
(5)   management services;
(6)   compulsory licensing;
(7)   financial control;
(8)   personnel and property management services;
(9)   accreditation of agents and maintenance of agent registers;
(10) contracting services;
(11) external relations with professional groups.

C. THE PATENT OFFICE

(a) Tasks

29.26 In the field of patents for inventions the main task of the Industrial Property Office consists of receiving applications for the grant of patents and deciding, separately for each application, whether a patent should be granted or refused. A further task of the Industrial Property Office is to deal with the renewal of the patents granted. Finally, an Industrial Property Office may have functions of disseminating technological information to the general public and deciding on cases of requests for compulsory licenses.

(b) Receiving the Patent Application and the Fees; Examination as to Form

29.27 Patent applications are usually prepared by professionals, that is, by patent attorneys or patent agents. Consequently, they are usually in the form required by the law or an applicable treaty. The Industrial Property Office nevertheless has to check that the requisite formalities have been complied with. This checking is called examination as to form. The Industrial Property Office will check whether the application is on the right size of paper, typed with the prescribed margins and containing all the prescribed elements of which the most typical are the request, the description and the claims. It will check whether the prescribed fees were paid. If there are defects and correction is permitted, it will invite the applicant to make corrections. If the defect is such that it cannot be corrected, the Industrial Property Office will refuse the application. Furthermore, the Office will examine whether the subject matter of the application is one which must be kept secret because of national security concerns.

(c) Publication of the Application

29.28 If the applicable law or treaty prescribes that applications be published, the Industrial Property Office will have to prepare the application for publication and

References for Section B
P. Trépanier, *Organization and Management of National Industrial Property Offices*, WIPO/RT/IP/TYO/90/1

make paper copies available to the public. The preparation typically consists of preparing the first page of a pamphlet that usually comprises the text of the application and any drawings that are part of the application. The first page shows, in a standard format, the so-called bibliographic data: name and address of the applicant, the inventor (if he is not the applicant) and the patent agent; title of the invention; date of the filing of the application; date, place and serial number of any earlier application filed abroad and whose priority is claimed. The Industrial Property Office will have to give each application a serial number and will have to assign to it a classification symbol showing the sub-division of the International Patent Classification (IPC) into which the claimed invention belongs. The resulting serial number and classification will be shown on the title page. Finding the right classification symbol is a task that requires familiarity with the IPC and understanding of the invention that is the subject matter of the application. It requires a high degree of professional skill, namely, that of a scientist or engineer. But if the application involves the priority of an earlier foreign application, it is usually safe, at this stage, to simply request that the applicant indicate the classification symbol given to the priority application by the foreign Industrial Property Office and to allocate the same symbol to the domestic application. Since many of the applications are of foreign origin and involve priority, such a method will solve, in most cases, the problem of assigning IPC symbols.

29.29 The number of copies to be prepared by the Industrial Property Office is a function of demand. The requisite number of copies may vary between a few dozen and a few hundred. Copies will be needed for exchange purposes with foreign industrial property offices and for sale to anyone who wishes to buy them. The copies are usually prepared by photocopying the first page prepared by the Industrial Property Office and the rest of the pages as prepared by the applicant and appearing in the application. In other words, there is no need for setting type. Photo-offset reproduction is typical. In addition to paper copies, the Industrial Property Office may also prepare and offer for sale copies on microfilm.

(d) Examination as to Substance

29.30 If the applicable law or treaty prescribes that applications be examined as to substance, then the Industrial Property Office will determine, for each application, whether it complies with the requirement of unity of invention and whether the invention claimed is patentable, that is, whether it is new, non-obvious and industrially applicable.

29.31 The carrying out of examination as to substance requires skilled professionals, engineers or scientists, called "examiners." They have to compare the claimed invention with the state of the art in order to determine whether the claimed invention represents a novelty, and a significant step forward in respect of the state of the art at the relevant filing date.

29.32 In order to know what the state of the art is, the Industrial Property Office must either have a collection of its own patent documents, scientific books and scientific periodicals, or it must have recourse to other means to receive the required information. Establishing and maintaining the said collection is an expensive undertaking even if it is determined that world-wide coverage is not necessary. But there are also means other than consulting one's own documentation to establish the state of the art. Patent applications filed under the Patent Cooperation Treaty are accompanied by so-called international search reports or international preliminary examination reports prepared by one of the leading industrial property offices of the world. Another method is to have recourse to one of the services offered to developing countries, in certain circumstances, by the World Intellectual Property Organization: the State-of-the-Art search reports program and the International Cooperation in the Search and Examination of Inventions (ICSEI). Finally, the Industrial Property Office may require, where the application involves the priority of a foreign application, that the applicant furnish the results of the search and examination carried out in respect of the said foreign application.

29.33 Irrespective of what method is used for establishing the state of the art, the Industrial Property Office will have to make a decision, in respect of every application, whether the claimed invention is patentable or not. Its decision may be facilitated by what is called an opposition procedure, provided for in the legislation of several countries. Under such a procedure, the application is published, and anybody may write to the Industrial Property Office opposing the grant of a patent. Hence, the expression "opposition." Opposition is usually based on an allegation that the invention is already in the state of the art and on producing evidence in support of the allegation. Thus, the Industrial Property Office receives the results of a search, carried out by the opposing party, on the state of the art, and then checks the correctness of those results and the conclusions deduced from them. All this may be done without a patent document collection of the Industrial Property Office itself.

(e) Refusal or Grant

29.34 Once the examination as to form is completed and the law or treaty does not require examination as to substance, and the examination as to form did not lead to rejection because of an uncorrectable or uncorrected defect, the Industrial Property Office will grant a patent. Where examination as to substance is also requested and the Industrial Property Office finds the claimed invention patentable, it will grant a patent. Otherwise, it will refuse the application.

29.35 The grant is expressed in a certificate that is signed and sealed by the Industrial Property Office and given to the applicant who, from then on, is called the patentee or the owner of the patent. Furthermore, the grant is inscribed in what is usually called the patent register, a register kept by the Industrial Property Office. The grant is also announced in the official gazette of the government or the special gazette of the Industrial Property Office. Finally, granted patents must be published and put on sale in sufficient numbers of copies, in the form of paper pamphlets, by the Industrial Property Office. The procedure is similar to the one mentioned above in respect of the publication of patent applications.

(f) Maintenance of Patents

29.36 Patents have a limited duration of validity, usually for a period of 15 to 20 years. But a patent once granted does not remain valid until the expiration of the said period unless it is "maintained" or "renewed." Maintenance and renewal usually require the payment of an annual fee by the owner of the patent. In several systems, the amount of the annual fee increases as one approaches the end of the maximum term of protection.

29.37 The tasks of the Industrial Property Office consist of receiving these fees and noting the receipt in the register of patents. In some systems, the resulting renewal is published in the gazette.

(g) Cost of Maintaining the System

29.38 Ideally, an Industrial Property Office should be able to cover the cost of its tasks from the fees it collects from patent applicants and patent owners. Those costs consist mainly of the salaries of the employees of the Industrial Property Office, the cost of publishing pamphlets containing patent applications or, at least, granted patents, and, where the Industrial Property Office has its own collection of documents, books and periodicals necessary for carrying out examination as to substance, the cost of creating and maintaining such collections.

(h) Compulsory Licenses

29.39 If the law provides for the possibility of granting compulsory licenses, that is, licenses to work the patented invention in the country even against the wish of the patentee where non-working by him or public interest justifies the grant of a compulsory license, the Industrial Property Office is sometimes entrusted with the task of receiving requests for the grant of compulsory licenses and of granting or refusing such requests after having heard the patentee and the requesting party.

29.40 This is a quasi-judicial function which requires a thorough familiarity with the economic policy of the government and the economic possibilities and needs for working the patented invention. It also requires the ability of judging the financial and technical capabilities of the party requesting the grant of a compulsory license. Because of the economic aspects of the question, government authorities other than the usual industrial property office, such as ministries of industry or planning, are generally better suited to deal with requests for compulsory licenses. Naturally, if a sufficiently, specialized staff is placed in the Industrial Property Office, the tasks may be performed by that office.

(i) Patent Information Services

29.41 Some of the industrial property offices provide technological information services based on patent documents. This means that a person may ask the Industrial Property Office to identify patent documents (and even provide copies thereof) that deal with the solution to a given technological problem. Such a problem will have to be described by the party requesting the information. Only those industrial property offices are in a position to provide this kind of information which either have a substantial patent collection themselves or which can access existing services, some of them on line, located in the same country or abroad. Derwent Publications Limited (London), International Patent Documentation Centre (INPADOC) (Vienna) and Pergamon Infoline Limited (London) are among the best known of such on-line services.

References for Section C
International Bureau of WIPO, *Administrative Structures in the Field of Industrial Property*, WIPO/IP/AC/86/9

D. THE TRADEMARKS OFFICE

(a) Tasks

29.42 In the field of trademarks and service marks, the main task of the Industrial Property Office consists of receiving applications for the registration of trademarks and service marks and deciding, separately for each application, whether registration should be effected or should be refused. A further task of the Industrial Property Office is to deal with requests for the renewal of existing registrations. Finally, an Industrial Property Office may be required to give information, upon the request of any member of the public, on the existence, in its register, of trademarks or service marks that are identical with or are similar to a sign in respect of which the said member of the public requests the information. The activity performed by the Industrial Property Office in this last respect is called "search" or "search for identical or similar trademarks or service marks."

(b) Receiving the Application for Registration and the Fees; Examination as to Form

29.43 An application for the registration of a trademark has to contain the name and address of the applicant and, if he is represented by an attorney or a trademark agent, the name and address of the latter. Furthermore, it has to indicate the word, drawing or other sign that is proposed to be registered as a trademark. Finally, it must list the goods and/or services for which the registration of the trademark is asked for. This list must be accompanied by the indication of that class or those classes—among the 42 classes of the International Classification of Trademarks—to which the goods and/or services listed in the application belong.

29.44 Trademark applications are usually prepared by professionals, that is, by trademark attorneys or agents. Consequently, they are usually in the form required by the applicable law or treaty. The Industrial Property Office nevertheless has to ensure compliance, a procedure known as examination as to form. The Industrial Property Office will check whether the application is on the required limits as to size and is of a clarity which allows reproduction. If colors are among the features of the trademark for which protection is claimed and publication is effected by the Industrial Property Office only in black and white, it is usually required that the colors be indicated in a special way on the black and white reproduction of the trademark as filed. Whether that special way is respected will, then, be also one of the requirements which will have to be checked by the trademark office.

29.45 The Industrial Property Office will have to check whether prescribed fees for registration have been paid by the applicant. Usually, the amount of fees varies according to the number of the classes in which the listed goods and/or services belong: the higher the number of classes, the higher the fees. This is one of the reasons why one has to indicate in the application the class or the classes to which the goods and/or services belong. The indications furnished by the applicant will be checked by the Industrial Property Office in order to determine the correct amount of the fees payable.

(c) Examination as to Absolute Grounds of Nullity

29.46 The Industrial Property Office is also required to examine the trademark as to whether there are absolute grounds which prevent its registration. Absolute grounds should be distinguished from relative grounds. Relative grounds are those that prevent the registration of a sign as a trademark because the sign is in conflict—is identical with or is similar to—another trademark that has already been registered for the same or similar goods and/or services, or because it is in conflict with a well-known trademark. In other words, a relative ground is formed by comparing the sign requested to be registered with an existing trademark. On the other hand, absolute grounds are not based on such comparison, and are independent from existing registrations. Typical examples of absolute grounds of nullity are that the sign requested to be registered as a trademark has no distinguishing character (is merely descriptive, is generic, etc.), or is offensive to the moral sense (for example, is pornographic), or is offensive to religious or patriotic feelings (for example, the mark uses for commercial purposes a religious symbol or the name or picture of a historic personality, or national ruler, a national flag or emblem). At this stage of the examination only absolute grounds of nullity are taken into consideration. If any are found, the application for registration will be refused by the Industrial Property Office.

(d) Examination as to Relative Grounds of Nullity

29.47 Not all laws require examination as to relative grounds of nullity. Where there is no such requirement, the registration will be effected, unless there is some defect in form or there is an absolute ground of nullity. Such registration, however, may be attacked by an interested person on the grounds of relative nullity and if such grounds are found by the Industrial Property Office or the court, the registration will be cancelled.

29.48 But where the law requires examination, prior to registration, of relative grounds of nullity, such examination will be carried out by the Industrial Property Office. This examination which may be called also examination as to possible conflict with existing marks, can be carried out either on the request of what is called an opposing party or *ex officio*, that is, independently of any such request. Where the law allows third parties to oppose registration, the trademark has to be published by the Industrial Property Office in what is called an "opposition" within the prescribed time limit, for example, three months from the publication in the gazette. Thus, in such a system, one of the tasks of the Industrial Property Office is the publication, for opposition, of the signs requested to be registered as trademarks. Where the examination for relative grounds of nullity is *ex officio*, such publication is not necessary. Where there is a system of *ex officio* examination, the Industrial Property Office has to keep indexes which allow it to effect the search for identical or similar trademarks. There are several indexes. One shows all the word marks in alphabetical order; another lists them according to characteristic endings or beginnings; yet another lists them according to the sequence of vowels. The indexing and searching of marks that have or consist of figurative elements are described by words, and the concepts go from the broader to the narrower. For example, where the sign is a parrot, the steps of indexing are "living beings," "animals," "birds."

29.49 The indexes have to cover all the registered trademarks whose registration is still valid. This usually means a relatively high number of entries and it means that the indexes must be kept up to date constantly, that is, every newly registered trademark has to be entered in the appropriate—usually several—indexes and every trademark whose registration ceases to be valid must be removed from all the indexes. This is a major task, requiring specially trained staff, usually called "trademark searchers."

(e) Refusal of Registration

29.50 Once the examinations are completed, the Industrial Property Office will either reject the application or allow it. In the latter case, it will inscribe the trademark in its trademark register, will give a certificate of registration to the applicant (who, henceforth, will be called the owner of the registration) and will announce the registration in the official gazette of the government or in the special gazette of the Industrial Property Office. The latter means work for preparation of each issue of the gazette and work for printing and distributing it. These activities require staff and equipment.

(f) Renewal of Registration

29.51 The initial registration of a trademark is usually valid for 10 or 20 years. The validity of any registration may be prolonged through what is called renewal. Renewal may be requested any number of times, each having a validity of a certain number of years, for example, 10 or 20.

29.52 Renewal must be requested and must be paid for, that is, the owner of the registration is required to pay the prescribed fee ("renewal fee") inside a prescribed period of time (for example, one year) around the date on which the validity of the previous registration would otherwise expire. The task of the Industrial Property Office consists of receiving the renewal fee, checking that it has been paid inside the prescribed period, checking that its amount is the required amount, inscribing the renewal in the trademark register, announcing the renewal in the gazette and issuing a certificate of renewal to the owner of the registration.

(g) Cost of Maintaining the System

29.53 As in the case of patents an industrial property office should, ideally, be able to cover the cost of its tasks from the fees it collects from trademark applicants and owners of trademark registrations. Those costs consist mainly of the salaries of the employees of the Industrial Property Office and the cost of publishing the gazette. More staff will be needed if the Industrial Property Office has to carry out the examination as to relative grounds of nullity, not only for purposes of undertaking such examination but also for keeping up to date the indexes required for this type of examination. The printing costs will be higher if trademarks having color features are published in color.

29.54 Experience shows that, if the fees are set at an appropriate level, it is relatively easy to make the trademark operations of an Industrial Property Office self-supporting, that is, to completely cover costs out of the collected fees.

(h) Search Service

29.55 Industrial property offices which administer a system providing for examination for relative grounds of nullity have, as already indicated, to maintain several kinds of indexes and will have to have staff that is skilled in searching in such indexes. Such industrial property offices usually maintain what is called a search service. Any person may request such a service to tell him whether a given word or other sign, that he presents to the service, is identical with or similar to one or more registered trademarks. The service is particularly useful for a person who intends to adopt a new trademark. Adoption of a new trademark usually means considerable investment, including heavy expenditure in advertising. The risk of adopting a trademark which might turn out to be in conflict with another trademark can, thanks to such service, be considerably reduced.

E. THE INDUSTRIAL DESIGNS OFFICE

(a) Tasks

29.56 In the field of industrial designs, the main task of the Industrial Property Office consists of receiving applications for the registration of industrial designs and deciding, separately for each application, whether registration should be effected or refused. In a few countries, including China and the United States of America, patents are granted for industrial designs. However, even in those countries, the tasks of the Industrial Property Office, in respect of industrial designs, differ very little from what is going to be described in the following sections. A further task of the Industrial Property Office is to deal with requests for the renewal of existing registrations for industrial designs.

(b) Receiving the Application for Registration and the Fees; Examination as to Form

29.57 An application for the registration of an industrial design has to contain the name and address of the applicant and, if he is represented by an attorney or industrial property agent, the name and address of the latter. Furthermore, the application must be accompanied by one or several drawings or photographs showing the design that is proposed to be registered as an industrial design. Furthermore, the application must indicate the object in which the industrial design is to be used, for example, "ashtray," "handbag," "fountain pen," "shoe," "necklace." If color or colors are regarded as essential elements of the industrial design, the drawings or photographs must show the color and the application must indicate that the color features are part of the industrial design.

29.58 The industrial property office has to check whether the application is in the required form, that is, in particular, whether it is made by using the form that the Industrial Property Office puts at the disposal of the applicants, whether the form is filled in all the applicable respects, whether the drawing or photograph is attached and has the right size, and whether the prescribed fee has been paid.

References for Section D
International Bureau of WIPO, *Administrative Structures in the Field of Industrial Property*, WIPO/
IP/AC/86/9

(c) Examination as to Admissibility

29.59 The Industrial Property Office is also required to examine whether there are grounds of morality or public order on which the application should be rejected, for example, because the design is pornographic, offensive to religious or patriotic feelings etc.

(d) Refusal of Registration

29.60 Once the said examinations are completed, the Industrial Property Office will either reject the application or will allow the application. In the latter case, it will inscribe the industrial design in its industrial design register, will give a certificate of registration to the applicant (who, henceforth, will be called the owner of the registration) and will announce the registration in the official gazette of the government or in the special gazette of the Industrial Property Office. The latter means work for preparation of each issue of the gazette and work for printing and distributing it.

29.61 It is to be noted that an industrial design that is the same as, or closely resembles, an industrial design that has already been published or registered, is not protected by law. Nevertheless, in most of the countries, industrial property offices do not have the task of examining to establish industrial designs whose registration is applied for in order to establish the existence or non-existence of prior identical or closely resembling industrial designs. The remedy that is available for the owner of such prior industrial designs consists of the possibility of asking for the cancellation of the registration of the conflicting industrial design. In most countries, such cancellation must be asked for from an ordinary court. In some countries, it can be asked for, at least in the first instance, from the Industrial Property Office. Where the latter possibility exists, the hearing and deciding of requests for cancellation are among the tasks of the Industrial Property Office, tasks for which that office will need to have qualified staff.

(e) Renewal of Registration

29.62 The initial registration of an industrial design is usually valid for five years but the validity of such registration may be prolonged, usually once, in some countries twice, for an additional period, or for two additional periods.

29.63 Renewal must be requested and must be paid for, that is, the owner of the registration is required to pay the prescribed fee ("renewal fee") within a specified period of time (for example, one year) near the date on which the validity of the previous registration would otherwise expire. The task of the Industrial Property Office consists of receiving the renewal fee, checking that its amount is the required amount, inscribing the renewal in the industrial property register, announcing the renewal in the gazette and issuing a certificate of renewal to the owner of the registration.

(f) Cost of Maintaining the System

29.64 As in the case of patents and trademarks an Industrial Property Office should, ideally, be able to cover the cost of performing its tasks from the fees it collects from applicants and owners of registrations. Those costs consist mainly of the salaries of the employees of the industrial property offices and of the cost of publishing the gazette. Experience shows that, with appropriate fees, it is quite possible to make the industrial design operations of an Industrial Property Office self-supporting.

F. INTERGOVERNMENTAL COOPERATION

(a) Introduction

29.65 The procedure for the grant and maintenance of industrial property rights involves the performance of administrative functions which are substantially the same or at least similar in a large number of countries. It is often the case, therefore, that the work done by industrial property offices in various countries is either exactly or nearly identical. Intergovernmental cooperation in the field of industrial property can accordingly lead to substantial economies in manpower and finances. For that reason, countries in several regions of the world have combined their efforts in order to make procedures relating to the grant of industrial property rights more efficient and economical. It is to be noted that intergovernmental cooperation is particularly easy in groups of countries which use only one language; the advantages of intergovernmental cooperation are, however, recognized even in groups of countries which have to take more than one language into account.

(b) WIPO's International Bureau

29.66 The International Bureau of WIPO administers three major systems of intellectual property registration from its headquarters in Geneva. These important systems, based on international treaties and conventions, greatly facilitate international cooperation in the administration of intellectual property. These three systems are outlined below.

29.67 The Patent Cooperation Treaty (PCT) is an international multilateral treaty for the filing of international patent applications. Under the PCT, international patent applications may be filed in any of the national industrial property offices of the member States, with the European Patent Office, or directly with WIPO. All applications, wherever filed, are processed by the international Bureau of WIPO. The international application has the same effect as that of national patent applications (that is, applications filed in the national offices or in the European Patent Office) for each country designated in the application. One of the largest patent offices of the world prepares a report on each international application, which report practically makes superfluous any examination as to substance in the national patent offices. Under the PCT, no patent is granted by a central authority; the decision on the denial or grant of a patent is made by the national industrial property office on the basis of the international application and the said report.

References for Section E
International Bureau of WIPO, *Administrative Structures in the Field of Industrial Property*, WIPO/IP/AC/86/9

29.68 The Madrid Agreement Concerning the International Registration of Trade Marks is an international multilateral treaty for the international registration of marks. Under the Madrid Agreement, any trademark that has been registered in the national trademark register of one of the member countries may be re-registered, on the request of the owner of the national registration, in the international register of trademarks. That international register is kept by the International Bureau of WIPO in Geneva. The effect of the international registration is the same as that of separate registrations in the national registry of trademarks of each of the other countries designated in the international application, except that each national industrial property office may, as far as its country is concerned, deny such effect if the trademark would not have been registrable in the registry of the national industrial property office had a national registration been applied for.

29.69 Under the Hague Agreement Concerning the International Deposit of Industrial Designs, industrial designs may be deposited in Geneva, with the International Bureau of WIPO. That deposit has the same effect as if the industrial design had been deposited separately, in the national industrial property office of each of the countries designated. States party to this Agreement may, but need not, establish a service for industrial designs in their national or regional offices.

(c) African Regional Industrial Property Organization (ARIPO)

29.70 Since 1973, WIPO and the United Nations Economic Commission for Africa (ECA) have been collaborating to assist the governments of English-speaking African countries in their efforts to harmonize and develop their industrial property systems to create the appropriate intergovernmental structures to this effect.

29.71 Those efforts resulted in the adoption, by a Diplomatic Conference held at Lusaka, Zambia, in December 1976, and at which 13 governments of English-speaking African countries were represented, of an Agreement on the Creation of an Industrial Property Organization for English-speaking Africa (ESARIPO). The Agreement entered into force on February 15, 1978. In December 1985 the Organization changed its name to African Regional Industrial Property Organization (ARIPO), by decision of its Council. At present the following 14 countries are members of ARIPO: Botswana, Gambia, Ghana, Kenya, Lesotho, Malawi, Sierra Leone, Somalia, Sudan, Swaziland, Tanzania, Uganda, Zambia and Zimbabwe. Membership in ARIPO is open to Ethiopia, Liberia, Mauritius, Nigeria and Seychelles, all of which participate in the Organization's activities. ARIPO has its headquarters in Harare, Zimbabwe.

29.72 The objectives of ARIPO are, *inter alia*:

(1) to promote the harmonization and development of the industrial property laws, and matters related thereto, appropriate to the needs of its members and of the region as a whole;

(2) to establish such common services or organs as may be necessary or desirable for the coordination, harmonization and development of the industrial property activities affecting its members;

(3) to assist its members in the development and acquisition of suitable technology; and

(4) to evolve a common view in industrial property matters.

29.73 Upon the request of (ES)ARIPO, WIPO, in association with the ECA, assisted the Organization in the establishment of a Patent Documentation and Information Centre, at its headquarters in Harare. The purpose of the center is to promote the objectives of ARIPO by providing member States with technological information available for patent and patent-related documentation in order to assist those States in the achievement of their development objectives.

29.74 The establishment of the center, after an initial preparatory assistance phase, commenced in 1981 within the framework of a UNDP financed project with WIPO, in association with the ECA, as Executing Agency.

29.75 Within the framework of its Committees for Patent Matters and for Trade Mark and Industrial Design Matters, the Organization has developed Model Laws on Patents and on Trade Marks to assist its member States in the strengthening of their legislation in those respective fields.

29.76 A Protocol on Patents and Industrial Designs Within the Framework of (ES)ARIPO, adopted at a Special Meeting held in Harare in December 1982, entered into force on April 25, 1984, initially among Ghana, Malawi, Sudan, Uganda and Zimbabwe. Since then, Botswana, Gambia, Kenya, Lesotho, Swaziland and Zambia have joined the Protocol, bringing the total to 11 member countries party thereto.

29.77 The Protocol establishes a system under which patent and industrial design applications are processed and granted or registered, as the case may be, on behalf of Contracting States designated in the applications, by the Office of ARIPO. The scheme established by the Protocol enables the technical processing of patent and industrial design applications, and the administration of granted patents and industrial designs, to be undertaken by a central authority. Any designated State has the right, however, where an application does not conform to the provisions of the Protocol or to those of its national industrial property legislation, to declare, prior to the grant of the patent or registration of the industrial design, that, if granted or registered, such grant or registration will have no effect within the territory of that State. Where no declaration is made, the grant of the patent or registration of the industrial design by ARIPO has the same effect as any grant or registration carried out under the national law of the States designated in the relevant application.

29.78 Part of the income generated from application and maintenance fees under the Protocol is used for the Office of ARIPO while the remainder is distributed among the Contracting States concerned.

29.79 On the occasion of its annual session held in Banjul (The Gambia) in 1993, the Administrative Council of ARIPO agreed on a Protocol on Trademarks under which it will possible to file applications with the ARIPO Office. Under the said Protocol, once in force, the ARIPO Office will have the competence to process applications and to register trademarks and service marks on behalf of Contracting States designated in the applications. At the 1994 annual session of the Council held in Kasane (Botswana), the said Protocol was signed by six member countries. It will enter into force three months after three member States have deposited their instruments of ratification or accession.

29.80 Also in 1993, the Administrative Council had, in principle, agreed that PCT applicants should be able to designate, for an ARIPO patent, States which are party to both the PCT and the Harare Protocol. In 1994, the Administrative Council of ARIPO adopted the necessary amendments to the Harare Protocol and its Implementing Regulations with effect from July 1, 1994. As a result, it will be possible from that date for PCT applicants to designate, for an ARIPO patent, the States of Kenya, which acceded to the PCT in 1994, Malawi and Sudan, the three Contracting States of the Harare Protocol which, as of now, are Members of the PCT.

(d) African Intellectual Property Organization (OAPI)

29.81 A system of intergovernmental cooperation in the field of industrial property among 12 French-speaking African countries was established by the Libreville Agreement of 1962 for the creation of an African and Malagasy Office of Industrial Property (OAMPI). The Libreville Agreement was subsequently revised by the Bangui Agreement Relating to the Creation of an African Intellectual Property Organization (OAPI, corresponding to the French name, Organisation africaine de la propriété intellectuelle), which entered into force on February 8, 1982. The Libreville Agreement established, among the member States, a common system for the grant and maintenance of industrial property titles (patents, trademark registrations, industrial design registrations) in accordance with uniform legislation contained in Annexes to the Agreement, which are applicable in each member State. At present, 15 countries (Benin, Burkina Faso, Cameroon, Central African Republic, Chad, Congo, Côte d'Ivoire, Djibouti, Gabon, Guinea, Mali, Mauritania, Niger, Senegal, Togo) are members of OAPI. The system provides for common formalities for the grant of industrial property titles by a central industrial property office, the African Intellectual Property Organization (OAPI), situated in Yaoundé (Cameroon), which acts as the industrial property office for each of the member States.

29.82 Under the system, titles granted by the central office have effect in all member States; there is no possibility of limiting the effect to only one or some of the member States. Applications are normally filed with the central office in Yaoundé; however, nationals of member States may file applications with national administrations, which then have to transmit the applications to the central office; national administrations cannot grant titles themselves.

29.83 The industrial property rights granted have the effect of national industrial property rights in each of the Contracting States, i.e., not of supranational titles of protection. Therefore, their invalidation has effect only in the territory of the member State or States concerned.

29.84 Apart from certain modifications in the uniform substantive law (e.g., the gradual introduction of examination of patent applications for compliance with the substantive requirements of patentability), the main features of the revision introduced by the Bangui Agreement include the extension of OAPI's field of competence to copyright and the protection of the cultural heritage, and the inclusion, in addition to patents, marks and industrial designs, of the following objects of industrial property: trade names, utility models, appellations of origin, indications of source and unfair competition. The uniform substantive law with respect to each object of intellectual property is set forth in separate annexes to the Agreement.

29.85 Upon the request of OAPI, WIPO has assisted it in the establishment, within the headquarters in Yaoundé, of a Patent Documentation and Information Department (Département de la documentation et de l'information en matière de brevets (DEDIB)). The aim of DEDIB is to contribute to the technological and industrial development of the member States by putting at the disposal of governments, research institutions, industry and other users of such information technological information based on a collection of patent documentation and to establish a network of national industrial property structures in the OAPI member States for liaison with the Organization. The establishment of DEDIB and of the network of national structures was accomplished with the assistance of the United Nations Development Programme (UNDP) under a project, covering the period 1979 to 1982, of which WIPO was the Executing Agency.

29.86 OAPI is financed entirely from the income it receives from fees it collects for the grant and administration of industrial property rights.

(e) Subregional Integration Agreement of the ANDEAN Group Countries

29.87 Under the above-mentioned Agreement, also called Andean Pact or Cartagena Agreement, which was concluded in 1969, the Commission of the Andean Group countries—Bolivia, Colombia, Ecuador, Peru and Venezuela—was given the power to take the necessary "Decisions" for the implementation of the Agreement. In the field of industrial property, "Regulations for the Application of Rules Concerning Industrial Property" were first introduced by Decision 85 of the Commission in 1974. That Decision established the basic framework for a common industrial property legislation. Decision 85 was replaced by Decision 311, shortly afterwards by Decision 313 and recently by Decision 344, which entered into force on January 1, 1994.

29.88 Decision 344 regulates, in particular, patents, utility models, industrial designs, industrial secrets, marks, trade names and geographical indications (appellations of origin). Even though matters not being treated by Decision 344 remain governed by the provisions of the national laws, the relevant articles of the Agreement regarding patents and utility models (Articles 1 to 57), industrial designs (Articles 58 to 71), industrial secrets (Articles 72 to 80), marks and trade names (Articles 81 to 128) and geographical indications (Articles 129 to 142) have led to a far-reaching harmonization of the industrial property laws of the Andean Group countries. In general, one can state that Decision 344 has considerably strengthened the protection of industrial property rights. Under the Decision (Article 143), Andean countries are expressly authorized to strengthen or enlarge the protection of industrial property rights through national legislation or by virtue of international agreements. The Andean Pact countries, however, maintain independent patent and trademark offices since no central Andean Industrial Property Office has been established yet, although this matter has already received some consideration.

(f) Central American Agreement for the Protection of Industrial Property

29.89 This Agreement, which was concluded on June 1, 1968, established uniform legislation in the fields of marks, trade names, advertising slogans or signs, geographical indications and unfair competition. The Agreement, which comprises

238 Articles and even prescribes common registration fees, has been in force in Costa Rica, Guatemala and Nicaragua since October 1975, and in El Salvador since 1988. Upon entry into force of the Agreement, the laws of each Contracting State relating to matters expressly governed by the Agreement ceased to have effect. Nevertheless, there is, as in the case of the Andean Pact countries, no regional Central-American office. The industrial property offices of the contracting States therefore continue to grant and administer the industrial property titles of protection dealt with in the Agreement. A Central American Agreement on Patents and Industrial Designs, which is mentioned in the Agreement of June 1, 1968, has not yet been concluded.

(g) North American Free Trade Agreement

29.90 The North American Free Trade Agreement (NAFTA) between the United States of America, Canada and Mexico entered into force on January 1, 1994. One of its main objectives is to provide adequate and effective protection and enforcement of intellectual property rights. At the same time, the Contracting States have to ensure that measures to enforce intellectual property rights do not themselves become barriers to legitimate trade. The Agreement contains, in its Chapter 17, provisions on intellectual property. Many of the provisions contained therein are similar to the provisions which form of the TRIPS Agreement. In addition to enforcing the provisions of Chapter 17 of the NAFTA Agreement, the contracting States must give effect to the substantive provisions of several international conventions and treaties administered by WIPO which deal specifically with the protection of intellectual property, namely the Paris Convention, the Berne Convention, the UPOV Convention and the Geneva Convention for the Protection of Producers of Phonograms. The negotiations for the NAFTA Agreement led, already in 1991, to a general revision and updating of the intellectual property laws of Mexico and, in 1993, to amendments to the Canadian intellectual property legislation which include, in particular, the repeal of provisions on the compulsory licensing of pharmaceutical patents. The United States of America have amended their patent law recently to eliminate discriminatory effects of Section 104 of its Patent Statute against Canadian and Mexican applicants for US patents. Consequently, [most of] the minimum standards of protection which are set by the NAFTA Agreement, are already provided under the current legislation of the Member States.

(h) Eurasian Patent Organization

29.91 On February 17, 1994, at the headquarters of WIPO in Geneva, representatives of ten of the twelve member States of the Commonwealth of Independent States adopted and initialled a multilateral treaty entitled "Eurasian Patent Convention." (Armenia, Azerbaijan, Belarus, Georgia, Kazakstan, Kyrgyzstan, the Republic of Moldova, the Russian Federation, Tajikistan and Ukraine.)

29.92 The Convention entered into force on August 12, 1995. As of October 1, 1996, there were nine States party to the Convention: Armenia, Azerbaijan, Belarus, Kazakstan, Kyzgyzstan, Republic of Moldova, Russian Federation, Tajikistan and Turkmenistan.

29.93 The treaty establishes a new intergovernmental organization called the "Eurasian Patent Organization" (EAPO).[1] Once operations have begun, the treaty allows nationals of any country to obtain patents of invention from the Eurasian Patent Office to be set up in Moscow. Such regional (Eurasian) patents will have effect in all countries of the Eurasian patent system.

29.94 The Eurasian Patent Convention not only provides for modalities of applying for and obtaining Eurasian patents but also for their legal effects: patented inventions can be used only with the authorization of the holders of the patents. Subject to the payment of a yearly renewal fee, any Eurasian patent can be maintained in force for 20 years.

29.95 The Eurasian patent system will be of great advantage both for local and foreign applicants. They will not have to apply for a patent separately in each country but with a single application, filed in the Russian language in Moscow, they can obtain, with a single act and a single payment, patent protection in all the States members of the new system. Foreigners shall be able to apply for Eurasian patents *via* the Patent Cooperation Treaty (PCT), which allows them to postpone the translation of their applications into Russian for 20 or 30 months.

29.96 Any country may become a party to the Eurasian Patent Convention, provided it is a party to two WIPO-administered treaties: the Paris Convention for the Protection of Industrial Property and the Patent Cooperation Treaty. Most of the States members of the Commonwealth of Independent States already fulfill this condition.

29.97 The Convention reflects the contemporary trends of patent legislation and administration and is compatible with the multilateral industrial property treaties administered by WIPO and the provisions on patents contained in the TRIPS Agreement concluded in the framework of the negotiations in the Uruguay Round of GATT.

(i) European Patent Organisation

29.98 Efforts to achieve intergovernmental cooperation concerning patent procedures in Western Europe started in the 1950s with plans aimed at avoiding duplication of the work of patent offices as regards the search and examination of patent applications. The European Patent Office (EPO) was established by the European Patent Convention, which entered into force on October 7, 1977, and which, at present, has 17 Contracting States (Austria, Belgium, Denmark, France, Germany, Greece, Ireland, Italy, Liechtenstein, Luxembourg, Monaco, Netherlands, Portugal, Spain, Sweden, Switzerland, United Kingdom). All those States are also party to the Paris Convention for the Protection of Industrial Property and the Patent Cooperation Treaty The EPO, which has its headquarters in Munich (Germany) and branch offices in The Hague, Berlin and Vienna, has almost 4,000 employees, organized in five Directorates-General. It processes and grants patents on behalf of Contracting States designated in the European patent applications. The EPO has been financially self-supporting since 1981.

---

1   Editor's note: the EAPO started its operations on January 1, 1996 (date from which PCT contracting States which are also party to the Eurasian Patent Convention could be designated for a Eurasian patent under the PCT).

29.99 Under the system of intergovernmental cooperation introduced by the Convention, it is possible to file a single patent application, in one of the three official languages (English, French and German), and thereby obtain a European patent with effect in one, several or all of the 17 Contracting States. Prior to the entry into force of the Convention, it was necessary, where protection of an invention was desired in a number of countries within the region, to file separate applications in each of those countries.

29.100 The Convention established a system of law common to the Contracting States and a uniform procedure for the grant of patents. The EPO undertakes the examination of applications as to formal requirements, the preparation of search reports and their publication and the examination of patent applications for compliance with the substantive requirements of patentability, namely, novelty, inventive step and industrial applicability.

29.101 The elimination of the duplication of the work involved in the processing of applications results in a reduction of cost not only for the applicant but also for the patent offices of Contracting States. The Contracting States nevertheless maintain national patent offices and process national applications filed with them.

29.102 In 1992, about 30,000 European patents were granted by the EPO. In the same year, about 59,000 applications for the grant of European patents were filed. Applications may be filed irrespective of the nationality of the applicant. They may be filed via the PCT, that is, any international application filed under the PCT may ask (also) for the grant of a European patent. Such applications are usually referred to as "Euro/PCT applications." In the single year of 1992, more than 12,800 of the applications for European patents were Euro/PCT applications. In the same year, there were altogether about 26,000 international (PCT) applications and in about 24,700 of them a European patent was (also) applied for. This corresponds to more than 95.28% of the total number of international applications of 1992.

29.103 The European Patent Office is one of the International Searching and Preliminary Examining Authorities under the PCT. It is also an intergovernmental industrial property organization which has certain functions under the Budapest Treaty.

29.104 An Agreement on working relations and cooperation was concluded by WIPO and the European Patent Organisation on May 17, 1978. The cooperation between the European Patent Office and the International Bureau has always been close. This is particularly needed in respect of PCT operations. Cooperation is very active also in the field of patent documentation and information. In the field of technical assistance to developing countries, cooperation is very generously given by the Office.

(j) Cooperation among the Member States of the European Union

(i) Community Patent

29.105 In addition to the European Patent Convention, the member States of the European Union have prepared a Community Patent Convention, which, however, has not yet entered into force. Under the Community Patent Convention, it will be possible to obtain a regional patent which will not only be granted by a regional industrial property office (the European Patent Office) but which will also have the effect of a regional patent instead of a bundle of national patents. As a consequence, such a patent can only be revoked in its entirety, i.e., not only with effect in one or some member countries. Provisions relating thereto form part of the Community Patent Convention and a Protocol on the Settlement of Litigation Concerning the Infringement and Validity of Community Patents. The Convention and the said Protocol provide for, in particular, the establishment of a Common Appeal Court which will take the final decision on the validity of the community patent.

(ii) Community Trademark and Approximation of Trademark Laws

29.106 In the field of trademarks, the long-lasting efforts to enhance the cooperation between the member States of the European Union were finally also successful. A proposal for a Council Regulation on the community trademark had already been made by the Commission of the European Union in 1980. In 1993, the remaining controversial issues were settled and a final agreement was reached. The Council Regulation (EC) No. 40/94 on the community trademark was adopted on December 20, 1993. It establishes a so-called Office for Harmonization in the Internal Market (trademarks and designs) which will be located in Alicante (Spain). The main parts of the said Regulations deal with the

(1) law related to trademarks;
(2) applications for community trademarks;
(3) registration procedure;
(4) duration, renewal and alteration of community trademarks;
(5) surrender, revocation and invalidity;
(6) appeals, community collective marks;
(7) procedure;
(8) jurisdiction and procedure in legal actions relating to community trademarks; and
(9) effects on the law of the member States and on the Community Trademarks Office.

29.107 On December 21, 1988, the Council of the European Union adopted the first Directive to Approximate the Laws of the Member States Relating to Trade Marks. The Directive deals, among other matters, with the signs which can constitute a mark, grounds for refusal or invalidity, including conflicts with other rights, sanctions for non-use and grounds for revocation. The process of implementing the said Directive has not yet been fully completed.

(iii) Counterfeit Goods

29.108 The Council Regulation (EEC) No. 3842/86 of December 1, 1986, Laying Down Measures to Prohibit the Release for Free Circulation of Counterfeit Goods lays down the conditions under which customs authorities must intervene in the case of goods entered for free circulation where they are suspected of being counterfeit, and the measures which must be taken by the competent authorities with regard to these goods where it has been established that they are indeed counterfeit.

(k) Uniform Benelux Laws on Marks and Designs

29.109 For some of the member States of the European Union, namely the Benelux countries (Belgium, Netherlands, Luxembourg), a close regional cooperation in the field of marks and industrial designs had already been established in the 1960s and the 1970s. The Benelux Convention on Trademarks, signed on March 19, 1962, came into force on July 1, 1969, and the uniform Benelux Law on Trademarks (which was appended to the said Convention) came into force on January 1, 1971. The Benelux Convention on Designs, signed on October 25, 1966, and the Uniform Benelux Designs Law (appended to the said Convention) entered into force on January 1, 1974, and January 1, 1975, respectively. According to Article 1 of each of the Conventions, the Benelux countries incorporated the uniform Benelux Laws on Marks and Designs into the national legislation. They also established administrative Offices common to their countries, namely the Benelux Trademark Office (BBM) and the Benelux Designs Office (BBDM), which have their headquarters in The Hague (Netherlands). These offices have, to a large extent, a combined administrative structure and are financially self-supporting. The registrations have effect in all three of the member States. There are no national procedures in the Benelux countries for the registration of marks or the deposit of industrial designs.

29.110 For the purposes of the international registration of marks under the Madrid system administered by the International Bureau of WIPO, the BBM has the same role as a national trademark office: regional registrations effected in the Benelux Trademark Registry may serve as a basis of international applications and, in international applications (based on non-Benelux registrations), the three Benelux countries may be designated.

29.111 As far as the international deposit of industrial designs under the Hague system administered by the International Bureau is concerned, the BBDM has the same functions as a national office. International deposits have automatic effect in the three Benelux countries. Nationals of the three countries may make international deposits.

29.112 The Benelux Offices participate in an observer capacity in WIPO meetings of interest to them, particularly the Assemblies of the Paris, Madrid and Hague Unions and in committees of experts dealing with the international registration of marks and the international deposit of industrial designs, as well as in meetings of working groups established under the auspices of the Madrid and Hague Unions.

29.113 Proceedings based upon the uniform laws are to be decided by the competent civil courts the decisions of which are also recognized in the two other states. The Benelux Court of Justice, staffed with Judges from each of the Contracting States, has to take cognizance of any question of interpretation of the uniform laws.

G. GOVERNMENT SUPPORT OF INVENTIVE ACTIVITY

(a) Introduction

29.114 Governments support inventors as their role in the development process is essential and vital. For their inventions, be they important or modest,

References for Section F
International Bureau of WIPO, *The Changing World of Intellectual Property: Regional and International Challenges: Issues in Regional Cooperation*, WIPO/ACAD/E/94/27
International Bureau of WIPO, *Administrative Structures in the Field of Industrial Property*, WIPO/IP/CAR/90/11

contribute to the birth and improvement of technology, the progress of industry and the increasing betterment of life.

29.115 It is, however, evident that the nature of government support to inventors and inventive activity will necessarily vary from country to country. Firstly, much depends on the level of development. Government support cannot be the same in a country with hardly any industry and a highly-industrialized one. Secondly, the importance of the support clearly depends on the nature of the socio-economic system prevailing in any given country. It will not be the same in two countries of similar industrial development, one having a market economy while the other a centrally-planned economy. Thirdly, the nature and level of government support will depend on political choices, based on other conditions, such as national priorities, objectives and interests.

(b) Protection

29.116 The major government policy in support of inventors and inventive activity is the legal framework which it provides for the protection of the rights and interests of inventors. The industrial property protection is the best stimulus for inventiveness because patents and other legal titles of a similar kind (known as inventors' certificates, utility models or certificates, certificates of invention and rationalization proposals) offer to the inventor a double incentive: material and moral; money received as contractual payment or reward, and recognition now and for posterity that something unusual, something springing from the creator's intellect, has been achieved.

29.117 The responsibilities of States towards inventors do not end with laws and treaties securing the substantive protection of inventions. Their administration must be effective and not over-expensive in order to avoid unnecessary obstacles between an inventor and his legal rights.

(c) Assistance

29.118 Government assistance to inventors differs very much from country to country. Some countries have established systems in order to assist individual inventors, small enterprises and non-profit organizations in the payment of the different kinds of fees due for obtaining and maintaining a patent.

29.119 Provisions contained in financial or tax laws creating favorable conditions for inventors and inventive activity could be summarized as follows:

(1) reduced taxes in respect of income stemming from licensed patents and know-how, as well as expenses in relation to acquisition and maintenance of industrial property rights;
(2) special loans or subsidies, including interest-free or low interest loans;
(3) grants for development of certain inventions and innovations;
(4) possibilities for concluding "research contracts."

29.120 With regard to government institutions offering assistance to inventors and support to inventive activity, the situation also differs very much from country to country. In some countries, the industrial property administration is the only governmental institution engaged directly in this respect, while in other countries, in addition to the industrial property administration ministries or departments, dealing with industry, trade and economic matters, science and technology could be involved in such activities.

29.121 In more and more countries, other specialized governmental institutions have been created to encourage inventive activity and also to promote the development, exploitation and to some extent the commercialization of local inventions, by providing the inventor with the relevant support.

29.122 For instance, in some countries individual inventors may get assistance and their inventions may be tested in government-owned or government-financed research and test laboratories and institutions. Usually it is done on a non-profit basis and in some cases restitution of the expenses is required if the invention has been successful on the market.

(d) Promotion and Reward

29.123 Exhibitions of inventions are an important support to inventors in as much as they highlight their inventions and assist inventors in establishing contacts in industry. In several countries, government agencies—including in some cases the industrial property administrations—organize or participate in the organization of such activities. In other countries, moral support is lent by government authorities, who extend their "patronage" to exhibitions and shows organized by private entities.

29.124 Special exhibitions and contests for inventions made by schoolchildren, students and young people, are held in several countries and are becoming more and more popular.

29.125 Another important means of action by governments for promoting inventive activity is the direct encouragement of inventors by public recognition. Non-material rewards (medals, diplomas) and sometimes financial rewards are granted not only to meritorious inventors, but also to potential inventors in the framework of youth science and invention contests. In some countries such moral awards and celebrations have even been established by legislation.

(e) Cooperation among Inventors

29.126 However important government support to inventors may be, it is necessary for inventors themselves to realize better than heretofore that they need to act collectively. They will be better heard, and their wishes will be better satisfied, if they form associations, if they are active in those associations and if their associations maintain closer relations with each other on the international level, that is, through the International Federation of Inventors' Associations (IFIA).

29.127 In fact several governments have given assistance to their local inventors' association or have supported the inventors of their countries in creating such an association.

References for Section G
International Bureau of WIPO, *Government Support to Inventors and Inventive Activity*, WIPO/IFIA/86/1

CHAPTER 30

Administration of Copyright

A. INFRASTRUCTURE FOR THE IMPLEMENTATION OF COPYRIGHT

(a) Introduction

30.1 Where laws do exist, their practical value depends on the extent to which they are effectively implemented. Adoption of the law is the first step. Its effective and efficient application is imperative. This could be achieved through the setting up of an appropriate infrastructure in the form of a suitable authors' organization for collection and distribution of authors' fees, particularly since individual efforts by authors to ensure the protection of their works might not yield the same results. Authors today face users who are large and powerful groups and combines, and need to put up a strong collective front. With the assistance of international conventions and reciprocal agreements between authors' organizations they are in a position to protect all the rights and repertoires managed by the other organizations and thus make available to their own public a much larger canvas of works and repertoire of creativity.

30.2 In the exercise of rights given to him by the law, it is thus essential that an author has the facility of an efficient infrastructure for ensuring the protection of his rights and for assisting him for the purpose.

30.3 Since the author or owner of copyright has generally the right to authorize or prohibit certain utilizations of his works or creations that are protected under the law, authors, creators and other rights owners protected under copyright laws have for quite some time established or joined in collective organizations created for this end.

30.4 Authorization of all kinds of non-dramatic musical works, or of mechanical reproduction of musical works, and collection and distribution of fees resulting from such use of the works, or from the application of statutory and other licenses, cannot generally be dealt with by the author himself. Take for instance the collection and distribution of fees for performance of music. There was a time, before the advent of sophisticated technology, when performances of music would take place before restricted and localized gatherings which no one except the immediate audience could enjoy. If others wished to hear the musical performance on a different occasion the musician or performer had to be subsequently hired and paid for. With the development of sophisticated communication technologies, and with the facilities for taping, recording, broadcasting and TV, performance of music and of works is no longer localized or ephemeral. The world has shrunk as a result, and dissemination to its furthest corners has been rendered easier. The result of all this on the copyright owners is far-reaching. Their works can not only be used at far-flung places, but the very same technologies have made extensive piracy also possible. In a situation like this it would appear quite impractical for an individual author or performer to obtain his legitimate dues for the use of his work or performance, without the assistance of specialized institutions for collecting and distributing the fees and royalties for their use.

30.5 The check over the use of works and their authorizations is relatively easier in respect of books (and generally the printed word) but more difficult when it comes to performances of dramatic or cinematographic works, and even more so in respect of musical works. In addition to the checks and authorizations involved, the infrastructural set up has to be responsible for collection and distribution of royalties for and to authors and their successors in title.

30.6 The protection of the interests of the authors in society, and their rights in connection with the use of their works, and also obtaining the most advantageous conditions for authors' works with the users' on just and reasonable terms, especially abroad, could best be done through specialist organizations established for one or the other kind of administration of authors' rights. These organizations are as a rule non-profit institutions. All sums collected by them are distributed to the authors and otherwise employed for the benefit of authors after deducting out-of-pocket expenses for the establishment and operational costs of the organization concerned.

(b) Objectives and Functions of an Authors' Organization

30.7 The essential role of an authors' society, therefore, is to collect copyright fees and to distribute the amount to the copyright owners after deducting the sum required to cover expenses, that is to say, without any possibility of making a profit.

30.8 Without the authors' society, the author alone, not being ubiquitous, cannot control all the uses of his works in his own country, to say nothing of their uses in other countries. It is therefore essential for authors to form a national society which, because of the extent of its repertoire, that is to say, the extent of the works in which it administers rights, will be sufficiently well organized to ensure that the interests entrusted to it will be safeguarded.

30.9 This is particularly true because a national society will provide for the administration and protection not only of its own national repertoire, but also of foreign repertoires, in view of the fact that contracts of mutual representation will be concluded with the societies of other countries. In return, its own repertoire will be administered and protected in each foreign country by the national society with which the contract of mutual representation referred to above has been concluded.

30.10 It should further be stressed that authors' societies, apart from their usefulness to authors, render services to users. In fact, without authors' societies, users would have great difficulty in discovering with any certainty the various owners of the authors' rights and, even if they succeed in discovering them, they would have to ask each one separately and individually for the necessary authorization to exercise those rights. Thus, in many cases, especially as far as works performed at concerts, variety shows, song recitals and dances are concerned, as well as, most importantly, in television and sound broadcasting, the organizers of such events would be obliged to ask for so many authorizations that they would practically give up the idea of seeking authorizations, and would consequently be infringing the law.

30.11 Due to the existence of authors' societies, to their organizations and to the contracts of mutual representation concluded between them, it will suffice for the user to turn to his national society alone to have all the necessary authorizations. Thus, in practice, he will obtain in one single operation through an all-inclusive authorization, the possibility of selecting freely, from a world-wide repertoire, the works which will make up the program of his choice.

30.12 The broad objectives and functions of an authors' organization or society, *inter alia*, would be to authorize use of works of their members, check on the utilization of their works, prepare model contracts for agreements between authors and the users of their works, collect royalties from the various users and distribute them to the rights owners, provide legal advice and assistance to authors and their heirs, collect and disseminate information relevant to the requirements and interests of their members; manage benevolent or social welfare funds for providing relief to authors in indigent circumstances, and contribute generally to the development of cultural life in the country. Such organizations have necessarily also to maintain elaborate documentation including lists of authors and their works not only in respect of their own members but also concerning foreign repertoires which they would manage on the basis of contracts of representation concluded with authors' organizations of other countries.

(c) Organization for the Protection and Administration of Copyright

30.13 In some developing countries there are both private and state organizations administering authors' rights, for example in Brazil, where besides a number of societies authorized by the National Council of Copyright (CNDA), a central office has been set up for collection and distribution of authors' fees. In certain other developing countries, where authors' institutions have been more recently established, only state organizations administer authors' rights. Thus in Algeria (ONDA), Morocco (BMDA), and Senegal (BSDA), state copyright offices have been established. In India there is the Indian Performing Rights Society (IPRS), and also an Authors' Guild which does not deal with the collection and distribution of authors' fees nor with licensing utilization of authors' works. The purpose of the Guild is to promote and protect the professional interests of its members in more general terms, both in India and abroad.

30.14 The institutions could be private, or public autonomous organizations or government offices undertaking these functions, depending on the circumstances, requirements or compulsions of the countries concerned. One view is that the State should exercise adequate control and supervision, and also render financial support to the extent required for the efficient functioning of such organizations.

30.15 While most of the initial institutions were set up in the form of societies under civil law, there are a number of developing countries which have preferred to establish bureaus or offices under public law for the administration of authors' rights. The choice seems to be for the reason that such an institution, in a developing country, operates well with government support and backing.

30.16 An important function of authors' organizations is also to take steps for the preservation, protection and encouragement of creative activities in the field of literature, art, music, etc. Apart, therefore, from the protection that effective implementation of copyright laws could provide, it is being increasingly realized that for encouraging and giving a fillip to creative activities, more positive steps are also necessary. Assistance or encouragement to creators of works, to the artists, by itself serves a larger social purpose apart from the fact that it also helps preserve and protect national culture. As is well known, the span of an artist's or musician's or dancer's active stage life is limited. Many of them face considerable economic difficulties when they are unable to sing or perform. The same could apply, in a different way, also to authors. And yet this is happening, especially in developing countries, where facilities for their assistance have not been organized. The creation of a properly administered fund could help mitigate hardship in such cases. Such a fund could be utilized for different kinds of financial assistance to authors and performers.

30.17 Certain countries have established special funds, statutory or otherwise, for the purpose of direct assistance to artists, musicians, etc. or for taking measures conducive to the protection, encouragement and promotion of creative activities. Thus, besides protecting and administering the rights and legal interests of authors, and of those who assist in disseminating authors' works, their organizations could be assisted to provide the requisite social security and financial assistance in the case of sickness, accidents, permanent or temporary disability, etc. The financial resources for such a support program could be obtained through contributions from users of authors' works and from owners of copyright, in proportion to the license fee or returns accruing from the use of works, as well as State and other grants.

30.18 Authors' organizations administering authors' rights themselves often establish one or more special funds for welfare and benefit purposes; the details of such funds are determined by an appropriate statute and the funds are financed by a part of the fees collected and/or from other sources, such as grants. For instance, in the Federal Republic of Germany, Article 8 of the Act of 1965 on the Administration of Copyright and Related Rights expressly requires collecting organizations to arrange welfare and assistance facilities for the owners of the rights or privileges administered by them. In France, the Society of Authors, Composers and Music Publishers (SACEM), covers quarterly payments for members older than 55 years; financial support by means of special funds to authors whose income has decreased in accident, sickness, etc; a mutual aid society reimburses all medical costs of the members. In Sweden, the statutes of the Swedish Performing Right Society (STIM) provide for a "benevolent fund" for making payments to members in case of sickness, and giving other temporary assistance, also to dependants. Different forms of benefit schemes are regulated by the Swiss Society For Authors' Rights in Musical Works (SUISA): savings account; aid to the aged members; pensions for retired members; aid and pensions for widows and orphans and allocations also for needy members.

30.19 The authors' societies in certain developing countries also provide for various benefit schemes. For example, the society in Tunisia (SODACT) provides in its rules for details concerning aid to retired members and for various other allocations. In Argentina, the statutes of their society (ARGENTORES) provide for mutual help through medical assistance, granting of subsidies, loans and pensions. In Mexico, fees are collected for the use of works in the public domain and those fees are administered by competent societies for welfare purposes.

30.20 There are only very few organizations established for the sole purpose of administering the rights of performers or other neighboring rights. Such organizations exist, for example, in Argentina (AADI), Czechoslovakia (OSVU), Mexico (ANDI), Sweden (SAMI), Switzerland (SIG). In Japan, the Council of Performers Organizations administers performers' rights; and in Norway there is the King's Fund for Performing Artists.

30.21 In Argentina, broadcasting revenues in respect of performers' and producers' rights are collected jointly by the performers and producers organizations, the latter getting a 33% share. The basis and the amount of remuneration for broadcasting or communication to the public of phonograms are fixed in various countries in different ways.

30.22 Besides performers' societies which collect and/or distribute performers' fees in respect of their rights, there are a number of organizations of other kinds, serving the purpose of protection of employed performers, to advance the interests of performers in more general terms, or, with respect to particular groups within them, to promote the activities of performers and the dissemination of their performances, or to assist needy performers; for example, performers' trade unions such as the Union of Swedish Artists and the Union of Swedish Musicians. There are also organizations functioning in some developing countries for the purpose, for example in Argentina, Bolivia, Chile, Costa Rica, Guatemala, Mexico, Peru, Uruguay.

30.23 As in the case of authors' organizations, performers' organizations may provide also for various benefit schemes.

30.24 There are few instances of legislative protection of performers, and even those laws which contain such rules do not in the majority of cases secure a share to performers in the fees paid in several countries for the broadcasting or communicating to the public of phonograms. Special stress is instead laid on collective agreements concluded between organizations of performers and organizations of producers of phonograms. Agreements between Independent Film Producers International Association (IFPIA) and the International Federation of Actors (FIA) and the International Federation of Musicians (FIM) at the international level, and similar agreements signed by the corresponding national organizations at national levels have achieved a certain respect for performers' interests also in some countries where legislation has not provided for it.

30.25 As for agreements with broadcasting organizations, the secondary use of their fixed performances represents for the performers an important source of possible additional income, compensating, to an extent, for the limited possibilities of live performance. Collective agreements with broadcasting organizations are, therefore, of particular importance for performers, whether these are concluded directly by their own organizations, or by organizations of producers of phonograms. Collective agreements with broadcasting organizations have been concluded, for example, in Austria, Brazil, Mexico, Norway, etc. An important area of collective agreements in favor of performers is the regulation of "needle time" restrictions. "Needle time" is understood in some countries as meaning the amount of use that may be made of commercial records for broadcasting purposes, usually fixed in hours for definite periods. Limitations on "needle time" in favor of transmitting live performances is motivated by the desire to safeguard the interest of the musical performers' organizations. At present, "needle time" provisions are included in the relevant contracts, for instance, in Barbados, India, Jamaica, New Zealand, Switzerland, Trinidad and Tobago, the United Kingdom.

(d) Organizations of Publishers

30.26 It may be mentioned here that in many countries of Western Europe the activities of authors' societies concern not only the safeguarding of the rights and interests of authors but also the protection of the interests of publishers, mainly in the case of the administration of musical performing and mechanical rights. In such situations, publishers of musical works take an active part in the management of the society, being normally members of its governing bodies.

30.27 The main objective of publishers' organizations is to protect the interests of the publishing industry and to promote its development, with particular regard to the printing and editing of and trading in books and periodicals. The purpose is to encourage the widest possible distribution not only at home but also abroad, since publishing activities are more and more international.

30.28 Several publishers' organizations also have programs enabling their members to be assisted in the administration of their companies or to be aware of government policies on matters of concern to publishers (taxes, trade conditions, censorship, etc. and also copyright). Publishers' organizations try also to strengthen public understanding of the role of books in the cultural, social and economic evolution of society.

B. COLLECTIVE ADMINISTRATION OF COPYRIGHT

30.29 Throughout the world, the rights of authors are known to be their personal rights. They form part of the individual rights provided for in Article 27 of the Universal Declaration of Human Rights of December 10, 1948. They are called exclusive rights in the Berne Convention for the Protection of Literary and Artistic Works.

30.30 Legislators and the writers of conventions draw inspiration from the notion that the author may either exercise his rights himself or have them exercised by others according to the rules of representation in the Civil Code. However, the development of the technical means of disseminating music has

References for Section A
International Bureau of WIPO, *Infrastructure for the Implementation of Copyright*, WIPO/CR/ ZOMBA/85/3

been such that the personal exercise of rights of performance and broadcasting by the composer himself has become an illusion. If for example a country has 500 radio transmitters daily broadcasting hours of music, composers find it impossible to authorize broadcasts of their works one by one. It would moreover be inadmissible to contemplate requiring a radio station that annually broadcasts the musical works of 60,000 to 80,000 composers from all over the world to approach each composer in turn for prior authorization!

30.31 Today, in the face of this mass consumption of music, the only way of safeguarding the rights of public performance and broadcasting of composers, songwriters, arrangers and translators consists in the creation of a link between the music "producers" and the music "consumers." The concentration of the rights of performance and broadcasting of musical works in the hands of one body in each country—which we shall call a collective administration organization here—and the blanket authorization to perform in public or broadcast protected music, granted by that collective administration organization, constitute the collective administration with which we are going to concern ourselves in this presentation.

(a) The Rights of Performance and Broadcasting Administered

30.32 The collective administration organization has to set out to secure all the rights of performance and broadcasting of musical works if it is to serve music users satisfactorily with a single blanket authorization. This aim of concentrating all rights may be promoted and furthered by the creation of a State monopoly. In itself, however, a monopoly does not confer any copyright on the collective administration organization: with or without a monopoly, the organization still has to persuade authors to assign their rights of performance and broadcasting to it.

(i) Assignment of Rights by Authors

30.33 The assignment or transfer of rights of performance and broadcasting normally takes place under a contract of association or management contract, signed by the author and his collecting society or collective administration organization. The legal form is dictated by the Civil Code and by the national copyright law of the country concerned. The best form is assignment, which enables the collective administration organization to represent authors without difficulty in both judicial and extra-judicial contexts. Some countries prefer the "fiduciary transfer" concept, which complicates the organization's representation of authors in its own name.

30.34 Assignments or transfers of rights are limited in time; at the end of the period of membership or on expiry of the mandate, the author recovers his rights.

30.35 The assignment or transfer of rights normally refers to all the musical works created by the composer. The composer may however have made his rights over to third parties before joining the collective administration organization. In such cases exceptions have to be allowed, with the composer being obliged for instance to declare those works in respect of which he is not assigning the rights of performance or broadcasting to the collective administration organization. The organization has to ensure that it respects those exceptions—except in cases where the publisher has acquired the rights and then assigns them in his turn. That case will be commented on below.

30.36 The practice is for authors to assign their rights also in future works, in other words for works that they will be creating during the term of their membership or during the currency of the mandate. In that way authors protect themselves against possible pressure from third parties, especially publishers, who might condition their willingness to publish the work on the securing of the rights of performance and broadcasting. The assignment of rights in future works is not recognized in all countries, however, and in that case the declaration of every newly-created work has to be combined with assignment of the performance and broadcasting rights in the work.

30.37 Assignments and transfers generally cover performances and broadcasts anywhere in the world. This territorial dimension of assignment and transfer enables the collective administration organization to sign contracts with foreign counterparts and thus to safeguard the national musical heritage at the international level. This does not rule out the possibility of certain authors—indeed often the best-known—being already registered as members or clients of foreign copyright societies before they apply to the collective administration organization in their country. It is advisable to respect these priorities when defining the territorial scope of each assignment or transfer. The idea of the collective administration of authors' rights is not threatened by the geographical subdivision of the assignments or transfers.

(ii) The Position of Publishers

30.38 Under a publishing contract signed with an author, the publisher is authorized to multiply the work and to sell copies to the public. He will also try to have riders written into the contract granting him the rights of performance and broadcasting, in the hope that this "second serving" of rights will add to his income.

30.39 If music publishers are kept out of the collective administration of rights of performance and broadcasting, the collective administration organization will not have access to the music publishing rights, which are in the nature of "extras" in the hands of publishers. This makes for serious gaps in the collective administration, because published works have a vastly greater audience than handwritten works. Experience has shown that collective administration without the incorporation of publishers quickly stagnates and loses its meaning. All the copyright societies of Europe and North America have therefore incorporated publishers who—as members or clients—assign all these "extra" rights to their collective administration organizations.

(iii) Foreign Counterparts

30.40 As mentioned above in connection with the possibility of territorial limitation of assignments or transfers, every collective administration organization assigns or transfers the rights acquired from its members and clients to its foreign counterpart for public performances and broadcasts in the latter's area of concern. In this way each collective administration organization controls the performance and broadcasting rights of the world music repertoire in its own country. This concentration of rights puts it in a very strong position.

30.41 Contracts signed between the collective administration organization or authors' societies of the various countries—called "reciprocal representation contracts"—correspond more often than not to the model drawn up by CISAC, the International Confederation of Societies of Authors and Composers. The member societies of CISAC are obliged to sign the contracts, and may neither compete with each other nor engage in restrictive practices against one of their number.

(iv) Rights of Unknown Authors

30.42 In the musical life of every country there are always works of unknown authors. Inasmuch as the works enjoy legal protection, the question arises whether the collective administration organization can or should concern itself with the rights of the authors of such works when they have not been either assigned or transferred to it. The answer to this question has tended to be affirmative in countries with civil codes that recognize the concept of agency without authority, so, under such provisions, the collective administration organization validly represents all unknown authors, and therefore includes their works in the authorizations issued to users, collects the royalties payable and keeps them at the author's disposal should he appear before the prescribed time limit.

30.43 One notes a correlation between the monopoly of the collective administration organization and the possibility of valid representation of unknown authors. If the collective administration organization is the only body competent to authorize public performances or broadcasts of protected music—in so far as the author is not exercising those rights himself—it goes without saying that it is likewise fully competent to act on behalf of unknown authors.

(b) Authorization to Perform Publicly or Broadcast Protected Music

30.44 All those who wish to perform publicly or broadcast protected music are given authorization for the entire world music repertoire at once. This greatly eases the users' job of respecting the rights of authors. Collective administration thus has to be looked upon as a considerable service to the world of music.

(i) Scope and Form of Authorization

30.45 The authorization is given the form of a contract under which the collective administration organization consents to a precisely specified use of the music, the user undertakes to pay the agreed royalty and submit accounts of the works performed or broadcast.

30.46 The world music repertoire cannot be defined precisely in a contract, but the collective administration organization can state:

(1) either that the world repertoire includes only music composed by authors who have assigned or transferred their rights to it or to a foreign counterpart linked to it by a reciprocal representation contract;

(2) or that the world repertoire includes all musical works save exceptionally those specially communicated to users.

In the second of the above two cases, the user is covered by the collective administration organization against any claims that may be made by third parties.

30.47 The authorization may relate to the exclusive or non-exclusive use of the music by the user. In the case of exclusive use, no other person may be authorized to make use of the same music. The practice is for authorizations given for public performances and broadcasts to be non-exclusive, with non-exclusivity being assumed in the case of doubt.

(ii) Royalty Scales

30.48 The author sets the monetary compensation for his authorizations at his discretion. Certain authors' societies have claimed the same freedom for their collective administration activities. These procedures are unreliable, however; any arbitrary action in a monopolistic management scheme is a short cut to anti-trust intervention. Equal treatment for users, and consequently the introduction of a clear and well-ordered scale of royalties, are indispensable elements underlying any collective administration of copyright.

30.49 The efforts directed towards the introduction of well thought-out and logical tariffs are reflected in the observance of certain basic standards for the charging of royalties. The most important standard—which is reflected in the CISAC recommendations—is the requirement that the author receive a ten per cent share in the revenue from the use of his work. In the case of the performance of both protected and unprotected works, the percentage is reduced in proportion to the performance time of the protected and unprotected works (the *pro rata temporis* rule). If the performance of the music is associated with the performance of a ballet, the composer of the music and the choreographer share the ten per cent royalty, each having a five per cent participation in the performance of the ballet (ballet rule). With these three rules it is possible to lay down all the tariffs for publicly-performed and broadcast music.

30.50 The tariff provisions have to be easy for both the collective administration organization and the users to apply. In order to avoid distortions, it is advisable to conduct tariff negotiations with the main unions or associations in each branch of users—for instance with the associations representing the hotel trade or cinemas—before laying down the tariffs and implementing them. The consent of a user's association to a proposed tariff can greatly facilitate its subsequent application. There too, experience has shown that agreement goes much further than disagreement.

30.51 In a great many countries, the representation monopoly of the collective administration organization requires State inspection of its tariffs to prevent any monopoly abuses. In such cases the approved tariffs are to be regarded as official tariffs, to be applied also by the courts in the event of dispute.

(iii) Accounts of Works Performed or Broadcast

30.52 If the royalties collected are to be distributed exactly—see below for the principles of distribution—users have to be made to provide accounts itemizing the works actually performed or broadcast by them. This obligation should be written into the contracts between the collective administration organization and the user as a condition of the grant of authorization.

30.53 It is often difficult and tiresome to draw up a record of works performed or broadcast. Satisfactory results are dependent on good cooperation between the collective administration organization and users, the latter including also the performers themselves.

30.54 The difficulty of procuring reliable records has led to the abandonment of this method in a number of countries; in such cases the collective administration organization records radio broadcasts itself on magnetic tape, and endeavors to identify the works broadcast from the tape. The experience gained with this method has not been encouraging; the procedure is very costly, and the percentage of works actually identified quite small.

(iv) Attitude to the Use of Music without Prior Authorization

30.55 Those who publicly perform or broadcast protected music without first having been authorized to do so by the authors or by the collective administration organization are guilty of copyright infringement. If these provisions were to be strictly and inflexibly applied, the collective administration organization would have to deal annually with thousands upon thousands of court cases, and would become bogged down in ruinous expenditure and lose all credit within the country. It is essential to offer delinquent users the possibility of rectifying their position after the event before taking them to court.

30.56 In the same context, it should be borne in mind that it is impossible to make the entire population of a country aware of copyright. The collective administration organization should not waste its energy incessantly explaining and commenting on copyright and the machinery of copyright administration, publishing brochures on the subject and continually organizing meetings and seminars without the remotest prospect of ever being able to lessen or discontinue that activity.

(c) Documentation

30.57 The word documentation is used in copyright administration to mean all the information concerning authors and publishers and their works, which is essential for the collection and distribution of royalties.

(i) Members and Clients of the Collective Administration Organization

30.58 The collective administration organization has to know with certainty, at all times, just which authors and publishers it represents. It therefore needs a register of authors and publishers, constantly kept up to date, preferably in the form of an electronic database. The data may be grouped in two categories:

(1) data serving as minimum characteristics for the identification of authors and publishers, both within the country and abroad: surname and first name or corporate name, membership of the authors' society, year of death where applicable (these are "CAE" data: see below);
(2) data pertaining to relations between the collective administration organization and its members or clients, such as addresses, bank or postal accounts, business information, etc.

(ii) CAE Documentation

30.59 The collective administration organization has to keep abreast of the foreign authors and publishers that it represents. This information is obtainable from CISAC'S CAE documentation, which is regularly brought up to date by SUISA, the Swiss Society for Authors' Rights in Musical Works (CAE stands for "Compositeurs, Auteurs, Editeurs" or Composers, Authors, Publishers). The

CAE documentation contains the data of approximately 1,300,000 authors and 250,000 publishers throughout the world, either belonging to 110 copyright societies or without any particular affiliation (NS authors = "non sociétaires" or non-members). These basic data consist, as mentioned above, of the following:

(1) surname or surnames, corporate name for publishers;
(2) forenames;
(3) affiliation (limited by rights or by territory where appropriate);
(4) year of death, where applicable.

30.60 The CAE documentation is presented every three months in revised and updated form on the following dates:

February 15;
May 15;
August 15;
November 15;

It is issued on magnetic tape, microfiche and (since the autumn of 1991) CD-ROM. CD-ROM will soon be replacing microfiches, whose bulk has made them difficult to handle.

30.61 The CAE documentation is in use in all societies and collective administration organizations. It is therefore advisable to enter the basic data on members and clients, and also any alterations and additions, as quickly as possible.

30.62 The spelling of authors' names is not always consistent in different language areas. In 1974 and 1975 the question arose of including the names of 36,000 Russian composers, written in Cyrillic characters, in the CAE documentation. On that occasion, the Slavonic Languages Institute of Zurich University devised a method of "multilingual transcription," which made it possible to present each name in two or more forms corresponding to the various linguistic regions of the world.

(iii) Declarations of Works

30.63 The collective administration organization has to make its members and clients declare all works created by them and accompany the declarations with supporting documents. Only in that way can the collective administration organization expect to have accurate information on the repertoire managed by it. Works not in written form may be declared in the form of a cassette recording. The obligation to declare works extends to publishers, who have to give notice of any publication that has taken place.

30.64 It is advisable to keep carefully not only declarations of works and supporting documents, but also copies of the contracts concerning works, especially publishing contracts. The collective administration organization thus becomes a treasury of national culture in the field of music. Its documentation will later be one of the main references for historical and scientific research, apart from which it will itself be in a position to intervene when documents are lost or mislaid.

30.65 The collective administration organization should not pay royalties to authors or publishers for works that have not been declared. Payments should be deferred until such time as the formalities have been completed.

(iv) WWL Documentation

30.66 Full documentation on the world music repertoire is impossible to compile; the existing data are not only fragmentary but also rapidly superseded. Because of this, cooperation between authors' societies in various countries is directed not so much towards the fullest possible mutual information as towards information limited to essentials, to avert the risk of a counterproductive flood of information. Instead of working solely on the basis of the documentation concerning works, the societies have recourse to the complementary input of the CAE documentation, which is much fuller. This auxiliary method is known as CISAC's "Warsaw decision procedure;" for all non-documented works, royalties are paid to the society to which the author, if identified, is affiliated.

30.67 The World Works List or WWL documentation corresponds to the idea that every authors' society knows the works in its repertoire that have succeeded in winning international recognition. The basic data of those works—the title of the work and name of the author or corporate name of the publisher, excluding data on any sub-editions—may be entered into CISAC's WWL system, which is kept up to date by the American authors' society ASCAP. The selection of the works to form part of the WWL documentation is left to the discretion of each society or collective administration organization, with the recommendation that care be taken not to overdo the quantity. The WWL system contains data on approximately 850,000 musical works.

30.68 The WWL documentation is available on magnetic tape and microfiche; CD-ROM will be added towards the end of 1992 or early in 1993, replacing the microfiches, which are awkward to handle. The documentation appears in two editions a year, in spring and autumn.

(v) International Fiches

30.69 Before the introduction of the WWL documentation, authors' societies obtained their information from international fiches on works that were not "mass" works, but possessed one of the following characteristics:

(1) they were internationally successful works;
(2) or works of exceptional length or with exceptional instrumentation;
(3) or works having appeared in a sub-edition.

Unlike the WWL documentation, the international fiches give information on the distribution scales applicable. This important additional information could well explain why the amount of international fiches sent every year has hardly decreased at all even since the WWL documentation became available.

(vi) Cue-Sheets

30.70 Cue-sheets contain the basic data of films, and more specifically of the music for those films. Unlike international fiches, cue-sheets are not sent automatically by authors' societies or collective administration organizations; this documentation is supplied on request, being addressed to the authors' society in the country of production of the film in the case of showings or television broadcasts in other countries.

(d) Distribution and Accounting

30.71 After collection of the royalties and after the accounts of works performed or broadcast have been received, the collective administration organization has to calculate the amount payable to each author and to each publisher. This operation is known as distribution, and is one of the most laborious jobs that the organization has to do.

(i) *Principles of Distribution*

30.72 Every author may demand to be paid the amounts corresponding to what the collective administration organization has charged for the works of that author or publisher, after deduction of management overheads and social and cultural expenses, which are dealt with in greater detail below. This *suum cuique* principle is not only the response to the firmly-rooted principles of authors and publishers; it also stems from the legal position of the collective administration organization as the trustee of authors and publishers.

30.73 The *suum cuique* principle cannot be respected unless the collective administration organization has been notified of the works performed or broadcast. The requirement of accounts of those works is therefore a *sine qua non* for the payment of his due to each author and publisher.

30.74 For all the goodwill that is shown, however, accounts of works performed or broadcast are never provided in full detail, and in certain cases it proves impossible to demand them, for instance in the case of the broadcasts relayed to the public or the use of jukeboxes. Royalties for such performances have to be apportioned on the basis of accounts of other performances of comparable music.

30.75 All authors and all editors are to be treated on a strictly equal footing, in the sense that no preferential treatment or privilege can be allowed. That applies in particular to relations between national authors and publishers and those of other countries. The Berne Convention provides in its Article 5(1) for the principle of equal treatment, and that principle has to be rigorously adhered to by any collective administration organization.

(ii) *The Matching Technique*

30.76 Works entered in accounts of music performed or broadcast have to be matched to the documentation on them, as a first stage in the apportionment process. This is a difficult and time-consuming task, which makes it a costly one, so costly indeed that authors' societies or collective administration organizations have made every effort to streamline it with computer technology. The technical applications developed for the purpose are themselves known as "title matching." By means of screens, memories and special indexes, the technique has been developed to such an extent that it is now possible to match a work mentioned in the account to the documentation on it in the space of 20 to 30 seconds. The research goes on, the aim being to introduce totally automatic title matching, but we must expect a degree of human intervention to be always necessary if errors are to be avoided.

(iii) Distribution Stages

30.77 Every collective administration organization controls its own system of distribution, but all systems are the same inasmuch as they are subdivided into three stages:

(1) establishment of distribution classes, that is, designation of the royalties to be distributed on the basis of a particular package of accounts of works performed or broadcast;

(2) calculation of the amount accruing to each work in each distribution class, and the total of those amounts;

(3) subdivision of the total amount by work between the authors and publishers of that work, using the distribution scale.

(iv) Accounts

30.78 The distribution work ends with the result of the calculations that award each author and each publisher an amount for each work performed or broadcast. The amounts then have to be grouped in an account by member, by client and by foreign counterpart. The sending of the accounts has to be accompanied by payment of the appropriate amounts to the beneficiaries.

30.79 Some collective administration organizations confine their accounts to a mention of the titles of the works performed or broadcast and the amounts accruing to those works. Others add figures for the performance or broadcasting of each work, broadcast dates, etc. Experience has shown that the interest of authors and publishers is not focused solely on the amount of the sums distributed; they are also interested in knowing how and where the works have been used. So the accounts of the collective administration organizations have to be regarded as their certificates of proficiency, serving as they do to create and strengthen the bonds of trust between the national administration and authors and publishers.

30.80 An annual rate of submission of accounts is considered a minimum service. Most copyright societies have gone further, sending their members and clients half-yearly or quarterly accounts. The effect of the delays in the sending of accounts may be offset by a system of advance payments. The rate of accounts submission has increased with the technical progress made with computer technology.

(v) Amounts Calculated but not Paid

30.81 Even the best collective administration organization will never be in a position to pay all the amounts calculated for distribution. Amounts accruing to unknown authors—and also to known authors not affiliated to authors' societies—the NS authors referred to above—remain on deposit in a special account held by the organization. This account is managed, in accounting terms, as if it were that of a foreign counterpart—a sort of society representing a fictitious country and grouping all unknown and unaffiliated authors as its members.

30.82 When those unknown or non-member authors subsequently make their appearance by joining a authors' society that has signed a reciprocal representation contract, the amounts on deposit should be paid to that society. The periods for the making of such subsequent payments are determined by the legal provisions on the lapse of claims, especially those applicable in connection with agency without authority.

30.83 In the event of a claim lapsing, amounts held on deposit may be put to another use. That use is however tied to the principle of equal treatment, which rules out any favor to members or clients and any crediting to cultural or social funds. Proper use is confined to the following two possibilities:

(1) the amounts are set aside for a subsequent distribution, and in that way are paid to national and foreign authors and publishers;

(2) the amounts are used for the payment of administrative costs, and thereby serve to lower the percentage deducted for expenses.

(e) Organization of Collective Copyright Administration

30.84 Because the rights involved, as mentioned at the beginning of this chapter, are personal rights of authors which are under collective management, it is important to ensure that the authors remain as closely associated as possible with the exercise of their rights by the collective administration organization. Administration without any reference to authors and or any influence exercised by them would come more under the heading of appropriation. The best structure within which to ensure the constant involvement of authors in the collective administration of their rights is the authors' society, composed of authors and formed and directed by them, and also for instance the cooperative society, with authors and publishers as members. This does not rule out the possibility, in other countries, especially African countries, of the task of collective administration being assigned to State bodies, but in such cases it is essential that the State bodies provide themselves with authors' committees to keep them constantly informed and advised. There are also composite structures, such as authors' societies with administrative boards partly appointed by the government.

30.85 The requirement that authors should not be kept out of the collective administration of their rights should not be interpreted to mean that authors absolutely have to concern themselves with all administrative work. Experience with authors operating as directors of societies—with a few happy exceptions—has usually been unsatisfactory. The author often succumbs to the temptation to abandon all impartiality, and amateurish management has ruined more than one society. Copyright management is a profession that cannot be exercised without sound legal, economic and technical skills. Adequate basic training is therefore essential for all those who are going to concern themselves with copyright management.

(i) Organizational Structure

30.86 Most collective administration organizations have major subdivisions in their administrative structures, with the servicing of authors and publishers grouped in one part, and the divisions concerned with users, including inspectors and regional and local agencies, in another.

30.87 Between these two groups—which correspond to the intermediary role between music "producers" and "consumers"—there are the more "neutral" departments concerned with documentation, distribution, accounting and computer systems. They can be assigned to one or other of the groups already mentioned, or alternatively grouped within a single technical department. Legal business and the handling of musicological problems are more often than not dealt with by the organization's "heads of staff."

(ii) Management Costs

30.88 Management costs are paid for out of the royalties collected. With the rights of public performance and broadcasting—unlike recording rights—the practice is for deductions to be confined to actual, genuine expenses. The percentage of deduction for expenses is therefore going to vary from year to year. Deductions that do not exceed 30 per cent are considered acceptable; rates have been following a downward trend in recent years.

30.89 The principle of equality of treatment, which has been mentioned several times, also operates in the area of deductions for expenses. National and foreign authors and publishers have to put up with the same percentage of deduction.

30.90 It is possible that a number of areas of collective administration will incur expenses in very unequal proportions. Allowance can be made for this by the application of different cost percentages in the various areas, with a higher percentage in the field of public performances, for instance, and a more moderate percentage in broadcasting. In that case the general expenses have to be distributed over the various categories.

(iii) Additional Receipts

30.91 Several months elapse between the date on which the royalties are collected and the date on which they appear in the accounts. During that time the money may be placed on deposit and may generate interest. Other additional revenue may be derived from the rental of offices or accommodation to third parties in premises belonging to the collective administration organization, or from work done on behalf of third parties on the organization's computer installation.

30.92 The additional revenue is closely related to the management of copyright, and therefore does not escape the equal treatment principle. It would be nonsensical to deprive authors and publishers of the interest produced by their money as they await their accounting breakdowns. These considerations limit the possible uses of additional revenue to the following two cases:

(1) it is added to a subsequent distribution;
(2) it is used to pay management costs and thereby serves to lower the percentage deducted for expenses.

(iv) Computer Systems

30.93 The introduction of a computer system is essential if the vast amount of music "consumed" nowadays is to be accompanied by accurate accounts, rapidly drawn up and circulated to authors and publishers. It is therefore advisable, when introducing collective administration of copyright for the first time, to have integrated computer systems available from the outset.

30.94 When the introduction of computer technology has to take place in stages, an order of urgency should be worked out. The area to be computerized as soon as possible, as mentioned above, is the distribution and accounting department. However, this area itself relies on databases with the particulars of authors and publishers and their works. This produces the following sequence of operations:

(1) database of authors and publishers;
(2) database of national works;
(3) distribution and accounting work;
(4) financial accounting;
(5) collecting work;
(6) other work.

This is also an illustration of the need to provide at all times for the later development of areas for computer applications.

30.95 The computerization of collective administration organizations is characterized by the need to have a vast storage capacity available. The data of a vast number of works have to be stored, but relatively few of them are later going to be performed or broadcast. Planning work thus has to include studies on the future enlargement of storage capacity.

30.96 There are few standards that could be used as guidelines in the computerization of collective copyright administration. However, with a view to the international cooperation with the copyright societies of other countries, and also with a view to the use of CISAC documentation, it is advisable to use the standards of the CAE documentation for the structuring of databases of members and clients, and to draw inspiration from the WWL documentation when designing databases of national works.

(f) Social and Cultural Activities

30.97 Every collective administration organization, in regular and close consultation with its members and clients, will do its utmost to promote their social welfare and publicize their music. In order to avoid conflict, in the pursuit of those aims, with the demands of equal treatment, CISAC has clearly and precisely demarcated the limits up to which royalties charged may be used to meet the social and cultural needs of members and clients.

(i) The Means

30.98 Under the CISAC Model Contract, a reciprocal representation contract between authors' societies of different countries, one-tenth of the royalties charged, after deduction of expenses, may be used for social and cultural purposes for the benefit of members and clients. This ten per cent deduction is made both from sums intended for foreign authors and publishers and from amounts to be credited to national authors and publishers. The deduction may be considered a "bonus," by way of recognition for the conscientious and efficient work of music authors and publishers in the interest of the world community.

(ii) Social Welfare

30.99 The collective administration organization is free to choose the structure and operation of its social welfare schemes; it also decides independently on how it should be financed. Systems in operation may be classified in two categories:

(1) one of them is noteworthy for its similarity to the schemes of insurance companies: the ten per cent deductions are regarded as each member's or client's contributions and, on the author's attainment of a certain age, the amount of his life annuity is calculated;

(2) the other endeavors to improve social welfare in the form of a guaranteed income for authors after they have reached a certain age. The insured amounts are calculated on the basis of the amounts resulting from previous calculations.

The advantage of the guaranteed income is that it comes into effect more rapidly, without the accumulation of a reserve of capital having to be awaited.

(iii) Cultural Activities

30.100 In the field of cultural activities, all initiatives and all new ideas are welcome. Solutions differ from country to country and include—among others—the following activities:

(1) music competitions, prizes and festivals;
(2) action to promote music publishing, launching of publication series and sets;
(3) disc or cassette production;
(4) recording facilities; provision of recording studios;
(5) publications on musical subjects, biographies, manuals and catalogues;
(6) financing of music gazettes;
(7) press service for musical matters.

References for Section B
U. Uchtenhagen, *Collective Administration of Copyright*, WIPO/CNR/CA/94/11

CHAPTER 31

The Patent and Trademark Attorney

A. INTRODUCTION

31.1 Industrial property agents deal generally with all matters in the field of industrial property, to the extent permitted by their national laws, and especially with the following three kinds of matters:

(1) the filing and prosecution of applications for patents for invention (and utility models, where applicable), trademarks and industrial designs, and the maintenance of their registration;
(2) advising in matters relating to industrial property rights, including unfair competition, licensing, know-how and transfer of technology;
(3) litigation in all fields of industrial property.

B. THE FUNCTIONS OF A PATENT AGENT

(a) Introduction

31.2 The professionals who practice the profession most commonly known as that of "patent agents" can also be called, depending on the circumstances and the particular country, "patent attorneys" or "industrial property agents" or "attorneys."

31.3 The basic function of the patent agent is to offer his professional services to the community. These services are:

(1) advice in the initial phase of the explanation and definition of the right;
(2) service and performance in the phase of the acquisition of the right; and,
(3) representation and advice in the phase of the maintenance and working of the right and in the phase of possible conflicts which may arise in connection with obtaining and/or protecting the right.

31.4 Generally speaking, the patent agent must give counsel and advice to three types of clients, namely:

(1) individual inventors;
(2) industry, consisting of small and medium-sized companies, as well as large and important industrial enterprises;
(3) foreign clients.

References for Section A
A. de Elzaburu, *Patent Agents: Their Role*, BLTC/19

(b) The Pre-Application Phase

31.5 In this phase, the prospective applicant will have to decide:

(1) whether it or he should seek patent protection for the invention or should try to keep the invention secret and not seek patent protection;

(2) whether it is probable that a patent for invention can be obtained for the invention;

(3) if the decision is to seek patent protection, the applicant must decide in which countries such protection should be sought;

(4) if protection is to be sought in several countries, some of which may be party to the Patent Cooperation Treaty or the European Patent Convention, the applicant will need to decide whether to file an international application under either of these two treaties or whether to file separate national applications.

31.6 Furthermore, in this pre-application phase, the application or applications will have to be written.

(i) Secrecy

31.7 If patent protection is desired, a patent application will have to be filed. The alternative is not to file an application and try to keep the invention secret.

31.8 The choice between these two possibilities requires careful consideration. One cannot keep an invention secret if one opts for seeking patent protection since the invention will need to be published either at the time of the application or when the patent is granted, depending upon national legislation. An invention for which a patent application has been filed will remain secret only if the application is withdrawn before the application is published or, under patent laws not providing for the publication of applications, if no patent for invention is granted either because the application is withdrawn by the applicant or because the application is considered withdrawn, or is refused by the Patent Office.

31.9 One seldom keeps an invention secret unless he believes that his invention will remain secret forever (which is theoretically possible), or for a long period, at least longer than the term for which a patent is granted, so as to have better commercial interest in keeping the invention secret than filing a patent application.

31.10 However, with rapid development of technology, it becomes increasingly difficult for a person to be very certain that his products embodying the invention will not be duplicated by others through products analysis or reverse engineering.

31.11 In addition, inventions may become known to persons other than the prospective applicant in various ways, for example, by inadvertence of the prospective applicant, or by indiscretion of the persons who work in the enterprise in which the invention is made or used, or of the persons to whom the prospective applicant has communicated the invention. Furthermore, where the prospective applicant is in negotiations with third parties about the use of the invention, particularly with prospective licensees, it will be inevitable that the invention be made known to such third parties.

31.12 Patent laws guarantee, in the case of patented inventions, that the knowledge which becomes public through the patenting of the invention cannot be used for manufacturing, etc., without the authorization of the owner of the patented invention. Consequently, publication of the invention which is patented usually does not contain any risk for the owner of the patent for invention. The risk which still exists is that if the grant of a patent for invention is refused after the application had been published, or if the granted patent is later invalidated, the invention is no longer secret. However, if the reason of such refusal or invalidation is lack of novelty, the alleged invention is not really an invention, and the fact that it is known to the public is not the result of the publication of the application or of the patent for invention but flows from the fact that it is part of the state of the art. This argument does not necessarily apply where the reason for the said refusal or invalidation lies in some procedural error or omission, for example, failing to pay the required fees to the Patent Office.

31.13 Another factor that one should consider when one has to choose between trying to keep the invention secret and trying to have it patented, is the risk that any applicant assumes in respect of what is called "inventing around" by third parties. "Inventing around" means that a third party will describe a solution which is essentially based on or "around" the ideas of the applicant's invention but still is sufficiently different from it so that the said solution will receive a patent for invention if sought.

31.14 In general, it is better and safer to try to obtain for the invention a patent than to try to keep the invention secret. This is so because the chances of not being able, in fact, to keep the invention secret are generally much greater than the risk of not getting a patent for an invention that is patentable.

(ii) Determining Patentability

31.15 The question whether the invention fulfills the conditions of patentability is decided by the Patent Office or, if the decision of the Patent Office is challenged in a court, by that court. The prospective applicant should also formulate a preliminary opinion concerning patentability because of the investment—in terms of time and money—associated with the filing and grant of a patent. How can the prospective applicant formulate an opinion on this question? The prospective applicant can do this only in the same way as the Patent Office, that is, by trying to know what the state of the art is, and once this is known, by comparing the invention with the state of the art: if the invention is part of the state of the art or if it lacks the inventive step it is likely that no patent for invention can be obtained; on the other hand, if the invention is not part of the state of the art and represents an inventive step, a valid patent for invention will be obtained.

31.16 Assisting the prospective applicant in identifying the state of the art and in comparing it with the invention is not necessarily among the tasks of an agent. The prospective applicant may decide not to ask for the opinion of the agent in this matter.

31.17 The prospective applicant may reach such a decision for a variety of reasons, for example because it or he is generally better informed about the state of the art than the agent. This may particularly be the case where the prospective applicant has great experience and knows thoroughly the field of technology to which the invention belongs. Or, the prospective applicant may not wish to spend the additional money which would have to be paid to the agent for checking the state of the art: such checking is time-consuming, requires specialists and carries with it a high degree of professional responsibility. All these factors will cause a considerable fee for the agent to be paid by the applicant. Another reason why the prospective applicant may decide not to ask the agent to formulate an opinion on patentability may be that the same invention was already the subject matter of a patent application in another country and the necessary checking of the state of the art has already been completely and correctly effected—at least in the opinion of the applicant—in connection with the other application.

(iii) Determining in which Countries to Seek Patent Protection

31.18 When it comes to the question in which foreign countries, if any, patent protection should be obtained, the prospective applicant and the agent have to compare and combine their respective experience and information about the situation prevailing in respect of each foreign country in which protection is contemplated. Is that country a potential important market for the products for which the invention will be used? Is that country likely one in which researches are being made for same or similar inventions? Is that country one in which there are likely licensees or assignees or in which there are potential competitors likely to try to exploit the invention if it is not patented there? If the answer to at least one of these questions is in the affirmative, patent protection should be considered.

31.19 Not only the local agent but also an agent in the foreign country in which protection is contemplated should be consulted on the question whether patent protection should actually be sought in that country. The foreign agent may be of the opinion that, for some reason flowing from the patent law of that country, an application, if filed, would probably not succeed. Or he may know of anticipatory publications, which were unknown to the prospective applicant, and which virtually exclude the possibility of obtaining a patent for invention in that country.

31.20 If the prospective applicant decides to seek patent protection in several foreign countries and if at least some of those countries are party to the Patent Cooperation Treaty (PCT) and/or to the European Patent Convention (EPC), the question will arise whether one should file an international patent application under the PCT and/or a European patent application under the EPC instead of filing national patent applications in each of the said countries.

(iv) Preparation of the Application

31.21 It is the agent who is primarily responsible for the correct preparation of the application. The practiced drafting of the key parts of the application, namely, the description and the claims, is important for the applicant to get adequate protection of his rights in the invention. Naturally, most of the facts that will be stated in the application are furnished to the agent by the prospective applicant, and it is the latter's responsibility that those facts be correct. But the expression of those facts in the application in a way that all the requirements of the law are fulfilled, and that nothing is omitted that must be included, or appears to be useful to be included, in the application, are the responsibility of the agent. All that the prospective applicant can do here, and only if there is a possibility of choosing among several agents, is that due precaution is used in selecting the agent. His professional qualifications and his reputation will be determinative in such a selection.

31.22 The responsibility for timely filing is shared by the prospective applicant and the agent. If the application is a first application, it should be filed, in most cases, as soon as possible. Such possibility will exist when sufficient clarity exists in the inventor's mind about the essence and the limits of his invention, when the prior art has been checked, and the application has been prepared. The preparation of the application by the agent should be done very quickly but since in the course of drafting it he may have to consult—sometimes repeatedly—the prospective applicant, prompt replies, or immediate availability for consultations, on the part of the prospective applicant, will be indispensable. And, once the preparation is completed, the filing should take place immediately. The urgency of any first filing resides in the fact that, according to the patent laws of almost all countries, when simultaneous applications are filed for the same invention, the patent will be granted to the applicant whose application was filed at the earliest date, or claims the earliest priority date, as the case may be.

31.23 Where the application is a later application in respect of which the applicant has invoked the priority of the first application, timely filing means filing before the expiration of 12 months after the filing of the first application. In respect of the chances of obtaining a patent for invention, it is immaterial when, during those 12 months, the application is filed because the relevant date for judging novelty and inventive step is the date of the filing of the first application and not the date of the filing of the subsequent application. It is the agent's responsibility to know the date on which the 12 months period will expire and to ensure that the application is received by the Patent Office no later than that date. But it is the responsibility of the prospective applicant to furnish all the data required of the applicant well before this date, so as to allow time for the agent to ask for additional information from the prospective applicant, to make translations where translations have to be made, and to exchange views with the prospective applicant on any unclear points.

(c) The Application Phase

31.24 This phase starts once the application has been filed and ends with one of the following events:

(1) the application is withdrawn by the applicant;
(2) the application is abandoned by the applicant;
(3) the application is refused by the Patent Office; or
(4) the application is accepted by the Patent Office, that is, a patent for invention is granted by the Patent Office.

31.25 Soon after having received the application, the Patent Office proceeds with what is called the "formal" examination, or the "preliminary" examination, of the application.

31.26 Such examination is called formal to distinguish it from the substantive examination. The latter is the examination which is mainly concerned with the patentability of the claimed invention, that is, whether the claimed invention fulfills those conditions of the patent law which concern patentability, namely, whether the claimed invention is new, involves an inventive step and is industrially applicable. The formal examination is concerned with most of the other conditions that the patent law prescribes for obtaining a patent.

31.27 The preliminary examination is characteristically designed to examine the following eight questions or groups of questions:

(1) Whether the application relates to an invention which is contrary to public order or morality or which concerns a type of invention which the patent law excludes from the possibility of patenting.

(2) Whether the application contains all the prescribed indications concerning the applicant and the inventor. Usually, what is required is that the application identify the inventor and the applicant (the two may, of course, be the same), and that the identifications are done by indicating their full official names (this is important not only for natural persons but also for legal entities and enterprises) and their addresses.
Omission of the name of the applicant is usually considered to be a mistake that cannot be corrected; a new application will have to be filed. On the other hand, omission of the indication of who the inventor is will usually be considered to be a correctable mistake. Incomplete indications of the name, spelling errors in the names and addresses, omission of the addresses and the indication of incorrect addresses are usually considered to be correctable mistakes. These mistakes may be discovered by the agent himself. If such mistakes are discovered by the Patent Office, it will invite the agent to submit corrections, and the agent should do so within the prescribed time limit.

(3) Whether an agent has been indicated in the application, and, if so, whether he is a person who has the right to act as an agent, whether his appointment has been duly effected by the applicant (by the applicant's signing the application or a separate "power of attorney," that is, a document appointing the agent) and whether the name and address of the agent are indicated fully.

(4) Whether the applicant is an entity or a person entitled to file a patent application. One of the usual requirements in this respect is that the applicant must be a national or domiciliary of the country where the Patent Office is located or a foreign country with which the said country has treaty relations. The matter is usually judged merely on the basis of the allegations concerning the applicant's nationality or domicile as contained in the application. But if the Patent Office has doubts about the veracity of those allegations it may ask for evidence. It will be the task of the patent attorney or agent to procure such evidence from the applicant and to submit it to the Patent Office.

(5) Whether the application contains all the parts prescribed by law. Patent laws usually require the following parts: request, description, claim or claims and abstract. They also usually require that the request contain a title for the invention and that the application contain drawings where they are necessary for the understanding of the invention.

(6) The Patent Office may examine the incompleteness of the priority declaration. "Priority declaration" is a statement, made in the request part of the application, to the effect that the applicant claims the priority right provided for in the Paris Convention on the basis of an earlier application. That earlier

application must be identified in the priority declaration by three elements: the name of the country in which it was filed, the date on which it was filed, the serial number which was given to it by the Office with which it was filed. As far as the serial number of the earlier application is concerned, most laws allow that it be furnished later, separately, within a prescribed time limit. They do so because the serial number of the earlier application may not yet be known to the applicant at the time the application under examination was filed. Here too, however, the agent will have to act spontaneously since most patent laws do not oblige the Patent Office to invite the applicant to furnish the missing serial number.

(7) Whether the application complies with what is usually—but not quite correctly—called the "physical" requirements. These requirements usually include the following: that the application be written on paper; that the paper be of a certain color, size and quality; that the writing on the paper be of a certain color and size; that the text is easily legible and reproducible by photographic methods; that the parts of the application be clearly separated; that each page have margins of certain dimensions; that the margins be left blank and that each page be numbered in a certain place on the page. These are true physical requirements. Other requirements, although not, strictly speaking, physical, usually include the following: that each claim be numbered, that each drawing be numbered and its number referred to in the description, that each part of the application indicate its title, that measurements be expressed according to the metric system and that temperatures be expressed in centigrade and that drawings indicate the scale of reduction or magnification.

Compliance with the physical requirements is usually the agent's personal and direct responsibility because usually it is he, and not the applicant who prepares the final copy of the application, that is the application as it is filed. The preparation of replacement pages or other corrections will also be his responsibility and in many cases may be effected without consultation with the applicant.

(8) Whether the necessary fees for filing the application have been paid to the Patent Office. Such official fees are paid by the patent agent who charges his client in the debit note.

Some Patent Offices permit agents to open what is called a "deposit account" with them. What is meant is that the agent sends a larger amount of money to the Patent Office but it is the property of the agent. When filing an application, the agent indicates the amount that should be transferred by the Patent Office from his deposit account with the Patent Office to that Office's own accounts. This method excludes the possibility of late payment. The method can be further developed to exclude even the possibility of an underpayment. Such development requires that the agent give a general authorization to the Patent Office to compute the amount of any fee concerning any application in respect of which he is the appointed agent and that the Patent Office transfer such amount, without any specific request by the agent, from his deposit account into the Patent Office's own accounts.

(d) Publication of the Application

31.28 The usual provision is that the publication must be effected promptly after the expiration of 18 months after the filing date of the application or, where the application claims the priority of an earlier application, the date on which the publication has to be effected is the date of expiration of 18 months after the filing date of the said earlier application. However, such a law usually also provides that the applicant may, at any time between the filing of the application and the expiration of the 18-month period, request the Patent Office to publish the application and that, in that case, the Patent Office has to publish the application promptly after receipt of the request.

31.29 The reason for an early publication may be that the applicant wishes that the technical solution described in the application should become part of the state of the art as soon as possible. If that solution was not yet disclosed to the public by other means than through the publication of the application—and barring the case of a co-pending application (where the filing dates will count)—then the solution described in the application may be made part of the state of the art through the publication of the application. Once that solution is part of the state of the art, applications filed later by others, in respect of the same solution even if filed in other countries, will in general,—or, at least, should—be unsuccessful. In other words, the earlier the application is published the earlier it will become an impediment for persons other than the applicant to obtain patents for invention for themselves for a solution which is the same as the solution described in the applicant's application. This is true also where the solution claimed as an invention by the third party is not the same as, but merely similar to that described in the applicant's application, but lacks the required inventive step. On the other hand, the earlier the publication, the earlier secrecy is lifted, the sooner others will have the opportunity to try to "invent around" the claimed invention or to use it as a basis for further inventions. The applicant, with the help of the agent, will have to decide what is better for him: a publication as early as possible or a publication as late as possible. If the decision is that an early publication is, on balance, desirable, it will be the task of the agent to request the Patent Office to effectuate a so-called early publication.

(e) Deferred Examination

31.30 Patent laws providing for a so-called "deferred examination" usually provide that the substantive examination, by the Patent Office, of the patent application starts only on the request of the applicant; such a request, however, has to be presented within a certain number of years from the date of the publication of the application. Until that request is made, substantive examination of the application is "deferred," that is, not started but delayed. It should be noted, however, that if the time limit is missed, that is, no request for the substantive examination is presented by the applicant, the application is considered withdrawn.

31.31 It is, therefore, one of the important duties of the agent to note the date on which the application *was* published and, when the expiration of the time limit approaches, to ask the applicant whether substantive examination should be requested. If the answer is that he should present such a request to the Patent Office, the agent will have to do it before the said time limit expires and, since the laws generally require the payment of a substantive examination fee within the same time limit, he will also have to see to it that the payment of that fee reaches the Patent Office within the same time limit.

(f) Opposition

31.32 Opposition is a request, presented by a person or entity other than the applicant, to the Patent Office to refuse the application. The request must indicate the grounds on which, according to the opposing party, the application should be refused. The typical grounds of refusal, are, that the applicant has no right to a patent for invention for reasons concerning its or his identity, that the invention is contrary to public order or morality or that it is in a field of technology excluded from the possibility of patenting, that the application lacks the required clarity and completeness so as to permit the carrying out of the invention by a person skilled in the art, that the invention does not fulfill the conditions of patentability, that is, novelty, inventive step and industrial applicability.

31.33 Pre-grant opposition often results in the period of granting a patent being considerably prolonged, and sometimes even causes the patent being paralyzed. In order to overcome these disadvantages, a growing number of countries have changed, or will change their law from pre-grant opposition system to administrative revocation (post-grant opposition) system.

31.34 What will be the role of the agent of the applicant? It is him that the Patent Office will notify of any opposition filed. The agent will then need to discuss with the applicant what counter arguments against the opposition should be communicated to the Patent Office. If the opposition relates to the novelty or inventive step, the refusal of the application may be avoided if the claims are amended.

31.35 Usually, not only the applicant but also the opposing party will need an agent.

(g) Substantive Examination

31.36 The substantive examination is carried out by the Patent Office. The aim of the substantive examination is to come to a decision on the question whether or not a patent for invention should be granted. If the application complies with the requirements of the patent law, the Patent Office must grant a patent for invention.

31.37 The substantive examination will consider all the possible grounds for refusal.

(h) Amendments

31.38 Most patent laws allow the applicant to amend the application. At the same time, they usually provide that no amendment may go beyond the original disclosure in the application as filed.

31.39 Most laws offer several occasions to the applicant to amend the claims. Typical such occasions are: first, just before the preparations for the publication of the application are completed by the Patent Office; second, at the time the request for substantive examination is filed, together with that request; third, during the substantive examination. The first two occasions, if used, will be the result of a spontaneous decision of the applicant. Using the first occasion may be motivated by a desire to disclose less than what the original application has disclosed. Using the second occasion may be motivated by a desire to reduce the risk of being attacked during later proceedings concerned. Amendments presented during the substantive examination are usually not spontaneous; they are usually inspired by the Patent Office when, through its examiner who carries out the substantive examination, it says to the applicant "if you amend the application in a particular way I shall grant you a patent; if you do not, I shall refuse the application." The suggested amendment usually consists of omitting one or more claims or restricting the scope of one or more claims, the reason being that only the remaining and restricted claims satisfy the conditions of patentability and/or are supported by the description. In such cases what actually happens is that a dialogue is carried on between the examiner and the agent; the latter tries to convince the former that the broader claims are allowable. In this dialogue, the respective views of the agent and the examiner may undergo changes in the light of the new arguments and new documents that they present to each other.

31.40 There is little doubt that this is one of the most challenging and interesting tasks of the agent. It is also a very responsible task because a patent for invention with too narrow claims may be worthless. Where the examiner insists on a restriction which, in the view of the applicant, is unreasonable, it does not have to be accepted by the applicant. The Patent Office will, in such an event, refuse the application. But such refusal does not necessarily mean that the application has been lost. Most laws provide for recourse to a higher authority—for example a review board—or to the courts. As a result of the recourse, the applicant may obtain the patent for invention with the claims as desired by him.

31.41 Since the task under consideration is such a responsible one, no agent will normally amend an application without the express and specific authorization of the applicant. Each proposed amendment is usually thoroughly discussed, orally or in writing, between the applicant and his agent.

(i) Role During the Life of the Patent

(i) Maintenance

31.42 Most patent laws provide that the owner of the patent for invention has to pay, once a year, a fee for maintaining the legal effect of the patent for invention.

31.43 Paying the maintenance fees on time is one of the important and responsible tasks of the agent. The agent will have to keep a record of the dates on which each payment will become due; he will have to make sure, in good time, what the desire of the owner of the patent for invention is: is maintenance desired or not desired? and he will have to make sure that he receives from the owner of the patent for invention in time the amount needed for the payment of the maintenance fee.

31.44 The responsibility of the agent is great because missing the due date will cause additional expense, namely, a surcharge. Missing the time limit of the grace period may also deprive the owner of the patent of all its or his patent rights.

(ii) Invalidation Proceedings

31.45 Most patent laws provide that any person may challenge the validity of a granted patent for invention before a court by bringing an action or lawsuit. The challenger is the plaintiff and the challenged party is the defendant. The latter, according to the laws of different countries, may be the owner of the patent for invention and/or the Patent Office, personified by its head (usually called, in English-speaking countries, "Commissioner," "Comptroller," "Controller" or "Registrar," and, in other countries the equivalents, in their languages, of the English "President," "Director General" or "Director").

31.46 The role of the representative of the challenger as well as the role of the challenged party is, of course, of paramount importance. He has, naturally, to be familiar with the history of the substantive examination and administrative revocation or opposition. He will also need to determine whether the same invention was the object of substantive examination or administrative revocation or opposition in the Patent Offices of other countries, or the object of infringement or invalidation actions in foreign courts, and, if so, what arguments were used and what the final outcome of the applications and actions was. Such information will be most useful for the representative.

(iii) Compulsory Licenses

31.47 The patent laws of a number of countries provide for the possibility of granting compulsory licenses. A compulsory license is a license given to an entity or person ("the compulsory licensee"), on its or his express request, by a government authority (for example, the Patent Office) to work the patented invention, and/or import products which include the patented invention; such license may be given against the will of the owner of the patent for invention.

31.48 The services of a representative, a specialist in patent law, will usually be needed by both parties. The party requesting the compulsory license will have to allege the non-working or the insufficient working, in the country, of the patented invention and the lapse of the three-year or four-year time limit prescribed by the Paris Convention. The applicant or the owner of the patent, if it or he wishes to resist the request for compulsory license, will either have to prove that the patented invention is sufficiently worked, in the country, by it or him or by persons or entities authorized by it or him, or it or he will have to specify and prove "legitimate reasons" for non-working or insufficient working of the patent.

(iv) Infringement

31.49 According to the laws of most countries, the owner of the patent for invention has the right to turn to the courts when an infringement has occurred and may ask for relief in one or more of the following forms:

(1) that the court order the infringer to stop its or his infringing acts;
(2) that the court order the infringer to pay damages to the owner of the patent for invention;
(3) that the court punish the infringer.

31.50 The preparation of any legal action will require the advice and assistance of legal and technical specialists. So will the preparation of the defense in a legal action. And so will the representation of both the plaintiff and the defendant before a court.

(j) Applications for Foreign Clients

31.51 The foreign patent agent will typically provide the required specification and particulars of the applicant and any priority claim under the Paris Convention but will have to rely on the local agent to:

(1) ensure that the application is filed by the specified deadline—usually the anniversary of the "basic" application;
(2) present documents in the proper form under local law and practice;
(3) advise on further information required;
(4) ensure that forms are correctly completed, and
(5) keep the foreign agent properly informed as to later deadlines for lodging supportive documents and meeting those deadlines when documents are forwarded by the foreign agent. Such documents include forms, formal drawings and "priority documents"—official certified copies of basic applications, with translations if necessary.

31.52 The foreign agent will also expect the local agent to advise of any particular difficulties which might arise under local law or practice, e.g. as to subject matter or format of claims, as to the nature of the intended application, or as to the adequacy under local law of the applicant's stated entitlement to file the application.

31.53 In the longer term, the key role of the local agent is to ensure that all deadlines affecting the application are advised, monitored and met, and to advise the foreign agent of peculiar requirements of local law and practice.

(k) Foreign Applications for Domestic Clients

31.54 The filing of the basic domestic application initiates the 12 month period provided by the Paris Convention. Within that period, the applicant will need to make a decision as to the countries in which he will confirm or extend his patent protection. An essential role for the agent in this connection will be to guide the applicant to ask the right questions and to assist him with clear information as to short and long term costs, and as to the situation in each country with the domestic application. The applicant himself will want to consider the market potential in each country; the possible modes of exploiting the patent, including licensing; and the level of technology in each country which will determine whether the invention can be put into use and, therefore, whether any additional protection can be obtained with a patent. He will also need to determine a total budget and to establish priorities.

31.55 It is very important that the agent keeps the applicant fully informed as to the costs he will incur: patent protection in multiple countries is quite expensive, especially if the invention is not a success, and many a patent applicant is caught by surprise by the medium and long-term costs of maintaining his patent protection.

31.56 Once the choice of countries has been made, the agent must undertake a number of steps in preparation for instructing the foreign agents. The first step is to select the agents who will act on his and his client's behalf in each foreign country. Many countries require at least local addresses for service for patent applicants but, in any event, it is much more practical for applicants to retain the services of a local skilled professional in each foreign country. This choice of agents is an important decision which should not be undervalued. Especially in countries where the language is not the same as the agent's or applicant's, the applicant will be relying upon the foreign agent to ensure that his interests are best looked after in that country. In making the choice, the agent will be considering matters of reliability, professional skill, and sound business judgment.

31.57 A further preparatory step for the agent is to determine what formal papers are required for each application as well as to prepare such papers. Most countries require a power of attorney executed by the applicant. Assignments may also be necessary. Application forms can usually be completed and signed by the local agent.

31.58 The next preliminary step is to prepare specifications for the foreign applications. In many cases these specifications will not be the final document as translation will need to be carried out into the foreign language. A skilled agent will not merely photocopy the local specification for use abroad but will consider whether he might fruitfully rearrange the language or structure of the claims to better suit the practice of each country, or perhaps augment or reduce the description.

31.59 Finally, taking careful account of the applicable convention deadline, the agent will forward full instructions to his selected overseas counterpart at the appropriate time.

C. CORPORATE PATENT ATTORNEYS

31.60 A patent department in a corporation usually consists of both technical and clerical staff and is, in many cases, headed by a patent attorney.

31.61 While the main function of a patent attorney's office is often limited to proceedings for the acquisition of industrial property rights the scope of the business of the corporate patent department covers a much wider field including business and commercial considerations:

(1) filing and processing applications;
(2) searches and monitoring;
(3) prior art documentation;
(4) coordination with the research and development division of the corporation and with patent attorney's offices;
(5) licensing and licensing negotiations;

References for Section B
A. de Elzaburu, *Patent Agents: Their Role*, BLTC/19
International Bureau of WIPO, *The Patent Agents' Tasks: Part l, Tasks up to the Filing of the Application*, BPAC/6 & 7
International Bureau of WIPO, *The Patent Agents' Task: Part II, Tasks During the Pendency of the Application*, BPAC/8 & 9
International Bureau of WIPO, *Patent Agents' Tasks: Part III, Tasks During the Life of the Patent*, BPAC/10
G. Noonan, *The Role of a Patent Agent*, WIPO/PS/KL/86/5

(6) maintenance of rights;
(7) training of any personnel who are or may become involved with industrial property matters;
(8) assignment of inventions for reward under remuneration systems;
(9) prosecuting and defending infringement suits.

31.62 Patent attorneys' offices become involved, or are consulted, in all the above areas. However, the patent attorneys' offices are, of course, in a passive position here as corporate patent departments take all initiatives, and issue their instructions for any work to be done by the patent attorneys' office.

31.63 Corporations which have a successful and planned patent management policy do recognize the necessity for the effective use of outside patent attorneys' offices with experts well qualified to handle particular matters, and which also have a sufficient number of back-up staff to assist.

31.64 Corporations also sometimes make use of outside patent attorneys' offices as if they were part of the corporation's own patent department, and discretion is given to the patent attorneys' office personnel to deal with and interview inventors directly, only reporting later any action taken, or results thereof, to the corporation's patent department.

31.65 Large corporations also have a liaison staff member for at least every separate technical department or laboratory within the corporation and sometimes the liaison staff may total 100 or more.

31.66 The main functions of a corporate patent department, as indicated above, include the following matters:

(a) Acquisition of Industrial Property Rights

31.67 The services of a patent attorney's office are utilized most for this type of work. The group of staff who handle such matters receive a draft specification or memorandum concerning an invention from the inventor(s). Some corporations, as a matter of policy, file patent applications by themselves, in which case the persons involved in the department re-draft or complete the specification, claims or drawings into proper form for filing. But, again, as a matter of policy, many corporations use outside patent attorneys for completing the applications for filing with the Patent Office. Also, there are many corporations which file applications with the Patent Office by themselves but use outside patent attorneys for making overseas filings. Some corporations make the domestic filings by themselves, and use outside patent attorneys for filing some of their foreign cases, while still doing some of their own foreign filings.

31.68 In any case, it appears that the business relating to acquiring rights is an area in which the corporate patent department can utilize outside services most, so that they can use their time more effectively for other policy or management affairs in the enterprise.

(b) Searches and Monitoring

31.69 The services of an outside patent attorney's office are utilized to some extent, but most of the business of this nature is handled by or within the corporate patent department. Nowadays, computer data-based searches or monitoring are increasingly being used.

(c) Prior Art Documentation

31.70 This involves the collection and documentation of patent Gazettes or other patent literature.

(d) Coordination with the Research and Development Divisions of the Corporation

31.71 The corporate patent department members join in the planning of research and development, and in the discussion and formulation of patent strategy, or in the study of patent strategy with the various divisions concerned.

(e) Licensing

31.72 Licensing patents or preparing various contracts is one of the most important functions of the corporate patent department. How the acquired rights can be effectively utilized is constantly examined. The corporate patent department is also involved in licensing negotiations.

(f) Maintenance of Rights

31.73 The keeping of records, and attending to the payment of annual fees for keeping the acquired rights in force, are also very important functions of the corporate patent department.

(g) Other Activities

31.74 The training of personnel who are, or will become, involved with patent matters is constantly carried out. Patent departments hold lectures and seminars for these personnel, or send them to outside courses or lectures. Patent department members are given the opportunity to observe the research facilities and actual research being carried out. All patent-conscious companies have some kind of remuneration system for rewarding employees for inventions. The patent department has a role in making assessments of the inventions which will be the subject of such remuneration.

31.75 Every time a new product is put on sale or is to be sold on the market, it is the work of the patent department to make a thorough search to ensure that there will be no infringement of patents already in existence. This is very time-consuming and a very important matter to be taken care of.

31.76 Another area wherein the corporate patent department becomes instantly involved is when an infringement action is taken against a third party or is to be defended.

References for Section C
K. Asamura, "Administration of a Patent Attorney's Office; Patent Policy and Management in an Enterprise" (1985) 10 *Intellectual Property in Asia and the Pacific*

D. ASSOCIATIONS OF PATENT AGENTS

(a) National

31.77 Associations of patent agents are, first of all, national in their scope. They group the professionals of a given country in a national association.

31.78 Such associations establish rules of professional conduct and supervise the ethics of that conduct. They impose penalties (or propose such to the competent governmental authority) when a member of the association fails to comply with the rules of the association.

31.79 Most national associations also undertake studies of industrial property with a view to improving their country's industrial property legislation. It is, therefore, customary for governments to seek the opinion of these associations when legislative reforms are contemplated.

31.80 Consequently, representatives of the professional associations are usually appointed as members of the official (governmental) committees constituted in the various countries for the drafting or revision of industrial property laws.

31.81 Every member of a national association must comply with the professional rules and regulations, and the association is an authority to which third parties can turn in the event of some irregularity committed by a member of the association.

(b) International

31.82 The principal international association of practitioners in the field of industrial property is the Fédération internationale des conseils en propriété industrielle (FICPI) (or International Federation of Industrial Property Attorneys).

31.83 FICPI was founded in 1906 as an association of industrial property attorneys in private practice and has its headquarters in Basel, Switzerland.

31.84 The principal aims of FICPI are the following:

(1) to enhance international cooperation within the profession of industrial property attorneys in private practice, promote the exchange of information and harmonize and facilitate business relations between members;
(2) to maintain the dignity of its members and the standards of the profession of industrial property attorneys in private practice on an international scale;
(3) to express opinions with regard to newly proposed international and national legislation, insofar as such legislation is of general concern to the profession, and to defend the interest of its members, in particular with respect to the maintenance and invigoration of the system of industrial property protection and of the position of industrial property attorneys in private practice.

31.85 FICPI was founded in Europe, although today its scope is universal. Present membership includes "National Groups" or "National Sections" in Africa, the Americas, Australia, Asia and Europe. In many countries in which there are no National Groups or National Sections, there are individual members of FICPI.

31.86 Another important international association, whose membership also includes attorneys in private practice, is the Association internationale pour la protection de la propriété industrielle (AIPPI) (or International Association for the Protection of Industrial Property).

31.87 AIPPI was founded in 1897 and is headquartered in Zurich, Switzerland. Its principal objectives are:

(1) to propagate the need for the international protection of industrial property;
(2) to study and compare existing laws with a view to taking steps to protect and unify them;
(3) to work for the development of international conventions concerning the protection of industrial property; and
(4) to distribute publications, to make representations, and to organize periodical congresses with the object of raising discussions and proposing resolutions on outstanding questions relating to industrial property.

31.88 AIPPI, like FICPI, has "national groups" throughout the world.

(c) Regional

31.89 In Europe among the regional associations of industrial property professionals is the Union of European Practitioners in Industrial Property (formerly the Union of European Patent Attorneys and Other Representatives Before the European Patent Office). It was founded in Brussels in 1961.

31.90 The membership of this association comprises almost a thousand practitioners plus professionals in the employment of industry in countries which took part in the elaboration of the European Patent Convention.

31.91 The general object of the Union is to study problems relating to the protection of industrial property and to the profession of the members of the Union in the European sector.

31.92 The Union is a private association, whereas the official body that groups all the professionals appearing on the list maintained by the European Patent Office is the Institute of Professional Representatives before the European Patent Office.

31.93 One of the objectives of the said Institute is to promote compliance by its members with the Code and Rules of Professional Conduct. The Code governs the conduct and other activities of the members insofar as such activities are related to the European Patent Convention signed in Munich in 1973.

31.94 There also exists in Europe an association of professionals not in private practice, but in the employment of companies. It is called the European Federation of Agents of Industry in Industrial Property (FEMIPI). There exists a similar association in the United States of America. It is called the Associate Corporate Patent Counsel.

31.95 A similar regional association in Asia, the Asian Patent Attorneys Association (APAA), is formed, among others, of patent attorneys from Japan and Australia.

References for Section D
A de Elzaburu, *Patent Agents: Their Qualifications and their Associations*, BLTC/20

E. THE FUNCTIONS OF A TRADEMARK AGENT

(a) Introduction

31.96 The trademark agent performs the same functions for trademark owners, as patent agents perform for patent owners. In some countries both groups of functions are performed by patent agents. In other countries the professions are separate.

31.97 In some cases, a trademark agent works with an enterprise as a member of the legal staff and is authorized to make final decisions on any matters concerning trademarks for the enterprise. In such a capacity, he give advice on trademark matters directly to executive officers and he carries out such business as the registration and renewal of trademarks, trademark licensing and the elimination of infringements.

31.98 In most cases, however, the trademark agent practices independently of any enterprise, and, as such, he represents a client enterprise in registration and renewal of trademarks, licensing of trademarks, elimination of infringements and other matters, and gives advice on any and all matters advantageous to his clients. Therefore, a trademark agent should basically refrain from representing a plurality of enterprises in competition with each other and also from contracting with them a position of legal counsel.

31.99 It has been said that one is qualified to be a trademark agent both in name and reality only if one is proficient in the selection and registration of trademarks, and their effective use in trade and commerce. Trademark agents need to be skilled in trademark management in a broad sense, including trademark licensing and treatment of infringement cases. As such, the trademark agent should have a sufficient amount of information easily accessible on trademark systems and practices prevailing in various countries since they vary from country to country. This makes it possible to protect trademarks or merchandise travelling to all world markets.

31.100 The trademark agent is specifically called on to perform the following functions:

(1)   to advise his clients in selecting new trademarks best suited to their businesses;
(2)   to deal with problems which will arise in various circumstances in the course of trademark registration, such as objections raised by the examiner or oppositions filed by a third party;
(3)   to advise his clients in an opportune manner as to good trademark practice and/ or use which will enhance the reputation of the trademark and maintain this as a permanent right;
(4)   to check points for serious consideration in trademark licensing, and advise his clients on such points, thereby keeping them from encountering difficulties on the way; and
(5)   to take for his clients the earliest and best possible measures against counterfeits which may affect their own trademarks.

(b) Choosing a Trademark

31.101 Although trademarks generally do not need to be registered before they can be used, and indeed some borderline trademarks can become registrable after many years of use, supported by evidence that they have become distinctive in the trade, it is preferable to choose trademarks which stand a chance of being registrable as devised.

31.102 The first step is to come up with a short list of possible trademarks to be applied to a particular product or range of products. Each of the marks on the list has applied to its tests shown. Of those marks which survive, as not being descriptive, misleading or pejorative (particularly when viewed as being foreign words of which the translation or transliteration into other important languages is unacceptable), a search is made through trademarks registered in the respective class(es) of goods. If a conflicting mark is encountered, then it has to be checked. If it is in use in the marketplace and the registration is in force, the would-be owner should reject his candidate. If the conflicting mark is in force, but no evidence can be found that it is in use, thought should be given to approaching its owner to see if he would be prepared to sell (assign) it, for a "fair" consideration. If it is not in use, and not for sale, then perhaps it could be expunged from the register on the ground of non-use. If that works, that would clear the way to the mark under investigation being registered in its turn.

31.103 If the risk of being sued for infringement is thought to be too high, then a fresh mark should be thought of, and the clearance process gone through again. If the risk is acceptable, an application should be made to register at least the new trademark against which there are fewest potential objections.

31.104 In most countries title to a trademark is based on registration. However, in some countries prior use is a condition of registration. In this event once a mark has been selected and adopted the intending user should produce appropriate packaging and advertising.

(c) Application for Domestic Registration

31.105 In most cases, the domestic application for trademark registration is filed prior to foreign applications. It is natural that the registration of a trademark should be made with a view to obtaining complete protection of the registered trademark.

31.106 Thus, it becomes necessary first to make sure that the registration does not conflict with any prior registered trademarks owned by others. In case an application is thus found to be registrable, the form of the trademark to be registered should be studied. In ordinary cases, it is considered that the simplest form of a trademark can enjoy the widest protection.

31.107 In arguing against the objection to the application (taken by the examiner in a Trademark Office) due to the trademark's lack of distinctiveness, the important point the trademark agent should consider is whether or not the trademark has long been commercially used in the country in which the application is made. In other words, the trademark agent should prove that the trademark has acquired a secondary meaning.

31.108 Generally speaking, judgments on the distinctiveness of trademarks are made by taking into consideration the current language in the country in which a trademark registration is applied for, and all other conditions concerned. Thus, it should be noted that the earlier the registration of the trademark in the applicant's country the earlier it may be considered in the country in which a later trademark application is filed.

31.109 On the principle of substantive examination in the country of trademark registration the examiner frequently issues objections to the effect that the trademark under application for registration is too similar and might be confused with a prior-registered trademark owned by someone else.

31.110 Such objections may be countered by limiting the designated goods to ones for which the applied-for trademark is actually used, or by submitting arguments opposed to the objection of the similarity of the trademarks.

31.111 Trademarks applied for are published for public inspection in the Official or Trademark Gazette before or after registration. This gives persons interested in such trademarks a chance to object or to initiate a cancellation action against the trademark registration.

31.112 Even when a trademark registration is opposed by a third party, the opposition is sometimes withdrawn in exchange for a concession the applicant makes, such as limiting the designated goods in the application to goods for which the trademark is actually used or restricting the form of the trademark in which it is used.

31.113 In case the examiner objects to the registration of the proposed trademark due to its similarity to a prior registered trademark, or in case a prior trademark owner brings an opposition proceeding on grounds of similarity, the trademark agent begins to examine trademarks similar to the cited trademark, so as to evaluate the examiner's objection and/or the oppositions raised by the said trademark owner.

31.114 In case there are no existing trademarks similar to the trademark cited by the examiner or by an opponent, and the cited trademark has long been used, it is understood that the prior registered trademark enjoys such substantial protection as to eliminate any possibility of registration of similar trademarks applied for later.

(d) Applications Abroad by Domestic Trademark Owners

(i) Introduction

31.115 In most countries foreign applicants must be represented in trademark procedures by a trademark agent or other qualified representative, for example, an attorney. In addition, an applicant may use the services of a trademark agent or attorney in his country in connection with trademark applications to be filed abroad.

31.116 It is necessary to prepare powers of agent for each country in which applications are to be filed and which require the appointment of a representative. For this purpose, normally a form is to be filled in, which is issued by the agent to be appointed. In each of the forms, it is necessary to fully identify the applicant, who has to sign the power of attorney. In other respects, the requirements may vary from country to country.

31.117 In all countries, the reproduction of the trademark is an essential requirement of an application for registration. Therefore, when the powers of attorney are prepared, it is also necessary, for most countries of the world, to order a printing block or print which is to be used for filing abroad.

31.118 Where rights to a trademark are derived by use, it is necessary to submit samples showing the manner in which the mark is used, as a condition for filing an application.

31.119 The decision to file a trademark application outside the home country can be made regardless of whether the mark in question has been used prior to filing and, in most countries of the world, there is no compulsory registration requirement. Thus, registration abroad is normally not a statutory condition precedent to use. However, registration has numerous advantages particularly in countries where trademark rights are derived by the act of registration. Registration affords the registrant the exclusive right to use the mark. It enables the rejection of confusingly similar marks and it becomes an important tool in licensing third parties to use the mark.

31.120 Where should the trademark agent file foreign applications? The countries in which trademark rights are acquired primarily by registration, or where rights of a prior user are not easily recognized, deserve the most adequate trademark protection. In countries in which the owner of the trademark intends to license the trademark to third parties and where the proposed licensed user must be registered, registration of a mark is a condition precedent to the recording of the licensee as a registered user.

(ii) Prosecution of Applications

31.121 The trademark agent will have the task of prosecuting the foreign trademark applications.

31.122 In all jurisdictions having an examination procedure, where any objection is raised, there is an opportunity to respond. In answering such objections it is advisable to submit arguments, relying on the administrative and/or judicial interpretations of the appropriate statute governing the objection.

31.123 It is advisable for the trademark agent to refer to the trademark statute in each country where objections are raised, so that a decision can be made, based on the statutory law of the country in question.

31.124 If the written arguments filed at the local Trademark Office fail to overcome the objections, the next step in the many jurisdictions whose procedure allows a hearing is to request such a hearing and submit oral arguments. If the application is not allowed on the merits of the case, it is necessary to consider whether the objection can be overcome by the submission of evidence of the mark having acquired distinctiveness by use in the country in question.

31.125 In certain cases, the trademark agent may decide to submit evidence of distinctiveness of use even if such evidence is not required to overcome an objection, and thereby attempt to obtain a "stronger" registration.

31.126 Apart from the question of the inherent distinctiveness of a mark, in many jurisdictions the applicant will encounter references to earlier registrations or applications which are deemed, by the local Registrar, to prevent registration of the mark. The procedure varies from country to country. In one group of jurisdictions, the citations are for informative purposes only, and it is possible for the applicant to insist that the application be published as allowed. Although the official report is informative only, the local practice may include the service of notice on the owners of the previous cited registrations of the allowance of the application or grant of the registration, affording the owner of prior marks actual notice of the opportunity to file opposition or cancellation actions.

31.127 In other jurisdictions it is necessary for the applicant to submit arguments to overcome the citations. In this area of the law, it is essential to know the pertinent sections of the statute and the court cases interpreting the statutes.

31.128 The possibility of seeking the consent of the prior owner whose registration has been cited should be explored. The direct approach to a prior registrant may place the prior owner on notice of an application of which the prior owner might otherwise never become aware. The timing of the approach, in relation to the progress made with applications in other jurisdictions, is essential before negotiations are begun.

31.129 It is also advisable to consider the relevant practice of "consents" before the local Trademark Office. In most jurisdictions, written consents are persuasive on the local Registrar to resolve the doubt in favor of the applicant. In some countries, such as Japan, consents are not deemed relevant, while in other jurisdictions, such as Sweden, a written consent is conclusive on the Trademark Office. The degree of cognizance of a written consent will be another important consideration in determining the advisability of negotiating for a consent. In other jurisdictions, a consent may not be essential, provided the applicant agrees, as a condition for allowance of the application, that notice of allowance of the application be served on the prior registrant who is thereby afforded the opportunity to file an opposition.

31.130 In order to obtain a consent, the trademark agent may consider limiting the specification of goods of the application. The owner of the prior registration may be satisfied if the list of goods to be registered and to be used by the applicant is sufficiently restricted. The trademark agent may conduct these negotiations directly with the owner of the registration or may prefer that the negotiations be handled by the foreign associate.

31.131 If, despite all effort, the application is still rejected, consideration may be given to amending the mark by the omission or addition of a single letter, which may result in the allowance without the necessity of filing a new application. Otherwise the addition of a distinctive device may achieve the desired result.

31.132 Finally, prior to an appeal to the court from a rejection of the application, it is necessary in some jurisdictions to request the Registrar's written opinion, which, in some cases, will result in an official action allowing the application, when there was no previous indication that the application might proceed to allowance.

(e) Licensing

31.133 If the applicant or registrant intends a licensee to use the mark in a particular country, it is essential to follow the registered user procedures to make certain that the use by the licensee or the intended use by the licensee inures to the benefit of the licensor.

31.134 In common law countries, the procedure usually followed is the recording of the licensee as registered user. If the licensor will not use, or does not intend to use, the mark abroad, and the licensee is the only party who will have the intent to use the mark, it will be essential to apply for the recording of the licensee as a registered user simultaneously with the application for registration of the mark. There are judicial decisions which hold that failure to apply for recording of the user as a registered user at the time of filing the application renders the mark and its registration invalid.

The papers usually required for the entry of a registered user are:

(1) authorization of agent for execution by licensor;
(2) authorization of agent for execution by licensee;
(3) joint application for registration of registered user;
(4) statutory declaration;
(5) statement of case;
(6) license agreement.

31.135 As regards the trademark license agreement, the first clause usually grants an exclusive or non-exclusive right to use the mark(s) subject to standards and specifications of the licensor. There is usually an inspection clause. The inspection is exercised by the trademark owner or by the authorized representative of the proprietor of the mark. The owner of the trademark normally has to review all written material prior to publication. A term or time limit for the agreement subject to termination by the proprietor is always provided.

31.136 With regard to licensing, the jurisdictions of the world can be divided into five major groups. In the first group of countries, it is advisable to record a license agreement with the local Trademark Office. In the second group of countries, a registered user document must be prepared and recorded abroad. In the third group, simultaneous registered user procedures must be filed—i.e., filing the trademark application must be simultaneous with the registered user application. The fourth group of countries includes jurisdictions where the entry of the registered user can be extended to other jurisdictions. In the last group of countries, the trademark use may jeopardize the validity of the trademark registration if the owner licenses the trademark to a third party.

(f) Maintenance of Trademarks after Registration

31.137 The trademark right is said to be a vulnerable right. This is because trademarks are always in danger of turning into the generic name of an article or being diluted. In fact, trademarks may easily turn into generic names, if the owner uses them in an inappropriate way, or if the competitors, consumers, or the mass media, such as newspapers or magazines are allowed to use them as if they were generic names. Among well-known cases are "cellophane" and "escalator".

31.138 If a competitor is allowed to use any similar trademark on goods of the same kind, or if the use of the trademark is overlooked even on goods other than the one for which the trademark has been registered, the artistic character of the trademark will be diluted, thus impairing its value.

31.139 It must be understood that in order to keep the trademark from turning into a generic name and/or becoming diluted, trademark management must be conducted intensively.

31.140 In such a situation, the trademark agent should check and keep watch on the use of the trademarks owned by the client and prevent them from being improperly used. In case such improper use is detected, the trademark agent should take appropriate action immediately or when the opportunity presents itself.

F. SKILLS AND KNOWLEDGE BY A PATENT AGENT

31.141 The profession of patent agency requires a combination of skills which are not readily available even in university graduates. It is worth considering systematically just what the requirements are for a qualified patent professional.

(a) Technical Background

31.142 Since patents, by their very nature, relate to new technology which is often at the very forefront of advanced scientific research, it is absolutely essential that the patent professional has a thorough understanding of the technical field concerned. Thus a university degree or a qualification of equivalent level in a science or engineering discipline is normally an essential pre-requisite.

(b) Literacy

31.143 It is quite essential for a patent professional to be able to express in reasonably clear and unambiguous terms the inventions to which the patent specifications which he drafts relate. In many countries, particularly with the early specialization in schools between the science and arts subjects, the applicant having the technical background required does not necessarily have the facility to do this.

(c) Legal Background

31.144 Whilst some knowledge of legal subjects would be helpful, it is found that this can be acquired. The greatest problem in this regard, particularly with people who are rather weak in item (b) above is the ability to comprehend the language in which much legal information is couched and, even if this can be achieved, the flexibility of thinking to approach matters in a legalistic as opposed to a scientific/technological manner.

31.145 It is believed that there is a very real difference in these approaches and that the technical graduate who for three or four years has been examining questions according to the scientific method, will often find it rather difficult to adapt to the methods of legal analysis. Often the legal points will seem to him to be rather trivial but, of course, the interpretation of patent claims and their scope does need an appreciation of such points.

References for Section E
S. Kimura, "The Role and Tasks of a Trademark Attorney" (1984) 8 *Intellectual Property in Asia and the Pacific*
International Bureau of WIPO, *Trademark Agency II (Asians Abroad)*, WILAW/BKK/83/L.XVI
K. Weatherald, *Patent Agents' Manual*, WIPO Pub. No.707(E)

(d) Personality

31.146 There is no doubt at all that, as in almost all other fields, a helpful, co-operative and understanding personality is a great asset. One must be able to communicate in a pleasant and effective way with a wide range of people ranging from factory operatives and research workers to legal counsel and including business executives who, above all, wish a rapid and clear exposition of problems and clear and unambiguous recommendations for their decision. Summarizing the above the potential patent professional must combine the actual or potential ability to communicate and express himself as a scientist, as a lawyer and as a business man and often to do all three of these simultaneously.

31.147 After a complete inventive teaching has been developed, it is the task of the patent attorney in conjunction with the inventor to formulate a corresponding patent application which should cover the invention in its broadest sense. The patent attorney should not rely on the inventor as to what he thinks he has invented. The attorney must extract the invention, in discussion with the inventor, from the scope of the special problem which the inventor was confronted with. Normally, the invention in its broadest meaning is then realized through this discussion, so that a correspondingly broad patent application can be formulated.

31.148 This important aspect of the work of the patent attorney cannot be taught in seminars or at the universities on a theoretical basis. The precise and comprehensive description of inventions in patent applications and the formulation of the patent claims is essentially a matter of practical experience, for which the patent attorney with his technical education has to be a real partner of the inventor in the discussions. For this reason, a technical degree from a university or an equivalent education is required. Furthermore, in most industrialized countries the profession of the patent attorney can only be practiced by persons who have passed an examination.

31.149 In addition to the absolutely necessary practical experience which a candidate must have, legal training is provided through which the candidate gains the required legal knowledge. This legal knowledge should include the legal provisions of the candidate's own country and of the most important industrial countries, as far as these relate to industrial property protection. This naturally also includes knowledge of the Paris Convention.

References for Section F
H. Bardehle, *The Profession of Patent Attorney*, WIPO/ACAD/E/93/20
R. Hurst, *Training to be a Patent Agent*, WIPO/PA/BKK/90/9

CHAPTER 32

The Teaching of Intellectual Property Law

A. INTRODUCTION

32.1 During the past decade, there has been a growing awareness of the importance of the intellectual property system to economic and cultural development. A renewed awakening of the role of intellectual property in the countries of the various regions of the world has led more recently to the adoption or revision of national legislation on patents for inventions, industrial designs, trademarks, copyright and the transfer of technology, as well as to the establishment or modernization of government structures that administer such legislation. At the same time, the legal profession, consisting of law officers in the various government ministries, judges and legal practitioners, are attempting to respond to the need for a better understanding of the problems presented by the new technologies and by the new technological means of communication of information and ideas and of their impact on industry and commerce and on the quality of life. In this process of change, professors and researchers at universities and institutes around the world are being called upon for inspiration, guidance and expertise.

32.2 The importance of intellectual property in the modern world goes far beyond the protection of the creations of the mind. It affects virtually all aspects of economic and cultural life. As a result, intellectual property education at the university level must have relevance for many areas of education and training.

32.3 The purpose of this chapter is to highlight the importance of intellectual property educational programs at the university level, and to give some guidance to university professors and administrators as well as governmental officials, on how to establish an effective university curriculum in intellectual property.

B. INTELLECTUAL PROPERTY TEACHING PROGRAMS

(a) Types of Intellectual Property Programs

32.4 The range of students that would benefit from intellectual property education is broad. It includes students of business, law, the fine arts, engineering, the sciences, journalism, etc. Naturally, a broad range of teaching programs should include intellectual property in their curriculum. However, of the many types of programs that might include intellectual property, three stand out as most commonly including intellectual property courses. First, almost all business programs include some overview of the basics of intellectual property. It is important for students who hope to go into business or government to have a basic understanding of the role that intellectual property plays in the modern concepts of economics and trade. Second, basic law degree programs offer intellectual property courses that give students a general understanding of the philosophy and application of intellectual property law. Even law students who do not intend to specialize in intellectual property should be familiar with the basic rights that are protected by intellectual property law. Third, specialized post-graduate (LL.M.) programs typically provide a more comprehensive, specialized knowledge of the theory and practice of intellectual property law. Such programs are intended to supplement the often fragmentary knowledge that a practitioner acquires in his practice, by covering all of the issues that are of importance to the protection of intellectual property.

32.5 Specialized intellectual property programs deal with three main aspects of intellectual property practice: (1) the nature and extent of rights that are available to protect intellectual property; (2) the process of obtaining and registering intellectual property rights (called "*prosecution*" where the filing and examination of an application is required), and (3) the process of protecting and enforcing intellectual property rights once acquired (most often this is done in the courts through civil "*litigation*").

32.6 Educational programs in business primarily focus on the first aspect—the nature and extent of the rights that are available to protect intellectual property. While such knowledge is only the starting place for an intellectual property practitioner, these are the most important aspects for business decision-makers and government policy planners. These programs give a basic understanding of the types of creative and technological products and processes that are protectable, the forms of intellectual property protection that are designed to protect each type of intellectual creation, and the effectiveness of the protection available. The student gains an understanding of the ways in which protection of intellectual property can enhance economic competitiveness. This understanding is even more important for the business planner or the economist who is concerned with the long-term economic health of his company or his country than for the author, artist or inventor, who is primarily concerned with the practical aspects of obtaining protection.

32.7 In addition to business programs, all basic university training programs for lawyers include courses in commercial law and property law, as well as courses dealing with civil and criminal procedures. Such courses are an indispensable foundation for a basic understanding of the concepts that are reflected in intellectual property law. Professors teaching such courses, particularly those of commercial, economic or property law, often include sections on various types of intellectual property protection, especially those which are of interest to the business or economics student.

32.8 Some university law schools include one or several classes, or even a complete program of classes, designed for students who intend to become intellectual property practitioners. These classes are designed to give future specialists a broad, if not deep, comprehension of the range of possible forms of intellectual property available. Such classes are valuable for the student who intends to help authors and inventors protect their works under national or foreign law, and for the student who, as a business attorney, will advise his client, the company, on this aspect of law which will have great importance for its viability and growth.

32.9 Students who enter a post-graduate specialized program in intellectual property (for instance an LL.M. degree program) will typically be intellectual property practitioners who are interested in deepening their understanding of the legal foundation of intellectual property law, and of increasing their skills in the acquisition and enforcement of intellectual property rights. Often, practitioners from one country will enroll in an LL.M. program in another country in order to gain a better understanding of the intellectual property laws in that country. Such programs go into great depth on the theoretical underpinnings of the law of intellectual property. But, being designed for practitioners whose daily work consists of the acquisition and protection of intellectual property rights, such programs will also include practical classes taught by experienced practitioners, covering actual techniques of prosecution of applications for intellectual property rights and litigation to enforce those rights.

(b) Intellectual Property Faculty

32.10 The quality of an intellectual property educational program will depend in large part on the level of experience and interest of the faculty. There are a number of full-time university faculty members in most countries who have made their specialty the study of one or more aspects of intellectual property. However, many universities do not have such specialists, and the education of students in intellectual property depends on professors who take an side interest in the field in addition to their main specialty. Recently, because of the increasing importance and popularity of the field of intellectual property, more and more professors are making this field their specialty. In addition, many practitioners who have had years or decades of experience in the practice of intellectual property law have decided to leave their practice of law and dedicate themselves full-time to the teaching of intellectual property. These former practitioners, once they have gained the necessary experience with the skills of university teaching, can make the most effective teachers of intellectual property law. Full-time law professors who decide to make intellectual property their specialty must undertake the unenviable task of mastering the maze of detailed knowledge necessary to the expert in intellectual property protection. However, the professor who undertakes this task finds in it a world of intellectual challenge and reward that makes the effort well worthwhile.

32.11 An interim source of qualified teachers that may effectively fill the vacuum left by the lack of full-time intellectual property professors consists of practicing attorneys who are willing to give part of their time (one or two nights a week) to teach intellectual property courses. Often called "Adjunct Professors", these instructors provide an effective and economical way of building a comprehensive and high-quality intellectual property program. This is a symbiotic process—it brings the benefit of many different qualified experts to a university program, providing a breadth of expertise that would not be available in a few individuals, at a fraction of the cost, and gives to the practitioner the prestige of being affiliated with a law school program, the motivation to keep current with new developments in the law, plus the stimulus and inspiration that comes from teaching to fresh minds who engage in re-thinking old problems. Students enjoy hearing stories about the practical experiences of the expert practitioner, and the practitioners enjoy sharing their expertise with an audience which (a rarity in the life of an attorney) is eager to listen and is ready to put its faith in what is said.

32.12 Basic intellectual property courses in a law school curriculum are best taught by full-time law professors who can dedicate the time needed to counsel and guide students through the program and into the specialty that they are most suited to. Ex-practitioners who become full-time professors have the advantage of their experience in the specialized job market of intellectual property law, and often acquire their counseling skills quickly. Experienced law professors have the advantage of understanding law education and the needs of law students.

(c) Teaching of Intellectual Property in Developing Countries

32.13 In the last decade, WIPO has taken a number of initiatives in order to bring about an awareness of the programs of teaching and research in the field of intellectual property that are being carried out in various developing countries and thus foster teaching and research in the field of intellectual property. These initiatives were designed to complement the activities of WIPO for the training of personnel, which are a part of the development cooperation program, in other words, the legal-technical assistance program, of WIPO.

32.14 In an endeavor to stimulate teaching and research of intellectual property WIPO published in 1970 two surveys, one on the teaching of industrial property law and the other on the teaching of copyright law. Those surveys described the number, subject matter, the level, the hours and the kind of instruction and related aspects concerning the courses given in various universities and other institutions of higher learning in some 30 countries of the world.

32.15 While the number of universities and institutions at which intellectual property law is taught has increased dramatically since that survey was made, the fact remains that in a number of developing countries, including some developing countries in the Asia and the Pacific region, intellectual property law has not yet been introduced as a course in the curriculum or is only taught as part of a course on commercial laws. This is largely because of scarce resources or because the number of students interested is limited.

32.16 There are, nevertheless, a number of universities and other institutions in developing countries which have introduced intellectual property courses. They have also organized periodically, in cooperation with the government bodies and the legal profession, interested organizations, and with the assistance of WIPO, general introductory courses on intellectual property law. Moreover, in some developing countries, special courses, as well as workshops and seminars have been organized on particular subjects of intellectual property law, directed to university students, researchers from institutes, government officials, legal practitioners and businessmen, and even members of the public, having a particular interest in intellectual property law. Symposia and other meetings have also been organized, devoted to a review of intellectual property laws in the light of current economic, technological and social developments.

32.17 At the forefront of these developments in the teaching of intellectual property law have been university professors who have had foresight and have realized that intellectual property is not an abstract concept but that it is an indispensable instrument in achieving desired economic and cultural objectives. Such professors need to be encouraged and accorded the means to bring their aspirations to fruition.

C. SELECTING INTELLECTUAL PROPERTY COURSES

32.18 Four types of intellectual property courses are typically taught at the university and law school level. These are: Survey Courses; Specialized Courses; Advanced Seminars; and Practice Courses.

32.19 *Survey Courses* are basic, broadly focused courses, which are intended to give an overview of the various fields of intellectual property law, with enough specific facts to "whet the appetite" of students who might decide on a specialty in intellectual property. Survey courses, which may be titled, for example, "Introduction to Intellectual Property" or "Patent, Copyright and Trademark Law," are popular with business and government students, who are looking for an economic perspective on the protection of the creations of individuals. The teaching of survey courses is especially suited for professors who are just starting to teach intellectual property—they may learn, along with the students, the breadth and complexity of intellectual property protection. However, many experienced professors who specialize in intellectual property enjoy teaching survey courses because they find that the interaction with students from a wide range of backgrounds continually broadens their perspective.

32.20 *Specialized Courses* are courses which focus in-depth on a single field of intellectual property. Specialized courses carry titles such as "Introduction to Patent Law," "Copyright Law and Practice," "International Trademark Law," "Intellectual Property Licensing," "Unfair Competition," etc. These courses convey the particulars of the field of law under consideration, including a study of the statute, regulations and procedures involved. Court interpretation of the law and judicial doctrines in common law countries, procedures for applying for and obtaining rights, and procedures for enforcing rights are some of the topics which would be addressed. After finishing such a course, a student should be familiar with all of the important doctrines of the field of law, and should have a good understanding of the most important standards for obtaining and enforcing rights.

32.21 *Advanced Seminars* are designed for students who have taken a specialized course in a particular field, and are prepared to learn more detail about one or more particular aspects of that field. An example of an advanced seminar in the patent field might be a course which examines the history of the protection of an invention, from the time that a patent application is filed, through the process of examination and issuance of the patent by the patent office, and through all stages of enforcement of the patent through litigation in the courts. In this way, the student would learn the practical application of the principles of patent prosecution and litigation that were learned in a general form in the specialized patent course. Another type of advanced seminar might examine an aspect of intellectual property law which does not arise often enough to make it the subject of a specialized course. For example, a seminar on "Antitrust Aspects of Intellectual Property Law" would fill in a gap that may have been left by the basic courses. Seminars can also give students the opportunity to prepare research papers on current issues for presentation to the rest of the class, or give the professor the chance to teach his own narrow specialty in depth, or to teach new and emerging fields such as biotechnology law or computer law.

32.22 *Practice Courses* focus on the actual steps that an attorney would take in practice to obtain and enforce intellectual property rights. Courses such as "Patent Office Practice," "Copyright Litigation" and "Trial Advocacy for Intellectual Property Attorneys" challenge students to do the very things that they will be asked to do in their legal practice. Practice courses are often best taught by practicing attorneys as Adjunct Professors, who will be teaching the very things that they are currently doing in their daily work.

32.23 The task of selecting the proper type of course to include in an intellectual property curriculum will depend on the nature of the students, the faculty, and the type of degree program offered. Most university programs, when they decide to incorporate intellectual property education, will begin with a modest program, offering a survey class and one or two specialized classes. They will gradually increase the number and complexity of courses as the level of student and faculty interest increases. Usually this happens quickly, and often the only limiting factor is the willingness to expand and to experiment with new types of courses.

D. CHOOSING TEACHING MATERIALS AND WRITING A SYLLABUS

32.24 One important, and in some ways the most difficult, aspect of teaching an intellectual property course is the selection of teaching materials. Of course, the types of materials chosen will be dictated to a certain extent by the form of the course to be taught. However, after choosing a course the instructor may discover that appropriate teaching materials simply do not exist in printed form, or that the materials needed exist in several different sources which must be combined. Where a satisfactory text is not available, where the presentation of a chosen text is to be re-arranged, or where several texts are used in combination, a proper "*course syllabus*" must be provided to facilitate the organization of the class and the effective education of the student.

(a) General Comments on Choosing Materials and Writing a Syllabus

32.25 Preparations for introducing a new course in the curriculum take time. Much labor must be exerted in compiling teaching material and reference sources on the particular area of intellectual property to be taught. Teaching materials used by other professors can be a starting point, and may even be used until the professor has had enough experience with the class to be able to choose his own materials. But some guidance and even some sort of starting material is needed. This section will aid the new or experienced teacher in selecting proper teaching materials for his or her intellectual property courses.

32.26 In all cases, a course text should be chosen which is compatible with the interests, expertise and teaching style of the professor. A new professor, or a professor who is teaching an intellectual property class for the first time, must choose a text which will educate and challenge, not only the students, but himself as well. An established text written by a recognized authority in the field will always be the safest choice for a beginning professor.

32.27 More experienced professors and practitioners, who are more familiar with the available texts, may decide to gather materials on their own, or combine resources from several different texts to reflect the course content and emphasis that they consider most appropriate. This allows the materials chosen to better reflect the instructor's own philosophy and teaching style, and prevents confusion between what is presented in class and what is read in the text. While differing points of view should always be presented, such differences are effective as teaching tools only when properly presented by the professor as such, and not when they appear to the student as differences between the professor and the text.

32.28 It is very difficult and time consuming to compile one's own course materials. However, given the relative lack of effective teaching materials available, sometimes this must be done. If at all possible, the class itself should not be used as a testing ground for the materials. Time should be taken in advance to carefully choose, review, edit and organize materials for presentation to the class.

32.29 A comprehensive syllabus covering the entire course should be presented to the students on the first day of class. A syllabus is a list of the topics to be presented in the course and the reading materials which correspond with each topic. The syllabus provides an "educational road map" for the students. An effective syllabus might separate the topics to be covered in the class in outline form, list the days that each topic will be covered, and give the names and page numbers of the reading materials for which the students will be responsible at each class. At its best, a syllabus will provide a coherent outline of the course, giving the students in advance an idea of the topics to be covered, and giving them in retrospect a guide for reviewing what they have (or should have) learned in the course. In scheduling topics for the various class sessions, it goes without saying that the amount of time spent on each subject should correspond with the importance or difficulty of the subject. However, some advanced subjects should only be mentioned in passing and should be left for more advanced courses. The choice of topics to be covered and the extent of coverage for each topic is a skill that the professor learns only with experience. One test for the effectiveness of a syllabus is to use it as an outline for introducing the content of the course on the first day of class, and for reviewing the content of the course on the last day. This follows the effective communication strategy of "tell them what you are going to say, say it, then tell them what you said."

(b) Choosing Materials for Particular Courses

32.30 Materials for *Survey Courses* are the most widely available of texts for intellectual property courses. In choosing a text for a survey course, the instructor should take the time to review all available texts. It is often advisable to contact teachers of the course at other universities and ask which texts are used and why.

A text should be chosen which gives, as much as possible, a balanced treatment of all topics. Each student in a survey course will have a different interest, and all students deserve to have their interests addressed. Intellectual property texts may also be supplemented with articles or texts which focus on the economic and political aspects of intellectual property. These may stimulate interesting discussions, and will deepen the student's understanding of the relation of intellectual property to the economic health of his nation.

32.31 Of particular interest with respect to survey courses, WIPO published, in 1988, a book entitled "Background Reading Material on Intellectual Property." This book, of which the present book represents a revised edition, consists of a collection of reading materials on various aspects of intellectual property law and administration. The text of this book is based on statements which appear in various publications of WIPO, for example, the commentaries to the model laws, the explanatory notes in the Licensing Guide for Developing Countries (which deals with technology transfer arrangements), the preparatory documents for, and the reports of meetings of, committees of experts and the papers prepared by the International Bureau for presentation at various seminars, workshops and symposia organized in various countries of the world. The book is intended to be used by students in courses of study at universities, in particular, by students in the developing countries of Asia and the Pacific, who are most affected by the unavailability of suitable teaching literature on intellectual property. The book is also useful to universities and other tertiary institutions in the developing countries of the region in the planning of appropriate curricula for the teaching of intellectual property law. While primarily intended for students, this book may also be of use as a reference work to government officials, attorneys and businessmen concerned with intellectual property law or its administration. To complement that basic reference work, WIPO has commissioned national supplements containing a commentary on the intellectual property laws of certain countries, so far, India, Malaysia, Pakistan, the Philippines, the Republic of Korea, Sri Lanka and Thailand. These supplements are designed to include the basic legislative texts, judicial decisions and other legal sources specifically oriented to the country in question.

32.32 Course materials for *Specialized Courses* are more difficult to find than those for survey courses. The reason is simple: there are fewer students taking specialized courses than survey courses, so that the writing and publication of specialized texts is not as well rewarded. However, excellent materials are often available, especially in the patent, trademark and copyright fields.

32.33 Where a specialized text is available, careful review of the text is necessary before selecting it. The instructor should check to see if the text is written by an expert in the field, whose work will have been checked by others knowledgeable in the field. He should supplement even the best of texts with current materials which update the text and make the abstract content of the text more approachable and more interesting. Copies of actual patents, copies of industrial design registrations along with samples of the product for comparison, samples of two product labels whose marks are confusingly similar, tape recordings of two songs which are substantially similar, all give life and reality to the principles that are conveyed by a text.

32.34 Where specialized texts are not available, the instructor may select a survey text which has a comprehensive chapter on the field that is the subject of the specialized class. Often a survey text which is not acceptable for a survey course because it does not give balanced treatment to all subjects will serve well as a specialized text for the subjects that are overemphasized.

32.35 Other materials which may be adequate as texts include hornbooks, annotated statutes, cases or journal articles. While these are usually more appropriate for advanced seminars or practice classes, there are many such materials which give an excellent overview of basic principles, and can be easily rounded out by a classroom lecture.

32.36 Choosing materials for an *Advanced Seminar* is often simpler than for a survey or specialized course, since the materials will be dictated by the subject matter of the seminar. Sample applications and court documents can be obtained from the relevant sources. In-depth articles and studies may be distributed as a basis for discussion. A single important case may, by itself, provide sufficient material for an entire seminar, supplemented of course with commentaries and subsequent cases relying on the main case.

32.37 *Practice Courses* should utilize the very same materials that are used by practitioners in the field. Statutes and regulations should be referred to directly. Manuals of procedure published by industrial property offices may be purchased and studied by the students. In litigation practice courses, actual court rules and procedures should be followed. The success, quality and usefulness of a practice course will vary directly with the similarity of the course to the actual practice in the field of law. If the course teaches litigation or appeals practice, the students might argue an actual case from court files, or might argue an appeal on actual briefs submitted by the parties to a case which has been decided by the appeals court. Where patent claim drafting is taught, using an invention from an actual patent will allow the students to compare their claims with those actually issued.

(c) Teaching Materials in Developing Countries

32.38 The availability of teaching materials on intellectual property in developing countries can be summed up this way: there is a dearth of teaching materials especially suitable for use in the developing countries. What material is available is likely to teach law and practice that may not be applicable to the developing country.

32.39 It will, therefore, in many cases, fall to the professor himself to choose the materials for an intellectual property course. The problem then lies in the process of making available to law professors in developing countries who are interested in planning and formulating a curricula on intellectual property law the necessary documentation which they could examine and from which they could build the desired teaching materials. That documentation could include the laws and regulations of other countries, the preparatory documents prepared by the International Bureau of WIPO on various intellectual property questions which have or are currently being studied and the various reports of the committees of experts which dealt with those questions, as well as the records of the diplomatic conferences at which new treaties were adopted or existing treaties were revised on the basis of those studies and reports. Each professor knows the limits of the resources of his faculty and its perception of any new curriculum matter that could be introduced, as well as other constraints, including the extent of the interest of the students in pursuing the topics of intellectual property law in competition with another topic or other topics, perhaps more attractive and even more rewarding in that a specialization in that other topic or those other topics could lead to a greater remuneration once the student enters the legal profession.

32.40 In addition to what has been said about the documentation of WIPO as a source of the kinds of questions and possible solutions that could be the subject matter of courses and teaching materials, attention is drawn to the papers presented at the annual meetings of ATRIP during the last ten year period. It has been a tradition at those annual meetings that the experiences of the professors in planning the curriculum and in devising teaching materials would be reported upon. Their presentations are reproduced at each such meeting. A list of those presentations, as of July 1, 1992, may be found in document BIG/307 issued by WIPO.

32.41 In addition to the book entitled "Background Reading Material on Intellectual Property," described above, a number of other publications issued by WIPO may be of particular interest to professors and researchers. These publications are listed in the WIPO Catalogue of Publications. It is the policy of the International Bureau of WIPO to meet the requests of professors for such publications, except those that have been issued in limited quantities and because of their length are rather expensive to produce. This is the case, in particular, as concerns the records of diplomatic conferences and the international classifications, especially the International Patent Classification. Except for these, publications are sent to the professor or the researcher, without charge, and the mailing cost is borne by the Organization. Also helpful is a list of documents issued by WIPO and ATRIP concerning teaching and research in intellectual property law. That list bears the code citation BIG/307 and includes the documents issued as of July 1, 1992.

E. TEACHING METHODS AND EDUCATIONAL STRATEGIES

(a) Methods of Teaching

32.42 Methods of teaching vary from country to country, from university to university, and from professor to professor. No one method of teaching will work for all instructors, and no one method will work for all types of students. However, in the legal field, there are two different basic approaches that are often used. These are the case method of teaching, and the problem method of teaching.

32.43 *The Case Method of Teaching.* The teaching materials which are rather well-known and widely used in the law schools of universities of the United States and the United Kingdom are based on the principles of the common law with its overlay of statutes and administrative regulations and interpretive judicial decisions. The teaching of that law is usually approached through the traditional "case method" of teaching calls for a certain disciplinary approach on the part of the professors and the students. That teaching is not unknown in other countries but it may not be practiced in those countries for a variety of reasons.

Some of those reasons are attributable to the fact that the nature of the legal system that exists in the various countries in the European continent and which influences a number of countries in French-speaking Africa and in Latin America, and to a certain extent in Asia, does not lend itself to this method of teaching. The use of such teaching materials devoted to intellectual property requires that the course be constructed on the basis of those principles of common law, statutes, regulations and judicial decisions, and often requires a detailed explanation of those legal sources so that they can be understood in the light of the legal sources of the legal system in the developing country concerned.

32.44 *The Problem Method of Teaching.* An alternative approach to the case method is gaining popularity even in the common law countries. Under the problem method approach, a professor will describe a particular set of circumstances which raise interesting legal problems. The students will be asked to apply the relevant principles of law to analyze and solve the problem. This requires of the student not only knowledge of the law, but also effort in thinking through all of the aspects of the circumstances and applying the law to achieve a just result. The general feeling among specialists who have looked into the question of teaching methods, in particular the working group established jointly by WIPO and ATRIP, have concluded that it might be possible in the international context to present samples or models of situations reflecting intellectual property questions and how those situations are treated under the various legal systems.

(b) Effectiveness Assessment

32.45 One of the most important and effective tools in teaching, yet one that is often overlooked, is the tool referred to as "effectiveness assessment." The most frequent method of effectiveness assessment, the final examination, is too often seen as a tool to evaluate only the student. In fact, it is an excellent tool for evaluating the instructor as well. One way to use the exam as an evaluation tool for the instructor is for the instructor to set specific goals at the beginning of the term, and to prepare exam questions that will test whether these goals have been achieved. The students' performance in answering these exam questions will give the instructor a good idea of how effective he has been in conveying his ideas.

32.46 A second means of assessing the effectiveness of the instructor is to request an anonymous evaluation of the instructor by the students. Such a survey, taken on the last day of the term, will allow the students to make suggestions for improvement of the class and of the methods of instruction, and will give the professor some much-needed objective feedback. To ensure anonymity and fairness, the surveys should not be filled out in the presence of the instructor, and should not be available to the instructor until grades have been distributed. Where the students are assured of the confidentiality of their comments, and that negative comments will not affect their grades, more objective comments will be encouraged. Questions about the quality and usefulness of the teaching materials and the syllabus are also helpful.

(c) Encouraging Student Involvement

32.47 Another often overlooked, yet highly effective, educational tool is to encourage practical student involvement outside of the classroom. Many law schools or universities allow student participation on publications such as law reviews or journals. Many of these journals specialize in aspects of intellectual property law, and most would welcome contributions in the field. Some schools also hold conferences on various topics of intellectual property. Participation, by attending or assisting in the organization of these conferences, can provide a student with a different perspective on the field. Finally, where the educational system allows students to engage in practical employment during law school, they may work part-time for judges, lawyers or government agencies involved with intellectual property.

F. CONTACTS AMONG PROFESSORS AND RESEARCHERS

32.48 Contacts among professors and researchers of different countries are an essential means for enhancing the role of intellectual property and for promoting intellectual property teaching and research. In a number of countries, professors and researchers often come together to form an association to advance their common cause. However, in the field of intellectual property research and teaching, such associations are rare.

32.49 Cognizant of this, WIPO embarked on a course of action to promote contacts among professors and researchers of intellectual property law with a view to promoting awareness of the need for intellectual property teaching and research. In 1979, WIPO organized a round table of professors interested in teaching industrial property law. The International Association for the Advancement of Teaching and Research in Intellectual Property (ATRIP), which was established in 1981, stems from a recommendation that was made at that 1979 round table.

32.50 ATRIP, whose membership has reached over 250, consists of professors and researchers throughout the world. It meets annually, once every two years at the Headquarters of WIPO in Geneva, and the other year in the country of its President, who is elected along with an executive committee for a two-year term. The Association has held annual meetings in other countries, in particular at the European Patent Organisation (EPO) in Munich, Germany, at the George Washington University in Washington, D.C., United States of America, at Trinity College, in Cambridge, United Kingdom, at the University of Costa Rica, in San José, Costa Rica, and at the University of Salamanca, in Salamanca, Spain. It held its most recent annual meeting in August 1993 in Stockholm, Sweden, under the presidency of Professor Gunnar Karnell of the Department of Law of the Stockholm School of Economics.

32.51 At each annual meeting of ATRIP, professors in each part of the world recount their experiences, their trials and tribulations in obtaining approval of the curriculum planning committee of their faculty for the introduction of one or more courses in intellectual property law and describe the scope of the course or courses, the amount of curriculum time devoted, the teaching material, the number of the students and the level, and the results that have been achieved. Those presentations provide a rich source of thought for the content of the courses, the teaching materials and the teaching methods upon which other professors can draw in planning or reviewing their own courses.

32.52 At the national level, in China, the Chinese Universities Society of Intellectual Property (CUSIP), was established in 1985. It consists of the representatives of institutions of higher learning in China, including universities and institutes of science and engineering. Its purpose is to promote the teaching and research of intellectual property.

32.53 In addition, study visits to meet with professors in other countries facilitate discussions of curriculum planning and course content, and observation of teaching methods. In the last five years, WIPO has organized study visits for professors coming from a number of developing countries. Such visits took place in France, Germany, the Netherlands, the United Kingdom and the United States of America.

G. THE ROLE OF PROFESSORS IN THE LEGISLATIVE PROCESS

32.54 National legislations and regulations in the field of intellectual property are being adopted in a number of countries and are constantly being reviewed in others. Such legislation and regulation need to take into account economic changes and the effects of technological advances. In most countries, the process of adoption and review is initiated by the executive branch, under which the industrial property office and the copyright office are placed and whose officials together with the law officers in the Ministry of Law or Justice usually prepare drafts of the legislation, and, subsequently, proceed to discussions among interested circles and ultimately, consideration as well as decision take place in the legislative branch.

32.55 In many developed countries, not only is there an expertise in the industrial property and copyright offices but such expertise exists in other government units, particularly, those concerned with trade matters, and also in the regulatory agencies that review or control television and radio broadcasting, or oversee the operations of firms that engage in various business practices.

32.56 In many industrialized countries, to assist the executive branch it is not unusual for it to establish a law reform commission or other special advisory body to make recommendations and even draft legislation.

32.57 Similarly, in industrialized countries, the parliaments are usually structured to include a committee or subcommittee specially devoted to intellectual property matters. The staff of such a committee are particularly knowledgeable of intellectual property matters and are constantly in contact with the interested circles to seek out and ascertain their views on the various policy questions and solutions to be considered in the process of legislative reform.

32.58 In contrast, in most developing countries, apart from a very few senior officials in the industrial property office or the copyright office, there is a relative lack of knowledge on the part of key government officials of the policy and implications underlying considerations and practical intellectual property questions. In those countries, it is more likely that legal practitioners and law professors in the universities will play a predominant role in the process of preparing and reviewing legislation. As general lawyers or practitioners and as professors who have over the years taught subjects in the area of commercial and economic law, they have developed a certain expertise in approaching legal questions which can be applied by them in working out solutions to intellectual property issues.

32.59 Increasingly, such persons seek to expand their horizons and knowledge of intellectual property questions by undertaking comparative studies of the laws of other countries dealing with intellectual property and related questions and by seeking consultations with government authorities and circles in other countries. And, since such persons will play a crucial role in the legislative process, it is not surprising that there is a natural thirst on their part for information concerning intellectual property laws and practices in other countries.

32.60 The international community attempts to respond to this need. Such persons can spend time at research institutes such as those listed in the section below, or visiting the capitals of other countries whose legislation in the field of intellectual property is well developed. Such persons can also benefit from study visits to Geneva to discuss current issues with the Secretariat of WIPO. Within the limited resources of the budget of WIPO, which is financed by the direct contributions of governments, funds have been made available to provide assistance to law professors wishing to undertake contacts with their counterparts in other universities and with the officials in industrial property and copyright offices in other countries. In a number of instances, such arrangements have also been made with the direct assistance and help of the universities and of the government in those other countries.

H. RESEARCH INSTITUTES FOR INTELLECTUAL PROPERTY LAW

(a) Introduction

32.61 Teaching at the university level is never fully effective without the opportunity for professors to undertake intensive individualized research. Such research, in the highly specialized field of intellectual property, can best be done in conjunction with other researchers with the same or related areas of interest. This explains the movement in recent years toward establishment of specialized centers of research on intellectual property law, or centers which combine both research and teaching, often as a part of the law school of a university.

32.62 Legal research centers in developed countries are of course a fairly well-known feature. While centers devoted exclusively to research in intellectual property law have not been very extensively established in industrialized countries, there are some very notable exceptions. The Max-Planck Institute for Foreign and International Patent, Copyright and Competition Law is one of the most famous, if not the most famous, center in the world for research on intellectual property law.

32.63 The objectives, structure and functions of an institution devoted to research of intellectual property law was first elaborated upon by Professor Friedrick Karl Beier, the Director of the Max Planck Institute, in a paper presented by him at the Regional Symposium on Intellectual Property Law Teaching and Research in Asia and Pacific, which WIPO organized with the State Education Commission of the People's Republic of China and the assistance of the United Nations

Development Programme (UNDP) in Beijing, China, in November 1987 (cited in the list of documents issued by WIPO and ATRIP, WIPO document BIG/307, July 1, 1992). Since then, the topic of how and what research should or can be undertaken in the field of intellectual property has been discussed at annual meetings of ATRIP and in seminars and symposiums organized by WIPO in developing countries and is included in the program of the present National Symposium here in the Philippines.

32.64 In the United States of America, one of the very first centers devoted exclusively to research in intellectual property was associated with the Law School of The George Washington University and was known as the Patent, Trademark and Copyright Foundation. It subsequently became a part of the Franklin Pierce Law Center where it has flourished with the support of the legal profession and industry.

32.65 Other intellectual property centers exist, though not exclusively for research. In North America, there is the Center for Intellectual Property Law at the John Marshall Law School, in Chicago, Illinois, which combines law school and post-graduate teaching of intellectual property with research and dissemination of intellectual property information. The Canadian Intellectual Property Institute, which was recently established in Hull, Canada, is very closely linked with the government authorities responsible for intellectual property matters.

32.66 On the continent, in Belgium, a Center for Intellectual Property Law has been set up at the Catholic University of Louvain. In Sweden, there is the Center for Intellectual Property and Media Law of the Stockholm School of Economics. In the United Kingdom, there is the Intellectual Property Law Unit of the Centre for Commercial Law Studies of Queen Mary College, at the University of London. In France, there is the Center for International Industrial Property Studies (CEIPI), at Strasbourg, (where WIPO, in cooperation with CEIPI, conducts each year a training course on industrial property for officials from developing countries). There is also the Institut de recherche en propriété industrielle Henri-Desbois, in Paris, the Centre universitaire d'enseignement et de recherche en matière de propriété industrielle (CUERPI) in Grenoble and the Centre Paul Roublier in Lyon.

32.67 In the Asia and Pacific Region, the Law Center at the University of the Philippines has been in operation for some years and has contributed to the analysis of intellectual property laws and has made studies on new legislation in the field of intellectual property. In China, an Intellectual Property Center was set up, jointly sponsored by the Patent Office of the People's Republic of China, the Trademark Office and the Copyright Administration of China. In the Republic of Korea, the International Intellectual Property Training Institute was set up, in Daiduk, in 1991.

32.68 In these centers mentioned, organized research and research projects are undertaken by individuals and research teams with defined tasks.

32.69 Students in attendance at university law schools also engage in research to the extent that this is a requirement of a certificate or diploma or other recognition of the successful completion of their studies. So also the professors, associated with a university, or a technical institute or with a center, themselves undertake individual research or are members of a research team. The scholars at these centers have specialized knowledge in given fields of intellectual property. While these centers are not devoted exclusively to research, or exclusively to teaching, they conduct excellent programs in research, teaching and training.

(b)   Establishing an Intellectual Property Law Institute and Library: The Chinese Example

32.70 Some years ago, consideration was given in Beijing to the establishment among interested universities of a joint program or a joint center or institute for the teaching of intellectual property law.   The idea was put forth by Professor Guo Shoukang, of the People's University of China, in Beijing, and he managed to advance it to the stage where serious consideration was given to it by the Ministry of Education which went so far as solicit the help of WIPO in outlining its establishment.

32.71 In responding to that request, WIPO organized for a team of specialists (consisting of Professor Dessemontet of the University of Lausanne, who also teaches at the University of Fribourg, François Curchod, who is currently Deputy Director General of WIPO and taught intellectual property law at the University of Neuchâtel, and Gust A. Ledakis, the Legal Counsel of WIPO) to go to Beijing for discussions with officials of the Ministry of Education and with the academic leadership (the President and Vice-Presidents and Deans of the Law Faculties of the Beijing People's University, Qing Hua University and Peking University) with a view to exploring how such program, center or institute might be established and financed.   It was contemplated that the program, center or institute would have associated with it universities in other parts of China, in particular in Wu Han, in Shangai and in X'ian. On that occasion, representatives of those universities came to Beijing to join in the discussions.   Professor Guo Shoukang ultimately succeeded in establishing an institute within the framework of the People's University of China, in Beijing. Arrangements with other universities have yet to be concluded.

32.72 Special mention should also be made of the Patent Law Research Institute which initially formed a part of the Patent Office of the People's Republic of China, principally because of the way it was established. That Institute has an extensive collection of legal materials on intellectual property. The driving force beyond that Institute is Professor Tang Zhongshun, who is probably the most preeminent expert in intellectual property law in China. Professor Tang was also a member of the committee which considered the type of industrial property legislation the People's Republic of China should adopt and participated actively in the drafting of that legislation and in its subsequent implementation.

32.73 Some years ago, Professor Tang had the idea of establishing a collection of legal materials in the field of industrial property that would enable the Patent Office and scholars wishing to do research, to keep abreast of developments in other countries, and to do so without having to incur the additional expense or the time to seek out such material in other countries. To assist him in his goal, WIPO provided Professor Tang with the opportunity to come to Geneva and to examine the legal materials in WIPO's very specialized intellectual property law library. Professor Tang prepared a list of the legal materials that he thought his Institute should have.

32.74 There remained to explore the ways and means whereby these legal materials could be acquired and put in place in Beijing. Of course, so far as the legal materials consisted of WIPO documentation, the International Bureau of WIPO made copies available and sent those copies to Beijing. On the other hand, in Professor Tang's list were publications issued by patent offices and copyright offices in the various countries of the world and publications which had been put on the market by a number of commercial firms, some of which were rather expensive and for which funds were not readily available to purchase. The International Bureau of WIPO wrote to each of the industrial property and copyright offices that had issued publications of interest to Professor Tang and those offices responded and sent their publications to Beijing. The expense was borne by the industrial or copyright offices concerned. Similarly, requests were made to a number of publishing firms and to universities with the hope that they too would be willing to contribute to the collection, particularly by providing gratis the publication and also bearing the transport costs. Many firms and universities responded, some with the latest edition of the work, while others were able to send at least earlier editions which they were about to discard. In this way a rather extensive collection of legal materials was established at the Institute.

32.75 In a similar, but more modest and reduced scale, WIPO may, at the request of an individual law professor, send to him or to her documentation consisting of preparatory papers and reports and of the publications of the International Bureau of WIPO. This has been done as a matter of course, without charge. As concerns other kinds of legal materials, not issued by WIPO, the experience of Professor Tang may serve as a guide to how they could be acquired.

I. CONCLUSION

32.76 Universities and other institutions have contributed and will continue to contribute to the training of the persons who will be the legislators, judges, administrative officials, legal practitioners, and even the teachers and researchers, of tomorrow. Research institutes have contributed and will continue to contribute to the analysis of the intellectual property system and make suggestions for its betterment. Present and future generations, one after the other, will be called upon to create, apply and improve that system. But to do so, each generation must have knowledge. But general knowledge, and even a legal knowledge, does not suffice. What is needed is specialization that is part of a legal education that is in turn based on a solid foundation of learning in the sciences and of humanities.

32.77 Further, greater support must be given to research institutes, so that a constant evaluation of the functioning of the law governing the objects of intellectual property can take place and lend support to the teaching process and serve as a foundation for legislators, judges and administrators officials to review the prevailing policies, principles and practices.

32.78 Universities and technical institutes must receive appropriate guidance so that their technological achievements are made more widely and rapidly known and be disseminated, not only to other researchers, but applied in industry, so that those results be recognized and an appropriate reward be received through their exploitation in industry and commerce for the skills, the time and other resources that have been used to bring about those results in technical achievements.

32.79 Finally, the process of intellectual property teaching and research can only be effective if resources are committed to teaching, to research and to the effective organization of educational and research programs. To fulfill those requirements, government and various sectors of the economy, as well as the educational community must work together. The tasks are too large for any one of them to proceed on its own. Each must help the other. Each must also offer to join their counterparts in other countries to identify their interests in common, so that the mutual assistance through international cooperation can be brought to bear.

32.80 The World Intellectual Property Organization (WIPO) stands ready to help governments and the educational and research community in the tasks of evaluating, selecting and applying the system of intellectual property law teaching and research that best suits the pursuit of the goal of government and the interests of industry and commerce in meeting the needs of the public, while preserving the traditional role of independent educational and research institutions as the bastions of learning and scientific investigation.

References for Section I
International Bureau of WIPO, *Universities and the Teaching of Intellectual Property: Syllabus and Methods for the Teaching of Intellectual Property Law in Universities*, WIPO/ACAD/E/93/21

PART VII

New Developments in Intellectual Property

CHAPTER 33

Protection of New Technological Developments

A. COMPUTER PROGRAMS

(a) Introduction

33.1 Computers—electronic machines capable of storing and/or processing data —have revolutionized our world. They have become indispensable tools in public administration, scientific research and industrial and commercial enterprises. They serve as memories for all kinds of data and as data processors, and, in particular, as calculators. They are also increasingly used for private purposes (home computers, computer games, etc.). In the language which has grown up around computers, the machines are called "hardware." The explanations, instructions and systems which have been developed in order to run the said machines are called "computer software."

33.2 The term "computer software" is understood to mean computer programs and other material prepared in connection with the use of computers. This includes program descriptions and explanatory material concerning the application of computer programs, for example, problem descriptions and user instructions. Computer programs, however, are the most important kind of computer software. They govern the operations of a computer in accordance with the objects to be achieved (for example, the storage and constant updating of data concerning stocks of merchandise kept by a commercial enterprise, the calculation of income tax by fiscal authorities, the control of a manufacturing process, the control of the flight of an airplane, etc.). The legal protection of computer programs raises complex problems which do not exist to the same extent in relation to the legal protection of other kinds of computer software.

33.3 In the preparation of a computer program, there are several stages. First, the program is written by its creator (the "programmer," or the team of programmers) in a programming language, i.e., in an artificial language consisting of specific symbols and established for expressing computer programs. This form of computer program is usually called "source code"; it cannot, however, be used by the machine as such, but must be transformed into a set of instructions that can be recognized by the central processing unit of the computer. Those instructions usually consist of only two different elements, symbolized by "0" and "1," which have the effect that the flow of electric current is either barred or permitted. In this machine-readable form of the program, which is usually called "object code," the instructions consist of extremely long combinations of these two digits.

33.4 Before a computer program can actually be written by the programmer, the task of the computer (for example, calculating income tax according to a series of legal rules and exceptions, etc.) must be defined, and the logical steps which are to form the basis of the program (the "algorithm") must be formulated. The definition of the task and the algorithm, however, are not considered to be part of the computer program.

33.5 In view of the preceding considerations, it is not easy to establish a generally accepted definition of the expression "computer program." The WIPO Model Provisions on the Protection of Computer Software, which were published in 1978, define a computer program as a set of instructions capable, when incorporated in a machine-readable medium, of causing a machine having information-processing capabilities to indicate, perform or achieve a particular function, task or result.

(b) Computers and Intellectual Property

(i) Introduction

33.6 In relation to intellectual property law, computer technology gives rise to three important questions:

(1) Where the information processed by a computer is expressed in a work protected by copyright, is the use of that work by the computer under the control of the copyright owner, and if not, should it be?

(2) Where a computer has been used to process information in such a way as to produce a work of a kind normally protected by copyright—for example, the processing of statistics so as to produce them in tabulated form designed to serve a particular purpose, or the use of a "synthesizer" to produce music— who is to be regarded as the "author", and hence the copyright owner, of the resulting literary or musical work?

(3) Is the software, often the product of great intellectual creativity (backed by considerable financial investment) protected against unauthorized use by others under any existing legal system such as patent law, copyright, breach of confidence, trade secrets, and so on; and if not, should it be, and if so, under what kind of system?

(ii) Computers and Protected Works

33.7 For the last two decades all three questions have been the subject of extensive study, both nationally and internationally; and in relation to questions (1) and (2) above there has been a very large measure of agreement as to what the answers should be. The general consensus on these questions is recorded in the Report of the Second Committee of Governmental Experts on Copyright Problems Arising from the Use of Computers for Access to or the Creation of Works— convened by WIPO and UNESCO in Paris in June 1982. The Committee, with one or two modifications, substantially endorsed a set of draft recommendations. The salient conclusions which emerged from these studies, as recorded in the report and the recommendations, may be summarized in the following way:

(1) the input of a protected work into a computer system includes the reproduction of the work on a machine-readable material support, and also the fixation of

the work in the memory of the computer system; and both these acts (i.e. reproduction and fixation) are governed by the international conventions (Article 9(1) of Berne and Article 4*bis* (1) of UCC);

(2) the output of a protected work from a computer system should be protected under copyright law, irrespective of the form of the output; for example, this might be—

    (a) a hardcopy printout, or

    (b) a fixation in machine-readable form, or

    (c) a transmission from the data base of one system into the memory of another system (with or without an intermediary fixation), or

    (d) making the work available to the public by audio or visual images presented on a screen,

(3) in amending or modifying national legislation to take account of computer use of protected works, care should be taken to ensure that authors' moral rights should continue to be exercisable in relation to computer use, and that the exemption and limitations on the copyright owner's right of control which computer technology might render desirable, do not exceed the limits on such exemptions permitted by the conventions;

(4) non-voluntary licenses in relation to the computer use of protected works should only be adopted when voluntary licensing is impracticable, and should, in any case, be in accordance with convention principles; and where a non-voluntary license is adopted by a national law, its effect should be confined to the territory of the country of that law.

33.8 In many countries the existing law appears to be regarded as implementing these general conclusions; but in some countries there have been specific amendments to the copyright law to put the matter beyond doubt. As an example, in the United Kingdom the Copyright (Computer Software) Amendment Act 1985 contain an express provision that:

> "References in the Copyright Act 1956 to the reduction of any work to material form, or to the reproduction of any work in a material form, shall include references to the storage of that work in a computer."

33.9 In relation to question (2) the general view which emerged from these studies is this: no matter how sophisticated a computer may be, it is only a tool, and the author of a work produced by the aid of a computer is the person who conceived the product which the computer was used to bring into being, and who gave the programmer and the technician the instructions to take the steps necessary to bring about the resulting product conceived by him. Neither the programmer who designed the program needed to operate the computer for the purpose of producing that work, nor the technician who operated the computer when carrying out the task, would be regarded as the author or a joint author; save that where the work of the programmer amounted to collaboration with the originating creative person to such an extent that the programmer contributed creatively in settling the form of the final product, he might be regarded as a co-author.

33.10 Question (3) has, perhaps, been the subject of more extensive examination than the other two questions; and is discussed below in detail.

(c) Protection of Computer Programs

33.11 Generally speaking, three types of legal protection of computer programs may be considered. The first is protection by patents, the second is protection by copyright and the third is protection by provisions against the violation of trade secrets.

33.12 With regard to patent protection, the question arises whether a computer program can constitute an invention. Inventions are usually understood to be solutions to a technical problem, which use scientific principles in the fields of physics, chemistry or biology. However, so-called "instructions to the human mind" are not normally considered to be inventions. A number of national laws therefore contain an express provision excluding computer programs from patent protection.

33.13 On the other hand, it may be that the program forms an integral part of a process in the field of physics or chemistry. In such a case, one could describe the invention as a "process controlled by a specific computer program" (for example, a chemical manufacturing process). If the program could be considered as forming part of the process, patent protection would be available, provided that the usual conditions of patentability (novelty, inventive step and industrial application) are fulfilled.

33.14 As regards protection of computer programs by copyright, the first question to be considered is whether computer programs are protectable "works" in the sense of copyright laws. There may be doubts as to this, since copyright laws usually contain lists enumerating categories of protected works and such lists normally do not mention computer programs. Computer programs do not readily fall into the categories of "writings," "books" or "scientific works" (categories of works protected by copyright). Therefore, some recent national laws, for example, the laws of France, Germany (Federal Republic of) and the United States of America, have overcome any doubts by expressly stipulating that computer programs are to be considered as works protected by copyright.

33.15 The second question which arises in connection with copyright protection of computer programs concerns the acts against which protection is needed. These ought to comprise not only the making of copies, but also the use of the program in the control of a computer. However, such an act of use is not normally covered by copyright protection, since copyright laws normally only confer protection against the making of copies and public performance of works protected by copyright (for example, theater or musical concerts), but not against the execution of the work in private (for example, playing of music in private). Nevertheless, it can be argued that the use of a program in a computer entails the making of a copy either in the central storage unit of the computer (because the speed of the magnetic tape that stores the program differs from the speed which applies in the use by the computer), or because the program is copied step by step during its use; whether either of these methods of copying occurs depends on the technical circumstances of each case. In order to ensure full protection against unauthorized use, it may be necessary to amend copyright laws accordingly. This was done, for example, in the copyright law of France by including a provision declaring unlawful any reproduction of the program other than the making of a back-up copy and any use not expressly authorized by the author.

33.16 As regards the third possible form of protection of computer programs, namely, protection against the violation of trade secrets, the decisive question here is how far such protection is available under the applicable national law. Moreover, it is clear that this form of protection is limited to programs which are communicated with an obligation of confidentiality.

33.17 Finally, it is to be noted that protection against copying may be afforded by contractual terms: for example, the user of the program may be bound through the contract with the creator of the program (the "software house") to use the program only for specific purposes, and not to communicate it to any third party.

33.18 In view of the problems existing with the protection of computer programs at the national level, the question of international protection of computer programs has also arisen. International protection means the protection of programs in a country in respect of which the creator or other owner is not a national or resident.

B. BIOTECHNOLOGY

(a) Introduction

33.19 Biotechnology is a field of technology whose importance has grown considerably in recent years. Indeed, it appears possible that biotechnological inventions will have a very significant effect on our future, in particular in the fields of medicine, food, energy and protection of the environment.

33.20 Biotechnology concerns living organisms, such as plants, animals and microorganisms, as well as non-living biological material, such as seed, cells, enzymes, plasmids (which are used in "genetic engineering") and the like. Biotechnological inventions fall into three categories. They are the processes for the creation or modification of living organisms and biological material, the results of such processes, and the use of such results.

33.21 While biotechnology has assumed increasing importance in recent years, it is nevertheless one of the oldest technologies. For example, the production of wine or beer involves processes using living organisms, and such processes have been known for a long time. Likewise, the selective breeding of plants and animals has an equally long history. However, as regards plant and animal breeding, there is no certainty as to the results because characteristic features of the organisms are transmitted from one generation to another according to the laws of heredity. These laws show that different combinations of features will produce a whole range of results.

33.22 Technology, strictly speaking, involves human control. Thus, processes which may be entirely controlled by man in a scientific way, or products which are made by man according to scientific principles involve the use of technology. The field of biology, however, was traditionally considered to be beyond the scope of technology as it could not be controlled in a predictable way by man.

References for Section A
International Bureau of WIPO, *Protection of Computer Software*, WIPO/IP/ND/87/3
D. de Freitas, *Impact of New Technologies (Reprography, Computer Use and Software Protection) on Computers*, WIPO/CNR/ND/86/6

33.23 In recent years, as a result of scientific discoveries, it has become possible to develop biological processes which manipulate living organisms. These processes may be entirely controlled by man. The most notable examples of such processes occur in the artificial modification of genes ("genetic engineering"). These processes are able to change the material determining the heritary characteristics of living organisms, and thus it is possible to create modified organisms which have certain desirable features. For example, the microorganism created by Chakrabarty (an inventor in the United States of America) is able to absorb oil pollution from oceans and rivers. It was the subject of a landmark decision of the Supreme Court of the United States of America, when it was recognized as patentable. Genetic engineering processes are also used in the modification of microorganisms for the production of new medicines. Biotechnology is expected to lead to important breakthroughs in medicine which may be effective in combating diseases such as cancer and AIDS. It may also lead to new opportunities for obtaining food and energy, and may provide solutions to the problems of pollution of the environment.

33.24 If it is possible to control a biotechnological process and to describe such a process in a way that experts in the field can carry it out on the basis of the description, then an invention in the field of biotechnology has been made. Traditionally, in scientific circles, the concept of invention was generally limited to the fields of physics and chemistry because living organisms were considered to be outside the scope of technology. However, with the possibility of controlling and describing processes in the field of biotechnology, the concept of invention will have to be enlarged to cover biotechnological inventions.

(b) Need for Protection

33.25 As in other fields of technology, there is a need for legal protection in respect of biotechnological inventions. Such inventions are creations of the human mind just as much as are other inventions, and typically they are the result of substantial research and inventive effort and investment in sophisticated laboratories. When decisions have to be taken on whether such investments for research are to be made, the question of the protection of the research may play an important role. Typically, enterprises engaged in research only make investments if legal protection is available for the results of their research. Thus, there is an obvious need for the protection of biotechnological inventions—as with other inventions—not only in the interest of inventors and their employers, but also in the public interest in order to promote technological progress.

33.26 Legal protection of inventions is normally effected through the grant of patents or other titles for the protection of inventions. However, inventors in the field of biotechnology are faced with several obstacles when seeking protection for their inventions. These obstacles do not exist to the same degree in other areas of technology.

33.27 The first obstacle is the problem of whether there really is an invention rather than just a discovery. If, for example, an as yet unknown microorganism is isolated by a sophisticated process, it may be argued that such a microorganism is not an invention but is a scientific discovery. The counter-argument would be that the isolation requires an important intervention by man using a highly sophisticated process, and that therefore the result is a solution of a technical problem.

33.28 Another obstacle faced by inventors of biotechnological inventions concerns the theory, mentioned above, that inventions can only be made in the fields of chemistry and physics but not in the field of biology because biological processes cannot be sufficiently controlled and described. This latter obstacle, however, now seems to belong to the past.

33.29 The third obstacle, which is the most important one, is the existence of express legislative provisions that exclude certain categories of biotechnological inventions from patent protection.   Those provisions have their origin in developments which took place in Europe, but have also influenced countries outside Europe.

(c) Existing Protection

33.30 Article 53(b) of the European Patent Convention stipulates that European patents shall not be granted in respect of plant or animal varieties or essentially biological processes for the production of plants or animals (with the exception of microbiological processes and the products thereof). This provision is to some extent the result of a provision in the Strasbourg Convention which was concluded in 1963 under the auspices of the Council of Europe and which concerns the unification of certain points of substantive law on patents for invention. According to Article 2 of that Convention, the Contracting States are not bound to provide for the grant of patents in respect of plant or animal varieties or essentially biological processes for the production of plants or animals (with the exception of microbiological processes and the products thereof). When the European Patent Convention was concluded in 1973, the Contracting States made use of their freedom under the Strasbourg Convention and did not permit the grant of patents for these particular categories of inventions.

33.31 There are two reasons for this approach. Firstly, it was considered that granting patents for inventions belonging to the categories referred to would create legal and administrative difficulties and that the newly created European system should not be burdened with such difficulties. Secondly, a special system of protection had been created in various countries with respect to plant varieties, and it was considered that this system should remain as the only applicable system with respect to that category of inventions.

33.32 The special system of protection for plant varieties is different from patent protection in that it only concerns the marketing of propagating material (seed, etc.) but not the growing and marketing of plants themselves. The system of plant varieties rights is also different in respect of the conditions for protection and the protected acts. The special nature of this system is demonstrated by the fact that an international convention was concluded for the protection of new varieties of plants which is administered by a special organization, namely the International Union for the Protection of New Varieties of Plants (UPOV).

33.33 The exclusion of plant and animal varieties and essentially biological processes for the production of plants or animals is a feature existing in a number of national laws, not only of the member States of the European Patent Convention, but also of other States such as Cuba, the German Democratic Republic, Mexico, Sri Lanka, Thailand and Yugoslavia. The patent law of China excludes animal and plant varieties, but not biological processes for their production.

33.34 In the United States of America, there are no such exclusions. Thus, for all kinds of biotechnological inventions, patents are available in addition to the plant variety rights which are available for varieties of sexually reproduced plants. For asexually reproduced plants, special patents, called "plant patents," are available.

33.35 It is to be noted that other countries with important research in biotechnology, for example Japan, do not have an express exclusion of certain categories of biotechnological inventions from patenting.

33.36 A particular category of biotechnological invention, namely, inventions concerning microorganisms (either the processes for obtaining a microorganism or the microorganism itself, or the particular use of a microorganism) are governed by special provisions. In view of the fact that it is difficult, if not impossible, to sufficiently describe a new microorganism, a system for depositing of microorganisms has been established. Thus, in many countries, applicants for patents do not need to describe a new microorganism but only have to refer to a deposit made with a recognized depositary authority.

33.37 This system is also the subject of an international treaty, namely, the Budapest Treaty on the International Recognition of the Deposit of Microorganisms for the Purposes of Patent Procedure, which provides for the setting up of international depositary authorities with which microorganisms can be deposited.

(d) Budapest Treaty on the International Recognition of the Deposit of Microorganisms for the Purposes of Patent Procedure

33.38 The Budapest Treaty on the International Recognition of the Deposit of Microorganisms for the Purposes of Patent Procedure (the Budapest Treaty) which is a special agreement under the Paris Convention, entered into force on August 19, 1980. At present, 38 States are party to the Treaty.

(i) Background to the Treaty

33.39 Disclosure of the invention is a generally recognized requirement for the grant of patents. Normally, an invention is disclosed by means of a written description. Where an invention involves a microorganism, or the use of a microorganism, which is not available to the public, such a description is not sufficient for disclosure. That is why in the patent procedure of an increasing number of countries it is necessary not only to file a written description but also to deposit, with a specialized institution, a sample of the microorganism. Patent offices are not equipped to handle microorganisms, whose preservation requires special expertise and equipment to keep them viable, to protect them from contamination and to protect health or the environment from contamination. Such preservation is costly. The furnishing of samples also requires specialized expertise and equipment.

33.40 When protection is sought in several countries for an invention involving a microorganism or the use of a microorganism, the complex and costly procedures of the deposit of the microorganism might have to be repeated in each of those countries. It was in order to eliminate or reduce such multiplication, in order to enable one deposit to serve the purpose of all the deposits which would otherwise be necessary, that the Treaty was concluded.

(ii) Summary of the Treaty

33.41 The main feature of the Treaty is that a Contracting State which allows or requires the deposit of microorganisms for the purposes of patent procedure must recognize, for such purposes, the deposit of a microorganism with any "international depositary authority" (Article 3(1)(a)), irrespective of whether such authority is on or outside the territory of the said State. In other words, one deposit, with one international depositary authority, will suffice for the purposes of patent procedure before the national patent offices (called "industrial property offices" in the Treaty) of all of the Contracting States and before any regional patent office (e.g., the European Patent Office).

33.42 What the Treaty calls an "international depositary authority" is a scientific institution—typically a "culture collection"—which is capable of storing microorganisms. Such an institution acquires the status of "international depositary authority" through the furnishing, by one of the Contracting States on the territory of which it is located, of assurances to the Director General of WIPO to the effect that the said institution complies, and will continue to comply, with certain requirements (Article 6(1)), including, in particular, that it will be available, for the purposes of the deposit of microorganisms, to any "depositor" (person, firm, etc.) under the same conditions, that it will accept and store the deposited microorganisms and that it will furnish samples thereof to anyone entitled to such samples but to no one else. The said assurances may be furnished also by certain intergovernmental industrial property organizations (Article 9(1)(a)).

33.43 The Regulations contain detailed provisions (Rule 11) on who is entitled—and when—to receive samples of the deposited microorganism. The depositor himself has a right to a sample at any time (Rule 11.2(i)). He may authorize any third party (authority, natural person, legal entity) to ask for a sample and such a third party will receive a sample upon producing such an authorization (Rule 11.2(ii)). Any "interested" industrial property office to which the Treaty applies may ask for a sample and will receive one; an industrial property office will mainly be regarded as "interested" where the microorganism is needed for the purposes of patent procedure before the said office (Rule 11.1). Any other party may obtain a sample if, roughly stated, an industrial property office to which the Treaty applies certifies that, under the applicable law, such a party has the right to a sample of the given microorganism; the elements of the certification are provided for in detail to ensure that the maximum extent of caution will be exercised by the industrial property office before it issues a certification (Rule 11.3(a)).

33.44 The Treaty and the Regulations also contain provisions allowing for what is called a "new" deposit where no samples of the originally deposited microorganism can be furnished (Article 4); permitting the termination or limitation of the status of international depositary authority at the will of the

Contracting States where the said authority does not, or does not fully, comply with its assumed duties (Article 8); requiring that all microorganisms deposited with an international depositary authority be transferred to another such authority if the former is about to cease functioning as such (Rule 5.1); regulating the content of the receipt that each international depositary authority is required to give to the depositor for the deposited microorganism (Rule 7); providing for the testing of the viability of the deposited microorganisms and the issuance of viability statements (Rule 10); allowing the international depositary authority to charge a fee for each deposit, the fee covering the minimum 30 years during which the deposited microorganism must be stored (Rules 9 and 12); providing for a special status and a special role for certain intergovernmental organizations (Article 9).

(iii) Main Advantages of the Treaty

33.45 The Treaty is primarily advantageous to the depositor who is an applicant for patents in several countries; the deposit of a microorganism under the procedures provided for in the Treaty will save him money and strengthen his security. It will save him money because, instead of depositing the microorganism in each and every country in which he files a patent application referring to that microorganism, he can deposit it only once, with one depositary, with the consequence that in all but one of the countries in which he seeks protection he will save the fees and costs that deposits would have otherwise entailed. In most cases, there will be at least one international depositary authority in the country of the depositor, which means that he will deal with an authority which is close to him, with which he can deal in his own language, to which he can pay the fees in his own currency and which he may even know from personal experience; in other words, he will be able to avoid dealing with distant authorities, in foreign currencies and in foreign languages. He will probably have a natural trust in the authority carefully preserving the viability of the deposited microorganism and furnishing samples only to those to whom it is supposed to furnish them.

33.46 The security of the depositor is increased by the fact that, for an institution to become an international depositary authority, solemn assurances as to the seriousness and continued existence of that institution must be given; such assurances must be given by a State or by an intergovernmental organization and they are addressed to all the member States of the Budapest Union. Consequently, it may be expected that the assurances will be strictly respected, all the more so since, if they are not so respected, the member States may take away from the defaulting institution the status of international depositary authority.

33.47 Finally, it is to be noted that adherence to the Treaty entails no financial burden or obligation for any Government.

33.48 The following 38 States were party to the Budapest Treaty on the International Recognition of the Deposit of Microorganisms for the Purposes of Patent Procedure as of October 1, 1996: Australia, Austria, Belgium, Bulgaria, Canada, China, Cuba, Czech Republic, Denmark, Estonia, Finland, France, Germany, Greece, Hungary, Iceland, Israel, Italy, Japan, Latvia, Liechtenstein, Netherlands, Norway, Philippines, Poland, Republic of Korea, Republic of Moldova, Russian Federation, Singapore, Slovakia, Spain, Sweden, Switzerland,

Tajikistan, Trinidad and Tobago, United Kingdom, United States of America and Yugoslavia.

C. INTEGRATED CIRCUITS

(a) Circuit Design

33.49 The question of the type of protection to be given to the layout-design of integrated circuits is relatively new. Although prefabricated components of electrical circuitry have been used for a long time in the manufacture of electrical equipment (for example, radios), large scale integration of a multitude of electrical functions in a very small component became possible only a few years ago as a result of advances in semiconductor technology. Integrated circuits are manufactured in accordance with very detailed plans or "layout-designs".

(b) Need for Protection

33.50 The layout-designs of integrated circuits are creations of the human mind. They are usually the result of an enormous investment, both in terms of the time of highly qualified experts, and financially. There is a continuing need for the creation of new layout-designs which reduce the dimensions of existing integrated circuits and simultaneously increase their functions. The smaller an integrated circuit, the less the material needed for its manufacture, and the smaller the space needed to accommodate it. Integrated circuits are utilized in a large range of products, including articles of everyday use, such as watches, television sets, washing machines, automobiles, etc., as well as sophisticated data processing equipment.

33.51 Whereas the creation of a new layout-design for an integrated circuit involves an important investment, the copying of such a layout-design may cost only a fraction of that investment. Copying may be done by photographing each layer of an integrated circuit and preparing masks for the production of the integrated circuit on the basis of the photographs obtained. The possibility of such copying is the main reason for the introduction of legislation for the protection of layout-designs.

33.52 Mention should be made, in this connection, of the concept of "reverse engineering." In the context of the integrated circuits industry, reverse engineering is the use of an existing layout-design in order to prepare an improved layout-design. It is considered desirable to permit reverse engineering even if it involves the copying of an existing layout-design, provided that an improved layout-design is

References for Section B
International Bureau of WIPO, *Industrial Property Protection of Biotechnological Inventions*, BIOT/CE/II/1 and BIOT/CE/IV/2
International Bureau of WIPO, *WIPO and International Cooperation in Relation to Patents*, WIPO/ PS/KL/86/1
International Bureau of WIPO, *Protection of Inventions in the Field of Biotechnology*, WIPO/IP/ ND/87/2
International Bureau of WIPO, *Guide to the Deposit of Microorganisms Under the Budapest Treaty*, WIPO Pub. No. 661(E)

thereby created—an advance of technology occurs which is in the general public interest.

(c) The Treaty on Intellectual Property in Respect of Integrated Circuits

33.53 In May 1989, the Diplomatic Conference meeting in Washington adopted a Treaty on Intellectual Property in Respect of Integrated Circuits. This was the result of an extensive preparatory phase that included four meetings of an *ad hoc* Committee of Experts, consultations with developing countries and the preparation of special studies by the WIPO Secretariat.

33.54 The preparatory meetings highlighted the critical attitude of developing countries, which questioned the need for a Treaty on this issue.

33.55 Developing countries considered that protection of investment in layout-designs for chips did not in itself justify the creation of a special intellectual property title. It was argued that not every creation justified departure from the principle of free competition. Because of the implications of absolute rights in an intellectual creation only certain specified intellectual creations should enjoy such treatment.

33.56 The weakness of the creative foundation on which exclusive rights would be based was also the subject of criticism since in the *sui generis* regime layout-designs for protectable integrated circuits did not require novelty nor inventive level. It was also pointed out that the creation and application of layout-designs for semiconductors presented a number of technological specificities that affected the legal context. For example, the growing use of computer design systems (especially silicon compilers) diminishes the individual contribution to chip design. The trend towards incorporating software (increasingly protected under copyright) in chips has also brought closer together protection of the former and possible protection of the latter.

33.57 As far as the draft Treaty itself was concerned, the main issues related to the definition of protectable objects, the ambiguity of the required provisions ("intellectual effort"), the scope of the requirement regarding "fixing" of the layout-design in a chip, failure to disclose completely, the duration proposed (ten years) and, especially, the content of the rights granted to the owner of the layout-design.

33.58 One subject of special concern was extension of the protection provided for in Article 4 of the draft Treaty to objects that incorporated an unauthorized copy of the microchip. It was considered that this would put developing countries in an extremely disadvantageous situation. Developing countries are net importers of electronic goods and local production capacity only exists in a few of them. To require such countries to assume responsibility for chips incorporated within equipment that they import would be to confront them with the almost impossible task of taking apart and verifying the origin of all the equipment's components. It would be far more reasonable to act against those who in the first place produce and distribute such equipment.

33.59 Taking into account the results of the preparatory work, the expectations of many observers with regard to the Washington Conference included, on the one hand, the hypothesis of relatively easy concordance among industrialized countries and, on the other hand, a defensive position (if not a blockade) on the part of developing countries. The reality was quite different. On the basis of an energetic stand by the Group of 77, Group B (developed countries) suffered an important division, mainly in connection with the provision on non-voluntary licenses. The United States and Japan voted against (the only two countries to do so), while the Treaty met with firm support from developing countries and the European Community.

33.60 Although, as mentioned above, the Group of 77 was far from seeking the adoption of a Treaty on the issue, it considered that the text negotiated represented a reasonable compromise, particularly with regard to the provisions finally adopted on non-voluntary licenses, "innocent offenders", the duration of protection and conditions of disclosure.

33.61 The Treaty lays down international norms approved by the majority of countries, even though they are rejected by the two countries that are currently the world's largest producers of semiconductors. The work carried out and the results achieved obviate the need to deal with the matter in other forums, for example, within the Uruguay Round. Moreover, reopening the discussion would be highly inadvisable and might incite a number of developing countries to reject *in toto* any form of protection for layout-designs of integrated circuits.

(d) Scope of Protection

(i) Object Protected

33.62 In accordance with legislation enacted in developed countries and with the Treaty adopted, layout-design of integrated circuits is protectable. United States law, influenced by the technology that predominated at the time of its adoption, refers to protection of the masks and not the layout- designs. The most recent laws in European countries, however, refer to the topography of integrated circuits, which gives an idea of their three-dimensional nature. In any event, the subject of protection is not the technology used to manufacture chips but the layout-design. The objective is to prevent slavish copies of integrated circuits, which can be done at low cost in comparison with the need to create a new design.

33.63 In conformity with a number of laws (although not those of the United States nor Japan) and the Treaty, protection does not depend on whether or not the layout-design is fixed in a semiconductor. The protection of layout-designs that are not fixed, therefore intangible, was considered by many delegations at the Washington Conference to be appropriate for the layout-design industry (as opposed to semiconductor manufacturing) emerging in some countries.

33.64 Legal control concerns layout-designs for both finished chips and intermediate chips such as gate arrays.

(ii) Protection Requirements

33.65 In conformity with legislation adopted and the Treaty, the only requirement for protecting a layout-design is that it should be original or considered to be the equivalent and should be the result of intellectual effort. In contrast to the patent system, therefore, neither novelty nor inventive level is required.

(iii) Type of Protection

33.66 It has already been stated that legislation adopted establishes a *sui generis* title. A number of developing countries questioned the need for establishing such special protection. For example, India considered that integrated circuits could be protected under copyright (a solution that was also proposed by Great Britain). Argentina argued that the provisions on unfair competition contained in the Paris Convention applied. In the case of Switzerland, it was stated that the Federal law of 1983 on unfair competition allowed the distortions resulting from unlawful copying of layout-designs of integrated circuits to be rectified.

33.67 The WIPO Treaty leaves each country free to decide on the legal framework (patents, copyright, etc.) under which protection is to be granted, subject to minimum rules laid down in the Treaty and, where appropriate, to international agreements governing the respective field (patents, copyright, unfair competition, etc.). In view of these restrictions, it is not likely that a country would choose any of these alternative forms of control because it would then have to respect not only the provisions of the Washington Treaty but also those of the other agreements concerned.

(iv) Rights Granted

33.68 In conformity with the legislation mentioned, the owner of a layout-design has the exclusive right to reproduce the design in question, to incorporate it in a chip and to market the semiconductors incorporating it. According to some laws (for example, the SCPA), the owner not only has the right to reproduce and market the chips but also the industrial goods incorporating the semiconductor concerned. This is one of the issues that met with the greatest resistance on the part of developing countries during negotiations on the Washington Treaty.

33.69 In accordance with the rules proposed for the Treaty, a person acquiring in good faith industrial goods incorporating an infringing semiconductor may be liable vis-a-vis the original owner of the semiconductor (and may have to pay fees). Although it is obvious that any importer of such goods does not in most cases have any real possibility of investigating whether or not the semiconductor incorporated is original, unless he takes the equipment apart, he is made liable for payment of compensation to the owner of the original circuit when the existence of infringement has been notified.

33.70 The final text of the Treaty makes it clear that protection is independent of "whether or not the integrated circuit is incorporated in an article" (Article 3.1(b)), although by not explicitly laying down procedures or penalties, it gives a certain leeway to national laws and judges to determine the legal effects of such a situation.

(v) Obligations of the Owner; Non-Voluntary Licenses

33.71 Unlike the patent system, which lays down the obligation to exploit the patent granted, the special protection mentioned does not include any form of obligation regarding exploitation or anything else.

33.72 However, some regulations (for example, the EEC Directive of 1987) provide for the possibility of granting non-voluntary licenses, as is the case in copyright laws under certain circumstances and in patent laws.

33.73 The WIPO Treaty also provides for this possibility in one of the articles that prompted the rejection of the Treaty by the United States. Article 6.3 provides the following:

"(a) Notwithstanding paragraph (1), any Contracting Party may, in its legislation, provide for the possibility of its executive or judicial authority granting a non-exclusive license, in circumstances that are not ordinary, for the performance of any of the acts referred to in paragraph (1) by a third party without the authorization of the holder of the right ("non- voluntary license"), after unsuccessful efforts, made by the said party in line with normal commercial practices, to obtain such authorization, where the granting of the non-voluntary license is found, by the granting authority, to be necessary to safeguard a national purpose deemed to be vital by that authority; the non-voluntary license shall be available for exploitation only in the territory of that country and shall be subject to the payment of an equitable remuneration by the third party to the holder of the right.

"(b) The provisions of this Treaty shall not affect the freedom of any Contracting Party to apply measures, including the granting, after a formal proceeding by its executive or judicial authority, of a non-voluntary license, in application of its laws in order to secure free competition and to prevent abuses by the holder of the right.

"(c) The granting of any non-voluntary license referred to in subparagraph (a) or subparagraph (b) shall be subject to judicial review. Any non-voluntary license referred to in subparagraph (a) shall be revoked when the conditions referred to in that subparagraph cease to exist."

(vi) Reverse Engineering

33.74 One important limitation on the rights granted under the laws and the Treaty is the admissibility of reverse engineering when it leads to the creation of a new integrated circuit. Reverse engineering has been accepted in practice as a legitimate method of competition in the semiconductor industry. However, it requires technological capabilities and resources that are beyond the majority of developing countries.

(vii) Disclosure

33.75 In this field as well the *sui generis* system is totally innovatory. In some laws, registration of the relevant documentation is not a requirement for protection because protection follows upon marketing of the product; in other cases, it is possible to withhold from registration any information that the owner considers confidential, thereby virtually making protection a system for protection of trade secrets. This also weakens one of the fundamental principles of industrial property, namely, the disclosure of knowledge, a principle that has been one of the cornerstones of the search for a balance between public and private interests involved in the granting of monopolies for inventions. In the case of integrated circuits, under some legislation it is up to the holder of the right to decide what information can be made available to the public and what he wishes to keep to himself.

33.76 Article 7.2 of the Treaty manages to achieve a certain balance:

"Any Contracting Party shall be free not to protect a layout- design (topography) until the layout-design (topography) has been the subject of an application for registration, filed in due form with the competent public authority, or of a registration with that authority; it may be required that the application be accompanied by the filing of a copy or drawing of the layout-design (topography) and, where the integrated circuit has been commercially exploited, of a sample of that integrated circuit, along with information defining the electronic function which the integrated circuit is intended to perform; however, the applicant may exclude such parts of the copy or drawing that relate to the manner of manufacture of the integrated circuit, provided that the parts submitted are sufficient to allow the identification of the layout-design (topography)."

(viii) Duration

33.77 The systems in force usually provide for a period of ten years from the date on which the layout-design was first commercialized (or an application for protection was made). If one takes into account the curve of obsolescence of many semiconductors, however, this period could be too long. The Treaty provides for a minimum duration of eight years, without specifying the moment at which the period begins (it could be from the time of the layout-design's creation).

(e) Implications of the Legal Regime

33.78 The *sui generis* regimes adopted in developed countries and in the relevant WIPO Treaty basically establish a right to prevent slavish copying of the protected layout-design. As we have seen, unlike patents they do not grant a monopoly for exploitation nor do they prevent independent development of layout-designs (even if they turn out to be identical to other designs already protected), nor "reverse engineering" based on a prior layout-design.

33.79 Paradoxically, cases of slavish copying of layout-designs of integrated circuits appear to be infrequent. In fact, despite the arguments put forward by the United States semiconductor industry in order to promote adoption of the SCPA, no case of copying such designs has been brought before United States courts. The only case brought before the courts under the SCPA concerned two United States companies (Brooktree and Advanced Micro Services) and the defendant pleaded a legitimate case of "reverse engineering".

33.80 The lack of effective application of the *sui generis* regime to semiconductors and the realization that copying is virtually non- existent led two United States experts to ask whether the SCPA was not in fact "a solution in search of a problem."

33.81 It is not possible to affirm with certainty that the situation described above will alter significantly in the future as a result of technological change.

33.82 Only a handful of developing countries are at present manufacturing integrated circuits and it is unlikely that many more will in the future embark upon a venture that requires considerable investment and is subject to a basically unstable market. Although the layout-design (but not the manufacture) of circuits is taking place in an increasing number of developing countries, it concerns designs for custom and semi-custom circuits, generally protected under contracts between the designer and the company interested in a special application (in the case of individuals).

33.83 Finally, it should be borne in mind, as we have already said, that "reverse engineering" requires a high level of technological capability and investment. It is outside the capabilities (and the interests) of the majority of developing countries.

33.84 While the protection of layout-designs of integrated circuits will probably not have wide-ranging effects on industrial development in the semiconductor sector in developing countries, it could have a considerable impact on trade in chips and the industrial products incorporating them. Conflicts between suppliers of chips could be transferred to the buyers through acts that prevent import or impose additional charges (through payment of fees) when such goods are acquired.

33.85 Developing countries certainly did not encourage the adoption of an international system in this field nor do they obtain advantages from it. However, the relative balance reached in the text of the Washington Treaty represents a reasonable point of departure (although it is far from being perfect) for achieving protection of layout-designs of integrated circuits in national spheres.

33.86 The Agreement on Trade-Related Aspects of Intellectual Property Rights concluded as part of the 1994 Uruguay Round of GATT (the "TRIPS" Agreement) incorporates many of the substantive provisions of the Washington Treaty. However, TRIPS does not include the compulsory license provisions of the Treaty. In addition, the following additional provisions are added by the TRIPS text:

(1) Members of the Agreement shall consider as unlawful the following acts, if undertaken without the authorization of the right-owner: the importation, selling or other distribution for commercial purposes of a protected lay-out design or an integrated circuit incorporating a protected design or an article incorporating such a circuit containing an unlawfully reproduced layout design;
(2) Members shall not consider as unlawful acts otherwise prohibited, where the person performing or ordering the act did not know and had no reasonable ground to know, when acquiring the integrated circuit or article, that it incorporated an unlawfully reproduced layout design;
(3) the term of protection shall be at least 10 years from either the filing of a request for registration or, where registration is not a requirement for protection, from the first commercial exploitation anywhere in the world; in any case it may be provided in national laws that the protection shall lapse 15 years from the creation of the layout design;
(4) the Agreement on Trade-Related Aspects of Intellectual Property Rights, Annex 1C to the Final Act Embodying the Results of the Uruguay Round of Multilateral Trade Negotiations, April 15, 1994.

D. REPROGRAPHY

(a) Reprography and Intellectual Property

33.87 Reprography is the generic term now used to describe all the kinds of photocopying equipment which are currently available, and which enable facsimile copies of documents of every kind indistinguishable from the original to be made

References for Section C
International Bureau of WIPO, *The Recent International Developments Concerning the Enforcement of Intellectual Property Rights*, WIPO-ASEAN/SEM/BKK/94/4
C. Correa, *Protection of Layout-Designs of Integrated Circuits*, WIPO/FT/MV/89/2

instantly and cheaply on apparatus which is simple to operate. Today, in almost all countries, no office, school or library is without such equipment, and a very large number of copies of literary dramatic, musical and artistic material are churned out through the use of reprographic equipment around the world.

33.88 Article 9 of the Berne Convention (Paris Act 1971) stipulates that "authors of literary and artistic works protected by this Convention shall have the exclusive right of authorizing the reproduction of these works, in any manner or form", and all contemporary copyright laws contain provisions implementing this principle. Paragraph (2) of Article 9, however, empowers national copyright laws to permit the reproduction of works in certain special cases, subject to two conditions:

(1) the permitted reproduction must not conflict with the normal exploitation of the work; and
(2) the reproduction must not unreasonably prejudice the legitimate interests of the author.

33.89 Photocopying on the scale which exists today, appears to conflict with the normal exploitation of those works which are copied in such large numbers; and such a volume of copying may unreasonably prejudice the legitimate interests of the author and, of course, his publisher.

33.90 A variety of solutions to the problem have been adopted in different countries.

33.91 In the 1970's, in some of the Scandinavian countries, a voluntary blanket licensing scheme, initially in respect of national works only, was instituted to cover photocopying in educational establishments. Subsequently, in the 1980's, in some of these countries the copyright law was amended so as to give statutory backing to this blanket licensing approach, and under the statutory provisions the ambit of the blanket license was extended to all copyright works, including foreign works, with a provision for arbitration to deal with disputes arising between the organization administering the blanket licenses and the educational establishments covered by them.

33.92 In the Federal Republic of Germany a more advanced and comprehensive system has been instituted by amendments to the principal Copyright Act. These amendments introduce a dual system—of statutory payments together with blanket licensing. The statutory payments are made by the manufacturers and importers of photocopying equipment, the amount of the payment depending on the speed of operation of the equipment. In addition, when equipment of this kind is used in educational establishments, in public libraries or in other institutions which make the equipment available to the public on payment of a charge, copying royalties are to be collected and distributed by collecting societies under the blanket licenses.

(b) Audio and Video Recording

33.93 Technological advances have made possible the high-quality copying of sound and audiovisual recordings. The copyright implications of this activity are the same as in the case of the copying of literary and other material by reprographic equipment—i.e. it is a potential infringement of the fundamental right protected by Article 9 of the Berne Convention and by the provisions in national laws which implement that Convention requirement.

33.94 Home recording has also been the subject of very considerable study at national and international levels; a number of countries have enacted or are considering legislation to deal with the matter.

33.95 Just as in the case of reprography, the various national solutions adopted are not identical, but they are all based on more or less the same approach which may be summarized in the following way:

(1) the basic idea underlining the approach generally adopted is that in respect of each unit of recording equipment or blank tape, of a kind likely to be used for home recording, and which is released to the public, a statutory payment should be collected;

(2) the rationale of this approach is that although it is not possible to identify each individual home user, nevertheless it is possible to identify the users as a class because they are those persons who buy the equipment and the blank tapes by means of which home recording are made; and it is not unreasonable, therefore, that as a class they should make a payment for the right to make home recordings—the payment taking the form of an element in the purchase price of the equipment and blank tape bought for the purpose;

(3) also, as it is the manufacturers and importers of the equipment and blank tape who, by making those items available to the public, make it possible for the public to use authors' works in this way, it is reasonable to require them (the manufacturers and importers) to collect the statutory payment and account for it to the copyright owners;

(4) under these schemes the statutory payments made—which in some countries are charged on the equipment only, in some on the blank tape only, and in some on both—are paid by the manufacturers and importers to collective agencies representing the various categories of interest entitled to share in the statutory payments; and those collective agencies are responsible for distributing the amounts so received.

33.96 The differences between the various national schemes relate principally to the following matters:

(1) the extent to which the total amount of statutory payments is distributed to individual right owners and other interested parties, or is applied to social purposes. In some countries virtually 100% is distributed on an individual basis, whereas in other countries a proportion, which in some cases may be 50%, is applied to general social purposes—e.g. the granting of scholarships to authors and composers;

(2) the extent to which the copyright owners of non-national works (but which are protected under the copyright law of the country) are entitled to participate in the distribution of the statutory payments; in some countries all national works from other countries belonging to the same Convention to which the

References for Section D
D. de Freitas, *Impact of New Technologies: Reprography, Computer Use and Software Protection,*
WIPO/CNR/ND/86/6

country in question belong, are entitled to participate; in other countries only national authors and other interested parties participate.

E. NEW COMMUNICATION TECHNOLOGIES

(a) Introduction

33.97 Communication technologies, which started with the transmission of sound only, began to serve the public on a significant scale in the first and second decade of this century. For thirty or forty years, thereafter, broadcasting was simply the transmission through the ether by wireless means of electromagnetic signals which, when received by suitable apparatus, could be converted into sounds and visual images audible to, and perceivable by, human ears and eyes.

(b) Satellites

33.98 In the middle of the century, a significant development took place in the field of broadcast communications. Instead of the electromagnetic signals emitted by the original broadcast travelling directly—that is, without any man-made intervening assistance—from the original transmitter to the receiver, the transmitted signals were received first by a satellite placed in orbit some 22,500 miles above the earth's surface. The satellite travelled at a speed and direction which kept it, in effect, motionless in relation to the earth in what is known as a geostationary orbit. From this satellite the received signals would then be transmitted back to earth where, at first, for technical reasons, they were receivable only by ground stations, but increasingly have become receivable by private receiving sets owned and operated by individual members of the public. This has meant that both radio and television programs originating in, and transmitted from, one country, are receivable in many other countries; indeed, some of the footprints of these satellites may cover as much as one-third of the earth's surface.

(i) Types of Satellites

33.99 Traditionally, one distinguishes between three types of telecommunication satellites: point-to-point, distribution and direct broadcast satellites, the first two of which are also referred to as communication satellites or fixed service satellites. Placed in geostationary orbit, these satellites are "anchored" at a specific point some thirty-six thousand kilometers above the Equator.

33.100 Point-to-point satellites are used for intercontinental communication between one emitting point and one or more receiving points. Their signals cover roughly one-third of the earth's surface, so that with the aid of three such satellites, placed over the Atlantic, Indian and Pacific Oceans, signals from any country in the world can be transported—if necessary via double hop—to just about any other country in the world, provided that the necessary earth stations are available. These earth stations must be very powerful and in consequence are very expensive.

33.101 Distribution satellites cover smaller geographical areas (e.g. Europe or part of the United States of America), and their signals are generally destined for a multiplicity of receivers (such as broadcasters or cable system operators) spread out over that particular area. The signal is more concentrated and more powerful than that from a point-to-point satellite, and in consequence the earth stations required for receiving signals from such satellites are considerably smaller—and cheaper—than those needed in a point-to-point satellite communication system.

33.102 Direct broadcast satellites are instruments which transmit programmes that are intended for direct reception by the general public. They are "ordinary transmitters hung up in space," with all the advantages that such a bird's-eye view carries with it.

(ii) Copyright and Satellites

33.103 Satellite broadcasting raises a large number of problems of considerable interest in the copyright field. Under the Berne Convention (Article 11*bis*(1)), broadcasting is the major form of wireless communication to the public. It is quite obvious that that Article of the Berne Convention also covers direct satellite broadcasting. However, we have to ask which act is in fact to be considered as an act of broadcasting; is the act of broadcasting simply the transmission of signals towards the satellite or does it comprise both the upwards leg (during which the signals are transported from the place of transmission to the satellite) and the downwards leg (during which the signals travel from the satellite towards what is known as the satellite's "footprint", that is to say the area in which the work may normally be received)? The term "normally received" means that the signals may be received on a dish aerial which is readily available to the public. We have all seen the dishes fixed on blocks of flats and used by a number of occupants of the same building or group of buildings. At present, there is an ever-growing trend in favor of interpreting broadcasting not only as transmission, but also as communication to the public, which would seem in line with Article 11*bis*(1).

33.104 To know what constitutes an act of broadcasting in the case of indirect broadcasting by satellite is important since programs are frequently put out from one country (or from international waters or other places located outside the jurisdiction of any country) and then transmitted to the public in a number of countries. There are also cases where the law of the country of transmission authorizes non-voluntary licenses, whereas such licenses are not authorized in the countries in which signals will be received by the public. In addition, the reply to the question where the act of broadcasting takes place also determines the identity of the person who is entitled to authorize that broadcast if the person concerned is not the same in the country of the place of transmission and in the country or countries in which the signals may be received.

33.105 Since copyright under the Berne Convention is a territorial right that subsists distinctly and independently in each country, it is the person who is the holder of copyright in a given country who may exercise that copyright in such country. Indeed, under Article 5(2) of the Berne Convention, "the extent of protection, as well as the means of redress afforded to the author to protect his rights, shall be governed exclusively by the laws of the country where protection is claimed." This means that in the case of direct satellite broadcasting under which a program is transmitted from one country and communicated to the public of one or more other countries, the provisions of at least two legislations have to be complied with, that is to say the legislation of the country of transmission and the legislation of the countries in which signals may normally be received. What happens if the owner of the right of broadcasting is not the same in each of the countries?

33.106 Views diverge at the present time as regards the applicable legislation and the exercise of rights by the various rightholders in the country of transmission and the countries of reception. It is to be hoped that a possible protocol to the Berne Convention will succeed in settling these divergences. At the second session of the Committee of Experts on that possible protocol, a large number of delegations favored the application of a single legislation which, in the case of a choice between the legislation of the country of transmission and that of the country of reception, was generally that of the country of transmission. The draft European Community Directive on cable distribution and satellite broadcasting seems to have adopted the same point of view. However, the draft excludes non-voluntary licenses in the case of satellite broadcasting. Thus, by establishing an exclusive right in all of the Community member States, the problem of differences between the law of the country of transmission and that of the country of reception would no longer arise within the Community.

33.107 A further possibility that was supported by several delegations and by observers from non-governmental organizations at the second session of the Committee of Experts was to adopt the law of the country of transmission, but with an important reservation. In those cases where the rightholders were not the same in the countries of transmission and of reception, an additional authorization would have to be obtained from the collective administration bodies or, in some cases, by a contract covering the countries of reception.

33.108 It would seem acknowledged that satellite broadcasting constitutes an act of broadcasting within the meaning of the Berne Convention since the program may be received directly by the public. Additionally, the idea of abolishing non-voluntary licenses for satellite broadcasting received broad support at the previously mentioned meeting. Finally, with regard to determining the law applicable to that type of broadcasting, several States seem to prefer the application of a single legislation and the majority of them tended rather towards the application of the law of the country of transmission despite the fact that a fair number of States had acknowledged the need to take into account the situation in the country of the footprint (or reception), either through collective administration or in some other way.

(c) Cable Distribution

33.109 Simultaneously with the development of the use of satellites for broadcasting, the cable distribution of broadcast programmes has also been evolving. This technology began in the United States originally in areas where, principally because of the mountainous terrain, the direct reception by domestic radio and television sets of broadcast programmes was very poor; and this led to the use of what in those days was called a "community antenna." This was a co-operative arrangement among neighboring house-holders who invested in a large aerial or other receiving device on a high point in the neighborhood where reception was good, from which the received signals were distributed by wire to the subscribers to the project. This arrangement was later regarded as having environmental value in that it eliminated the need for each individual household to have an aerial; and indeed, today there are a number of communities in Europe where municipal regulations prohibit individual household aerials and only permit the reception of radio and television signals via community antennae of this kind.

33.110 However, from these early origins of a purely co-operative local community service, cable distribution technology has evolved into large commercial enterprises both in North America and Europe. Cable companies establish ground stations which can receive not only national broadcast services but a large number of broadcast programmes from other countries which reach the ground station by satellite; and the cable operator then distributes these programmes, which could be as many as 60 different channels, to subscribers to his cable services, so that the subscribing household, instead of having a choice of one or two or maybe half-a-dozen national television programmes, may be able to tune in to a wide range of programmes from many countries.

33.111 Along with this technical development, the member States of the Berne Union have felt it necessary to carry out several revisions of the Berne Convention, of which the original text was signed in 1886, to accommodate the changes and the new relationships that it has instituted. Acceptance of a right of rebroadcasting dates back to the 1928 revision in Rome during which a new Article 11*bis* was added to the Convention to afford to authors an exclusive right of authorizing communication to the public by broadcasting. This right was subject to a number of conditions that are set out in paragraph 2 of that Article. The Article was subsequently revised at the 1948 Brussels Conference where numerous other acts were added in addition to broadcasting as such and also to provide for what are known as ephemeral recordings made by broadcasting organizations for later broadcasting of a work that has been temporarily recorded. It is that 1948 version of Article 11*bis*, adopted in Brussels, that is to be found almost word for word in the 1971 Paris Act, that is to say the most recent Act of the Berne Convention.

33.112 As far as cable broadcasting is concerned, Article 11*bis*(1)(ii) refers to broadcasting by wire "when this communication is made by an organization other than the original one." Although the Convention does not define the term "wire," it is generally accepted that the word in fact means "cable." Cable comprises considerable advantages over other forms of dissemination, particularly since it does away with those enormous aerials and dishes that are to be seen increasingly on blocks of flats and hotels. In addition, cable provides the user with access to a larger number of programs. Finally, where the cable is of sufficient technical quality, as for example optical fibers, the quality of the broadcast is greatly improved in comparison to broadcasting by electromagnetic waves and, as we shall see at the end of this paper, even allows digital broadcasting.

33.113 From the legal point of view, the Berne Convention does not deal with all programs broadcast by cable in the same manner. In the case of cable distribution of broadcasts originally put out by electromagnetic waves or by direct broadcasting satellite, distribution can be considered a secondary use. Thus, a broadcasting organization that has obtained permission to broadcast a work by wireless means will not need an additional authorization to broadcast the same program by cable since Article 11*bis*(1)(ii) of the Berne Convention affords that exclusive right only where cable distribution is made by "an organization other than the original one." However, if cable distribution is made by an operator who is not the original organization, the author of the work distributed will enjoy the exclusive right under that Article.

33.114 It may be added that the Berne Convention allows non-voluntary licenses to be imposed for cable distribution, except for programs that are diffused for the first time by cable, that is to say where they do not constitute a rebroadcast. However, at international level, the current trend is towards the elimination of non-voluntary broadcasting licenses and, at the second session of the Committee of Experts on a Possible Protocol to the Berne Convention, held in Geneva in February 1992, a fair number of States supported a proposal that this type of license be suppressed. We may therefore consider that such non-voluntary broadcasting licenses are in the process of disappearing.

33.115 The limitation of copyright under non-voluntary broadcasting licenses was authorized in 1928 on the grounds that there was a need to make works available to the broadcasting organizations who claimed that, failing such a possibility, they could fall victim to societies of authors enjoying a monopoly situation. Experience has since shown that those who feared they would not be able to readily use works for broadcasting had exaggerated the risk. Where problems of that kind have arisen, they have been settled by the establishment of appropriate collective administration systems. The argument that the societies of authors could possibly abuse the situation has proved to be unfounded. In the field of public performance rights, there is no doubt that it is not necessary to have recourse to non-voluntary licenses to prevent the collective administration societies from abusing a possible monopoly position which they would enjoy *de facto*. The advent of new significant forms of communication of works to the public (such as cable-originated programs) has also thrown new light on the matter of non-voluntary broadcasting licenses under Articles 11*ter*(1), 14(1) and 14*bis*(1) of the Berne Convention. The holders of copyright have the exclusive right to authorize communication by cable of their works to the public in a cable-originated program, that is to say a program that is not simply a simultaneous and integral retransmission of a broadcast program, thus excluding the institution of compulsory licenses. The function of a cable-originated program is exactly the same as that of programs broadcast over the air, which are indeed frequently retransmitted by cable together with cable-originated programs. Generally, these two differing types of program are in competition; there would seem no reason to favor one of the competitors (cable rather than broadcasting over the air) by giving him the advantage of possible non-voluntary licenses. There is entire justification, therefore, in envisaging the suppression of such non-voluntary broadcasting licenses.

33.116 Where the programs transmitted by broadcasting services in one country are received, via satellite, by a ground station in another country, and are thence distributed by cable to the public in that country, there is an additional dimension to the copyright implication. In this scenario the interests of the owner of the copyright in a work incorporated in the broadcast programs may be prejudiced for various reasons, for example:

(1) in the country where the cable operator is situated, there may be no copyright law or the law may not give a copyright owner rights against a cable operator;

(2) although there may be a law which gives the copyright owner rights in respect of cable distribution, the law may be ineffective because for any one of many reasons it may not be possible for the copyright owner to enforce his rights.

33.117 In this scenario it is clearly reasonable and indeed necessary that the copyright owner should be able to look to the original broadcaster to protect his interests. This in turn means that the action of the originating broadcaster in transmitting a copyright work embodied in one of his programs via a satellite and destined for reception by ground stations in other countries, should be regarded as an act of broadcasting within the copyright owner's control; in other words, the copyright owner must be in a position to hold the original broadcaster responsible. This situation has been the subject of much debate and broadcasters have been reluctant to accept responsibility. However, there is growing acceptance that when a broadcaster transmits signals directed to a satellite from which their downward onward transmission will make them receivable in foreign countries, that act of initiating the transmission must be within the copyright owner's control.

F. DIGITAL DISTRIBUTION SYSTEMS

33.118 The most recent technical developments in the field of broadcasting aim to increase the quality of the carrier signals, which also means that reception by the public has improved, as also the user-friendliness of the systems. As far as the improvement in diffusion quality is concerned, various countries are currently working on the introduction of high-definition television systems that are expected to lead to fully digitized television. At the same time, work continues on setting up distribution networks for musical, audiovisual and other works on fully digital media. By making available to the public recordable digital media it becomes possible to make digital-quality copies (like compact discs) of works which can then be disseminated, either by cable (optical fibers) or by an equivalent system.

33.119 There are significant differences between the two systems. High definition, and then digital, television will remain a form of mass broadcasting intended for a broad public receiving the same program at the same time, but, when compared with present day television, will make it possible to produce a digital copy and not a video cassette whose quality deteriorates with use and with the number of generations of copies made. From the point of view of copyright, the problem will then arise of the reproduction and distribution of copies made at home by private individuals without the authorization of the rightholders.

33.120 The digital distribution of musical and audiovisual works on request raises the same type of problem, but on a quite different scale. Using these

References for Section E
International Bureau of WIPO, *The New Communication Technologies and Copyright*, WIPO/ACAD/E/93/23
D. de Freitas, *Impact of New Technologies: Reprography, Computer Use and Software Protection*, WIPO/CNR/ND/86/6
W. Rumphorst, *Broadcasting and Copyright*, WIPO/GIC/CNR/GE/86/13

systems, which are currently being developed in the United States, Japan and, shortly, in Europe, a user at home may at any time ask to receive a film, a musical work or possibly even a computer program, a text or any other type of work that can be digitized, that is to say any work transferred to a binary computer format enabling a computer to process the work in the same way as simple data, in digital quality. That data can then be manipulated, reproduced a very large number of times without any loss of quality, and then transmitted by telephone, cable or copied onto a diskette.

33.121 If it becomes possible to obtain at home any type of musical or audiovisual work, computer program or any other type of work from an enormous central database, which itself could be linked to other similar databases throughout the world by satellite, the user will have at his disposal practically all creations available anywhere in the world. He will be able to make copies on a digital medium and subsequently reproduce that work an infinite number times or, with the help of a computer, could manipulate it, transform it and create a derived work or, at least, a work inspired by the original. This activity is known as sampling and is already very wide-spread, consisting basically in manipulating and modifying by computer the human voice or a musical performance.

33.122 The impact of this type of distribution of works on copyright and neighboring rights will be gigantic. It will cause a major change in the distribution chains since users will no longer have to acquire conventional media, as is today the case when acquiring compact discs, videocassettes or other records. It will lead to a radical transformation of the financial flows since retailers trading in such media will no longer represent the main source of revenue for producers or, upstream, for authors and performers. Furthermore, each user will be able to become a source of piracy while producers of works are using a simple computer and creating a work on the basis of an existing, copyrighted work. It will likewise be very easy to produce multimedia works by combining music, images, texts and the like.

33.123 As a remedy to the first mentioned problem (modification of the financial flows), it will be necessary to envisage the collection of substantial royalties on blank media on which the users will make copies at home of works disseminated through digital distribution systems. The collecting of such royalties would be carried out by the collective administration bodies and that remuneration would be paid to the manufacturers and importers of recording equipment and media. Those manufacturers and importers are able to recover all or part of the amounts involved through the price of their products, meaning that remuneration would be paid by the persons who effectively copy the works. Subsequently, the collective administration bodies would share the remuneration between the authors and other rightholders whose works may legitimately be presumed to have been reproduced for private purposes. The techniques for sharing out the amounts collected vary from one country to another but, in general, distribution is based on sampling which is one of the techniques most frequently used by the collecting societies dealing with musical performance rights. Although this technique is not perfect, it nevertheless ensures a relatively fair distribution between the various authors and rightholders and is basically representative of the true use made of the works concerned. Various studies have shown that, in the case of sound recordings made at home, the two major sources of reproduction are sound recordings (phonograms) and radio programs. It is possible to determine the effective structure of home recording activities using the data provided by radio stations of the figures for sales of records and from other similar data. The royalties may then be distributed between the authors and other rightholders with practically the same precision as for other conventional categories of royalty concerning the right of performance, at an extremely low cost. As far as home video recording is concerned, that consists in most cases of directly copying television programs, it is difficult to identify the most frequently used works but an appropriate sampling technique nevertheless makes it possible to obtain fairly equitable results.

33.124 This remuneration is due with respect to the most basic form of use of literary and artistic works, that is to say their reproduction. It is therefore owed to the authors and other holders of rights in those works. It is obvious that this right and the relevant remuneration depend on the concept of the rights of authors in their works and that, in Article 5(1) of the Berne Convention, those rights are subject to the principle of national treatment.

33.125 Nevertheless, at present, the application of national treatment to such royalties is not uniform and the countries party to the Berne Convention may be split up into four categories: (i) those who give national treatment in accordance with the Berne Convention; (ii) those who generally afford national treatment but whose legislation provides for the allocation of a certain percentage to collective purposes or for the promotion of culture; (iii) those who refuse national treatment and apply a principle of reciprocity and (iv) those who simply refuse national treatment. That means they acknowledge only the rights of their nationals.

33.126 The above analysis shows that refusal of national treatment in respect of remuneration for home recording is contrary to the principle of national treatment and to the relevant provisions of the Berne Convention. As regards the allocation of a certain percentage of the remuneration to collective purposes or for the promotion of culture, this is lawful if authorized by the supreme organ of the collecting society with respect to nationals and, in the case of foreign rightholders, by bilateral agreements concluded between the collecting societies concerned.

33.127 With the advent of digital technology, private reproduction for personal purposes, which already constitutes one of the most important forms of reproduction will certainly become *the most* important form. This again shows clearly the absurdity of any attempt to put aside the application of national treatment of this right to remuneration by attempting to remove it from the scope of copyright and by denying its true legal nature. We may therefore conclude that the principle of national treatment must be applied to this right to remuneration as to other rights comprised in authors' rights and that any attempt at national level to put aside this rule could one day be sanctioned under a dispute between States submitted to a competent international body.

References for Section F
International Bureau of WIPO, *The New Communication Technologies and Copyright*, WIPO/ACAD/E/93/23

CHAPTER 34

Proposed International Treaties and Conventions

A. THE DRAFT PATENT LAW TREATY

(a) The Origins of International Patent Law Harmonization

34.1 International harmonization of legislation on patents began more than 100 years ago with the adoption of the Paris Convention for the Protection of Industrial Property (hereinafter referred to as the "Paris Convention"). While stressing the independence of national patent systems and the territorial limitations of rights granted under those national systems, the Paris Convention nevertheless contains some basic norms, such as the principle of national treatment, the right of priority, the prohibition of the forfeiture of a patent by reason of importation of the patented product, the time limits and the requirement of non-exclusivity in respect of compulsory licenses for non-working and the temporary protection of inventions disclosed during exhibitions. These norms were extended during the various revisions of the Convention but they still cover only some aspects of patent protection.

34.2 In the 1950s, discussions started within the Council of Europe concerning the creation of a European patent system and the harmonization of patent laws. This led to the adoption of the Convention on the Unification of Certain Points of Substantive Law on Patents for Inventions of November 27, 1963. This Convention represented the achievement of a high degree of unification of substantive law on patents in Europe. Several of its provisions served as a basis for the European Patent Convention (EPC) of 1973, which entered into force on October 7, 1977, and established a unified procedure of a grant of European Patents, and for the Luxembourg Convention on the European Patent for the Common Market of 1975 aimed at the grant of European Patents for the European Community in its entirety.

34.3 Other examples of regional agreements which have achieved harmonization or unification of substantive and procedural patent law, or cooperation on patent granting procedures, can be found in Africa and Latin America. The Agreement on the establishment of an African Intellectual Property Organization (OAPI), concluded in Libreville in 1962 and revised in Bangui in 1977, and the Harare Protocol adopted in 1982 in the framework of the African Regional Industrial Property Organization (ARIPO), unify a number of points of substantive patent law and provide for the centralized grant of patents by regional patent offices. In Latin America, the Andean Group countries (Bolivia, Colombia, Ecuador, Peru and Venezuela) adopted Decision 313 which contains, *inter alia*, uniform substantive and procedural patent provisions.

34.4 The harmonization of patent laws was an aim frequently mentioned by delegations in the negotiations which led to the adoption of the Patent Cooperation Treaty (PCT) in 1970. The PCT is an agreement for international cooperation with regard to the filing, searching and preliminary examination of patent applications and the dissemination of technical information contained in patent applications. The PCT, which is administered by the World Intellectual Property Organization (WIPO), contains elements regarding patent applications for which there is worldwide consensus.

(b) The History of the Patent Law Treaty

34.5 The history of the Treaty Supplementing the Paris Convention as far as Patents are concerned ("the Patent Law Treaty") started with a proposal made in June 1983 by the Director General of the WIPO to the Governing Bodies of WIPO (and, in particular, the Assembly of the Paris Union), for a study on the legal effects of public disclosure of an invention by its inventor prior to filing an application. The "grace period," as it is usually called, has the effect that certain disclosures made by the inventor during a specified period prior to the filing or priority date of an application do not affect the patentability of the invention claimed in the application. The proposal was adopted and the question was considered in May 1984 by the WIPO "Committee of Experts on the Grace Period for Public Disclosure of an Invention Before Filing an Application." Provisions on the grace period are found in Article 12 of the Basic Proposal for the Patent Law Treaty.

34.6 It was soon realized that the question of a grace period could not be dealt with in isolation, since it necessarily involved other issues that would have to be agreed upon at the same time as the grace period. In particular, such issues were the identification of the inventor (since the grace period primarily covers disclosures of the invention by the inventor) and the requirements of a filing date of the application (since the grace period is counted from the domestic filing date or the priority date). These issues were considered for the first time in the second meeting of the Committee of Experts, held in July 1985, and are addressed in Articles 6 and 8, respectively, of the Basic Proposal.

34.7 In recognition of the expanded scope of the task, the name of the Committee was changed to "Committee of Experts on the Harmonization of Certain Provisions in Laws for the Protection of Inventions." That name was retained throughout the preparatory work for the proposed Patent Law Treaty. The Committee continued to meet during the six years between 1984 and 1990: once in 1985, once in 1986 and twice in each of the subsequent four years (1987 to 1990), making a total of 11 preparatory meetings. At many of those meetings, the scope of the proposed Patent Law Treaty grew as the Committee considered additional substantive subject matter for inclusion in it.

34.8 Through this gradual process of growth of its scope, the proposed Patent Law Treaty came to address many important issues in the field of patents upon which there is great divergence in treatment among national and regional laws, but for which harmonization is desired. It is the intention of the Treaty to simplify and render more effective and more economical the previously established means of obtaining patent protection in the various countries of the world, for the benefit of patent offices, inventors, industry and their professional representatives.

(c) The Basic Proposal for the Treaty

34.9 The "Basic Proposal" is the current official version of the proposed Patent Law Treaty. The Basic Proposal was presented to the first part of the Diplomatic Conference held in The Hague, in June 1991. The Basic Proposal includes 20 substantive articles. Twelve of them are accompanied by draft Rules which form the Regulations and are considered to be part of the Basic Proposal.

34.10 The substantive provisions of the Basic Proposal deal with the following subjects:

(1) disclosure and description (Article 3; Rule 2);
(2) claims (Article 4; Rule 3);
(3) unity of invention (Article 5; Rules 4 and 5);
(4) identification and mention of inventor; declaration concerning the entitlement of the applicant (Article 6; Rule 6);
(5) belated claiming of priority (Article 7);
(6) filing date (Article 8; Rule 7);
(7) right to a patent (Article 9);
(8) conditions of patentability (Article 11);
(9) disclosures not affecting patentability (grace period) (Article 12);
(10) prior art effect of certain applications (Article 13);
(11) amendment or correction of application (Article 14);
(12) publication of application (Article 15; Rule 8);
(13) time limits for search and substantive examination (Article 16);
(14) changes in patents (Article 17; Rule 9);
(15) administrative revocation (Article 18; Rule 10);
(16) prior user (Article 20);
(17) extent of protection and interpretation of claims (Article 21);
(18) starting date of the term of a patent   (Article 22(2));
(19) enforcement of rights (Article 23).

34.11 These substantive provisions relate to patent application and examination procedures, standards for obtaining a patent, and rights and remedies under a patent. The draft Treaty also provides definitions for some of the terms used in the Basic Proposal. Other provisions relate to the administration of the treaty itself. Individual provisions of the Basic Proposal are discussed in more detail below.

34.12 In September 1992, the Assembly of the Paris Union recommended decided that six Articles be removed from the Basic Proposal under consideration by the Diplomatic Conference. Those articles were Article 10 (Fields of Technology), Article 19 (Rights Conferred by the Patent), Article 22(1) (20-Year Term for Patents), Article 24 (Reversal of Burden of Proof), Article 25 (Obligations of the Right Holder) and Article 26 (Remedial Measures Under National Legislation).

34.13 In May, 1995, a Consultative Meeting for the Further Preparation of the Diplomatic Conference for the Conclusion of the Patent Law Treaty was convened by the Director General of WIPO following a decision made by the Assembly of the Paris Union in October 1994, in order to try to recommend solutions to the principal issues involved in the PLT.

34.14 The Consultative Meeting adopted a recommendation which reads as follows:

"The Consultative Meeting,

Considering that, in the absence of consensus on the basic proposal that was before the diplomatic conference in The Hague in 1991, a continuation of that conference may either not be the best approach or not be opportune,

Believing that harmonization of patent laws on a number of subjects is of the utmost benefit for patent protection of inventions,

Recommends to the Director General of WIPO to seek decisions from the September 1995 session of the General Assembly of WIPO and the Assembly of the Paris Union on another approach for promoting harmonization, particularly of matters concerning the formalities of national and regional patent applications including matters such as signatures, changes in names and addresses, change in ownership, correction of mistakes, observations in case of intended refusal, representation, address for service, contents of at least the request part of the application, and use of model international forms, and that two or more sessions of a committee of experts to discuss such matters should be organized by WIPO before the September 1997 sessions of the said Assemblies,

Is of the view that the question of having a diplomatic conference, with what agenda and when, should be considered in the said sessions of the said Assemblies."

B. THE PROPOSED PROTOCOL TO THE BERNE CONVENTION AND A POSSIBLE NEW INSTRUMENT ON THE PROTECTION OF THE RIGHTS OF PERFORMERS AND PRODUCERS OF PHONOGRAMS

(a) Introduction

34.15 Probably, it is not an exaggeration to state that the international copyright and neighboring rights system, since its very birth, has never undergone more fundamental and multiple changes than now. This is mainly the consequence of the spectacular technological developments in the fields of creation, dissemination and protection of works, but the recognition of the economic importance of copyright and neighboring rights and their increased role in trade relations and economic integration also have contributed to this.

34.16 In the last decade, WIPO convened a number of meetings and prepared a number of studies and documents which dealt with the impact of new technologies on copyright and neighboring rights on the basis of which guidelines, recommendations and model provisions were worked out for national laws. Those guidelines, recommendations and model provisions had a non-negligible influence on the development of national legislation, but they were not binding.

References for Section A
International Bureau of WIPO, *Draft Patent Law Treaty*, WIPO/ACAD/E/94/17.A
International Bureau of WIPO, *Report, Consultative Meeting for the Further Preparation of the Diplomatic Conference for the Conclusion of the Patent Law Treaty*, PLT/CM/4

In the absence of binding international norms, there was increasing danger that national legislators might choose differing solutions to the new problems, that this might lead to increasingly divergent trends in the international copyright and neighboring rights system and that, as a consequence, this might also undermine the delicate balance between the minimum level of protection determined by the Berne, Rome and Phonograms Conventions, on the one hand, and the principle of national treatment, on the other.

(b) The Proposed Protocol to the Berne Convention

34.17 The recognition of the danger of such possible developments led WIPO to include in its program the preparation of a possible protocol to the Berne Convention. Such a protocol, in addition to responding to the challenges of the new technologies, was also intended to serve as a bridge between the two basic copyright systems, the "civil law" (or "continental") and the "common law" (or "Anglo-American") systems, first of all in respect of the protection of sound recordings (phonograms). The first four sessions of the Committee of Experts were held in November 1991, February 1992, June 1993 and December 1994, all in Geneva.

34.18 A memorandum of the International Bureau established the issues to be discussed by the Committee of Experts on a Possible Protocol to the Berne Convention as the following:

(1) computer programs;
(2) data bases;
(3) rental right;
(4) non-voluntary licenses for the sound recording of musical works;
(5) non-voluntary licenses for primary broadcasting and satellite communication;
(6) distribution right, including importation right;
(7) duration of the protection of photographic works;
(8) communication to the public by satellite broadcasting;
(9) enforcement of rights; and
(10) national treatment.

34.19 Two areas considered by the Committee of Experts—computer programs and data bases—were the really important ones. At the first session of the Committee, there was practically unanimous agreement that computer programs—both operation system programs and application programs, and both in source code form and object code form—are to be protected by copyright and that the obligation to protect such programs, at the same level as literary works, may also be deduced from the present text of the Berne Convention. By and large the same can be said about the outcome of the discussions concerning data bases. Article 2(5) of the Berne Convention provides for the protection of collections of literary and artistic works that, by reason of the selection and arrangement of their contents, constitute intellectual creations. That is, the reason for the copyright protection of such collections is the original way of selecting and arranging the works included in them. However, not only literary and artistic works but also simple unprotected data may be selected and arranged in an original manner. Therefore, the original collections—compilations—of simple data are also to be protected under the Berne Convention. Although all this may be deduced from the Berne Convention on the basis of an extensive interpretation of the Convention, it is obvious that a clarification in the possible Protocol to the Berne Convention would create a much clearer situation without any legal uncertainty concerning the obligation to protect such creations.

34.20 As far as non-voluntary licenses for the sound recording of musical works and for primary broadcasting and satellite communication are concerned, there was a fairly general agreement, at the second session of the Committee, that such licenses allowed under the present text of the Berne Convention are out-of-date and should be abolished. Some delegations, however, hesitated; thus, these items should still be further considered.

34.21 The last item that really has any importance separately from the other items is the term of protection of photographic works. The Committee agreed that such works deserve the same term of protection as the other categories of literary and artistic works—that is, the term should be 50 years following the death of the author—and, thus, that the provision of the Berne Convention providing for a shorter term for photographic works—25 years after the making of the works—should be eliminated.

34.22 The reference in the preceding paragraph to "the last item that really has any importance separately from the other items" includes the implicit statement that the last two items "already discussed"—the rental right and communication to the public by satellite broadcasting—do not have such importance. The right of rental is actually an element—a sub-right—of the right of distribution. Satellite broadcasting does not have importance as a separate item because it seems that it is only the elimination of compulsory licenses, in respect of such broadcasting, which is a sufficiently important aspect and on which there is a hope for agreement.

34.23 Concerning "distribution right, including importation right," the memorandum contained a thorough analysis on the basis of which it proposed that the protocol state that, under the present text of the Berne Convention, it was obligatory to protect the exclusive rights of the author or other owner of copyright to authorize the first distribution and the importation (for distribution) of copies of works, since those rights, although not mentioned in the Convention, were corollaries to the right of reproduction expressly mentioned in the Convention.

34.24 The memorandum suggested that, after such clarification, the protocol provide the following:

(1) the author of, or other owner of copyright in, a work has the exclusive right to authorize the distribution of the original or copies of the work, through sale or other transfer of ownership, or through rental, public lending or other transfer of possession;

(2) subject to Article 14*ter* of the Berne Convention (*droit de suite*), any national legislation may provide that this right is not applicable in respect of the original or a copy of the work which has been sold, or the ownership of which has been otherwise transferred, by or pursuant to an authorization of the author or other owner of copyright;

(3) however, this faculty provided for national legislation does not apply in case of rental [or public lending] of the original or copies of musical works in the

form of graphic notation, audiovisual works, works the performances of which are recorded in phonograms (sound recordings), computer programs, and any other kinds of works stored in electronic (including digital) format.

34.25 The memorandum also proposed that the right of importation be recognized (with the exception of importation for personal and non-commercial use, as part of personal luggage).

34.26 The Committee had reservations concerning the interpretation that the obligation to grant a first distribution right and an importation right could be deduced from the 1971 Act of the Berne Convention. However, as far as the right of distribution, including a right of rental, was concerned, in general, the Committee agreed with the proposals included in the memorandum. It seems that further discussions will be needed concerning the coverage of the proposed rental right surviving the first sale of copies (that is to which categories of works it should be extended) and concerning the recognition of the right of importation. At the same time, the Committee was of the view that it would not be appropriate to deal with public lending rights in the protocol.

34.27 Concerning enforcement of rights, the memorandum contained two sets of proposals: first, the proposals of the International Bureau, and second, at the request of certain governments, the relevant part of the draft GATT/TRIPS agreement. Both sets of proposals concerned provisional (conservatory) measures, civil remedies, criminal sanctions, "border" measures, and general procedural safeguards. The proposals of the International Bureau also extended to measures to be applied for abuse in respect of technical devices (more particularly, for circumventing copy-protection or copy-management systems) and for illicit manufacturing, importing, and distributing devices for the reception of encrypted programs.

34.28 At the third session of the Committee of Experts, all participants who compared the two sets of proposals felt that the WIPO proposals were clearer, legally much more precise and better suiting the purposes of enforcement of rights. Nevertheless, the draft GATT/TRIPS text was accepted as a basis for the further preparatory work because it was taken into account that it formed part of a complex negotiated draft agreement and it was felt that "renegotiating" it separately would not be appropriate.

34.29 Finally, as far as national treatment is concerned, the memorandum contained three proposals. First, the protocol should not introduce new exceptions to the obligation of granting national treatment, in keeping with Article 5(1) of the Berne Convention. Second, the protocol should provide explicitly for the faculty of countries party to it not to grant national treatment in respect of rights granted for the public lending of books and similar printed publications (a faculty which so far only exists on the basis of a *de facto* agreement among the member countries of the Berne Union). Third, the protocol should oblige the countries party to it to provide that national treatment be fully respected also where rights are exercised through the collective administration of rights and, further, that no remuneration collected by collective administration organizations and due to foreign authors and other foreign owners of copyright be used without the authorization of such authors or other owners of copyright—authorization given directly or through persons or bodies representing them—for any purposes other than distributing such remuneration (after deducting the actual costs of administration) to the authors or other owners of copyright concerned.

34.30 At the meeting, a restatement of the principle of national treatment, without qualification, received general support. Several delegations expressed the wish, however, that the question of national treatment be revisited at an appropriate future moment when the contents of the future Protocol is further clarified. The majority of the delegations appeared to be of the opinion that there was no need to recognize the right of lending (for example, of books, by libraries) and it was permissible for a country to regulate the question of public lending as a matter outside the scope of copyright. The majority opposed the proposal of the International Bureau that the Protocol should contain rules on the collective administration of rights. The Director General expressed his regrets over this attitude since the rights of foreign authors were particularly susceptible of disregard in the case of collective administration arrangements.

34.31 As indicated above, the International Bureau of WIPO proposed the reinforcement of the principle of national treatment. It is important to note, however, that the principle of national treatment under the Berne Convention has always been coupled with the obligation of the countries party to the Berne Convention to grant certain rights specially prescribed by the Convention. The minimum level of protection under the Convention has been regularly updated at the various revision conferences.

34.32 Since 1971, however, the Berne Convention has not been revised, although since then probably many more important developments have taken place in the fields of creation, exploitation and protection of works than between 1886—the year of adoption of the Berne Convention—and 1971. Since the level of protection has thus not been updated, serious discrepancies now appear among national laws, not only at the margin, but in the very center, of copyright protection, in respect of new categories of works and new rights of great importance. This has created new strains and contradictions around the principle of national treatment; the more generous countries recognizing certain "new" rights try to use any reasonable—and sometimes even not quite reasonable— excuses not to assume what they consider the unjustified unilateral burden of granting national treatment to the nationals of those countries which do not grant the same rights.

34.33 Therefore, the reinforcement of national treatment in the proposed protocol should be linked to an appropriate updating of the minimum level of protection. The question is whether the list of items determined by the Assembly of the Berne Union in September 1992 which the protocol is to cover is sufficient for such updating. It is true that the other two "new" items—"distribution right, including importation right" and "enforcement of rights"—are important and that any agreement on them would be essential elements of an updating of the minimum level of protection under the Berne Convention. As we have seen, of the seven items "already discussed," only two—computer programs and data bases—are of similar importance; one of them—rental right—is actually covered by one of the "new" items ("distribution right, including importation right"), while the other four "old" items are not among the most urgent questions of international copyright protection.

34.34 At the same time, various questions that—on the basis of the memoranda prepared by the International Bureau—were discussed at the first two sessions of the Committee of Experts (such as the recognition of computer storage as reproduction, the questions relating to private copying of sound recordings of works and audiovisual works, the questions of reprography, the recognition of a right of public display, the definition of "public") do not appear on the list determined by the Assembly of the Berne Union in September 1992. Those questions relate to new ways of exploiting works, and their importance is growing with the rapid spreading of the use of the new technologies involved. There are ever greater discrepancies among national laws in the ways they try to respond to those questions; consequently, some of those questions are also in the center of the contradictions and disputes around the application (or non-application) of the principle of national treatment.

34.35 If the principle of national treatment were reinforced without responding to all those controversial questions through an appropriate updating of the minimum level of protection under the Berne Convention, this would seriously upset the traditional balance between the principle of national treatment, on the one hand, and sufficiently detailed and harmonized provisions concerning minimum obligations, on the other. Therefore, it would seem desirable to reconsider the list of questions to be settled in the protocol and to extend it to all important problems of contemporary copyright law.

34.36 Actually, many participants in the third session of the Committee expressed their wish that the terms of reference of the Committee be revised and essentially extended again.

(c) Possible New Instrument on the Protection of the Rights of Performers and Producers of Phonograms

34.37 The memorandum prepared by the International Bureau of WIPO for the Committee of Experts on a Possible Instrument on the Protection of Performers and Producers of Phonograms contained proposals concerning the protection of unfixed performances and of phonograms, both in respect of producers of phonograms and in respect of performers for their performances fixed in phonograms. In waiting for the decision of the Governing Bodies of WIPO whether or not the terms of reference regarding the new instrument should extend to the protection of performers in respect of audiovisual fixations, the memorandum included no proposals concerning such protection.

34.38 In the latter respect, there was consensus in the Committee that nothing in the terms of reference of the Committee precluded a discussion on the question of possible provisions on the rights of performers in audiovisual (as opposed to purely sound) fixations. The Governing Bodies were in agreement with this at their sessions in September 1993. The International Bureau would, consequently, prepare a working document in due time on the rights of performers in audiovisual fixations.

34.39 The memorandum proposed new definitions for "performers," "phonogram," "fixation," "producer of phonograms," "publication," "reproduction," "rental," "public lending," "communication to the public" (a notion which according to the proposed definition would also cover broadcasting) and "public performance." The new definitions are needed mainly because of the new technologies (particularly, digital technology) having a decisive impact on the creation, exploitation and protection of phonograms. The Committee, at its first two sessions, did not discuss those definitions separately but only in connection with the provisions on the rights concerned.

34.40 Digital technology makes it possible, *inter alia*, to re-master the fixations of performances (such as removing noises and "bad notes," strengthening, lengthening, shortening or otherwise altering different parts of performances) and also to use pre-fixed performances or parts of performances in new combinations in new contexts.

34.41 This development strengthens the position that performers should also be granted moral rights more or less similar to the moral rights of authors. The memorandum proposed that such rights be recognized. The proposal received substantial support, but it also met with some opposition.

34.42 For unfixed (live) performances, the memorandum suggested that the same rights (extending to the communication to the public and to the fixation of such performances) be prescribed as those provided for in the Rome Convention. It also proposed, however, that these minimum rights be granted not as a right to prevent (as in the Rome Convention) but as an exclusive right to authorize (or to prohibit). The Committee, in general, agreed with these proposals.

34.43 Of course, the most important part of the memorandum related to the economic rights of performers in respect of their performances fixed in phonograms and to the economic rights of producers of phonograms in respect of their phonograms.

34.44 Let us first talk about the copy-related rights. The memorandum suggested an exclusive right of performers and producers of phonograms to authorize the reproduction of phonograms as well as exclusive rights to authorize first distribution (distribution until the first sale) and importation of copies. Furthermore, since rental of phonograms (mainly of compact disks) had become a major form of exploitation in certain countries, the memorandum also proposed an exclusive right to authorize rental and, as a possible alternative, also public lending of phonograms which would "survive" the first sale of copies. These proposals, with the exception of the recognition of a public lending right, were supported by the Committee.

34.45 Home taping, of course, is also a very much copy-related issue. The memorandum suggested that, as a minimum obligation, a right to remuneration be recognized in the form of a levy to be paid by manufacturers and importers of recording equipment and material, to be collected by collective administration organizations and to be distributed to the performers and producers concerned (in parallel, of course, to a similar right of authors and other owners of copyright). If one considers the quite controversial nature of this issue, it was surprising that the great majority of the delegations supported the proposals included in the memorandum. Further work is, however, necessary concerning certain details.

34.46 Due to the possibility—and actual practice—of manipulating and transforming phonograms and, thus, producing adapted versions, a right of adaptation in favor of both performers and producers was also proposed. Views were divided at the first session of the Committee whether or not the recognition of such a right is justified. It will be further considered.

34.47 Finally, as a starting point, exclusive rights were suggested for both performers and producers also for communication to the public (including broadcasting) and for public performance. It would be a matter for national legislation to restrict this right to a mere right to remuneration. This faculty would not apply, however, to communication to the public (including broadcasting) by digital means. Through digital transmission (digital delivery), phonograms can be received, enjoyed and (by means of digital audio tape (DAT) recorders) reproduced in perfect CD quality. With the advent of (digital) fiber optic networks, the use of phonograms may—and certainly will—become "interactive," which means, *inter alia*, that any person linked to such a network will be able to listen to a recording at a time of his choice. Those developments may—and certainly will—undermine and replace the copy-related forms of exploitation (reproduction, distribution) of phonograms. Therefore, to maintain the possibility for producers of phonograms—and for performers concerning their performances fixed in phonograms—to control the basic forms of exploitation, it seems indispensable to grant them exclusive rights for digital communication to the public (including broadcasting) of phonograms. At the second session of the Committee, there was an intensive discussion on these proposals. It seems that there is an agreement that, at least, in the case of interactive digital cable services, an exclusive right is needed. In respect of digital broadcasting, the discussion will be continued at the next session of the Committee.

34.48 The remaining proposals included in the memorandum can be summed up as follows: (i) the minimum term of protection for performers should be 50 years from the date of the fixation of their performances, and, for producers, as a general rule, from the date of the publication of their phonograms; (ii) no formality should be allowed as a condition of protection; (iii) the same provisions should be applicable for enforcement of rights, *mutatis mutandis*, as those proposed in the memorandum concerning the protocol to the Berne Convention in respect of copyright; and (iv) full national treatment should be prescribed. The proposed criteria for eligibility for protection under the possible instrument are similar to the criteria for eligibility under the Rome Convention. Of these proposals, only the question of national treatment was discussed at the second session of the Committee. The other above-mentioned proposals were considered generally acceptable, and it was decided—without discussion in detail—that they should be included in the "next generation" of working documentation. No final decision was taken about the principle of national treatment either. It was felt that the extent of application of this principle depended on the level of protection to be provided for by the new instrument and, thus, the eventual contents of the instrument should be first seen.

34.49 The Committee only discussed the proposed economic rights of performers in their unfixed (that is, "live") performances and some of the proposed economic rights of performers in their performances fixed in phonograms and of producers of phonograms in their phonograms (namely, the rights of reproduction, distribution (including importation), rental, public lending and adaptation). The Chairman summarized the discussions as follows: "A general right of distribution for performers and producers of phonograms had received broad support, subject to a carefully-worded provision on the application of the principle of exhaustion of the said right. The proposal for a public lending right had not received sufficient support, but the right to authorize public lending as a means of exercise of the right of distribution subject to exhaustion should be maintained. The right of rental had received broad support, and a majority expressed the preference for an exclusive right rather than a right to remuneration. The transition period from a right to remuneration to a full exclusive right of rental, in those countries whose legislation provided a right to remuneration when the new instrument comes into effect, should be as short as possible. The exercise of exclusive rental rights by different right owners should be studied. A number of speakers expressed opposition to or reservations concerning the proposed right of importation. There was, however, also substantial support for the recognition of such a right, and the support by non-governmental organizations was particularly strong. The right of importation should be further studied."

34.50 The relationship between the possible protocol to the Berne Convention and the possible new instrument was not yet discussed in the memoranda prepared for the forthcoming sessions of the two committees of experts. It seems quite obvious, however, that for a well-balanced updating of the international copyright and neighboring rights standards, some kind of substantive link between the protocol and the new instrument would be necessary. This may be similar to the link between the Berne Convention (and the Universal Copyright Convention) and the Rome Convention, in the sense that no country may accede to the latter without being party to the former, or it may consist of the condition that a country must accede to both the protocol and to the new instrument at the same time. This link, however, may be even stronger through the obligation to grant national treatment not only separately (within the framework of the protocol, on the one hand, and the new instrument, one the other), but in a parallel and interrelated way (extending to both the protocol and to the new instrument, and through them, to the protection of both authors' rights in literary and artistic works and to the rights of performers and producers of phonograms). The latter solution would truly make the new instrument—as it is frequently referred to—a "bridge" instrument.

C. REVISION OF THE HAGUE AGREEMENT CONCERNING THE INTERNATIONAL DEPOSIT OF INDUSTRIAL DESIGNS

(a) Introduction

34.51 The system of international deposit of industrial designs administered by the International Bureau of WIPO has been established by the Hague Agreement Concerning the International Deposit of Industrial Designs, which was concluded in 1925. At present, procedures under the Hague Agreement are governed by two different Acts, namely the London Act of 1934 (hereinafter referred to as the "1934 Act") and the Hague Act of 1960 (hereinafter referred to as the "1960 Act").

References for Section B
International Bureau of WIPO, *The Proposed Protocol to the Berne Convention and a Possible New Instrument for the Protection of the Rights of Performers and Producers of Phonograms*, WIPO/ CNR/CA/94/3

The 1960 Act, which entered into force in 1984, now governs the large majority of all international deposits. Although the system of international deposit of industrial designs has functioned for more than 60 years and serves a useful purpose, the number of States members of the Hague Union is relatively small.

(b) The Need for Revision

34.52 It appeared that the number of international deposits could be increased and additional States could join the Hague Union if certain problems in respect of the system of the Agreement currently in force could be solved. Those problems are of three kinds: the first kind comprises problems of the users of the system; the second kind is a problem of the industrial property offices of the designated States; the third kind is a problem of any regional system that does not replace national systems (for example, a Community Design Office which could be established by the European Communities).

(i) Problems Faced by Users of the System

34.53 There are three problems that are faced by users of the system; one concerning the form of deposit, one the fees to be paid by the depositors and one the deferment of publication of the deposit.

34.54 As regards the form of deposit, Article 2(1) of the 1934 Act permitted the deposit of industrial designs either in the form of a graphic representation or in the form of an industrial product incorporating the design. This was modified by the 1960 Act, Article 5(1) of which requires depositors to submit one or more photographs or graphic representations of the design. At the time when this change was made, it was considered that the deposit of industrial products incorporating designs was cumbersome for the International Bureau, because the later had to store the deposited products. Therefore, and also in view of the fact that it had become much easier to take photographs of industrial designs, the possibility of depositing only an industrial product (and not a photograph) was abolished (but it is still possible, under Article 5(3)(b) of the 1960 Act, to add a sample of the industrial product to the deposit). However, following the entry into force of the 1960 Act in 1984, certain branches of industry, in particular some representatives of the textile industry, said that they preferred a system, as provided for in the 1934 Act, under which they could, at their choice, submit either a specimen of the industrial product incorporating the design or a drawing, photograph or other adequate graphic representation of the design. According to that view, it is by far more expeditious to deposit a specimen of the product (for example, a textile tissue incorporating a particular design) than to prepare a graphic representation (of course, for the purposes of publication under the 1960 Act, a representation is needed, but that could be prepared without pressure of time by the International Bureau).

34.55 A possible solution to this problem would be to allow—as an exception under certain well-defined circumstances—the deposit of industrial products incorporating designs. In order to avoid the problems resulting for the International Bureau from a requirement to store cumbersome articles, for example, fenders of automobiles, the possibility of depositing industrial products could be limited to two-dimensional articles not surpassing certain maximum dimensions. Moreover, the International Bureau could be compensated through a special fee for the additional work caused by the preparation of a reproduction for the purposes of publication.

34.56 Concerning the fee system, currently, the applicable fee for the deposit of one design covers a term of protection of five years. It has been suggested that, in certain branches of industry, in particular, in the textile industry where designs apply to certain articles which rapidly change because of changing fashions, there is no need for protection for more than two to three years. Under the 1960 Act, the initial period of validity of an international deposit is five years, and there is no option for a shorter duration. Consequently, it is felt that the cost of multiple deposits is too high. According to the opinion referred to, it should be considered establishing a shorter initial period of validity with a correspondingly lower fee, thus making the system of international deposit more attractive for the branches of industry referred to.

34.57 A possible solution to this problem would be to allow payment for the initial period in two instalments, each covering a period of 30 months, and to allow, in the case of a multiple deposit, a limitation of the multiple deposit to only some of the deposited designs at the time when the second instalment is due. This could result in substantial savings in the specific cases referred to, without, however, establishing an exceptional treatment for certain branches of industry. Such an exceptional treatment would be undesirable for several reasons, in particular, the difficulty of precisely defining the branch of industry concerned.

34.58 As regards deferment of publication, Article 6(2) of the 1934 Act permitted a deposit under sealed cover for a period of five years, whereas Article 6(4) of the 1960 Act limits the possibility of requesting deferment of the publication of the international deposit to a maximum of 12 months. This limitation is based on the consideration that protection of industrial property rights should always be made dependent on the publication of the creation or invention to be protected. However, in respect of certain kinds of products, in particular, those subjected to rapid changes of fashion, it is argued that the publication of the deposited industrial design facilitates counterfeiting just at the time when there is a large demand for the products incorporating the industrial design. According to this opinion, the maximum of 12 months provided for in Article 6 of the 1960 Act is too short and should rather be replaced by a longer period, which would avoid premature dissemination of new fashion designs.

34.59 A possible solution to this problem would be the replacement of the maximum of 12 months provided for in Article 6(4)(a) of the 1960 Act by a maximum of 30 months, which would correspond to the period covered by the first instalment of the fees. It is to be noted, however, that, according to one of the basic principles of industrial property law, publication of an intellectual creation is considered to be a condition of protection. This was the reason for the change made at the Diplomatic Conference in The Hague in 1960, when the possibility of a five-year deposit under sealed cover was replaced by a maximum time limit of one year for deferment of publication. On the other hand, recent developments in intellectual property law seem to indicate that, under particular circumstances, exceptions to the requirement of publication as a condition of protection appear to be acceptable.

(ii) Problems Concerning Industrial Property Offices

34.60 As regards the problems concerning industrial property offices, the time limit of six months for a notification of refusal of protection provided for in Article 8(1) of the Agreement may be too short. Indeed, it is certainly too short for the offices which examine industrial designs as to novelty. Therefore, a prolongation of the six-month time limit might have to be considered. Moreover, the possibility might have to be considered of providing, in addition to a general extension of the time limit, for an additional special extension where a refusal of protection results from an opposition. In this connection, it is to be noted that, among the States at present not party to the Hague Agreement, in particular, Brazil, Denmark, Norway, Portugal, Spain and Sweden, appear to provide for the possibility of opposition before the registration of an industrial design.

34.61 A possible solution to this problem could be found by prolonging the six-month time limit to 12 months and by allowing Contracting Parties providing for an opposition procedure to apply an even longer period, for example, up to seven months from the date on which the opposition period begins.

(iii) Regional Systems

34.62 As regards regional systems for the registration and protection of industrial designs, the 1960 Act only provides for the case that two or more Contracting States replace their national system of registration of industrial designs by a common (regional) system. This provision, contained in Article 30 of the 1960 Act, obviously was adopted with the Benelux Designs Office in mind and for which at the time of the 1960 Diplomatic Conference at The Hague preparatory work had started. However, at present, there exist not only regional systems that replace the national systems (such as the Benelux Designs Office or the Organisation africaine de la propriété intellectuelle (OAPI)), but also at least one system which offers, in addition to the possibility of obtaining the registration of an industrial design with a national Office, the possibility of regional registration, namely, the African Regional Industrial Property Organization (ARIPO) which, under the Harare Protocol of 1982, functions as a regional office for the registration of industrial designs with effect in 11 States. In the future, the European Communities may set up a Community system for the registration of industrial designs following the model of the envisaged Community trademark system. Such a Community system would permit the registration of industrial designs with effect for all member States of the European Community but would not affect the existing national systems for the registration of industrial designs.

34.63 Article 30 of the 1960 Act does not take into account a regional system that coexists with national systems. In order to establish the—desirable—possibility of using the international deposit system under the Hague Agreement with effect for all existing and future regional systems, it would be necessary to provide for the possibility that intergovernmental organizations such as the European Communities and the African Regional Industrial Property Organization could join the Hague Agreement and could thus be designated in the international deposit of an industrial design under the Hague Agreement.

(c) The Committee of Experts

34.64 A Committee of Experts, consisting of representatives of States members of the Hague Union and, as observers, other States, intergovernmental organizations and non-governmental organizations, has met to consider the advisability of revising the Hague Agreement to introduce into the system further flexibility in order to encourage States not yet party to the Hague Agreement to join the system, and to make the system easier to use for applicants. As of 1995, the Committee of Experts has held five sessions (one each year in 1991, 1992, 1993, 1994 and 1995).

D. THE WIPO DRAFT TREATY ON THE SETTLEMENT OF DISPUTES BETWEEN STATES IN THE FIELD OF INTELLECTUAL PROPERTY

(a) Introduction

34.65 The interpretation and application of treaties governing relations among states, in the field of intellectual property, may give rise to disputes between States. In the absence of a governing treaty provision, such disputes, in accordance with the relevant principles of general international law, would have to be settled by means agreed by the parties to the dispute. The establishment of effective procedures for the settlement of such disputes would contribute to the effort to strengthen the protection of intellectual property.

34.66 Disputes concerning intellectual property may be between private parties. The present document refers only to disputes between States and it does not cover disputes between private parties and the activities of WIPO to facilitate their settlement on the matter (i.e., the WIPO Arbitration and Mediation Center).

34.67 A number of treaties in the field of intellectual property do not establish procedures for the settlement of the disputes that may arise from their interpretation or application (e.g. the Madrid Agreement Concerning the International Registration of Marks). Other treaties, including certain treaties administered by WIPO, contain provisions for the settlement of disputes. Those treaties contain provision calling upon the States party to those treaties to resolve their dispute through negotiations and provide for resort to the International Court of Justice. Article 28 of the Paris Convention for the Protection of Industrial Property and Article 33 of the Berne Convention for the Protection of Literary and Artistic Works provide that any dispute concerning their interpretation or application, not settled by negotiations is to be brought to the International Court of Justice. Similar provisions exist in other treaties administered by WIPO (e.g. the Patent Cooperation Treaty (PCT) and the Rome Convention for the Protection of Performers, Producers of Phonograms and Broadcasting Organizations) and in other multilateral treaties not administered by WIPO (i.e. the Universal Copyright Convention).

References for Section C
International Bureau of WIPO, *Possibilities of Improving the System of International Deposit of Industrial Designs*, H/CE/1/2

34.68 Past experience demonstrates that States have not resorted to the International Court of Justice to settle disputes relating to intellectual property. The jurisprudence of the International Court of Justice shows that not a single dispute on intellectual property has ever been submitted to the Court for its decision.

34.69 In view of the existence of a vacuum in some intellectual property treaties, as far as dispute settlement provisions are concerned, and the lack of adequate procedures for a settlement of disputes in other intellectual property treaties, the Governing Bodies of WIPO decided, in 1989, to establish a Committee of Experts on the Settlement of Intellectual Property Disputes Between States, with the mandate of examining whether a treaty on the matter should be prepared and, if so, to consider its contents. It was understood, from the outset, that a possible treaty should not abrogate the existing provisions on the settlement of disputes in the treaties in the field of intellectual property.

34.70 As of August 1995, the Committee of Experts has held seven sessions; the first and second in 1990 and one every year thereafter. The first session considered a memorandum which contained issues to be solved in a possible treaty on the settlement of intellectual property disputes between States (see documents SD/CE/I/2 and 3). The second session considered a memorandum containing principles for a draft treaty for the settlement of disputes between States in the field of intellectual property (see documents SD/CE/II/2, and 4). The third session examined a memorandum containing provisions of a draft treaty for the settlement of disputes between States in the field of intellectual property (see documents SD/CE/III/2 and 3). The fourth, fifth, sixth and seventh sessions considered a memorandum, which was revised for each meeting, entitled "Draft Treaty for the Settlement of Disputes Between States in the Field of Intellectual Property" (see documents SD/CE/IV/2 and 3; SD/CE/V/2, and 6; SD/CE/VI/2 and 6, and SD/CE/VII/2 and 7). The fifth, sixth and seventh sessions also considered memoranda containing draft Regulations under such a draft Treaty (see documents SD/CE/V/3, SD/CE/VI/3 and SD/CE/VII/3).

34.71 It is on the basis of the draft Treaty, as revised, that the Committee of Experts has conducted its work in its last four sessions. The comments that follow are based on the draft treaty that was presented for the consideration of the Committee of Experts at its last session in May-June 1995. In the following paragraphs, the said text of the draft Treaty on the Settlement of Disputes between States in the Field of Intellectual Property is referred to as "the Treaty". Since the said text corresponds to a draft—and only to a draft—this currently under consideration, the comments that follow do not prejudice, in any way, the final outcome of the work undertaken by the relevant bodies of WIPO or, subsequently, by the Diplomatic Conference that may be convened to adopt the Treaty.

(b) Objective of the Treaty

34.72 The objective of the Treaty is to promote the protection of intellectual property by furthering the enforcement of international obligations in the field of intellectual property and by securing the uniform interpretation and application of international rules concerning such obligations.

34.73 To achieve that objective, the Treaty would establish, within the framework of the World Intellectual Property Organization (WIPO), procedures for the settlement of intellectual property disputes between States or between States and intergovernmental organizations.

34.74 In addition to promoting, as such, the protection of intellectual property, the Treaty would be a further step in promoting the progressive development of international law.

(c) Sphere of Application of the Treaty

34.75 Article 2 of the Treaty establishes the rules governing the sphere of application of the Treaty. Paragraph (1) sets forth the general rule governing the applicability of the Treaty; paragraph (2) sets forth special rules providing for the extension of the sphere of applicability of the Treaty when the parties to the dispute specifically agree, paragraph (3) establishes exceptions to the applicability of the Treaty, paragraph (4) deals with the question of the relationship between the dispute settlement system of the Treaty and other dispute settlement systems, and paragraph (5) deals with the matter of exhaustion of local remedies.

34.76 As concerns the entities, being party to a dispute, to which the Treaty applies, paragraph (1) provides that the Treaty shall be applicable to disputes between Contracting Parties. The term Contracting Party is defined in Article 1(i) and it encompasses only a State or an intergovernmental organization party to the Treaty.

34.77 The Treaty applies neither to disputes between private parties nor to disputes between one or more private parties and a Contracting Party. Such disputes are subject to the jurisdiction of the competent domestic tribunals of the States or to such other procedure permitted by national law for the settlement of disputes, as for example, arbitration. However, nothing in the Treaty precludes the submission by a Contracting Party to the procedures established by the Treaty of a dispute concerning the treatment by another Contracting Party of individuals, particularly foreign nationals. Such a submission would be subject to the applicable general rules of international public law, including the rule of exhaustion of local remedies.

34.78 Article 1(ix) defines the term "dispute" as a disagreement between parties as to the existence or breach of an obligation that relates to the matter or to matters of intellectual property. That provision, read in conjunction with Article 2(1), makes it clear that the Treaty will be applicable to the dispute only if the dispute relates to intellectual property and requires the interpretation or application of one or more provisions binding upon the parties to the dispute in a multilateral treaty. Three elements are involved in that definition and each calls for an explanation: the subject matter of the issue to be decided upon (an intellectual property matter and only that); an obligation, the existence or breach of which is in dispute (binding on the Contracting Party against whom the complaint is made); the source of that obligation (any multilateral treaty or certain multilateral treaties).

34.79 As concerns the *subject matter* of the issue or issues to be decided upon, the paragraph under consideration, when read in conjunction with the definition of dispute (Article 1(ix)), requires that the issue or those issues relate to "an intellectual property matter." Consequently, the Treaty would not apply to a dispute that has nothing to do with intellectual property. However, the Treaty would apply to a dispute which involves issues other than an intellectual property matter, but in such a case, the Treaty would apply only to the issue or issues involving an intellectual property matter.

34.80 It should be noted that the treaties administered by WIPO contain, in addition to provisions concerning intellectual property, provisions of an administrative nature and final clauses that might give rise to disputes. Such disputes would not fall under the sphere of application of the Treaty since those provisions or clauses do not ordinarily involve intellectual property matters. For example, if a country does not pay the contributions it is obliged to pay to WIPO under the provisions of a source treaty, such a breach would not be recognizable under the Treaty.

34.81 The Treaty requires that the provision or provisions whose interpretation or application is in question, be the basis of an obligation. In other words, that provision or provisions must be binding upon the parties to the dispute. The Contracting Parties may be bound by a provision in a source treaty either because they are both parties to the source treaty or because the Contracting Party against whom the complaint is made is bound by the obligation imposed by that provision even though it is not a party to the source treaty. Normally, the parties to the dispute will be parties to the source treaty; but there are situations where a party to a dispute may be bound by provisions of a source treaty to which it is not a party. Such is the case of an intergovernmental industrial property organization which has accepted certain obligations pursuant to Article 9 of the Budapest Treaty on the International Recognition of the Deposit of Microorganisms for the Purpose of Patent Procedure yet is not a party to that treaty. Such is also the case as concerns a member of the Berne Union that has not ratified or acceded to Articles 1 to 21 and the Appendix of the Paris Act (1971) of the Berne Convention but has filed a declaration under Article VI of the Appendix of that Act.

34.82 As concerns the treaty which may be the source of the obligation to which the dispute must relate, the Treaty contains four alternatives (A, B, C and D).

34.83 Alternative A would encompass within its scope a treaty that, without being in the field of intellectual property, contains obligations concerning an intellectual property matter. For example, Article 36 of the Treaty [of Rome] Establishing the European Economic Community and Articles IX, XII:3(c)(iii), XVIII:10 and XX(d) of the General Agreement on Tariffs and Trade (GATT 1947) might be regarded as provisions setting forth obligations concerning an intellectual property matter but those obligations are not in a treaty "in the field of" intellectual property.

34.84 Under Alternative B only a multilateral treaty in the field of intellectual property could be a source treaty. All the treaties administered by WIPO are, for example, treaties in the field of intellectual property. There are a number of multilateral treaties not administered by WIPO which are nevertheless in the field of intellectual property, as for example, the Universal Copyright Convention.

34.85 Under Alternative C, the source treaty would have to be a multilateral treaty which is administered either by WIPO alone or by WIPO in association with one or more other intergovernmental organizations. The Geneva Convention for the Protection of Producers of Phonograms Against Unauthorized Duplication of Their Phonograms is an example of a treaty administered by WIPO in association with one other intergovernmental organization (Unesco), whereas the Rome Convention for the Protection of Performers, Producers of Phonograms and Broadcasting Organizations is an example of a treaty administered by WIPO in association with more than one (namely two: ILO and Unesco) intergovernmental organizations.

34.86 Under Alternative D, the source treaty would have to be a multilateral treaty that is administered by, and only by, WIPO. Examples are the Paris Convention for the Protection of Industrial Property and the Berne Convention for the Protection of Literary and Artistic Works.

34.87 Article 2(2) makes the provisions of the Treaty applicable to a dispute that relates to an intellectual property matter and that is not otherwise within the scope of Article 2(1) the General Rule, if the source treaty so provides, or the parties to the source treaty so decide, or where the source treaty so permits or is silent on the matter and the parties to the dispute so agree. The agreement or decision of the parties to make the Treaty applicable to a dispute not covered by Article 2(1), can be concluded at any time, either before or after the dispute has arisen.

34.88 There are two cases where, expressly, the Treaty does not apply. The first exception is where the parties to a dispute, by agreement among them, exclude the application of the Treaty to their dispute. The second exception, is that the Treaty would not apply where the dispute must be settled according to a procedure other than the one provided for in the Treaty, that is, where, according to another treaty, to which the parties to the dispute are parties, recourse to any other procedure than the one provided for in that treaty is excluded. All the potential source treaties in the field of intellectual property, that are presently in force, have provisions on dispute settlement that would allow recourse to the envisaged procedures under the proposed Treaty.

34.89 Article 2(3) addresses the question of the applicability of the dispute settlement procedures of the Treaty in cases where other dispute settlement procedures may also be applicable and prescribes that, in the absence of an agreement as to which system is to be resorted to, the procedures of the Treaty would, as a general rule, prevail. At the seventh session of the Committee of Experts, different views were expressed as to whether the Treaty should include a provision on the matter and, if so, as to its content.

(d) Means for the Settlement of Disputes

34.90 The Treaty establishes four means for the settlement of disputes that are available to the parties, namely, consultations; good offices, conciliation and mediation; panel procedure and arbitration.

34.91 Consultations followed by a panel procedure are the means of settlement generally applicable to disputes falling under the scope of the Treaty. Good offices, conciliation and mediation are, with one exception—to be explained shortly—optional to the parties to a dispute. Arbitration is always optional. By optional, it is meant that those means can only be resorted to if the parties to the dispute so agree. The exception concerns disputes to which a developing country is a party. The good offices, conciliation or mediation of the Director General of WIPO can be resorted to upon the unilateral request of a developing country.

(e) Consultations

34.92 Consultations are aimed at giving to the parties to the dispute the opportunity to reach an amicable settlement without the participation of intermediaries. It is believed that, even in cases where consultations do not lead to a direct settlement of the dispute, consultations are useful since they provide the parties with an opportunity to clarify the nature and extent of their dispute as well as the issues involved.

34.93 Consultations are normally a first and a necessary step preceding the establishment of a panel. Consultations will, in fact, be the only step of a dispute settlement procedure if, during the consultations, a settlement is reached. Consultations will not be a necessary step preceding the establishment of a panel if the parties to the dispute agree not to have consultations in respect of a given dispute, or agree to replace the procedure of consultations by good offices, conciliation or mediation, or in the case where a developing country party to the dispute requests that the procedure of good offices, conciliation or mediation replace the consultations. The fact that consultations, unless so dispensed with, are an essential condition to a procedure before a panel does not mean that the consultations as a procedure, as well as the other dispute settlement procedures established by the Treaty, are not equally important but that in terms of the stages in the process of dispute settlement, the one procedure (consultations) is required to be pursued before the other (the panel procedure) can be engaged.

34.94 The Treaty contains the basic rules governing the consultations (e.g. invitation, reply, notifications, time limits) whereas the procedural details are covered by the Regulations which may be amended by the Assembly.

(f) Good Offices, Conciliation and Mediation

34.95 The Treaty does not define the terms "good offices, conciliation and mediation". By and large, those three means for the settlement of disputes refer to procedures that have essentially the same characteristics: what each attempts is the settlement of the dispute with the intervention of an intermediary; in none of these procedures can the dispute be settled by a decision emanating from the intermediary. Instead, each of the procedures contemplates the participation of a third person who tries to bring about an agreement between the parties to the dispute. Such a third person is called "the intermediary" but he could just as well be called a "conciliator" or a "mediator." The intermediary could be the Director General or another person, an entity or even a State.

34.96 As a general rule, good offices, conciliation and mediation can only be resorted to if the parties to the dispute so agree. The agreement will necessarily identify the subject matter of the dispute and the intermediary.

34.97 The Treaty contains a special measure in favor of developing countries. In accordance with paragraph 1(b) where a party to a dispute is a developing country, it has the right to request, unilaterally, the good offices, conciliation and mediation of the Director General of WIPO. This measure is based on a similar measure adopted by the Contracting Parties of GATT.

34.98 The basic rules governing good offices, conciliation and mediation are set forth in the Treaty whereas the procedural details are covered by the Regulations.

(g) Panel Procedure

34.99 The submission of a dispute to a procedure before a panel for its consideration, findings and recommendations with a view to settling the dispute is the central element of the system for the settlement of disputes envisaged in the Treaty.

34.100 The Treaty provides for a right of a Contracting Party to submit a dispute to a panel for examination and for making recommendations by it to the parties to the dispute. It is to be noted that the establishment of a panel is automatic in the sense that it does not require a decision of the Assembly or other such body to set up the panel. This feature is different from other dispute settlement systems. For instance, under Article 14 of the Treaty on Intellectual Property in Respect of Integrated Circuits, it is the Assembly which decides on the establishment of the panel.

34.101 As a general rule, the establishment of a panel can only be requested after the parties to the dispute have resorted to consultations. If the parties fail to reach a settlement through consultations within a specified time limit, any of the parties may request the establishment of a panel. In cases where good offices, conciliation and mediation have been resorted to, any of the parties to the dispute may request the establishment of a panel after a specified time limit has elapsed. The specification of a time limit ensures that the panel proceedings are not delayed in cases where agreement in the consultations or the good offices, conciliation and mediation is not forthcoming and also ensures that a party reluctant to cooperate may not unwarrantably block the timely establishment of a panel.

34.102 Unless the parties agree otherwise, the panel would be composed of three members. The panel would be constituted separately for each dispute. The composition of any given panel would normally be different from the composition of any other panel. The Assembly would establish the roster of potential panel members. The details—for example, who (any Contracting Party, the Director General) may propose candidates for inclusion in the roster and what qualifications candidates must have—would be governed by rules in the Regulations. The roster would be revised from time to time. The members of any panel would have to be persons whose names appear in the roster, unless the members are designated by common agreement of the parties to the dispute.

34.103 The designation of the members of the panels is to be made, in the first instance, by agreement of the parties to the dispute. The parties to the dispute would be assisted in this task by the Director General. If the parties do not agree on the members, within a specified period of time, any of the parties to the dispute may request the Director General to designate those members. The Director General would designate members from among persons on the roster who are not nationals of the countries party to the dispute and who have expertise in the field of intellectual property. It is to be noted that the Treaty does not provide that the members be designated by the Assembly of the Contracting States as is the case in other forums. It is believed that this designation by the Director General, as opposed to the approach adopted in other forums where the contracting parties are entrusted with this task, will ensure that the procedure would not be delayed or hindered by lack of agreement.

34.104 As concerns the task of a panel, the Treaty does not require that a mandate or terms of reference be established for each panel as and when a panel is set up. The dispute is defined by the request, that is, by the allegation of the existence and breach of an obligation relating to a matter or to matters of intellectual property and the factual information and legal argumentation set forth in the request to establish a panel and in the submissions of the parties to the panel. Experience in other forums has revealed that, where terms of reference must be decided upon by a Governing Body, the establishment of a panel may be unwarrantably delayed.

34.105 The report is to be adopted by a majority of the members of the panel. If all the members of the panel cannot agree, the report must state the opinion of those that did agree and state separately the opinion of the others.

34.106 If the panel is of the opinion that a party to the dispute has breached an obligation, it must make a recommendation to the responsible party to bring its legislation and practices into conformity with its international obligations. The Treaty does not provide that the panel or the Assembly established by the Treaty may impose sanctions or authorize retaliatory measures.

34.107 The powers of the Assembly in respect of any dispute consist exclusively of the possibility of having an "exchange of views" in and by the Assembly about the report of the panel. The Assembly is not empowered to adopt, endorse or reject the report of the panel, not to modify the recommendations of the panel.

34.108 No provision of the Treaty precludes the applicability of relevant general principles and norms of international law governing the consequences of a breach of an obligation arising out of any source treaty. Such principles and norms could include the measures set forth in the Vienna Convention on the Law of Treaties concerning the termination or suspension of the operation of a treaty as a consequence of its breach (Article 60) or in the rules of international law on international responsibility.

34.109 As concerns international responsibility, it is to be mentioned that the principles and rules governing the matter recognize that a State whose conduct constitutes an international wrongful act has the duty to perform the obligation it has breached and to cease the conduct that constitutes the international wrongful act and that an injured State is entitled to obtain from the State which has committed the international wrongful act reparation in the form of restitution in kind, pecuniary compensation for the damages caused by that act, satisfaction (an apology, nominal damages and damages reflecting the gravity of the infringement) and assurances and guarantees of non-repetition of the wrongful act (see the draft articles on the topic of State responsibility, being prepared by the International Law Commission, Report of the International Law Commission on the work of its forty-fifth session (May-July 1993), United Nations document A/48/10) or, perhaps, to apply as against that State countermeasures (see Report of the International Law Commission on the work of its forty-fourth session (May-July 1992), United Nations document A/47/10), in particular, suspending operations under the source treaty or terminating it (see Article 60 of the Vienna

Convention on the Law of Treaties, United Nations document A/CONF.39/27 1969) or not performing one or more other obligations towards the said State (see Article 11 of the draft articles on State responsibility, referred to above).

34.110 Each of the parties to a dispute must submit reports to the Assembly on the recommendations made by the panel.

34.111 The Treaty contains the basic rules governing the panel procedure (request, answer, notification, establishment of the panel, intervention) and leaves certain procedural details to the Regulations, to be adopted with the Treaty, but which can be amended by the Assembly.

(h) Arbitration

34.112 The Treaty does not define arbitration for the purposes of this Treaty. Arbitration may be characterized as a means of settlement of a dispute by a third person or a group of persons—called an arbitrator or arbitrators—who decide on the basis of the source treaty and in accordance with international law, and that entails a binding and final decision.

34.113 Parties to a dispute, or a possible future dispute, may prefer arbitration to the panel procedure, and this Article provides for satisfying such a preference. They may prefer to do so because they could freely choose the persons who would examined and decide on their dispute, because the dispute would be defined by agreement (in the terms of reference of the arbitration tribunal) rather than on the basis of the request of the complaining party, and because they could entrust the arbitration tribunal with broader powers than merely the power of making findings and a decision. They could, for example, entrust the arbitration tribunal with the power to determine damages or other sanctions. Naturally, all this would require agreement between the parties to the dispute. Such agreement is not required in the panel procedure, and this is the advantage—at least from the viewpoint of the complaining party—of that procedure over arbitration.

34.114 Recourse to WIPO arbitration is optional—and not mandatory—since the parties to the dispute must agree to arbitration; otherwise there cannot be arbitration. Their agreement could be concluded at any time, either after or before the dispute has arisen, either before or during or after the consultations or the good offices, conciliation or mediation, or even during the panel procedure. Further, the arbitration agreement may be expressed either with reference to a specific dispute or with reference to all disputes or a specified category of disputes.

34.115 Since recourse to arbitration is optional, any dispute falling within the sphere of application of the Treaty could be submitted to arbitration, including any dispute arising out of a bilateral treaty or involving a non-Contracting Party provided that in such a dispute at least one of the issues to be decided concerns intellectual property.

34.116 Recourse to arbitration is to the exclusion of the other procedures provided for in the Treaty. Consequently, after the agreement to submit the dispute had been concluded, neither of the parties to such agreement could submit that very dispute, and in respect of any of the parties to the said agreement, to any the procedures set forth in the Treaty. Nor may any such procedure in progress be continued.

34.117 The arbitration procedure is governed by the rules agreed upon by the parties. In the absence of such agreed rules, the procedure is governed by the Treaty and Regulations. The Treaty establishes that, unless the parties agree otherwise, the Director General of WIPO appoints the arbitration tribunal and that the tribunal decides its award on the basis of the source treaty or any other source of international treaty establishing the obligation giving rise to the dispute.

(i) Administrative Provisions

34.118 As it is the case of most treaties administered by WIPO, the Treaty provides for the establishment of a Union of the Contracting Parties. The Union has an Assembly composed of the Contracting Parties to deal with various matters in implementation of the Treaty and the maintenance and development of the Union.

34.119 Among the most important tasks of the Assembly, is its power to amend certain provisions of the Treaty and the Regulations. That power enables the Assembly to make changes in certain provisions of the Treaty and Regulations when experience or circumstances indicate that they are so required.

(j) Future Work

34.120 In view of the need to consider further certain questions that are still outstanding (in particular, the question mentioned in paragraph 34.89, above), the Committee of Experts suggested that a new session of the Committee be convened and, thereafter, that the Governing Bodies take a decision as to whether a diplomatic conference for the conclusion of a treaty on the settlement of intellectual property disputes should be convened and when.

References for Section D
The International Bureau of WIPO, *The WIPO Draft Treaty on the Settlement of Disputes Between States in the Field of Intellectual Property*, WIPO/ACAD/E/94/19.

Index